RICHARD WAGNER

The Man, His Mind, and His Music

Robert W. Gutman was born in New York and received his B.A. and M.A. from New York University. He was one of the founders and directors of the Master Classes at the Bayreuth Festival, where he was lecturer on Wagner and his works. He is a member of the faculty of the State University of New York, and he has taught at The City College of New York and The New School for Social Research. He edited and wrote the preface to William Morris' translation of *Volsunga Saga* and has written on music for periodicals.

Robert W. Gutman

RICHARD WAGNER

The Man, His Mind, and His Music

A Harvest Book
Harcourt Brace Jovanovich, Inc.
New York

Printed in the United States of America
A B C D E F G H I J

The author thanks Alfred A. Knopf, Inc., for permission
to quote material from *Cosima Wagner* by Richard du Moulin-Eckart,
translated by Catherine Alison Phillips; and Macmillan Publishing Co., Inc.,
for permission to quote material from *Letters of Richard Wagner:
The Burrell Collection,* ed. by John N. Burk,
copyright 1950 by Macmillan Publishing Co., Inc.

Library of Congress Cataloging in Publication Data

Gutman, Robert W
Richard Wagner; the man, his mind, and his music.

(A Harvest book, HB 272)
Bibliography: p.
1. Wagner, Richard, 1813–1883.
[ML410.W1G83   1974]   782.1'092'4[B]   73–12381
ISBN 0–15–677610–3

In memory of my parents

Contents

List of Illustrations

ix

Preface

Wagner wrote of the "incomparable magic" of his works; music was their most powerful charm. A Prospero with book and wand who sought rule over a world of inferior spirits, he used music to sway the senses—to captivate, subdue, and lecture an audience rendered unquestioning. His music compelled belief, its marvelous instrumentation, as Nietzsche remarked, working upon the nervous system, having the power to "charm the spinal marrow" and "persuade even the bowels." And like his Lohengrin, whose motto was "Never question me," Wagner wished his origins to remain mysterious. He required the romantic dream of the artist as lonely inventor and superman.

In his autobiography, *Mein Leben,* he began to create his own myth, a fantastic Passion of suffering and resurrection. He was a god, tortured by the world, yet forgiving. Cosima, his mistress and then his second wife, to whom he dictated the book, was moved by "the gentleness" with which he judged "everybody's abominable behavior toward him," although, prudently, she delayed a public printing until well after the turn of the century, when most recipients of his sweet forbearance would be in their graves, unable to protest.

His prose, like his operas, attacked the emotional, not the critical, faculties. In *Siegfried* the Wood Bird sings, "Only those who yearn can grasp my meaning!" Arraying instinct against reason, Wagner demanded a faith permitting disciples to view the world through spectacles hazy with Wagnerian steam. "Lay aside your doubts," Lohengrin tells Elsa as she vainly seeks to discover whence her mysterious lover came. "My origins lie in radiance and ecstasy." She was the first unsuccessful Wagnerite and Nietzsche's forerunner.

Wagner's own methods inspired the disingenuousness of his early biographers, their task no doubt made easier by a Victorian delight in bringing ethical standards to bear upon artistic affairs. It was comforting to equate great art with the good life, and, seemingly, many held it a duty to ignore facts that might disturb this sentimental balance. Glasenapp, working under the eye of Cosima, faced the difficult task of constructing from the evidence before him a Wagner answering the majesty of his works. The capacity of a devoted disciple for self-deception is considerable, and no doubt Glasenapp could justify to himself his remodeling, disregarding, and, perhaps, ever destroying documents. Such methods probably appeared to him not only an obligation toward a genius' memory, but toward society itself. The temptation was strong to ignore the least attractive of the great man's adventures or to touch them up, much plain ugliness being distorted into characteristic charm.

Perhaps recalling Wagner's hatred of scholarship and its lack of "spontaneity," Cosima's biographer, Moulin-Eckart, implied that the future of Wagnerian writings lay in novels about members of the composer's circle. The "official" biographies having been written, those in Haus Wahnfried, seat of Wagnerian empire, evidently thought it best for future generations to tiptoe around the awesome subject, to treat it indirectly, through fiction; rigorous research would shake down the house of myths so laboriously raised.

In his essay "Religion and Art," Wagner had warned against the lies of reality taught by historians; he, the poet-priest, alone revealed ideal truth. Houston Stewart Chamberlain, Wagner's son-in-law and biographer, declared the composer's frivolous way with fact to be of no matter, for, regardless of his premises, he penetrated to a higher verity. Such was the intellectual basis of most early Wagnerian studies. Konrad Heiden observed, "With Richard Wagner in mind, Chamberlain foreshadowed a whole school which falsifies facts and calls the result higher truth."

Primarily to the brilliant music critic and historian Ernest Newman fell the task of freeing Wagnerian biography from both the artful and crude overpaintings of the composer himself, Glasenapp, Chamberlain, and their successors, a deliverance still deeply resented by zealots committed to the consoling legends of Cosima's Wahnfried. From Wagner's portrait he began scientifically to erase coats of thick Victorian varnish and flattering but inexcusable restorations. The face that began to emerge at first horrified him, perhaps because it was even more blemished than suspected. But he was at peace with what had come to view by the time he set to work on his *The Life of Richard Wagner,* those four monumental volumes to which anyone writing on the composer must be incalculably indebted.

Newman observed that Wagner's freedom from ordinary concepts of morality enabled him to survive the unending emergencies of his life and to complete and leave to posterity a series of masterpieces. But Nietzsche had earlier surmised the heavy price posterity would pay for the gift. Wagner's magnification of instinct—specifically, German instinct—made him seek material for his dramas in myth and legend, the age-old creation of what he held to be the Folk's unfailing natural tendencies; this doctrine of the unerring impulses of the German Folk led him into the dark waters of collective right and freedom in which individualism and dissimilitude are subdued in a fated mass destiny and also to the perilous concept of an infallible leader as symbolic extension of the Folk's wisdom. When the time came for settling the Wagnerian patrimony, so heavily encumbered with such fraudulent items, the cost proved so appalling that not only were the man and his political beliefs cursed, but his art and fatherland, too. Ethics and aesthetics were again confused.

The ruthlessness and fanaticism characterizing certain aspects of Wagner's personality and works are not restricted to one nation or time. Croce saw Wagner as standing outside the great idealistic German tradition of Beethoven and Schiller and to be rather a strange survival from some earlier, more violent age, like that of Cellini. The matter from which an artist shapes his work may grow in unwholesome climates, and, to a larger extent than one would wish, the great Wagnerian operas are sublimations of ignoble ideas and instincts. In *Toward a Genealogy of Morals* Nietzsche spoke of the artist as "after all, only the presupposition of his work, the womb, the soil, at times the dung and manure on which and out of which it grows—and, accordingly, in most cases, something one must forget if the work itself is to be enjoyed." But what Wagner helped accomplish in the world of practical politics so shocked civilization and remains so close a terror to those who suffered directly from his teaching and bear its mark that at this time his art can be divorced from his personality and credo only with difficulty.

Yet the effort can be made, and, like any great art, Wagner's may be appreciated as a pure aesthetic experience. To admire the Segnatura frescoes or the Sistine ceiling requires no knowledge of the elaborate philosophical and theological programs they embody. Nor will a single fact of their painters' lives or beliefs quicken appreciation of the sheer artistic qualities of these masterpieces. Yet, understanding of the symbolism of certain groupings, personages, and objects does add another dimension to the spectator's comprehension. One cannot dismiss iconography without at the same time renouncing the attempt to grasp the whole intellectually as well as artistically. And, though many who find Wagner's "iconography" embarrassing or repulsive either ignore or deny it, such considerations are the essence of critical biography.

Nietzsche implied that Wagner the man must be forgotten if Wagnerian opera is to be enjoyed. But enjoyment is often innocent of understanding. Nietzsche himself declared in *The Gay Science* that his eye became "ever sharper for that most difficult and most risky form of *retrospective inference* in which the most mistakes are made—the retrospective inference from the work to the author, from the deed to the doer, from the ideal to him who *needs* it, from every manner of thinking and appraising to the commanding necessity behind it." What the worthy Tovey called the "vulgar entanglements" between the artist's work and life—interrelationships that often dangerously confuse biography and assessment—are of inestimable importance for seizing the cultural totality of Wagner's achievement. He fed on himself and is to be found on nearly every page of his operas. If nothing were known of his personality, its basic traits could be reconstructed from their evidence.

To grasp the nature of Wagner's creations fully, one cannot dismiss his character and theorizing simply as troublesome side issues. This is the stratagem of those who, seeking to make of Wagner something he was not, sum up his sung tracts in terms of what Shaw labeled "the love panacea." Love in terms of Beethoven's universal brotherhood was exactly what Wagner did not preach.

Unhappily, a proto-Nazism, expressed mainly through an unextinguishable loathing of the Jews, was one of Wagner's principal leitmotifs, the venomous tendrils of anti-Semitism twining through his life and work. In his final years, his hatred reached out further to embrace those with black and yellow skins. This attitude cannot be shrugged off as an unfortunate whim or a minor flaw in a musical hero. Those who lament that the genius who could create the noble Hans Sachs and the Christian Parsifal is wronged when his name is linked with Hitler's have never opened or have hastily closed the volumes of letters and essays in which Wagner unmistakably expounds his political program. This book will examine this program and attempt to assess Sachs's particular kind of nobility and Parsifal's quite special Christianity to determine whether such characters do stand against the perilous main current of Wagnerian thought.

In *The Gay Science* Nietzsche held an artist's philosophy of little importance if it remained only a "supplementary" element, leaving the art itself uninjured. In Wagner's case the works did sustain serious ideological corruption. Yet his music provides beauties to admire even after those elements formed by hatred are recognized, understood, and suffered for what they are. Certainly he would refuse to disassociate his dramas from the ideas that fed them. His stage works were for him projections into the realm of art of all he wished to accomplish as a social and political reformer.

Toward the close of his days he seemed unable to think, write, or talk on any subject other than the Jews, and ended not far from insane on the question of their imagined danger to Germany's future. The sections of this book dealing with *Parsifal* become almost a case history of someone maddened by anti-Semitism. That the opera is on one level a symbolic dramatization of the atrocious racial theorizing of his last articles (Nietzsche called the work "an outrage on morality"), on another, an allegory of a soul's maturing, and, most important, one of the musical peaks of the century, summarizes that mystery called Wagner.

Ernest Newman could not bring himself to look squarely at the late Wagnerian essays; obviously, he could not bear what he glimpsed. Moreover, another problem troubled him. The fourth volume of the masterly *Life* shows fatigue, haste, and a certain cantankerousness. A large part of it was transplanted from an unfinished book on Nietzsche started by Newman but abandoned. For him to confront Wagner's final prose works critically would have involved the complete recasting of his material on Nietzsche. And so, in this writer's opinion, he closed his eyes to the significance of the late articles and fobbed his readers off with what is almost unthinkable for this great biographer—sentimental evasions. He refused to see that in Wagner's closing period his essays and his art were as intricately intertwined as in earlier days and that *Parsifal* is many things, but certainly not "the supreme song of love and pity. . . ." Only age and a desire to be done with his task can explain Newman's blindness on this matter, his strange approach to the break between Nietzsche and Wagner (an attitude involving a series of amazing self-contradictions that must be scrutinized), and his comments on Hanslick, which unjustly parrot the abusive vocabulary of Wagnerism.

But these points are exceptions. A multitude of facts discerned by Newman's keen mind invariably yielded a high factor of common sense; the more tangled the threads, the greater his ability to lead them into meaningful patterns, an ability especially to be admired in his analysis of the Wagner-Cosima-Bülow affair. Here, the present volume ventures some steps beyond Newman by maintaining that this involved relationship becomes completely understandable only when one recognizes the simultaneous demands of both men upon Cosima as a sexual partner. But even though the intertwined histories of Wagner, the Bülows, and Ludwig of Bavaria cannot be related without legitimate recourse to the detail of scandal, this book's primary aim is to relate Wagner to the history of ideas.

And many currents of thought converged in this fascinating figure. His derivative art ended as a compendium of the finest and worst elements of a great, turbulent period stretching from Byron's *The Giaour* and the picturesque cardboard filigree of the early Gothic Revival to the sultry era of Abbot Sebastian Kneipp's baths and the sinuate vegetation of Art Nouveau. The tendencies of the entire century hold reunion in his final work. A strange battle is joined in Klingsor's garden. Victory is borne away by Parsifal, the new Redeemer, a rosy-cheeked, blond simpleton, ready for his ominous *Lehrjahre*—a blunt cog manufactured to improve the failing machinery of natural selection. Scientific Determinism gains the day and, in an almost unimaginable, intellectual Salmagundi, Darwinian optimism, refashioned by Wagner, leads the way toward the Schopenhauerean vacuum. *Parsifal* was Wagner's gigantic summing up. And the world has yet to recover from the catastrophe that followed when the malefic forces that helped shape this phantasmagoria suddenly broke the thin bonds of civilization holding them in check. *Parsifal* remains a marvel and a despair.

And Wagner remains an artistic fact and an artistic challenge. Caught in the currents of evolutionary thought, he had seen himself as the fittest. Once Darwin had won his victory over the first chapter of Genesis, a fascination with evolutionary theory led to its application to aesthetics. Wagner flew up to perch upon the highest bough of the evolutionary tree, whence he fell low indeed.

His works jarred music into alignments remaining relatively stable until early in this century, when Diaghilev's Russian ballet held out a quite different and more varied artistic experience. Clarity, humor, and wiry intellect supplanted the ponderous aesthetic based upon Teutonic instinct. Epigram replaced rhetoric. The mammoth Wagnerian opera suddenly seemed strangely oppressive, sentimental, even provincial. Those thick German mists began to dissolve before the Franco-Slavic civilization of St. Petersburg as the fleshy, leaden-footed gods of Walhall gave way before Stravinsky's lithe Apollo. The spell of Bayreuth was broken.

Respect for the Wagner operas, declining among intellectuals for some time, had been thoroughly undermined by the incredible nonsense of the journals of Wagnerism, led by the composer's own *Bayreuther Blätter,* Dujardin's *Revue Wagnérienne,* and Ellis' *The Meister.* The less sense Wagnerites made, seemingly the more they understood one another. In his autobiography, Eduard Hanslick had correctly predicted that not many decades would pass before such writings would "be looked upon in amazement as the relics of an intellectual plague."

During the composition of the *Sacre du Printemps* Stravinsky was invited by Diaghilev to join him at Bayreuth for *Parsifal.* To Stravinsky, the atmosphere seemed lugubrious. He was dismayed by "this comedy of Bayreuth, with its ridiculous formalities," and by an uncritical audience, dedicated to a "sacrilegious" concept of art as religion and the theater as temple. "But is it at all surprising that such confusion should arise at a time like the present . . . ? People are . . . apparently fully aware of the sort of monster to which the world is about to give birth, and perceive . . . that man cannot live without some kind of cult."

The "present" of which Stravinsky spoke was the time of his autobiography—the nineteen-thirties.

In February, 1933, to commemorate the fiftieth anniversary of Wagner's death in Venice, Thomas Mann delivered a lecture on him at the University of Munich. He who had immortalized a craving spirit bursting from discipline and finding strange release and death in the city of lagoons was unconsciously saying farewell to his native land, now disposed to cast off civilization. He elaborated upon the vital enchantment of Wagner's art, but warned against projecting his intellectual views into the present. Mann, who ever and again reassessed a devotion to Wagner not unmixed with fear, could never bring himself to consider Wagnerian politics or aesthetics seriously. The hour was late. Germany seized the goblet, poured away the precious liquid of her culture, and prepared to quaff its heady and corrupting dregs.

That Wagner as a political and social thinker was a link between Jahn and Hitler cannot be denied. Hitler especially revered Wagner's prose works, emulated their turgid style, enthroned him as artistic god of the Third Reich, and carried to their logical and appalling conclusions many of the ideas implicit in the composer's essays and dramas. The art-work was swallowed by its hypotheses. What the best of Wagnerites had condoned as of trifling significance developed into the world's most frightening reality. Bayreuth became the spiritual capital of an unparalleled villainy, and many turned from Wagner in horror.

Though he has returned as a classic, entitled to a place among his peers, his art has yet to recover fully from the blight his theories have put upon it. Music alone cannot preach; it can reveal nothing about a composer's character; it is either good or bad. But Wagner's great music is often allied to texts and episodes typifying the despicable points of view elaborated in his essays. Nonetheless, his ability to set up highly dramatic situations in which characters express themselves in elusive verse enveloped by a music that interprets and insinuates opens the doors to many constructions. As a supreme cultural irony, Freud has come to Wagner's rescue.

In an age of psychoanalysis, his operas are regaining interest through his shifting levels of meaning and through that mysterious Wagnerian sortilege which, attacking the senses, provokes the subconscious. Many dramas simultaneously play in works that may be explored on more recently discovered avenues of the mind. Bayreuth has perceptively exploited this new outlook. Its stylized productions came into being not for superficial reasons of economics or publicity; rather, it has done Wagner the service of attempting symbolically to separate the prose works from the dramas by throwing the political, social, and racial concepts built into the latter into deep shadow and illuminating their other, more tolerable—indeed, frequently universal—aspects.

The reaction against Wagner's operas was also, in part, the cyclic revolt of one generation against what its fathers most highly prized. But Wagner, in addition, presents special problems of performance in today's more critical climate, which has appreciably raised the level of what a discriminating audience will tolerate in the name of the *Gesamtkunstwerk*. The old magic no longer benumbs the judgment.

Notwithstanding their assured and ponderous exteriors, Wagner's music dramas are strangely delicate. Apart from *The Flying Dutchman,* they show none of the youthful resilience of Verdi's operas, with their power to triumph over haphazard production. Even in the old Verdi there is no *fin de siècle* languor. In comparison, Wagner's torpid stage works must be nursed lest they wilt.

Yet Wagner survives, and primarily because he was a great musician. His ripe late-romantic style retains much of its allure. In an intellectual climate happily alien to his mentality and his complex aesthetic of tonnage, a music of almost unparalleled eloquence and intimacy keeps his works on the stage. Nietzsche, in *The Gay Science,* described Wagner's "genius for finding the tones peculiar to the realm of suffering, oppressed, tortured souls. . . . No one equals him in the colors of late autumn, in the indescribably moving happiness of a last, ultimate, all-too-short pleasure. He knows a tone for those secret and uncanny midnights of the soul when cause and effect seem out of joint, and when every moment something may arise 'out of nothing.' He draws sustenance, most auspiciously, from the lower depths of human happiness and, as it were, out of its drained goblet, where the bitterest and most unwholesome drops, for good or for ill, have finally mixed with the sweetest. . . . Yes, as the Orpheus of all secret misery, he is greater than anyone." In *The Wagner Case* Nietzsche spoke of the composer as "our greatest melancholist in music, full of flashes, tenderness, and words of solace in which none has anticipated him, the tonal master of a sad and indolent happiness."

This gift is, for many, ample indemnity for his less praiseworthy aspects, his music seemingly giving his works, like the spears that pierced Telephus and Amfortas, the power to heal wounds they have opened.

Newton repeated the ancient remark that a successor sees farther than his predecessors because he stands on their shoulders. My indebtedness to such writers as Ernest Newman, Paul Bekker, Julius Kapp, Otto Strobel, Alfred Einstein, Jacques Barzun, Jack Stein, Arnold Hauser, Joseph Kerman, Walter Kaufmann, and—the greatest name in Wagnerian studies—Nietzsche will be apparent to anyone in command of the essentials of a bibliography so vast that no one can claim to have exhausted it. And, though after decades of studying a subject one can rarely be sure that an idea, opinion, or phrase is one's own or has emerged from some corner of the memory, the reader will discover new facts and certainly many new interpretations of familiar ones.

Acquaintance with the plots of the standard Wagnerian operas is assumed. A chronological presentation of Wagner's life is generally adhered to, while, with only few exceptions, the poems, music, and essays are discussed at the periods they arose in their creator's mind or where they have most significance for his artistic development. Wagner's aesthetic theories, closely bound to his political utterances, are considered, especially the fascinating fact, first observed by Nietzsche in *Toward a Genealogy of Morals,* that, after the composer's study of Schopenhauer, there ensued "a complete theoretic disagreement between his earlier and later aesthetic faith," a subject later pondered by Bekker and then explored in detail by Stein. Only the chapter on musical form and the leitmotif stands as a separate unit, though appearing at the point where the composer's use of the latter device had reached its most characteristic phase. This section must cut across chronology, its self-sufficient nature permitting the reader not interested in specifically musical questions to pass over it without losing biographical continuity, though the jump will be taken at the cost of a more complete grasp of Wagnerian theory. Technical language has been used with discretion, so that all sections on music may be meaningful to laymen. I hope to fulfill a need for a comprehensive, one-volume biography of the composer combined with critical discussions of his works. Essentially, the purpose of the book is to see Wagner in terms of ideas—of cultural history.

The logic of Wagner's musical mind found no parallel in his handling of words. His struggle with his native language often led him into mazelike sentences from which only a stronger grammatical gift than his might have offered hope of rescue. The *stylos* was literally the scribe's burin or graver, and Wagner's was an exceedingly blunt instrument. Not only a poor style but also his essential discomfiture in the realm of abstract thought, in which he nonetheless forced himself to wander, frequently make his verse and prose bristle with difficulties formidable for the reader and at times insurmountable for the translator. Most of Wagner's words herein quoted are newly put into English. However, such readable and reliable English versions of his letters as Burk's notable edition of the Burrell Collection have been gratefully quoted, as has Catherine Phillips' admirable translation of Moulin-Eckart's Cosima documents.

In rendering proper names and titles in a foreign tongue, consistency is not necessarily a virtue. In this book ear and custom guided the choice of particular forms; one will encounter Frederick the Great and Ludwig—not Louis— of Bavaria, *The Twilight of the Gods* and *Die Feen.* Musical examples have been omitted, since scores and phonograph recordings of Wagner's works abound; even his *juvenilia* are now easily accessible. Notes are generally restricted to amplifications of the text, the main sources consulted being indicated in a selected bibliography at the end.

This book grew out of a series of lectures given at the Bayreuth Festival Master Classes. Over pitchers of Bayreuth white wine, whimsically called *"Weiberschreck,"* students and colleagues generously prompted the enterprise. At the worst, the *Weiberschreck* can be blamed; it has undone many.

For her encouragement I must especially thank Mrs. Richard Fried. Friends have been generous in placing their libraries at my disposal: Mrs. Herbert Janssen, Dr. Stoddard Lincoln, Paul Creamer, Jon McLain, Dr. William

Preface

Kimmel, Robert Zarbock, Dr. A. F. R. Lawrence, and the late Max Friedlander. The latter's death at the time of the completion of this manuscript
underscored how much I owe to his lectures at Bayreuth, his conversations,
and his friendship. Above all, I owe an extraordinary debt of gratitude to
Ted Hart, so generous with his formidable musical and literary knowledge;
his critical eye fell upon every page of the manuscript, and the entire task
was made lighter by his understanding help.

R. W. G.

New York City
December 1967

Such welcome and unwelcome things at once
'Tis hard to reconcile.

Macbeth, Act IV, Scene 3

I

Childhood in Saxony

Cannonades preluded the birth of Richard Wagner in Saxony during the spring of 1813. This German kingdom was overrun by the troops of Napoleon Bonaparte striving to reassert dominance over a Europe no longer intimidated by the legend of his invincibility. The previous autumn his forces in Russia had begun a disengagement that ended in flight; the Grande Armée had melted away, and at the end of 1812 the Emperor was back at the Tuileries levying new troops for the resubjugation of Prussia. By March, 1813, French soldiers were once again advancing toward the Elbe.

The main action of this new campaign unfolded in Saxony, which Bonaparte planned to use as a base for his immediate goal—the capture of Berlin, the Prussian capital. Since the Peace of Posen (1806) Saxony had been part of the French Confederation of the Rhine. But the calamities of the Russian adventure had shaken the confidence of the Saxon king in Napoleon, and when in 1813 the Allies—the combined Prussians and Russians—entered his realm to meet the advancing French, King Friedrich, refusing to join against Napoleon, withdrew his troops and fled to Prague. He was somewhat reassured by the French victory at Lützen, where early in May, 1813, the Allies took flight. Later that month they were again defeated at Bautzen. There, however, Marshal Ney's too punctilious observance of instructions permitted them to retire in excellent order. When the smoke cleared at Bautzen on May 21, the Emperor had neither trophies nor multitudes of prisoners to betoken his victory. Wrecked guns, the wounded, and the dead were his prizes. Recollections of abandoned Moscow may well have crossed his mind.

On the following day Richard Wagner was born in Leipzig, the Saxon metropolis situated fewer than one hundred miles west of the battle. These military operations markedly influenced the course of his life.

The Allies continued to fall back, and Napoleon was unable to coax them into action. Lengthening supply lines and a shortage of cavalry caused him to negotiate an armistice that lasted until mid-August. During this interval he hastened to fortify the Saxon capital of Dresden, where on August 27 he overcame the combined might of Prussia, Russia, and Austria. But this was the last of his great victories. In October the "Battle of Nations" was fought before Leipzig; Saxon troops, betraying their king, besieged within the city by the Allies, deserted both him and Napoleon, whose vanquished forces were soon fleeing toward Mainz and the confines of France itself. The Empire was crumbling, and within half a year Paris was to fall.

The legal father of the infant Richard was Carl Friedrich Wagner, a Leipzig police official whose knowledge of French made him valuable to Saxony's imperial ally. Exhausted by duties greatly increased during the campaign and the Allied attack on the city, he was vulnerable to an epidemic of typhus that flared as a result of the carnage. He died on November 23, 1813, six months after Richard's birth.

The mutiny of King Friedrich's troops exemplified popular Saxon feeling. The French were detested, and stories of Napoleon's rape of Germany undoubtedly were part of Richard's childhood. His hatred of France remained a lifelong obsession, which rose to the surface in unexpected places. He mars, for example, his human and often universal *Die Meistersinger* by a brief, unexpected, and irrelevant anti-French diatribe delivered by Hans Sachs.[1] Of course, Wagner's late play, *A Capitulation,* remains the most gross witness to an undying Francophobia, which in this case gleefully celebrates the misery in Paris after the fall of the Second Empire.

In more quiet days Carl Friedrich Wagner's avocation had been the theater. He occupied himself with amateur histrionics and frequented the licensed troupe managed by Franz Seconda, which performed alternately at Dresden and Leipzig. These interests brought him into contact with the volatile and multitalented Ludwig Geyer, whom economic necessity had driven from serious studies in law and art to hack portrait painting and finally to the stage. Geyer became an intimate of the Wagner family circle and when in Leipzig lodged at Carl Friedrich's house.

Not only the art of Goethe and Schiller engrossed Carl Friedrich but also those who gave life to this art, namely, actresses. To them, particularly to Friederike Wilhelmine Hartwig, he paid his addresses while pretending

---

[1] Hans Sachs warns of French rule bringing with it French humbug and trifling that might submerge serious German art. For "French," Wagner uses the adjective *"welsch."* In the destruction of the Hohenstaufen line through Charles of Anjou's beheading of Conradin, Wagner saw mankind bereft of the last fiber of its natural racial origin. In his opinion, the Capetians were racially impure, nonsense he elaborates at length in his essay *The Wibelungs.*

to his knowing wife that pressing documents delayed him at the office. But Frau Johanna Wagner was not without consolation in the person of young Geyer, who frequently filled the place of his absent friend.

Napoleon's campaign of 1813 had given Seconda second thoughts about his regular Leipzig summer season, and he moved his base to the Bohemian spa of Teplitz. There, as usual, Geyer was with the company. During the actor's unwonted absence from Leipzig, Richard was born to Johanna.

Unlike his elder brother, Albert, who was baptized five days after birth, the infant was deprived of this sacrament for several months. Johanna was religious; surely there must have been particular reasons for delaying the important rite. Wagner's statement in his autobiography that he was christened two days after he was born was written either in ignorance or in an attempt to deceive.

Actually, he never knew the most fascinating tale of his early childhood; his mother certainly believed that the secret would die with her. When her strength returned after confinement, she quit husband and children—six without counting Richard and Albert, the eldest, a pupil at Meissen— and undertook the extremely difficult journey of one hundred and fifty miles to seek out Geyer at Teplitz. Whether or not the infant Richard went along is not certain, but he probably accompanied her. In the early nine- teenth century not only was this trip considerable for an unescorted woman, with or without baby, but also, at this particular time, Johanna had to traverse territory in upheaval. Although the truce was in operation, she, a subject of pro-French King Friedrich, had to pass through Allied lines. Moreover, the armistice had not put a halt to chaos, pillage, and hunger, and the Czar's cossacks preyed upon all. An urgent need drove her on; despite hazards she made her way to Teplitz to take up residence there a little past the middle of July in the very building in which Geyer was housed.[2]

Evidently Carl Friedrich wanted no part of the new child. Johanna had to discuss the problem with Geyer and perhaps wished to show him his offspring. What other reasons can be brought forward to explain this strange trip, kept secret for more than a century and then betrayed by a fortuitous perusal of an 1813 visitors' registry in Teplitz?

Something was worked out; Frau Wagner returned to Leipzig and her family. On August 16, when almost three months old, the boy was baptized Wilhelm Richard in St. Thomas', whose most famous cantor, Johann

---

[2] The Napoleonic campaign also caused inconvenience to the infant Verdi, born five months after Wagner. During 1814 the armies of Russia and Austria appeared on the Paduan plain, then part of the Taro, a French transalpine department. Local legend recorded that the child's mother fled with him to safety in the tower of the church at Le Roncole.

Sebastian Bach, might still have been remembered by the eldest in the congregation. For the child who was to create *Die Meistersinger,* baptism at this font was of a doubly spiritual significance.

Thus Richard was acknowledged by Carl Friedrich as his own. Three months later Leipzig was invested and Carl Friedrich died of typhus. Nine months after this, Geyer married Frau Johanna and took upon himself the burden of maintaining her and her seven children.[3] A girl, Cäcilie, was born to them in February, six months after their wedding. This younger full sister was Richard's favorite, the playmate and companion of his childhood.

Through the years tender feelings persisted between them. When Wagner had become famous, both were eager to preserve family mementos. For Christmas, 1869—Wagner was then at work on *The Twilight of the Gods* —her present to him consisted of copies of letters in her possession that had passed between Geyer and Johanna more than half a century earlier. In acknowledging the precious gift, Wagner wrote to her that the "sacrifice (*Selbstaufopferung*) on the part of our father Geyer"—that is, Geyer's willingness to assume responsibility for Carl Friedrich's entire family—was deeply touching, the letters having afforded Wagner a glimpse into the relationship between the pair during difficult days. Though he found it hard to put his views into words, he remarked that Geyer's sacrifice could be perceived as an attempt to make amends for a guilt. Though this "guilt" may be interpreted as referring either to Johanna's extramarital liaison with Geyer that produced Richard or to their prenuptial relationship that resulted in Cäcilie—or to both—this letter, among other evidence, leaves little doubt that Wagner believed himself to be Geyer's son. In fact, he confided this belief to friends, one of whom was Nietzsche.

Nor at the height of his fame was he reluctant to make similar private revelations to his patron, the Bavarian king. On Wagner's birthdays pantomimes in his honor were frequently performed by his children. He dearly loved these somewhat foolish ceremonies. Describing the one of 1879 to Ludwig II, Wagner wrote that his son, Siegfried, posing as a painter, represented Ludwig Geyer "significantly reborn." The phrase was well chosen, for in later life the gentle Siegfried showed talent for the fine arts (Geyer's avocation) as well as for the theater and for music; moreover, Wagner's choice of phrase throughout the description clearly underscores his belief in the Geyer paternity.

Yet, what led him to dissemble in his autobiography, *Mein Leben,* in which he declared himself the son of Carl Friedrich? Nietzsche was

---

[3] In January, 1814, a daughter, Maria Theresia, had died at nearly five years of age.

shocked to discover the creator of Siegfried, the superman, unwilling to reveal to the world the truth about himself. Despite Wagner's claim that his book's justification was its unadorned veracity, much of *Mein Leben* was propagandist and twisted facts for its own ends. The horrified Nietzsche dubbed it *"fable convenue,* if not worse." That pioneer of Wagnerian scholarship, Mrs. Burrell, could not believe Wagner was responsible for this "miserable book." His second wife, Cosima, was held to account for its lies and evasions. But time has proved Wagner its undisputed author.

A clue to the reasons for Wagner's duplicity concerning his paternal parentage may well lie in Nietzsche's famous play upon words to the effect that a Geyer is almost an Adler. In German *"Geyer"* means "vulture," while *"Adler"* is the word for "eagle"; and both names representing birds are also frequently encountered German-Jewish names. Nietzsche in the first postscript to his *The Wagner Case* (1888) flatly declared Wagner to be the son of Geyer. He resented Wagner's fear of admitting the possibility of a Jewish origin. Yet such a public disclosure on Wagner's part would indeed have required courage, for by the time of *Mein Leben* he was one of Europe's most articulate anti-Semites. But this bigotry and his reluctance to speak out probably sprang from common roots.

He was known as Richard Geyer at least until his confirmation at the age of fourteen, six years after Geyer's death; sometime thereafter he re-adopted his legal name of Wagner. Not only had the Norns of destiny in a malevolent hour given the boy a Jewish name; they had also placed his birth on the Brühl, the center of the Leipzig Jewish quarter, and had, to crown their mischief, given his features a hawklike cast with prominent nose, pointed jaw, and high, intellectual brow; his oversized head was perched upon a stunted but energetic body at an angle suggesting to Mrs. Burrell a close escape from deformity; in short, the boy had physical characteristics which ignorance and prejudice associate exclusively with the Jews. It is not unlikely that young Richard Geyer was considered Jewish by various classmates and townsfolk and that his denial was expressed by a vigorous anti-Semitism.

Ironically, research has so far failed to produce a single demonstrably Jewish ancestor on the Geyer family tree. But Richard could not know this. That hysterical anti-Semitism which continued unabated throughout his life may well have grown from attempts to evince an Aryan purity. Nonetheless, despite his efforts, part of intellectual Europe continued to consider him Jewish, and the belief persists. His confidences to intimates had not remained private, and journalists and cartoonists delighted in irritating him by exploiting the open secret of his supposed Jewish background.

Throughout his life Wagner was consumed by a strange love-hate for the Jews. He often delighted in them in particular but always loathed them in general. His friendships with Jews extended from his childhood sweetheart, Leah David, and his school chum, Lippert né Levy, to those close and emotional but ambiguous relationships of his final years with Joseph Rubinstein, Hermann Levi, and Angelo Neumann.

Yet, unsympathetic preoccupation with the Jews as a group forms one of the cornerstones of Wagnerian thought in art and politics; vicious as it was, lethal as its inheritance has been, and painful as it is to observe in such a genius, it cannot be ignored if a full picture of the man is to emerge.

2

He loved Geyer. At what point in his life he came to realize that this charming artist was his real father is not known. Was there a period of uncertainty for him as a young man? It is clear that his mother, who was even coyly taciturn about her own origins, kept her peace. She was actually an illegitimate daughter of Prince Friedrich Ferdinand Constantin, brother of Grand Duke Karl August of Weimar. A rather self-indulgent young nobleman with a talent for music, Constantin fathered Johanna before his sixteenth birthday. It was Dorothea Erdmuthe Iglisch, a tanner's daughter, who, after a decade of marriage to the baker Herr Pätz of Weissenfels, was honored by the princely attentions that produced Johanna. The propagation of bastard children by the German nobility was not in the slightest way unusual, and, to the young aristocrat's credit, he arranged for the infant's acceptance by Herr Pätz and also provided for her education. (Interestingly, Constantin was the model for Goethe's Lothario.)

This affair was an open secret. In *Mein Leben* Wagner writes that his mother spoke with some embarrassment and even uncertainty about her maiden name, and he also mentions the princely friend who aided her family. But, of course, a few hints about a royal strain in the Wagnerian blood would be on the credit side. Semitic blood was quite another matter; the Geyer he loved had to be denied. How striking that to work wonders Lohengrin must hide both name and race and that the pronouncing of his and his father's name destroys the knight's happiness and forces him to depart.

It is strangely moving to observe Wagner in 1870 asking Nietzsche, who was looking after the publication of *Mein Leben*, to order a vulture (*Geyer*) engraved as a decorative emblem for the autobiography. And Wagner takes special pains to urge that this bird be drawn with the characteristic vulture ruff about its neck so that it be easily recognized for what it represented.

The *Geyer* had in fact become Wagner's crest, and his need of this device seems as private as Lohengrin's of an embroidered swan. Symbols, especially words as symbols, fascinated Wagner, and the power of his poetry often rests upon allusion latent in the phrase; much is covert and much implied. Often he sets up a stage situation whose externals mime one tale while his sinewy and punning diction unfolds another.

It is tempting to believe that in *Mein Leben* he wished, at least subconsciously, to hint at the Geyer paternity. He need not have described Carl Friedrich's late evenings at the theater, and certainly, had he wanted to, he could have expressed somewhat differently that clause which relates how on these nights "the estimable actor generally filled his [Carl Friedrich's] place in the bosom of the family." The phrase is suggestive enough in English, but the German way of turning it is to say *"im Schosse seiner Familie"* or "in the lap of his family." Since the word *"Schosse"* must in German do double duty for "lap" and "womb," it is difficult to imagine that the Wagner who was one day to make even his Kundry speak in puns was completely unaware of the implications of the idiom he chose to employ.[4]

By the end of Wagner's life rumors had spread about his dubious paternity,

---

[4] There are those who cite as evidence that Wagner was Carl Friedrich's son the strong resemblance between Richard and his older brother, Albert, born before Johanna and Geyer knew one another. But could not these traits in common have descended through Johanna, that is, through Prince Constantin or the Iglisch family? It is easy to fancy Richard's facial characteristics in Auguste Böhm's water color of Johanna as an old woman. But arguments based upon photographs, paintings, and sculpture are often inconclusive. The resemblance between Richard and Carl Friedrich's brother Adolf, has been frequently asserted, but one might as easily imagine the prototypal Wagnerian nose and chin in both the pastel and bust of Prince Constantin at Weimar. In matters of this sort investigators on both sides of the question usually quite sincerely find just what they are looking for. To take up the problem of the likenesses or lack of them between Wagner and his various sisters is pointless for this reason and also because, although Geyer was not resident in Leipzig between 1805 and 1809, no one knows when the intimacy between him and Johanna began. Did Geyer sire any of the other Wagner children? This question clouds any discussion of the talent shown by the sisters. Although Luise and Klara were born in 1805 and 1807 respectively, in their cases as well as Albert's the musical inclinations of Prince Constantin at least balance Carl Friedrich's sorties into the theater. Again, inquiries of this nature are at best specious. How often great talent springs from barren ground.

Geyer's letter to Johanna of January, 1814, in which he refers to his presence in Leipzig the year before in no way precludes his having performed at Teplitz during the summer of that same year. On June 6, 1813, he had written urging Johanna to persuade Carl Friedrich to make a summer excursion with her to Teplitz. There the Seconda troupe started performances on June 11. Of course, some scholars find it in no way astonishing that the husband remained behind in Leipzig while Johanna set out to visit her friendly erstwhile boarder.

It remains to be observed that possibly Johanna and Carl Friedrich were never legally married. Glasenapp's date for the ceremony is probably one of his convenient and pious inventions. According to Pank, as quoted by the editor of the Burrell Collection, no record of the union can be found in the Leipzig church register.

and an attempt was made at one time to fabricate a myth that Geyer at first disliked the young Richard. But the survival of a few of Geyer's letters makes nonsense of the idea.

A certain wildness of temperament, called "divine" by Geyer, earned the boy the nickname "Cossack" when only a few months old. The fierce troops sent by the Czar to stop Napoleon were terrorizing the German countryside; the nickname was most topical. With the naïve pride of a young father, Geyer thus referred to the infant in a Christmas letter of 1813: "Light a beautiful tree for the Cossack—I should like to rough it up with that lad on the sofa."

In August, 1814, Johanna married Geyer at Pötewitz bei Zeitz, and in September the Wagner family took up residence with him in Dresden, where he was occupied with the regular Seconda winter season. By 1816 the troupe no longer played at Leipzig during the summer. (It had been during these appearances that Geyer had lodged at Carl Friedrich's house.) In fact, Geyer's theatrical duties in Dresden being far from arduous, he found time to turn to painting as a means of supplementing the family income. Occasionally, he was called to other companies as a guest artist, and once, when at the Munich court theater, he was invited to do portraits of the Bavarian royal family.

Richard, fascinated by his father's studio, tried his hand at the brushes. But this gift he had not inherited; to him, rather, had come the manifold legacy of Geyer's intelligence, volubility, articulateness, acting talent, and literary ability.

Several of Geyer's plays were performed, and his last, *Der bethlehemitische Kindermord,* earned posthumous fame and Goethe's praise. Moreover, Geyer's tenor voice was serviceable enough for the Dresden conductor Carl Maria von Weber to draft him for duty in various Singspiele and operettas. He appeared in Méhul's *Joseph,* Weber's first operatic production in Dresden.

But music was the last of Geyer's many aptitudes looked for in Richard. When Weber, on meeting the nine-year-old Richard, politely asked him whether he wanted to be a musician, Frau Johanna informed the great man that, though the lad was mad about *Der Freischütz,* she had noticed no indication of musical talent. He was the only one of her children not to be given regular music lessons, perhaps because Johanna feared losing him to the stage toward which so many of the others were drifting. In any case, Richard's enthusiasm for the *Freischütz* overture eventually led him to finger it and other favorites for himself at the keyboard.

While attending school in the village of Possendorf, not many miles from Dresden, he had been hurriedly summoned home in September, 1821, to witness Geyer's final struggle with the tuberculosis that had brought him to his deathbed. Frau Johanna asked Richard to play the piano in the hope of diverting Geyer. After he had heard the boy's rendition of the folk song, *"Üb' immer Treu' und Redlichkeit,"* and also the *"Jungfernkranz"* from *Freischütz,* he remarked, "Is it possible he has musical talent?" On May 22, 1873, at a special performance of Geyer's *Der bethlehemitische Kindermord* in Bayreuth's baroque opera house, Wagner ordered the folk tune played by an orchestra between the two acts. The performance of play and song in the new Wagnerian capital was an affecting gesture of fondness for Geyer's memory.

Fathers—vague, unidentified, vanished, dying, and dead—form an important theme in Wagner's works. He based an early attempt at building a drama upon a fable according to which Odysseus perished at the hands of his son by Circe (Wagner confused her with Calypso in *Mein Leben*). The action of "Leubald," the gory tragedy Richard started in his fourteenth year, proceeds from the death of the hero's father, whose ghost he longs to join. In *Die Feen,* Wagner's first completed opera, Arindal laments his father's death in a section that the young composer enthusiastically described to his sister Rosalie: "My rich, royal garment is woven from my father's shroud." Siegmund in *The Valkyrie* describes how his lupine father disappeared, leaving behind only an empty wolfskin; that this wolf-father was really Wotan is disclosed by the orchestra in one of the most majestic moments of the *Ring*. Siegfried, lying in the shadow of a lime tree, speculates upon what his father looked like, for his suspicion that he is not the son of Mime, the dwarf, as he had been raised to believe, has been confirmed. Gamuret, Parsifal's father, is an obscure figure, a warrior who fell in combat; and Parsifal's mother strives to hide any knowledge of him from the boy. Old Titurel, father of King Amfortas, occupies a weird middle world between the quick and the dead, lying entombed, though living, in a vaulted niche in the temple of the Grail. And Tristan, recalling that he came into the world "out of father's need and mother's woe," hears again the plaintive folklike tune that sounded at their deaths: "Oh, solemn song of old lament that, fearfully moving through the night, once told the child of his father's death." Possendorf, Geyer's death, and the folk song are reflected in this noble passage.

3

Geyer left behind a family, mostly stepchildren, devoted to his memory. Upon the advice of Weber, who thought much of his tenor voice, Albert, the eldest son, had abandoned his medical studies to take up an operatic career. At Breslau his beautiful trill, fine technique, and powerful voice made him leading tenor. Richard's other brother, Julius, was apprenticed to Geyer's brother, a goldsmith in Eisleben; Rosalie, the eldest daughter, had made her stage debut in Geyer's play *Das Erntefest* (1818) and became a member of the Dresden court theater. Sister Luise, trained as an actress by Carl Friedrich Wagner's old love, Frau Hartwig (the first "Jungfrau" in Schiller's play), had procured an engagement at Breslau. Johanna's Dresden household included: Rosalie, the breadwinner; Klara, a gifted vocal student who was to make her operatic debut in 1824 as Angiolina in *Cenerentola;* and the small children, Ottilie, Richard, and Cäcilie.

Richard, too, had made an early stage debut. A *pièce d'occasion, Der Weinberg an der Elbe,* with special music by Weber, was concocted to welcome his Saxon Majesty back from captivity. Less than a fortnight before Waterloo, King Friedrich, seized by the Allies, had returned to a Saxony forced by the Congress of Vienna to forfeit large areas to Prussia. If the political situation was not amusing, perhaps the King was cheered by the sight of young Richard Wagner, sewn into tights with wings on his back and gracefully posed as an angel. His reward was an iced cake intended especially for him, he was assured, by the King.

Less reliable but more inventive was his performance at the age of four in Schiller's *William Tell,* with Geyer as Tell and sister Klara as Walther, the elder son. Because of the illness of the regular child actor, Richard was pressed into service as little William, the younger brother. As Tell bade farewell to his wife and started to depart with Klara, Richard, who, according to Schiller, was supposed to declare his desire to stay with mother Hedwig, blurted out instead, "Klara, you're going? I'll go, too." He exited to great applause. Scholars do not know whether he collected the cream puffs promised him during the make-up ritual. In any case, little Richard was not above filching sweets, and it was an ominous augury when he persuaded a confectioner to charge marshmallow paste to the account of his unknowing parents. He was five when he attended his first opera, Grétry's *Bluebeard,* after which he regaled the family by rendering *"Ha, die Falsche!"* accoutred with a paper helmet of his own manufacture.

For a while after his father's death, Richard lived with Geyer's younger bachelor brother, Karl Friedrich Wilhelm, the Eisleben goldsmith. The lovely old town in which Luther was born and died visited Wagner's dreams often in later years. Perhaps memories of it helped him create the Nuremberg of *Die Meistersinger.* More immediate, however, was the boy's enthusiasm for the fact that in Eisleben resided a famous tightrope walker, Kolter. Richard applied himself to learning the rudiments of this art, and a passion for acrobatics remained with him. As late as 1871, when he was almost sixty, he astounded a group gathered in his drawing room by standing on his head. Karl Friedrich Wilhelm's sudden decision to marry ended the boy's residence at Eisleben after about a year, and for several days in 1822 he stayed at the Leipzig home of Adolf and Friederike Wagner, brother and sister of his long-dead legal father.

He then returned to his mother in Dresden. She was augmenting the family revenue by letting spare rooms, and the famous composer Louis Spohr was for a while her tenant.

At the end of 1822 Richard was enrolled as Wilhelm Richard Geyer in the Dresden Kreuz School. He took some kind of piano instruction from Herr Humann, a Latin tutor, but spent his time playing theater overtures by ear and could not manage a scale correctly. Studies could not compete with the excitement in a home frequented by actors and musicians. The stage and its magic filled his thoughts, and he started a chivalric drama for performance in his own puppet theater. To be near props, scenery, and costumes lifted him into a feverish world of imagination. From the stair window he spied mocking devils, who ceaselessly changed shapes. Ghostly visions troubled his sleep; the furniture in his room seemed to come to life, and he would shriek aloud during the night.

Living in the fantastic world of the *Freischütz,* the boy watched with awe as Weber on his way to the theater passed the Geyer house and, as has been noted, occasionally stopped in to chat with Frau Johanna.

King Friedrich, after his return to Dresden, had been persuaded to found a German opera to parallel the illustrious Italian troupe of his court. In a sense, the tradition of Italian opera in Saxony reached back to the very birth of that art form in Tuscany. In the early seventeenth century, Heinrich Schütz, court musician of Johann Georg I of Saxony, procured the music of Peri's *Dafne,* the very first *dramma per musica* (Florence, 1597?). But, unable to adjust it to the German translation of Rinuccini's famous text (made by no less a poet than the imperial laureate, Martin Opitz), Schütz wrote new music, the performance taking place at the castle of Hartenfels in Torgau (1627). The history of Italian opera in the capital of Dresden extended from the work of Bontempi (*Il Paride,* 1662), through the golden age of the eighteenth century associated with the glorious names of Porpora, Hasse, and Faustina Bordoni, right down to the Italian company of King Friedrich directed by that estimable Perugian, Francesco Morlacchi. Despite the court's preference for fashionable Italian opera and notwithstanding Friedrich's distaste for the composer who had set lyrics of the "revolutionary" poet Körner, Weber had been called to the task of forming the new German company at the end of 1816. The little boy in the Geyer house was one day to develop this German national opera to its mightiest point and, in a touching act of reverence for his hero, was to be instrumental in bringing back to Dresden Weber's remains from their first resting place in England.

The spring of 1821, which saw the death of Napoleon, had also witnessed the birth of a fervent German nationalism that followed the première in Schinkel's new Berlin theater of Weber's *Freischütz* on June 18, 1821, the sixth anniversary of Waterloo and a good omen to Weber. *Freischütz,* the great product of his work in Dresden, was (more than Mozart's *The Magic Flute*) the foundation of the German romantic *opera seria.* The next stone in the edifice was his *Euryanthe.* On these works of Weber rested the framework of the early Wagnerian opera: *Die Feen, The Flying Dutchman, Tannhäuser,* and especially *Lohengrin.* That romantic German mood and sound of the young Wagner was first heard in the Bohemian forests of *Freischütz* and the Nivernais landscape of *Euryanthe.*

Dresden first heard *Freischütz* early in 1822, and, despite the coolness of the court, the enthusiasm of the public for the new opera knew no bounds. And upon none did its romantic spell eventually work to greater advantage than upon the nine-year-old Richard Geyer.

II

Youth and Apprenticeship

I

In the fall of 1826 Richard at thirteen remained behind in Dresden, the other children accompanying Johanna to Prague, where Rosalie had a promising engagement. The Geyer home in Dresden was broken up, and Richard boarded at the home of the Böhmes, the family of school chums. During the winter Johanna came to Dresden and took him back to Prague for a brief holiday. Sister Ottilie had made friends with Jenny and Auguste, daughters of wealthy Count Pachta, once Weber's patron and Geyer's friend. Richard's susceptibility to feminine charm, already awakened in the Böhme household, was heightened by these handsome girls.

Prague's Catholic mystery enchanted the youth raised in the more sober towns of Lutheran Saxony.[1] And in Prague he made the literary acquaintance of E. T. A. Hoffmann, whose eerie tales were much to his taste. Hoffmann's influence had seemed foreordained. Within hours of Richard's birth this odd and multifaceted genius had entered Leipzig to assume the duties of *Kapellmeister* in the New Theater situated not many steps from the Red and White Lion, in which house the boy had been born. Subsequently Hoffmann became a friend of Carl Friedrich Wagner, of his brother Adolf, and of Geyer.

The attraction of Bohemia's capital was enormous, and the next spring (1827) Richard and his friend Rudolf Böhme set out from Dresden on a walking tour to Prague. Richard begged funds as more retiring Rudolf hid in a ditch. They caroused, drank the local wines, and slept on straw. Sunburned and attired in an outrageous traveling outfit of blue and bright

---

[1] Since Augustus the Strong's conversion to gain the Polish crown (1697) a Catholic court in Dresden had ruled Protestant Saxony. Geyer kept his faith despite promptings from the palace that court servants embrace the established religion.

red,[2] Richard was mortified to meet the Pachta girls in the outskirts of Prague as they passed in their splendid coach. He hastened to his mother's house and for two days applied poultices of parsley to his scorched face. This beauty treatment over, he was ready for the Pachtas and Prague society.

Reluctantly he returned to Dresden and the Kreuz School, where only Greek mythology and Greek history had held his interest. The ancient language fascinated him, but he did not have patience enough to master its grammar.

By the time of *Mein Leben* he seemed to have incorrectly recalled the limited extent of his Greek. Cosima, first his mistress and later his second wife, also posed as an accomplished student of the classics. Although Richard's genius made their home a rendezvous of some of Europe's greatest minds, in such company he was at times inwardly defensive. When embarrassed by his sketchy education, he frequently compensated for ignorance with bluster and intellectual hocus-pocus. Yet, so magnetic was his personality and so involved his expression, that many who should have protested accepted meekly his most idiotic pronouncements. His painfully sophomoric "Open Letter to Friedrich Nietzsche" of 1872 makes reference to his tutelage under Sillig, a Kreuz School teacher who encouraged his philological and literary interests and also stimulated him to try his hand at a dramatic poem inspired by the ancients. But the letter reveals how little Greek he ever learned.[3] Throughout his life he was a wretched linguist.

As a youngster Richard enjoyed a reputation as a rhymester. His earliest verse had caused much mocking merriment in the Geyer household. Later, when a schoolmate died, it was Richard's eulogy—stripped by Sillig of youthful extravagances and some plagiarism from Addison—that appeared as a tribute to the lad's memory.

At this first success pious Johanna had folded her hands in thanks. Poetry was obviously Richard's calling, and at least one of her brood besides Julius was to be saved from the stage. Indeed, the devotion between Johanna and Richard makes it difficult to grasp her willingness to leave the young adolescent unsupervised in Dresden while she went off to Prague. Perhaps

[2] Over three decades later his color sense was still shocking. In Paris he appeared at an audition of *Tannhäuser* wearing a blue jacket with red braid and completed this costume with a yellow cap trimmed with green fringe. But this attire would only do for his rendition of the first part of the opera. He vanished before the startled eyes of the impresario Carvalho to reappear at the piano in a yellow coat with blue braid and a red cap with yellow edging.

[3] The "Open Letter" does provide his preposterous etymological derivation of the Rhine Daughters' *"Weia! Waga!"*

Geyer's "Cossack" was already impossible to manage, and Johanna decided to leave matters in the hands of that Providence in which she had so much trust.

Richard, giddy with dreams of coming literary celebrity, neglected the Kreuz School. In fact, he quit the Böhme home to rent a cramped attic, where, alone and sustained by notoriously weak Saxon coffee, he turned his attention to the composition of a giant tragedy, "Leubald."

But Dresden bored him. During a summer excursion in 1827 he had visited Leipzig, the bustling city of his birth, and there renewed acquaintance with his uncle Adolf, who not only received him cordially but presented him with a part of Carl Friedrich's library.

What attracted Richard most in Leipzig was its university students, arrogantly strutting in the outfits and insignia of their various clubs. The theatrical wardrobe of his sisters had provoked and stimulated him even as a child. He was never to be free from the allure of costume and outlandish clothing. To be part of a Leipzig fraternity and parade its colors became an immediate goal.

To the Kreuz School authorities he presented a trumped-up excuse to the effect that his family had called him to Leipzig, and he shook the now-provincial dust of Dresden from his heels. True, his mother had left Prague and resettled in Leipzig, where Luise had accepted an engagement at the theater. Nonetheless, at Christmas, 1827, Johanna was surprised to find the "Cossack" at her door with news that he had burned his Dresden bridges. But, anxious about his unrestrained life, she lovingly welcomed him.

It was about this time that he reclaimed the name of Wagner. In addition to the reason already suggested, the Semitic associations of "Geyer," perhaps Adolf Wagner's influence may be seen in this move. Whatever inspired the change, it certainly could not have been particularly successful in Dresden, where Richard had always been known as Geyer. But Leipzig was to be the scene of new friendships, new experiences, and new literary triumphs with "Leubald." And in this city Adolf Wagner, whom he was doubtlessly pleased to call "Uncle," enjoyed a kind of celebrity—albeit modest—as a man of letters, respected for the seriousness of his scholarship, criticism, and translations, if not for the graciousness of his style. Adolf's obtuse and needlessly complicated sentences may well have formed the baleful model that to this day often sends even German-born readers in search of foreign translations of his nephew's infamous prose. An entry in E. T. A. Hoffmann's journal ironically refers to Adolf's vast knowledge of languages and his maladroitness in using them.

But in the eyes of young Richard the Wagners of Leipzig were associated with a literary reputation of which he might be proud. Possibly Adolf, who had never approved of Geyer, urged the boy to reaffirm his legal name. The presentation to Richard of Carl Friedrich's books was a strong patrimonial gesture. In June of 1826 Weber had died in London. Richard found in Adolf a new idol, whose influence was the more decisive because it reached him while he was living unchecked by any control. It may well have been as Richard Wagner that he appeared at Johanna Geyer's door at the end of 1827.

2

Early in 1828 he entered Leipzig's St. Nicholas' School. It was a jolt when a poor showing on the entrance examination caused him to be placed in a class lower than the one he had quit in Dresden. Considering his haphazard attendance, the demotion should not have been surprising. But the Wagnerian ego, already formidable and probably nurtured by Johanna, had been injured; his uniqueness remained unrecognized; he found no new Professor Sillig. His St. Nicholas career was over as soon as it started. In his maturity he enjoyed belaboring what he held to be the pedantry and incompetence of his Leipzig teachers. Yet, considering his appalling record of absence, it is hard to believe that he gave them much opportunity to do him injury.

He indulged in the usual dissipations of adolescence but devoted many hours to visits and walks with Uncle Adolf, who could speak of literature, philology, and philosophy and also of the men who touched his life—Schiller, Goethe, Fichte, Tieck, Jean Paul, and August Apel, the *Freischütz* poet [4] whose son was to become Richard's friend.

And all the while the secret labor on "Leubald" continued. It progressed best when Frau Johanna was ill in bed. Then Richard would cut classes and lock himself in his room to work. Only in Cäcilie [5] did he confide; she was permitted to hear some of the play's most demoniacal passages, histrionically declaimed by the poet.

[4] Friedrich Kind worked Apel's material into a libretto for Weber.

[5] Although in *Mein Leben* Wagner twice mentions Ottilie in this role, it is possible that after more than three decades he confused the sisters and really meant Cäcilie. Henry T. Finck cites an article by her son, Ferdinand Avenarius, that appeared in the *Allgemeine Zeitung* of Munich, in which are discussed particulars of "Leubald" obtained from her. According to these remembrances, it was she who was witness to Richard's secret work on the tragedy. It is true that Richard found both Ottilie and Cäcilie with Johanna when he arrived in Leipzig at Christmas, 1827. However, Ottilie moved in with her sister Luise after the latter's marriage to Friedrich Brockhaus during the following year. It would appear that Cäcilie was that "only confidante" left in Johanna's house to whom Richard recited his drama.

"Leubald" was a heady combination of bits and pieces mainly from Shakespeare's *Hamlet, King Lear, Macbeth,* and *Richard III.* Some elements of Harry Hotspur also entered, as did resemblances to Goethe's *Götz von Berlichingen* and Kleist's *Familie Schroffenstein.* Like Hamlet, Leubald sought vengeance for the murder of his father, interestingly named Siegmar. Less dilatory than the Dane, Leubald killed the enemy's entire family save one, a daughter whom Richard called Adelaïde after Beethoven's song. Leubald then fell in love with a maiden who proved to be this very girl. Pursued by battalions of ghosts, among them the shades of his victims, he went mad, stabbed Adelaïde, and expired transfigured over her bleeding body as she caressed him with her last strength.

Thus, embryonic elements of the mature Wagner can be perceived in his first literary works, while his early musical attempts might have been made by any modestly talented student. His literary and theatrical style was already coming dimly into focus before he even felt a need to compose. Some of the verse of "Leubald" could be slipped into a reading of *Tristan* with not too many people being the wiser; certainly Astolf's apostrophe to Leubald has the cadence of Kurvenal and Mark.

Richard sent the finished manuscript of "Leubald" as an offering to his belletristic colleague, Uncle Adolf. Along with it went a message indicating that a burgeoning literary career was not to be hindered by such limiting considerations as attendance at school; Adolf was expected to explain this to Johanna. Manuscript, message, and situation—all horrified Adolf and the family. In "Leubald" was seen the fruit of ill-advised pursuits encouraged in an immature boy.

His grand strategy to impress the family thus failed. But in theater and concert hall he was absorbing experiences that gradually revealed to him where "Leubald" had miscarried and why it was as yet incomplete.

3

Like Dresden, the city of Leipzig offered opportunities to see a repertory of operas and plays. The line between the two was not always sharp. Music and song often had a significant part in the drama; Weber, for example, contributed scores to Schiller's *Turandot* and Wolff's *Preciosa,* among others, and the Singspiel, a form between play and opera, had a worthy history in Leipzig.

In 1829 its theater was reorganized as a royal establishment. The Wagners were well represented. Although Luise had quit the stage in 1828 to marry the wealthy Leipzig publisher Friedrich Brockhaus, Rosalie returned to her home town to join the new company in its opening Shakespearean production. In some roles she was preferred even to the reigning actress-singer of Germany, Wilhelmine Schröder-Devrient. In Dresden, Rosalie's musical background had permitted her to play Preciosa under Weber's baton. Leipzig applauded her as the mute in Auber's *Masaniello* (*La Muette de Portici*), a work which deeply impressed Richard as did the new romantic operas of Marschner. Through Rosalie he attended many performances at the theater.

His most overpowering theatrical experience in Leipzig was the appearance of Schröder-Devrient as Leonore in Beethoven's *Fidelio* during 1829. This highly dramatic singing actress, who was to play a significant role in Wagner's career, had a remarkable background. Her mother had been the "Sarah Siddons of Germany," the actress Antoinette Sophie Bürger; her father, the baritone Friedrich Schröder, renowned for his Don Giovanni, had been the first to perform this part in German. Wilhelmine combined the talents of her parents. She acted in Shakespeare and Schiller at Vienna's Hofburg Theater and, in addition, developed a singing voice flexible enough to realize both such lyric parts as Pamina and Agathe (she sang the latter *Freischütz* heroine under Weber's direction) and also the heavier and more dramatic Leonore. Huddled in a cloak that hid all but his gleaming eyes, Beethoven had observed her performance at the 1822 Vienna revival of *Fidelio*. She won from him a smile, an affectionate pat, and (extraordinary) his unkept promise to create a role especially for her. Schröder-Devrient's embodiment of the noble wife established *Fidelio* on the German stage and always gained encomiums. Later, when her voice began to fail (she, like Albert and Klara Wagner, had studied with the Dresden chorus master Mieksch, and all of them had been encouraged to sing too much while too young), she could still hold an audience by the authority of her acting. Early training in ballet had given her remarkable assurance and grace of movement.

She was twenty-four in 1829, and Richard experienced her art in its prime. Overwhelmed, he dashed from the theater to pen her a note of adulation. Some years later he was moved to hear her recite this ebullient message by heart. She was to him at the beginning of his career what Schnorr von Carolsfeld was later to be, a model of the gifted, intelligent, and earnest actor-singer. Her Germanic beauty, ample but shapely figure, and Hoffmannesque mastery of the passionate (Londoners dubbed her the "Queen of Tears") made an unforgettable impression on Richard. He wished to create something worthy of her.

In the field of instrumental music Dresden was eclipsed by Leipzig with its Gewandhaus concerts, whose establishment in a private house as *"Das grosse Concert"* dated from the time of Johann Sebastian Bach. Mendelssohn's brilliant stewardship of the orchestra was still a few years in the future, but, under the direction of Pohlenz and his blue baton, Richard heard much music both new to him and important for his development. Memorable for him were performances of Mozart's *Requiem* and Beethoven's Seventh Symphony. In Richard's pantheon Beethoven now shared the high seat of Shakespeare. In *Mein Leben* he wrote, "In ecstatic dreams I met both, saw and spoke to them, and upon awakening found myself in tears."

As Goethe's *Egmont* had been transfigured by Beethoven's incidental music, so "Leubald"—Richard now thought—needed only the addition of a similar score to achieve its own perfection. Perhaps he envisioned Schröder-Devrient as Adelaïde. Beethoven had died in Vienna only recently. Did mourning Richard feel the mantle of greatness slipping over his modest frame as he set himself the task of becoming such a composer? That he had no musical training did not dishearten him. In his sixteenth year he willed that he compose in order to realize his dramatic genius fully. From these somewhat droll circumstances the great poet-musician was born.

4

His natural endowment for music was, of course, enormous; but how was he to tap these resources and give them shape? He played the piano badly, a most meager background for a composer wishing to project the manifold passions of "Leubald." Presciently he desired to give an individual musical color to each of his various ghosts so as to differentiate their characters!

He knew that he needed help but dared not tell Johanna and his sisters in which direction his ambition now inclined. He had been ridiculed as a dramatic poet; how would his hopes as a musician be received?

And so for the first time, and certainly not for the last, Richard Wagner went into debt for the sake of his art.

From the circulating library of Friedrich Wieck he borrowed the *Method of General-Bass,* a musical text by Johann Bernhard Logier. Wieck, a piano pedagogue for a while interested in Logier and his revolutionary system of piano instruction, perhaps recommended the latter's harmony book. Richard was unable to pay the rental. Months went by. Finally Wieck had to press for payment, and Frau Geyer learned of the accumulated fees. Thus to Wieck's distinctions—he was the teacher of his daughter, one day to be Clara Schumann, of Schumann himself, and also of Hans von Bülow—must be added that of being possibly the first in the long line of Wagnerian creditors. It might be added that he fared better than most of his followers; Johanna evidently paid what was due.

Now the secret was out; the "Cossack" had turned to music. Unable to make sufficient progress with the Logier book by himself, he had, in addition to the Wieck affair, run up a bill for secret harmony lessons with Christian Gottlieb Müller, a theater violinist. Müller also conducted the Leipzig Euterpe Society, a private group of amateur and professional musicians who gave concerts.

But most of what Richard learned about music at this time he acquired by himself. As soon as a few technical difficulties, such as the transposition of clefs, were resolved, he could read scores as easily as prose and thus began to initiate himself into the repertory and craft of the masters. He studied *Don Giovanni,* which he had formerly disparaged because of its Italian text. From the days when the Geyer home was visited by Sassaroli, castrato of Dresden's Italian court opera, Richard loathed the sound of this language. Perhaps because Hoffmann used *Don Giovanni* as the basis of one of his most original tales, in itself an exposition of Mozart's genius, Richard turned again to this opera and perceived its mastery.

During the summer of 1829, profiting by his family's absence, he began to compose a sonata, a quartet, a song, and, most important, a score, suggested by Beethoven's Sixth Symphony, to his own pastoral play inspired by Goethe's *Laune des Verliebten.* Of this ambitious schedule of works, nothing has survived.

In the drama he created text and music simultaneously. Significantly, he commented in *Mein Leben,* "While I wrote the score on one page, I had as yet not even considered a text for the following." Is it too much to assume that as the music proceeded it drew forth the words? However primitive this piece, Wagner's method as an opera composer was possibly already present as he wrote. Music always shaped his words, although he enjoyed pretending that the poet in him was master. For example, months before he started his libretto of *Tristan,* the music was already thrusting itself upon his attention. And while at work on *Tannhäuser* he wrote to the Berlin critic Karl Gaillard, "Before starting to write a verse or even to outline a scene, I must first feel intoxicated by the musical aroma *(Duft)* of my subject, all the tones, all the characteristic motives are in my head." Though they in turn helped crystallize his musical ideas, the verses must be considered only as an extension of a musical inspiration. In 1856 he wrote to Liszt, "Curiously enough, it is only during composition that the real essence of my poem is revealed to me. Everywhere I discover secrets which had been previously hidden from me."

An experimenting and largely self-instructed young composer, Richard had problems akin to those of Robert Schumann, whose brief life was to be intertwined with his. After attempts at literary expression and desultorily pursued studies in law, Schumann decided late in adolescence that music was to be his profession. But, unlike Wagner, he had shown remarkable musical gifts very early. Unfortunately, plans to study with Weber fell through, and his attempts at composition remained for a time unguided. He set his own poems to music, Jean Paul and Johann Sebastian Bach being to him what Hoffmann and Beethoven were to Richard. In 1830, when he was twenty, Schumann left Heidelberg for Leipzig to take up piano studies with Wagner's first creditor, Friedrich Wieck, but permanently lamed his right hand by using a contrivance he invented to achieve greater finger dexterity. Only then did he turn seriously to composition. Though he, too, seeking to augment a piecemeal knowledge of theory, sought instruction from Richard's teacher, Herr Müller, and studied counterpoint with Heinrich Dorn (like Mendelssohn, a student of Zelter), Schumann, like Wagner, had irregular training and learned in his own way.

The appalled Wagner-Geyer clan soon learned that Richard had been cutting classes for half a year. The family had changed. Luise was now Frau Brockhaus; Klara had wed Heinrich Wolfram, a singer. Brockhaus was consulted as to what to do with Richard. The family, reconciled to his musical career, insisted that at least he learn to play an instrument so as to assure himself of a living. This was solid middle-class thinking. Generous Brockhaus suggested that he study with Hummel, one of the most dazzling pianists of the day, once a protégé of Mozart and, like Beethoven, a pupil of the legendary Albrechtsberger. Was not little Clara Wieck making a name for herself by her performances of Mozart and Hummel concertos?

Conscious of his digital limitations, Richard rejected the idea. At an early age he had "conceived a great abhorrence of all rapid passages." Composition and conducting were his goals. But he did agree to take lessons from Robert Sipp, a violinist in the Gewandhaus orchestra. In later years Wagner mused upon the "unutterable torture" he must have visited upon his family by practicing. The indefatigable Mrs. Burrell sought out Sipp, still alive in 1889. He remarked that Wagner "caught on quickly but was lazy and unwilling to practice. He was my very worst pupil." This was all probably true and was Sipp's favorite joke about his "once small and later great pupil." In 1876 Wagner invited the old fellow to attend the first Bayreuth festival.

5

Richard was fortunate in his sympathetic brothers-in-law. During a visit to Magdeburg in the summer of 1829 Klara's husband, Heinrich Wolfram, gave him a manuscript copy of Beethoven's late E-flat Quartet. Musicians of the time prevalently thought of a quartet as a piece for solo violin with trio accompaniment. To comprehend the unity of a late Beethoven quartet, to have its parts assembled, and to present a copy of the resulting score to the young man speak highly for Wolfram's musicianship and also for his opinion of Richard's.

The works of Beethoven's final period were looked upon by most as the lamentable result of deafness. In fact, what first drew Richard to the Ninth Symphony was the popular and rather Hoffmannesque view of it as a vast, fantastic, and unfathomable aberration of a deaf and perhaps mad genius— a judgment reinforced by the chaotic performances it generally received. The open fifths of its first phrases took Richard back to childhood, when the tuning of an orchestra or the mere sounding of a fifth had appeared to him as a spirit message, and ghosts seemed conjured by the magic interval. From such early associations and from the spectral qualities he found in the first measures of the Ninth was to develop the mysterious theme of the Flying Dutchman, that most Hoffmannesque of his characters.

He not only copied the score of the symphony but also reduced it to a piano version, which he twice offered to the house of Schott, the Mainz music publishers. The arrangement was not issued, for there was insufficient interest in the supposed eccentric work. But Schott kept the manuscript, in payment for which Richard received some Beethoven scores he requested. In 1872 Betty Schott was instrumental in having the manuscript returned to Wagner, and he rewarded her kindness by the dedication of a well-meant but rather insipid *Albumblatt* for piano, composed in 1875 after his exhausting labors on the *Ring*. The creditability of Richard's transcription of the symphony demonstrates how quickly the seventeen-year-old had gained considerable technical knowledge.

New harmony lessons from the pedantic Müller, now no longer an unpaid and *sub rosa* tutor, proved as valueless as Richard's promises to apply himself to academic studies. His tremendous natural talent, suddenly awakened and inspired, needed more than pedestrian guidance. Richard floundered, and his frustrations were to lead to some excessive adolescent indiscretions. One morning he awoke at home to find himself possessed of the fragments of a red curtain, a painful reminder that the preceding night he had joined a frenetic crowd of students in an attack upon two houses of prostitution. His early opera, *Das Liebesverbot,* was to open with just such a scene of tumult and destruction.

In June of 1830 he had entered St. Thomas' School; he dared not show his face at St. Nicholas', whose teachers would certainly never have co-operated with his plan to enter Leipzig University. Some private tuition and a few months at St. Thomas' would, so the long-tried family hoped, qualify him for higher studies. But to Richard the university had but one meaning —fraternity life.

Impatient, he helped organize a club at St. Thomas' over whose initial meeting he held sway fantastically gotten up in white leather breeches and jack boots. To regular school work he paid scant attention, although he did not completely neglect his music.

Richard was not altogether dependent upon his mother. Brockhaus was bringing out a series of history books and gave Richard an opportunity to earn money by proofreading the volumes on the Middle Ages and the French Revolution. From this work he gained a deeper appreciation of history and some realization of how vague his education was. He became a catholic and voracious reader.

The most exciting events of his days at St. Thomas' were the disorders generated in Saxony by the July Revolution in France. There were strong ties between the two nations; the fecund Saxon Princess Maria Josepha, daughter-in-law of Louis XV, had given three kings to the French. The last, obstinate Charles X, had been forced to abdicate. By August, 1830, Louis Philippe, son of a regicide, was seated upon the throne, which he pretended to reupholster as a bourgeois *fauteuil;* the lilies of France vanished from the royal coach. It appeared that the accession of this Prince of the Revolution, now "Citizen King," was a blow at absolutism. The rioters in Saxony hoped for a similar victory. Their disturbances were a stage on the journey of this reactionary kingdom toward constitutionalism.

In Leipzig, the traditional hostility between police and students was annulled, the authorities calling upon student organizations to come to the protection of private property menaced by an uneasy mob. The young men answered the call. Inns and taverns apparently required an extraordinary number of protectors. Brockhaus' printing presses were safeguarded by the cream of the university corps, eagerly responding to the lavish hospitality of the publisher, whose ubiquitous young brother-in-law, delirious with the drama of a world turned topsy-turvy, snatched at this opportunity of ingratiating himself with the town's most renowned young bloods.

Masaniello was playing in the streets; young Richard's proofreading on the French Revolution had come to life. In the wonderful confusion of his mind he saw Brockhaus as a Saxon incarnation of Lafayette, the almost mythical French general who but recently had publicly embraced the tricolor-draped Louis Philippe at Paris' Hôtel de Ville. When Richard heard of the elevation of liberal Prince Friedrich to be coregent of Saxony with King Anton, he composed an overture which tonally progressed from the somber colors of oppression to an exultant climax representing political liberty. When in later Dresden days he was summoned before this cultured and generous prince, then Friedrich August II, his mind wandered back to the youthful piece based on the motto of *Friedrich und Freiheit.*

At the end of 1830, revolution came to Warsaw, challenging the authority of "iron" Czar Nicholas I, who a year earlier had seated himself on

Poland's throne. Since the days when Augustus the Strong of Saxony and his son had worn the elective Polish crown (the latter's coronation at Cracow a century earlier, in 1734, had been celebrated in Leipzig with a festive cantata hastily concocted by Bach), Saxony and Poland, even though no longer united by a common obedience, were yet linked by emotional ties. As Russia re-established control over the rebellious land, Polish troops and exiles streamed into Saxon cities.

In Germany, the insurgent cause elicited such sympathetic response as Platen's *Polenlieder*. Among Leipzig students, however, a prevailing indifference to serious matters baffled Richard, whose heart beat fast when he espied in the Gewandhaus foyer the expatriate revolutionary leader Count Tyszkiewicz, a heroic figure in laced coat and red velvet cap.

6

At this time, in addition to his political composition, Richard wrote three works that also have not survived—an Overture in C Major, an overture to Schiller's *Braut von Messina,* and a piano Sonata in B-flat Major for four hands, which he orchestrated. An overture in the latter key is often cited as his first work performed in public; actually, it was the second.

A year before, at sixteen, Richard had come under the spell of a gaunt character named Flachs who haunted the city's concerts. Blind to the fact that he was befriending an object of general derision, Richard mistook Flachs's strangeness and eccentricity for depth of soul and mystery. The boy believed that in him *"Kapellmeister* Kreisler" had stepped from the pages of Hoffmann. Flachs arranged one of Richard's airs for band, and it was performed at a garden concert at Kintschy's Swiss Chalet, a popular place of refreshment. Thus did Wagner first step before the public.

Flachs had money; a woman seeking it pretended to fall in love with him. Her first device was to close Flachs's house to her rival, who was shocked when he grasped the situation. The bizarre friendship was over.

There seemed to be a turning point when Heinrich Dorn showed interest in his work. Dorn was the young conductor of the Leipzig theater whom Schumann later described as "the man who first gave a hand to me as I climbed upward." By the time of *Mein Leben,* when Wagner and Dorn were enemies, Wagner was suspicious of the latter's motive in accepting the B-flat Major Overture for public performance. But there can be no doubt that a combination of Rosalie's promptings and Dorn's concern for youthful talent, and not his desire for fun at a neophyte's expense, led to the disaster at the benefit concert for the poor during Christmas of 1830.

The overture was the strange result of Richard's study of Beethoven's

Ninth Symphony and the mystic messages he received from it. Just as he had wished to characterize musically the individual ghosts in "Leubald," so now he desired readers and performers of his overture to be made aware of the occult differences he projected into the various choirs of the orchestra. Toward this end he planned to note each instrumental group in its own color of ink—brass and tympani in black, strings in red, winds in green. A want of green ink almost wrecked the esoteric plan, but nonetheless at rehearsal there was no lack of astonishment as the musicians contemplated the work. After a proclamation by the black brass, a red allegro theme for strings fell into a four-measure phrase, followed by a fifth measure on the second beat of which a boom sounded from the black world of the kettledrum. This unusual five-measure unit was heard quite a few times before the green world of the winds communicated its own mystic message. At the performance the audience began to reckon the inevitable return of the boom, and at each stroke the snickers grew louder, swelling to outbursts of mirth. Richard cowered in his seat; it was a nightmare. The theater echoed to guffaws until the piece, for which Richard had scorned to write the usual formal close, suddenly stopped. Now there was neither laughter nor hisses nor applause. An incredible amazedness, if not stupefaction, reduced all to silence. In misery Richard stole from the theater. Fortunately, the overture had been billed anonymously; but he was long to remember the quizzical look on the face of the doorman, to whom he had revealed himself as the composer in order to gain free admittance.

After this catastrophe his interest in composition lagged. "Leubald" was forgotten. He sketched some music to Goethe's *Faust,* but now his main purpose was to don the uniform of a university club.

7

Realizing that a recommendation from St. Thomas' was as unlikely as one from St. Nicholas' and that he could never qualify for regular matriculation at the university, Richard decided upon an adjunct relationship with the institution which would accord the only privilege he really coveted, that of joining a fraternity. At the end of February, 1831, he enrolled in Leipzig University as a music student (*studiosus musicae*), for which the exacting requirement was the payment of fees, and then rushed to request admission into the popular Saxonia Club. The gates of heaven opened; he appeared all over Leipzig in Saxonia colors, paraded in the form of a fantastic cap emblazoned with silver.

The early part of *Mein Leben* is the best. In dealing with the days before he took to polemics, Wagner found little need to juggle facts as he remembered them, and his recollections of his youth are recounted with what is for him a startling lightness of touch and vivacity. He laughs at the foolish and pretentious boy he was, and nowhere is he more amusing than in those paragraphs touching upon his rash and almost insane behavior as a Saxonia member. Completely inexperienced as a swordsman, he challenged some of the university's most dashing bloods. Before the appointed contests gracious Providence, perhaps looking forward to the *Ring,* removed these opponents from his path.

A feature of the German educational system was the passage of the student from the strict, even harsh, discipline of the Gymnasium to the intellectual and social freedom of the university. Richard had instead effected a transition from self-indulgence to profligacy. He drank heavily and gained a taste for gambling. His case was not unique but forms a strong contrast with that of Schumann, who in 1828 had matriculated as *studiosus juris* at Leipzig University, where he found club life coarse and shallow.

From acquaintances Richard seemed to derive little intellectual stimulation, although a certain Schröter introduced him to the works of Heine. He lamented that he was incapable of forming close friendships, an inability deriving from his habit of talking at, rather than to, people and from his intolerance of views contrary to his own. Even before his university days, fellow students had avoided his cutting remarks, irritability, and impetuosity. Moreover, his extremely thick Saxon accent (Weingartner, who met him some months before his death, was fascinated to discover that the famous master still spoke the unvarnished dialect of his birthplace) and obstreperous presentation of his thoughts stupefied listeners. When finished with a tirade he often wondered why its sequel was silence. Endorsement of his ideas was Richard's concept of conversation. This attitude was suffered when he became eminent, but fellow students were hardly likely to tolerate such presumption.

Wagner and Schumann did not know one another during these Leipzig days. However, an anecdote related by Hanslick concerning a later time tells of Schumann's complaint that Wagner talked incessantly and of Wagner's grumbling that Schumann was quite impossible, sitting as if struck dumb and letting him hold forth. One may imagine gentle Robert's difficulties in interjecting a word and also his reluctance to arouse the Wagnerian temper by opposition. In 1848 Wagner and Liszt so upset Schumann in his own home (it was during a discussion of the relative merits of Mendelssohn and Meyerbeer) that he lost control and fled to his bedroom.

The family, especially Rosalie, though unaware of the full extent of Richard's dissipations, held him in contempt as a wastrel. Increasing debts drove him to the extremity of gambling with his mother's monthly pension, which he had collected for her. All but one thaler was lost. Frightened, he wagered his future on the next play and miraculously won, his luck continuing until not only the sum of the pension was regained but enough to liquidate his other obligations.

The next morning he confessed to ever-forgiving Johanna, who, never having lost faith in Geyer's conviction that something might be made of the "Cossack," had been deeply troubled to observe him drifting. She had sought help from Christian Theodor Weinlig, one of Germany's most learned contrapuntalists and since 1823 cantor of St. Thomas', upon Weber's recommendation. Johanna interested him in Richard, who, however, rebelled at the exercises in strict harmony scheduled at the beginning of the course. Weinlig was ill and, in no mood to tolerate a novice's perversity, gave him up. This was the period of Richard's drinking and gambling. The shock he experienced in almost injuring the mother he dearly loved restored his equilibrium. Richard sought Weinlig's forgiveness. Perhaps Johanna again appealed; one morning the summons came to start studies again. Parsifal was to blame himself for dalliance with the Flower Maidens and a foolishness that made him unmindful of mother and mission: "Dolt and coward, I rushed on to wild, boyish escapades."

8

Weinlig was a disciple of Marpurg, and the heart of his teaching was the fugue. Though doubting that Richard would ever write fugues or canons professionally, he held study of their complexities indispensable for achieving independence in any style of composition. Interestingly, what pleased Mendelssohn most in *Tannhäuser* was the canonical treatment of the second-act duet, *"Gepriesen sei die Stunde."*

Weinlig had been a student of Abbate Mattei, himself a favorite pupil of illustrious Padre Martini. Mattei was also the master of Rossini, Donizetti, and Morlacchi, who was later Weber's rival at Dresden. Grounded in this fertile Bolognese tradition, doubtlessly passed on to Richard, the Saxon Weinlig, who had assumed a post held less than seventy-five years before by Bach, must also have known something of his music.

How much did Richard learn of Leipzig's almost lost Bach heritage? His work with Weinlig started less than three years after the revival in Berlin of the *St. Matthew Passion* under the baton of twenty-year-old Mendelssohn. Interest in old Bach's forgotten music was being pursued in the highest intellectual circles. Hegel had become an admirer of Bach, whom he discussed in his lectures on aesthetics. In the spring of 1830, Mendelssohn, while visiting Goethe, played for him the *Inventions* and much of the *Well-Tempered Clavier*. This last work had been the Bible of

Beethoven, who around the turn of the century had interested himself in financially aiding Bach's last surviving child, the impoverished Regine Susanna. Leipzigers themselves seemed to have forgotten that great Sebastian had died in their service.

Of course, during his lifetime Bach's fame rested not upon his compositions, but mainly upon his virtuosity as an organist and his reputation as a theorist. By the end of his career his serious, mystic, and involved creations—the climax of the German baroque—were considered old-fashioned by an age fast losing historical perspective. The new *style galant* of the rococo, embraced by his sons and even by his contemporary, Telemann, together with the fashionable philosophy of Enlightenment, seemed to doom his weighty, pietistic utterances to eternal sleep. His pupil Doles became St. Thomas' cantor in 1756, but only rarely gave performances of Bach, whose manuscripts gathered dust. When Mozart visited Leipzig in 1789, he heard one of Doles's sporadic renderings of the motet, *Singet dem Herrn;* his joy at direct contact with Bach's genius makes one of music history's touching anecdotes. Wagner was to conduct this piece during a series of concerts in Dresden in January, 1848.

But the enthusiasm of Mozart and Beethoven was unwonted. Doles's successor, Johann Adam Hiller, spoke of Bach's "crudities." It was the era when zealots of the Enlightenment proposed pulling down the Gothic cathedrals, finding such architectural complexities uncouth. Only in the new century could a historian like Forkel, a critic like Rochlitz, and a musician like Zelter, by calling attention to the beauties in Bach's neglected scores, set in motion the movement that culminated in Mendelssohn's revival.

Wagner's mature opinion of Bach was respectful but condescending. Although taking up Forkel's appeal to honor Bach's contribution to Germany's cultural patrimony, Wagner's article *Jewry in Music* (1850) patronizingly viewed Bach's musical language as standing in the same relationship to the music of Mozart and Beethoven as the Egyptian Sphinx to a sculptural rendering of man by the ancient Greeks: "Just as the Sphinx strives to free its human head from an animal body, so Bach's noble countenance seeks to come forth from under its wig." This foolish judgment, to some extent inspired by rancor, Wagner wrapped in a suitably absurd image. (Late in life he was to declare that Bach was to music as Sanskrit to language, something estimable, "complete, incomparable," but defunct.)

He could not bear unreservedly to praise the musical god whose neglected altars the Jew Mendelssohn had reconsecrated. With the personal expressiveness of Beethoven he unfavorably compares the formal quality of Bach, this comparison following the observation that the confusion induced by the luxurious musical taste of the day had beguiled the public into esteeming the two styles equally. *"Luxuriös"* is but one of many Wagnerian euphemisms for Jewish. Although acknowledging that Bach's genius embraced some substance of personal statement *("das Was")*, Wagner continues that this master's works must nevertheless be grasped mainly in terms of technique *("das Wie")*, an element easily aped by Mendelssohn, for Jews, though incapable of true Germanic utterance, are clever imitators. But, although unwilling to forgive the old cantor his posthumous cult, in many ways Wagner was one of his heirs in respect both to *"das Wie"* and *"das Was."*

Like Bach, Wagner was a master of tone painting, especially of nature. Bach's device of investing a text with instrumental and vocal representations of phrases inviting musical realization is more pictorial and external than Wagner's usual technique of achieving a tonal correlative of the emotions in his words, which changes with every inflection. Of course, motives such as those of his *Ring* menagerie have a literalness not second to Bach's, and Wagner's vocal line abounds in pictorializations of individual words similar to those in the cantatas and Passions. But, more profoundly, both men could penetrate to the essence of a poetic idea and translate it into musical terms. Their fusion of tone and word most often seems fated. Since Bach did not write his cantata and Passion texts, his achievement in this area is even more extraordinary than that of Wagner, who had already conceived his music as he wrote the poem. Both Bach and Wagner on occasion elevated some rather indifferent verse to a beauty far above its intrinsic worth.

One might, in Wagner's specialized vocabulary, describe his own imitative genius in *Meistersinger* as "Semitic." He turned to a diatonic idiom and adapted the apparatus of Bach counterpoint to represent the conservative aesthetic values of Nuremberg's guilds; to their established ideas, he opposed Walther von Stolzing's revolutionary viewpoint, which he cast in the uneasy chromaticism of *Tristan.*[6] The opening choral of *Meistersinger* is worthy of Bach himself, while the technical address of the fugato riot in the second act, wherein both tonal languages are combined, is unique even for the consummate craftsman that Wagner was. What indeed would Mendelssohn have said of this ensemble which turns into a kind of chorale fantasia with the melody of the serenade functioning as *cantus firmus?*

In yet another respect Wagner was a musical descendant of St. Thomas' mightiest cantor. Through almost inexhaustible melodic, harmonic, and

---

[6] The device is also found in *Rhinegold,* where the rule of Wotan, built upon the major triad, is threatened by the dissonant and chromatic harmonies of Loge and Alberich. In *Tannhäuser,* Venus and the hero present a similar contrast of idiom in the grotto scene, just as in *Parsifal* the sinuous chromaticism of Klingsor's domain serves as foil for the triads of the Grail temple.

rhythmic transformation of themes he, as much as Mozart, Beethoven, Schubert, and Brahms, was a master of the variation form which had reached its German baroque climax in Bach. Moreover, Bach's great arches of unbroken vocal and instrumental melody seem to have found a stylistic echo in Wagner.

One wonders whether his half year with Weinlig did not include some perusal of the wealth of Bach material lying on the shelves of St. Thomas' School. The Bach revival was in crescendo, and Weinlig's immediate predecessors at St. Thomas', August Eberhardt Müller and Johann Gottfried Schicht, had shown an increasing interest in his works. Certainly Weinlig could not have been unaware of what was going on around him; and Bach's influence is felt in Richard's early fantasia, his most significant piece of *juvenilia* composed under Weinlig. In 1848, while en route to Vienna, Wagner stopped in Breslau to visit Mosewius (an old friend of Geyer's) expressly to look at his copies of Bach cantatas, and during the *Parsifal* period he lectured friends on the preludes and fugues during frequent "Bach evenings."

9

Bach's eighteenth-century baroque spirit pervades the sixteenth-century Renaissance setting of *Die Meistersinger*. In the third act an autobiographical touch adds yet another era as Cantor Weinlig and Richard—that fervent product of the romantic century—converse in the cobbler's studio.

"How do I begin in accordance with rules?" asks Stolzing. By homely parallels and with gentle patience Hans Sachs (Weinlig) teaches Stolzing (Richard) that his poetic and musical speech, impassioned but as yet amorphous, will gain clear utterance only when guided by the logic of form. He advises the young knight that the rules of the masters will truly guide and preserve the ardent, instinctive inspiration of youth. The delicious give and take between forbearing teacher and mercurial pupil echo the hours of counsel at St. Thomas'. How often must Weinlig have heard from Richard the equivalent of Walther's impulsive *"Genug der Wort'"* ("Enough talk"). Certainly it must have been difficult to cope with the wounded pride of the composer of the kettledrum overture who, like Stolzing, had heard his earnest effort ridiculed and himself declared *"versungen und vertan!"* Weinlig saw deeply into both the musical and the personal problems of his charge. The two learned to love one another, and, refusing Johanna's money, Weinlig found sufficient recompense in the pleasure of instructing a gifted pupil. Most successful was Weinlig's method of having him create strict imitations of masterworks they had analyzed together, and then of rewarding his diligence by permitting a more free expression. So remarkable was Richard's progress that within six months the course was completed to mutual satisfaction.

The lateness of Wagner's serious musical training has already been compared with the case of Schumann. A parallel with Verdi also suggests itself. His first score, performed when he was fifteen, made Busseto's village folk deem him an accomplished musician. But wiser heads thought his training incomplete. He had studied with Parmesan counterparts of Humann and Müller. In June, 1832, some months short of nineteen, he sought admittance to the Milan Conservatory. Rejected mainly because he was over the required age, he found his Weinlig in the person of Vincenzo Lavigna, who privately instructed him in fugue and canon. Verdi remarked that no one taught him either orchestration or the manner of handling dramatic situations. Like Wagner, he learned such matters from the example of the masters, and the opera house was his training ground. The similarity of their situations is striking.

10

Wagner's fragmentary student career closed with its only successful phase —the months with Weinlig. Houston Stewart Chamberlain, Wagner's son-in-law and an official of Cosima's Propaganda Ministry, wrote that "of all the really great masters of the musical art Wagner is the only one who enjoyed a thorough classical education." Tolerantly observing that "nobody will think the worse of a Bach, a Mozart, or a Beethoven because their general education was scanty," he added that "Richard Wagner enjoyed essentially the same kind of education as, for instance, Goethe and Schiller." Although Goethe did enter into the distractions of Leipzig student life, this is the only point of comparison; to analogize with Schiller, educated at the strict school of Duke Karl Eugen, is preposterous. Wagner in his *Communication to My Friends* (1851) writes sweepingly of his "anarchic" education: "Life, art, and myself were my only teachers." Actually, Verdi's formal education was more "classical" and complete.

There were, however, a few days during Wagner's university career when a twinge of conscience urged him to attend lectures. A single session in philosophy ended his attempts to grasp its principles. He was present at two or three talks on aesthetics given by an abstracted young professor named Christian Hermann Weisse. Known for an obscure style, he defended it by declaring that weighty matters could not be comprehended by the rabble. Weisse was a friend of Adolf Wagner's, at whose house Richard heard this justification of abstruseness. With Weisse's example added to Adolf's, he adopted an impenetrable prose. So complicated was the diction of a letter he sent to brother Albert that the latter was alarmed concerning the boy's sanity.

II

In a letter dated March, 1832, to Ottilie, who was visiting in Denmark, Richard announced the end of his studies with Weinlig, although he added that the master would stay at his side as advising friend. Weinlig released him from tutelage much as a master his apprentice, an incident recalled in that enchanting moment in *Meistersinger* when Sachs sings to David, *"So mach' ich den Burschen gleich zum Gesell!"* ("On the spot, I'll turn the lad into a journeyman!")

A piano Sonata in B-flat Major had secured Richard his new status. Weinlig not only accepted the dedication but interested Breitkopf and Härtel in issuing the youthful work—an indulgent act Wagner was to regret in maturer days. The same publishers also engraved his Polonaise in D Major (four hands), an effective little piece based upon Weber. Youthful pride suffuses the letter to Ottilie; his exchanges with the family reveal a warm and loving side of the complicated boy.

In the sonata exercise Weinlig had asked for something on the model of Pleyel, Haydn's pupil who died in Paris during November, 1831, only a few weeks after Weinlig and Richard started their studies. Though superficial features of Mozart and Beethoven appear, the mechanical, rattling quality of late Pleyel dominates the composition, which represents an efficient aping of the devices of others without a trace of individual spirit. Like much student work, it is a shell without a core. An enthusiasm for Bellini is reflected in the closing movement's second theme. Elephantine and ludicrous as is its striving for lyricism, it yet anticipates those enveloping melodic arcs Wagner was able to inscribe from *Die Feen* on.

A piano Sonata in A Major which followed is of interest because Wagner put some of its thematic material to use again in the torso of an E-Major Symphony attempted in 1834. The sonata seeks weight by parroting Beethoven; but it abandons the more usual scherzo and substitutes instead a three-part fugue framed by rhapsodic passage work. Optimistic ears might detect intimations of *Tannhäuser* at the close of the second movement. The infectious lilt of Rossini, perhaps an echo of Weinlig's Bolognese musical background, characterizes the final movement.

Weinlig now encouraged Richard to compose unrestricted by set forms. The result was an F-sharp Minor Fantasia for piano, some of whose material reappears in his first completed opera, *Die Feen*. The chromaticism of the Fantasia encourages the unearthing of all manner of germinal ideas for themes in later Wagner works; certainly the progressions of *"zu König Markes Land"* from *Tristan* and the motif of Tannhäuser's misery are spelled out clearly, and one hears melodic prefigurations of the final act of *Valkyrie.* There is a striking phrase with a mordent rising to the sixth, a favorite idiom of Wagner's from *Rienzi* to *The Twilight of the Gods.* (Without the decisive leap, the turn paints Amfortas' sufferings in *Parsifal.*) Parodies of Beethoven sonatas flit by, and a primary inspiration of the piece is Bach's *Chromatic Fantasy.* Nevertheless, in this rambling work Richard says a few things of his own. The sonatas have hard, polished surfaces but no content; the Fantasia, diffuse and less finished, has at least a minimal substance and thus represents a tentative step toward individual expression.

12

His concert Overture in D Minor, written under Weinlig's scrutiny, had a friendly reception at a Gewandhaus concert of February 23, 1832. That his local star was rising was no doubt owing to the easygoing ways of Leipzig subscribers, the friendship of Pohlenz, and, above all, the estimable place his family held in the city's cultural life. The public had not forgotten Geyer (the Germans have always been sentimental about their artists), Luise's interpretations of Preciosa, Silvana, and Amine were fresh memories, and Rosalie reigned as the most famous Gretchen of the day.

Richard returned to his abandoned "Faust" music. The songs and choruses reveal dramatic effects achieved through modest means; some touches call to mind Schubert, who had died in Vienna only four years earlier. Yet it is doubtful that Richard knew his work at this time; similarities probably stem from a common Beethoven heritage.[7] Hopes that the young composer's music would be heard at Leipzig performances of *Faust* were unrealized, but Rosalie determined to force an opportunity for him at the theater.

[7] In coming years the songs of Schubert (and those of Wagner's contemporary, Schumann) with their meticulous union of text and music contributed toward the Wagnerian ideal of word realized through tone.

Wagner was to borrow direct inspiration from several Schubert works. The posthumous Quartet in D Minor was to provide both the motif of the Nibelung smithies and the contour of Mime's music; the *"Erlkönig"* became the model for the tempestuous introduction to *Valkyrie;* and, as Ellis has shown, Sieglinde's dream derives from the piano Sonata in B flat, as does the Valkyrie's annunciation of death motif from the fifteenth and sixteenth measures of *"Trockne Blumen"* (*Die schöne Müllerin*).

By the time of his overture's success, she was playing Lucia in Raupach's *König Enzio*, a sentimental Hohenstaufen tragedy with a plot not unlike Beethoven's *Fidelio*. Through her efforts Richard's overture and incidental music to this play were performed under Dorn's direction. The kettledrum overture had evidently not been forgotten, an announcement of the new music and of its composer's name not appearing until the wary management was certain that the audience manifested no dissatisfaction. In the middle of March his name was printed on a theater bill for the first time. The D-Minor Overture had its inspiration in Beethoven's *Coriolanus; Fidelio* is the dominant influence on the *Enzio* music, put together with a growing confidence and obviously benefiting from the poetic inspiration of a literary work.

With Mozart of the "Jupiter" Symphony as his guide, Richard next completed a large concert Overture in C Major. The work, its young creator conducting, appeared on a program of the Euterpe Society. Its fugato finale did not please his mother, who remarked that Beethoven's *Egmont* music, played at the same concert, had moved her more than her son's "stupid fugue." Perhaps Frau Johanna had penetratingly observed the musical emptiness beneath the learned form. At the end of April the overture achieved a hearing at the Gewandhaus. (As part of Wagner's sixtieth-birthday celebration at Bayreuth in 1873, Cosima arranged for its surprise performance. At first unrecognized by Wagner, who tried to guess the composer, it drew from him humorous remarks about a piece recalling both Beethoven and Bellini and obviously by neither.)

Rosalie and Dorn zealously promoted their protégé, for also in April of 1832 a "Scene and Aria" of his was sung in the theater by Dorn's pupil Henriette Wüst, later the first Irene in *Rienzi*. Mrs. Burrell believed that the selection possibly formed part of *Die Feen,* on which Richard might already have been working.

Richard's first real friend was Theodor Apel. Two years younger than Richard, he, too, had been a student at St. Nicholas'. An interest in poetry and music united them, and Theodor's wealth and generosity made him a yet more attractive companion. Within the decade it was to him that Wagner's desperate wife was to turn with appeals for funds to free her husband from a Parisian debtors' prison (1840). In 1832 Theodor was at Heidelberg. In a letter to him dated December 16, 1832, Richard revealed that he had composed a symphony within a period of six weeks, his "most powerful work to date." Created during the early part of the summer, its models were Mozart and Beethoven.

Richard also made friends at Brockhaus' home with the Polish revolutionary Count Tyszkiewicz, whose person and costume had so attracted him at the Gewandhaus. Tyszkiewicz was determined to risk a return to Galicia and planned to travel there via Brünn. He offered to take Richard with him as far as the Moravian capital, from whence the boy could proceed on his own to Vienna. Taking with him the scores of his overtures and his as yet unperformed symphony, Richard set out for the leading musical city of the German-speaking world.

Cholera had appeared at Brünn, and Richard passed a night of Hoffmannesque horror in his hotel. His childhood hallucinations reappeared. The disease incarnate stood before him; he could see it and grip it with his hands. The ghastly apparition lay with him in bed and embraced him. Next morning he arose, surprised to find himself whole and healthy.

Those were pleasant weeks in Vienna's sultry summer heat. He visited the theaters and was especially impressed by the magic play, a type of work loved in Vienna and best represented in opera by Mozart's *Magic Flute* and in drama by Raimund's *Zauberpossen*. This Viennese genre and its conjurations remained forever part of Wagner's dramatic vocabulary and form an ingredient in practically every one of his plots from the transformations of *Die Feen* through Ortrud's witchcraft and Alberich's tricks to Klingsor's wizardry. A performance of Gluck's *Iphigenia in Tauris* not only disappointed but also bored him. He missed the fire of Schröder-Devrient.

Vienna echoed to Strauss waltzes and the tunes of Hérold's *Zampa* (or *The Marble Bride*), a work making its triumphant way through Europe. (It had earned a Viennese parody by Nestroy—*Zampa . . . or, The Plaster Bride*.) Hérold's opera was to become something of a bête noire to Wagner, but he did come to owe it a curious debt. Its enchanted statue, whose fingers close over a ring as its arm threateningly rises, reappears transmuted in that revelatory moment at the end of the *Ring* when Siegfried lifts his hand in death. To keep Hagen from ripping the Nibelung ring from the defenseless corpse, Wagner fell back upon this *Zampa* idea, mixing it with elements from the brothers Grimm.[8]

During his visit to Vienna a kind effort of the Conservatory Orchestra to read through his D-Minor Overture failed. In *Mein Leben* he remarks that some debts run up at this time were repaid when he became *Kapellmeister* in Dresden—more than a decade later!

He turned toward home and, while crossing Bohemia, visited the Pachtas at Pravonin, their estate a few miles from Prague. He stayed until autumn, renewing his friendship with the lovely and flirtatious girls and falling in love with one of them, Jenny, as was expected of him. However, following the advice of their mother (the Count's mistress, Frau Raymann), they reserved serious coquetry for more eligible and aristocratic suitors. Richard's

---

[8] The raised hand appeared as early as the 1848 prose scenario of the *Ring*.

self-conscious, Werther-like sufferings led him to set Apel's poem, *"Abend-glocken"* (*"Glockentöne"*), to music. The December letter to Apel contains what was to become the closing theme of many Wagnerian love affairs—*"Sie war meiner Liebe nicht wert"* ("she wasn't worth my love").

In November he proceeded to Prague, where he cajoled Dionys Weber, a pupil of Vogler and founder and director of the conservatory, into giving his symphony its first performance.

In romantic Prague, nursing a disappointment in love, he turned a histrionic grief into literature and produced his first opera book, *"Die Hochzeit"* ("The Wedding"). Or was it the other way around? Perhaps he found in Jenny someone with whom to act out dramatic ideas within him. In later years, his famous affair with Mathilde Wesendonk was the result, not the cause, of the *Tristan* theme coursing through him. His life was always to follow the path of his art. Richard dramatized his annoyance with Jenny's other suitors and created violent scenes in the Pachta home. He wrote to Apel, "My idealizing eyes beheld in her everything they desired to find; therein lay my misfortune!" *"Die Hochzeit"* was taking form. In December he returned to Leipzig with his precious manuscript.

About the middle of the month Clara Wieck sent a letter to Robert Schumann that warned, "Listen, Mr. Wagner has soared beyond you." She was referring to Richard's symphony, which had been accepted for performance at a Gewandhaus concert (at which she was to play a concerto) by the famous Rochlitz with the hope that it first be attempted by the Euterpe Society. Richard had easy access to this group, founded by Sipp, his former violin teacher, and directed by Müller, his first harmony master; indeed, the Society had already tried out one of his overtures. It was Richard's success at the Euterpe reading, despite what he lamented as a poor performance, that inspired Clara's letter to her friend Robert, who she hoped would get along more quickly with his own symphonic writing.

When they met, Wagner's youth amazed Rochlitz, whose perusal of the technically finished score had led him to expect an older composer. Richard's knowledge was on display. Themes were constructed to dovetail contrapuntally, and the final movement was fugal. Like so much of Wagner's *juvenilia,* the symphony's polished exterior sheltered a vacuous content. Some years later he set material from the andante to work again in a New Year's Cantata performed at Magdeburg.

The "Faust" music, which alone rises above the counterfeit level of his youthful achievement, ironically received no performance. An expressive melody from Gretchen's *"Ach neige, du Schmerzenreiche"* was again taken up in *Die Feen.* The songs state something personal. Thus, quite early appears Wagner's need for a text to kindle his genuine musical impulse. The utter inanity of the late *Albumblätter* and marches shows how helpless his muse was—even when he was at the summit of his powers—when not inspired by the word. As early as 1846 the young critic Hanslick observed that Wagner required a developing dramatic situation as a basis for his music. The situation awakened musical ideas, to which a text was often simultaneously fitted. Wagner spoke of composing as a process of recollection.

III

The Journeyman: Lehr- *and* Wanderjahre

The book of *"Die Hochzeit,"* a product of Richard's Bohemian stay, quickened his musical pulse and, like "Leubald," contained rudiments of later developments in his art.

Two families determine to end their years of enmity. Ada, daughter of Hadmar, is to marry Arindal, and as a symbol of reconciliation their former enemy, Morar, is invited to the wedding. Too old to undertake the journey from his far-off land, the latter sends his son, Cadolt, accompanied by a vassal, Admund. They arrive as the bridal procession passes, and Cadolt's melancholy and magnetic glance falls upon Ada. The principals join in a septet: Hadmar welcomes the moody youth in the spirit of concord; Cadolt, lamenting that he came, is urged by his Kurvenal-like companion to trust no one, while Hadmar's retainer has similar advice for his master; Arindal and a lady of the court sing of love; Ada, transfixed by Cadolt's glance—much as Senta was to be by the Dutchman's—is filled with apprehensive presentiments. She then retires to her tower chamber to await the bridegroom. Suddenly, through the window she perceives the fearful eyes of Cadolt, who has climbed to her apartment. As he seizes her passionately, she is able to tilt him backward over the balcony to his death. His followers, finding him in the courtyard, demand revenge for the presumed betrayal. A general slaughter is averted when Hadmar summons the relatives of the victim. It is hoped that God's judgment will fall upon the guilty one during the obsequies. Ada, showing indications of madness, flees Arindal to lock herself in her tower. She appears at the funeral, and, as avengers break into the chapel calling upon the malefactor to show himself, she sinks lifeless upon Cadolt's body.

Wagner had originally planned to make a short story of this material derived from both Büsching's book on chivalry and Karl Immermann's

Cardenio und Celinde (1826), that tragedy derided by Platen in his *Der romantische Oedipus* (1829). Richard's earlier project seems to have contained more obvious and naïve references to Pravonin and his disconsolate love for Jenny than do the surviving musical fragment and summary of the libretto. They indicate a tighter utilization of the material and, notwithstanding some Grand Guignol sensationalism, outline an uncompromising and remarkable creation.

Despite Weinlig's high praise for the transparency of the septet, Wagner relates that on his return to Leipzig from Prague he ceased to work on *"Die Hochzeit"* in deference to Rosalie's disapproval of its nocturnal and gloomy mood. Early in 1833 he wrote Apel, "I have renounced and torn up my opera text." Actually he probably found himself incapable of continuing—of finding a musical garb suitable to it. He was still almost completely dependent upon the example of other composers, and his too original literary creation had left him with no operatic model to emulate. He scorned the use of florid decorations foreign to the seriousness of his story. Vouchsafed a vision of his future music drama, he lacked the inspiration and inventiveness to follow it.

Only in a section sung by the women (it hints at the Messengers of Peace from *Rienzi*) does the chorus of welcome to Cadolt depart from an embarrassing dependence upon *Fidelio*. The recitative between Admund and Cadolt is remarkably assured and filled with those swift changes of mood characteristic of later Wagner. A melodic fragment derived from questioning figures of the Fantasia (and anticipating similar themes in *Tristan* and *Valkyrie*) threateningly appears under this conversation in the manner of a leitmotif, rising a fourth at each repetition to heighten the tension. But the following septet reveals a young composer in search of a style. Its musical weakness perhaps discloses the real reason for his readiness to desert the entire project. Nor was it to be the last time he set aside a book after having found his emotional and musical resources too limited to express fully what was dormant in his words. From the beginning, the musical concepts that gave birth to his texts were deep within him. But often he had to await the spiritual and technical maturity needed to show forth his vision. Through inner development, study, and assimilation, his powers of expression in sound were to grow steadily from *"Hochzeit"* to *Parsifal.*

Although he never returned to *"Hochzeit,"* the diction of its verse, its bridal procession, the idea of its ensemble, and Ada's appearance, "pale and silent at the head of her women," come back transformed in *Lohengrin.* In "Leubald" and *"Hochzeit"* the basic situation of guilty love shared but unacknowledged until too late—a love in conflict with the social order— points to both *Tristan* and *The Twilight of the Gods.* And the motive of the Hoffmannesque glance reappears in *Dutchman, Die Sarazenin,* and *Tristan.*

After abandoning *"Die Hochzeit,"* Richard turned to the magic opera, for which models were at hand in works of Mozart, Weber, and Marschner. But he was not to pursue this direction in his native land.

2

Did the author of "To the German Army before Paris" (1871), a malicious poem lauding the victory of a renascent German kaiserdom over the French, ever recall that a desire to escape military duty played a part in his decision to quit Saxony early in 1833? Certainly his career in Leipzig was progressing extremely well. Though he was young and unknown, his works were being heard. And Rosalie had interested yet another of her admirers in him. She was idolized for her interpretation of Gretchen by the brilliant critic Heinrich Laube, whose good will soon extended to her young brother. Laube was writing a libretto on Kosciuszko intended for Meyerbeer. Impressed by Richard's C-Major Symphony, he asked·him to set this book to music. But from the time of "Leubald" it had been instinctively clear to Richard that he must be his own poet. An invitation from Albert Wagner to visit Würzburg permitted him to put a diplomatic distance between himself and Laube and to live in the neighboring Kingdom of Bavaria free from fear of conscription. This evasion of military service was to make it difficult for him to procure a regular passport for many years.

Albert, not only leading tenor but now also stage manager of the opera, was able to get his brother the position of chorus director and coach at the Würzburg theater and to encourage performances of his compositions in the town. Richard was no longer completely dependent upon Rosalie for funds. He plunged into study of a repertory largely unfamiliar to him and began to build what was to become a formidable practical knowledge of the stage and of the conductor's art. In dealing with this Würzburg period in *Mein Leben,* he deplored a decline in his taste which permitted him to admire Meyerbeer's *Robert the Devil,* attributing the lapse in part to the influence of Albert, who sang the title role.

Singers commonly cut, altered, or added to operatic parts they considered ineffective. Albert was no exception. Richard's first task for him, that of transplanting an aria from one Bellini opera to another, was not a success because of an inappropriate orchestration. But approval was won by the new extended ending he tacked on to Aubry's *"Wie ein schöner Frühlingsmorgen"* from Marschner's *Vampyr* (September, 1833). Richard's frenzied words and music (the latter containing an astounding prefiguration of the flight motif from the *Ring*) are in the idiom of Prince Arindal's *"Wo find ich dich?"* from the first act of a new magic opera, *Die Feen,* on which he had busied himself since the beginning of the year. He had brought his libretto from Leipzig, and by January, 1834, three large volumes of the completed score testified to his industry.[1] Ambition to complete this work probably made him, to the family's chagrin, turn down a position as conductor in Zurich. Moreover, it was problematical to obtain a passport without having fulfilled the military obligation.

Despite his labors, Richard had not forgotten how to play. Distractions of the tavern and an occasional drunken brawl were still enjoyed. And he had discovered that, though he was far from handsome, his intensity and impetuousness held an attraction for certain women. His first conquests were a chorister, Therese Ringelmann, daughter of a gravedigger, and then Friederike Galvani, a mechanic's daughter, whom he shabbily stole from her fiancé, the first oboist of the theater orchestra.

Evidently, he sought amusement at the nearby watering places. A superb adagio in Weber style for clarinet with string quintet accompaniment has been ascribed to him by Julius Kapp, who believed it written for the clarinetist Rummel during a visit to Kissingen.

Richard was apparently not rehired for the full fall opera season but stayed on in Würzburg to complete *Die Feen.* In December he had been able to write Rosalie that its composition was finished, only some work on the orchestration remaining. At a Würzburg concert, excerpts were tried out.

Rosalie was already attempting to smooth the way for a Leipzig première. Her importance to the theater manager was sufficient to extract his disingenuous promise to mount a work which, as the following months were to show, he really intended to relinquish by means of those vacillations, objections, and postponements which are the weapons of an unwilling impresario. Ironically, by the time it had become clear that the manager, Ringelhardt, was playing him false, Richard had turned away from the Weber-Marschner Germanism of *Die Feen* and was seeking another style.

Die Feen, his first completed opera (it was never performed during his lifetime), deserves the attention of anyone studying the Wagnerian drama. Its plot, taken from a story by Gozzi, *La donna serpente,* Wagner freely varied. Adolf Wagner, known as a translator of Gozzi, must certainly have led his nephew to the works of the Venetian writer. Wagner carried over from *"Die Hochzeit"* the Gaelic names of the leading characters. Like Goethe, Chateaubriand, Byron, and Mendelssohn, he had been infatuated with the Ossianic poems, those literary frauds of Macpherson that almost succeeded in giving Scotland a Homer.

In pursuit of a doe, Prince Arindal of Tramond plunges into a river and

---

[1] The score was finished on January 1, 1834, the overture later the same month.

loses consciousness. He awakens in the castle of Ada, a surpassingly beautiful woman. They pledge their love, and he agrees to her stipulation that for eight years he make no inquiry concerning her origin. When the time has passed, he poses the question, and Ada and her castle vanish midst thunder. Arindal is found by courtiers from Tramond, who, advising him that he has been thrall to a wicked enchantress, urge his return home. During his absence his royal father has died of grief, and Lora, his sister, now defends the last city of the realm still free from the invaders' ravages. But Ada is really a benevolent spirit deeply in love with Arindal. Her problem is not unlike that of young Strephon in *Iolanthe,* who was but half a fairy. Like his father, hers, too, was a human (though hardly the Lord Chancellor of England), and she longs to shed her immortality and join Arindal as his earthly wife. To accomplish this end both must undergo harsh tests; she must torment him with terrible acts. If he prove steadfast, her reward is mortality; if he curse her, then she must be metamorphosed into stone and so remain for a full century. She sets about her disagreeable tasks, and Arindal, confused and uncomprehending, execrates her. Appalled by his inconstancy and her own future, she reveals the purpose of the trials. Arindal sinks into madness. But with the help of the magician Groma, he gathers his resources and penetrates into the underworld, where he overcomes its guardian spirits. To the tones of a magic lyre and with the warmth of his love song, he disenchants the cold stone, and Ada stirs to life. He becomes immortal and mounts Fairyland's throne with her at his side.

In Gozzi's tale the heroine becomes a Mélusine-like serpent, whom the hero must kiss to exorcise the charm. Wagner's alteration permitted a more musical treatment of her deliverance in the tradition of Gluck's *Orfeo* and Shakespeare's *The Winter's Tale.* Yet, the great importance he later attached to this change suggests that it also had psychological roots. One is reminded of Ruskin's recurrent nightmares of snakes and his struggle to repress the satanic serpent-tempter.

The libretto abounds in fertile motives that re-emerge in later Wagnerian operas—especially the last, *Parsifal.* Quite like its hero is Arindal, who fails to recognize the significance of his first probation but, gaining strength through further trials, finally breaks the evil spell. Ada, mercurial of mood as she is forced to execute tasks distasteful to her, is a precursor of Kundry. Groma, the invisible spirit whose voice echoes through palace wall and deep cavern, suggests Titurel. And the death of the grieving King of Tramond after Arindal's disappearance calls to mind Herzeleide and Parsifal.

Elements of *Lohengrin* are foreshadowed. The fulcrum of its action is also an injunction concerning identity. Most interestingly, Ortrud's scheme that her husband, Telramund, destroy Lohengrin's magic by cutting even the smallest joint of his finger is elucidated by the *Romanze* sung by Arindal's vassal in the earlier *Feen.* It relates the tale of Frau Dilnovaz, a witch whose disguise as a maiden falls away when her little finger bearing a magic ring is severed. The tale of Frau Dilnovaz in *Feen* antecedes Wagner's reading of *Der jüngere Titurel,* in which are pursued the adventures of Loherangrin *(sic)* after his departure from Antwerp. He marries a woman who is told that his steadfastness can be assured only by her consuming flesh cut from his body. Mutilation, suggested in *Feen, Lohengrin,* and the *Ring,*[2] was to assume commanding importance in the plot of *Parsifal.*

Ada's deathlike imprisonment, broken by her lover, looks back strikingly to *Orfeo* and forward through *Valkyrie* to that mighty descendant of *Parsifal,* Hofmannsthal's and Strauss's *Die Frau ohne Schatten.*[3] Elements of Arindal's madness—especially the musical delineation of his calling to remembrance the hunting hounds in pursuit of the doe—astoundingly anticipate Sieglinde's frenzied scene in the second act of *Valkyrie.*[4] But most noteworthy is the fact that *Feen,* like the famous dramas that were to follow it, is a tale of the human spirit and its trials.

A few examples will show that the young Wagner's timid employment of the leitmotif is at times noteworthy. When the text alludes to deceitful magic, the main theme of the Dilnovaz *Romanze* sounds again. Most telling is its return as Arindal prepares to curse his wife as a witch. Her anxieties are portrayed by the kind of falling figure that was one day to picture Alberich's woe. The poignant thirds, first heard representing Arindal's voice echoing Ada's name through the wilderness, recur at the

[2] The Norns reveal that Loge, once tamed by Wotan's spear, sought his freedom by biting through its shaft. In punishment, Wotan forced him to blaze as fire around Brynhild's rock. On the last day of the gods Wotan was to plunge the splinters of his shattered spear into the fire god's breast. From it would issue flames to kindle the ruins of the world ash tree heaped about Walhall.

An Indian tale that Wagner especially recommended to Frau Wesendonk (he had taken Holtzmann's edition with him to London in 1855) was that of King Usinar, who ransomed a dove from a hawk by paying with flesh cut from his own thigh.

[3] The story of *Die Frau ohne Schatten,* which tells of a supernatural woman who, like Ada, longs to become human—to cast a shadow—has other fascinating resemblances to *Die Feen.* Consider the punitive transformation into stone of the emperor. He, like Arindal, met his wife (daughter of the spirit ruler, Keikobad) while hunting. A gazelle he pursued fell to the ground and changed into the beautiful peri whom he then made his empress. Of course, Eastern myth teems with the motives found in both works.

[4] *Die Feen* also indicates that a characteristic Wagnerian diction was forming. Lora's ecstatic *"Den Busen fühl' ich hoch sich heben,"* sung during a Weber-like outburst, is an unfortunate phrase reappearing in Elizabeth's entrance in *Tannhäuser.*

moment his mind begins to give way after the curse and again at the height of his madness as he sinks down on the steps of his throne. Of course, Wagner does not yet develop his motifs, but merely repeats them at a dramatically appropriate spot in a convenient key.

Feen abounds in melodic turns and harmonic colors that anticipate *Dutchman, Tannhäuser,* and *Lohengrin.* The "magic" E major of Mendelssohn's Overture to *A Midsummer Night's Dream* (and of the later Venusberg music) characterizes Ada's fairy realm, a tonal foreshadowing of the Circean court into which Tannhäuser would stumble. And in *Feen* Wagner also puts to use a Tristan-like *Steigerung* or mounting tension achieved by the reiteration of brief phrases.

In general, Wagner borrows his vocabulary from Mendelssohn, but the score also rests heavily upon Weber and his follower Marschner.

In 1827 the latter had become *Kapellmeister* of the Leipzig theater, where two of his operas were first heard, *Der Vampyr* (1828) after Byron—or, rather, his physician-secretary, Dr. Polidori—and *Der Templer und die Jüdin* (1829), based upon Scott. The former was to inspire the first numbers Wagner composed for *Dutchman;* the plan for the opening act of *Lohengrin* came from *Templer,* with its trumpet calls for a champion at last answered by Ivanhoe's appearance to defend guiltless Rebecca against Brian, who falls even before the righteous sword touches him.

Richard wrote to Rosalie from Würzburg expressing great disappointment in Marschner's latest effort, *Hans Heiling* (1833). (Thematic material for the death-prophecy scene of *Valkyrie* was to be borrowed not only from Schubert but also from the Mountain Queen's great aria in *Heiling.*) Perhaps what really disturbed Richard was that, although based on a folk tale of the Erzgebirge, the substance of the Lohengrin-like plot of *Heiling* was not dissimilar to that of *Feen.* Its libretto by Eduard Devrient had, in fact, originally been intended for Mendelssohn. With *Heiling* filling the Leipzig theater, it is not surprising that Ringelhardt had no real intention of indulging Rosalie's younger brother by producing his comparatively clumsy work. Original Marschner was available; he did not need an imitation.

3

Thus, the hopes harbored by Richard upon his return to Leipzig early in 1834 gradually declined. But renewed friendship with Laube compensated for the weeks of uneasy waiting. Though not resentful over the rebuff to his Kosciuszko libretto, Laube made no effort to hide his contempt for the tradition of murky German romanticism that *Die Feen* prolonged. Laube had become one of the most admired iconoclasts of progressive German youth. Devouring the first part of his novel *Das junge Europa,* Richard was swayed by the opinions of a new idol.

Having already observed in Würzburg the simple lyric means with which Latin opera made its effects, Richard now saw its German counterpart as labored, pedantic, contorted. The month of March determined his new course, for then Schröder-Devrient appeared in Leipzig as Romeo in Bellini's *I Capuletti ed i Montecchi.* Richard had created Ada with Devrient in mind. In the physical presence of her emotional interpretation of the Sicilian master's warm score, his own work seemed bloodless. Turning his back upon "the eternally allegorizing orchestral bustle" of his compatriots, and blaming old Bach's instrumental obbligatos for the German practice of swamping and restricting the singer in a sea of sound, Richard embraced cantilena and the sensualism and simplicity of the Italians.

These sentiments, strange from the future creator of *Tristan,* formed the burden of two articles he wrote in 1834, the first appearing anonymously in June in Laube's *Zeitung für die elegante Welt* and the second in November in the *Neue Zeitschrift für Musik,* Robert Schumann's new periodical. What Richard had venerated in the past now confused him. The wretched performances of Beethoven and Weber he had often endured now led him to wonder whether his high estimate of their worth had been mistaken. Although the second article touched upon the Latin tradition's deficiency in respect to the psychology and motivation of its characters (and also executed a hasty bow in the direction of Gluck and Mozart), there was no doubt that the young composer had made a complete about-face.

During the spring of 1834, while awaiting a decision about the production of *Die Feen,* he and Theodor Apel had set out on an excursion to Bohemia. This was hardly the frugal journey of seven years before with Rudolf Böhme. Theodor evidently paid the bills; there were private carriages and excellent food, wine, and accommodations. The friends had in common not only their enthusiasm for art but also the liberal ideas of Laube and Heinse. It was the Mediterranean sensualism of the latter's *Ardinghello und die glückseligen Inseln* (1787), whose hero founds a Utopia in the Grecian isles, that made the blood of these "Young Germans" course faster. Heinse's *Musical Dialogues* extolled music as a universal language "understood by the Iroquois as well as the Italian," and he was an admirer of Gluck. It is amusing to observe Wagner returning to the reveries of Ardinghello during the Laussot crisis of later years, which included plans for a flight to Greece.

The Bohemian trip was a lyric idyl closing Wagner's youth. In retrospect, he even enjoyed the violent arguments with Theodor, which sometimes drew crowds beneath the open windows of their hotel room. One morning in Teplitz, the spa where years before Johanna had sought Geyer, he slipped away from Theodor to breakfast alone and to make the rough draft of a new libretto, *Das Liebesverbot*.

After trying the thermal baths, they journeyed to Prague, where Theodor was introduced into the Pachta household. Relishing Frau Raymann's vain attempts to capture the wealthy Apel for one of the girls, Richard felt an old affront requited. Completely freed from his former infatuation, he played the madcap. A serious word could not be drawn from him. His tomfoolery seemed inexhaustible. After bawling the forbidden "Marseillaise" into the night air of the provincial Hapsburg capital and climbing in a state of undress from one window ledge to another of his fashionable hotel—the acrobat of Eisleben had evidently been reawakened by spirits—the young hero was invited to visit the police. He was released after questioning.

Sensing that he was saying farewell to his youth, he wrote to Rosalie from Prague, "Are the happy days I'm now enjoying about to venge themselves on me . . . for with this coming winter the chill of life will seize me, too."

4

At home in Leipzig the Opera had found an opportunity of ridding itself once and for all of *Die Feen* and its persistent composer. The Magdeburg theater, managed by Heinrich Bethmann, was in need of a conductor and turned to Leipzig for a recommendation. Richard sprang immediately to mind; with him permanently out of town, the *Feen* project, by this time really dead, could be properly buried. Although discerning intrigue in the apparent benignity, Richard, probably to placate the family, agreed to investigate the offer. But he had no intention of joining a plot aimed at himself.

During the summer months the Magdeburg company played at the Thuringian watering places, Rudolstadt and Lauchstädt. Carl Friedrich Wagner had taken Johanna to the latter spa for the première of Schiller's *Braut von Messina* (1803). Its theater had been designed by Goethe. Despite this modest fame, the town filled Richard with misgivings upon his arrival there to visit Bethmann. The impresario, always in financial trouble, survived on a pension from the King of Prussia, a reward for having suffered the first Frau Bethmann, a famous actress, to receive royal favors of a very personal sort.

At the moment of Richard's arrival matters were highly confused. A performance of *Don Giovanni* was scheduled for the next Sunday; but the municipal band of Merseburg, which made up the theater orchestra, was unable to appear for the Saturday rehearsal. Richard appraised the situation and quickly decided not to become in any way involved with this sordid group. But he needed a room. A young actor suggested a lodging, at whose door Richard encountered the beautiful *jeune première* of Bethmann's acting company—Minna Planer.

He immediately changed plans and rented quarters directly under Minna's. Agreeing to make an operatic debut conducting the ludicrous *Don Giovanni* performance, he hastened back to Leipzig to fetch some linen. There he learned that Laube was being harassed by the authorities, notwithstanding that his energies were devoted more to aesthetics than to politics. He had just returned from an Italian journey undertaken with Karl Gutzkow, another leader of "Young Germany." Within a short time Laube was to enter a Berlin prison, forbidden to read, write, or smoke; not long after, Gutzkow was confined at Mannheim. The forces set in motion by the July Revolution were meeting a strong reaction.

Richard hurried back to Lauchstädt, where he observed with delight his growing abilities as a conductor. And the gentle Minna (Christiane Wilhelmina), the cause of this new career, increasingly fascinated him not only by her beauty but also by her genuineness. Between three and four years his senior, she was circumspect and decorous. Yet, evidently first startled and then amused, she tolerated the ardent advances of the little *Kapellmeister.* At night she took the precaution of having the landlady lock her door. One memorable evening a good burgher of Lauchstädt up sufficiently late might have observed him standing on his window sill like a lovesick Cadolt seeking Ada in her tower.

His many attempts at seduction were good-humoredly rebuffed. He often wondered whether she responded to the importunities of others as negatively as to his. By the time Bethmann's company set out for its season at Rudolstadt, Richard had learned that Minna was romantically attached to an impecunious young nobleman. This news, added to the fact that he was receiving but part of his wages and this fraction in irregular installments (Frau Bethmann's lover, the bass Kneisel, was the only performer to pocket a full salary), soon led him back to gambling and liquor, his old medicines for frustration. He was externalizing his *Liebesverbot* with its theme of revolt against hypocrisy and its mood of mutinous boisterousness. Having attempted and abandoned a symphony in E major that used material from the second piano sonata, he had turned to versifying this operatic plot sketched some weeks before in Teplitz.

When the company gathered in Magdeburg for its winter season, it was agonizing for him to observe Minna pursued by aristocrats. Was it to be the story of the Pachtas again? In any case, his local reputation as a conductor was keeping pace with his waxing dissipations, cultivated, one suspects, not only to answer his erotic needs but also to soften Minna's heart by under-scoring the extremes to which her refusals had brought him.

A combination of solicitous and resentful emotions led her to accept an invitation to his New Year's Eve party in 1834. Recently he had been enjoying the company of an actress of scandalous reputation. Perhaps she was the "Toni" mentioned in one of his letters to Apel. Minna felt it wise to appear. More and more she was conscious of the gifts and mounting success of this young musician. His new cantata, *Beim Antritt des neuen Jahres,* was to be heard at the gala on the next day. A plentiful supply of alcohol gradually undermined the propriety of his guests, whose in-hibitions vanished in the glow of the heady punch. Only Minna retained her composure. But Richard's triumph was near.

He soon contrived to enter her apartment, where he had been invited for tea, at such a late hour and so intoxicated that she had no choice but to let him collapse on her bed. Awaking at dawn, he entreated. He adored her; she both admired and pitied him. They parted as lovers. "Then take me, oh, tempestuous youth," cries Isabella in *Liebesverbot* as she capitulates to the wild Luzio.

Old friends turned up in Magdeburg. Apel had arrived for the per-formance of his play, *Columbus,* accepted by the wily Bethmann not by reason of Richard's spirited recommendation (Uncle Adolf, too, had blessed the work) but because Theodor contributed money toward scenery and costumes useful in other productions. Richard composed an overture (Jan-uary, 1835) more successful than the drama it preceded and subsequently scheduled at a Gewandhaus concert in Leipzig by Pohlenz, who had played the *Feen* overture the year before. Richard's almost hysterical enthusiasm for the play coincided suspiciously with his request for a two-hundred-thaler loan from its accommodating author. At least Theodor had the pleasure of seeing his *Columbus* on the stage. Within months he would be seriously injured by a fall from his horse and then completely blind.

Richard persuaded Schröder-Devrient to sing such roles as Romeo and Desdemona (Rossini) under his baton. So fond did she become of him that she offered to perform at his benefit concert, an evening of great importance to him, inasmuch as its proceeds were an only hope of satisfying his many and demanding creditors. He had no clear idea of the total sum owed but was certain that a concert including the appearance of Germany's greatest prima donna would bring rich receipts. Preparing an ambitious program that included Beethoven's *Battle Symphony,* he arranged for special apparatus to project its artillery effects and for an augmented orchestra.

In Magdeburg his prestige as a young conductor was high. His un-precedented accelerandi in finales drew intoxicated applause. But evidently his personal integrity was less esteemed. Certainly there was gossip in the small city about his luxurious tastes, his tailors' bills, his delight in entertaining with fine wines, and the fact that this extravagance was maintained by a prodigious accumulation of debt. He was being pressed by tradesmen, whom he termed "the cursed rabble of Jews." The citizens of Magdeburg simply did not believe that Schröder-Devrient would return so soon to the provinces to sing a few selections at the benefit of a talented but unknown and irresponsible musician. That he raised ticket prices confirmed suspicions that a ruse was contemplated. When the great lady arrived on the night of May 2, she was startled to find a most meager audience.

Moreover, Richard had miscalculated the acoustic effect of his enlarged orchestra and ordnance machines in the small hall of the hotel, Zur Stadt London. A performance of his brash *Columbus* overture with its six trumpets evoking the New World had his few auditors quailing. This but anticipated the rout precipitated by the *Battle Symphony.* After her solos Schröder-Devrient had taken a seat in one of the first rows. But not even this trouper could withstand the auditory assault that Richard now unleashed. She fled, followed by what remained of the public. The piece finished to an empty room. The receipts were insufficient even to pay the musicians.

The morning after this disaster he had to face his creditors. They stood two by two in long rows. He was saved by one of them, a Madame Gottschalk, whom he described as "a Jewess one can trust." She cajoled his assembled victims with reassurances that seemed to rest upon his connection with the Brockhaus fortune. When later attempting to regain what was due her, she reaped the usual harvest of Wagnerian execrations.

The Magdeburg season was over. Bethmann's financial situation was as perilous as that of his conductor, who in May in the company of an intelligent brown poodle named "Rüpel" (Boor), his only perceptible emolument, retreated to his family in Leipzig. He penned extravagant love letters to Minna, who had remained in Magdeburg to conclude the dramatic troupe's performances. On her way home to Dresden she paid him a visit.

He had found Leipzig's musical taste altered. Mendelssohn had been summoned to assume conductorship of the Gewandhaus concerts. Gone was that amateurism characterizing the tenure of Pohlenz—that musical naïveté which had, in fact, permitted a composer of young Wagner's inexperience and artlessness to gain a hearing. Now the *Columbus* overture, conducted by him at a concert of the singer Livia Gerhardt, made little impression on an increasingly sophisticated public. He longed for the return of what he later styled Leipzig's "pre-Judaic age" (*"in der christlichen Vor-Jetztzeit Leipzigs"*). His resentment of Mendelssohn had started. Within the year he was to send his symphony to this young master, who never acknowledged its receipt or alluded to it when they later met. This remissness fed Wagner's rancor against Mendelssohn as much as the latter's musical classicism and religious origin. To the composer who had written his overture to *A Midsummer Night's Dream* at the age of seventeen the C-Major Symphony of Richard Wagner could hardly seem a testimony of youthful talent. Renowned for his tact, Mendelssohn perhaps felt silence to be the courteous course.

Mendelssohn, born the same year as Minna, so near Richard's age and yet so far ahead in fame and achievement, roused the younger musician's jealousy. He wrote to Apel in October, 1835, "Perhaps I shall do as well as Mendelssohn; however, I am only in Magdeburg while he is in Leipzig— that's the difference. But I haven't finished yet! I feel full of vigor!" Almost five decades later he was still grumbling about Mendelssohn's old affront to his genius.

5

By chance Richard met Minna and one of her sisters journeying back to Magdeburg. With youthful enthusiasm and characteristic irresponsibility he used borrowed money for a holiday with the girls and Rüpel at Schandau in the Saxon Alps. This episode was one of the happiest of his life. Almost a quarter of a century later, when he and Minna were living apart, he was to write her from Venice of their youthful pranks at Schandau on the Elbe, evidently the scene of some mighty adventure of Rüpel's with a tortoise.

After months of detention Laube had been set free provisionally and was recuperating at Bad Kösen, whither Richard traveled to show him the *Liebesverbot* verses and beguile the days while awaiting tidings of his contract renewal at Magdeburg. He had little hope of money; to be with Minna would be ample compensation.

Bethmann had extraordinary news. The talents of his first wife must have been phenomenal, for the Prussian king had come to his aid with a liberal new subsidy. Back in Magdeburg Richard enthusiastically volunteered to search Germany for vocal talent answering the dignity of the theater's new footing. Extravagantly, he offered to undertake this quest on his own, his recompense to take the form of a benefit performance. The boy had learned nothing, and Bethmann, running no risk, solemnly blessed the enterprise.

In Leipzig he presented the scheme to Brockhaus, who remained indifferent to investing further in Richard by advancing money for travel.

And evidently Friedrich delivered a homily on the relationship between work and income. Forgetting past favors, Richard, in a letter to his mother, vowed never to forgive this humiliation. He wrote that only her love healed and sustained him. His material sustenance, however, came mainly from the purses of Rosalie and Apel. Friedrich finally relented and contributed enough for Richard to set out on his tour.

He visited Bohemia and then, crossing the Fichtelgebirge, paused to admire the lovely city of Jean Paul—Bayreuth—lit by the evening sun. In Nuremberg he persuaded his sister Klara Wolfram and her husband, who were employed at the local theater, to join the Magdeburg troupe. From an earlier visit on his way home from Würzburg Richard had taken away pleasant memories of Nuremberg's tavern life. Now he was amused at an inn by the hilarious singing of a talentless and vain master carpenter. Baiting of this simpleton by a crowd of drunken merrymakers continued outside through winding lanes of the old town. The clamor reached its height in a near riot, which broke off when, as if by magic, the multitude melted into the surrounding maze of alleys. In the clear moonlight tipsy Richard incredulously contemplated the hushed scene where but a moment before all had been tumult. Memories of this night live on in Beckmesser's serenade and the cudgel scene in *Die Meistersinger.*

His tour continued as far as Wiesbaden and Frankfort, where, stranded without funds and forced to surrender his baggage as security for an unpaid hotel bill, he started with unassailable confidence in his future to jot down notes for an autobiography in a red copybook. Having selected his singers, he turned back to Leipzig, where he learned of Uncle Adolf's death, gathered up his poodle, and went on to Magdeburg, arriving there on September 1, 1835.

Among his newly engaged artists were Minna's sister Amalie, whose pliant mezzo was one day to influence the creation of Adriano in *Rienzi,* and an old flame of his Leipzig days, Marie Löwe, a formidable harp player and singer, perhaps best known for giving birth in 1848 to Lilli Lehmann. With a strengthened orchestra Richard started a season that included Auber's *Lestocq,* Bellini's *Norma* and *I Capuletti ed i Montecchi,* and Spohr's *Jessonda.* An October letter to Apel reveals that his feelings against German opera had, if anything, heightened. "The opera [*Jessonda*] again fills me with utter disgust; the soft Bellini is a true Hercules compared with this great, lengthy, pedantic, sentimental Spohr." Along with aesthetic commentaries he bombarded Theodor with requests for money.

The score of *Liebesverbot* occupied him throughout 1835. He curtailed his drinking and worked. Bethmann had agreed to mount the opera at the end of the regular season. Because of the expense involved the management was to take the proceeds of the première; the second night was to constitute Richard's benefit. Bethmann had outwitted him again.

The success of the work was now as important to Minna as to him. Early in November she had suddenly left the company to accept an offer from Herr Cerf (born Karl Friedrich Hirsch), manager of the Königstadt Theater in Berlin. Her absence drove Richard to write her frenzied love letters that included a formal marriage proposal. "Minna, all my faith is leaving me; a pitiful theater intrigue, sure to blow over soon, is important enough to you to destroy our living together, brought about by many sacrifices on my part." Again the next day he wrote, "Here I accepted the job only for the sake of possessing you," and two days later, "Oh, if you would recognize the unceasing strength and endurance of my love, your ice would melt, and you would be compelled to throw yourself into my arms." He forced Bethmann to restore to her those roles pre-empted by Madame Grabowsky, the stage manager's wife whose plots had caused Minna's departure. She returned.

Despite generous royal support, once again bankruptcy terminated Bethmann's opera season before schedule. Out of good will toward Richard the artists agreed to stay on and learn *Liebesverbot*. But the ten days available were hardly sufficient to master a complicated ensemble opera with a difficult text. Richard felt that he could depend upon his extraordinary ability to conduct orchestra and singers while simultaneously indicating stage business. Helpful as this technique was at rehearsal, the exigencies of performance reduced the scope of his vocal and semaphoric cues. The first performance (March 29, 1836) foundered. The leading tenor, as his memory failed, hid behind an enormous feather boa and came up with bits and pieces of Auber and Hérold to fill the gaps. Inasmuch as no printed libretto was available, the mystified but not unfriendly public could not even grasp the intent of the plot. Word of the fiasco traveled.

On the second night—his benefit—Richard glanced into the auditorium some minutes before curtain time and counted an audience of three, all Jews. With her husband sat Madame Gottschalk; a Polish Jew in full regalia completed the trio.

Suddenly there was an uproar backstage. The husband of the leading soprano (Frau Pollert, from St. Petersburg) was attacking the dashing second tenor, who was suspected of being her lover. As the victim fled, dripping blood, she, racing in to stop the fracas, also received her husband's hand and immediately succumbed to convulsions. It was announced to the select audience that *Liebesverbot* could not be given that night. So ended the benefit.

Richard's situation was desperate. With his hopes, his poodle, too, had disappeared. Creditors, no longer put off, sought his arrest. He attempted to have his work produced in Leipzig, but the Opera's director rejected it, finding the subject matter too licentious. As Richard prepared to leave his native city, Rosalie seized his hand, saying presciently, "God alone knows when I shall see you again!" The months of life remaining to her were few.

Minna was his strength in this crisis. He returned to Magdeburg and hid, but it was obvious that they must leave. Fortunately, her talents were in demand, and she came to terms with the Königsberg theater (as did Marie Löwe) on condition that a position as conductor be made available to Richard. The management held out such a possibility, and she left for East Prussia while he, in the middle of May, tried his luck with *Liebesverbot* in Berlin until the time his Königsberg job should materialize.

In Berlin Herr Cerf of the Königstadt Theater toyed with him, promising much and then breaking off negotiations. Luckily, Laube was in town to comfort the young man, highly overwrought by the uncertain status of his career, by separation from his mistress, and by claims of creditors like the Gottschalks, who evidently were threatening to press Minna about her lover's obligations.

In Laube's company Richard heard Spontini's *Ferdinand Cortez,* conducted by its composer at the Hoftheater. The heroic scale and showiness of grand opera immediately appealed to Richard, who took up an overture, *Polonia,* conceived in his Leipzig days after a drinking bout with the Polish exiles, and finished it in pompous style. Spontini was to be a major influence on his development.

This encounter with the art of the Prussian king's Italian *Kapellmeister* gave Richard's stay in the capital its only compensation. Though he lived fairly comfortably, he was short enough of money to save postage by compressing onto two sheets of paper a letter of over five thousand words to Minna in Königsberg. His expectations had come to nothing, and his humiliation can be read in the hysterical correspondence with which he overwhelmed her. These letters, filled with a morbid, uncontrolled self-pity, reveal that effeminate aspect of his nature (*"eine zu weibliche innere Beweglichkeit"*) which he was frankly to concede in a fine letter of September, 1841, to Johanna. His enormous capacity for lamentation would one day be turned to great art in the creation of Tannhäuser, Tristan, and Amfortas. But at the moment Minna's devotion must have been severely tried. *Liebesverbot* was unwanted, and he needed her strength.

6

Das Liebesverbot, an adaptation of Shakespeare's *Measure for Measure,* was a dramatic exposition of Wagner's new anti-German and pro-Italian sentiments, which embraced not only preference for an operatic style but also enthusiasm for the national temperament that gave it birth. Shakespeare's play rested indirectly upon an Italian tale related by Giraldi in his *Hecatommithi,* first published in Sicily in 1565. To this island Wagner transferred the action that Shakespeare had placed in a fanciful Vienna. And during the move south Wagner let go the ethical and social issues upon which Shakespeare's main plot turns and reduced the whole to the rowdy level of an Elizabethan subintrigue. Angelo was transformed into Friedrich, agent of a German royal power ruling Sicily (the historical Hohenstaufen sway over southern Italy would have made the situation credible to the German public), and this variation gave Wagner the opportunity of contrasting what he held to be the Puritanism and narrowness of the Teutonic spirit with the sensualism and freedom of the south. Friedrich's German hypocrisy is the villain of the piece, Sicilian candor its hero.

Shakespeare's Angelo, a man "whose blood is very snow-broth" and whose "urine is congealed ice," now, as Friedrich, becomes the target of Laube's disciple:

> The German fool . . . laugh him to scorn . . .
> Send him back to his wintry home;
> There may he be temperate and chaste.

How full of the iconoclast's contempt for pedantry is Friedrich's dialogue with himself as he discovers his austerity completely undermined by Isabella's beauty: "Wretch, whither has sped away that system so carefully established by you? A hint of her warm breath and it melts like a cold winter dream."

To Richard, Italy summed up warmth, freedom, and the forsaking of outworn shibboleths. About the time he was setting to work in earnest on *Liebesverbot,* he had been "reading Laube about Verona, about Vicenza and its Palladio." And then almost despairingly he wrote to Apel, "Oh, let us but get to Italy, and may God grant us strength!"

Wagner's conversion of *Measure for Measure* into light farce—really *opera buffa*—is remarkable. One is only too ready to believe his admission that little care went into the versification of *Die Feen.* On the other hand, *Liebesverbot* represents his unique success in the realm of the well-made play. His only other attempt in this field, *Meistersinger,* is a drama of depth and perception. But its mechanism is flawed by inconsistencies of construction that yield logical fallacies even more disturbing than those of the *Ring,* which, unlike *Meistersinger,* at least makes no pretense to being "well made" in the Scribe sense.

Wagner, of course, had other and more important aims for his art. But his dramaturgy is often more slipshod than need be; his dependence upon music to make the illogical seem logical often led him to downright literary carelessness. *Liebesverbot* is a fascinating document showing what Wagner could do by varying and accommodating a pre-existent play to his needs. He obviously benefited by having a model from the hand of a master poet, but he never again returned to this method.

Excepting *Rienzi*, whose excellent libretto owes much to the example of Bulwer-Lytton's novel, Wagner laboriously hammered subsequent opera books out of a variety of sources—many relatively obscure—in verse and prose. His abilities were never equal to achieving a unified result, completely satisfying from the literary point of view. Claims of the old Wagnerites that he was as great a poet and playwright as a musician are, of course, absurd. Wagner's music usually carries forward triumphantly the ingenious but cumbersome machinery of his librettos, which would otherwise sputter and stall. Together they make a kind of foreordained and inevitable progress, rewarding to those with patience enough to follow.

These observations, however, hardly apply to the music of *Liebesverbot,* described by Einstein as "a piece of impertinence and shameless imitation," a hodgepodge of Beethoven, Hérold, Auber, Rossini, Bellini, Marschner, and Meyerbeer. Since the operas from which Wagner purloined material are no longer in the general repertory, *Liebesverbot* seems more original today than it did at the time of its creation. In this strange stew at least one ingredient was worth salvage, and the nuns' off-stage *Salve Regina* was later put to better use as the motif of Heavenly Grace in *Tannhäuser.* This theme, which in the orchestra opens the cloister scene, represents Wagner's first use of the Dresden Amen, here transformed as it is known in *Tannhäuser.* In *Parsifal,* following Mendelssohn's example in the "Reformation" Symphony, he returned to the original floating form as found in the Dresden liturgy.

Wagner's mature judgment of *Liebesverbot* was "atrocious, abominable, nauseating." Few would dispute him. In general, the music, more chromatic than *Feen,* is terribly busy and has a frequent and astounding irrelevance to the dramatic situation. Leitmotifs, hinted at in the *"Hochzeit"* fragment and turned to modest account in *Feen,* are more boldly manipulated. The long dark theme picturing Friedrich and his inflexible law is often fragmented and used cleverly throughout the opera. There is a penetrating harmonic alteration of Isabella's motif when for the moment she finds herself defeated by Friedrich's villainy, the phrase regaining its major luster as he recalls her beauty in the recitative to her aria. As in *Feen,* there are canonic sections to warm Papa Weinlig's heart and moments when the bloom of the melodic line pleases even in the face of either its triteness or the composer's unembarrassed plagiarism.

Despite the work's harmonic turgidity, one must wonder at its temerity, its self-confidence, and the adroitness involved in expressing relatively so little musically by so many notes. The monstrous length of the ensembles already indicates a lack of concern for proportion, throughout his career one of Wagner's major artistic failings.

It remains to be observed that the motive of redemption, Wagner's favorite literary device, already toyed with in Die Feen, assumes clear form in Das Liebesverbot, wherein Isabella, having taken upon herself the cleverness and ambiguous humanity of Shakespeare's Duke (banished by Wagner from the action), emerges as the prototype of the resourceful Wagnerian virgin, busily preparing salvation for an undeserving male.

It is not surprising that Richard's derivative score did not impress the musical world of Berlin. There were polite comments, easy and insincere promises, but only someone gifted with prophecy could have seen that the work was by a great composer.

7

In Königsberg, Minna had made her usual success. Richard, his Berlin hopes gone, was able to join her there in July of 1836 through Laube's financial help. The Königsberg conductor's desk was still not free. Ludwig Schuberth was temporarily occupying it until the Riga theater, in the process of reconstruction, was ready to receive him. At the moment, enjoying an affair with the prima donna of Königsberg and in no mood to return to his wife in Livonia, he resented Richard's presence as a constant reminder that he must one day tear himself from the allurements of Madame Henriette Grosser. He sought to rid himself of the interloper. But when Minna threatened to leave for Danzig, where she could obtain work for both herself and her lover, the Königsberg management set April, 1837, as the date for Schuberth's withdrawal.

With financial stability in sight—the main consideration to the cautious Minna—the couple planned to marry. And the theater offered them a wedding benefit of Masaniello, with Richard conducting and Minna miming the part of the mute, Fenella.

All was not tranquil. Richard's violent temper exploded whenever he found indications of former lovers in Minna's life. Much about her past was hidden. Moreover, he was becoming ever more conscious of the cultural gap between them. Upon entering the shabby world of provincial theater, he had been forced to neglect intellectual pursuits. Laube had been concerned to observe this. But, deep down, a finer life continued—Richard's own secret from Minna. Still, when he considered her beauty and felt the warmth of her concern, doubts vanished. Things would work out.

In the parsonage of the suburban parish of Tragheim they squabbled as one rainy and miserable morning they arrived to make arrangements for their wedding. The economical Minna was on edge; to her horror, Richard had furnished a comfortable dwelling for them entirely on credit. And the Magdeburg debts were pursuing him from the Elbe to the Oder and across the Frisches Haff.

On November 24, 1836, they were married. Minna's attire was selected by Richard. (Over four decades later he would steal time from work on *Parsifal* to choose gowns with matching shoes for Cosima.) He was encouraged by the pastor's assurance that an unknown friend would remedy whatever trials might lie ahead; another Apel was what Richard needed. But hopes were shattered when the good genius was identified as Jesus.

The morning after his wedding he had to appear before a magistrate in connection with the claims of his Magdeburg creditors. The groom, pleading infancy under Prussian law, startled the court; on the preceding day he had been permitted to marry without parental consent by claiming to have attained his majority according to the statutes of his native Saxony. The stratagem devised by one of Minna's Königsberg admirers, Abraham Möller, at least gained a brief respite.

While awaiting Schuberth's departure, Wagner wrote the *Rule Britannia* overture in his new inflated style, projected a piece on Napoleon, and from a tale in the *Arabian Nights* developed a sketch for a two-act comic opera, *"Die glückliche Bärenfamilie."* Taking the measure of the Königsberg troupe, he planned a work musically less demanding than *Liebesverbot;* the light French idiom of Adolphe Charles Adam (remembered today for his ballet *Giselle*) characterized the fragment of it he composed. There are allusions to his family in the libretto: a jeweler styled Julius Wander after his goldsmith brother, who once roamed as far as Paris, a dancing bear called Richard—really the goldsmith's lost brother in disguise!—and the bear's master, Gregor, whose name reminds one of Geyer and who is another lost father, here fortuitously restored to his son.

As the Lenten season to be crowned by Schuberth's farewell approached, it was obvious that the Königsberg company faced financial embarrassment. The situation demanded salary cuts which in turn brought catastrophe to the Wagner household, mortgaged to local merchants and besieged by creditors from distant cities. The young couple quarreled hideously. And they were not alone in this crisis. Natalie, aged eleven, known to the world as Minna's young sister, was living with them.

Richard was by now fully aware that Ernestine Natalie was Minna's daughter, the illegitimate child of Ernst Rudolph von Einsiedel, an officer of the Royal Saxon Guards who had seduced Minna when she was in her fifteenth year. ("Half rape and half seduction" brought her to his arms,

Wagner later recorded.) Her pregnancy had forced her to leave home. This timely disappearance, in addition to the sympathetic connivance of her mother and some miracle of feminine persuasion and masculine vanity, had led Herr Gottlief Planer to believe that the new baby belonged to him and his wife.

The experience accounted for much that was mysterious and contradictory in Minna. Richard's full acceptance of the child as his sister-in-law (she herself probably did not learn her true identity until old age) and his willingness to continue the masquerade evidence a generosity the passing years were to make ever more difficult to detect but which could still be called forth even to the end of his days in the right circumstances.

Late in May he returned home from the theater to find that Minna had fled with Natalie. Moreover, he learned that Dietrich, a wealthy Königsberg merchant who had often shown an annoying interest in Minna, was no longer in town. After an abortive attempt at pursuit, Richard dejectedly returned and could leave the city again only by stealth, so surveillant were his creditors.

He found Minna at her parents' home in Dresden and was ashamed of his suspicions, for he had, in fact, initiated a petition for divorce. It seemed that her nervous system simply could not stand the financial uncertainty of life with him. This forthright bourgeoise was unable to cope with summonses on the front door and creditors at the back. But he brought news of the possibility of a good position as conductor in Riga that might even free her of the necessity of working on the stage any longer. A trip to Berlin, where he met with Holtei, the new Riga manager, yielded a contract, and Richard and Minna attempted a reconciliation in the Elbe countryside at Blasewitz near Dresden. Here he read Bulwer-Lytton's novel *Rienzi,* in Bärmann's translation.

The reunion appeared to him to be going well; his unusual patience and reassurances were ostensibly calming her. Then, on the pretext of joining an old friend and her family on a short excursion, she vanished again. From Abraham Möller, his confidant in Königsberg, he learned that Dietrich had recently been in Dresden. The conclusion he drew was numbing.

Fortunately, in the beautiful Grosser Garten near Blasewitz lived his sister Ottilie and her scholarly husband, Hermann Brockhaus,[5] a younger

---

[5] In one of those strange errors, the nightmare of the historian, the treacherous standard English translation of *Mein Leben* seemingly misled Ernest Newman in his monumental *Life* into at times combining Hermann and Heinrich Brockhaus into one personage. Heinrich was a bookseller and a representative in the Saxon Diet. His role in *Mein Leben* is ungrateful, as one who stood aloof from the starving young Richard in Paris and as the confiscator of his Dresden library for debt. For Hermann, on the contrary, Wagner had an abiding affection.

brother of Luise's husband, Friedrich. Sympathy, affection, and the intellectual companionship of Hermann, an authority on Eastern languages, helped Richard revive. His restored energies went into sketching an opera book on the Rienzi theme cast in the grand Spontini-Meyerbeer tradition. He attended performances of Halévy's *La Juive* and Spohr's *Jessonda* at the Dresden Opera and spent the remainder of the summer in a state of mounting artistic exaltation. He was always able to recover quickly from the many crises of his life.

Grand opera's high abode, Paris, had been much on his mind. Throughout his letters to Apel was the dream of escape to Europe's greatest metropolis. "I shall compose a French opera in Paris—and God knows where I shall be then! I know *who* I shall be, certainly no longer a German Philistine!" (Magdeburg, October, 1834.) From Königsberg, his "Prussian Siberia," he had written to Schumann in Leipzig, seeking information about the Opéra-Comique, to which he wished to submit *Liebesverbot;* and he had sent the plan of a big opera based upon Heinrich König's novel *Die hohe Braut* to the great Scribe, librettist for Auber and Meyerbeer, offering him—Paris' most lionized dramatist—use of this literary material with the stipulation that he adapt it for production at the Opéra with music to be composed by one Richard Wagner. Could the naïve young man know that for a book Scribe asked as much as twenty thousand francs, a fee that eclipsed that of Rossini, whose agreement of 1829 with the government of Charles X guaranteed him fifteen thousand francs for a new opera? As a sample of Richard's talent Scribe also received from him the score of *Liebesverbot* along with the diffident suggestion that its merits be judged by either Auber or Meyerbeer. Taking no chances, he recommended himself to the latter in a deferential letter. He was not one to hide his light. Had he not sent from Magdeburg an enthusiastic review of his own work to Schumann's magazine? He was willing to do anything to consummate a *mariage d'esprit* with Scribe and also implored him to turn to account the *Liebesverbot* material howsoever he would. Through the writer and publisher August Lewald, Richard soon would be offering him his new grand opera, for flexible Rienzi could "sing French at a moment's notice." Also during the summer of 1837, with an eye on London, he posted the *Rule Britannia* to Sir George Smart, president of the Philharmonic Society.

Late in July he prepared to leave for his Riga engagement. A foolish but understandable fear of embarrassment made him shun his mother and Rosalie in Leipzig. Johanna had warned against an early marriage. Always hoping for news of Minna, he made his way via Berlin and Schwerin to Lübeck. The young man who had scoffed at Frankfort on the Oder as the ultimate in provincialism was setting sail for the most remote outpost of German civilization.

8

Riga, the main city of ancient Livonia, had sheltered a German enclave since the days of the Teutonic Knights. Governed at the time of Richard's arrival by the Russians, who he feared could read Polish sympathies in his features, the city with its Hanseatic flavor and its theater's German atmosphere made him welcome. Holtei had hired him because of his youthful enthusiasm for Bellini, Adam, Auber, and Donizetti. In addition, the Geyer-Wagner family connections had worked their old magic. The opera had sound financial support from the German colony, and only Minna was lacking to complete his well-being.

In need of a prima donna, he wrote to Minna's sister Amalie,[6] with whom he had recently wept at a Berlin performance of Beethoven's operatic essay on conjugal fidelity. After this renewed contact with her in Dresden, a message from Minna followed. Ill and dejected at her parents' home, she wrote of her love and of her desire to join him again. He answered quickly in several letters, "Forget everything, my poor wife; I take no heed of the past, no heed of the present . . . ; only *one* burning desire, one longing is still alive in my heart; I count every minute until I can hold you in my arms." He was almost beside himself. Since they as yet had no children, he bought two black poodles, whom he planned to name "Dreck" and "Speck." "And now, in heaven's name, let me stop; I can't sit still on the sofa any longer; I must do a bit of dancing around the room."

It must be cautioned that it was Wagner, fed on rumor by his Königsberg gossip, Möller, who recorded the Dietrich episode. It might very well have been true. However, Natalie's descriptions of his unjustifiable and overmastering jealousy are reminiscences which, even if exaggerated, clearly show that Minna's beauty and celebrity were sources of unreasonable uneasiness to him. His violent and often hysterical reactions to what he unwarrantably considered affronts to his dignity certainly had much to do with Minna's flight. An unprepossessing mien evidently made him vastly insecure. From Berlin he had written to her in Königsberg, "Where you are there are said to be some handsome men. Be careful, Minnachen, do you hear? Don't look at them!" A magnificent letter to her written during the *Tristan* period (May 18, 1859) acknowledges this obdurate jealousy in Königsberg and, incidentally, also strongly supports suspicions of Minna's infidelity.

---

[6] Though in Riga Amalie sang both soprano and mezzo parts (Donna Elvira, Norma, Romeo), she was essentially in the lower category. With the aid of transpositions, she bravely filled a breach in personnel until Frau Pollert (of *Liebesverbot* fame!) arrived to take over the high roles.

In addition, her applauded career had rankled in a man who was suffered in the Königsberg theater only because he was his wife's husband. The tasteless observations in *Mein Leben* that neither Rosalie nor Minna ever had any real acting talent are contradicted by much evidence to the contrary; one is forced to conclude that, dearly as he loved these women in his own egoistic way, his old resentment of their modest artistic success was still alive more than a quarter of a century after the burial of one and the retirement of the other.

In October the Planer girls, having picked up various Wagnerian household objects in Königsberg, journeyed across the wastes to Livonia. Richard promised never to remind Minna of their recent difficulties and, to his credit, except for the above-mentioned letter to Minna written over twenty years later and a loving account of a dream about her disappearance (in a letter of June 25, 1856), he kept his word. Though the sisters quarreled, the couple could have enjoyed relative calm and security had not Richard come into conflict with Holtei by suddenly veering from the limited aesthetic the manager thought they both shared.

Heinrich Dorn, once sponsor in Leipzig of Richard's kettledrum overture and now Riga's municipal director of music, was at first amazed at what the teachings of Laube and Gutzkow had done to the former young idolizer of Beethoven and Weber. But, little by little, preoccupation with the Rienzi theme was restoring his earlier seriousness. And news of Theodor's illness and of Rosalie's death in October, 1837, had confirmed a growing sobriety. Other than some incidental music for the theater, a setting of Scheurlin's *"Der Tannenbaum,"* and a broad concerted hymn in praise of the Czar, the weighty affairs of Rienzi occupied most of his writing hours.

Shakespeare again elated him as much as *Die glückliche Bärenfamilie* now offended. Holtei's admiring eye had been drawn to this libretto which Wagner now cavalierly presented to his assistant, Löbmann. The light Franco-Italian repertory bored Riga's *Kapellmeister,* and his feelings were certainly known to the company.

The grubby theatrical world of small cities now seemed to him not only to have brought to pass the decline of his taste but also to have sown the seeds of his recent marital difficulties. Despite the blow to his income, he determined to keep Minna from the stage and to cut himself off as much as possible from contact with shallow vaudevillians. This new Olympian attitude hardly increased his popularity with his fellow artists. Moreover, the gigantic proportions *Rienzi* was assuming made it clear that Paris or Berlin were his immediate, if fanciful, goals and that for the limited resources of the local stage he had only contempt. Despite his months in Riga, he remained almost a complete stranger there, although his unusual taste in dress did impress those citizens who in mild weather could glimpse the strange figure at the window in dressing gown and Oriental fez.

In the course of two seasons at Riga, Wagner gained valuable conducting experience. He had a fine, if limited, group of singers and instrumentalists and the opportunity and desire to rehearse them whether or not he admired the work being prepared. Many of the now almost forgotten operas he studied and conducted in Magdeburg, Königsberg, and Riga contributed a filament here and a fibril there toward that glorious fabric of threads and patches—the Wagnerian opera. For example, extraordinary echoes of Boieldieu's *La Dame blanche*—with which he made his Riga operatic debut—sound through his works from the spinning scene in *Dutchman,* the *Tannhäuser* march, and Lohengrin's arioso, to the St. John motif in *Meistersinger* and Isolde's outburst, *"Da die Männer sich all ihm vertragen."* (In 1874, while completing the *Ring,* he delighted in burying himself in the score of *Dame blanche.*)

Wagner was looking with interest at the notable achievements of French opera, which stretched from Lully through Gluck and Méhul to Cherubini and the Auber of *Masaniello* and, at the time, seemingly culminated in Meyerbeer. The tradition was largely the creation of nonnatives, often the case in French art. Of course, Wagner's admiration for and imitation of French opera was to some extent inspired by opportunism. For the past decade he had been an impressionable traveler attempting to straddle divergent paths. At this point the most auspicious route seemed to be that of Meyerbeer. Its direction was clear, its rewards rumored to be fantastic. But, although Richard had been roused by tales of the profits earned by *The Huguenots* (1836), the score itself had greatly impressed him. In his eyes Meyerbeer had lifted the restricted tradition of French opera into the universal by the admixture of German spirit and rumination. Richard inwardly realized that his ever more critical situation in Riga would shortly force his withdrawal. The next attempt at success would be in the Continental capital itself, where Richard Wagner, the new Meyerbeer, the Saxon Rienzi, would appear as a musical Camillus ready to command the Rome of the Seine.

As the months passed his position became increasingly difficult. Holtei openly showed his antipathy and met with scorn his conductor's demands for a more serious repertory. And the Magdeburg and Königsberg creditors were seeking justice from imperial Russia. Minna's retirement had had its effect on the family income, and fresh debts were accumulating. His passport, secured with difficulty, was seized by the authorities on behalf of creditors he had too often evaded by flight. In March of 1839 he learned that his contract was not to be renewed. His final performances were to take place in June during the summer season at Mitau. Holtei, before his own resignation, had selected Dorn to follow Wagner as conductor under a new manager, the tenor Johann Hoffmann.

Later, to explain his predicament to Ludwig of Bavaria (for whom *Mein Leben* was professedly written), and, of course, to posterity, Wagner fell back upon one of his favorite devices—character assassination. Everyone was against him. He accused Holtei, a well-known actor, poet, and novelist, of having been a homosexual and a pimp who had made advances to Minna in order to deceive people as to his real nature. And Dorn emerged as a traitor operating under the cover of friendship.

It is, however, obvious that the theater could hardly depend upon the services of a conductor who might at any moment be either imprisoned or forced to flee. And Dorn was his most logical successor—an excellent musician resident in Riga. Since Dorn and Holtei were old friends who had, in fact, collaborated on an opera (*Die Bettlerin,* Königsberg, 1828), it is probable that Dorn had actually first been offered Wagner's post; he had evidently declined, recommending his young protégé,[7] who had written him an imploring letter from Königsberg in August, 1836, seeking information about the position in which Schuberth apparently no longer had any interest. And how ironic that Wagner should indicate to King Ludwig that sexual inversion was the basis of what he held to be Holtei's inadequacies!

Obviously, too, Dorn and Hoffmann attempted not only to protect the theater but also to help the menaced Wagner by seeing that sufficient salary was advanced to provide funds for escape.

It was surprisingly easy for him to prepare Minna for the idea of a flight to Paris. She saw her darling as he saw himself—the victim of treachery. And had he not in June of 1837 received a polite note from Scribe? Recently, through sister Cäcilie's fiancé, Eduard Avenarius, employed by the Brockhaus firm as manager of its Paris branch, he had learned that Scribe not only could recall his name but could also be prodded into vague recollections of various enclosures received. The ingenuous Minna, persuaded that her husband was in touch with the highest operatic circles of Paris, fell in with an adventure holding so much promise. Richard hastened to insert a Parisian-style ballet into *Rienzi*'s second act, whose composition was completed before their departure, and started his lifelong struggle with the French tongue.

Money for the voyage had to be raised. There was a benefit concert, and Minna returned to the stage for a few guest performances that drew good receipts. She then sold part of her elaborate theatrical wardrobe and many household furnishings. Wagner's creditors were not alarmed by these activities. After all, he could not go far; he had no passport. And who

[7] It was Dorn's half brother, Schindelmeisser, who first put Wagner into contact with Holtei.

would be foolish enough to attempt to cross the heavily guarded Russian frontier without official permission?

Old Möller arrived from Königsberg with a battle plan. It was really an outflanking maneuver, whose dangers Amalie's betrothed, the Russian officer, Carl von Meck, revealed to Minna too late for retreat. Möller's strategy rested upon a friend living in Prussia near the Russian border; he was willing to assist.

It was decided to exit from Mitau. From this small town, some thirty miles southwest of Riga and thus nearer the Tilsit plain, a more circumspect departure could be made.

In July, Möller, Richard, and Minna set out in a coach traversing the luxuriant Courland summer landscape. But they were not entirely alone. Richard had been adopted by a gigantic Newfoundland dog, who trotted beside in the hot sun. Not for long could Richard watch the exertions of the animal, for he was soon invited into the carriage, which he filled to overflowing with his giant frame and shaggy coat.

When the frontier was reached on the second day, Möller's friend was found waiting. He drove Minna, Richard, and the dog, now named "Robber," through devious lanes to a smuggler's inn filled with Polish Jews who somewhat alarmed Richard. There a guide took the fugitives in charge and at sundown led them to the boundary line protected by a ditch and patrolled by Cossacks. Möller's arrangements had so far been remarkable. But even though he had managed to bribe several sentinels, the danger was at its height. At a change of guard Minna and Richard ran down a hill, hurtled across the ditch, and raced for their very lives. Even when on the Prussian side, if observed by any soldier uncorrupted by Möller, they would have been shot. At this critical point a single bark from Robber might have deprived the world of much great music. When they were out of gun range, the carriage of their Prussian ally approached and conveyed them to the anxious Möller.

Reaching the village of Arnau the next day, they rested from a harrowing experience, the extent of which Richard had not anticipated. But the worst was yet to come. En route to the port of Pillau on the Frisches Haff, where a boat was to take them to London, they traveled by back roads in order to avoid Königsberg, whose police had an interest in the runaway. The primitive coach from Arnau overturned. Richard ended in a heap of manure, Möller was shaken up, and Minna, caught under the coach, was so badly injured that, according to Natalie, she lost the child she was carrying. The few days of waiting for the sailing gave the poor woman some respite.

Captain Wulff of the Prussian-owned *Thetis* had agreed to take the couple on board without papers. But the harbor watch had still to be outwitted. One morning before dawn Minna, Richard, and Robber crawled through wet and high grass to a dinghy that glided to the *Thetis.* Robber again kept his peace. But now the giant beast had to be hoisted up the side. Once aboard, they hid among the cargo in the hold for hours until after the final official check. The *Thetis* set sail, and the fugitives breathed more easily.

IV

Paris: Reconnoiter and Retreat

I

The voyage recalled to Wagner the legend of the Flying Dutchman. Nature seemed in rebellion; unfriendly winds and deceptive calms were followed by hurricanes with towering waves. Shelter was sought in the Norwegian fjords. One of them, the bay of Sandvika, was to appear as the opening setting of *The Flying Dutchman,* in whose pages echo rhythmic cries Wagner heard from the mariners as they anchored and furled sail.

The water's anger had torn the figurehead of Thetis from the bow, and a trunk of Minna's containing silver and clothing was washed away with the wooden nymph. The crew, acquainted with the tale of Vanderdecken, the dread flying Mynheer, perhaps suspected their Saxon passenger also of bearing some powerful curse that turned a routine eight-day sail into the Thames into a dangerous misadventure lasting over three weeks.

Young Victoria's capital overwhelmed the Wagners. Its size, its crowds, and the Regency splendor of John Nash's still-new city were to make Paris—not yet rebuilt by Haussmann—seem to them cramped and mean by comparison. Robber disappeared for a couple of hours but returned, and the family was together at a boardinghouse in Old Compton Street.

Having failed to contact Sir George Smart of the Philharmonic, Richard next attempted to locate Bulwer-Lytton, Lincoln's parliamentary representative, in order to discuss the operatic adaptation of *Rienzi.* At the Palace of Westminster he learned that Lytton, like Smart, was out of town. Posterity thus missed what might have been an interesting encounter between the elegant, urbane man of letters and the provincial young *Kapellmeister.* Conversation would have been possible, for Lytton knew some German. Richard, on the other hand, was discovering that a few words from Shakespeare did small service in dealing with his landlady.

After a week of rest and sight-seeing he, Minna, and Robber crossed the channel to Boulogne on August 20. On board the steamer he met Mrs. Manson, a Jewess traveling with her daughter. They were acquainted with Meyerbeer, who, to Richard's fortune, was at the moment residing at Boulogne, and a letter of introduction was provided. Richard took modest quarters on the outskirts of the city in order to profit by the coincidence and to put final touches to the orchestration of *Rienzi's* second act. There was no need to rush to Paris; he had discovered in London that people of quality did not return to town until mid-September.

Meyerbeer, once a fellow pupil of Weber under Abbé Vogler, affably received his compatriot, patiently listened to more than half the libretto of *Rienzi* recited by its poet, and complimented the meticulous calligraphy of the two completed acts of the score, which he kept to examine at leisure. Generously, he promised Richard recommendations to Duponchel and Habeneck, manager and conductor respectively of the Grand Opéra, and introduced him to Moscheles, the Jewish virtuoso pianist, and his famous pupil Marie Blahetka. Luck had brought Richard into contact with some of music's most lustrous names.

Eduard Avenarius, Cäcilie's fiancé, had been requested to find quarters in Paris for the Wagners. On September 16, 1839, after almost a month in Boulogne, Richard struggled to lift Robber to the roof of a diligence and then set forth with Minna for the city of the Opéra and Eugène Scribe.

2

During Richard's residence at Boulogne a libretto from Scribe was being solicited by Hector Berlioz, who, having recently failed at the Opéra with his *Benvenuto Cellini* (1838), hoped that a book by the master of the *"coup de théâtre"* might redeem the setback. Of the reception of *Cellini* it was cruelly said that the audience slept and awoke hissing.

The Grand Opéra was the center of French musical life. Though, like the great lyric institutions of today, this theater founded by Louis XIV was a vulnerable target for humor and vilification, there is nevertheless no doubt that it was the finest in Europe.

In 1826 Weber had been impressed by what he experienced in the great hall on the Rue Le Peletier—a superb orchestra technically beyond the imaginings of a German *Kapellmeister,* lavish stage resources, and the magnificence of the house itself. Even at the less ostentatious Théâtre Feydeau he found Parisian singing, orchestral, and acting standards unknown in Germany.

Two years after Weber's visit, the art form known as "grand opera" was born in Paris with *La Muette de Portici (Masaniello)* by Scribe,

Delavigne, and Auber. But the union of Scribe's talents with those of the Prussian Jew Meyerbeer in *Robert the Devil* (1831) really set the triumphant course of this international, ingenious, and calculated operatic genre of historical pageantry accompanied by music. Its character and purpose departed from the tradition of the *tragédie lyrique,* that Gallic *opera seria* nourished by Gluck which, in Cherubini's and Spontini's finest moments, had survived the excesses of the French revolutionary style. Action and character were realized through a music whose intent was the articulation of drama. In contrast, the protagonists of grand opera were usually costumed figures performing vocal stunts before a background of stupendous scenic paraphernalia. The true ambitions of such a work usually did not rise above the decorative. But, unlike the opulent art of baroque opera, which had answered the glittering but tasteful needs of an aristocratic society, grand opera was, rather, a pretentious charade or variety show responding to the ambitions of a wealthy but culturally impoverished bourgeoisie. To grasp this difference, one need only compare those noble courts of the Louvre inspired by the Medici and the Sun King, with its theatrical pavilions in the style of the third Napoleon.

The contrived craft of Eugène Scribe and the hybrid art of Giacomo Meyerbeer (born Jakob Liebmann Beer at Berlin in 1791, he concocted his name, like his music, from various sources) seemed compelling to the parvenu society of the July Monarchy and the Second Empire. Parades, dances, and songs offered something for everyone whose taste was not penetrating. Moreover, thanks to its impressive historical framework, grand opera had, in the eyes of its public, the twofold virtue of appearing serious while, at the same time, not taxing the mind. That Parisians applauded Scribe's banal verse and Meyerbeer's empty music and frequent assaults upon the prosody of their language, reveals the extent to which taste had coarsened. In the time between Gluck and Meyerbeer, Paris had gradually declined from an art to an entertainment capital.

The new form did produce an opera of genuine merit, *La Juive* of Halévy (1835). His music transformed Scribe's well-carpentered but ponderous book into a moving, human work, under whose spell Wagner had already come in Dresden. The next year saw Meyerbeer's most sustained effort and chief recommendation to posterity, the magnificent fourth act of *Huguenots.* Rossini had attempted to embody elements of the new all-conquering grand opera in his *William Tell* (1829). But the revolution of 1830 altered his official position, and, perhaps sensing his more aristocratic era to be over, he capitulated and renounced operatic composition.

The dissimilarity between the personalities of Charles X and his successor, Louis Philippe, parallels the contrast between the patrician art of Rossini and Meyerbeer's accomplished, but less wellborn skill for accommodation, for bringing the Industrial Revolution to music. It was Rossini who had first introduced a work of Meyerbeer's to Paris, and, somewhat bitter in retirement, yet still venerated as *Illustrissimo Maestro,* he scorned the unvocal quality of "modern music" and looked forward to the day when "the Jews had finished their Sabbath." But, like Charles X, he had known when to abdicate and stylishly to withdraw.

Wagner's unquenchable drive for success made him adopt the aesthetic and methods of grand opera which his genius was to transform into art. Not only *Rienzi,* but also *Tannhäuser, Lohengrin, Meistersinger, The Twilight of the Gods,* and *Parsifal* reveal in their mixed heritage strains that descend, as does Verdi's *Aida,* from Meyerbeer's Parisian grand opera. In this form lay buried (and, of course, not yet worked up into swollen artistic theory) the seeds of Wagner's *Gesamtkunstwerk,* that all-embracing work of art which, despite the pretensions of Wagner's pamphleteering, is really the child of his flirtation with Meyerbeer and not, as he claimed, the aging Beethoven's legitimate offspring, nourished and reared by himself. As did Berlioz, Wagner studied Meyerbeer's instrumentation, praised by the famous Gevaert and so highly developed that, for the most part, it often camouflaged a relative poverty of musical thought.

It was the intimate knowledge of the Opéra's organization, gained by Wagner during the *Tannhäuser* production of 1861, that provided an important model for the festival house at Bayreuth. And the Opéra's new realism in décor, inspired by Ciceri, designer of *Robert the Devil,* became the Bayreuth ideal. Wagner's lament in later years that he had neglected to make his stage as well as his instrumentalists invisible is not to be taken as presaging Appia's Spartan aesthetic. On the contrary, the composer was deploring his failure to find in Germany the equal of Ciceri, his disciples, and their Parisian technicians.

3

The young provincial, his coach surmounted by a giant Newfoundland, was approaching Paris. Money was his goal. Opera composers were treated penuriously in Germany, where each theater paid a modest fee for a première, with neither royalties nor commissions following if the work entered the repertory. A right in perpetuity was sold for a pittance, and the creator of a successful opera might live in want as box offices profited from his labor. Such, for example, was the lot of Lortzing with his *Czaar und Zimmermann* (1837).

But in Paris fees accumulated with each performance, and a work that enjoyed repeated presentations at the Opéra constituted an annuity for its composer. Even during the establishment's earliest years the despotic Lully had paid his composers liberally for the first thirty representations. An international army of hopeful musicians besieged this incomparable theater. Its financial rewards for success explain why a genius of Berlioz's integrity and literary refinement would for a moment forget himself and consider collaboration with Scribe, even forgoing an appointment with Delacroix in order to propitiate the poetaster by accompanying him on a fishing trip. Eventually Berlioz received and then returned to him the libretto of *La Nonne sanglante;* it then became Gounod's dubious inheritance.

Wagner, bearing his *Liebesverbot* and *Rienzi* fragment, felt prosperity within his grasp. Paris was to be a cruel frustration, but he gained immeasurably from his stay. He saw superior operatic productions, heard for the first time truly professional orchestral playing, and had contact with genius of the rank of Heine and Berlioz. The latter made him feel like a schoolboy, and he discovered how meager his own accomplishments were. As his old idealism reawakened, simultaneously he found his true voice. In Paris, the great Wagner of history took his first steps.

Inroads had been made upon the money smuggled out of Russia. Möller intended to send funds to Paris, but uncomplimentary remarks allegedly made about him by the Wagners were repeated, and, indignant, he ignored their distress.

What Richard really intended to live on in Paris for his immediate needs remains as mysterious today as it then seemed to his soon-to-be brother-in-law, Eduard Avenarius, whom he promptly put under financial contribution. Busy with affairs of the Brockhaus firm and with preparations for his coming marriage in Leipzig to Cäcilie, Avenarius had taken time to find for the Wagners a small but agreeable *chambre garnie* on the narrow Rue de la Tonnellerie in the old Quartier des Halles.

Through Avenarius Richard met Gottfried Anders, a learned German working in the music division of the Bibliothèque Royale. Nervous, impractical, and enfeebled, this man in his fifties had an assumed name (*anders* means "otherwise"), and he claimed to be a ruined Rhenish aristocrat. Effeminate in nature, he shared his tiny book-lined bachelor's quarters on the Rue de Seine with a consumptive Jewish-German philologist named Samuel Lehrs. Wagner never forgot the latter, a gentle and grave scholar who first drew him to serious consideration of medieval poetry and of philosophy.

Intellectual interests, the German tongue, and poverty were the common bonds of this trio of new friends who were joined by young Ernst Kietz, a portrait painter from Dresden studying in Delaroche's classes. Wagner came to love the amiable Kietz (at the height of the Wesendonk crisis in 1858 he conceived the bizarre idea of adopting the middle-aged Kietz as his son), who was nevertheless a source of anxiety because of a too frequent surrender to moral weakness. A note to him from Richard ends with the blithe but protective injunction, "God be with you. Don't do too much pederasty!" Minna mothered this somewhat less than hardy band of aesthetes, which later admitted Kietz's fellow student Friedrich Pecht.

Wagner's poor progress in French confined close friendships to Paris' German community.[1] In addition to this linguistic problem, his rough provincial manners and difficult personality made impossible his rise in the world through fashionable drawing rooms. He barely attained the periphery of Parisian literary and musical society, at whose center was the flamboyant Liszt, for whose social and material good fortune he felt the contempt born of envy. He wrote to his mother in 1841 concerning talent for the salon, "I have felt bound to despise whomever I have seen succeed in this way!"

Friedrich Brockhaus, in Paris for a while, was joined by his wife Luise in November of 1839. It was she who introduced Kietz to her brother. To Friedrich, Richard's French adventure appeared preposterous. He was, after all, an unknown composer of two operas with but one disastrous performance of the second on record. *Rienzi*, on which so much hope rested, was unfinished. It seemed clear that Richard's talent as a composer was limited, and that his most prudent course would be to find another niche as *Kapellmeister* in a comfortable German town. At least his ability as a conductor was proved.

He had so far survived in Paris by borrowing from Avenarius and by pawning his and Minna's valuables and then selling the tickets. Minna let go the remainder of her magnificent theatrical wardrobe, Richard especially mourning the sacrifice of a blue dress embroidered in silver with a grand train. One desperate day their wedding rings, too, were relinquished.

Soon after his arrival he was delighted to discover Laube and his wife living on the Boulevard des Italiens. Laube undertook to communicate with Friedrich on Richard's behalf, and the generous brother-in-law and sister agreed to send him funds over a period of half a year to be dispersed through Avenarius. Despite doubts the family rarely failed Richard. Moreover, Laube also persuaded a friend, the wealthy Jewish merchant Axenfeld of Leipzig, to contribute a similar gift.

Avenarius was back in Paris with his bride in the spring of 1840. An estrangement arose between the young couples when Eduard's purse, in reality far from full, was again boldly attacked by Richard, whose pleas were always accompanied by pious promises that each new demand would be the last.

Meyerbeer's letter of introduction had secured from Duponchel, the

---

[1] In 1855 Wagner's ignorance of English was similarly to debar him from contact with London society and account for his strange concepts of English life, largely garnered from the misinformed opinion of German refugees in the capital.

Opéra's director, an interview that was really only a gesture, a respectful response to a famous signature. And Richard learned that an attempt to contact Scribe would be considered rash at this time. But Habeneck, conductor of the Opéra (and son of a German musician), indulgently accepted upon Meyerbeer's urging the dreadful *Columbus* overture for performance at a rehearsal of the Société des Concerts du Conservatoire, which he had founded in 1828. An excellent musician responsible for introducing Beethoven's symphonies into France, his interpretation of the Ninth rekindled Richard's veneration for the master. Through Habeneck and his marvelous orchestra he for the first time experienced aurally the immensity of Beethoven's late orchestral style. The older Wagner, who speculated on German racial superiority, evidently forgot that he owed this revelation to French musicians.

To bring his name before the world he turned to the salon song, air, and vaudeville chorus, producing a group of works of rather despicable quality, some of which he unsuccessfully peddled to famous singers, among them Pauline Garcia (later Viardot), Malibran's sister. As a youth in Würzburg he had fashioned a new coda for an aria in Marschner's *Vampyr;* in Livonia he had not only added an air to a Singspiel but had contributed a new bass aria with male chorus to *Norma,* the opera of his first Riga benefit. Now in Paris he attempted to persuade Lablache to interpolate a Wagnerian pseudo-Bellini solo into the part of Oroveso. The renowned bass diplomatically declined.

Though Wagner, using texts by Heine, Hugo, and Ronsard, among others, cast his Parisian songs in a style combining touches of Berlioz with what he imagined to be a fashionable salon idiom, rhythmic and thematic anticipations of later works are here and there observable. Climaxing this series is an air for Mary Stuart, a setting of a noted poem by Béranger, which, along with Victor Hugo's play *Mary Tudor* (1833) had made the British queens popular literary subjects in France. During its incubative stage, for example, Berlioz's *Harold in Italy* had been called *The Last Moments of Mary Stuart.* Wagner's contribution to this royal literature may well be the worst.

4

His prospects at the Opéra were visionary. But through Meyerbeer he was recommended to the Théâtre de la Renaissance, where interest was expressed in producing *Liebesverbot.* Only an audition of excerpts was necessary to assure its acceptance, and Meyerbeer's influence persuaded singers from the Opéra to prepare three of its numbers already translated into crisp French verse by Anders' friend Dumersan.

On the strength of these hopes, Laube's financial arrangements, and Lehrs's impractical counsel, Richard during the spring of 1840 moved to expensive quarters on the Rue du Helder near the Boulevard des Italiens. His first visitor was Anders bearing the ominous news that the Théâtre de la Renaissance was bankrupt. Wagner later suspected himself a victim of Meyerbeer's machinations, but practically anyone who ever helped Wagner was to have as reward a formidable ingratitude expressed in slander and recrimination.

In order to salvage something from the catastrophe, Wagner prevailed upon Edouard Monnais, new provisional director of the Opéra, to listen to the three selections from *Liebesverbot*. At a hearing in the green room of the great theater, Scribe magnanimously appeared in response to Wagner's invitation. After the audition (over which Wagner presided at the piano!), polite and hollow remarks were directed at the work, in which no one, least of all the composer, was at all interested. As the music unfolded, Richard had felt rather ashamed of its superficiality. Beethoven once again possessed him, and a serious composition—a "Faust" symphony—was forming in his mind; its opening section depicting the solitary philosopher had been completed in January, 1840. Unhappily, the poor impression made by the *Columbus* destroyed any expectation that Habeneck would accept his new work.

He came to realize that, even with Meyerbeer's help, an unknown might at best float a small-scale work in Paris. Meyerbeer advised a modest contribution to a ballet score, but Richard had drafted a compact one-act opera on the theme of the Flying Dutchman to be used as a curtain raiser to a night of ballet. Such a procedure was not infrequent, having origins in baroque practice. In the summer of 1840 he submitted his sketch to the Opéra, and during the following winter, having completed *Rienzi* in November, he worked out the poetry (turned into French by Emile Deschamps) and music of Senta's ballad, the song of the Norwegian sailors, and the chorus of ghosts. Both text and music were indebted to that classic *Schaueroper, Marschner's Vampyr.* He was ready for auditions, which, alas, were never called.

By fall, financial disaster had threatened at the Rue du Helder. His stipends exhausted, Richard wrote to Heinrich Schletter, one of Rosalie's old admirers in Leipzig, and extracted money from him. The Wagners confined themselves to a few rooms and, when possible, sublet the rest of their apartment. Beautiful Minna, once the artistic protégée of Emil Devrient, performed all chores, even the most menial. A serious breach with Eduard and Cäcilie was near; during an encounter in the Champs Elysées the latter warned Minna that Richard's financial demands must cease. Natalie joined the forlorn household in November, 1840, in time to witness the low point of its distress.

It was almost a year since Robber's disappearance. Upon arrival in Paris the handsome fellow had become a *flâneur,* a frequenter of the Palais Royal gardens, and an artist drawing admiring crowds to his baths and formidable exhibitions of diving and retrieving in the Seine. Perhaps he had been stolen, but more likely he had decamped to find a new master able to keep flesh on his giant bones. Now, in the autumnal mists, Richard caught sight of voracious Robber, who recognized him and fled. He vanished in the fog near the church of St. Roch, that great confessor of Montpellier so often painted and carved in the company of his faithful dog, and Richard trembled at what seemed a fearful portent.[2] Perhaps he intended this anecdote related in *Mein Leben* to symbolize the climactic point of his wretchedness, his imprisonment, tactfully left unrecorded.

Late in October of 1840, at the insistence of a creditor who would no longer be fobbed off, Wagner was jailed for debt. *Rienzi* was possibly finished during this confinement. He hastily drafted a letter of appeal to his old friend Apel, which Minna then copied and dispatched as if it were her own. The preceding month Wagner had written to Apel and begged for money. But the blind Theodor did not reply directly to the old chum who had neglected him for years only to break silence with a familiar request. Nonetheless, he did send Richard funds through Laube, known to function as the clearinghouse for Wagnerian alms.

The style of the October letter must have betrayed its true author to Theodor, who, perhaps suspecting exaggeration or even a hoax to extort money, indicated that little more could be done. Minna wrote him a second letter on November 17, an ingenuous creation of her own in which she touched upon sacrifices she once had made to provide her brother with an education. Evidently moved by her nobility and guilelessness, Apel responded to her entreaties. *Mein Leben* seeks to cloud the events of this embarrassing period, but it seems that by early December Wagner was no longer behind bars.

With good reason the New Year was welcomed by a frenetic celebration during which Richard mounted a table to deliver a drunken harangue lauding the attractions of the New World, where, one assumes, he felt debtors could not be tracked.

Next morning he was up early working on arrangements of Donizetti's *Favorita* for various vocal and instrumental combinations, a tedious but remunerative task given him by a friend of Meyerbeer and Berlioz, the German-Jewish music publisher Moritz Schlesinger. His kindness was ill

[2] In Wagner's short story, "An End in Paris," a Newfoundland, stolen by a wicked Englishman, recognizes yet flees his old master. But the contrite dog later returns to mourn at his grave.

rewarded in *Mein Leben*. Even if he profited by such labor, his fees did sustain Wagner, whose only means of earning money were musical hack work and journalism. Schlesinger sympathetically endeavored to provide opportunities for both. As early as the summer of 1840 Wagner sent articles to the *Gazette musicale,* a magazine owned by Schlesinger, in lieu of payment to the latter for engraving "The Two Grenadiers," a song into which Wagner, like Schumann, introduced the "Marseillaise." Once the obligation was met, Wagner was paid for subsequent contributions. Thus started a series of articles, more or less watered Hoffmann in style, including some of the little Wagnerian prose of any intrinsic literary merit. Of course, Wagner wrote in German, which was translated into French.

His name was becoming known to the *Gazette*'s readers, and, when this publication sponsored a concert on February 4, 1841, Schlesinger invited him to participate. Unsure of his new "Faust" music and with nothing else in the cupboard—his incarceration had cost him an opportunity of trying out the newly completed *Rienzi* overture—again he foolishly fell back upon the *Columbus*.

At the rehearsal he was humiliated by the presence of Berlioz—through his careworn smile he managed to murmur something politic—and by an orchestra and conductor certain they were playing trash. Not surprisingly, the performance failed. Poor emaciated Minna almost broke down when she heard the hisses. One can find no fault with the Parisian taste that rejected what Wagner offered. If the city of Meyerbeer did not recognize depth, it at least demanded adroitness. Wagner had as yet demonstrated neither. Meyerbeer's continuing interest in him can only be attributed to an obliging nature and to the fact that he had seen part of *Rienzi*.

Berlioz's association with the *Gazette musicale* (he had been its official editor until some four years before) made the failure of the piece yet more painful for Richard, who not many weeks after his arrival in Paris had been overwhelmed at one of the première performances of *Romeo and Juliet.* Subsequently, he heard and admired the *Symphonie fantastique, Harold in Italy,* and the *Funeral and Triumphal Symphony.* Berlioz's works were to be for him a mine of thematic material and orchestral effects. Though his attitude toward this music was not uncritical, he revered much of it, especially the *Romeo,* elements of which emerge in his own scores as late as *Parsifal.* In his *Memoirs,* Berlioz speaks of Wagner of the Paris days as a young man known through articles in the *Gazette,* generously making no mention of having been exposed to the *Columbus.* Liszt had been present at the première of the *Symphonie fantastique* (1830), and, through him and Wagner, Berlioz's influence was to permeate the musical achievements of the century.

Glasenapp invented the legend that the title page of the *Dutchman* manuscript was inscribed, "in night and misery." The motto might have been as suitably applied to *Rienzi,* probably completed in jail and without a future in the city for which it was conceived. Wagner's only hope now was that it might prove a passport back to Germany. He had sent the score to the Dresden Opera right after his release from prison. The theatrical connections of the Wagner-Geyer clan might again prove valuable, and his old friend Schröder-Devrient, the theater's prima donna, would doubtless contribute her influence. Moreover, Nourrit's suicide in 1839 left Dresden in possession of Europe's greatest dramatic tenor—Devrient's protégé, Tichatschek. It was for such a rare instrument that the title role of *Rienzi* had been written.

5

Rienzi's prodigious length is not vindicated by an analogous musical distinction. Thematic material, often commonplace, reaches, in ballet and procession, the quite intolerable level of Wagner's Leipzig piano works. Monotonously repeated marching rhythms, coarse instrumentation, crudely employed reminiscence motifs, and much clumsy recitative assault the ear. Yet a sufficient number of splendid moments free of the fustian of his mock-Spontini-Meyerbeer style do justify generously cut and edited productions of the opera.

In the second act the Mendelssohnian Messengers of Peace chorus (derived from the *"Hochzeit"* fragment) diffuses the sweet light of *Lohengrin.* A hand growing in facility more flexibly molds recitative and motif and enriches the orchestra's role in the last three acts. They include the poetic lament for the slain (Wagner's first great ensemble and a passage especially dear to Tichatschek),[3] the hero's prayer, which rightly gained Berlioz's praise, and the final tableau, wherein themes identified with Rienzi's triumphs sound in irony through the uproar of his fall. And throughout, dominating even the inferior numbers, is an unmistakable authority. Wagner had not as yet the marvelous craft of the Meyerbeer of *Huguenots,* the masterpiece against which he obviously wished *Rienzi* to be measured. But it is not surprising that the elder composer paused when in Boulogne he first scanned even the less accomplished Riga portions of the work.

The opera's book is admirably constructed to provide extravagant situations obviously selected with an eye on Scribe's libretto for *Masaniello.* Rienzi, his sister Irene, and Adriano, the young aristocrat, parallel Masa-

---

[3] It begins with the text, *"Jungfrauen, weinet!"*

niello, fisherman-king of Naples, Fenella, his sister, and Alfonso, son of the Viceroy. Masaniello's treacherous friend, Pietro, furnished Wagner with a model for Cecco and Baroncelli, and Rienzi's leniency toward the nobles merely repeats the unwise example of Masaniello, another commoner driven to take power by an oppressed and then inflamed populace.

Rienzi's disposition is the more theatrical. His appearance "in fantastic and sumptuous attire" before the Peace Messengers calls to mind Richard's sybaritic tendencies. In the character of the Roman tribune may be glimpsed traits of the coming line of Wagnerian heroes, those generally offensive and self-assertive creatures who are nevertheless curiously alien to their environments, being for the most part either malcontents or reformers providentially sent to order the affairs of the uncomprehending. On the other hand, in Irene one perceives her dramatic descendants—Senta, Brynhild, Isolde, and Eva—heroines who, though excited to defiant behavior, yet are more subtle, moving through Wagner's symbolic worlds with relative ease. In ascribing the failure of his elopement with Jessie Laussot in 1850 to her lack of revolutionary resolve, Wagner wrote, "He is mine who rebels through the power of love, though rebellion spell his ruin. And, if this love be for me, then it could only content me if it worked my ruin as well."

The ruin of Rienzi, victim of the mob's shifting allegiance, awakens little sympathy. The bumptious idealist is human only during his prayer and in what is almost a love scene with Irene, his sister. Having with Valkyrie-like strength renounced Adriano, her suitor, to perish in the arms of Rienzi, Irene inspires him to their joint immolation in the fiery hall, a survival of the second act of *Feen,* in which corseleted Lora rouses her brother as their palace is stormed. Adriano, tracking Irene through the Capitol ringed by the ungrateful rabble, is recognizable as a descendant of Leubald, that fantastic literary product of Richard's adolescence. Adriano, deranged by conflict between hatred for his father's slayer, Rienzi, and love for this enemy's sister, attempts to abduct her by force. Like Ada in *"Hochzeit"* she summons superhuman might to repulse him and then joins her brother in death. Adriano's agony is Leubald's and Tristan's, a torment born of conflicting duties to kin and beloved. Irene, like her operatic offspring, Sieglinde, is a monument to Wagner's sister Rosalie. When Sieglinde's husband threatens Siegmund's life, she, too, proclaims a desire to die at the brother's side. Her *"Haltet ein, ihr Männer! Mordet erst mich!"* derives from Irene's ecstatic *"Ermorde mich—ich lass' dich nie!"*

The libretto of *Rienzi* so admired by Meyerbeer was not without influence on his own work. The situations agglomerated by Scribe for *Prophète* (produced in 1849) came from the public arsenal of operatic effects and were an attempt further to turn to advantage the theme of *Masaniello*. Yet the accumulation in one work of interjections of Latin chant, battle alarms, a triumph song, an assassination planned at a feast, and a final scene in which mother joins son in death as a palace burns and collapses suggests a debt to *Rienzi* greater than Scribe himself admitted. The prophet is another revolutionary leader beguiled by pride into believing himself God's instrument and then abandoned at the height of his grandeur by those who had created and used him.

6

In *Prophète* Meyerbeer and Scribe employed the theatrical curse tellingly. But in Wagner's hands this timeworn stage device was to become singularly implicative. From *Feen* to *Parsifal* he was fascinated by the dramatic motive of a curse frequently followed by madness and a journey, often expiatory, that in turn led to redemption through a lover's act of benevolence. The essentials of this structure remain clear throughout Wagner's work, though the integrants are freely varied.

In *Feen* Arindal execrates Ada, for a time loses his senses, and then roams the underworld, where his love song finally breaks the charm holding her. The raging Dutchman, banned by Satan to eternal voyaging, is freed by his encounter with Senta's devotion. In *Tannhäuser* these themes are presented with multiple force, for three curses and two journeys are involved—Venus' curse of insatiableness upon the hero, the malediction of the Thuringian court outraged by the revelation of his sensuality, his first journey (the pilgrimage to Rome), an imprecation from the mouth of the Pope, the knight's straggling return over the Alps, seeking readmittance into the goddess' underground realm, and, finally, his absolution in death as Elizabeth's intercession in heaven ironically makes the Pontiff's taunting words a very proof of divine pardon.

The Wagnerian malediction reached a dramatic peak in Alberich's outbursts in *Rhinegold,* in which he cursed love and those who would steal from him the rewards of this renunciation. Siegfried, heir to Alberich's curse, ranged valley and mountain to find, though guiltless, a betrayer's death ennobled by his incestuous wife's suicide in the flames. Did Rienzi and Irene return to Wagner's mind as he conceived the conflagrant finale to the *Ring?*

Tristan's curse on the potion during his delirium, a curse on himself, climaxes his suffering; his journey is the fearful psychological one of self-inquiry. Like Irene, Isolde seeks out the hero to share and crown his death. By the time of *Tristan,* redemption, love, and death were synonymous to Wagner, an amalgam already clearly forming in *Tannhäuser* but, indeed, suggested from the time of his earliest works. The most famous of love-deaths [4] is but a refinement of the closing tableau planned for *"Hochzeit."* And, like Elizabeth's position in *Don Carlos,* Isolde's (though somewhat ambiguous) as consort to a patriarchal rival colors the situation with a tint of Wagnerian incest.

Parsifal transfigures and presents most elaborately the composite motive of curse, derangement, journey, and redemption. The ban directed by Christ's glance to Kundry has caused her to drift as a transmigrator through the centuries, unable to weep or die, a wretch suffering fits of raving and delirium. Her deliverer is a chaste young male to whom she transfers her curse in a masterly superposition of symbols (*"Irre! Irre!"*—"Wander! Wander!"). He must then wander till the spell is lifted on that day when full understanding [5] of Monsalvat's tribulation comes to him. This knowledge annuls the proscription, and Kundry gratefully sinks to rest before the altar of the Grail in the ultimate convolution of the love-death. In *Parsifal* Wagner intertwined the multiple motive of the curse not only with crude political intimations but also with subtle psychological nuances foreshadowed as early as in *Dutchman.*

The Dutchman frees himself from his curse through an awakening to the need of another. He, like Kundry a wanderer through the ages, comes ashore every seven years recklessly to find and woo a girl whose fidelity might release him from Satan's ban. Numberless maidens have already proved unequal to the test, and to them, like Kundry's to Parsifal, his curse has been extended. Clearly, he is as much destroyer as destroyed. But Senta has awakened his tenderness, and for the first time he loves and pities a victim of his matrimonial experiments.[6] Wrongly suspecting her faithfulness, he nevertheless releases her from her vow. At this moment of newborn compassion the curse lifts. Her plunge into the sea unites her with a soul already redeemed. Here is Wagner's innate comprehension of Schopenhauer's *Mitleid* as the mainspring of morality, the germ of the idea of wisdom and redemption through intuitive suffering that would one day make Siegmund's misery turn the pitying goddess, Bryn-

[4] At the end of Fouqué's and Hoffmann's opera *Undine* (first performed in 1816) the hero Huldbrand suffers what is described as a *"Liebestod."* This knight, though a baritone, is an ancestor of all those Wagnerian heroes redeemed by love.

[5] Donington sees the *Ring* as an allegory of character-building and growing awareness, a tale of Wotan's maturing.

[6] Lord Ruthven in Marschner's *Vampyr* is compelled by supernatural forces to woo and destroy three maidens within a year. Though he, too, passes his curse on to others, the libretto suggests that at times he somewhat regrets their fate. Wagner used elements of Ruthven in constructing his Dutchman.

hild, into a woman [7] and Amfortas' wound burn deep within Parsifal. In *Rienzi* Wagner put the curse to use only in its simplest grand opera form but in two highly effective stage situations. As Rienzi proceeds in pomp to attend what he expects to be a *Te Deum,* he is driven back from the Lateran's doors by a chant of excommunication. And in the final moments of the opera he calls down a dreadful imprecation upon Rome.

Completed during Wagner's darkest days in Paris, the last act of *Rienzi* is really his curse upon the French capital. From Dresden he wrote to Cäcilie in 1843, "Ah, how I hate Paris, vast, monstrous—alien to our German hearts." Paris taught him to loathe large cities. At the time of the Franco-Prussian War he maintained that they must pass away, for in them was spawned the un-German rabble! Was this, then, the lesson of *Rienzi?*

7

Through ignorance of Parisian rent laws, Wagner found himself burdened with the flat on Rue du Helder for another year. Happily a tenant for it was found, and in April, 1841, Richard and Minna moved to Meudon, a village right outside the gates of Paris where an inexpensive summer house could be rented and, most important, where Parisian authorities were handicapped in exercising their powers of arrest for debt.

His prospects were dark. There was no hack work from Schlesinger, and he managed to alienate people at the Opéra by an article in the *Gazette* criticizing music he had neither seen nor heard, the recitatives

---

[7] A poignant theme appearing in the *Faust Overture* paints not only this moment of sympathy in *Valkyrie* as Brynhild melts before the defiant hero with drawn sword but also the forbearance of Isolde, who, sword poised over Tristan, helpless on his sickbed, suddenly condoles with him (Isolde's narrative, Act I). *Tristan* and *Valkyrie* are thus interlocked by a musical motif representing a kind of Schopenhauerean *Mitgefühl.* (This philosopher's influence on Wagner will be discussed in the following chapter.) Ellis, who so perceptively remarked these interconnections, also cites the theme's presence in *Siegfried*. The hero sings it as he discovers Mime's plan to hack off his head (*"Im Schlafe willst du mich morden?"*), and probably at this point decides to return the compliment by slaying Mime first.

In the examples from *Valkyrie* and *Tristan,* pity was born of a sudden, intuitive reversal of opinion in an atmosphere of elevated swords and contemplated murder. Possibly subconscious memories of the last two elements prompted the composer to give the theme to Siegfried in the scene at the cave. The boy's retarded mind was hardly capable of compassion. Perhaps the sudden comprehension of another's soul (given him by the dragon's blood) is the psychological link binding all the incidents together. In any case, the superman's magic perceptiveness is short-lived; for the rest of the cycle he is led about like a donkey.

being prepared by Berlioz for the coming première of *Freischütz* at this theater (June, 1841). But he did admit that if Weber's masterpiece had to be remade into grand opera—ballet as well as recitatives were being added—Berlioz's genius could best effect the change. If Richard could have looked into the future to see himself making over *Tannhäuser* for the same house, patching his youthful work with the gorgeous fabric of *Tristan,* perhaps his tone would have been less superior. The article earned George Sand's approval.

One work of Richard Wagner's had captured the interest of Léon Pillet, new director of the Opéra—the draft of *The Flying Dutchman.* Pillet was outspoken. Obliged to provide operatic subjects to composers under contract, he wished to purchase the *Dutchman* sketch but wanted no part of Wagner the musician. He indicated to Wagner that it would be foolish for him to be difficult about the matter, for obviously no one had exclusive rights to a legend; in fact, Victor Hugo's brother-in-law, Paul Foucher, stood ready to work up a libretto on the same subject for the management. Pillet's candor was admirable; if he had so chosen, Wagner's rights could have been ignored. Pillet informed him that musical works already commissioned filled the needs of the Opéra for the next seven years, after which time Wagner might find an opening as a composer. Ironically, this was the period the Dutchman had to sail the seas to win respite on land.

In July, 1841, Richard accepted a handsome fee of five hundred francs for the sketch and returned to Meudon to resume the musical setting of his *Dutchman* poem (the verses had been completed in May, 1841), now intended for Germany. The Paris dream was over.

His pen flew. By August 22 the romantic opera was composed and lacked only its full score and overture. Whatever alchemy transforms talent into genius worked its mystic transmutation in Wagner during the late summer of 1841. At Meudon he enjoyed the company of Monsieur Jadin, a Hoffmannesque fellow with a passion for fantastic clothes of his own creation, wigs of every color, and quantities of costume jewelry. Wagner had found another Flachs. The old man, who remembered Pompadour, busily practiced the harpsichord for his musical friend's edification. Jadin was to appear in Wagner's anecdotal "Parisian Fatalities" as the author's eccentric landlord.

Wagner had entered into an exchange of favors with an old family friend, Hofrath Winkler of Dresden. Winkler, known under the pseudonym of Theodor Hell as writer and translator, had years before formed part of a famous group at Dresden's Café Eicheltraut which included Friedrich Kind, librettist of *Freischütz,* and E. T. A. Hoffmann. Winkler had, in fact, been present with Tieck when Minna made her stage debut as Lady Milford in *Kabale und Liebe* at Dresden. In return for his aid in urging *Rienzi* on the Dresden Hoftheater, of which he was secretary, Richard, for his part, sent articles on the Parisian scene to the *Abendzeitung,* a failing newspaper edited by Winkler. These essays attempted to emulate the lively style of Heinrich Heine. Laube had introduced Richard to this poet whose treatment of the Flying Dutchman legend had greatly influenced his own. Wagner's journalistic methods were, as he admitted, deplorable. Having neither inclination nor money to attend Parisian musical events, he depended for material upon secondhand gossip retailed by Anders and Lehrs.

Meyerbeer wrote a letter generously recommending Wagner to Baron von Lüttichau, director of the Dresden Hoftheater. A decision to produce *Rienzi* was communicated by Winkler's committee in June, 1841. But from his experience with *Die Feen* Richard knew that an announced intention did not necessarily result in a performance.

Autumn's chill filtered into the unsubstantial summerhouse, and by mid-October Richard's teeth were chattering. The five hundred francs from the Opéra were gone, but Kietz, for a time part of the Meudon ménage, somehow raised enough money to permit the Wagners to return to Paris. At the end of October they settled in small quarters on the Rue Jacob. Eduard Fechner, Kietz's uncle, provided sustenance while the scoring and overture to *Dutchman* were being completed, and late in November the finished opera was dispatched to Berlin.

The successful première of Halévy's *La Reine de Chypre* in December, 1841, benefited Richard, who was hired by Schlesinger to make various arrangements of the score. An admirer of Halévy, Wagner lavishly praised his music's concentrated energy, intense thought, and affinity with the German spirit (the Tarnhelm and potion motifs in the *Ring* owe much to a phrase in *La Reine de Chypre*), and enjoyed conferring with this "honest and frank" composer whose Semitic skepticism he particularly relished. Halévy's incredulity was evidently directed toward the merits of Meyerbeer, with whom Richard, too, was becoming less enchanted. The skillful orchestration and décor of *Huguenots* had fascinated him, but somehow he wished never to hear the music again.

Work for Schlesinger and a Christmas loan from Schletter eased his financial cares. German history, especially Raumer's *Geschichte der Hohenstaufen,* now commanded his interest, and he sketched a drama about Manfred, which he called *Die Sarazenin*. It was not the first time he had concerned himself with the affairs of the Hohenstaufen. Raupach's *König Enzio*, for which he had provided music in 1832, told a tale of Manfred's half brother, the Sardinian King. And in *Liebesverbot* the shadow of Hohenstaufen authority was cast over *Measure for Measure*.

Liebesverbot and *Die Sarazenin* share a noteworthy treatment of sister love, a motive manifest in Wagner's works from the time of *Feen*.[8] Young Richard's sexual instincts had been aroused very early by his sisters. After adolescence the reformed profligate especially wished by his artistic creations to propitiate Rosalie, his chaste protector. In *Feen* Arindal's sister is a Rosalie who dons armor to protect the home while her brother languishes in indecision. What drew Richard to *Measure for Measure* was the idea of a noble sister's sacrifice for an erring brother. Rosalie's brief married life ended in death through childbirth, movingly recalled in *Siegfried* when Mime sings of the bride-sister's last agony.

It has been observed that an almost incestuous love between brother and sister dominates *Rienzi*, whose hero has evidently never been concerned with another woman. (Significantly, Wagner on this point departs from Lytton's novel, in which Rienzi has a wife.) *Volsunga Saga* was one day to inspire Wagner openly to sing the praises of incest (*Valkyrie*), an impulse already present in the outline of *Sarazenin,* in which a physical love grows between Manfred and his half sister, daughter of Friedrich II and a Saracen maid. As in Wagner's *"Hohe Braut,"* where highborn Bianca has as lover her foster brother Giuseppe, the steprelationship in *Sarazenin* was especially pertinent to Wagner's problems of identity. The situation recalls *Feen:* a sister rouses her brother from womanish lethargy; then, like Irene in *Rienzi,* she dies a sacrificial death for him.

As yet insufficiently mature to cope with this strange fantasy he had elaborated and uneasy about the incestuous motive, Wagner put *Sarazenin* aside when there came into his hands material on the Venusberg and Tannhäuser, the minstrel contest on the Wartburg, and Lohengrin. He was being directed by Lehrs toward this storehouse of medieval literature and through him learned of Professor Lucas' writings, which were to influence the fusion of the Venusberg and Wartburg tales in the libretto of *Tannhäuser*. Failure of the French adventure had made Richard return nostalgically to things German, and E. T. A. Hoffmann again enchanted him. Upon Schlesinger's recommendation, a Jewish composer, Dionys Weber's pupil Josef Dessauer, whom Wagner had met in Prague, commissioned him to write a libretto in *Dutchman* style. For a fee of two hundred francs Wagner sketched an opera based upon Hoffmann's *Die Bergwerke zu Falun,* a tale of prophetic dreams, subterranean caverns, and a hero torn between a mysterious mountain queen and a faithful earthly maid, whose love goes beyond the grave, the very conflict the composer was to treat again in his *Tannhäuser*.

[8] The puzzling relationship between Elsa and her younger brother in *Lohengrin* was discussed by Max Friedlander in a paper read at Bayreuth during the season of 1962.

Reports came of new delays in Dresden concerning *Rienzi*. Despite an arduous correspondence with the staff of the Hoftheater, the affair would perhaps come to nothing without his presence. When in March, 1842, he received notice that the Berlin Opera had, at Meyerbeer's suggestion, accepted *Dutchman,* he felt he must return home. Friedrich Brockhaus, who had indicated that his patience and subventions were at an end, was now sympathetic to the necessity of Richard's pursuing his improved prospects at close hand. He sent funds for traveling. The wheel of fortune was swinging round, propelled by Meyerbeer's generous hand.

In April, Richard and Minna said tearful good-byes to Eduard and Cäcilie (with whom they had been reconciled and to whose care Natalie was entrusted), Anders, Lehrs, and the precious Kietz, who slipped his last few francs into Richard's hand as the coach set out on the five-day journey to Dresden—to the mother Richard had not seen in six years and the grave of beloved Rosalie.

V

Kapellmeister *in Dresden*

By that famous evening of October 20, 1842, when Dresden received *Rienzi* with unexampled enthusiasm, Richard had been back in Germany six months, a period of rest, consolidation, and poetic employment that was to produce *Tannhäuser*. Friedrich and Hermann Brockhaus, the latter now Professor of Oriental Languages at Leipzig University, held it a duty to support him for this half year, after which, it was hoped, an income from *Rienzi* and *Dutchman* would be forthcoming.

The trials of Paris had told upon Minna's frail constitution. During June of 1842 she improved by taking the saline Eger waters at Teplitz. Sentiment now made the Parisian misfortunes take on a winning mellowness, and in letters to Cäcilie and Eduard she and Richard lamented separation from the great city and friends left behind. In their longing for a child they had developed a touching attachment to little Max, the Avenarius heir. Richard wrote: "As we still have no prospect whatever of *human* young, we have to do the best we can with dogs. We've another now, only six weeks old, a funny little beast named *Peps*. . . . I'd much rather have a Maxel."

At the end of June he left Minna at Teplitz and set out on a solitary hike in the Bohemian mountains. On the Schreckenstein at Aussig, with elements from his own *Hohe Braut* and *Sarazenin* and from works by Hoffmann, the Grimm brothers, Fouqué, Tieck, Bechstein, and Professor Lucas, he began to outline a three-act opera, *"Der Venusberg,"* and jotted down several musical themes for it. In a sense he was continuing the work of Weber, whose friend, Brentano, had begun to fashion for him a libretto on the Tannhäuser legend but unfortunately had laid it aside.

A bit past mid-July Wagner was back in Dresden, spurring on preparations for *Rienzi*. Signs of success were clear. Tichatschek adored a role affording so many occasions to trumpet forth in his best range and to appear in the splendid costumes Ferdinand Heine, an old friend of Geyer's, was devising. Schröder-Devrient, though a little disappointed with the relatively secondary role of Adriano—and her now impressive girth made her assumption of such a trouser part a trial for her admirers—yet showed good will by lavishly praising the opera. Orchestra and chorus, the latter prepared by the enthusiastic Wilhelm Fischer, delightedly responded to the challenge of the score. And the worthy conductor and composer Karl Reissiger was cleverly propitiated by Richard, who offered him the *Hohe Braut* as a libretto on which to exercise his own musical genius.[1] Only one reservation was harbored by Fischer, who wished to cut the work. But Richard could find few sections to drop without, in his opinion, prejudicing the integrity of the whole.

The measure of the opera's triumph may be taken from the fact that Dresdeners sat through a première that started at six and ended well over five hours later. As the opera progressed, Richard could no longer ignore its monstrous length and nervously expected the Roman Capitol to flame and crash before an empty house. Almost beside himself, he stopped the clock over the stage. But, except for an old man in the parquet, not a soul stirred, and Richard acknowledged the full crowd's thunderous final ovation.

He hurriedly devised cuts for subsequent performances. But Tichatschek would not suffer the loss of a note, and omissions brought protests from artists and audience. A somewhat abbreviated *Rienzi* was tolerated by its voracious public only after three attempts at presenting it cyclically on two consecutive evenings (acts I and II, "Rienzi's Greatness," and acts III, IV, and V, "Rienzi's Fall") caused resentment when the thrifty Saxons realized that they were paying double admission for one opera.

From this time on Wagner was never unwilling to cut his works when practical reasons demanded curtailments. Nor, starting with Schröder-Devrient's Senta, was he, at particular productions, averse to altering a part to fit the resources of an individual interpreter. When it had appeared that a coloratura, Madame Marr, might sing Irene in *Rienzi*, he had even faced the unhappy possibility of her injecting *fioritura* of her own into his score. To accommodate Tichatschek and Niemann he consented to alterations in the second act of *Tannhäuser*, and for his

---

[1] Frau Reissiger, suspicious of Wagner's willingness to renounce the libretto, persuaded her husband not to set it. Wagner passed the book on to his old Prague friend, Kittl, who composed it under the title of *Bianca und Giuseppe, oder die Franzosen vor Nizza*. During the fateful year of 1848 the opera achieved in Prague the reputation of being a Bohemian *Masaniello*, a revolutionary air from it becoming quite popular.

niece, Johanna Wagner, he shortened the prayer in the third. (She could never negotiate this aria, according to both Bülow and Minna.) In 1861 by cuts, transpositions, and text changes he recast the part of Tristan to meet the limitations of the panic-stricken Viennese tenor, Ander. Unhappy with his Wotan after the first Bayreuth festival, he wished the role to be assumed by the bass Siehr, whose anxieties over its great range he allayed by assurances that high notes might always be lowered. His fretting over unauthorized suppressions at the early Weimar performances of *Lohengrin* was born of misgivings that in his enforced absence the work might be mangled rather than cut.

2

In the light of *Rienzi*'s triumph his fee was especially augmented. But a man who knew Paris and its ways found it paltry. Nevertheless there would be other theaters and, of course, publishing rights. He and Minna suddenly found themselves lionized. The only shadow was that Dresden wasn't Paris—it wasn't even Berlin. He had been contemptuous of the Opéra during his last days in France, but by comparison even Semper's handsome new Dresden theater seemed insignificant.

The management, coveting another Wagnerian triumph, sought Berlin's rights to the première of *The Flying Dutchman*. They were readily relinquished. Meyerbeer's friend Count Redern was retiring as Berlin director, his place being given to Küstner, who had already rejected *Dutchman* while manager at Munich. Küstner felt the opera unsuited to German taste, ironically merely a way of saying that it was not sufficiently Italian or French in style. The eagerness of Dresden could hardly compensate Richard for the loss of Berlin with its large fees and far-reaching influence.

The première of *Dutchman* took place in Dresden on January 2, 1843; it was given in three acts. Schröder-Devrient, in the midst of a tumultuous rearrangement of her love life, brought to Senta a blazing intensity that threw into shadow Herr Wächter's elementarily acted Dutchman. This was Wagner's opinion; but Berlioz, in Dresden on his first German tour, noted, in recording his impressions at a later performance, her affected posing and frequent resort to speaking the notes; for Wächter's vocal mastery he had the highest praise.

Berlioz found the orchestration of *Dutchman* excessive, an opinion Wagner evidently shared, for he revised the scoring in 1846 for a Leipzig performance that never took place, subdued it again for the Zurich production of 1852 (at which time he first overhauled the coda of the overture), and patched it once more during the *Tristan* period. In November, 1843, *Rienzi* had reappeared on the Dresden boards with its instrumentation similarly polished. When Wagner heard his early works, he was distressed by the too massive effects in the brass, a miscalculation he particularly wanted to correct when later retouching what he had completed of his Parisian ".Faust" Symphony. Berlioz also criticized Wagner's overindulgence in sustained tremolo effects in both *Rienzi* and *Dutchman*.

The latter work had been presaged as early as that inchoate seascape, the *Columbus* overture. Yet, as Spohr perceived, Berlioz was the immediate influence on the opera, which was not, in fact, Wagner's first attempt at poetic, literary music in the manner of the French master. The surviving opening movement of that "Faust" Symphony of early 1840 [2] depicts an oppressed, restless hero akin to the despondent artist of the *Fantastique*. But, like his Columbus, Wagner's Faust is comforted by an optimistic motif while Berlioz's young man finds solace in narcotic dreams.

Berlioz's example dominates Wagner's "Faust" music, whose accents ripened into the turbulent idiom of *Dutchman*, its D minor, the key also of Beethoven's Ninth, becoming the characteristic tonality of Vanderdecken's wandering, until his redemption in the parallel major. Thus, in the fashioning of *Dutchman*, three heroes of the youthful Wagner played a part—Beethoven, Columbus, and Berlioz. Wagner's *Art-Work of the Future* (1849) was to fuse the first two by celebrating Beethoven as a musical Columbus exploring the seemingly shoreless sea of absolute music to gain undreamed-of coasts. Somewhat later, Wagner's book *Opera and Drama* was to make the analogy more personal by implying that Beethoven, seeking a different route to a long-known land, discovered instead a new world—the Wagnerian drama! On the other hand, the role Berlioz played in his development Wagner minimized as he came to look upon the elder master as a rival. Nevertheless, the "Faust" fragment, a pivotal piece in Wagner's works, bears witness to his desire to embrace Berlioz's aesthetic and techniques.

Possibly *Dutchman* preserves material from the abandoned second movement of the "Faust" Symphony in some of the music of Senta, whose theme of redemption has the long line and lyricism of Berlioz and expresses confidence in deliverance through Goethe's Eternal Feminine.

An interest in Goethe was but one of many parallels between Wagner and Berlioz. Neither composer was an instrumentalist, and both were

---

[2] This first movement, revised at the time of *Valkyrie*, is known as the *Faust Overture*.

littérateurs who experienced hapless first marriages to actresses. As youths they came under the spell of *Faust,* a fact more noteworthy in the case of the Frenchman. Young Gérard de Nerval's translation of the first part of Goethe's poem came into Berlioz's hands at a turbulent time, when a new, free, resonant universe had been opened to him by *Hamlet* at the Odéon with Kemble and, above all, Harriet Smithson. Goethe's Shakespearean range stimulated Berlioz to use the lyrical parts of *Faust* for eight musical scenes comprising nine songs. Completed in 1829, this French counterpart to Wagner's more modest effort of three years later became the heart of the *Damnation of Faust* (1846). The daemonic aspects of Goethe's *Faust* also left their mark upon the *Symphonie fantastique.* Berlioz, as in the majestic *"Nature immense"* of *Damnation,* showed remarkable grasp of the issues of Goethe's drama.

Charles Lamb placed the Gretchen theme in proper perspective in Goethe's masterpiece by asking just what Margaret had to do with Faust. Goethe primarily sang of man who errs as long as he ventures, who earns freedom and existence by daily conquest. Wagner seized mainly upon the poetic drama's recondite and theatrical ending. Its *chorus mysticus* in praise of the woman-soul helped form the closing moments of *Dutchman, Tannhäuser, Tristan,* and the *Ring.* Only the character of Tannhäuser (significantly, he shares with Faust as well as with von Ofterdingen of the Wartburg legend the first name of Heinrich) shows Wagner turning to account some of the substance of Goethe's play.

3

Dutchman disappointed many who awaited another *Rienzi.* Their objections were similar to those of the wealthy host in Strauss's *Ariadne auf Naxos,* displeased that his magnificently appointed mansion be the scene of an opera set on a desert island. Moreover, *Dutchman* harked back to a German romanticism that seemed outdated after Meyerbeer's new historicity. Furthermore, unlike *Rienzi,* it was concisely constructed, proceeding with few of the digressions beloved of grand opera.

Despite a disturbing alternation between the facile, florid style of Franco-Italian opera and the new-found eloquence of the main characters at their most impassioned, the work found appreciation among sensitive souls like the wife of Prime Minister von Könneritz and Ida von Lüttichau, the Intendant's wife, who sensed the direction that this gloomy, poetic work indicated for its composer. Wagner, fully realizing his dilemma, that his new and local fame rested upon *Rienzi,* whose style he had abandoned, felt, nonetheless, that with the strength of youthful genius—he was not yet thirty—he could lead on a new path. For the moment, however, he did waver and considered another five-act, spectacular grand opera. Schröder-Devrient's Senta inspired him to complete especially for her the discarded *Sarazenin* libretto. But she, finding some of its text embarrassing in relation to her publicly followed private life, discouraged its composition. The finished book is economically built and, like *Tannhäuser,* was to open with a ballet. The scene depicting Fatima awaiting Manfred at the gates of Luceria touches greatness.

Wagner had conducted *Dutchman,* but it was not his first appearance on the royal podium. Karl Reissiger, like Marschner once a pupil of Schicht at St. Thomas' and Weber's successor at Dresden, was finding his duties increasingly burdensome. At the sixth presentation of *Rienzi* (December 12, 1842) he had relinquished the baton to Wagner, who, in addition, conducted Weber's *Euryanthe* within days of the *Dutchman* première.

A week after the first performance of *Rienzi* Francesco Morlacchi, on leave from his Dresden post, had died at Innsbruck while en route to Italy, and in mid-November the theater suffered another loss in the sudden death of Joseph Ritter Rastrelli, a secondary conductor. Although sounded as to accepting Rastrelli's subordinate post, Wagner declined. He was becoming conscious of his unique role in the history of German opera, and, incensed by Schumann's just observation that in *Dutchman* a flavor of Meyerbeer was still to be distinguished, late in February he was to describe himself as nauseated by the odor of this particular operatic spring, although acknowledging a personal debt to Meyerbeer. (Surprisingly, the honest Schumann did not comment on some rather obvious indebtedness to the mood and thematic material of Mendelssohn's *Hebrides* overture.) It was a declaration of independence from a young man infuriated by the popular idea that he was Meyerbeer's pupil. He had felt himself second to no one when declaring that he would have Morlacchi's place on an equal footing with Reissiger or nothing. The *Euryanthe* performance had been in the nature of an examination of his abilities with repertory pieces. Frau Caroline, Weber's widow, took up his cause; old Hofrath Winkler was theater secretary and guardian of Weber's children; the King, an excellent musician, admired *Rienzi* and *Dutchman,* though not uncritically. Technicalities were waved, and early in February Richard Wagner became Royal *Kapellmeister,* a lifelong position at fifteen hundred thaler.

After the *Rienzi* triumph Minna had written to Eduard and Cäcilie, "Children, I am too happy; my utmost wishes are attained!" Now her cup was full. Senta's fidelity had seemingly earned an earthly reward. She and her wanderer were at rest. The cursed ship had sunk beneath the waves.

4

In the first version of *Dutchman* its heroine was called not Senta but Minna. As *Rienzi* had celebrated Rosalie, so *Dutchman* paid tribute to the love of Wagner's life. His devotion to Minna throughout the early, trying years of their marriage brought out the best in him. He could forgive with grace. Her fidelity and sacrifices during the Riga and Paris calamities bound them closely. As part of a birthday greeting to her in 1841 he wrote, "One who has such a good reputation with God can expect many good things in the future as a reward for faithfulness and confidence." One recalls the irony of Henry VIII's dance before Catherine of Aragon with the emblem "Loyal Heart" embroidered in gold upon his tunic.

Unfortunately, Wagner dictated his autobiography to Cosima. Otherwise a different Minna would certainly have emerged from its pages. His lack of taste in retailing the very sort of gossip about Minna that he held in reserve about himself is sad witness to the characterless ogre Wagner had become by the eighteen-sixties. Cosima and he, each married to someone else, were producing illegitimate children at the time they penned and then mercilessly published the tragic tale of adolescent Minna's seduction. Yet, notwithstanding Cosima's influence, *Mein Leben* contains some lovingly recalled episodes of life with Minna at his side.

Though no one can doubt the strong bond between Wagner and Cosima, her relationship to him often appears to be that of a curator to a historical monument. By the time she entered his life, he was a famous artist and royal favorite. But so hardened and gnarled had his nature become and so thickened his hide that only a forceful, well-directed blow could draw the mighty beast's attention to the fact that others still lived in the world and objected to being trod upon. Nonetheless, there would always be the Cosimas to stretch themselves prone.

While Cosima loved the genius and his glory, Minna loved the man. And there was still something to hold dear in the fiery young composer. He was excitable and voluble, luxury-loving and spendthrift, conceited and intolerant. But he knew how to endure the faults of others and could admit his own. The Wagner to whom Cosima allied herself was a master to be revered, but a man more worthy of pity than love. And, like Alexander the Great, he developed toward the end of his life a taste for Oriental court etiquette, although the ceremonies at Bayreuth inspired more ridicule than deference. In her palace career Cosima moved from major-domo to mistress to wife to priestess. Her character, temperament, and psychological problems were not unlike his. Fortune created for the self-anointed god a guardian of the gates, his female Cerberus.

Wagner's lifework was completely planned before his final separation from Minna. Cosima appears only indirectly in the dramas as that spirit of abundance saturating the end of the *Ring* and perhaps as reflected in the sexual abandon of Kundry. The purely instrumental *Siegfried Idyll* is his testimony to her fecundity, that vital quality in which Minna had failed him. The latter lives on in four operas. The young wife of Riga and Paris is Senta of the *Dutchman,* defying the bourgeois world, putting her fate into the hands of an unknown, cursed wanderer, and, by her sacrifice, gaining immortality. The more mature Minna of Dresden appears as the doubting Elsa of *Lohengrin* and then is seen as the righteous, practical Fricka of *Rhinegold* and *Valkyrie,* she who would pull from her husband the cloak of speciousness in which he attempted to wrap himself. Such was Wagner's disappointed view of Minna's character development from faith to doubt to censure. The noble and the pragmatic, qualities at times in conflict, were reconciled in Minna's personality, and this combination makes Fricka fascinating. Unfortunately, she is often interpreted as a scold, and, indeed, it was to this state that Wagner had reduced Minna by the close of their Dresden adventure.

5

The court appointment magnetized his creditors, some of whom threatened publicly to embarrass the new royal retainer whose position could be jeopardized by scandal. Schröder-Devrient had pressed a loan upon him to quiet the most vociferous.

Hopes that his last two works would quickly find their way into many other German opera houses remained unrealized. *Rienzi* was beset by the eternal problem of finding adequate heroic tenors. Its lamentable production in Hamburg in March, 1844, made Wagner heartsick. Königsberg did attempt the opera in 1845, but other houses were reluctant. Perhaps because of the King's interest, Berlin flirted with it, but no performance took place until 1847. There was only one Tichatschek.

Just as Bellini and Donizetti shaped many of their tenor phrases with Rubini's voice in mind, so after *Rienzi* Wagner wrote his tenor parts for the incredible instrument that was Tichatschek's. Even Siegfried was created with the sound of this voice in Wagner's ear. The difficulty of finding another such singer pursued Wagner throughout his career and still follows those attempting to cast his operas. Moreover, he admitted that *Rienzi* and *Tannhäuser* tried even robust Tichatschek terribly.

Although during the spring of 1843 reports came of successful mountings of *Dutchman* in Kassel (by Spohr) and in Riga (by Dorn), its critical

Berlin production in January, 1844, was disparagingly received by the press. From the beginning Wagner's relationship with journalists was unfortunate. To his credit, he was generally reluctant to stoop to the flatteries and bribes that at times assure benevolent reviews. Upon his return to Germany he did attempt to court the dreaded Berlin critic Rellstab; the latter discouraged any intimacy, perhaps being aware of the violent attack upon him that Wagner in 1836 had unsuccessfully attempted to publish in Schumann's magazine under the pseudonym of "Wilhelm Drach." Rellstab's disapproval doomed *Dutchman* in Berlin and, because of the city's influence, subsequently in most provincial towns. Ironically, Rellstab was to acknowledge that the opera became accessible with repeated hearings. Wagner approached him again at the time of *Rienzi*'s Berlin production (1847) but once more met with a rebuff.[3]

If the Fates had seasoned Wagner's genius with more tact, his way would certainly have been easier. His growing arrogance seemed to court needless enmities. Even brother Albert flung at him the charge of haughtiness. Although the proposed *Dutchman* première in Berlin had involved him in fruitless trips there and to Leipzig, yet the manner in which he threateningly repossessed the score for Dresden had been outrageously overbearing.

His close friends in Dresden were few: Ferdinand Heine, Fischer, Anton Pusinelli, a physician and member of the Dresden *Liedertafel* filled with a presentiment of Richard's greatness, and August Röckel, Wagner's assistant (he was related to both Hummel and Lortzing, and his father had sung Florestan in the revised *Fidelio* of 1806), who became the prototype of those dedicated disciples willing to set aside personal ambitions to serve Wagner's cause. Theodor Uhlig, a young violinist in the theater orchestra, became an adherent and one of the most perceptive of the early Wagnerites after experiencing the composer's interpretation of Beethoven's Ninth and studying *Tannhäuser*.

Considerably less friendly to Wagner was Karl Lipinski, concertmaster of the Dresden orchestra, who was dedicated to Hector Berlioz. Like Vieuxtemps, Lipinski had met Wagner while giving concerts in Riga. The eminent Pole's reputation as a virtuoso was linked with Paganini's, and Schumann had dedicated the *Carnaval* to him. Young Bülow received his first ticket to *Rienzi* from Lipinski. The latter admired the opera but, suspicious of Wagner's character, unjustly imagined an attempt on his part to sabotage Berlioz's Dresden concerts of 1843. On the contrary, Berlioz attested to Wagner's good will.

[3] A decade later Cosima was able to flatter Rellstab into a more kindly attitude toward Liszt and Bülow.

Berlioz could not sufficiently praise Lipinski's musicianship. But Wagner found virtuoso temperament and style hardly ideal in a concertmaster. Personal and professional friction between the two was inevitable and came to a'climax in a controversy over Wagner's unusual tempi in Mozart.

During Wagner's seven-year stay in Dresden a number of gifted people were resident there. Chief among them were the architect Semper and Robert and Clara Schumann, whose circle included the painters Bendemann and Hübner (brothers-in-law and both distinguished pupils of Schadow), Eduard Devrient (the theater's dramatic director and a member of the famed German acting family), Weber's widow, Lipinski, the poet-painter Reinick, and Ferdinand Hiller, the conductor and composer to whom Schumann dedicated his piano concerto and who in his Paris days had preceded his friend Berlioz in the affections of the obliging Marie Félicité (Camille) Moke, later Madame Pleyel.

Many artists visited the city: the prodigy Joachim, Mendelssohn, Gade, Berlioz, Spontini, Liszt, Meyerbeer, Jenny Lind, Hanslick (in the Dresden days an admirer of Wagner), the painter Moritz von Schwind, Hebbel, and the youthful Hans von Bülow, whose parents had settled in Dresden. Artists and intellectuals frequently gathered at Engel's restaurant on the Postplatz or met in private salons. Evenings at Hiller's house were especially enjoyed because of Polish Frau Antolka's hospitality. Life was leisurely in the matchless "Florence on the Elbe." In fact, Schumann had moved to the capital at the end of 1844 as an antidote to Leipzig's too energetic tempo.

Richard attempted to fit himself into this new social pattern. His observation that not a soul at these meetings seemed particularly interested in anyone else was probably a projection of his own attitude, for he missed those Parisian evenings of old when his faithful band would assemble mute before his soliloquies. Pecht did turn up in Dresden, but it was Kietz for whom Wagner longed and whom he strove to lure from Paris. He frequently saw Kietz's brother Gustav, a student of sculpture. Dresden was possessed of an important group of sculptors, including Hähnel and Rietschel, young Gustav's master.

Wagner was ill at ease in surroundings in which the fine arts were as earnestly discussed as music and literature. That colossus of German romantic art, Julius Schnorr von Carolsfeld, became director of Dresden's Kunstakademie in 1846 and joined the Saturday group at Engel's.

Only the polemic of fiery Gottfried Semper gave Wagner genuine pleasure. He seemed impressed by Berthold Auerbach, the novelist of the Black Forest, who arrived in Dresden to take up quarters with the Hillers. Both Auerbach and Hiller were evidently submissive enough for Wagner to forgive them their Jewish parents.

Wagner and Schumann were never able to draw near one another. Even before the century was half over, the line, though faint, was already drawn between the early German romantics, of whom Schumann after Mendelssohn's death in 1847 was the last great representative, and the romantic realists, who were to be led by Liszt and Wagner. The marriage of flesh and spirit to be achieved by the latter was announced in *Rienzi* and *Dutchman* and effected in *Tannhäuser*. Schumann might admire the daring of the union but could not feel at ease in the couple's presence. Like Mendelssohn's estimate of Liszt's life, *Tannhäuser* fluctuated between scandal and apotheosis.

Schumann longed to write a successful opera. He considered many subjects, among them *Eulenspiegel*, the *Nibelungenlied*, the Wartburg contest, *Hermann and Dorothea*, *Faust*, Byron's *Corsair*, and the omnipresent Mary of Scotland. He finally settled upon the tale of St. Geneviève of Brabant, already treated in literature by Tieck and Hebbel, and ended by concocting a libretto of his own that leaned most heavily on Hebbel's drama. He read it to Wagner, who suggested some changes especially concerning the visions conjured in a magic looking glass by the witch Margaretha. But he sensed that Schumann resented suggestions, and let the matter rest.

Wagner's attacks upon Schumann were to come in his final, irascible years. In 1843 he had written him expressing the hope that their artistic tendencies might converge. *Meistersinger*, from Wagner's middle period, embodies a subtle reference to the writings of the composer-critic. Schumann's commentaries on music were often set forth as opinions of the fictitious *Davidsbündler*, a group representing the Davids of the arts forever letting fly at the benighted Philistines. Not by accident is Hans Sachs's apprentice called David, he who cudgels Beckmesser, that rather pathetic spiritual compatriot of Goliath who is routed twice, first physically by David and then artistically by Stolzing. David's name is Wagner's tribute to the old combative ideals of Schumann's *Neue Zeitschrift*, the journal he termed, in an enthusiastic letter of 1835 to Schumann, "a splendid battleground." The riot scene was the germ from which grew all of *Meistersinger*, on its highest level a sagacious essay on the reconciliation of what is precious in both the old and new. Is not Stolzing stormy Florestan and Sachs poised Master Raro, those pen names under which Schumann engaged in aesthetic discussions in his magazine?

Wagner took pains to indicate to posterity that Schumann preferred his conducting to Mendelssohn's. Perhaps he was misled by a tactful compliment on the part of Schumann, who, in fact, often found Wagner's musical approach incomprehensible. Schumann was not unlike those Renaissance artists who beheld with misgivings the fearful world opened by Michelangelo. The elements making up the new art were familiar, but the novel assemblage was disturbing. Musicians like Zelter had tampered with Bach and envisioned him nodding approval in heaven, but Wagner was perhaps the first great virtuoso conductor who felt it his right completely to remold the repertory in his own image. To him, history as a record meant nothing and had value only for the treasure to be yielded for his own use. At times he "modernized" by reorchestrating and by changing tempi, dynamics, and even harmonies to fit his highly personal conception of the drama of a particular piece. He filtered the works of others through his theatrical genius. By taking literally Beethoven's broad, figurative, and private use of the word "picture," Wagner was coming to see Beethoven's major compositions as attempts to represent actual subjects, the obstacle to their understanding lying in the fact that most conductors (Mendelssohn in particular), being unaware of the master's involuntary error in omitting the key to his "tone poems," interpreted them in purely musical terms. Only another tone poet of capabilities equal to Beethoven's—dare one guess his name?—might divine the subject, thus grasping the emotional "what" of Beethoven's creations for which the formal "how" was but the means of expression.[4] Thus came into being what Dorn later called *"ver-wagnerter Beethoven."*

Although Wagner's Dresden notes for the Ninth Symphony (1846) "explained" it quite simply by quoting appropriate lines from Goethe that were to guide the listener toward an emotional understanding of the work, by the opening of the new decade he had arrived at the startling conclusion that Beethoven's symphonies were program music. As his own inclinations led him more and more from the realm of pure music toward that of literature, of necessity he came to believe in similar tendencies in Beethoven justifying his course. Preposterous as it may seem today, Wagner also felt that certain of Bach's preludes and fugues needed words, which he actually contemplated providing. His subjectivity was opposite to Mendelssohn's relatively cool detachment, and it was the latter whom Schumann admired, though not slavishly.

Wagner was a master of rubato, a veritable Chopin of the orchestra whose

[4] Coming from notes handed over to Uhlig in 1852, these ideas are strongly akin to many in the contemporary *Jewry in Music*. In contrast, it is interesting to find in Wagner's short story "A Happy Evening," written during his first Paris stay, the opinion that music can communicate only abstract concepts. The two points of view did not necessarily appear contradictory to Wagner, whose Swiss essays were to reconcile them, at least to his satisfaction. He saw himself as an interpreter uniquely gifted to recapture Beethoven's "lost" images or dramatic visions and also as the creator whose mission was the destruction of the Italian number opera by the harnessing of Beethoven's universal orchestral music to the concrete images of the vocal drama. In "A Pilgrimage to Beethoven" (Paris, 1840) Wagner had given the master a vision of such a composite work.

mode of expression seemed to the Dresden critic Carl Banck a series of irresolutely sustained tempi. It was Wagner's seeming vagueness of beat and intensity of shading that Mendelssohn and his French counterpart in conducting, Berlioz, abhorred. (However, neither Berlioz nor Schumann was always happy with Mendelssohn's occasional precipitate tempi in Beethoven, though even Wagner had to admit the detested Jew's technical refinement.) When Londoners in 1855 had the opportunity of hearing both Wagner and Berlioz conduct during the same season, Berlioz's strict and precise interpretations in the manner of Mendelssohn gained the encomiums.

Wagner wrote to Liszt that he was "little edified" by Berlioz's Mozart, which seemed to him mere time-beating—completely without "depth," Minna was told—while Berlioz felt no pleasure in Wagner's "free" style of conducting, which he likened to Klindworth's piano playing.[5] To Davison of the London *Times* Wagner's changes seemed "perpetual and fidgety," his "capriciousness" in slackening the time making him, at intervals, the orchestra's tormentor rather than conductor. The more friendly critic, Hogarth, made reference to the unusual effects produced by retardations and accelerations. Here is the basis of Lipinski's struggles with Wagner, whose pliant phrasing in Mozart had elicited critical reproaches from Dresdeners.

It is to be recalled that what Wagner hailed as intensity in Schröder-Devrient's Senta, Berlioz deplored as exaggeration. The two men had fundamentally different artistic ideals. Berlioz continued the French classic tradition, as did his elder contemporary in painting, Ingres. Although, unlike the latter, Berlioz hardly disparaged color, for which he showed the enthusiasm of a true romantic, he used it to strengthen and clarify his linear patterns. In contrast, Wagner usually loaded his canvas thickly with the brilliant pigment of Delacroix, often applied with Courbet's palette knife; contour tended to yield to an assault of glowing paint in Wagner's compositions and evidently in his interpretations, too. He wrote that piety never inspired him to follow musical directions literally when, as in Beethoven's Ninth, he held the score's markings to be erroneous, thus misrepresenting the effect he was sure Beethoven really intended! He felt free, for example, to add brass to passages originally given to the more mellow wood winds and, in general, attempted to effect what he termed a *"restitutio in integrum"* of the symphony's design. An admirer of Mozart's instrumental embellishment of *Messiah,* he certainly saw himself accomplishing a similar task "in the general interest of art," and it is all the more amusing to call to mind his indignation in Paris during 1841 when

---

[5] Earlier, Berlioz did find some kind words for Wagner's energetic and punctilious conducting of his own music.

Adolphe Adam reinforced the brass in Grétry's *Richard Coeur de Lion*. Believing Beethoven to have fallen short of his intentions because of deafness and the technical limitations of contemporary instruments, Wagner set about "restoring" the work with the same marvelous and smug Victorian self-assurance with which Viollet-le-Duc renovated the abbey of St. Denis or Gilbert Scott the cathedral at Salisbury. At the height of his career in his article on the Munich music school, Wagner was still deploring the "bland" and "soulless" kind of performance resulting when a conductor restricted himself to the markings in a master's score, and called for the "instinctive" interpretation of "a musician of feeling."

6

From the time of *Rienzi*'s première Wagner's fame grew. Selections from the opera were given under his baton about a month later in Leipzig as part of a benefit for Schröder-Devrient's famous actress-mother, the aging Sophie Schröder. Laube had again taken up editorship of Leipzig's *Zeitung für die elegante Welt*, to which Wagner contributed an autobiographical sketch (February, 1843). In Dresden on his thirtieth birthday he was serenaded by sixty lantern-bearing vocalists from local singing societies. He had found himself elected to the committee of the Dresden Liedertafel (January, 1843), whose president and founder, Professor Löwe, conceived the idea of convening a union of Saxon choral societies in Dresden's baroque Frauenkirche. Wagner was asked to write a composition for the festivity, and on July 6, 1843, he conducted a Berlioz-like concourse of twelve hundred male voices and an orchestra of one hundred (concealed behind the singers) in his *Love Feast of the Apostles,* a work exploiting the relationship between architectural and musical structure, a principle he would one day turn to magnificent account in the temple scenes of *Parsifal*. Most dramatic in the *Love Feast* are the *"Stimmen aus der Höhe"* sung by about forty singers whom Wagner placed in the cupola of the church. Their comforting words, climaxing many pages of *a cappella* singing, are followed by the striking first entrance of the hidden orchestra with tremolo strings, tympani, and winds, painting the descent of the Holy Spirit as the disciples sing, *"Welch Brausen erfüllt die Luft?"* This "Biblical Scene" the composer dedicated to Frau Weinlig, widow of that "unforgettable teacher" who had died exactly a month before Richard's departure from Paris.

He took over another of Professor Löwe's projects, that of effecting the removal of Weber's remains from St. Mary's Chapel, Moorfields, London. On the evening of December 14, 1844, the dead composer was greeted on

Kapellmeister *in Dresden*

Saxon soil with funeral strains for winds and muffled drums composed by Wagner from *Euryanthe* themes. The next day he delivered an oration over the grave and conducted the singing of a poem written and composed by him for male voices. Particularly eloquent, he certainly remembered little Richard Geyer peering with awe at Weber through Johanna's curtains and pleasant picnics of the Geyer circle in which the master had joined.

During June of the preceding year, Wagner had written the first of those occasional pieces required of him as a composer to the crown. In Matthäus Daniel Pöppelmann's architectural miracle, the Zwinger, a monument by Rietschel to the late King Friedrich August I, Napoleon's unhappy ally, was unveiled to Wagner's cantata for male voices. At this same ceremony a composition by Mendelssohn was also heard, but Wagner assured brother Albert and Minna that the simplicity of his contribution, contrasting with Mendelssohn's pomposities, bore off the palm!

On the occasion of his royal master's return from England in August, 1844, Wagner hastily composed a musical welcome (it was the germ of the *Tannhäuser* march and chorus in praise of the Landgraf), gathered and rehearsed one hundred and twenty instrumentalists and three hundred singers, and in the mists of early morning packed them into a river boat that set out for the royal seat at Pillnitz. The organizing hand that created the Bayreuth festival was already visible.

But despite theater and chapel service, his musical duties were not arduous, and there was time for his own work. In urging Albert to send his adopted daughter, Johanna, to sing at Dresden, he promised that her beautiful young voice would not be overworked, stressing the leisurely pace at the opera.[6]

In October, 1843, with the help of a loan he and Minna were established in a spacious, well-appointed apartment with a view of the Zwinger on the fashionable Ostra-Allee. Peps, the tyrannical spaniel—his presence on an upholstered stool near the new grand piano ordered from Breitkopf and Härtel was necessary when Richard composed—had been joined by a gray parrot named "Papo," a gift from the Hamburg impresario. Papo was coached by Minna in vocal selections from *Rienzi*.

And Minna now had a maid. Her health appeared to be slowly returning, thanks to long vacations with Richard in their beloved Bohemia, periods, as will be seen, significant to his creative development.

The new Wagnerian affluence was possible only because Richard, as usual, was living on the future. Lawsuits had been averted by assuaging

[6] Johanna started her Dresden career in the spring of 1844. At first she was a mezzo capable of sailing into the high soprano range. She had already made her debuts as both actress and singer.

creditors with freshly borrowed funds. Moreover, even had the self-indulgent young man been debt-free, it would have been impossible for him to live within his comfortable salary. He reasoned that, since his operas would soon be in the repertories of many theaters, he might spend freely with the certainty that multiplying fees would presently set his tangled affairs aright. What delayed this happy situation, he felt, was that no printed full scores or piano arrangements of *Rienzi* or *Dutchman* existed. Having failed to come to an agreement with Breitkopf and Härtel, he had contracted in June of 1844 to have these works brought out at his own expense by the publisher Meser, who was to receive a commission on sales. Necessary capital was promised by Schröder-Devrient's generous agreement to underwrite the enterprise.

When the day arrived to collect the first installment, Wagner learned to his consternation that the diva's slender, dashing, and military new lover had taken over management of her finances and evidently had more personally profitable investments in mind. She maintained that she no longer controlled her money and could be of no service. Meser's engraving was well under way, and with it the pattern of future disaster was clearly being traced.

7

Wagner's experience with the repertory was generally humdrum. The orchestra was content, as was he, to hold few rehearsals for standard pieces. But he particularly regretted conducting underrehearsed Mozart operas as stopgaps in the schedule. Yet there were also gratifying occasions, as when he led the Dresden première of *Armide* in March, 1843. Edited by him in respect to tempi and dynamics and sumptuously mounted, it gained him a reputation as an interpreter of Gluck, its heroine providing one of the molds from which was cast the *Tannhäuser* Venus. During this first year Mendelssohn, visiting Dresden to conduct his *St. Paul* at the annual Palm Sunday concert, impressed Wagner with a work that also left its mark on *Tannhäuser*. In February, 1844, he presided in the pit over the first Dresden performance of *A Midsummer Night's Dream* with Mendelssohn's incidental music, a score which was to help shape the first-act finale of *Lohengrin* and from which many years later he was to borrow a theme to be put to use in *Meistersinger* as the poignant motif of Sachs's resignation.

More colorful than Mendelssohn's visit was that of Spontini during the winter of 1844. On Wagner's initiative he had been asked to superintend a Dresden production of his *Vestale*. In 1819 the contract had been signed by which Friedrich Wilhelm III of Prussia had lured him from Paris with a munificent salary and the title, among others, of chief *Kapellmeister*. The

King's death in 1840 portended the end of a long and tempestuous musical reign in Berlin. Spontini's tactless arrogance involved him in an indictment for lese majesty and earned the royal reprimand of Friedrich Wilhelm IV. Cries of *"Hinaus!"* greeted the maestro's attempt to mount the podium, and in 1842 a dethroned musical monarch quit Berlin. During the following period of wandering and indecision he received the invitation to Dresden.

Wagner vividly recalled Spontini's disciplined production of *Cortez* in Berlin and over the years absorbed many of his practices. Not infrequently did Spontini's rehearsals last eight full hours to secure, from principals down to supernumeraries, perfection of musical and dramatic detail. His conducting favored precise entries, sharp accents, and bold contrasts. Dorn described his forte as a hurricane, his piano as a breath.

Brandishing his baton like a field marshal, more as a sign of authority than as a truncheon for beating time, he transfixed his musical troops with withering glances, although he could barely discern their positions. Extremely shortsighted, he felt that eyeglasses would detract from the spectacle of predominancy he wished to present. This vanity made him insist that instrumentalists always occupy the same relative positions in any orchestra he conducted, and the Dresden band, to Wagner's pleasure, was reseated along the lines of Berlin's, in which the strings were evenly distributed on either side of the conductor, and a more balanced tone resulted.

A modest *succès d'estime* rewarded *Vestale,* which the public attended out of curiosity to see the famous and cadaverous musical tyrant. The performances, late in 1844, aggravated the growing rivalry between Schröder-Devrient and Wagner's niece Johanna. The former was no longer able physically to suggest a virgin of Vesta, a dilemma accentuated by the latter's youthful appearance in the senior role of the high priestess. The Devrient was well aware of the unvoiced opinion of many that the roles ought to have been exchanged.

Another musical luminary's visit followed Spontini's. Marschner returned to Dresden when his *Adolf von Nassau* was given its first performance by Wagner in January, 1845. From the hero's address to his knights in the opening scene was to be born King Henry's speech to the nobles assembled before the judgment oak in *Lohengrin.*

Dresden's Palm Sunday concerts provided the opportunity of revealing Wagner's qualities as an interpreter of scores other than operatic, among them the "Pastoral" Symphony, Haydn's *Creation,* and, in 1846, Beethoven's Ninth, given successfully by Mendelssohn in Leipzig and by Nicolai in Vienna, but still unappreciated in Dresden. Wagner was deeply affected as he studied this work, so important to his earliest artistic development and musical reawakening in Paris. Possibly he recalled his plan to write with Anders a definitive book on Beethoven.

To fit his concepts of proper balance and mood he revised instrumentation, dynamics, and tempi and inspired his orchestra and a chorus of three hundred (he evidently had these vocalists proclaim rather than sing the most ecstatic phrases) to a performance of the Ninth that had enormous success, especially with what he honestly identified as the nonprofessional public. Musicians like Hiller believed he had gone too far in modifying the printed score, although Niels Gade felt richly rewarded for his trip from Leipzig to hear the general rehearsal, being especially moved by the famous recitative for low strings. In this passage Wagner sensed a point of decision where Beethoven's instrumental style, pressing toward articulateness, could of necessity but call to its aid the human voice and thus prepare the Wagnerian synthesis. Among the auditors at the performance were two boys whose destinies were to be linked to Wagner, Hans von Bülow and Ludwig Schnorr von Carolsfeld, son of the painter. So successful was Wagner's effort that he was requested to repeat the Ninth at the concerts of 1847 and 1849.

One of his most enthusiastically received productions was that of Gluck's *Iphigenia in Aulis* (February, 1847), which he subjected to drastic dramatic, textual, and musical emendations. As he edited the score, he interpolated an aria and freshly composed instrumental passages, dovetailed sections to achieve a more romantic "forward" movement, added new recitatives and rewrote the old, changed harmonies for dramatic effect, altered the vocal parts, and completely revised the plot and instrumentation. By the final act he had all but thrown away the original and was writing entirely new music to his own text. What remained of Gluck was dressed in Wagnerian costume. Iphigenia emerged as Elsa and Achilles as Lohengrin. Dresdeners, particularly their king, applauded the transformation. But Schumann, not terribly grateful for Wagner's additions to the score, wrote, "In the case of Wagner's operas, Gluck would probably have employed the opposite process —subtracted, cut out." Robert's pen could be very brittle.

8

Wagner had begun the music of *Tannhäuser* while he and Minna were vacationing at Teplitz during July and August of 1843, the poem having been completed during the spring. In a fury of creative impotence, he smashed the strings of the piano specially installed in his pension. The weak opening scene in Venus' grotto bore witness to this struggle until its revision in Paris over seventeen years later. He wrote to Pusinelli lamenting his lack of inward or outward harmony.

During the hours devoted to his cure he carried a flask of mineral water to the most sheltered and deserted groves of the Thurn Gardens, where he settled down to peruse Jakob Grimm's *German Mythology*. The fragments of a forgotten world both confused and provoked him.

After a trip to Prague with Minna (inquiring after the Pachta girls, he learned that they had married well), he returned to Dresden in August. Despite a schedule during the following year and eight months that included, in addition to his regular conducting duties, the Berlin *Dutchman*, the Hamburg *Rienzi*, Spontini's visit, and the Weber funeral ceremony, he managed to complete *Tannhäuser* by April, 1845. He had gathered capital to continue his printing enterprise by begging funds from, among others, Pusinelli and artists of the theater, and one hundred copies of the full score of *Tannhäuser* were lithographed by Meser. On his advice the original title, *"Der Venusberg,"* was altered, for it had already given rise to raw jokes among Dresden's medical students. A sign of Wagner's waxing fame was the presence of both Spontini and Meyerbeer at the twentieth presentation of *Rienzi* in September, 1844, while during May, 1845, the King of Prussia heard the twenty-fifth.

Exhausted by his labors, Wagner in July, 1845, again set out with Minna for a Bohemian vacation-cure, this time in Marienbad. He suffered from hemorrhoids, and his bowels were often in a disastrous state. With him traveled Simrock's and San-Marte's modern German versions of Wolfram von Eschenbach's poetry and the anonymous epic of Lohengrin, which had attracted him at the end of his Parisian stay.

Rather than finding rest, he entered a state of growing disquietude. To divert himself from the serious subject of Lohengrin, which had taken complete dramatic form within his mind and was seeking to break forth, he sought distraction in sketching a light comedy about Hans Sachs and the Meistersinger, a subject that had fascinated him since his reading in Gervinus' *Geschichte der poetischen Nationalliteratur der Deutschen*. It was to be a satyr-play following the tragedy of *Tannhäuser*. The song contest on the Wartburg was to find its humorous analogue in the Nuremberg meadow. Comedy was the genre most likely to open the doors of German theaters. But *Lohengrin* could not be suppressed, and one day, to the annoyance of his doctor, Wagner sprang from his medicinal bath and closeted himself to outline the opera.

He was in Dresden again by the middle of August. *Tannhäuser,* already in preparation, had the outward features of popular success. Its framework was that of a Meyerbeer grand opera, its pages including an exotic ballet, a transformation scene, and a splendid procession with regal paraphernalia. The delighted management, anticipating a return to the box office of the *Rienzi* queues, ordered scenery from Paris. Moreover, the figure of the noble Landgraf, obviously patterned upon Count Ottokar in *Freischütz,* and the ensemble voicing his virtues, composed of musical material derived from the

Pillnitz tribute, were compliments to Wagner's beloved King Friedrich in the tradition of *La clemenza di Tito,* an opera of homage, that genre more recently revived by Spontini. And the Catholic court, somewhat uneasy in Protestant Saxony over the unflattering role the Vatican played in *Rienzi,* could feel consoled by the fact that, despite Pope Urban IV's overhastiness in Tannhäuser's case, heaven had nonetheless inclined to set him right. Wagner even had to cope with rumors that the Catholic Party had bribed him to write the opera.

Only Schröder-Devrient perceived the composer's intentions to be deeper than the opera's tinseled, politic exterior. Tannhäuser with his Faustian contrariety was not a stock tenor hero like Rienzi. Rather, he was for the operatic stage of the time a relatively complicated portrait of an immature man at odds with himself and in open revolt against his environment. Ambivalence distinguished the best of Marschner's characters (Heiling and the Templar), and from him Wagner had learned the dramatic richness to be exploited in such figures.

Madame Devrient asked Wagner whether he seriously expected Tichatschek's simple mind to grasp and convey Tannhäuser's part. And did Wagner believe that the inexperienced Johanna could comprehend the complex emotions agitating Elizabeth—a character embracing elements of Fatima, heroine of *Die Sarazenin?* Moreover, Schröder-Devrient evidently realized that the role of Venus was inchoate and incommunicable, as Wagner was to admit years later in a letter to Mathilde Wesendonk. Devrient's notorious private life made the part somewhat embarrassing for her, and the aging prima donna pointedly demanded to know how she was to costume her voluminous figure as the goddess—"in only a belt?" [7] In the end the resourceful artist devised eloquent classic gestures that wove some kind of illusion.

As rehearsals progressed, Minna foresaw the audience's disappointment. The orchestration lacked the brilliant if obvious effects of *Rienzi.* And the song contest in the second act was insipid despite Wagner's rationalizations. How astute the old trouper, Minna, was! At the première the audience slumbered through this section, which would one day be considerably shortened for Paris. Hanslick, too, was to find the effectiveness of the scene damaged by too much uninspired declamation. Furthermore, the denouement could be grasped only by those who had carefully studied the poem. Rather than underlining the outcome of the plot, the stage action and circuitous diction of the text only hinted at it. One critic observed that, rather than ending, the opera evaporated. A claque of friends was required to teach Dresdeners that Tannhäuser's angel was the very Elizabeth whom they had seen in the flesh but minutes before her ascent to God's throne.

---

[7] *"Mit einem blossen Gürtel geht es doch nicht."*

But *Tannhäuser* revealed musical progress. In *Rienzi* Wagner had relied upon a well-carpentered libretto and stage effects to rescue him from the musical morass into which he frequently stumbled; in *Tannhäuser* he depended upon the poetry of his music to make convincing a libretto whose mechanics he seemed unable to master.

Vainly hoping that Wagner would reconcile himself to using the new hall painted for Weber's *Oberon*, Lüttichau had delayed ordering a Parisian setting for the interior of the Wartburg. Its tardy arrival made necessary at the première the unhappy substitution of the *Oberon* décor with which the public was already familiar. Thus, many factors made the first *Tannhäuser* (October 19, 1845) something less than a triumph. It was a tribute to the discernment of musical Dresden that the awkward but poetic work gradually made its way to join *Rienzi* in a secure position in the repertory. The unfortunate *Dutchman* had disappeared from the boards early in 1843 and was not heard in Dresden again for over twenty years. There was occasional interest in reviving the work, but Johanna disliked a heroine requiring so simple a wardrobe.

Of course, most applauded in *Tannhäuser* were the septet and march, frankly old-fashioned numbers. But such sections were more artfully linked with surrounding material than had been the case in *Dutchman* and tended to continue rather than interrupt the plot's movement. On the whole, even the stage effects appeared dramatically justified. The transformation scene was more than the usual well-applauded manipulation of painted gauze. The change from the Venusberg to the Wartburg valley provided a musical and scenic antithesis comparable in dramatic mastery to the passage from Hades to Elysium in *Orfeo*. The piping of the shepherd of Eisenach shows that the floating winds in Gluck's roundelay of the blessed spirits helped Wagner find the means of painting a tranquillity all the more exquisite for the contention preceding it.

Both interpreters and audience found difficulty in fathoming those sections cast in Wagner's new style, in which a recitativelike melody grew out of an orchestral harmony, in itself a tonal interpretation of the text. Here classical phrase formation often gave way to a naturalistic declamation, vibrating to every inflection of the words. Such methods had been foreshadowed by Weber and Marschner but had never been pushed so far. Spohr, who was enthusiastic enough about *Tannhäuser* to plan a production at Kassel soon after its première (opposition at the Electoral Court postponed the event until 1853), nevertheless criticized Wagner's frequent forsaking of rounded periods, his occasional radical modulations, his evasion of cadences, and a certain rhythmic monotony—the last a most modern-sounding criticism. Indeed, immediately after his Kassel production of *Dutchman,* Spohr had written Wagner to recommend "fewer difficult figurations for the strings, less brass, less modulation, and the development of more pleasant-sounding harmonies and melodies." It would seem that in *Tannhäuser* the abandonment of the niceties of traditional form under the pressure of the dramatic moment somewhat further disconcerted the elder *Kapellmeister,* who nevertheless admired the work's seriousness of purpose.

Tannhäuser's eloquent recital of the failure of his Rome journey had suddenly thrust auditors into that world of overwrought suffering that was to be the mature Wagner's unique domain. Even the Dutchman's tale of his unsuccessful attempts at suicide, Senta's morbid fantasies, or Erik's prophetic dream were but generalized emotions compared to the passionate self-pity unleashed in this jagged narrative. And it was precisely here, in the free arioso engendered by the searing text, that Tichatschek was most helpless. But Wagner had cast the quotations from the Pope in the style of Rienzi's curse on Rome. The tenor's prodigious tones subduing the brass redeemed the situation somewhat. Nineteen successive E flats, followed by eight repeated G flats and crowned by a pair of G naturals, constituted a passage Tichatschek could grasp.

After the first performance Wagner set to work revising his own miscalculations and cutting those portions of the score his artists were unable to project. During 1846 and 1847 he strove to contrive a new ending and in desperation fell back upon a solution inspired by the dramatic materialization of the Mountain Queen at the conclusion of Devrient's and Marschner's *Heiling.* Venus was made to hover in the sky to contend with heaven for Tannhäuser's soul. Elizabeth's body was borne on stage to the chagrin of many of Wagner's friends, who wondered at the swiftness of medieval Thuringian burial procedure.[8]

But despite the opera's many flaws, it was obvious that a giant artistic brain was at work. The tasks Wagner set himself in *Tannhäuser* were not fully accomplished until the time of *Parsifal.*

9

The problem of ending a work pursued Wagner. He once exclaimed to Kittl, "Do you know what the closing of an opera is? *Everything!*" Believing that, in general, an audience had no need to ponder a denouement, he wrote, "If the right aspect is drastically set before it, [the ordi-

---

[8] At Karlsruhe in 1855 Eduard Devrient solved the problem by having Elizabeth's corpse borne on a litter of rough boughs by the older pilgrims, the implication being that she had fallen dead before gaining the Wartburg.

nary public] receives the right impression by instinct." Nevertheless, the dramatic incoherence often proceeding from such an attitude, which trusts only in effects, as well as frequent doubts in his own mind as to what the proper "impression" should be, gave rise to problems perplexing to him throughout his career.

Though effective, the final scene of *Dutchman* is logically unconvincing, the hero's pompous self-identification being superfluous, for he and Senta have already exchanged confidences during the duet. Yet Wagner makes him spell out his name after having dragged Erik on stage (he is a dramatic remnant from an earlier draft of the work) as an agent to incite the Dutchman's jealousy and thus set in motion the canvas waves of a grand opera finale. Certainly Fenella's vault from the terrace in *Masaniello* inspired Senta's gymnastics.

Wagner revised the wording of Rienzi's farewell curse. The strange diction of its final version may be attributed to the difficulties of reconciling a change demanded by the Dresden censor with an existing vocal line, but the hero's prediction of his return in the manner of Barbarossa was a new idea, unrelated to Wagner's earlier conception of the tale. His difficulties in terminating *Tannhäuser,* already touched upon, reappeared as he reworked *Iphigenia in Aulis,* which he finally concluded by throwing away Gluck's finale and turning again to the example of *Heiling.* To the horror of purists, he made Artemis appear poised in the air above the altar to deliver herself of a Wagnerian proclamation. In order to avoid the predicament of another altered ending, he consciously started setting the last act of *Lohengrin* first, so that the completed final scene would be a *fait accompli* toward which he could then peacefully work. Prompted by his subconscious, he began with the text of the final segment of his *Ring* cycle, and then, layer by layer, penned the poem backward, ending with the completed first drama, *Rhinegold.* But when he proceeded to set the words musically by working forward from *Rhinegold* toward the end, the old *Tannhäuser* dilemma reappeared, but on a giant scale. The clumsy textual revision of the two final *Ring* dramas to conform with the new plan of an expanded cycle was simply a matter of dramatic craft, of which Wagner was unfortunately not a master. Not the many loose ends which he never folded in, but dissatisfaction with the dramatic resolution in the final moments tormented him for decades as he repeatedly altered the words of the peroration.

While at work on the music of the *Meistersinger* finale, he came to think of the text of Sachs's political address as having an awkward relationship to the preceding prize song. Indeed, Walther's *"Will ohne Meister selig sein!"* is about as infelicitous a joint as can be found in Wagner. He had more or less determined to scrap the contemplated diatribe and end with the tenor aria and bestowal of the prize when Cosima, then his mistress, made a piteous face, talked for hours, and persuaded him to abide by the earlier plan. But to the last moment he was obviously uncertain just what "impression" of the complicated play he wished to leave in the public mind. Wagner's opera and reputation would have benefited had Cosima retired earlier that evening.

But in the case of *Lohengrin* he adhered to his original conception of the ending, despite goodly cuts and minor changes, even though it cost him the greatest anxiety. With friends he debated his decision that Lohengrin must leave Elsa. He grieved at the tragic necessity of the lovers' parting and was deeply sympathetic to Elsa, who could love but thus and not otherwise. Before this "glorious woman," rushing to her doom for the sake of love, the uncomprehending Lohengrin had to vanish.

10

In the form of Lohengrin the Dutchman had returned from over the seas, not in black attire aboard his ancient ship impelled by storm winds but now in radiant armor, standing in a bark gently drawn over the waves by an enchanted swan. He no longer raged; more contained and obviously now a successful man, he spoke in assured, gentle tones. But he was still the marvelous stranger guarding the secret of his fate. Both Senta and Elsa had invoked the visionary lover by phantasmagoria, Senta by that *"Schwärmereï"* ("ecstatic reverie") deplored by Erik, and Elsa by her more tender fantasy described by Telramund as that of a "visionary" as early as the Marienbad prose sketch of *Lohengrin*. Senta had given hysterical, unquestioning love. The more mature and womanly Elsa did not share this adolescent fever. Despite evidence of her lover's deeds and accomplishments, she would know, him better so that she might share his danger and protect him.

One may interpret Dutchman-Lohengrin's secret either as an unquenchable drive toward more experience—Venus' curse upon Tannhäuser—that propels man to a Faustian search, or as the mystery of artistic creation never to be comprehended by the layman; the two concepts were inextricably united in Wagner. It became clear to the Senta who had matured into Elsa that the same mysterious, faith-born forces that had brought the stranger to her over the waters might one day tear him from her if faith were weakened by the trials of marriage. With horror she suddenly comprehended that the Dutchman's boat had not forever sunk beneath the waves. "The swan, the swan! . . . You call to him and he comes drawing the skiff." Lohengrin had begged the question by maintaining to Elsa that their happiness was in her hands. Beside herself with anxiety, she in turn put their future up to him and asked the question he most dreaded and which few can answer and fewer withstand: "Who are you?" Lohengrin fled, and Elsa sank down. With *Lohengrin,* the only major work of Wagner's to end without some transfiguring reassurance, it was evident that Wagner would leave Minna.

It is difficult to determine just when strain developed between them. After their return from Paris Minna felt a need to live apart from him for a while at Teplitz. But in this decision matters of health and economy perhaps played important parts.

In a frank letter to Dr. Pusinelli of October, 1859, Wagner discussed the gradual discontinuance of sexual relations between him and his ailing wife. He does not date the beginning of this *"Liebesverbot,"* but evidently the decline in their intimacy began during the *Tannhäuser-Lohengrin* years, and Minna resented a restraint Wagner claimed to have initiated only for reasons of her health. He wrote her from Berlin in September, 1847, how splendid it was to find themselves calling one another "old Minna" and "old Richard"; "what is a young passion beside so old a love?" He was thirty-four, she thirty-eight! He seemed determined to persuade her that their relationship had passed beyond the sexual.

The success of *Rienzi* had exhilarated him, and he entered a period of sensual gratification. Even without this disclosure in his essay *A Communication to My Friends,* Wagner's *Tannhäuser,* that marvelous study in disquietude, tells its tale of zealous indulgence followed by luxuriant guilt. This opera, forever on his mind, achieved a kind of predestined consummation in *Tristan,* a work born over a decade later midst the turbulence of conjugal transgression. Its somewhat better-mannered hero descends from the ambiguous Tannhäuser. In 1854 Wagner contemplated interlocking his fully planned life's works further by bringing the wandering Parsifal to Kareol to present an example of renunciation to the dying Tristan, himself so striking a precursor of the wounded, suffering Amfortas. In his *Communication,* penned years before the *Tristan* project, Wagner wrote that *Tannhäuser* depicted a longing for release from the present, for absorption into an endless love which, though denied on earth, was yet to be reached through the gates of death. The meaning, in fact, the very diction, of *Tristan* was already present in this description.

Soon after completing *Tristan,* Wagner again turned to *Tannhäuser* and rewrote much of it. His recast Venusberg scene anticipated the second act of *Parsifal,* a work in which he offered at the close of his life a final version of the Tannhäuser theme, transforming the Venusberg into Klingsor's garden and the righteous Wartburg into the castle of Monsalvat. The motive of sex followed by guilt thus came full cycle.

Tannhäuser tells of a man who, unhappily and guiltily finding himself incapable of accepting a love in which the spirit signified more than the body, plunged instead into a kind of adolescent sexuality. There seems no doubt that in Dresden Richard's love for Minna imperceptibly changed into affection based upon habit. In addition to being older than he, she had aged before her time, her beauty remaining, but signs of the heart disease that would claim her already evident.

Much has been made of the intellectual gulf between Richard and Minna. But who among his women was not distant from the workings of his colossal brain? He never sought intellectuality in those he desired to sleep with. His ardor past, he subjected the rather foolish Mathilde Wesendonk to ridicule; at Penzing he delighted in Marie, his housemaid and companion, after pursuing her less acquiescent sister; and his numerous other affairs, especially during those vigorous days at Biebrich, brought him no female Nietzsches. Cosima's cleverness was his dividend in their association. Her ability to hold him consisted mainly in her highly charged sexual nature and fertility, her idolization of him, and a capacity for submission enabling her to forget an immediate cruelty and live for his art and those days when a more generous side of his nature might assert itself. Unlike Minna, she learned that with Wagner acquiescence was often the route to domination. One thinks of Fletcher's sequel to Shakespeare's *The Taming of the Shrew*, which was called *The Woman's Prize or, The Tamer Tamed*.

In Dresden, coincident with Wagner's growing reputation, the first members of his female coterie appear. Mention has been made of Maria von Könneritz and Frau von Lüttichau. The reader to Princess Augusta of Prussia, Alwine Frommann, became a Wagnerite, as did Madame Kalergis (niece of Count von Nesselrode, the Russian chancellor) and Jessie Taylor, a young Englishwoman living in Dresden with the wealthy Frau Julie Ritter. The latter and her young son Karl were devoted to Wagner's art, and in the company of Hans von Bülow, at the time a law student at Leipzig University, Karl occasionally visited the Wagner home. Hans and Jessie Taylor had been fellow piano students of Fräulein Schmiedel of Dresden. One would like to know the nature of their conversations when they met in Italy in later years, after Wagner had damaged Jessie's and ruined Hans's life.

Minna strove to keep Richard with the only means still left her, those domestic arts in which she had come to excel. He celebrated her *baba* as a delicacy that posterity must laud. She had agreed to expensive quarters on the Ostra-Allee for much the same reasons that inspired Fricka to encourage Wotan's Walhall project. Fricka sings, "Concerned about my husband's fidelity, I sadly pondered how I might bind him when he was lured forth. A well-appointed, stately home, I thought, would tempt him to tarry."

But Wagner-Wotan smiles and answers, "Woman, if you would contain me within walls, then you must not begrudge the captive god his conquest of the outside world. All who live love change and variety; such distractions I cannot forgo."

II

Schröder-Devrient's professional jealousy of Wagner's niece Johanna turned against him, and, regretting her former generosity, the diva suddenly took legal steps to force him to repay her old advance of funds. The palace, through Lüttichau, permitted him, in an unprecedented action, to dip into the theater's pension fund in August, 1846, for a loan of five thousand thaler at interest, the risk being secured by a policy on his life. The Wagnerian power of survival was strong; it was the pensioners' misfortune that his probity in money matters could not be insured.

A favorite topic of Dresden gossip was his indebtedness, daily aggravated by a growing obligation to Meser, the publisher, forced to keep his fatal investment in the score business alive by more borrowing. Relatively few copies of the scores were sold, for the operas had not spread from Dresden to other theaters. The Berlin première of *Rienzi* (October, 1847) under the composer had had little success, and royalties from Berlin had been among the last hopes of a man chronically threatened with litigation. The Prussian monarch, unable to attend the première of *Rienzi* in his own capital, journeyed to Dresden to hear *Tannhäuser*. But from this irresolute man little was to be won.

During the winter Wagner, in audience with the Saxon king, entreated for aid. Again Lüttichau came to the rescue by persuading Friedrich in February, 1848, to grant his problem *Kapellmeister* a temporary increase in salary to extricate him from his most pressing obligations. A reprimand accompanying the royal favor dumfounded Wagner, who, moreover, felt affronted to find the supplement valid for only one year. That the court would extend itself to make so many exceptions for this recalcitrant musician shows the extent to which his genius was appreciated.

In January of 1848 Johanna Geyer had slumbered into death. A letter of Albert Wagner to his daughter Franziska describes the dissolution of this last link binding Richard to Saxony. Albert observed him at the bier "quite the old Richard again, who was so fond of his mother, you know, in days of yore." Although in her senility Johanna's nagging had forced him, in his own words, to "fly out at her," a deep filial love enriched his music. Among the most affecting moments in Wagner are Siegfried's musings on Sieglinde's beauty, his speculation that the sleeping Valkyrie is perhaps this mother, who had not really died but only slumbered, and Parsifal's shattering cries to the mother destroyed by his departure from home.

Wagner's relationship with his niece Johanna was worsening. Accompanied by her stepfather and teacher, Albert, she had been sent by the Saxon king to study half a year with Garcia in Paris. Her fame was growing, and, inasmuch as her uncle's operas were unfortunately restricted essentially to one stage, she naturally began to specialize in the international French and Italian repertory. Her enthusiasm for the role of Valentine in *Huguenots* especially exasperated Wagner, who repudiated her and especially her manager-father as materialists. Wagner had always detested Johanna's mother, the soprano Elise Gollmann.

In an effort to cut expense and avoid gossip, in April, 1847, the Wagners had moved to the suburb of Friedrichstadt and taken up residence on an upper floor of the municipally owned Marcolini Palace, a building that had once housed Napoleon and later been broken into apartments. At Grossgraupa near Pillnitz, where they had vacationed during the spring and summer of 1846, the music of *Lohengrin* had been sketched. Upon their return to Dresden, detailed composition began with the third act. Interrupted by his renovation of Gluck's *Iphigenia in Aulis*, Wagner completed the orchestral sketch of this act in March, 1847, and worked on the first two in his garden haven at the Marcolini, where he also read Aeschylus' *Oresteia* in Droysen's translation.

Its situation and characters deeply indebted to Weber's *Euryanthe* and the rescue scene in Marschner's *Templer*, the libretto of *Lohengrin*, completed in November, 1845, remains, with that of *Parsifal*, Wagner's finest poetic achievement. It was well known and admired in Dresden. He had recited it before the group at Engel's restaurant. Schumann, he would have one believe, was at a loss to comprehend how it could be set musically until Wagner at a later reading playfully divided his recitation in the manner of operatic numbers. That the old poet Tieck raised such questions [9] when Wagner discussed the libretto with him in Berlin is understandable, but it seems hard to accept that Schumann—who in a contemporary work, *Genoveva*, was to go even farther than *Lohengrin* toward the integrated form of the music drama—could have been so unimaginative about a matter with which he himself was actively concerned. Cosima's remarks in later years about Schumann reflect Wagner's views. She claimed to be appalled by the vulgarity, coarseness, and traits of Meyerbeer in *Genoveva*. But her opinion clearly grew from prejudice. *Genoveva* is a work of extraordinary musical beauty. Despite Wagner's well-known partiality to dead composers, with

---

[9] Dramatic director of the Dresden theater at the time of Weber, Tieck had described *Freischütz* as a "din."

the passing years his hatred of Schumann grew into an extramusical obsession, and whatever he or his followers have to say about Schumann must be considered with this fact in mind.

As early as his Parisian short story "A Pilgrimage to Beethoven," Wagner had dreamed of a lyric drama in which the old operatic divisions would dissolve. Not until *Rhinegold* would he approach this ideal. But *Lohengrin* went far beyond *Tannhäuser* in this direction. Not many vocal *"morceaux"* may be easily detached from a score in which whole stretches are made up of eloquent musical phrases subtly molded by verbal inflections. In such passages (as in Tannhäuser's narrative) there is neither aria nor recitative, but an expression combining both.

Except for an excerpt played at a concert in September, 1848, Dresden was to wait long to hear the music of *Lohengrin,* that glory of the German romantic opera. Exhaling an exquisite lyricism obviously derived from Schumann, it climaxed the work of Weber and, moreover, contained the seeds of romantic realism within its second—and last-composed—act.

As he worked on this tale of the remote hero (so like Marschner's and Devrient's tortured Heiling torn between the earth he longed for and the miraculous realm of his origin), Wagner gradually adopted toward his official duties a contemptuous attitude similar to the Jovian pose of his last days at Riga. His conducting became careless. The excellent Baron von Lüttichau, who strove to prevent the ruin of Wagner's public career, fared little better in *Mein Leben* than Dorn and Holtei, although a certain admiration for this honorable aristocrat at times comes through the acrimonious pages. Lüttichau could hardly know that for Wagner the world of Monsalvat was real and the affairs of the theater committee chimerical. With the rejection in 1847 of his sensible scheme for improving the theater orchestra ("Concerning the Royal Orchestra," 1846), Wagner had washed his hands of Dresden's artistic affairs and turned in upon himself. His feud with Gutzkow, Eduard Devrient's successor as the theater's dramatic director, was even more bitter than his wrangling with Lüttichau.

From Wagner's remarks one would scarcely gather that Karl Ferdinand Gutzkow was that gifted and influential journalist, pioneer of the social novel, and admired playwright who with Laube had been a leader of *"das junge Deutschland,"* the political and literary movement that included Heinrich Heine and had once been so enthusiastically espoused by the youthful Wagner. In 1846 Dresden produced Gutzkow's finest play, *Uriel Acosta,* a plea for religious liberty based upon the life of this famous seventeenth-century Jewish apostate to both Christianity and Judaism. Wagner was not unimpressed by the work but, looking askance at its few beggarly musical effects, lectured Gutzkow upon the union of music and drama. The latter, however, was of the opinion that opera was one genre and pure drama quite another. There was nothing left for Wagner to do but declare him a blockhead. Certainly Gutzkow's unconversant observations on opera were no more foolish than Wagner's on the spoken drama and many other subjects about which he fulminated and knew even less.

At the time Wagner was at work finishing the full score of *Lohengrin*, France's King Louis Philippe and his queen made a hasty exit from a back door of the Tuileries. The rule of the citizen-king who had attempted to couple the Revolution and the *ancien régime* collapsed in February, 1848, and the succeeding Second Republic, though chaotic, inspired hopes in liberals all over Europe. With the July Monarchy romanticism died, and *Lohengrin* was one of its final monuments. No longer would men flee reality by seeking the past; the future—"progress"—beckoned in a new direction.

Wagner seemed to relive the ecstatic Leipzig days of 1830. He felt that the peril to Germany now lay to the east and wrote a poem calling for a crusade against Russia (*"Der alte Kampf ist's gegen Osten"*), an echo of King Henry's tirade against the Hungarians in the opening scene of *Lohengrin*. The court at Dresden began seriously to suspect the loyalty of a royal servant indiscreet enough to publish revolutionary writings and actually to deliver an address on the subject of the relationship between republic and monarchy (June, 1848) before several thousand members of the Vaterlandsverein, a political organization engaged in forwarding a plan to arm the populace. Although Wagner, perhaps harking back to the optimistic young days of Louis Philippe's reign, set forth in this foggy harangue his thesis of the king as first democrat of the land, his open attack upon the courtiers (he had poor Lüttichau especially in mind) created a storm when the printed address started to circulate. The next performance of *Rienzi* had to be canceled to forestall public demonstrations. Until then the court had ignored the fact that had made Donizetti back away from Lytton's novel as operatic material: *Rienzi* was obviously susceptible of an interpretation unfriendly to any aristocracy.

Mein Leben presents Wagner's political activities with much injured innocence. The book intended for the royal eyes of Ludwig of Bavaria explained his presence at revolutionary meetings as a combination of curiosity and coincidence—"like attending a play." But there is not the slightest doubt that he was up to his neck in political intrigue. He was soon to be over his head.

12

A segment of the orchestra's personnel was bent upon his dismissal. Casting about for a new position, he felt that Vienna, where the revolutionary spirit was high (in May Emperor Ferdinand, fitfully insane, had been forced to flee his capital for Innsbruck), offered scope for his activities. Pretending to Lüttichau that he was in desperate need of reviving his overwrought mind and body at a spa, he instead set out for Vienna in July, 1848, to seek a position as manager of the Kärntnertor Opera. The city again bewitched him; he described it to Minna as another Paris, but "more beautiful, gayer, and German." With him he brought a program (somewhat similar in spirit to his controversial "Draft for the Organization of a German National Theater for the Kingdom of Saxony," written some two months before) in which he envisioned a union of the various Viennese theaters under one administration. It was a period when universal programs of reform were being drawn up all over Europe, and the essays of Dresden's *Kapellmeister* were just another not very distinguished contribution to an enormous literature. But the unsettled times were not suited to the consideration of idealistic schemes in art, and he returned disillusioned to Dresden and a court well aware of his activities in Austria and his bad faith in requesting a vacation.

Financial pressure was mounting as creditors, hearing rumors of his heedless involvement in culpable political activity, called in loans. In vain had he pleaded with Breitkopf and Härtel and with Liszt to purchase his publishing venture from Meser and secure the copyrights of *Rienzi, Dutchman,* and *Tannhäuser*. Typically, it escaped Wagner's memory that he had already conveyed to Pusinelli ownership in his published works as collateral for loans. He was even to ask the doctor to purchase a second time this very security that was becoming his by default! That the rights to *Tristan and Isolde* were later given him as general compensation did not stop Wagner from subsequently negotiating their sale to Breitkopf and Härtel. Nor was Pusinelli to be the only submissive victim of such chicanery. Otto Wesendonk, who bought the publishing rights to *Rhinegold* and *Valkyrie* in 1859, had wide experience with Wagner's character and was perhaps not too startled to learn that *Rhinegold* was soon sold again to Schott of Mainz without any intention on Wagner's part of repaying the original advances. As requital Otto was granted the rights to *The Twilight of the Gods*—an unwritten work! But in 1865 Wagner demanded that Otto without reimbursement give up all claims to the *Ring* (he had also paid for the incomplete *Siegfried*) and even surrender—"amiably and generously"—the autograph orchestral score of *Rhinegold,* his only remaining asset of these transactions, to the *Ring*'s newest proprietor, the Bavarian king. The climax of double dealing came after the first Bayreuth festival, when King Ludwig's ownership rights, for which he had paid untold thousands of marks, were ignored by Wagner, who proceeded to sell the *Ring* to individual theaters for his own profit. It was only the pursuit of gold by Frenchmen and Jews that Wagner found seriously immoral.

Amazingly Wagner's creative work continued throughout the turbulent year of 1848. While finishing *Lohengrin* (completed April, 1848), he was deep in studies for a Nibelung tragedy and in the following months was devouring the *Volsunga Saga,* the *Nibelungenlied,* the Eddic poems, the writings of the brothers Grimm, and other works on the Nordic tales. He must have been digesting much of this material during his visit to Vienna. At the end of summer he produced his essay *The Wibelungs,* by the opening days of October the consequential scenario to be called "The Nibelungen Myth as Scheme for a Drama," and later in the autumn a poetic play, "Siegfried's Death," wherein a sylvan Lohengrin, supernatural but spared full knowledge of his origin and curse, suffers more than the repudiation accorded Tannhäuser or the retreat of Lohengrin. Siegfried, the redeeming hero, dies an innocent victim of man's hate. Early in 1849 Wagner further pursued this pessimism concerning a reformer's earthly recompense by sketching a drama, "Jesus of Nazareth," in which a god—created by a marvelous father who was not his putative parent—wills his own destruction. The Magdalen frankly asks whether he desires Judas' work to be accomplished, she alone divining his mission; Wagner had to give even Jesus an Eternal Feminine.

Confronted with a materialism he cannot demolish to build his new order, Wagner's Jesus, who is more the son of man than the mystic Christ,[10] longs for death as an act of disowning the loneliness encompassing him. He stands solitary midst the loveless throng.

Not until 1854 did Wagner become acquainted with Schopenhauer's works. Their immediate fascination for him lay in the fact that they clearly expressed a philosophy he had been intuitively following. Schopenhauer's *The World as Will and Idea* (issued in 1818) saw the self-determining will as transcending the world of phenomena, outsoaring causality, space, and time, forever warring against itself, and buying evanescent instants of self-realization at the cost of other aspects of fulfillment. To Schopenhauer the cosmic will presented an unending, senseless pattern of self-destruction, born of disillusionment and dissatisfaction, its guerdon being surfeit, misery, then fresh craving, and all to no end. Release from this insane cycle he saw in the will not to will; redemption was to come through the extinguishing of desire. Only by thus striving to triumph over the limitations of his nature could man rise to contemplate the eternal and universal. Schopenhauer's nirvana was influenced by Buddhism.

Wagner had laid out the same path for his artistic creations. It led from

---

[10] Wagner, like Goethe, put to literary use the mythology of a religion which he not only disbelieved but, at the time, actually found repellent. Soon he was to give his entire attention to the Eddic gods. His return to Christian symbols in his final drama was to give rise to its most serious flaw. *Parsifal* could not repeat the miracle of the second part of *Faust.*

Eisenach, scene of Tannhäuser's struggles, to Antwerp's citadel, in which Lohengrin abandoned earthly joy, through the Cornish garden of Mark's castle, where Tristan and Isolde sang their hymn to divine oblivion, past the fire-rock beneath which Wotan willed his own destruction; it went by the Nuremberg cobbler's shop that witnessed Sachs's wise renunciation, and ended in Klingsor's domain, where Parsifal vanquished Schopenhauer's foe of foes—sex—and thus prepared himself for the holy temple.

Many of Wagner's characters were disciples of Schopenhauer before their creator grasped the doctrine guiding their steps. By denying his ego and participating in the sufferings of another, the Dutchman had performed that manner of deed which alone was of moral value to Schopenhauer. Only after reading the Sage of Frankfort could Wagner fathom his own Wotan's will to ruin, a longing not to be checked by the finale Wagner had penned to "Siegfried's Death," in which the god, having consecrated the flames consuming the hero's corpse, awaited his spirit's victorious arrival in Walhall. Here Wagner attempted to convert the burden of his Vaterlandsverein speech into an operatic denouement. All-father (King Friedrich), liberated by the hero, was to rule a new order. Such, too, was the ending sketched in the earlier scenario. Wagner, having written "Siegfried's Death" while elatedly anticipating revolution in Dresden, was misled by a tendency to inflate his domestic and professional problems into transcendent political and moral issues. He saw in the revolutionary movement engulfing Europe hope for a change that might jumble his personal life and career into some kind of tolerable pattern.

"Jesus of Nazareth" was to open with a conversation between Judas Iscariot and Barabbas in which the latter, contemplating a Judaic rising against Rome, pointed to the unusually weak position of the imperial soldiery and expressed his certainty that the Folk could be goaded to insurrection.

At the end of 1848 all preparations for the production of *Lohengrin* had been suddenly halted. Considering the unsettled state of most Continental governments at this time, the countermanding of an elaborate operatic première was not an unnatural step. But the order also served to put the rebellious composer in his place. Moreover, it must have been well known to the court that since late 1845 he had unsuccessfully attempted to bypass Dresden and achieve this première in Berlin.

Embittered, he flung himself deeper into revolutionary activities. In his poem *"Die Noth"* (March, 1849) he saw visions of the old order going up in flames and cities reduced to skeletons. The fervor and obscenity of the poem bear witness to his impassioned state of mind. He was losing faith in King Friedrich and returning to the insurgent mood of *Liebesverbot,* where he had felt Shakespeare's Duke unequal to solving the complications of the plot. Revolution alone could unloose the knot. Notes for a never-completed essay disclose his conviction that, with the coming communistic order, such historical fictions as monarchy and hereditary possessions would disappear.

Reeling under his mountainous load of debt, he clutched at this possibility of avoiding his usual stealthy flight from the nest he had soiled. Somewhat like a failing pupil longing for his school to burn, he strove to bring down ruin upon the capitalistic society to which he was liable. "Jesus of Nazareth" abounds in references to the protection of private property as an act to shackle love! Thus did Wagner philosophically dispose of his creditors.

Minna could no longer grasp what he was doing as his activities seemed less and less pertinent to music. Indeed, *Lohengrin* already presents a relationship between a couple with a minimum of semantic communication.

"Die Noth" reflects the thinking of Mikhail Bakunin, the Russian anarchist who, after involvement in the Prague Whitsun rising of 1848, had sought refuge in Dresden. He took up residence with Wagner's disciple and musical assistant, Röckel, now an ardent revolutionist, and patiently awaited the full frenzy of the political conflagration. Wagner, both perplexed and arrested by Bakunin's commanding personality and his doctrine of annihilation, saw enticing visions of Europe's mighty capitals as smoldering rubbish heaps. The promise in *"Die Noth"* of life springing anew after universal ruin echoes Wagner's reading of the *Völuspâ* in the *Elder Edda,* the seed of the *Ring*'s eventual finale.

As has been remarked, research and studies for "Siegfried's Death" had occupied him throughout the second half of 1848. This heroic drama had been conceived for "the theater of the Revolution." It was clear to Wagner that his Dresden career was near its end. Hoping for insurrection, he described himself as ready to surrender to the stream of events, indifferent to their direction. But the artistic reasons leading him toward revolution were as impelling as his financial-political dissatisfactions; and all became intertwined to form the Wagnerian concept of the hero's "highest need."

As with his marriage, he had approached his post at the royal Opera with certain doubts, shying from possible restrictions upon his time for composition. But in the end his frustration in Dresden had not arisen from discontent with his achievement. He knew the value of what he had created, and his recognition by public and court was unprecedented for so young a man. Rather, his real lament was that, despite outward success, what he held to be the essence of his work, its drama, had not been comprehended. For the most part, Dresden audiences accepted *Tannhäuser* much like *Huguenots* or *Rienzi,* and those sections in which he most radically departed from old models were those least esteemed. He sadly acknowledged that he commanded a vogue based upon a misconception of his aims and that the projected *Lohengrin* would but aggravate his perplexity. This recognition forced him to search for a means of changing the indolent German operatic audience into a dedicated assembly whose cultured demand for his works would end his financial cares. He came to regard the socialist revolution as the magic instrument of transformation.

13

The Wagner of "Siegfried's Death" saw himself in the role of a hero redeeming a materialistic and base world through art. Earlier flirtations with revolutionary themes in *Liebesverbot* and *"Hohe Braut"* had been, in the first case, an expression of adolescent rebellion and, in the second, a practical desire to emulate the success of *Masaniello*. But now in the Eddic tales of corrupted gods he had found a parallel to the philistine and degraded officialdom of Europe, especially of his native Saxony, ready for regeneration. The Wagner of 1848 did not wish authority to wither away; reform was sufficient, though perhaps it had to be imposed by strong methods. Despite his dalliance with socialism, his friendship with Bakunin and Röckel, and his infatuation with cleansing fire and destruction, Wagner always remained essentially a monarchist and an authoritarian.

For months before writing "Siegfried's Death" he had realized that his career in Dresden would never bring artistic satisfaction and that his life's goal, the revitalizing of German culture through reform of the theater, could come about only by political upheaval. His practical program for the improvement of the Opera orchestra had been rejected, and his plan for a German national theater ignored. Disillusioned, he believed the courtiers guilty of betraying their trust; in their unqualified hands was what he believed to be the divine instrument of German rebirth, the opera house; if recast along Wagnerian lines, it could fulfill its lofty mission and bring to the German Folk that same sense of dedication with which the works of the Athenian playwrights had once inspired the ancient Greeks. Like Rousseau, he saw mankind as fallen from an ideal condition which it must regain. He alone knew the route.

At this time Wagner believed in the innate virtue and noble instincts of the Folk; it was the degenerate courtiers and Jews who had misled both Folk and king and who formed the main stumbling blocks to his proposals. The elimination of these parasites would bring freedom, and in some vague, romantic, marvelous, and Wagnerian way the Germanic world, purged of its enemies and redeemed by its theater, would be a happy land in which monarchy would be eradicated and kinghood simultaneously emancipated. Not surprisingly, such nebulous ideas inspired in Bakunin, a friend of Marx and Engels, contempt for Wagner's so-called "politics." Like Lohengrin, Wagner frequently longed to retire from a world that did not comprehend his artistic charge; in this mood he had sunk himself into Teutonic poetry—the Eddas and sagas.

As a result of the revolution in Paris and risings in Vienna and Berlin, a parliament had been convened in St. Paul's Church at Frankfort on the Main during the spring of 1848 to frame a constitution for a united Germany. Wagner felt that, if his ideas were adopted, the Folk would soon be free, and the Wagnerian Utopia might rise in Saxony. He did not hesitate to send suggestions to the august body. In his Vaterlandsverein speech in June he optimistically peered into the future to perceive the Germans, resembling gods, busy at their task of civilizing the globe, hardly the vision Heine had seen in his *Deutschland, ein Wintermärchen.*

During the summer of 1848 Wagner's cloudy rhetoric reached mystic heights with the writing of *The Wibelungs,* a determined but confusing attempt to organize and clarify his reading and thinking on the Rhenish myths of Siegfried and the Nibelung hoard and their relationship to German history.

The Wibelungs, an outgrowth both of a spoken drama on Barbarossa he had sketched in the fall of 1846 and of the Vaterlandsverein address, identifies Friedrich Barbarossa as the reborn sun god, Siegfried; [11] the Nibelung hoard mysteriously ascends, is transmuted in the process of time into the Holy Grail (an act accomplished, Wagner insists, in the German consciousness), and becomes the object of the Emperor's last journey to the East. Despite the turgid prose, a reader with knowledge of the completed cycle of Wagner's masterworks is thrilled to perceive in this essay what the struggling young genius could himself only dimly apprehend, the unparalleled path that lay before him from *Rhinegold* to *Parsifal,* a road that was to lead from the theft of the treasure in the river's depths to the reunion of spear and grail in the temple of Monsalvat.

In 1848 Wagner made additions to his Barbarossa play but then abandoned it in favor of an operatic work on Siegfried; he renounced, so he thought, the historical, with its dependence upon interpretation, and embraced the mythical, whose source is his favorite theme, the noble intuition of the Folk. Concluding that, because it was addressed to the understand-

---

[11] This thought is anticipated in *Die Sarazenin,* where the Maid declares Friedrich II to have been neither Christian nor Mussulman but a god reverenced as such in the East.

ing, history was unsuited to drama, he saw in myth, arising from the pathos of man, the only material meet to stir emotions in the theater, a frankly sensuous purpose, which, in his judgment, alone justified the stage. Along with the Barbarossa and Jesus of Nazareth projects, he forsook the spoken drama and, like a petulant lover, soon declared this former object of his trifling unworthy of a serious person's interest. Intuitively he recognized not word but tone to be his vital medium of artistic expression and began grappling with ideas that would lead to the synthetic *Gesamtkunstwerk*.

Since Friedrich, Siegfried, Baldur, and Christ appeared to him as manifold manifestations of a single god, his subject but changed garments and the outward circumstances of his struggle. Wagner's Siegfried always remained mixed with his vague and muddled concepts of Emperor Barbarossa, the German leader, and universal kingship. Like his Jesus and Siegfried—and, indeed, like Lohengrin, his ideal of Teutonic knighthood— Wagner's Emperor was ultimately to have been subdued by the forces he strove to master. When finally transferred from Siegfried to Wotan, this motive reached its Wagnerian apogee.

"The Nibelungen Myth as Scheme for a Drama" of October, 1848, was an attempt to reduce his impressions of the sagas, Eddas, and compendiums of myths into some manageable and cohesive form of his own; this wide-ranging prose outline or scenario, which embraces practically all the substance of the present *Ring*, was one practical result of the vague ramblings of *The Wibelungs*. Parts of it, the sections dealing with Siegfried's and Brynhild's tragedy, he developed into "Siegfried's Death" (November, 1848, but revised early in 1849), that dramatic poem he intended to set musically as "a grand heroic opera."

In "Siegfried's Death" Wotan, although he does not appear in the action, survives; the gods are saved through the hero's deed. The prediction of the Third Norn in the opening scene is realized; a joyful hero whose will is free defiantly fights for the gods (a topical reference to the *Landwehr* or Folk-arming to which Wagner was deeply committed) and, by triumphing over the dragon, wins the curse thenceforth deflected from Walhall. Gained is the victorious peace promised by the very name of Siegfried.

The poem reflects Wagner's optimism that the degraded society he deplored might yet be reborn through sacrifice and art, a German art that would turn his countrymen, led astray by the quest for gold and the seductions of French and Jewish pseudo art, back to the essential greatness and profundity of the German spirit. He passionately believed in the theater as a temple of Germanic art where mystic rites might redeem the erring and exorcise the Semitic demons Mendelssohn and Meyerbeer. (The latter had joined Felix in the Wagnerian Gehenna.) And need one ask whose works Wagner imagined should form the Proper and Ordinary of this cleansing ritual? He had found in the Teutonic myth the elements he would consecrate for the new sacrament. His offering for the redemption of the German Folk, "The Nibelung's Ring," a work whose consummation was more than a quarter of a century in the future, had begun to shape itself within his teeming brain.

Wagner and those who anticipated quick political change had been over-optimistic. The constitutional labors of the Frankfort Parliament were rejected by the Saxon government; the populace revolted, and the King sought refuge at his fortress of Königstein, where he awaited deliverance and the restoration of order by Prussian troops dispatched by that admirer of *Rienzi* and *Tannhäuser,* Friedrich Wilhelm IV.

During several days of civil war Wagner was in the center of revolutionary activity. In any case, he was near the end in Dresden both professionally and economically, and flight from the city would have been inevitable within a short time. Having nothing to lose and seeing only advantage in turmoil, he welcomed the exhilaration of the barricades. The rising failed. By a providential escape he eluded capture, indictment for treason, and a possible death sentence.

VI

Switzerland: The Prose Years

I

Franz Liszt now actively entered Wagner's life. They had first met in Paris, but Liszt could never recall the encounter. Late in 1842 Schröder-Devrient brought them together again in Berlin, and Wagner discovered indications of depth in someone he had earlier repudiated as a shallow virtuoso. In 1844 Liszt attended a specially arranged performance of *Rienzi* and then lauded it all over Europe.

He was determined to withdraw gradually from his bravura career and devote himself to serious music making and composition. In 1844 he entered upon duties at Weimar in response to Grand Duchess Maria Pavlovna's invitation to reside there for part of the year as a kind of *Kapellmeister* in Extraordinary. For well over a decade this modest Thuringian capital was to be Europe's musical center. Here were created those symphonic poems that in turn transformed Wagner's harmonic idiom. Russia heard Liszt's final commercial concert at Elisabethgrad in 1847. He returned to Weimar, where, joined by his new mistress, Princess Carolyne Sayn-Wittgenstein, whom he had met in Kiev during February of the same year, he began the momentous second phase of his career.

Early in 1849 news had come to Wagner that Liszt felt sufficient confidence in his position in Weimar to begin turning to reality his dream of uniting his and Wagner's names in the city's artistic history much as Goethe's and Schiller's had been joined under Grand Duke Karl August. In Weimar Liszt was arranging the first production of *Tannhäuser* outside Dresden, and at his invitation Wagner planned to observe a performance during the second week of May. After his return from Vienna, Wagner had briefly visited Weimar to see Liszt, who at that time probably came under the opera's spell.

On the last day of April King Friedrich's order dissolving both houses of the Saxon Diet was effected and thereby a signal for the Dresden rising unwittingly given. The sudden display of royal courage had rested on Berlin's assurance of military aid should it be needed, and within days it was clear that the insurgents must inevitably yield to speedily dispatched Prussian might. It was not as a visiting dignitary but as a fugitive that Wagner made his way to Weimar.

With indecision, dejection, and exhaustion mounting among the revolutionists, Wagner had recognized the prudence of establishing a base outside Dresden. He ordered his troops—the appalled Minna, the dog, and the parrot—to proceed with him to the house of his sister Klara in Chemnitz. He then turned back once more to Dresden in hope of a miracle. Sent from there on courier duty by the self-styled "provisional government," he soon found himself in the van of its retreating leaders, Bakunin and the valiant Heubner. Wagner's erroneous report on the strength of the insurrectionary cause in Vogtland helped form their disastrous decision to set up new headquarters in Chemnitz. But a remarkable instinct for self-preservation led him to quit their company at the crucial time. He contrived to arrive alone at Chemnitz, where he took his rest at an inn other than the one at which they stopped. In their sleep, Bakunin and Heubner were seized by the police. They were subsequently doomed to death, a sentence eventually lightened to lengthy imprisonment. Wagner, on the other hand, left his room in the early morning hours to make his way to Klara's house in the suburbs.

The account in *Mein Leben* of his movements abounds in prevarications not sufficiently artful to mask his rather obvious intentions. His endeavors to explain separation from his comrades and to stress the extraordinary efforts made to rejoin them are feeble. While they were attempting to strengthen their purpose with declarations that their cause might yet be won and war waged from the mountain fastness of the Saxon Erzgebirge, Wagner, who knew a botched job when he saw it, slipped away.

However, the record of his actions before and during the turmoil could not be erased. He had attended meetings of the inner revolutionary council, helped plan its strategy, directed publication of the radical *Volksblätter* after its editor, Röckel, had been forced to flee to Bohemia, attempted to incite disobedience among royal troops, stood watch on the tower of the Kreuz Church, and been deeply involved in ordering hand grenades from a Dresden brass founder.

In Chemnitz he did not yet fully realize the seriousness of his position, for he hoped for a quick general amnesty. Nonetheless, his immediate concern was to leave Saxon soil and jurisdiction. At night his brother-in-law Wolfram clandestinely conveyed him via Altenburg to Weimar, where, indeed, he had an invitation from Liszt to the opera. Neither the reigning Grand Duke Karl Friedrich nor his son, Hereditary Grand Duke Carl

Alexander, was aware that, because of the indiscretion of a tanner's daughter some decades before, it was a cousin who now sought safety in their capital. Liszt and the Princess were eager to be rid of their guest. To reach Weimar Carolyne herself had raced across the Russian border. Although separated from her husband for some time, she had now technically deserted him, carrying off their daughter Marie. The Czar was displeased, and Weimar's Grand Duchess was his sister. Although her broad-mindedness was well known, the lovers hardly desired to test its scope by openly sheltering a political outlaw.

Wagner attended a *Tannhäuser* rehearsal and was astounded to recognize his second self in Liszt on the podium. Though only at the start of his conducting career, Liszt was able to draw from his orchestra that variety of color he commanded at the keyboard. Like Wagner's, his beat was considered erratic, and as Europe's most famous improviser he was hostile to interpretations in strict time.

The Grand Duchess ordered the creator of *Tannhäuser* fetched to Castle Eisenach so that she might behold him before the inevitable arrival of a writ for his extradition. At Eisenach he first visited the Wartburg. Seven years before, its storied towers had flashed their greeting across the valley as he traveled back from France. Now within its walls, he faced the fact that his days in his homeland were numbered.

From Dresden Minna wrote of police visiting their apartment with instructions to search his papers and of the preparation of a warrant for his arrest. A letter found on Röckel's person (upon hearing of the rising, he had returned to Dresden and been apprehended) linked Wagner to insurgent plots by evidence of his own hand.

Flight from Germany was his only course, and, fortunately, Weimar officialdom was willing to assist. He could not risk showing himself at the *Tannhäuser* performance. Taking the name of a Berlin admirer, Professor Werder, he journeyed thus incognito to the village of Magdala, where Minna arrived on his birthday. He had written her in an attempt to justify his actions and lay some foundation for his future with a woman to whom he was tightly bound by the ties of shared ordeals: "In a state of extreme discontent with my position and almost with my art, groaning under a burden which, unfortunately, you were not really willing to understand, deep in debts . . . I was at variance with this world, I ceased to be an artist, I frittered away my creative powers, and became a mere revolutionary; . . . that is, I was seeking in a wholly transformed world the ground for some new art creations of my spirit." He continued that a man of his type was not destined for the "horrible" work of a revolutionist; destruction no longer attracted him, but "the formation of something new." He cried, "You see. Thus I am parting with the revolution."

The avowals of guilt—they seem to call for musical setting—were only partially true and the summation thoroughly dishonest. In addition to many extraordinary achievements as *Kapellmeister* during seven years in Dresden, he had also composed two masterpieces, achieved premières for three of his operas, sketched a vast Nibelung drama, outlined *Meistersinger,* and had within him the germs of *Tristan* and *Parsifal.* The genius who had planned almost a whole life's work can hardly have "frittered away" much energy. One wonders where he found time for both the marvelous and foolish projects that occupied him. The claim, advanced to Liszt as well as Minna, that he was sundering himself from radical politics was, however, pure dissimulation and primarily meant to raise his wife's courage by minimizing his involvement in illegal activities and simultaneously to supply her with appropriate phrases and explanations to pass on. But during the early days of his exile he opened his soul to Uhlig in a correspondence so frank that in later years it was severely censored by Cosima before publication.

Immediately after the flight from Dresden his radicalism, if anything, increased. He foresaw 1852 as the year of revolutionary flood, once again returning to that vision that so often enticed him—the burning of Paris. He maintained that solely in a revolutionary context could his Nibelung drama and concept of the theater of the future be apprehended, the heirs of the coming "fire cure" being those for whom his work was meant. "From the ruins I shall then find those whom I need. Then I shall erect a theater on the banks of the Rhine and issue invitations to a great dramatic festival." Religion had become "poison" to him. He had probably read some of the writings of Marx and Engels as well as those of Ludwig Feuerbach on the subjective origin of theological dogma, and he felt that atheists alone were fit to be part of his artistic program. With the passing months of exile this mood of fiery reform was spent, and in his ensuing melancholy state of mind the poem of "Siegfried's Death" began to transform itself slowly into *The Twilight of the Gods,* though in neither art nor life could he clearly divine the nature of the finale.

At Magdala Minna was near a breakdown. At any moment she expected the police to burst in. How often in the past had she heard and read his voluminous self-accusations, declarations of reform, and entreaties for understanding. Now he could only offer desperately conjured hopes, envisioning her ensconced on one of the Weimar ducal estates with money pouring in from Liszt, the Princess, and the Duchess. But Minna no longer believed his dreams. Wantonly he had shattered the only important one that had come true for her; no longer was she *Frau Königliche Kapellmeister.*

At this time few besides Liszt foresaw Wagner's higher mission. One must not think Minna alone in believing he had thrown away his finest, perhaps unique, opportunity. Their painful parting came at Jena on May 24. Middle-aged, ill, tired, and angry, she turned back to Saxony; not a step farther would she go until he could point to the next roof that would shelter her. Liszt and the Princess had filled him with thoughts of London and Paris, where his growing reputation might be profitably exploited. Perhaps *Lohengrin* would first be given in English translation or the Opéra at last commission a new Wagnerian work. His safest route to Paris lay through Switzerland. Equipped with the passport of a Tübingen professor, funds from Liszt, and—should he be questioned—a feigned Swabian accent to accord with his papers, he made his way to Zurich via Lindau and the Bodensee.

2

Zurich appealed to him. The handsome capital of German-speaking Switzerland seemed a promising haven. He looked up Alexander Müller, once a drinking companion of his youthful sprees in Würzburg's beer gardens and now a respected music teacher. His official connections secured Wagner a Swiss passport. At the end of May he set out for Paris by way of Basel and Strassburg and, like *Tannhäuser,* shut his eyes against the distractions of scenic beauty, concentrating on his goal alone. The journey was made to please Minna and Liszt. Aware of their concern for his outward fortune, he struggled to suppress inner misgivings.

Paris seemed to him "a dark image out of a terrible, long-buried past." He wrote Minna, "It was with a pang that I saw Kietz and Anders again [Lehrs had died in 1843]; . . . they made an almost specterlike impression on me, and I felt as if I myself were just where I was ten years ago." He met as fellow refugees Semper and Ferdinand Heine's son Wilhelm, the lad who had devised scenery for the abandoned Dresden production of *Lohengrin.*

Liszt's article on *Tannhäuser* in the *Journal des Débats* in May, 1849, had stirred up interest in Wagner. But the great theaters were no less difficult to storm than before. And now he was without his influential patron. By this time Meyerbeer had certainly guessed the identity of the critic of the *Neue Zeitschrift* who, hiding behind the initials "H. V.,"[1] had many years ago (February, 1842) described the composer of *Huguenots* as a *filou* (pickpocket). It was no consolation that he had also called

---

[1] The choice of these initials was vicious. Henri Valentino had conducted the disastrous performance of the *Columbus* in February, 1841. Wagner was paying him back by attempting to compromise him with the most influential musician of Paris, whose name Wagner did not spell out but coyly abbreviated to "M."

Liszt a buffoon. Moreover, many of Wagner's contemptuous remarks about Meyerbeer's religious descent and talent had undoubtedly reached his ears, and he recognized Wagner, so obsequious when a favor was to be asked, as a hopeless ingrate. Furthermore, a man in Meyerbeer's position could not associate with a flagrant revolutionary.

Cholera was daily claiming lives in stifling Paris, and Wagner was happy to forsake it and his disagreeable mission by vacationing in the country with Liszt's secretary, Belloni. He was establishing a connection for Wagner with Gustave Vaez, a poet induced to turn into suitable grand opera form whatever sketch the composer might fix upon. Belloni was to oversee negotiations with the Opéra. Wagner decided that his own part of the work might be more pleasurably accomplished in Switzerland, whence he could speed to Paris whenever necessary on the soon-to-be-completed railroad. He had faced the utter unlikelihood of his achieving anything in London and was content to toy for a while with Liszt's Parisian scheme. From France he wrote to Minna, pleading that she join him in Switzerland: "I must have tranquillity of spirit, and that is possible only when I am near you! . . . I would keep writing new works with joy and love; . . . if success should fail to come, I would still be happy in the process of writing them, having you always at my side." On July 6 he was back in Zurich awaiting her decision.

3

Minna, not sanguine about her husband's prospects, was further depressed to learn that he planned to live on the charity of friends: "Don't take this amiss—it is very doubtful whether you will ever be able to pay it back since you never adapt yourself to the world as it really is but demand that the whole world adapt and form itself according to your ideas." She wrote explaining that her hesitancy to quit Dresden was due to no lack of affection but, rather, to her health, which had suffered much from the recent excitement, and she no longer felt "like serving as a goodhearted bootblack." She would bring Natalie along to help in whatever home might be pieced together.[2] Her pen was brittle and bitter, but she acknowledged her love for him and the intention, once domestic affairs in Dresden were settled, again to link her destiny with his.

[2] Natalie, left behind in Paris in 1842, subsequently returned to Saxony, where she lived in Zwickau with Minna's sister Charlotte Tröger. The movements of Minna's unfortunate daughter remain something of a mystery. According to Glasenapp she formed part of the Wagner household in Riga. How did she get there, and then by what means did she make her way to Paris? During the Dresden years she again joined Minna for a time.

In the meantime Wagner had few unoccupied summer hours in Zurich. He produced a series of articles on art and society. Wigand of Leipzig was glad to pay well for them, considering the sensational title, *Art and Revolution,* and the author's notoriousness. Relaxing with Alexander Müller and his friends, in whose company both conversation and wine were unusually stimulating, he returned to the drunken boisterousness of an earlier period. It was time for Minna to claim her own as she had in Magdeburg some fourteen years before.

The day came for Peps to be shut in his dog crate and for Papo's stand to be dismantled and packed. Early in September, 1849, the curious family, set in motion by one hundred thaler remitted by Liszt, arrived at Rorschach. Later that month on a pleasant street, the Zeltweg, in Zurich's suburban Hottingen commune, a new Wagner household was established. It included the Breitkopf piano Minna had managed to salvage from their Dresden effects; the library, however, was retained by a creditor.[3]

To his sister Klara, Wagner wrote that without Minna he wouldn't care to live: "The knowledge of her necessity to me gives her great strength to endure all with me, notwithstanding her inner resentment." His love for her was, he declared, the bond still joining him to the world. Now his task was to fulfill what she expected of him.

The preposterous idea of converting his dramatic sketch, "Jesus of Nazareth," into a Parisian opera kept recurring. At Weimar Liszt had suppressed his reservations about the plan, but Princess Wittgenstein wisely showed open disapproval. Achilles, whose adventures had preoccupied Wagner during the Dresden revolt, seemed a more practical subject for the purpose, but by the end of 1849 he had decided upon the tale of Wieland the Smith.

He had no real faith in the French project and felt that his true catastrophe had not been the flight from Germany—which had, in fact, given him the sensation of being a bird aloft above the quagmire—but rather this venturing again into the international operatic market place, a decision he now considered to have been unfairly forced upon him to please Liszt and propitiate Minna during those anxious days at Weimar. He would play the game for a while, but he was inwardly determined not to follow a path divergent from his true artistic direction. A letter to Uhlig (August, 1849) implied that the method in the madness with which he had pursued the idea of a Parisian libretto based upon the life of Jesus was to so dismay Vaez that their partnership would be abandoned.

Already a shadowy vision of the *Ring* was hovering before his mind's eye. With the second act of *Lohengrin* he had opened a new phase in his creative life, and he knew there was no turning back. But he was resigned to go through the motions of working for Paris. He was financially de-

[3] See Chapter III, note 5, on page 58.

pendent upon Liszt and had held out a triumph at the Opéra as the bait with which to lure Minna across the Bodensee. Only the fine fee he had received for *Art and Revolution* reconciled her to watching him spend weeks at a new essay, *The Art-Work of the Future,* completed in November and dedicated to Feuerbach, whose philosophy and style had great influence on him at the time. Feuerbach was a hero to many revolutionists of the late eighteen-forties.

By the close of 1849 it was apparent that Liszt, with all his good will, did not command sufficient resources to support the Hottingen household. In Paris he was supporting his mother and three bastard children (at this early date Liszt's daughter Cosima and Richard, her future lover, were both receiving allowances from the same purse), and in Weimar he had to maintain a standard befitting his position and that of the Princess. She was threatened by the Czar with sequestration of her vast estates for refusing to return to Russia. Of course, in Germany she was poor only in contrast to what she had left behind. But her stingy streak invited Liszt to tease her with the nickname of "Harpagon."

In the belief that patrons might "spontaneously" contribute funds for his needs, Wagner appealed to Ferdinand Heine in Dresden to form a kind of relief committee. (That his own hand had stirred up these solicitations Wagner wished to keep secret, especially from Minna; he contemplated a "discreet circular.") For a while he had similarly fancied that a few members of Germany's princely houses might, for Liszt's sake, grant him an annuity. In these areas there was no immediate success. How black his reputation was at home he was only beginning fully to grasp. He was even accused of being the incendiary who had put the torch to Dresden's old opera house during the insurrection.[4]

By January, 1850, a sketch of "Wieland" was on paper, and Minna gave him no rest until he betook himself to Paris early in February to pursue the plan further with Belloni and Vaez. He was in a state of extreme nervous exhaustion.

In Paris a proposed performance of the *Tannhäuser* overture was postponed because of the tardy arrival of the orchestral parts, and his attendance at the forty-seventh representation of Meyerbeer's *Prophète* at the Opéra confirmed his sense of artistic isolation. He could not bear this second *Rienzi* and realized that such a "show" would be expected of him were he to gain the Opéra's stage. Perhaps on this evening the germs of *Jewry in Music* began to infect his system, although a draft of a letter of Minna's (May 8, 1850) in the Burrell Collection would indicate that such an essay had al-

[4] It is remotely possible that in his fury he had attempted to organize a group to burn down two royal residences. Flames always fascinated him.

ready been sketched in Dresden. Only in letters to Uhlig could he confide his true political-artistic plans.

To escape the merciless demands of the material world was his only dream. It was at this time, when he observed those he most loved unwittingly conspiring against his innermost convictions, that Jessie Taylor again entered his life.

Before recounting the tragicomedy that followed, it would be valuable to examine the text of Wagner's Paris libretto.

4

"Wieland the Smith" was the bizarre confection he ostensibly fashioned for Paris. This potpourri of Teutonic myth and Wagnerian symbol was, of course, completely alien to French taste, and he could never have seriously hoped for its acceptance. Obviously, the sketch was written to exhibit diligent activity on a "practical" opera project. But it also enabled him to outline an allegory of his personal dilemma and thus come to terms with himself. "Wieland" is one of Wagner's most frankly autobiographic libretti.

Once a maiden was wooed by a prince of the spirit world (*"der Fürst der Lichtalben"*), who approached her in swan form. They marry on condition that she never seek to learn his origin. Though she keeps her peace for three years, growing curiosity finally leads her to put the question. Thereupon the prince, who has returned to human guise, appears once again in plumage and, rising on great pinions, disappears into the clouds. The abandoned mother raises her three daughters. Their periodic tendency to sprout swans' wings somewhat alarms her, and she crops the feathers as they grow, putting them aside.

Irked by the arrogance of the Neiding tribe, who have been attempting to conquer her Norse homeland, she one day returns the feathers to her daughters, bidding them to become Valkyries and streak through the air to warn and inspire the threatened Norsemen. On such a journey her daughter Schwanhilde suffers a spear wound, falls into the sea, and is rescued by Wieland, the famous wonder-smith. She puts aside her wings to become his wife upon learning that his devotion is no less even after she removes from her finger a magic ring compelling love and victory.

Soon after, Princess Bathilde of the materialistic Neiding arrives with an army to subject to her family's autocratic sway Wieland's proud clan, which has always lived in an idyllic, protocommunistic state. By magic she enters the room of the sleeping Schwanhilde, whose wound is healing through the care of Wieland's brother, the surgeon Helferich,[5] and steals

---

[5] Wagner's son was to be named Siegfried Helferich.

the ring, coveted for so long. Wieland returns to find his home burned and, discovering no sign of Schwanhilde, sets out in pursuit of the raiders.

At the Neiding court he forgets the avenging of his wife as he falls under the spell of Bathilde, the ring's new mistress. Its magic makes him forge weapons for his enemies. In jealousy he slays a rival for Bathilde's affections. Attempting to shield the victim from the blow, she finds her finger grazed and the magic stone loosened from its setting. To punish his rashness, Wieland is maimed so that, though powerless to flee, he is yet able to forge. In his prison-smithy the crippled hero is at length visited by Bathilde, who entreats him to repair the ring upon whose power her family's victories now depend. Once she slips it from her finger, he remembers Schwanhilde. Weeping, he denounces Bathilde, who, moved by his wretchedness, for the first time understands the depths of human love and misery. She repents her wickedness and reveals that Schwanhilde has escaped the burning house.

Wieland then perceives a way to rise, even with crippled legs, above the world's treacheries, jealousies, and distress. From his stock of swords he fashions wings, fastening them with the magic gem. Schwanhilde's voice is heard echoing down the chimney shaft.

When the Neiding come to gloat over Wieland and to examine the products of his forge, he appears in his mighty wings and fans the flames. The smithy, catching fire, collapses, burying the Neiding horde. Swinging himself higher and higher, Wieland rises above the smoke to join the hovering Schwanhilde and fly with her into the distance.

The book combines motives known in *Feen, Lohengrin, Tristan,* the *Ring,* and *Parsifal.* A swan is artfully associated with the idea of the disappearing father of mysterious origin. Again a doubting wife and a forbidden inquiry cause a husband to desert. The Valkyries appear in their classical Norse form as Swan Maidens. Spear-wounded Schwanhilde recalls both the swan and Amfortas in *Parsifal.* That opera and *Tristan* are prefigured in the healing ritual, here, as in *Tristan,* of one who has drifted over waters. Parallels to the magic ring are obvious, and its ravager, Bathilde, combines characteristics of Alberich and Ortrud with Kundry's repentance. As in the later cycle the ring appears here in the double form first suggested in the essay *The Wibelungs;* though like the Nibelung treasure it is capable of inspiring the basest actions when misused, in essence the gold is noble. Wagner had pictured the ancient hoard becoming the Holy Grail. The finale of *Wieland* blends the ascension of Senta and Vanderdecken with the inevitable collapsing palace of Parisian grand opera. And echoes sound of *Feen's* Frau Dilnovaz with her severed finger and magic ring and the motive of maiming. The Neiding who destroy Wieland's home with fire are identified in Siegmund's narrative in the first act of *Valkyrie* as the tribe who burned the nest of his father, Wolfe.

Wagner's book has moments of great beauty. Wieland's dialogue with Schwanhilde, who flies above the house, certainly played a part in forming the Wood Bird scene in *Siegfried,* its text having thrilling, Eddic strength. The concept of Wieland as Wagner and of Schwanhilde as his muse is significant. At their first encounter she implores him to hide her wings, warning that one who has tasted of soaring can never tear this yearning out. Wagner's genius for the poignant suffuses that scene in which the lamed smith, longing to leave his impotent body, calls for wings with which to mount above his foes and cleave the clouds. The artist who in happier days had worked with joy in his heart for a free society, finding himself forced to smite out chains for his own body as well as arms and idle trappings for others, rebels and rises through his own genius in pursuit of the ideal. Ironically, Wagner's so-called "Paris libretto" was a declaration that he would never again seek terms with the commercial world of art.

5

A proposal had been advanced that set Wagner's hopes soaring. Uhlig's and old Ferdinand Heine's solicitations had at last reached willing ears. Frau Julie Ritter of Dresden planned to join forces with a certain Laussot family of Bordeaux to provide Wagner an annual allowance of three thousand francs. He was touched to receive this news at the end of 1849. It confirmed his belief: "With women's hearts it has always gone well with my art."

Jessie Laussot was the former Jessie Taylor, a shy English girl who had lived with Frau Julie in Dresden. She had sent Karl Ritter to beg Wagner's autograph on her *Tannhäuser* score soon after the work's première. Wagner hardly knew her, although she had called upon him in Dresden in 1848. The paths of master and admirer, now turned benefactress, evidently crossed again in Paris. He had Kietz do his portrait and dispatched it to her home in Bordeaux, where she lived with her wine-merchant husband, Eugène, and her wealthy Scottish mother, Ann Taylor. Wagner was duly invited to visit their home and set forth in March of 1850. Early that month he had written Jessie from Paris of his decision never to deal with the Opéra. The Ritter-Laussot pension had given Wieland wings. Minna was informed of his trip, and both he and Jessie wrote to her to lessen this good bourgeoise's sense of guilt about accepting charity.

The plan permitting Wagner to create "in complete accord with the inspiration of his soul" was one of Jessie's few satisfactions from her mother's fortune. The young woman's position was not enviable. An extraordinary business and personal relationship bound Ann and her handsome young son-in-law. She had not only bought him out of impending bankruptcy but had enjoyed his amorous attentions before passing her daughter on to him as a kind of bill of exchange. Into this tense *ménage à trois* Wagner entered. He read Jessie his "Wieland," and she saw herself as the swan-appareled maiden leading his genius. But he had renounced the wonder-smith along with the Opéra, and his mind, filled with Siegfried, was already apprehending the outlines of the entire *Ring*. He found himself playing the embryonic first act of *Valkyrie* much as he had performed *"Hochzeit"* for the Pachtas many years before. One day he was to impersonate the Volsung with greater assurance in Otto Wesendonk's parlor, but at this Bordeaux dress rehearsal the scenario was surprisingly complete. Storm-driven Siegmund had stumbled into the hut where Hunding "made love to a wife who without her consent had been delivered to him by villains." Spring forced open the doors; Richard and Jessie fell into one another's arms, and the first-act curtain was at hand. They would not flee into the woods, but determined to escape together to the Grecian isles of *Ardinghello* and to the Orient. The feverish state of Wagner's mind is shown by his imagining that Hunding and his clan would forward an allowance to the absconding couple.

Jessie was the first of four married women Wagner desired during the incubation and creation of the *Ring*. The betrayal of Hunding by the Volsung twins and of Gunther by Siegfried was mirrored in the wooing of Jessie Laussot, Mathilde Wesendonk, Blandine Ollivier, and her sister Cosima von Bülow.

"Hochzeit" and *Dutchman* prefigured the idea of foreordained lovers forced by a Feuerbachian *Notwendigkeit* and *Bedürfnis* (urgency and necessity) to cheat a husband or fiancé whose claims were worldly rather than ideal and thus invalid to Wagner. *Tristan* raised this motive to its most palatable level. Composed during an intermission during the labors on the *Ring,* it continued the turn the theme had taken with "Siegfried's Death," in which the beguiled spouse was also the hero's intimate. Wagner lived on amicable terms with Laussot, counted Otto Wesendonk among his most generous patrons, asked all manner of favors from Ollivier, and was father and friend to Bülow. How often during the personal intrigues that paralleled his operas must Wagner have longed for those drinks of oblivion with which the valiants of legend and saga had been generously provided. Not only were the husbands caught in his affairs, but also that tragic figure he would most gladly have forgotten—Minna. Life had betrayed him; heroes were supposed to be free. She haunted his thoughts throughout the Laussot episode. Quitting Bordeaux, he returned to Paris early in April to think matters through and await Jessie's arrival.

From Montmorency, a town about ten miles from Paris, he wrote Minna in the middle of the month to announce that they had become strangers and lacked a faith in common. "You cling to the peacefulness and permanence of existing conditions—I must break them to satisfy my inner being. . . . You cling to people, I to causes; you to certain human beings, I to humanity. . . . I can thrive only in the company of kindred souls. . . . For the sake of the love which still remains between us I say, *Let us remain separated!* . . . Don't inquire about me! But I shall always do everything to find out whether you are well." He proposed to share his now largely figmental allowance with her and claimed he was departing for he knew not where. That he would have a charming twenty-two-year-old traveling companion he did not confide to his old "Mienel." From the fact that Ann was the widow of a jurist he soon concocted the fiction of "a new protector," an eminent English lawyer who had stepped forward to place funds at his disposal. He reproached his wife for being incapable of "unquestioning love"; Lohengrin was awaiting the swan boat that would tug him away.

Minna was thunderstruck. There had been occasional quarrels, but nothing to justify this dramatic farewell, though she realized that perhaps she had been driving him too hard to leave pamphleteering and get on with work for Paris. Recently a new point of contention had arisen. She was horrified by his mounting intolerance, which was fast approaching the maniacal. On May 8 she wrote, "As for your spiritual development, I was happy in the knowledge that you were close to me while you created *all* the *beautiful* things. . . . You always made me so happy, sang and played almost every new scene for me. But since *two years* ago, when you wanted to read me that essay in which you *slander* whole *races* which have been fundamentally helpful to you, I could not force myself to listen; and ever since that time you have borne a grudge against me and punished me so severely for it that you never again let me hear anything from your works." Like Nietzsche and Ludwig of Bavaria after her, she found his anti-Semitism abhorrent.

She divined the cause of his latest crisis and hurried from Zurich to Paris. Alarmed by news of her presence, he forced Kietz to deceive her by assurances that the errant husband had already left town, the ruse giving him time to escape to Villeneuve on Lake Geneva, there to seek word from Julie Ritter, now the confidante of the new lovers. Her son Karl joined him. An agitated letter from Jessie suddenly revealed that all had been discovered. Foolishly she had confided her purpose to Ann, who naturally revealed it to Eugène. He threatened to shoot Wagner on sight. Hunding was calling together clan and hounds.

Wagner immediately wrote Eugène to point out the immorality of restraining an unhappy wife and to announce that eagerness to settle matters would compel him to set out for Bordeaux without awaiting endorsement of his passport by the French Embassy. Laussot passed this last information on to the police, and he and Ann dragged Jessie off to the country. They saw that she received no messages from Wagner. In fact, she was unaware of his second visit to Bordeaux, where he had been greeted by the authorities with a strong recommendation that he take his invalid papers and leave as soon as he had rested. Jessie, with every right to consider herself abandoned by her lover, promised to reconsider her course. Ann had at first encouraged the affair to afford Jessie some consolation, but the separation of her "children" had not figured in Mother's plans.

Dejectedly, Wagner turned back to Switzerland and Karl. Frau Ritter, arriving with her daughter Emilie to celebrate Wagner's thirty-seventh birthday, was determined to continue whatever her means permitted toward his support. After a week of diverting excursions with him in the superb Rhone landscape, the ladies returned to Saxony, leaving Wagner and Karl to seek solace together on an Alpine vacation.

A final, bitter word from Jessie delivered through Karl restored Wagner's senses. Wieland would never rise on his wings,[6] but Siegfried would swing "Nothung," the sword of necessity. The weapon's change of name from the "anointed" ("Balmung") in "Siegfried's Death" to the "needed" ("Nothung") in the later *Ring* was not without significance. During the coming months Wagner would dare face a return to his cosmic scenario of 1848 for a complete Nibelung drama. But to accomplish what was stirring within he needed the tranquillity of a home; for this, reconciliation with Minna was an immediate requisite.

He had been deeply upset by the wounds dealt his wife. Her abortive trip to Paris to reclaim him was as pathetic as his letters of explanation, which, though sophistical, cannot be read without emotion. From Karl he learned that she had taken a house on the Lake of Zurich and was awaiting his return. Certainly she remembered how generously he had received her in Riga after the Dietrich episode. And in a strange way they still loved one another.

She had set up modest quarters on the second floor of a house (christened "Villa Rienzi") in the Enge district. Here early in July, 1850, Wagner took up the threads of his domestic life. Papo, calling, "Richard," would flutter into the study where the composer worked under Peps's watchful eye. Minna and Natalie bickered as ever, the latter unaware, of course, that the too-authoritative "elder sister" had every right to a maternal manner. Minna never referred to the immediate past, and, in general, life was peaceful. Yet Wagner's greatest joy made him despondent. *Lohengrin* was to be given, and he could not hear it.

---

[6] Wagner, in the autumn of 1850, sent his draft of "Wieland" to Princess Wittgenstein in hopes that Liszt might set it. When he declined, Wagner wished him to offer it in turn to Berlioz!

On April 21, 1850, at the height of the Laussot affair, he had written Liszt entreating him to get *Lohengrin* produced. Despite reservations in respect to the work's effectiveness as a stage piece, Liszt dramatically scheduled the première on Goethe's birthday as part of Weimar's Herder festival in August. Wagner instructed him to give *Lohengrin* uncut except for the omission of fifty-six bars originally forming a concluding exposition to the knight's narrative, describing how Elsa's brother, in swan form, swam to Monsalvat for aid. (Even so, the section appears to have been sung at the première.)

To indicate his concept of the décor he sent sketches—perspective presented Ludwig Geyer's son with insuperable difficulties!—and requested that Liszt cajole the Grand Duchess into issuing him a safe conduct to her capital. He even pondered the possibility of arriving incognito. Neither plan was feasible, and during the summer his thoughts frequently wandered to Weimar and the score he longed to hear. Its first performance on August 28 before an international audience established him as the most significant German operatic composer of the day.

6

Wagner was determined never again to be placed in the dilemma presented by the Parisian opera scheme, that of seeking a popular success of a kind that awakened his inmost artistic aversion. "I must come myself, and those who are interested in my artistic being must come with me, to a clear understanding; else we shall forever grope about in hateful twilight. . . ." He would make his position clear in a series of articles. "It is most essential that I should accomplish this work and send it into the world before going on with my immediate artistic productions."

The Swiss essays were to be the dubious monuments of his first years in exile. "The real art-work cannot be created now but only prepared for, yes, by revolutionary means, by destroying and beating down all that deserves to be destroyed and beaten down." And Wagner in his prose did undertake a mighty work of destruction whose cadaverous shadow fatally fell upon the present century.

His critical prose actually started in 1834 with the two essays on German opera and continued with the "Bellini" of three years later, a brief notice intended as an *avant-courrier* of *Norma,* his Riga benefit. However, these writings, with their *Liebesverbot* mood of antagonism to German music, remain alien to the fundamental content of a critical system remarkably of a piece from the time of an aspiring young composer's first Parisian stay to the very last day of a wearied master's life in Venice. The prose works include the series of journalistic articles and reviews begun in France and also the ambitious speculative and polemic treatises anticipated by *The Wibelungs* but really embarked upon in Switzerland.

The heart of Wagnerian thought is revealed in four tracts written soon after his flight from Germany: *Art and Revolution* (1849), *The Art-Work of the Future* (1849), *Jewry in Music* (1850),[7] and *Opera and Drama* (1851). They set forth in Wagner's tortuous style a complicated, historically inaccurate, and speciously reasoned dialectic of dramatic and musical art.

The first discussed the Athenian drama, which had brought together the arts of poetry, music, drama, dance, and design in a profound civic and religious expression; only revolution, claimed Wagner, could free Germans from a materialism hindering the emergence of such a great communal utterance in their midst. The Greek art-work could not be reborn, but its spirit could be born anew. The role of the chorus in *Lohengrin,* that of a unit commenting recurringly upon the action, had been a result of this long-held enthusiasm for ancient drama.

The second essay described Wagner's amorphous conceptions both of the Folk (the epitome of all who feel a *gemeinschaftliche Noth,* i.e., a common and collective want) and of the nature of the Greek dramatic synthesis, after whose decline and disintegration, he asserted, the individual arts went their egoistic, separate ways; having in his time reached the limits of these divided routes, they longed to reunite, languishing for absorption, dissolution, and redemption in the universal art-work, whose true creators, the Folk, he apostrophized, comparing it to Wieland of the saga: "Weld thy wings and soar on high."

The notorious *Jewry in Music* arraigned the Jew as a materialist, hindering the pure instincts of the German Folk from realizing the art-work of the future through some Teutonic Aeschylus. The Jew, Wagner reasoned, must, therefore, be eliminated from German life.[8]

The final link in this speculative tetralogy surveyed operatic and dramatic history with a sweep uninhibited by the hesitations that specialized knowledge might inject, and then proceeded to describe the philosophy and technique of his coming composite art-work, with its close relationship between word and music and its expanded orchestral eloquence that would utter the unspeakable.

Opera and Drama postulated a compound formed of verse and its parallel

[7] *Jewry in Music* was launched by Wagner under the extraordinary pseudonym of "K. Freigedank" (Free Thought); its style was immediately recognized, and Wagner admitted authorship. He always preferred to attack from ambush.

[8] Perhaps the ultimate evaluation of his prose works was given by Wagner himself, who in his humble and repentant petition (1856) to Friedrich's successor, King Johann of Saxony, described these literary exercises as a method of voiding the poison in his system.

vocal melody. The verse, the poet's part, presenting the conceptual elements, would beget the musician's vocal line; the latter was to interpret the text emotionally through artfully calculated juxtapositions of rhythm, accent, pitch, and key relationships. A resulting congruity of verse and musical phrase was to be further confirmed both by an orchestra providing harmonic modulations and instrumental color appropriate to the stage situation and by dramatically compatible contributions on the part of singing actors. The orchestra with its many tongues would take over the traditional operatic tasks of the chorus. Throughout its length, the art-work was to be unified by a system of motifs, reiterating and stressing the conditioning forces of the drama. Toward this end certain musical phrases were to be abstracted from their positions under their correlative verses and repeated by voice or orchestra in later dramatic situations whenever ideas associated with the original words had particular pertinence. (And, as well as recalling the emotional content of past thoughts, the motif could awaken foreboding.) Accordingly, through a subtle integration of word and tone, the conceptual was to be conveyed in terms of the musical. As will be seen, Wagner's actual use of the device departed greatly from his theoretical program.

In *The Art-Work of the Future,* he had claimed the new all-embracing dramatic form as an extension of Beethoven's Ninth Symphony, imagining the Wagnerian synthesis anticipated in that finale in which a symphonic web discoursed on sung poetry. *Opera and Drama* espoused the myth as the worthiest subject for such discourse. Only what came from the Folk was proper matter for the poet, and through him the unconscious genius of a people might rise to consciousness. Wagner intended to impart such artistic awareness to the Germans through *The Nibelung's Ring,* a work meant to satisfy tribal emotions rather than the "disturbing" demands of the intellect.

There was dignified literary precedent for his theory of the myth. Recommending that the spirit of the Greek tradition be used by new creative hands and that German poetry, like the ancient, derive its vitality from myth, Herder himself had held up the Edda as the source of a mythology suited to the Germans.

But the day of myth was done. What Wagner provided, mainly through the magic of his music, was the illusion of myth—the myth as symbol—as he bent the ancient heroic tales to embrace an alien content.

Opera and Drama discussed the poetic language of Wagner's new national drama, the old alliterative verse called *Stabreim.* Banished was the elegant diction of *Lohengrin,* terminal rhyme, and all formal metrical patterns. In pithy accented first syllables and explosive consonants Wagner saw a return to language's simplest roots. Certainly the condensed manner in which he used *Stabreim*—at times only too faithful to his theory of being more sensory than sensible—gave him a compensatory opportunity for musical expansiveness.

7

Karl Ritter's arrival at Villa Rienzi in July provided the household with some distraction. Clearly, the lad's whims, moods, and impractical ambitions were generously tolerated only because, along with Liszt, the Ritters contributed Wagner's main subsidy. Nonetheless, the composer took pleasure in Karl's often charming company, especially during these early days on the lake when he was a worshipful disciple. Goethe's Faust had had his Wagner, and Richard Wagner, as in the case of Kietz, also found need for a somewhat ludicrous famulus. For a while Karl did nicely in a part in which Wagner later mistakenly attempted to cast Cornelius and Nietzsche.

Schumann, Karl's theory teacher, had commended his musical capacity and sure ear. But a premature talent had become arrested, and, vainly seeking to force his languishing endowment, he had come to Wagner for help. His uncertainties, however, were not restricted to musical problems; his homosexuality is more than hinted at in *Mein Leben*. Perhaps Frau Julie Ritter felt that in Wagner he would find a father. It is ironic that Wagner himself called her "Mother" in turn. As matters ended, Karl had to fight to free himself not only from the hold of a magnetizing mother but also from the galvanic attraction of Wagner's personality.

Because of Karl, Wagner unintentionally found himself back in the opera house. Oddly enough, no test of the boy's practical musical abilities had been made before Wagner's recommendation brought him an appointment as conductor at the Zurich theater. The management, wisely cautious in view of his youth and inexperience, made Wagner guarantee his own appearance in the pit should his protégé encounter difficulties. After hearing Karl play the opening work, *Freischütz,* at the piano and observing his meaningless gestures on the podium, Wagner realized that his own Zurich début was at hand. It had never been his intention to appear at an institution whose resources and importance he felt to be beneath his dignity. The removal of young Ritter from the conductor's desk was not easily accomplished. But with delight Zurich finally heard under Wagner performances such as it had never before experienced.

Hans von Bülow arrived in October, having defied a parental wish that he avoid Wagner's company and devote himself to law and diplomacy. Roused by a letter from Wagner—surreptitiously delivered by Karl—urging him to become an artist, he had fled his father's home and made his way to Villa Rienzi. Wagner set the untried conductor to work at the theater. He displayed such remarkable skill that Wagner's mind was set at ease concerning the rest of the season. He did conduct again out of a sense of responsibility toward the management and so that his two pupils might benefit from his example. But friction between Hans and the prima donna—it is fortunate that he had quit diplomacy—ended the unusual arrangement in December, and the boys, who had set up housekeeping together, went off to gain more experience with the wretched company at St. Gall. Here Karl suffered another contretemps while conducting a Gluck overture, but Hans matured to such a point that at Easter, 1851, he set out to study with Liszt at Weimar, bearing the blessing of Wagner and also of Frau von Bülow, who wished her son far from the man she considered his depraver.

8

Uhlig had added to his heavy duties with the Dresden orchestra those of being the exile's amanuensis in Germany. Occupied with Wagner's printing and music-copying errands, he also arranged *Lohengrin* for piano, prepared its full score for a coming Breitkopf and Härtel edition, and with the composer's long-distance instructions revised and forwarded scores of *Dutchman* and *Tannhäuser* to theaters showing a growing interest in these works. Moreover, Uhlig, like Bülow and Liszt, wrote magazine articles to advance the cause of Wagner, to whose already notorious political reputation the appearance of *Jewry in Music* had given the extra fascination of infamy.

Liszt proposed that "Siegfried's Death" be completed for a Weimar première. But reports indicated to Wagner that because of its limited resources the Grand Ducal company had only hinted at the substance of *Lohengrin*. He wished to send his Siegfried into the world in better fashion.

During the winter of 1850–51 he realized that the time had come to develop into theatrical and poetic form his scenario of 1848, "The Nibelungen Myth as Scheme for a Drama." There he had outlined the myth's gigantic sequences. "Siegfried's Death" had been an attempt to represent its crowning catastrophe; the vast train of events which led to this crisis and which alone gave the protagonists their immensity were there set forth in rather perplexing narrative. That the first sketch of "Siegfried's Death" demanded too much foreknowledge on the part of the public had been indicated to him in Dresden by Eduard Devrient, and his observation had led Wagner to write the expository, albeit laconic, prologue to the drama.

Now in Zurich he acknowledged that Devrient's criticism had to be even more vigorously examined. (The weight of the latter's influence as man and artist upon Wagner is hardly indicated in *Mein Leben*.) The poem of "Young Siegfried" was written in June of 1851, and for a while Wagner intended substituting this lighter work at Weimar for "Siegfried's Death," the tragedy it was intended to introduce and elucidate. Prompted by a simple statement of Brynhild in the *Volsunga Saga,* he had associated young Siegfried with the boy of the old German story who was too stupid to learn fear, a motive which had interested him since Dresden days but which he was never able felicitously to incorporate into the Volsung myth. "Siegfried's Death" had been written for the revolutionary public of the future but did not go beyond the resources of the grand opera stage as it existed. However, as his Nibelung plan expanded, he saw himself actually withdrawing from the theater of his day. Reveling in the wealth of situations his imagination was sweepingly bringing together, he further recognized that in tiny Weimar a production of either "Siegfried" would be absurd. He was resolved never again to endure the martyrdom of things done by halves.

During July and August of 1851 Uhlig visited Wagner, and they set out on a vigorous walking tour of the Tell country. Karl Ritter, terrified by heights, had dropped out of an earlier expedition and declined to join them again. But Wagner, the old acrobat of Eisleben, was invigorated by the danger, and Uhlig pushed his consumptive body to follow the vertiginous paths. Within a year and a half the handsome musician, so like one of Schiller's young men, would be dead.[9]

Spurred on by Uhlig, who was desperately seeking means of repairing his wasting frame, Wagner, too, became a fanatic about water cures and spent over two months in the autumn of 1851 at a hydropathic establishment at Albisbrunn, where he brooded over his expanding concept of the Nibelung theme. (The landscapes of the *Ring* owe much to the lofty Alpine surroundings in which a good deal of it was first visualized.) Suffering from constipation and shingles, he persuaded himself of the brutal regimen's efficacy. The fervor of a convert and a nature that would tolerate no contravention made him insist that his friends, too, seek salvation through water. Karl kept him company during the ordeal.

Soon after Uhlig's return to Dresden (August 10) Wagner had completed an autobiographical essay, *A Communication to My Friends,* which he described as a decisive work. Even before its publication Uhlig knew of the prodigious plan ultimately revealed to the public in those closing sentences rushed to the printer late in 1851. In October and November Wag-

[9] He may well have been an illegitimate child of King Friedrich of Saxony, whom he closely resembled.

ner had written his friend from Albisbrunn to announce his vision of the giant mythical argument in terms of three dramas and a prologue. He missed Dresden's royal library and pleaded with Uhlig to smuggle him its copy of the *Volsunga Saga*.

If the betterment of his health was illusory, he did return to Zurich at the end of November in improved financial condition. The Ritters, further enriched by a new inheritance, had settled an augmented allowance upon him equal to approximately half his former Dresden salary. Scores for him and silver for Minna rained down upon their little household.

In Albisbrunn he had taken advantage of this development to return the honorarium accepted in advance from Weimar for the composition of a new opera and to write frankly to Liszt of his skepticism concerning the little town's ability to produce any of the projected Nibelung dramas, the grand plans for which he eloquently unfolded. Liszt, for his part, must have felt delivered from what he knew to be an impossible situation. His request to Berlioz in July, 1851, that he revise *Cellini* for a Weimar production had irritated Wagner, who saw his patron unwilling to devote his energies exclusively to Germanic and Wagnerian purposes.

Liszt really had little enthusiasm for Wagnerian aesthetic philosophy, his admiration being confined to Wagner's music. The creed of redemption through the German opera house was irreconcilable with Liszt's growing belief that the stage restricted rather than incited the imagination and also with his international background and interests.

Early in 1852 Wagner wrote to him, "Nothing that lies within the possibilities of representation on the stage should be only thought or indicated, but everything should be actually shown." [10] In contrast, Liszt was attempting in his symphonic poems to join poetry and music in an alliance he held to be more spiritual and intimate than that possible in the opera. The goals and personalities of the composers were worlds apart. An association endured between the aristocratic, generous Liszt and the raucous, self-seeking Wagner solely through the former's appreciation of an overwhelming musical talent and the exercise of a diplomacy for which he was famous.

Prose sketches for the prelude (originally called "The Rape of the Rhinegold") and first Nibelung drama occupied Wagner through the spring of 1852, the wealth of his material growing almost to excess. By the end of May Liszt learned from him that the tetralogy was completely designed. At a pension on the Zürichberg, where he and Minna were vacationing, the

---

[10] During the era of Wieland Wagner, the productions at Bayreuth largely denied his grandfather's aesthetic and, ironically, on occasion attempted to convert his operas into staged oratorios in the manner of Liszt's *Legend of St. Elizabeth*.

poem of *Valkyrie* was brought into existence during June and July, that of the prelude being completed early in November. After a summer journey to the Ticino and Piedmont at Liszt's expense, the titles had been proclaimed to Uhlig: *The Nibelung's Ring,* a stage-festival play to be performed in an introductory evening and three successive days—*The Rhinegold, The Valkyrie,* "The Young Siegfried," and "Siegfried's Death." By the end of 1852 Wagner had reworked the poems of the last two dramas to make them accord with the expanded concept of the *Ring,* revision and adjustment of their detail, however, being hastily and carelessly accomplished. In "Young Siegfried" some narration was jettisoned because it appeared as action in the newly written preceding dramas. Only three scenes in "Siegfried's Death" were created afresh: the colloquy of the Norns, Brynhild's dialogue with her eight sister Valkyries (they were reduced to only Waltraute), and the finale. On the whole, both Siegfried dramas, quickly retouched and edited by excisions and additions, were made to do. Wagner was caught in a dilemma. Writing antecedent plays intended, in part, to explain those that followed, he at the same time felt constrained to retain tracts of repetitive narrative in each of the works in order to permit them quasi-independent lives on the stage. From this difficulty were born the celebrated *longueurs* of the *Ring.* But even before completing the enormous literary work, Wagner declared it "the greatest poem ever written."

In September, 1850, he had whimsically pictured to both Uhlig and Ernst Kietz a plan for producing "Siegfried's Death" in a temporary theater of planks to be erected in the fields near Zurich; after three performances the building was to be demolished and the score burned. A little over a year later he had foreseen an immense Nibelung cycle played during a series of four days in a Wagnerian festival theater raised on the banks of the Rhine.

The *Communication* had ended as an appeal for help in bringing the new project to reality. But, as the passing months made his pardon by the Saxon king appear increasingly unlikely, he at times let himself be beguiled into believing that his *Ring* festival might yet take place in Switzerland. An article, "A Theater in Zurich" of April, 1851, had touched upon a reform of this modest institution which he dreamed might one day contribute toward his goal. But sober reflection would force him to concede that the resources of a town of little over thirty thousand citizens were insufficient. The one hundred thousand francs he blithely announced as necessary for the construction of a temporary theater for his *Bühnenfestspiel* must have thoroughly alarmed the good burghers, the very arrogance of the demand, however, revealing the extraordinary celebrity he enjoyed.

9

In Switzerland Wagner found himself a revered *"Meister."* His reputation grew through his own polemic writings and the efforts of a newborn Wagnerian guard, which filled publications with articles on him, thus spreading his name across Europe. In Paris Gérard de Nerval, who had attended the *Lohengrin* première, took up the cause in the *feuilleton* of the *Presse,* hailing the composer as "an original and bold talent . . . which has as yet uttered only its first words."

Occasionally Wagner was prevailed upon to conduct Zurich's modest symphonic society. These highly anticipated appearances, at which he specialized in Beethoven, were climaxed by a Wagner festival coinciding with his fortieth birthday. Musicians traveled from Germany to contribute their services. On hearing his *Lohengrin* prelude for the first time, he had to make an effort not to break down. Pelted with flowers, he modestly declined the laurel crown.

Liszt's Weimar productions of *Tannhäuser, Lohengrin,* and then *Dutchman* (February, 1853) had demonstrated that Wagner's operas, though difficult, were nonetheless practicable on modest stages. Despite official antagonism toward his personality and politics, German theaters were acquiring his scores, that of *Tannhäuser* being the most popular. Even tiny Zurich forced him to consent to productions of *Dutchman* (1852) [11] and *Tannhäuser* (1855), his guidance enabling these performances to transcend severe physical limitations.

Yet, despite this waxing fame he had to admit that because of his enforced absence from Germany the representations of his works multiplying over the land were certainly travesties of his intentions. Nonetheless, he did not wish to discourage new Wagnerian productions, for their fees made a comfortable addition to his income from the Ritters. More to salve his conscience than to solve the artistic dilemma, he wrote a pamphlet, *On Performing Tannhäuser,* in August, 1852, and at the end of the year another on the mounting of *Dutchman.* These were dispatched to the theaters concerned. Their interest in the poet-composer's recommendations may be epitomized by his discovery years later that six copies of the *Tannhäuser* brochure, once hopefully forwarded to the Munich Opera, had remained pristinely uncut. [12]

---

[11] His new treatment of the overture's coda also served the opera's final moments, for which the Zurich theater's program indicated a complete change of scene: "Final transformation—Apotheosis."
[12] Here and there men like Schindelmeisser read and were influenced by Wagner's suggestions.

In the fall of 1852, during the creation of the *Rhinegold* poem, Belloni, Liszt's secretary, sought him out to discuss a possible French première of *Tannhäuser*. A campaign against Wagner had been under way in the Paris press for several months. The result, ironically, was an appetite on the part of many Parisians to hear his works. Delighted, he wrote brother Albert's daughter Franziska that he had "suddenly become famous in Paris, or at least very interesting." Belloni believed Meyerbeer to have been behind the contemptuous comments of the critic Fétis in a pamphlet serialized in the *Gazette musicale* during the summer. It accused Wagner of creating by system rather than inspiration. But Meyerbeer would have had to possess the Tarnhelm to accomplish all the mischief credited him by the old Wagnerites.

That same autumn Prince Wilhelm of Prussia and his consort, Augusta,[18] had attended a *Lohengrin* performance given in their honor at Weimar. The Prince expressed hopes for a Wagnerian success in Berlin, Meyerbeer's second stronghold, where the theater was coquetting with *Tannhäuser*. In 1851 Botho von Hülsen had followed Küstner as Berlin's opera director. As one of the Prussian officers sent in 1849 to suppress the Dresden revolt, he at first found repugnant any direct relations with a man he considered an escaped criminal. Wagner's brother Albert, who was with Johanna in Berlin (she was the city's reigning diva), was called upon to act as intermediary.

The plan came to nothing because of Wagner's insistence that Liszt, as his plenipotentiary, supervise the production, a demand probably intended, in part, as an insult to Dorn, now a Berlin *Kapellmeister* and Nicolai's successor. Certainly Wagner was unconcerned about who oversaw the work when it was mounted in other cities, putting to rest his oft-justified fears by the optimistic dispatching of his pamphlets.[14]

10

The Zurich friends were staunch and dedicated. In the fall of 1851 Wagner had quit his remote retreat on the lake and moved back to the

[18] As Wilhelm I, Kaiser of the new Reich, he was to attend the initial Bayreuth festival; Augusta was the daughter of Maria Pavlovna of Weimar.

[14] Liszt did remind him that Berlin was a decisive field to conquer and that it was important for his operas to be well produced there. Yet obviously the Prussian capital would eclipse the standard of small towns where *Tannhäuser,* with its creator's blessing, was already in the repertory. Wagner admitted that his instructional brochures were but advance protests against poor performances. In 1857 he did not scruple to throw *Tannhäuser* to a Viennese variety theater.

Zeltweg in the Hottingen quarter. As always, his house was a meeting place. Conversations with Jakob Sulzer, a cantonal secretary, gave him much pleasure, their friendship surviving both the young man's frank objections to his habit of speaking authoritatively on matters about which he knew nothing and his unremitting demands upon Sulzer's modest fortune. (There was perhaps a method in Wagner's unusual forbearance.) A Hegelian, Sulzer turned him toward philosophic speculation, a discipline into which Lehrs had attempted to initiate him during the early Paris days; Wilhelm Baumgartner, a local piano teacher, had rekindled his interest in Feuerbach; and acquaintances also included Professor Ettmüller, an authority on the Germanic sagas, who had a hand in shaping some of the details of the *Ring,* and, a little later, Vischer, the renowned Tübingen aesthetician, whose article of 1844, *Suggestion for an Opera,* had already played its role in drawing Wagner toward the Nibelung subject. Vischer had gone so far as to concoct the scenario for a Nibelung libretto in cyclic form.

The most famous, and to the spies of the German police the most notorious, of his new friends was the urbane Georg Herwegh, the exiled Swabian poet of the revolution, who familiarized Wagner with the works of Byron, Shelley, and the Persian Hafiz. Not far from Zurich was Mariafeld, the comfortable estate of Herwegh's friends Eliza and François Wille, the latter an old school chum of Bismarck's. At Mariafeld, which Wagner delighted in frequenting, Herwegh introduced him to Schopenhauer's works, and here, to the Willes and their circle, Wagner first read aloud the poem of the *Ring* (December, 1852).

Thus the main interests of his companions in Switzerland were philosophic, political, and literary. He had a growing sense of isolation from German music; an inner despair over exclusion from his homeland was heightened by the realization that, until the ban was lifted, he could not hear a full performance of *Lohengrin.* Moreover, instead of softening its attitude, the Saxon police had, in the spring of 1853, reissued the warrant for his arrest should he dare touch upon German soil. Faithful Uhlig, whose visit and letters had kept him in touch with German operatic life, had died during the first week of 1853. In February Wagner wrote to Liszt, "I stand in a desert and feed on my own vitals; I *must* perish"; and later, in March, "My whole intercourse with the world is entirely through paper."

It was with an almost hysterical enthusiasm that he looked forward during July of the same year to a week's visit from Liszt, who found him like Vesuvius in eruption, falling on his friend's neck twenty times a day, rolling on the ground, fondling Peps and whispering nonsense into his ears, and cursing the Jews, a Wagnerian noun Liszt discovered to be of most elastic meaning. As Wagner developed at length that favorite theme of his sufferings, Liszt could not avoid observing the fairly luxurious disposition of his home (in April he had moved into more spacious quarters in a neighboring building), its silver, crystal, velvets, sumptuous red hangings, and especially the splendid wine cellar. At the piano Liszt played some of his symphonic poems, an event of great importance in the coming expansion of Wagner's harmonic style.

After Liszt's departure Wagner fell into a state of deep depression. There was reason enough for his melancholy. At times he must have doubted whether he would ever compose again.

II

Since the *Lohengrin* prelude of August, 1847,[15] Wagner had written no music of importance. During the summer of 1850, immediately after the collapse of the Laussot affair, he attempted to sketch a setting of "Siegfried's Death" but lasted only through the Norns scene and a bit beyond, breaking off when not far into the lofty Eddic colloquy of Siegfried and Brynhild on the mountain. Inspiration failed. Perhaps, as in the case of *"Hochzeit"* long before, he stopped upon finding his musical language and technique as yet deficient in the means to set forth the sounds heard in his inner ear. Certainly it is difficult to call to mind another major composer who suffered so long a musical drought.

No doubt *Ring* motifs were shaping themselves in his imagination. Fafner's theme and Siegfried's horn call seem to have come to him quite early. In the musical fragment of "Siegfried's Death" there occurs a descending phrase foreshadowing the treaty motif, and the Norns sing a tune clearly recognizable—pallid though it is—as the embryo of the Valkyrie ride. The music of one set of Erda's daughters was shifted to the other within the year, for there exists a version of the ride dated July, 1851. But a change of this kind was the exception. Not only the musical outlines, but details, too, were at times strikingly clear to Wagner at the moment he devised his dramatic situations and words. On stylistic grounds, Edward Downes has astutely suggested that the opening of the Gibichung hall scene in *The Twilight of the Gods* may preserve an original musical conception dating from the period, that of *Lohengrin,* when the text came into being. (On the other hand, the musical fragment of "Siegfried's Death" reveals a vocal line that attempts to escape the rhythmic monotony of the *Lohengrin* style.) Even before commencing the actual composition of *Rhinegold,* Wagner had played some of its motifs to Liszt, and the

[15] Work on the manuscript of the *Lohengrin* full score occupied him until April, 1848.

opening phrase of Siegmund's *"Winterstürme"* cavatina was written down spontaneously when the Austrian poet Hermann Rollett, expressing enthusiasm for the just-completed lines, asked Wagner how he intended to set them.

But such work was fragmentary; impotent to gather his full musical resources, he found reasons to justify postponement, a state of affairs disquieting to friends who nervously observed the new hero of modern music powerless to compose. Liszt's letters urged him to set aside secondary matters and to take composition of the Nibelung operas seriously in hand. But to the Wagner of the early eighteen-fifties an immediate choice of activities limited itself to the question, was it to be "a poem, a book, or an essay"? Music was only mentioned in terms of the future. He maintained that his "deadly enemy" was winter, when he could hardly be expected to compose. And during the more clement months he sought relief from gastric and nervous troubles in travel and water cures. Significantly, his health returned as soon as he was able to put *Rhinegold* on paper. But this was to be in the fall of 1853. For six musically fallow years he endured a despair that a proud arrogance could not always hide. At times his letters to Liszt were dithyrambs of distress.

He was awaiting inspiration. It came in Italy. Following Liszt's departure from Zurich in July, 1853, a midsummer trip in the company of Herwegh brought him to the Upper Engadine. After vainly seeking to strengthen his nerves with St. Moritz's carbonic waters and mountain climbing, he returned to Zurich. Then late in August, seeking the Italian sun, he fled to the Ligurian coast by way of Mont Cenis. But his indispositions increased. Weakened by dysentery, he staggered into a hotel in Spezia (September 4).

In childhood and adolescence he had been subject to hallucinations and seizures, and during his speech before Weber's grave at Dresden he had entered a cataleptic state. At Spezia he fell into a deep trance and seemed engulfed by water whose rushing sound made the tonality of E-flat major swirl in his ears. The triad was broken and reverberated with ever-increasing motion.

The hour had come. What for years had been fermenting deep in the unconscious was rising to the surface. From the heroic triad poured forth the motif of the primeval flood, of nature and its mother goddess. He was ready to give musical shape to his universe of water, vapor, and fire. The task was formidable; the vision seen in a dream had to be evinced by the will. *"Wie im Traum ich ihn trug, wie mein Wille ihn wies . . ."* ("as glimpsed in my dreams, as shaped by my will"), sings Wotan, contemplating the completed Walhall. Wagner turned back to Zurich to "die or compose."

But before he could settle down to work, he fulfilled a promise to rendezvous with Liszt at Basel. Fresh from triumphs with his and Wagner's works at the Karlsruhe festival, he arrived on October 6 in the buoyant company of Bülow, Joachim, Cornelius, Pohl, Reményi, and Pruckner. The group was joined by Sayn-Wittgenstein and her daughter, Princess Marie, almost seventeen years old, who was to be in Wagner's mind as he created the music of Freia. With the ladies and Liszt, Wagner set out by way of Strassburg for Paris. There he read aloud part of his *Ring* poem to, among others, a doubtlessly bewildered Berlioz, dined with an old admirer, Madame Kalergis, and made the acquaintance of Liszt's three children—the dazzling Daniel and the shy girls, Blandine and Cosima, the latter being almost a year younger than Princess Marie. He found Kietz and Anders flourishing, and by chance met some Zurich friends, the handsome couple Otto and Mathilde Wesendonk.

Minna had been summoned to join the improvised holiday and by late October was back in Zurich with a puzzled husband who wondered what had prompted him to go through so much money. He sat down to *Rhinegold* on November 1 and finished the composition sketch by the middle of January, 1854, the orchestration occupying him until the end of May. *The Nibelung's Ring* was well on its way.

VII

Switzerland: Personal and Artistic Crisis

I

Naïvely, Wagner and his disciples expected *Faust,* the national poem, to yield its place to the *Ring.* The latter did come to occupy a significant position in Germany's culture, but disappointed hopes and the example of the composer's curiously indecisive attitude toward Goethe led commentators on Wagner for the most part to ignore the extent of his debt to Germany's greatest poet, of whom he could write to Mathilde Wesendonk, "He did what he could, and—honor be to him for that!"

Possibly the young Wagner already knew Goethe's *Clavigo* when drafting *"Hochzeit."* The works are related through elements in their funeral scenes, the blood and thunder of youth, and a common debt to the saturnine melancholy of Shakespeare's Dane. Certainly Rienzi, that late straggler from *Sturm und Drang,* has qualities of both Götz and Egmont. Tannhäuser, though lacking Tasso's inherent innocent nobility, finds himself in the very role given the Italian poet in Goethe's *Torquato Tasso,* that of a vain, rash, poorly mannered, self-pitying artist whose refusal to compromise with life's realities—the Ferrarese court being no different from that of the Wartburg—leads him to shipwreck against the rock of established society. In both cases the reef against which the hero crashes provides, at the same time, a route to safety.[1] Vacillating Weislingen and demonic Adelheid in *Götz* may well have contributed to the figures of Telramund and Ortrud,[2] and Brynhild has in her much of Goethe's high-souled Iphigenie, who matures before the spectator's eyes. Brynhild, too, sprang from a sordid lineage to develop majestically into a figure of compassionate humanity,

[1] Wagner discussed *Tasso* in a letter of April 15, 1859, to Mathilde Wesendonk.
[2] Lysiart and Eglantine in Weber's *Euryanthe* were more direct models for this pair.

though the vengeful virago of the middle act of *The Twilight of the Gods* has no affinity to the priestess of Tauris whose *"stille Grösse"* ("hushed greatness") the Valkyrie attains only occasionally. But against the background of the gods' treachery she shines all the more brightly. Ethical growth is, of course, also the burden of *Dutchman, Tristan,* and, in a sense, *Parsifal.* *Iphigenie* not only anticipates such idealism but also embodies that mother goddess,˙ the Eternal Feminine, praised in the finale of *Faust.* And along with this motive of the redeeming woman Wagner appropriated the theme of renunciation that flows quietly through Goethe's works, as well as his repeated striving for a denouement that is coincidentally a *Verklärung* (transfiguration).

As in *Iphigenie auf Tauris,* the moral values Goethe presents in contention are not necessarily incompatible. An exception is the collision of the contrary worlds of Faust and Gretchen, as hopeless of reconciliation as those of Wotan and Fricka or of Richard and Minna Wagner. Goethe, a child of the German *Aufklärung* and spiritual heir of Lessing, usually sought a constructive adjustment, avoiding purely tragic endings. Wagner, the late romantic, tended to see only in terms of black or white. Rapprochement is impossible between Wagnerian adversaries; one must annihilate the other.[3] The Nibelung's ring and the magic ring of God's favor described by Lessing's Nathan the Wise form a striking symbolic antithesis.

Wagner embraced the tragic—his optimism was always theoretic, his essential nature pessimistic—tempering it with his own adaptation of the *Verklärung,* a sentimentalized, negative, but theatrically effective variation of Goethe's motive of assertive optimism. Nietzsche wittily observed that Wagner, adroitly taking the part of the cultured German maiden of redemption, saved even Goethe.

Only in *Meistersinger* does Wagner's mood more consistently resemble Goethe's. As in *Faust,* solemnity and wit join hands, doggerel elbowing poetry. (Wagner even makes his Nuremberg tailors parody *"Di tanti palpiti."*) *Meistersinger* seeks to solve an aspect of the dilemma propounded in *Egmont,* the reconciliation of joyous, youthful freedom with the cautious and often wise experience of tradition. Sachs's elegiac *Entsagung* (renunciation) is truly Goethean. He would conciliate by the noble but costly act and, having called Walther's dream into reality, summons the young poet to enter the world. Walther, though as stubborn as his ancestors, Tannhäuser and Siegfried, is at least able to take instruction and learns that the romantic artist must leave isolation and adjust to society if he

---

[3] Tasso's quarrel with Antonio seemed relatively uninteresting to Wagner since it admitted of adjustment. But of Tasso and the princess he wondered, "How will these opposites be reconciled?"

would have not only its applause and rewards but, most important, its comprehension. Again one feels the influence of *Tasso*. Tannhäuser, in the guise of Walther, has been housebroken and can now enjoy a fuller life in contact with the community. But, whereas Tasso sees his unique genius as forever setting him apart, Walther, who has thoroughly revised his style, prepares to become a good bourgeois. In *Meistersinger* Goethe's humanity and rationality have inspired a denouement that is wondrously moving, even though illuminated by the not always flattering light of Victorian self-satisfaction.

Despite many points of contact it must again be stressed that Wagner, in general, rejected the essence of Goethe, being content to appropriate various odds and ends of his work. Goethe's characters strive for life, Wagner's for death, a contrast in which early and late romanticism stand opposed. Wagner's letter of April 7, 1858, to Mathilde Wesendonk, so famous because it was intercepted by Minna, was in part a commentary on the character of Faust, whom he judged stupid for having turned from redemption through a woman's love only to rush headlong into the world to explore and comprehend experience. For Wagner, a Gretchen offered all the world had to teach. Siegfried's departure from the mother goddess on the mountain led to his ruin; Faust's inquisitive wanderings brought him salvation.

Both Goethe and Wagner put themselves and their problems on the stage and often tended to write expanded monologues masquerading as dramas, individual episodes being so persuasively handled that the observer is most often unaware that what passes before him is a series of rather imperfectly dovetailed incidents and not a unified dramatic design. The *Ring* occupies among Wagner's works a place analogous to that of *Faust* in Goethe's. Each took decades to find a final form, underwent startling changes and additions during the long course of creation, and remains the undisputed centrum of its author's output. Starting as relatively modest efforts—the one, as a heroic grand opera, the other, as a satire on pedantry combined with a romantic tragedy—with the years they grew to gigantic proportions to become vehicles of cosmic allegory, both betraying in their patchwork nature a not always successful agglomeration of segments revised here and affixed there. But from the point of view of structure the two works are basically dissimilar.

Faust does not even pretend to a central plot. To see how unnecessary, indeed, inimical, such a device is to the essentials of this drama one need only glance at the well-made version of the Gretchen tragedy ground out by Messrs. Barbier and Carré as a libretto for Gounod. Goethe's poetry and ethical concerns always compensate for occasional imperfections in his overall designs, but for the tale of the Württemberg doctor he fashioned an irregular, unaccustomed form that, especially in the *Urfaust* and its subsequent expanded versions, works marvelously well.[4]

When it suited his purpose, Goethe could chisel iambics with which to build the closer plan of his "classic" *Iphigenie* (a reaction against the freer forms of his earlier works) or force a reluctant German into hexameters in the pseudo-antique poetic idyll, *Hermann and Dorothea*. But in *Götz, Faust,* and *Egmont* he called to his aid in dialogue and plan the spirit of an open, so-called "Shakespearean" approach answering the sonority of these romantic themes. His versatility was enormous, his poetic and dramatic forms following the function of the material at hand. He could turn from wrestling with the homeric style of his ill-fated *Achilleis* to continue the "gothic" *Faust*.

Unfortunately, Goethe's bold example in evolving unorthodox forms had little effect on Wagner when he constructed libretti from the immense, impassioned stuff of the Nibelung legends. The swift pace of the first *Ring* scenario (1848) suggests that perhaps he originally hoped to carry out the work as a succession of freely disposed, quickly brushed Goethe-like pictures. The formal diversity of *Faust* is dazzlingly modern, its almost Brechtian kaleidoscopic series of images lifting it above concern with time, space, or causality; a scene materializes, makes its point, and fades to be replaced by another, a technique Maeterlinck and Debussy were to follow in *Pelléas* and Ibsen in *Peer Gynt*. The *Ring* material would have benefited from such a flexible approach, dispensing with Wagner's compulsive, cumbersome explanations of matters often defying elucidation. Though Goethe, like Wagner, luxuriated in the monologue, he could also represent a scene economically by means of swift, masterly touches, a literary facility denied the composer, whose heavy hand could do no better, in the end, than set the cycle within grand opera's ponderous walls with their realistic Louis Philippe and Second Empire decorations. There was nothing essentially new in the ground plans of the four *Ring* dramas, although the marvelous music and liberal doses of tinted compressed steam led spectators to believe that they were experiencing unparalleled theatrical innovations. Right up to *Parsifal* Wagner's aesthetic remained that of the Rue Le Peletier, and it is really not surprising that the Opéra opened its gates to *Tannhäuser* and shut out Berlioz's *Trojans*. Too often muscle, strain, and visible ropes are needed to fly a Wagnerian fantasy, while Shakespeare's, Goethe's, and Berlioz's creatures materialize and vanish, ordered by unseen cords of the imagination.

Having chosen a grave, respected architecture, Wagner found himself

---

[4] The overwhelming second part of *Faust,* being a poetic, philosophic closet drama, leaves the world of the theater.

unable to force his variegated material to take the requisite shape. An antagonism between, on the one side, a vigorous poetic content unbounded in breadth and, on the other, the sophisticated, ennuied, restricted form into which it was crammed, as well as Wagner's changing attitudes toward this material during the quarter of a century of the *Ring's* creation, led to embarrassments in construction that not even the technical address of a Scribe could have remedied. Instead of eluding the exigencies of plot, Wagner let himself be overtaken by them. During the writing of the *Ring*, haunted by the specter of relevance, he wandered in a maze of conflicting detail from which he never quite emerged. And though he ended by exclaiming in bewilderment and some anger that, after all, the *Ring* was not to be judged in terms of a well-made play and examined in a legalistic, caviling spirit, he was certainly aware that a rigid literary anatomy hindered it from moving with the confident spontaneity of its Eddic models.

But an incomparable musical eloquence, in its own way probing as deep psychologically as Goethe's diction, compensates for constructional imperfections and oft-found foolishness and inconsistencies in the texts. If these flaws belie the composer's pretensions to propounding the ethical values of a Goethe, and if most Wagnerian characters do lack great human qualities, especially humor,[5] nonetheless his music probes a wide range of emotions with astounding penetration. Goethe's words invite one to consider the highest aspects of man's conduct; Wagner's music, lying beneath less lofty words, explores the recesses of the soul.

Surely he had in mind the epic plan of *Faust* to lead the spectator "from heaven through the world to hell." The vast Nibelung drama extends from Walhall by way of the Rhine to the sulphur caverns of the underworld. But it was Wagner's incomparably persuasive music that brought into being a unique universe, a tonal cosmos in which one can believe despite the fact that its literary course seems somewhat less than eternally fixed.

2

Erda's warning toward the end of *Rhinegold* points up the insoluble problems of adjustment and revision Wagner faced in 1851–52. In the original Nibelung scenario of 1848 the Norns (called *"Schicksalsfrauen"*) premonished Wotan of the gods' downfall should he withhold the Ring from

---

[5] However, in *Rhinegold* one must admire the manner in which Wagner uses Loge's sarcasm as a foil for Wotan's pomposity, a device obviously following the pattern of Mephistopheles vis-à-vis Faust. It is a pity that Loge does not accompany the god throughout the cycle.

the giants and thus fail to complete payment for their building of Walhall. By heeding this advice to surrender the cursed Ring, Wotan escaped ruin. When Wagner in his Zurich days added the figures of Freia [6] and Loge to his plan, a *"dea ex machina,"* Erda, replaced her daughters, the Norns, as Wotan's mentor.

But such changes were insignificant compared to the entirely new concept of the gods' fate toward which Wagner had been veering. Gradually he had come to see that no stratagem could mitigate Wotan's guilt in the rape of the gold. Wagner had chosen to write a political finale to "Siegfried's Death" and ignore the fact that the concept of the gods' fall lay buried in the prose of the 1848 scenario. There one reads that, when they endowed man with divine attributes and also with a free will and a free conscience to work the annulling of their crime, the eternals risked their own destruction. Wagner picked up this almost forgotten idea again by the spring of 1851. At that time he penned both a new ending for "Siegfried's Death," in which Brynhild apprised the gods that extinction would redeem them from fear (*"Machtlos scheidet die die Schuld nun meidet"*), a passage Ellis believed conceived as early as the days immediately before the Dresden insurrection, and also wrote an outline of the Erda scene in "Young Siegfried," wherein the gods' twilight was preluded.

Wagner realized that at the moment in *Rhinegold* when Wotan declared, "I must possess the Ring!" the curse, though yet unuttered, unalterably descended upon him and ordained his doom. (To August Röckel, the composer remarked that Alberich's magic ring would have been powerless against the gods had they remained uncorrupted.) But Erda was not informed of the drastic change in Wagner's apprehension of the plot. Surfacing to declare the emergency on the heights disquieting to her cosmic slumber, she still repeated in the final version of *Rhinegold* the substance

---

[6] According to Wagner's scenario of 1848, the Volsung twins were the issue of a marriage that had remained barren until their parents ate one of Holda's apples. The idea derived from the marvelous incidents surrounding King Volsung's birth as described in *Volsunga Saga*. In this tale the goddess of the magic fruit is called Freia. Her presence in the *Ring* under another name was thus faintly foreshadowed in Wagner's first plan. In *Rhinegold* she is called both Freia and Holda, the double appellation permitting him to indulge in some dreadful punning. In "Wieland" Wagner refers to the goddess of youth as Iduna, but Holda's name had already appeared in *Tannhäuser*, where the shepherd extols her as the goddess of fertility. Here Wagner used one of those implied analogies in which he delighted. The shepherd sings, "Lady Holda stepped forth from her mountain to wander through field and meadow." Having been led but instants before to the Thuringian landscape from the cavern of Venus, the audience inevitably makes an association between her and Holda. In Norse mythology Freia-Holda at times played the role of Wotan's (Odin's) wife and thus was occasionally identified with Fricka or Frigg. In the *Ring* Freia and Fricka are sisters.

of the Norns' message of 1848, by this time, alas, a canard: "Yield, Wotan, yield; flee the curse of the Ring. Retain it and dark ruin without deliverance will be yours." The implication was clear: relinquish the token and be freed from the evil it breeds. She dangled hope of rescue. For what other reason did the god toss the Ring to the giants?

Wotan is deceived by a false confidence that Loge, a figure created for the new *Rhinegold,* slyly attempts to confirm. Erda's message, originally intended to be delivered by her daughters, is left over from an earlier draft and has no relationship to the revised *Ring.* As the gods prepare to cross the rainbow bridge to Walhall, Loge, observing that they but hasten toward their end, foresees their destruction by his flames, though, fortunately, not his own mutilation by Wotan. The latter, caught between two antithetical versions of the *Ring,* remains perplexed throughout the cycle. As late as *The Twilight of the Gods,* Waltraute reports him still clinging to hope of escape from his doom should the Ring find its way back to the Rhine.

Wagner did sense a want of coherence in the situation, but, despite attempts, a bold remedy seemed beyond his energy or powers. In a sketch for *Rhinegold,* Erda, as messenger of the Norns, had told Wotan that, while the gods must in any case slowly decline, retention of the Ring would only accelerate their fall—an ingenious solution, but its very baldness and lack of theatrical mystery may have led to its abandonment. As late as 1854 Wagner was still tinkering with Erda's eloquent utterance, which at the end made sense only in respect to the early, triumphant conclusion to *Siegfried's Death.* He sought a solution in obfuscation, but, despite her cryptic mutterings about the world's end and the dusk of the gods, Erda remained an allegorical monitor of 1848 addressing Friedrich of Saxony, her warning still implying that, if the Ring of materialism be ceded, its curse might be shunned. A perceptive listener of today, knowing *The Twilight of the Gods,* might conclude that in *Rhinegold* the mother goddess, claiming knowledge of the future, is misinformed, a fraud, or perhaps a mischief-maker.

The scope of the *Ring* can be fully valued only by those willing to examine its preliminary studies, since many references have relevance to material missing from the final version. Repeatedly Wagner put his hand to the texts, especially when he set them to music. But his revisions often only aggravated the perplexities. Especially in the two final dramas, fascinating stratas of the cycle's literary formation lie pell-mell like abandoned rock in an exhausted quarry.

The dramatic incoherence in which the *Ring* abounds raised many eyebrows as the poem circulated. Though Wagner pretended to be amused at Princess Wittgenstein's "mathematical" queries as to the fate of the gods, she had obviously touched a sensitive spot. He had attempted to expunge from his Nibelung plan ideas that too clearly marked its origin as an allegory of the 1848 revolutionary movement. But Uhlig's plainly fatal illness was a blow that weakened Wagner's failing health, and his pitch of interest in consolidating the tetralogy seems to have lowered considerably. Interconnections were perfunctorily, if not carelessly, accomplished. It was the *Tannhäuser* story again. A cloak of music would envelop and render inconsequential his dramatic floundering.

Vigorous dramatic coherence was difficult for Wagner under the best of circumstances; it was thoroughly impossible in this bulky work so long in creation. Moreover, the Wagner who finished the main revision of the poem late in 1852 was no longer the firebrand of Dresden.

3

The political optimist of 1848 had gradually fallen into a mood of resignation, later reinforced by reading Schopenhauer. Moreover, Louis Napoleon's *coup* of December, 1851, which prepared the Second French Empire, further deepened his despair of Europe's artistic and political future.

The pessimism that had led him toward the destruction of Wotan built a most extraordinary bridge. For some time an inner compulsion had been urging him toward an almost mystical synthesis. From the very beginning, his conception of the myths had bound the destiny of gods and Volsungs closely together. From hints and vague allusions in Edda and saga he fashioned a tightly woven relationship between happenings in heaven and on earth. The Valkyrie, Brynhild, spanned these two worlds. But nowhere in the ancient tales is the death of Siegfried (Sigurd) connected with the twilight of the gods. Now, since Wagner wrote the *Ring,* it is difficult to separate the events. It was he who made the flames of the hero's funeral pyre rise to ignite Walhall itself. By this union of *Volsunga Saga* with the prophetic utterances of the Eddic *Völuspâ* a new and fateful mythology was created.[7] The title of the revised "Siegfried's Death" was eventually changed to *The Twilight of the Gods,* and Brynhild's apocalyptic *scena* underwent many variations before reaching its incomparable ultimate form, in which Wagner, at the height of his powers, painted in purely musical terms the majestic ruin of the gods and the emergence of a new order after the cataclysm.

His poetic article of 1849, "The Revolution," had promised a new Europe.

---

[7] Earlier, a similar merger of two unrelated legends had been effected in *Tannhäuser.*

To the jubilant strains of shrill, warlike music, a paradise was to rise from the devastation of a volcanic upheaval. But in the finale of the *Ring,* hostility gives way to a calm resignation, knowing neither defeat nor victory. Brynhild bids her father, Wotan, rest to music of infinite sadness, and the old world sinks down because it can no longer bear its load of deceit and treachery. Hagen, preaching Bakunin-style violence to the end, is pulled into the depths of the cascading river by the Rhine Daughters. But, though they happily ride the crest of destruction with their restored treasure, no new Eden can follow. Alberich is still at large, and the new world may well be as troubled as the old.

At the end of both the first Nibelung scenario and "Siegfried's Death," Brynhild gave assurance that the dwarf would never again possess the Ring and, in fact, promised freedom to him and all the Nibelungs from their enslavement to gold's power. The final stage direction of "Siegfried's Death" describes the inconsolable and obdurate fellow as he "sinks down with a gesture of woe." It seems mute evidence of Wagner's growing pessimism that in *The Twilight of the Gods* not only does Brynhild pass over the dwarf's fate in silence, but the action fails to dispose of him in any way. His survival is obviously not due to an oversight, but to acceptance of the changing complexion of a work that in the end renounced all intellectual coherence.

Moreover, Wagner's manner of working could hardly result in a coherent dramatic design. In view of the scope of the cycle and his method of construction, it is amazing that the *Ring* gives at least a surface impression of unity. He assembled his plots by what psychologists call "association." From his vast reading, bits and pieces of legends accumulated in his febrile brain, where they were further fragmented, mixed, transformed, and then reshaped into a completely "new" mythology. Any attempt to follow his creative path is, of course, hypothetical. Yet it might be helpful to guess at how he fashioned, for example, the main symbol of his drama, the cursed and powerful Ring.

In the nineteenth adventure of the *Nibelungenlied* there is casual reference to the fact that on the hoard lies a magic wishing rod with the power to make its discoverer master of the world. This alluring bit of information is never put to use by anyone in the tale, but Wagner evidently seized upon it; by combining this rod with the ring cursed by the dwarf Andvari in *Volsunga Saga,* he forged the famous and dreaded Ring of the Nibelung, a symbol of unlimited and cursed power that could dominate the universe.

Perhaps, while creating the psychologically profound scene in *Siegfried* in which Wotan bars the hero's access to the sleeping Brynhild, there hovered in Wagner's mind remembrance of that moving fragment of old Low

German poetry called the *Hildebrandslied* (ca. 800), wherein a conflict to the death is spurred by a hasty and suspicious youth who does not recognize his opponent as his parent.

The *Vegtamskvidha,* the fifth section of the *Elder Edda,* in which the disguised Odin descends to the underworld and by his magic compels a great *wala* or prophetess to awaken and unravel the mystery of Baldur's fearful dreams, became the model for the encounter between Wotan and Erda in the third act of *Siegfried.* Indeed, stretches of Wagner's *Ring* text are lifted wholesale from the Eddic poems, which were themselves formed of a commingling of inconsistent details and traditions.

How far afield Wagner wandered to gather ideas may be seen in his own acknowledgment that a farce by Hopp, *Dr. Fausts Hauskäppchen,* contributed toward the scene in *Siegfried* wherein the hero divines the malicious thoughts beneath Mime's unctuous melodies, an incident in which memories of Hoffmann's "Meister Floh" also played a part. Moreover, a story by Dumas, *Les Aventures merveilleuses du Prince Lyderic,* evidently influenced the construction of the *Ring.* Nor did Wagner hesitate to borrow from himself. Brynhild's appearance before Siegmund was certainly inspired by that atmospheric scene in *Sarazenin* in which Fatima, on a jutting crag silhouetted against the clouds, materializes before the eyes of Manfred.

4

Rhinegold presents a striving god, his distrustful, chiding spouse, and their well-meaning but simple relatives. Wagner's gods are a bourgeois lot, closer to *verismo* than to *opera seria.* Wotan's far-reaching plans are thwarted by lower spirits, stupid giants unable to grasp his vision of a newly ordered universe with himself at its center, and also by Alberich,[8] a clever Nibelung dwarf who grasps the plan all too well. The giants, Wotan believes, can be beguiled into serving his ends; at worst, their doltishness would render ineffective any eventual hostility. But the dwarf is a substantial threat; this swarthy underworld prince has gained power by dedicating himself and his kingdom to unrelenting labor at amassing a golden hoard with which he plans to win the world. He cries out to Wotan, "Beware the army of night; from silent depths the Nibelung hoard shall rise to daylight!" He is a masculine parody of Ortrud, one who, abandoning all hope of love, turns to a fearsome destructive fanaticism, and Wotan clearly sees what he

---

[8] The name, found in the *Nibelungenlied,* is also reminiscent of Albert, the brother Wagner despised as a materialist. Alberich has in him something of Devrient's and Marschner's Heiling.

deems his racial superiority threatened by the ruthless sovereign of an inferior breed.

This Wagnerian contest for dominion opposes Wotan, the Alberich of light, to Alberich, the Wotan of darkness, the one conceiving prideful thoughts and expansive plans, the other heaping up riches. In view of obvious autobiographical elements in the book, not surprisingly Wagner desired the perverse Nibelungs to speak a kind of Jewish-German and to gesticulate in a manner he held to be characteristically Semitic. One must be grateful that he did not specify that Alberich be made up and costumed as Meyerbeer.[9]

Early in 1854 Wagner's need for money was at its periodic peak, and as usual he blamed his predicament on the Philistines and Jews. On January 15, immediately after completing the *Rhinegold* composition sketch, he wrote to Liszt, "The only thing I want is *money;* that at least one ought to be able to get. *Love* I abandon, and *art!*" Of course, he was ironically playing Alberich. His finances were in so extreme a state that he halfseriously contemplated flight to America, whence came flattering accounts of Wagner evenings in Boston.

By the end of 1853 about twenty German theaters had purchased the privilege of producing *Tannhäuser.* But his fees were only for premières, the first wave of the opera's popularity was already receding, and there was little interest in *Lohengrin,* especially in the wake of its near-disastrous production in Leipzig during the first week of 1854, a failure costing him the opportunity of selling the performance rights for a lump sum. Thus, honorariums had all but ceased, and in order to augment the Ritter allowance, Wotan set about duping the many indulgent Zurich giants, easily cajoled into lending a hand toward the raising of Walhall.

Luxurious surroundings were necessary for his work. "I cannot sleep on straw and drink bad whisky. I must be coaxed in one way or another if my mind is to accomplish the terribly difficult task of creating a nonexisting world. . . . Before all, I must have *money* . . . but what is the good of hundreds where thousands are needed?" The joy of creation past, his nervous disorders returned, and he was drained by the mechanical labor of turning sketches into a finished *Rhinegold* score. But hope for his wearied arm and exhausted purse was beckoning in the figure of the lovely Mathilde Wesendonk. He wrote to Liszt in the summer of 1854, "Do not look out for a copyist. Madame Wesendonk has given me a gold pen of indestructible power, which has once more turned me into a calligraphic pedant." She was to give him much more.

[9] In *Meistersinger* he almost went this far in respect to the role of Beckmesser and its prototype, the critic Hanslick.

He had spoken of her in a letter to Uhlig of February, 1852: "Some new acquaintances have forced themselves on me; the men are highly indifferent to me, the women less so. A rich young merchant, Wesendonk . . . settled down at Zurich some time ago and in great luxury. His wife is very pretty and seems to have caught some enthusiasm for me after having read the preface to the three operatic poems." [10]

A performance of the *Tannhäuser* overture on March 16, 1852, had surpassed all his expectations, especially in respect to its effect on the audience. "The women in particular were turned inside out . . . taking refuge in sobs and weeping." The *Ewig-Weibliche* filled him with sweet illusions. "The moist, shining eye of a woman often saturates me with fresh hope."

The twenty-three-year-old Mathilde had been among these deeply afflicted ladies. It was probably she who persuaded Wagner to mount *Dutchman* in Zurich. And, by the time of the concerts in honor of his fortieth birthday, he could speak of laying the festival at the feet of a beautiful woman. Her husband, Otto, picked up the bill.

5

Otto Wesendonk was called upon increasingly to pay the price of his wife's enthusiasm as Wagner exhausted his resources of borrowing among older Zurich friends. It was now Wesendonk who staved off those frequent financial catastrophes threatening the Wagnerian household on the Zeltweg. To efforts of this sensitive and extremely generous man systematically to order Wagner's chaotic money affairs, he responded by affecting every subterfuge that might prevent a complete picture of his indebtedness from emerging. Perhaps he himself dreaded the truth. He had fled Dresden owing funds in excess of twelve times the total of his comfortable *Kapellmeister's* salary, and every week in Zurich brought to light more local debts.

Otto had confidence in Minna. In his role of new Wagnerian patron he would have insisted that she alone control all family income had not a reluctance to embarrass Wagner made him drop the stipulation. The idea was certainly circulating among Wagner's friends, and even he admitted to Liszt the wisdom of putting Minna in control.

She was seriously declining, the face and figure of the former leading lady inevitably bowing to the ravages of heart disease. In September, 1854, Wagner gave out that she was returning to Germany for a brief period

[10] The *Communication to My Friends* was issued as a preface to the poems of *Dutchman, Tannhäuser,* and *Lohengrin.*

because of her health and to visit relatives. Actually he had dispatched his theater-wise wife to negotiate with Hülsen of the Berlin Opera over its revived interest in a production of *Tannhäuser*.[11] Berlin paid royalties, and Wagner, as he quaintly put it, was ready to throw his pre-Nibelung operas to the Jews. Now eager to hand the score to the hated Heinrich Dorn, to whom he had indirectly sent messages of good will, he really longed to drop his old unrealistic condition that Liszt supervise preparation of the work in Berlin. The problem was that Liszt took seriously the pious protestations of artistic idealism with which Wagner's correspondence had overwhelmed him and, standing on what he thought to be mutually held principles, would not step aside. Moreover, Wagner had unwittingly maneuvered him into a position from which retreat without humiliation would be difficult. Despite Minna's and Hülsen's ingenious stratagems,[12] matters came to a standstill.

Except for an impromptu Alpine trip with the Wesendonks, Wagner was mainly occupied during Minna's absence with the fair copy of the *Rhinegold* score and the composition of *Valkyrie,* begun at the end of June. (His letters to her in Germany attempted to allay her obvious uneasiness about the developing Wagner-Wesendonk relationship.) Also during this fall, as an outgrowth of his introduction at Mariafeld to Schopenhauer's speculations, there had germinated his first conception of *Tristan.* In December, 1854, he wrote to Liszt, "since I have never in life tasted the actual happiness of love, I must raise a monument to the fairest of all dreams, in which from beginning to end that love shall be thoroughly satiated. I have in my head *Tristan and Isolde,* the simplest but most full-blooded musical conception; with the 'black flag' that waves at the end of it I shall shroud myself to die."

He had read Gottfried von Strassburg's Tristan epic in Hermann Kurz's modern German version, received further information from Friedrich von der Hagen's volumes on the minnesinger, and doubtless was acquainted with many variants of the tale. The reference to the black flag in the letter to Liszt would indicate that Wagner at first planned to include in his work the two Isoldes whom legend had given to Tristan—his Uncle Mark's

---

[11] Minna was enormously stimulated by *Lohengrin* in Weimar despite the sad fact that the hero was sung by "a voiceless big booby." She regretted that the performance sped by so fast, for she would have liked to hold it up, the better to enjoy the opera's exquisite detail. In Frankfort *Tannhäuser* moved her to tears, the papers commenting on her evident emotion.

[12] Minna journeyed to Dresden and appealed to King Johann (he had recently inherited the Saxon throne upon the death of his brother, King Friedrich) to pardon Wagner. She and Hülsen reasoned that if Wagner might safely visit Berlin, Liszt's presence could be dispensed with gracefully. But Johann denied the petition.

wife, the Irish Princess, Isolde the Fair, whom he loved passionately but secretly, and also Isolde of the White Hands, a Breton noblewoman whom he wed after being compelled to flee Mark's kingdom of Cornwall. The Irish Isolde was renowned for her knowledge of philters, and, having received a deadly poisoned wound, Tristan sent for his beloved to cure him. Isolde, his wife, however, overheard the plan—if her rival agreed to journey to Brittany, the ship bringing her would hoist a white banner; if she were not on board, a black sail would fly. Immobile upon his bed, the knight asked Isolde of the White Hands to scan the sea for an approaching sail and report its color. As the ship neared with white floating from the masthead, the wife, moved by jealousy, told Tristan that the flag was black. He then turned his face to the wall and died. Isolde the Fair, arriving too late, fell upon her lover's body and joined him in death.

That Wagner's earliest conception of *Tristan* included elements of this famous situation involving the two Isoldes and the flag is evidenced not only by the letter to Liszt, but also by some vestigial remains of this first scheme still embedded in the completed opera. Upon his deathbed, Tristan beholds Isolde's ship in a feverish vision: "It comes, it comes with courageous speed, the flag fluttering from the mast." And when his servant, Kurvenal, finally sights the actual vessel, Tristan questions him about the flag and is told that "the banner of joy" flies "happily and brightly." These allusions to the flag and its nature have no relevance to anything left in the text of the opera. When Wagner reduced his stock of Isoldes from two to one, quite typically he neglected to remove all traces of the earlier plan.

Considering Wagner's usual difficulty in deciding upon a close for a dramatic work, it is unlikely that he had at this time fixed upon an ending for *Tristan* other than that of tradition—certainly none that Liszt could be expected to have knowledge of. And, since the black flag waving at the end exists only in the hero's deluded mind, one must assume that the composer's reference to it is a convenient if inaccurate figure for dramatizing his own melancholy mood.

It may also reveal how deeply immersed in Schopenhauer and the story he already was. He had known the poem since Dresden days, but only after reading Schopenhauer did the possibilities of its material become clear to him. He then saw in Tristan a figure to be interpreted in terms of the theory of disaffirmation. Overlooking the myriad trivial adventures in which the hero was involved, Wagner concentrated his gaze on the main outlines of the tale and in the deaths of Tristan and his royal mistress found a Schopenhauerean triumph. (One day Wagner even contemplated sending the philosopher a letter on the subject of the joint suicide of lovers.) Tristan, tired of life's sham and illusion, turned his back to the light and willed that he expire. Clearly, in Wagner's view, not the poisoned wound but the account of the black flag decreed Tristan's end and led Isolde to follow him into Schopenhauer's nirvana of nonwilling. The white flag on the mast was one of reality's deluding specters; the black promised salvation, the subjection of individuation through a kind of euthanasia of consciousness. Wagner had conceived the main symbols of his opera, the realms of day and night, and, in the dark folds portending self-extinguishment, Wagner, so he dramatically announced to Liszt, planned to enclose himself.[18]

As was usual when a legend seized his imagination, he was closely identifying himself with its hero. Not only was he stripping a medieval tale of its picturesque detail, extracting its tragic essence, and bringing it into harmony with nineteenth-century romantic philosophy, but he was also simultaneously associating himself with the hero's woes and beginning to act them out in reality. Such a mood always threatened danger to his intimates, and his "Tristanizing" was to bring about a major crisis in this career of alarms and emergencies.

Tristan believed the flag black, and so did Wagner, who doubtlessly imagined himself as the helpless, betrayed man, deprived by a resentful woman, more companion than wife, of a healing love. Indeed, in some versions of the legend the Breton Isolde is Tristan's wife in name only. The Tristan theme was gradually taking complete possession of the composer and at times drove from his mind the robust Nibelung music [14] and replaced it with intimations of those chromatic harmonies of passion and sorrow inseparable today from the very idea of Tristan and his beloved. Late in 1856 he wrote Otto, "I can no longer attune myself to Siegfried, and my musical perception already roams far beyond it into that realm of melancholy befitting my mood." And as this Tristan atmosphere enveloped Wagner more and more, he dramatized in life his discontent with the aging Minna of the White Hands and a growing delight in Mathilde the Fair, whose flaxen tresses enchanted him much as that single golden hair from Isolde's head had captivated Mark, when a swallow brought

[18] That the route to salvation lay through death was Wagnerian embroidery upon Schopenhauer, who held that, since the will had never been born, it could not die. Meditation, compassion, renunciation, and ascetic discipline were his instruments of redemption. Wagner created his own rather extravagant version of Schopenhauer and, not surprisingly, never heard a direct word about the copy of the *Tristan* poem that he dispatched to the old philosopher. Not only must its diction have offended a great stylist, but, when proudly sending off this paean to love, Wagner was obviously unaware that his idol was a confirmed misogynist whose soul had found its mate in a white poodle.

[14] The Tristan of legend was another manifestation of Siegfried. Wagner eliminated mention of Tristan's victorious combat with a dragon that had been the scourge of the Dublin suburbs.

the shining thread from Dublin to Tintagel. (Wagner was appalled to learn later that Mathilde-Isolde had her own set of magic bottles enabling her to change the color of her hair at will.) As in the legend, Wagner's infatuation was for the wife of his greatest benefactor. He later declared, with specific reference to his *Tristan,* that poetry anticipates events, reality later confirming the poet's vision.

The immediate route to *Tristan* lay through the first act of *Valkyrie;* Siegmund, Sieglinde, and Hunding were metamorphosing into Tristan, Isolde, and Mark. And Wagner was now playing both dramas, Richard, Mathilde, and Otto constituting the fatal trio.

A sonata written for Mathilde in June, 1853, among the trifles that were Wagner's only compositions between *Lohengrin* and *Rhinegold,* holds interest not for its shallow music but rather for an echo of the Norn text written on it as motto: "Do you know what will follow?" ("*Wisst Ihr wie das wird?*") Mathilde received the sonata while vacationing at Bad Ems and hastened to send thanks in a letter to Minna, assuring her that the motto was difficult to fathom!

A manuscript of the first act of *Valkyrie* presents cryptic allusions, set down in a kind of shorthand, to Wagner's passion for Mathilde. In the titanic second act of the opera Fricka strides on stage to demand the ruin of the Volsung lovers. With Wagner, life followed art, and inwardly he must have known that Fricka-Minna would contrive an ending to the Wesendonk drama and thus answer the sonata's question.

6

It has been pointed out that *Valkyrie* and *Tristan* share a significant musical motif,[15] and the emotional, autobiographic links between them have been touched upon. Though Gottfried's poetic model makes *Tristan* a courtly drama, it is nonetheless an undisputed child of the wild and at times boisterous *Valkyrie*. Remarkable in both is Wagner's ability to strip an old tale of its many superfluous and bewildering incidents and to hew out of it a relatively concise plan preserving what is essential. Siegmund's tragedy and the inexorable love of Tristan and Isolde are no less moving in the sagaman and Gottfried; but in these early writers one must cut through much that is accessory to reach the kernel.

[15] See Chapter IV, note 7, on page 80. *Lohengrin* and *Tristan* are also united by a theme in common. In the final act of the latter opera the shepherd asks about the state of the knight's health. In reply, Kurvenal silences all questions, echoing his master's response to Mark in the second act: "That you can never come to know." Kurvenal's melodic line, as Ted Hart has pointed out to the writer, is a version of Lohengrin's imperious advice to Elsa: "Never question me."

A significant change takes place, however, during Wagner's process of reduction. In contrast to the vitality of his sources, Wagner's dramas are curiously inert and passive, his stage on the whole being occupied by characters chronicling past events and expressing their reactions to the generally woeful situations in which they discover themselves. They narrate, argue, meditate, or lament, but rarely act.[16] In Wagner a decisive movement or bit of stage action often has the force of an event. His supreme artistic moments are those of subjective deliberation for the very good reason that they provide the major opportunities for a music that turns seemingly unhistrionic cogitations into powerful drama. Whether this approach makes for viable theater can be argued; that it produces great theatrical experiences in the tradition of Goethe's poetic monologues cannot be disputed. Indeed, few other than Shakespeare could master equally both external and internal drama.

Wagner's difficulties when forced to deal primarily with events rather than with those inner struggles that drew dramatic music from him are revealed in *Rhinegold*. Though he made valiant efforts to concentrate its prodigious variety of episodes, his concepts, so poetic, vast, and all-embracing in earlier studies, tended to contract and lose focus as he reduced a titanic action to the dimensions of the opera stage. For example, the clash of two entire races opposed in goals and temperament, the giants and the gods, shrank to less than half a score of costumed creatures striking attitudes.

Rhinegold, crowded with incident, leaves a short measure of Wagnerian self-searching. Moreover, despite Alberich's disquieting activities, the fresh, youthful optimism of a new world suffuses the work, affairs having not yet reached those crises of agonized pondering that could draw forth the finest from Wagner's musical pen. *Rhinegold* ended as a curious magic opera relying rather too heavily on a marvelous talent for descriptive music and calling to mind that passage in *Faust* wherein the director recommends a full complement of stage machinery and abundant effects of water, fire, and walls of rock.

On the other hand, in *Valkyrie,* as later in *Tristan,* Wagner devoted himself mainly to depicting the mental attitudes of his characters and could happily tarry in that world of protopsychology in which he was most at home.

The example of Greek tragedy had suggested to him a means of consolidating his resources by dwelling upon the conflicts of a limited number of personalities in a series of encounters. Psychological motives were to be gathered into a few powerful images condensed in form and thereby magnified in effect, a point of view much in the spirit of Gluck and Calzabigi,

[16] In addition to its probing monologues, *Meistersinger,* an anomaly in Wagner's works, boasts humor of a kind as well as considerable action.

not unknown in the works of Spontini, but generally abandoned when grand opera re-established a taste for restless changes of scene and excessive action.

Monologue and duet as principal mediums of expression had been hinted at in Wagner's work as early as *Dutchman,* but in *Tannhäuser* and *Lohengrin,* returning to the pattern of *Rienzi,* he again cast some of his most effective moments in grand opera ensembles. He returned to the path of *Dutchman* in that prophetic middle and last-composed act of *Lohengrin,* where, despite the presence of the entire apparatus of Meyerbeer, the drama makes its main points in a succession of deeply etched confrontations. The turnabout was completed at the time of *Opera and Drama,* wherein ensemble was frowned upon and, with Metastasian austerity, the chorus banished, *Valkyrie* being the first seasoned product of this spirit, *Tristan* its apogee.[17]

Valkyrie's very bulk conceals a plan which, constraining an episodic action within a circumscribed time span, pours a flood of movement over the boundaries of the acts. Because of its vastness and the insufficiency of most performances, few realize that *Valkyrie* has been made to submit to the classical unity of time.

Similarly, as Wotan announces in his splendid *"Abendlich strahlt,"* the last three scenes of *Rhinegold* unfold between the morning and evening of a single day, this large unit being preceded by the prologue in the river's bed that takes place outside of time. But despite the rigorous traveling of Wotan and Loge between the scenes there is little forward movement in a work that is essentially expository. Moreover, excepting Loge and Alberich, its characters seem strangely two-dimensional.

In contrast, though the mechanism hinging the acts of *Valkyrie* is the well-worn device of pursuer and pursued, so overwhelmingly does Wagner reveal his characters' passions that during the intermissions the spectator mentally pictures the twins in flight from Hunding and Wotan searching the clouds for disobedient Brynhild. Significantly, the swiftest action transpires while the curtain is down. Were it not for impossible demands upon the stamina of artists and public, *Valkyrie,* like *Dutchman,* would cry out for performance without pauses. Because the pathos of the characters grips the listener, this drama that mixes narration, emotional analysis, and dialectic discussion progresses with relentless inevitability. The shadow of Greek tragedy does fall on *Valkyrie.* And it sweeps forward despite a formidable hindrance arising in the second act, so often a crucial and vulnerable point, as in *Lohengrin, Siegfried, Tristan,* and *The Twilight of the Gods,* for Wagner's system of construction.

[17] This, despite the chorus of Warrior Maidens in *Valkyrie* and the brief choral passages in *Tristan.* (See the following note.)

He was troubled by the imposing mass of Wotan's monologue, that centrally located peak toward which a chain of dialogues mounts and then descends.[18] The act is a series of encounters, its first part propounding Wotan's dilemma, the second half similarly setting forth that of Brynhild. Both predicaments arise from the equivocal attitudes of father and daughter toward Siegmund. Wotan's monologue, originally intended to bridge the two main divisions, rises instead like a barrier, its weight throwing out of balance the drama's center, which appears hippopotamic, especially in contrast to the perfectly proportioned opening act.

Though the critic Hanslick admired the spaciousness Wagner could achieve by reducing his action to a few episodes which occasionally attained the serenity of statuary, he nonetheless wondered how a theater-wise man could at times so abuse the device that all sense of proportion was lost, his works seemingly coming to a halt. To Hanslick the middle act of *Valkyrie* appeared especially vulnerable to such criticism, and Wagner's correspondence reveals that during the creation of the opera he himself inwardly had these very misgivings about Wotan's extensive monologue.

He was often at the point of suppressing the problem scene but finally in desperation persuaded himself that correct interpretation would justify it. That Wotan was displacing Siegfried as hero of the *Ring* was becoming clear to him, and he seemed paralyzed by the change. Moreover, without Wotan's recapitulatory exposition and his reactions to the problems it poses, *Valkyrie* would lack ostensible links to the preceding *Rhinegold*. As has been noted, Wagner's sketches were usually magnificent, combining a clever abridgment of material with breadth of treatment. It was in their mechanical development that he so often stumbled. He really had little choice; the monologue remained.

His feeble dramatic craft would lead to a somewhat similar pass in connection with Mark's soliloquy in the second act of *Tristan*. Much in both passages is noble in diction and music, magnificently presenting the very

---

[18] The duet as constructive unit also dominates the final act, the polyphonic Valkyrie scene notwithstanding. Brynhild's sisters are even less characterized as individuals than the Rhine Maidens. Flosshilde is at least somewhat brighter than her companions. But the Valkyries, like the Grail Knights in *Parsifal,* are a well-indoctrinated, anonymous military force, their scene with Wotan being really an exchange between two characters. Only in *The Twilight of the Gods* does Waltraute detach herself from the group. Perhaps because he looked upon them as forming two collective units, Wagner let Rhine Maidens and Valkyries sing in ensembles without considering the strictures of his Swiss theories violated. In contrast, the Norns communicate their personal and weighty messages in a series of solos, their half-dozen measures of unison singing serving to announce their imminent disappearance.

What Donington calls the hysterics of the Valkyries forms one of the weakest musical sections of the *Ring,* and the brief sailor choruses in *Tristan* have a similar distinction in that masterpiece.

essence of a tragic dilemma. But they are placed in theatrically untenable positions. Moreover, though one knows a good deal of Wotan's tale only too well, both he and Mark impart some rather important new information to the audience, but, unfortunately, at a time when it is least likely to appreciate their labor. In Wotan's long recitation, repetitive narrative, fresh exposition, and emotional revelations mix uncomfortably. What during an earlier age could have been tidily disposed of in recitative had to be relentlessly through-composed under the conditions of Wagner's Zurich system, and at such times he is often justifiably accused of sporting with his themes, of aimlessly paddling in a sea of musical motifs.

Yet nothing can dam the inspiration of *Valkyrie*. The hesitations, indecisiveness, and stylistic hodgepodge of *Rhinegold* have vanished. Pathos pervades every scene as most of the text is shaped by a musical eloquence that seemingly gives each phrase an inevitable form. The longed-for ideal balance between voice and instruments holds for the first act. Then gradually the weight inclines toward the pit as the orchestra grows more assertive, a tendency that was to accelerate and leave *Valkyrie* the last Wagner opera, until *Parsifal,* in which most of the words may be apprehended clearly. As Wagner's taste for instrumental counterpoint grew and his orchestral tone became riper, the text, though often scrupulously set, tended to recede behind a curtain of sound not to be completely raised even by his heroic gesture at Bayreuth of depressing the instrumentalists beneath the stage. Only at the very end, in *Parsifal,* did the transparency of the flanking acts of *Lohengrin* and the opening act of *Valkyrie* return. A thickening texture in the last half of *Valkyrie* prefigures the dense weave of the *Tristan* score.

During his middle period Wagner's growing delight in interweaving musical strands was to lead him back to the vocal ensemble itself in *Tristan, Meistersinger,* and the end of the *Ring,* and at times one regrets that a temporary respect for *Opera and Drama*'s censure of vocal combinations restrained him in *Valkyrie* from blending the voices of the Volsung twins. But, following the example of Tristan, their son was destined to join vocal forces with his beloved Brynhild, and together they were to become sufficiently brave to attempt snippets of imitative counterpoint.

The relatively loose framework of the concluding acts of *Valkyrie,* markedly dissimilar to the concise architecture of the first, also reveals a proclivity to throw up rambling units so imposing in depth and length as almost to defy endurance. *Tristan* continues in this direction. Wagner's structures were becoming like those sprawling baroque palaces that the eye cannot embrace within a single view. It is difficult both to appreciate the rich passing detail as a segment of a larger part and also to grasp the over-all pattern articulating the edifice. As will be seen, in Wagner, a mastery of joinery, if not of proportion, is what informs the whole.

He sought to justify the maladroit elements in his works by maintaining that he wrote for those who could stand something, not the weak and incapable. He was determined to raise not only a new race of singers but also of theatergoers. Travail on the part of the public seemed to him included in the very nature of his art, an extraordinary rationale that was to become a leading precept at Bayreuth. Handel had tailored his oratorios to a special audience; Wagner, in contrast, would fashion the audience itself.

7

Early in 1855 Wagner reworked the *Faust* fragment of his Paris days. Then, in hopes of making money and also of perhaps creating an opportunity to mount *Lohengrin* under his own baton, he broke off the scoring of *Valkyrie* late in February and journeyed to London in response to an invitation to conduct a series of concerts for the Old Philharmonic Society. After attempting in vain to hire Berlioz and then Spohr, its management had turned to someone whose international notoriety might prove of value at the box office even if his music and conducting talent were unknown quantities to the English.

"What will one not do for money?" Wagner asked Minna in a letter from London soon after writing Liszt of his decision to cede *Tannhäuser* unconditionally to Berlin. Liszt, who was now to have no official connection with the project, answered rather caustically, expressing trust that another occasion might present itself when he would be "neither superfluous nor inconvenient." Although their letters soon regained the old warm style, from this time the gradual ebb in their romantic friendship may be dated.

For Wagner, the London experience was harrowing. That its critics, nurtured on the Mendelssohn tradition, did not respond to his interpretations has already been mentioned, as has his friendly rivalry with Berlioz, who was for a time simultaneously conducting the New Philharmonic at Exeter Hall. As usual, Wagner was too often tactless and tasteless. In order to show contempt for Mendelssohn's "Italian" Symphony, he conducted it in kid gloves, dramatically removing them when proceeding to Weber's *Euryanthe* overture. And this in a city where *Jewry in Music* stuck in many throats. Since even so hardened a Wagnerite as Ellis could not condone such barbarity, he conveniently dismissed the story as a malicious myth. But Wagner's letters, to Minna of April 17 and to Kietz of April 27, describe this very incident frankly and proudly as a calculated act of malice. Evidently, he felt constrained to strike at the Mendelssohn cult. The London press, he wrote Otto Wesendonk, was "a pack of vagabond Jews (*Juden-Gesindel*). . . . Mendelssohn is to the English exactly what Jehovah is to the Jews. And Jehovah's wrath now strikes me, an unbeliever."

Living costs ate away fees he hoped to take back to Minna, and he was obliged to conduct so much mediocre music that he often thought himself back in harness at Dresden. At the end of his stay, there was an awkward encounter with Meyerbeer, the two composers eying one another without exchanging a word. Wagner had hoped to finish the scoring of *Valkyrie* in London, but the climate, his inability to get properly warm indoors, and a complete lack of harmony and sympathy with his environment made work difficult and slow. He seemed almost to have forgotten his composition and had to ask himself what this or that meant in his sketches. For a time, his "inner memory" betrayed him, and *Valkyrie* appeared "a complete stranger." He hated the city, his only hope being that "time may quickly slip by." He wrote, "The misery I feel in having to live in these disgusting surroundings is beyond description." He lodged in a cozy house that looked across the Regent's Canal to the park.

Despite vexations, he somehow persisted through the four months of his stay, much to the relief of friends who had regarded as a foreboding augury the abrupt manner in which he had bolted from conducting at the little Swiss festival at Sitten the preceding summer.

He found compensation for a wretchedness, no doubt exaggerated to entertain those at home and gain their sympathy, in again working with a first-rate orchestra—although he held English musicians to be only "clever machines . . . artisanship and the tradesman spirit stifling everything." Translated from the Wagnerian, this simply meant that the orchestra, used to playing in strict time, found difficulty adapting itself to his famous rubati. He took pleasure in his acquaintance with Karl Klindworth, a Liszt pupil who played for him that master's B-Minor Sonata. The handsome young man—"just like Uhlig," Wagner wrote Minna—was soon set to work at a piano version of the first act of *Valkyrie*.

Wagner's greatest satisfaction came during the intermission of his seventh concert; a message summoned him to meet Queen Victoria and Prince Albert. In the face of public opinion they had come to the old Hanover Square Rooms to hear the *Tannhäuser* overture.[19] The Queen inquired whether his operas might not be translated into Italian so that she might hear them! Evidently, not too much had changed since Handel's day. Wagner diplomatically rejected the well-meant idea. Certainly he knew that Meyerbeer's *L'Etoile du Nord* had been given in English at Drury Lane in March and that Victoria was only tarrying in her capital in order to hear its July production as *Stella del Nord* at Covent Garden's Royal

---

[19] It had already been introduced to London by Lindpaintner at the New Philharmonic. Harold Truscott has pointed out the debt Wagner's early style owed the work of Lindpaintner, especially to his *Faust* music and his opera *Der Vampyr*. Perhaps the respected composer from Coblenz was amused to recognize himself as a contributor to the music of the future.

Italian Opera. Her brother-in-law, Ernst II of Coburg-Gotha, was a Wagner devotee,[20] and the royal couple had come to Hanover Square to investigate this enthusiasm. Their solid, conservative taste for Meyerbeer and Mendelssohn could hardly encourage the visitor's hopes. But there was no doubt that Wagner was a very famous man, and the Queen and her husband were obviously curious about him.

8

On the last day of June he was back in Switzerland. The end of 1855 brought him friendship with Gottfried Keller, the poet-novelist, who had returned to Zurich from Berlin, where his celebrated *Der grüne Heinrich* had been written.

New ideas jostled *Valkyrie* as Wagner worked at its orchestration, not only the *Tristan* plan but also a project for an opera based on an incident from the Buddha's life. Despite attacks of erysipelas, he completed *Valkyrie* in the spring of 1856, and by the middle of May a sketch of the Buddhistic drama, "The Victors," was drafted.

The second half of the month was enlivened by a visit from Tichatschek. But a new eruption of his ailment sent Wagner in search of absolute rest. By making inroads into a thousand francs sent by Liszt as a subsidy for the expenses of score copying, he was able to undergo a new Alpine water cure at the establishment of a doctor allusively named Vaillant (summer, 1856). His sole companion was Fips, a spaniel presented him by the Wesendonks as successor to poor departed Peps.[21]

He was not yet ready to start the third *Ring* opera—about this time (June) it had been renamed simply *Siegfried*, and "Siegfried's Death" had become *The Twilight of the Gods*—and spent his time considering his Buddhistic plan and poring over Liszt's symphonic poems, which revealed to him ever new harmonic subtleties. He longed to hear them. Toward the end of August he was again at home, and in September music for the opening act of *Siegfried* was under way.

In October, after returning from Hungary, where his Mass had dedicated Gran (Esztergom) Cathedral, Liszt paid Wagner a second visit in Zurich.

---

[20] He had, in fact, wished Wagner to orchestrate and put the finishing touches to one of his amateur operas. The offer was rejected and with it a handsome fee. For his part, the royal composer did fear that Wagner might insist on too many alterations in his masterpiece!

[21] Papo, the parrot, had died early in 1851 and had been replaced by Jacquot. Old age claimed Peps in July, 1855, soon after Wagner's return from London. Pets were vital emotional links between the childless Wagners.

It was not as auspicious as the first. With her daughter, the Princess joined the company. Her eyes had long been open to Wagner's practice of relentlessly discarding people for whom he no longer had use. She knew that on that day when either Liszt's efforts on his behalf ceased or the Liszt-Wittgenstein purse snapped closed, the "eternal" friendship would die. But for a while one need kept it going. She watched Wagner devour her lover's creations. Her rancor grew from an innate realization that this opportunistic magpie had the almost unparalleled capacity for assimilation of a Shakespeare and that the styles of others, once incorporated within his own musical body, emerged transformed by a genius that threw most of his contemporaries into his shadow. Much as he admired and studied Liszt's symphonic works, he never encouraged their public performance. At the end of Liszt's visit both participated in a concert at St. Gallen, where *Orpheus,* which Wagner considered a masterpiece, and *Les Préludes* were heard. But at this time he was yearning to hear the notes known to him only on paper. There is little doubt that he wished his musical obligations to remain hidden. When the critic Richard Pohl wrote that *Tristan* was harmonically indebted to Liszt's example, Wagner felt himself the victim of a friend's indiscretion. The "secret," he believed, should have been kept strictly among professionals. While the second act of *Tristan* was germinating, he had a young pianist play Liszt for him frequently. One cannot overemphasize this composer's influence on the creation of the opera, as well as that of Chopin's harmonic vocabulary. Moreover, loving recollections of Berlioz's *Romeo* suffuse the score.

Wagner had shown annoyance with the latter's importance on Weimar programs. Princess Carolyne was thrusting him forward as counterbalance to Wagner. By neutralizing these two mighty forces, she hoped to find a place for Franz. During the second famous "Berlioz Week" at Weimar, in February, 1855, her contagious enthusiasm had been directed toward stimulating Berlioz to plan *The Trojans,* a cycle she hoped might checkmate the *Ring.*

There were, of course, glorious hours during Liszt's visit of six weeks; he played his "Dante" Symphony and read through much of *Valkyrie,* with Wagner interpreting the male parts. But both men, worn by illness, had difficulty keeping their masks of good-fellowship from falling occasionally. Moreover, Princess Carolyne exasperated Wagner. She had no patience with his dogmatic sermons, and doubtlessly he knew that she characterized his prose works as *"grosses bêtises."* So rickety was Wagnerian "thought" that a puff of derisive criticism, so easily exhaled by the brilliant Carolyne along with the smoke of her cigars, was sufficient to make it tumble down. Confirming his suspicion, she had opened Liszt's eyes to the true value of Wagner's ramshackle theorizing. Ironically, in later days she was to become

a scribbler as inveterate as Wagner and to compile her own series of monumental *"bêtises."*

In Zurich she was soon surrounded by the leading professors of the university, and in such company Wagner was obliged to surrender his usual
claim to omniscience, an eclipse he could not forgive. And even in less
competitive surroundings he was rivaled in multiloquence by a woman
whom Liszt held alone equal to the fiery assaults of Wagner's conversation,
which at times continued in monologue form for six to eight hours. On
one famous occasion he became so upset to discover himself not leading
the discussion and in fact to observe his guests quietly chatting with one
another that to regain their attention he simply opened his mouth and
screamed. At times he showed the emotional maturity of a four-year-old.

The crisis of the Liszt visit developed over Karl Ritter, that boy who
passed in and out of Wagner's orbit. After enjoying a romance with a
youthful actor in Stuttgart, he had embarked upon what Wagner called a
"curious" marriage, whose success he strongly doubted. Indeed, at the ill-
fated Sitten festival, Karl was in the company of a new enthusiasm, wealthy
young Baron Hornstein. Karl eventually brought both his wife and Hornstein to Zurich (although the latter soon fled after being upbraided by Wagner
for failing to supply his table with champagne) and again formed part of
the group at the Zeltweg. Karl, as Wagner observed, enjoyed making their
relationship into a Socrates-Alcibiades ritual.

Liszt had already met Karl and pronounced him "absurd." Perhaps vexation that Wagner would apparently tolerate someone for reasons of money
rankled and grew into Liszt's abusive outburst, which sent Karl storming
from the house. It would seem that Liszt's exasperation against Wagner had
been deflected to Karl. Wagner attempted to make peace, for with alarm he
correctly foresaw the end of it all in a suspension of his allowance. For a
while the incident poisoned his relationship with Karl and Frau Julie, who
took it in ill part that her boy had been left undefended. Matters became
so strained that Wagner felt he could no longer accept the Ritters' annuity.
In any case, he now had security in Otto Wesendonk's generosity.

After the departure of Liszt and Carolyne, Wagner worried about the
impression he had made. By letter he implored them to forget the unpleasant things about him, remembering only the kindness of which they
thought him worthy. Perhaps he feared he had betrayed his longing to see
their visit end. He was eager to take up work on *Siegfried*.

9

Beneath the cordial friendship uniting the Wesendonk and Wagner households simmered that dangerously increasing affection between Richard and

Mathilde. For years he had been careful to avoid any open action that might compromise the good will of her husband. Matters changed, however, when Mathilde contrived that Wagner live only fifty yards from her. The Wesendonks undertook to construct an ostentatious villa overlooking Lake Zurich on a ridge called the "Gabler" (later named the "Green Hill" by Wagner) in the suburb of Enge. By purchasing a modest house that adjoined the property, Mathilde saw a way of gratifying Wagner's oft-expressed wish for a home of his own with a garden. As a delicate gesture to assure his feeling of independence, she arranged that he pay a token rent.

Otto wisely kept his wife in Paris for many months during 1856 and 1857. Indeed, he had heartily recommended the earlier London journey to Wagner, whose growing influence on the exquisite and impressionable young Mathilde he already feared. (Anti-Semitism "aroused the disgust"—in Wagner's phrase—of the cosmopolitan North German who was as much at home in New York as in Paris.) Using all the weapons of her considerable feminine arsenal, she forced Otto, against his will, to buy the neighboring premises for the composer and from Paris wrote to Minna, "May this little house become a true refuge of peace and friendship." This naïvely optimistic averment gave the dwelling its name of "Asyl."

Wagner and Minna entered their new home late in April, 1857. *Mein Leben* relates that he awoke on Good Friday in a sun-filled room to find the garden in spring green and birds singing; reflecting on the day's significance, he rapidly conceived and outlined in prose a drama in three acts, *Parsifal.* There is, however, disagreement concerning the date of this sketch. Good Friday of 1857 had already passed when Wagner removed to the Asyl. It has been conjectured that his memory tricked him and that the event took place the following year, when he passed his only Good Friday on the Green Hill. On the other hand, the peaceful, optimistic mood in which he assures us the drama was born is difficult to reconcile with his turbulent spring of 1858, and an entry in his annals indicates that the idea came to him during a visit to the hill at the earlier date, when he inspected the renovations of architect Zeugherr. No matter the year, a joyous day doubtless led him to contrast its warmth with the cutting frost of that Good Friday when, as related in Wolfram's poem (Book IX), the wandering Parzival rode through the snow toward Fontane la Salvatsche and the hermitage of his uncle, Trevrizent, who was to become, in part, the model for Gurnemanz.

Wagner could work in the Asyl without disturbance. On the Zeltweg the noise of neighboring musicians and of a tinker had almost maddened him. Moreover, next door lived Frau Heim, an amateur soprano studying Sieglinde and Brynhild under his tutelage for those informal renditions of *Valkyrie* given among friends. Minna doubtlessly did not object to moving some distance from this beauty whose windows opened but inches from her own.[22]

By August 22, when the Wesendonks took possession of their estate—they first called it "Hochwyl," though Wagner coined and preferred "Wesenheim" —the orchestral sketch of the second act of *Siegfried* was complete, at which point Wagner had determined to interrupt work on the *Ring*. He wished to devote his flowing creative energies to *Tristan,* which with its dependent theme of *Parsifal* now consumed his thoughts. Negotiations with Breitkopf and Härtel over the publication of the *Ring* had failed. Not having appeared before the public with a new work in seven years, Wagner desired to make known his more mature style as well as to start a new flow of royalties. The *Ring* seemed doomed to a long paper life. So great was his need of revenue that he permitted his old colleague of Riga days, Johann Hoffmann, to produce *Tannhäuser* during the summer of 1857 at an ill-equipped theater in the Vienna suburbs. (Nestroy immediately composed a parody.) There was the illusion of deliverance when Wagner was contacted by a representative of the Brazilian emperor, who wished him to work in Rio, and it is amusing that for a while *Tristan* appeared to him as likely to satisfy the Italianate taste of Dom Pedro II.[23] The South American plan, of course, collapsed.

Deeper, less worldly reasons also led Wagner to leave Brynhild un-awakened on her fire rock. The first act of *Siegfried* shows his inspiration for the Nibelung subject losing its edge. And perhaps he believed himself unready to depict musically the goddess turned woman, for with precisely such a portrayal he had already failed in *Tannhäuser.* Subconsciously he laid out a sure but circuitous route to the awakened Brynhild; it was to travel by way of the impassioned figures of Isolde and the Paris Venus. Moreover, his embracing of Schopenhauer had, for the moment, run the *Ring* aground. How the whole affair was to be brought to a conclusion was painfully unclear. It took Wagner some time to see his way out of the difficulty by, in Nietzsche's words, claiming "the reef on which he was wrecked . . . as the *goal,* as the real end, as the true meaning of his voyage." In the meantime he gratefully felt the pressure of *Tristan* ripe within and ready to burst forth.

[22] Frau Pollert, the chastised Isabella of the *Liebesverbot* première, now an artist at the Zurich Opera, took over the reading of *Valkyrie.* Wagner had tailored the role of Brynhild to the prodigious vocal talents of his niece, Johanna, who had recently vexed him by appearing in Dorn's *Die Nibelungen* (Berlin, 1854). In 1857, Wagner unsuccessfully attempted to lure her to Zurich, obviously hoping to hear her essay Brynhild.

[23] This enlightened and modest ruler later turned up at the first Bayreuth festival, where, according to tradition, he dutifully indicated his occupation by inscribing the simple noun "Emperor" in the hotel registry.

With him as neighbor the Wesendonks, as Mathilde surely anticipated, found their lives rotating on a Wagnerian axis. Otto indulged his wife in her new role as muse to Wagner, whose rudeness soon reached the insufferable point of taking in ill part Otto's presence in his own drawing room. Mathilde emphasized to her husband the ideal, artistic bonds linking her soul to Wagner's. Having confidence in her virtue and appreciation of Wagner's genius, he awaited the day when her enthusiasm should spend itself. Minna also watched. But to her no explanations were vouchsafed, nor did she share Otto's faith.

He despised Wagner. But Mathilde's candor and her suicide threats made temporary compliance and patience Otto's only possible stratagems. He even agreed to give up his conjugal rights and to show an amicable face to the interloper. Otto rightly reasoned that the children were a bond that would one day bring his wife around, and, indeed, the shock of little Guido's death late in 1858 helped recall her to reality. Like her predecessor, Jessie Laussot, she enjoyed play acting and, though thrilled by the idea, was in very truth not eager to renounce day and enter Tristan's realm of night.

One cannot reproach Minna for believing that the incessant visiting, exchanges of billets-doux, and languishing attitudinizing on the part of Richard and his muse betokened something more than spiritual communion. He read Mathilde his complete prose works, and, what is more astounding, she listened.

They became artistic collaborators late in 1857 when he began to set five poems she had written under the influence of the *Tristan* text (completed in September). The first of them, *"Der Engel,"* celebrated him as an angelic redeemer come to bear the spirit upward.[24] Its music combined recollections of *Rhinegold* with intimations of *Tristan,* whose love duet in Mark's garden grew from the setting of the second poem, *"Träume,"* its verses evoking the unique reality alone shared by lovers. In *"Schmerzen,"* the third, Mathilde played with the day and night imagery of *Tristan,* mixing it with elements of Buddhistic rebirth. Wagner's monologues in Otto's parlor had fallen upon at least one pair of receptive ears. The Buddhistic sketch of "The Victors" was to become the focus of the lovers' later Venetian correspondence. The first chord of *"Schmerzen"* is the very dissonance that was to open the introduction to the second act of *Tristan* in its revised form. (Originally, it began with what is today the ninth bar.)

Wagner broke off work on the poems to complete his composition sketch of the first act of *Tristan,* which he had begun in October, and then suddenly

[24] Certainly Wagner saw Mathilde and not himself in this role when he set her text. The composition draft of *Tristan*'s first act is dedicated to "the angel who has lifted me so high!" The songs are here numbered in order of composition.

in mid-January, 1858, left for Paris under the pretext of a business trip to protect his French copyrights.

The Wagner-Wesendonk situation has been called a triangle by those who forget Minna. It was actually an impossible piece of geometry, about to be pushed into a yet stranger shape by emotional pressures. Wagner's absence of a few weeks served to reduce the stress.

In Paris, where he lived on money borrowed from Liszt and other friends, Wagner read Calderón, visited Liszt's daughter Blandine and her husband, Emile Ollivier (in 1870, as the statesman outmaneuvered by Bismarck, he was "with a light heart" to point his nation toward disaster), and met with Berlioz, who read him the text of *The Trojans*. Not surprisingly, Wagner judged it harshly, for it was antithetical to his concept of the epic, being, despite its vastness, a work of Gallic concision, far from the expansive Teutonic deliberations of the *Ring*. He wished never to see Berlioz again. Least of all did he wish to meet him within the precincts of those very few theaters capable of coping with works the size of *The Trojans* and his own cycle.

10

After a brief visit with Ernst Kietz at Epernay Wagner returned to Zurich on February 6 to find the Green Hill still enveloped in an uneasy atmosphere. Toward the end of the month the fourth Wesendonk song, *"Stehe still,"* came into being. In it the robust idiom of the opening act of *Siegfried,* here painting the striving of the universe, yields to the silken musical language of *Tristan*'s second act as Schopenhauerean self-extinction and the oblivion of love are invoked. A superb peroration depicting man, made wise through love, solving the riddle of nature anticipates in harmony, and, in fact, in its very pitches, that moment in *The Twilight of the Gods* when Waltraute describes Wotan's emotional remembrance of Brynhild.

Mathilde grew increasingly careless in manner and of reputation. To the haughty, condescending tone she at times adopted toward Minna the latter quickly gave answer. Taking her duties as muse most seriously, Mathilde saw no place for the plebeian wife even on the lowest slopes of the new Helicon at Enge. Clandestine visits to Wagner's rooms on the second floor of the Asyl could not remain hidden despite Mathilde's admonishing the household servant of the wisdom of silence. And, obviously, it was when Otto was absent from his villa that Wagner found the time most propitious to cross through the greenery to refresh himself at the spring of Hippocrene.

The intrigues did not bother Minna as much as their lack of subtlety. Even if the meetings were as ideally platonic as pictured in Wagner's Venetian diary (written after the fact and as much for posterity as for Mathilde), the lovers showed utter grossness in respect to the sensibilities of a wife willing to look away from their liaison were it conducted with some delicacy. She wrote, "Only the mean insults, the slights ought to have been spared me, and my ridiculously vain husband ought to have concealed everything from me." She was seriously ill, the drugs prescribed for her vulnerable heart and insomnia steadily undermining all nervous control. And the years with Wagner had not made her callous to hurt.

The inevitable crisis came when she intercepted a servant carrying a letter to Mathilde concealed by Wagner inside the rolled pencil sketch of the *Tristan* prelude. His extreme nervousness had betrayed that something was afoot. Undoubtedly letters as little or as much compromising as this one had passed between the houses before. But Minna, at the end of her endurance, found sufficient cause in its abstruse diction and, above all, in its familiar tone to confront her husband with an offer to leave if he wished to take Mathilde openly.

Wagner was thoroughly frightened; all the characters in the play were necessary to maintain his well-being: Minna's domestic talents, Mathilde's youthful beauty, love, and inspiration, and Otto's money—all were needed. Something had to be done quickly before an eruption rocked the sacred mount.

He sought to set right what he declared to be Minna's misconstruction of his letter. And as in that delicious scene in Rossini's *Barber* wherein the intrigants persuade Basilio that he should to bed, so Minna was prevailed upon to leave for a rest cure at nearby Brestenberg. Certainly Wagner's Saxon eloquence must have risen to dizzy heights of persuasiveness. But he foresaw that this new precaution would indeed be vain should she have contact with Mathilde before the departure. His fears were justified, for, though Minna promised silence, behind his back she made her way up the hill for some plain talking with Frau Wesendonk, an act which—so Wagner wrote his sister Klara—"in a crude and vulgar way struck at the delicacy and purity" of his relationship with Mathilde. The muse, pulled down to inferior spheres, was genuinely horrified to discover that Wagner had not confessed their love to his wife. And Otto was pleased to see in these developments the beginning of the end. He took Mathilde to Italy for a month to avoid the tide of tattle soon mounting from the town's *Kaffeeklatsche*.

Early in May, three weeks after Minna's precipitate actions had induced the crisis, Wagner set *"Im Treibhaus,"* thus completing the cycle of Wesendonk poems, a monument of the German lied. *"Treibhaus"* speaks of the cleft between a lover's natural yearning and the artificial environment in which society demands he live. Mathilde's text again called into play the

Tristan symbols of day as love's foe and of night as its friend, imagery hardly uncommon in German romantic poetry. The *Night Hymns* of Novalis (d. 1801) present almost literal parallels to such lines in *Tristan* while Friedrich von Schlegel's romance *Lucinde* (1799) is equally famous for anticipating the Wagnerian concept of day's delusion and the fulfillment of night. The music of *"Treibhaus,"* anticipating the introduction to the final act of *Tristan,* is built largely on a permutation of the second half of the opening phrase of the opera's prelude. This chromatic germ, which had appeared in Wagner's work as early as the recitative passages of his adolescent fantasia, here reaches an ultimate melancholic expression.

Wagner passed delightful hours in the Asyl with Karl Tausig. Liszt had sent his brilliant pupil, not yet seventeen, to play on the grand piano inveigled from Widow Erard by Wagner during his recent trip to Paris, a prize, Wagner proudly observed, listed in a catalogue at five thousand francs. The house sounded with Liszt. It is strangely affecting to read of the childless Wagner's solicitude for the eating, drinking, and smoking habits of the little Jewish lad from Warsaw who, after Mathilde's return, came to function as emissary between the separated lovers. Professedly, communication was broken for a period between the households. And all the while work on the garden scene of *Tristan* proceeded.

At Brestenberg Minna's enlarged heart pounded dangerously. But, though racked with fury and misery, she was ready to forgive. There were reassuring letters and visits from Richard. Upon her homecoming a devoted servant prepared a floral arch of welcome. Minna instructed that it be left standing, wishing to broadcast to the gossips of Zurich the triumphant nature of her re-entry. Mathilde was appalled by a gesture touching her prestige. How illusive were Wagner's hopes that time, working remedial wonders, would outwardly reconcile his women, offer some *modus vivendi,* and thus preserve the Asyl. But the furious muse had really expected Minna to have conveniently vanished by this time, leaving Wagner the Wesendonks' sole and untroubled tenant.

The finale was lento, prolonged by the mitigating bustle of summer guests. Wagner welcomed them enthusiastically, knowing that, when the last visitor had departed, he would quit the Asyl. His position was untenable.

Hans von Bülow and his bride, Liszt's daughter Cosima, had visited him on their honeymoon less than a year before, when they witnessed the birth of the *Tristan* poem after its long gestation. Now they returned, and, upon Tichatschek's vacating the guest room, Hans and Cosima, as during their earlier stay, slept under Richard's and Minna's roof, with Mathilde and Otto but yards away.

Klindworth arrived and accompanied Wagner's singing of *Rhinegold* and *Valkyrie*. Karl Ritter, reconciled with his master through Bülow, also appeared—Frau Ritter had restored Wagner's pension at the time he moved into the Asyl—as did Countess d'Agoult, Cosima's mother and Liszt's former mistress. Her presence probably helped keep him from Zurich at this time of crisis in Wagner's life. The Weimar circle was certainly aware of the turbulence over the Green Hill.

In mid-August, when the troubled company dispersed—the storm-charged atmosphere could not be ignored, despite some wonderful hours of music making and conversation—Wagner set out for Geneva, where difficulties over his passport detained him about a week. Then, via the Simplon, he made his way to Italy, entering Venice on August 29, accompanied by Karl Ritter, who had given up his experiment with matrimony. Minna remained in Zurich long enough to salvage what she could of the furnishings before creditors, hearing of Wagner's latest flight, swooped down upon his effects. Her destination was Dresden, where she was to put herself under the care of Dr. Pusinelli. After a calming separation, she and Richard planned again to take up life together. So troubled was he about her health that, while on his way to Venice, he sent her five telegrams, in addition to letters, within a single week.

Minna, firing a final salvo, wrote Mathilde, "Before my departure I must tell you with a bleeding heart that you have succeeded in separating my husband from me after nearly twenty-two years of marriage. May this noble deed contribute to your peace of mind, to your happiness."

II

Although incorporated into the Austrian monarchy after Napoleon's fall, Venice was not properly part of the German Confederation. Wagner knew that his movements would be under close surveillance but felt no real danger of being seized. In June he had called upon Grand Duke Carl Alexander of Weimar during the latter's stay in Lucerne. Certainly this prince, who at the time had asked that the *Ring* première be reserved for his capital, would extend a protective arm should difficulties arise in Austrian Italy.

To complete *Tristan* Wagner had to draw strength from solitude. Minna had written Mathilde, "Now Wagner will go back to his work, from which, to my great sorrow, he has long been so shamefully kept." As retreat he chose Europe's most quiet city, although journalists were perhaps not entirely wrong in guessing that the Venetian expedition also permitted him gingerly to put a toe into the sea of German politics and test its temperature.

He took up quarters in a stately, melancholy *palazzo* (one of the Giustiniani) on the Grand Canal. An abscess in the leg and old gastric and nervous symptoms for a time delayed the progress of *Tristan*. Breitkopf and Härtel were anxiously awaiting the remainder of a manuscript they had already started engraving, and Eduard Devrient, now Intendant at Karlsruhe, was arranging for the première in this Baden capital. The Erard piano, for a while held hostage by Wagner's Zurich creditors, had been hauled over the Alps and set up in his spacious palace apartment, whose walls he ordered covered with dark red hangings. Police Councilor Crespi, instructed to report all unusual activities of the notorious visitor, dutifully made complete notes, even leaving a record of the composer's color preferences. Ever since that boyhood adventure when he had helped pull such draperies from a Leipzig house of prostitution, they had kept strong associations for him. Apparently, they both shut out the world and could awaken those erotic feelings that had to be stimulated during his creative periods. As he grew older and excitement had to be whetted increasingly by artificial means, he surrounded himself with an ever more exotic décor of hangings, portieres, and counterpanes, about which he wandered in costumes that, by the time of *Parsifal,* approached the fetishistic.

On October 15 he had resumed work on the orchestral sketch of *Tristan's* second act, which had been broken off at Brangäne's observation, "I deceived my mistress but once." He wrote to Liszt that music flowed from his spirit like a gentle stream. Intensive work was interrupted only for a daily gondola ride to St. Mark's Square, where he dined with Karl Ritter and then promenaded through a city that excited him as a marvelous piece of stage scenery.

From Liszt came indications that his ties with Weimar were breaking. The scandalous reception given Peter Cornelius' *Barber of Bagdad* (December, 1858) by an organized segment of Weimar's public had been a demonstration against Liszt's private life as well as the music he stood for. In the sparkling opera, indebted to the influence of Berlioz, Cornelius' musical brilliance was complemented by his poetic talent. The delectable libretto, whose insufferable barber, Abul Hassan, is obviously in part a satire on Wagner, shows Cornelius as an admirer of the composer sufficiently independent to evaluate his pretensions at their just worth. Peter's sense of humor always hindered his becoming a true Wagnerite. Abul Hassan describes himself as dancer, mime, poet, musician, and great dramatist, and sums up his talents as those of a "total genius" (*"Gesamtgenie"*). Peter has him speak a jargon that is a delicious, highly polished mockery of Wagner's, and, when he salaams to Nureddin, the Wagnerian turn is heard.

The victim of a theatrical cabal, the work did not receive a fair hearing until after its composer's death. Although the dour Liszt preferred serious subjects, he was captivated by the *Cellini*-like elegance of the score, and he and certainly the Princess must have been diverted by the launching of a barb that, ironically, was to bring about a public display against their relationship.

They were nearing the end of their patience with Wagner, who lamented his poverty as he lived in palatial splendor on his restored allowance from the Ritters. And he had made it clear that in his opinion Liszt's Weimar duties were relatively trivial and should not be permitted to conflict with his responsibilities toward Richard Wagner.

At the beginning of 1859 Liszt exploded; a misunderstanding had arisen over a fee for a projected Weimar production of *Rienzi*. A complete break was avoided by facile explanations on Wagner's part, and their correspondence resumed its friendly but ever more self-conscious tone. Wagner now recognized the Princess as a clever, implacable foe. Moreover, with Liszt's impending departure from Weimar, his immediate usefulness, especially his intimate contact with the Grand Duke, was over. Wagner's brother Albert had already rebuked him for showing consideration to people only when they might be of service; their helpfulness over, they no longer existed for a man with a poor memory for past favors.

12

In Venice work on his score impelled Wagner toward *Parsifal* as Tristan metamorphosed into Amfortas. Their wounds of shame are closely affined, though Wagner, his faith in Goethe's redeeming woman seemingly withdrawn, was not dispatching an Isolde with healing arts to cure the afflicted Grail King. A youthful male virgin took her place. Wagner, though he did not yet realize the fact, was through with Mathilde and already conjuring Ludwig, his young Bavarian prince. To Mathilde he observed, "My poetic conceptions have always been so far ahead of my experiences that I can only consider these conceptions as determining and ordering my moral development."

A bridge between *Tristan* and *Parsifal* is formed by the sketch of "The Victors," whose completion Ludwig in later years was repeatedly to urge, its glorification of sensual renunciation evidently succoring his attempts to combat an ever more insistent homosexuality. In Venice, years before the appearance of Ludwig at his side, the tale of ecstatic resignation formed a similarly curious link between Wagner and Mathilde. Moreover, "The Victors" provided material for the most valuable commentary in his love letters to her, which so often have the tone of a schoolmaster lecturing a somewhat disappointing pupil. In them the inflections of Sachs instructing Eva are already discernible.

When Wagner in the final year of his life described "The Victors" as "related in a weaker sense to *Parsifal*," he was perhaps seeking to justify the abandonment of a plan not really completely relinquished until his last opera was under way with elements of the earlier Buddhistic project safely incorporated within it. *Mein Leben* still contemplated the eventual realization of the fragment that Wagner at another time considered completing as a poetic legacy to his son, who, so he thought, might one day set it to music. This whimsical idea shows how deeply he regretted failure to find a musical point of departure for his sketch. Not until its Indian asceticism was, in *Parsifal,* converted into his own neoromantic version of medieval mysticism could he find the musical vocabulary with which to express his drama of spiritual "becoming," beside which even the musical refinements of *Tristan* seem blatant.

"The Victors" remained unwritten because, among other reasons, Wagner could not conceive it operatically. A literary exercise without musical stimulus, the quiescent tale resisted translation into grand opera's language.[25] On the other hand, as had been the case with *Lohengrin,* he was immediately able to apprehend the Parsifal subject in terms of what might be called the Meyerbeer Romanesque, that genre of *Robert the Devil.* It at least furnished a starting point; thereafter he could refine his conception and camouflage its patent origins.

Nonetheless, despite artful dovetailing and polishing, exotic veneers do not fully mask either the joints in *Parsifal* or its core of solid, grand opera deal. (The bells of Monsalvat ring out the opening theme of the composer's first success, *Rienzi.*) Parisian devices abound—the rolling scenery of the Odéon, those ever-effective ecclesiastical processions of Scribe, the collapsing splendors of a magic palace, one of the perdurable effects of Parisian machinists (and in this case obviously inspired by the climax of Gluck's *Armide*), the Opéra's inevitably tolling church bells, and even, *horresco referens,* traces of the Passover scene in Halévy's *Juive.*

Parsifal, that wonderful patchwork, grew from mixing such elements with bits of Wolfram von Eschenbach's romance and pieces of Wagner's own sketches for both "Jesus of Nazareth" and, especially, "The Victors." The latter, first conceived when his love for Mathilde seemed doomed to remain unfulfilled, returned to his mind in Venice after the ruin of their romance.

The sketch of 1856 pictures Ananda, a disciple of Buddha, hospitably given well water by a maiden. She falls deeply in love and seeks out his master (like the Emperor in *The Wibelungs,* he is on his last journey) beneath a tree at the city gate to ask permission for union with Ananda. The Buddha reveals her identity in a former incarnation as an overproud

---

[25] A theme constructed for "The Victors" did find its way into the *Ring* and significantly sounds its promise of regeneration as Wotan, in the final act of *Siegfried,* resolves to face extinction with joy. Seemingly, the theme was also to appear in a quartet Wagner planned at Lake Starnberg in 1864.

girl who scorned the love of an unfortunate, an arrogant act she must now expiate by experiencing the torture of unsatisfied passion. Only by sharing Ananda's vow of chastity may she stay at his side. Grasping this condition of salvation, she joyfully agrees, and Ananda receives as his sister one who has risen to his own level of self-denial. Elsa no longer questions but acquiescently follows Lohengrin, whose abstention on his wedding night has become a rule of life. In the figure of the maiden, who was one day to become Kundry in *Parsifal*, Wagner sought finally to resolve his concern with the motive of incest.

In one sense Mathilde Wesendonk was the Rosalie of his middle age, a respectable young woman who gave him not only love and inspiration but also financial security. As with Jessie Laussot, he encouraged her to play the role of Sieglinde, the bride-sister. And Mathilde was also adept in representing the less bellicose moods of Brynhild, the wish-maiden to whom the god could address monologues of unprecedented length. As the creative passion unleashed in *Valkyrie* had channeled itself into *Tristan*, Mathilde assumed the trappings of Isolde, while poor Otto, who would have preferred the avenging hounds and spear of Hunding, found himself forced by his wife to assume the permissive mien of Mark.

Before the move to the Asyl, Wagner saw resignation as the only solution to his infatuation for Mathilde. "The Victors" was a product of this frame of mind. His restricting union with Minna he dramatized by picturing himself in correspondence as "an outlaw, an impossible person," in short, as Siegmund, whose ancestor, Sigi, the *Volsunga Saga* described as "a wolf in holy places." The triangle in *Tristan* was but a more sophisticated extension of that in *Valkyrie,* and Wagner enjoyed viewing himself as the self-pitying Volsung. There are few more obviously autobiographic passages in Wagner than Siegmund's recital of his sadness, tinged with some surprise, that the world obstinately refused him comprehension: "Evil lay upon me. What I held right, others considered arrant. What appeared wrong to me, others cherished. Feuds arose wherever I appeared. My presence kindled animosity. Striving for joy, I but awakened woe." (His letters to Mathilde abound in "Siegmundisms": *"Dorthin, von wo ich mir Trost holen wollte, brachte ich Unruhe und Leiden."* ["Where I sought solace, I brought anxiety and harm."]) Without doubt Wagner-Siegmund's puzzlement was sincere. Why, when he approached, did the Hundings of this world feel inclined to lock up their wives and cupboards and bolt the door? Had Otto studied *Valkyrie* carefully, he would have realized earlier that Hunding's fatal error had been to grant an unwelcome guest the shelter of his roof.

Like the prelude, the finale to Richard's and Mathilde's personal drama was languid and renunciatory. The music of the acts between can be only tentatively reconstructed from passages in incompletely issued diaries and letters. Here is found an *agitato,* there, *con amore* or *dolce,* and *pastoso* characterizes many a page. But, bearing in mind Wagner's dishonesty in autobiographic matters, one can only with difficulty decide whether or not there was an *attacca subito.*

In a long letter of October 19, 1861, he declared to Minna that though passion had entered into his "originally delicate and pure" relationship with Mathilde, temperance had prevailed. A more sure guide in this matter is certainly the score of *Tristan,* which, paralleling, indeed, inspiring, the lovers' conduct, grew on the Green Hill in an atmosphere of real suffering too often cheapened by that self-conscious posturing Wagner brought to human relationships. But the master dissembler could not lie in his works.

In Mark's garden, Tristan and Isolde, in the manner of Richard and Mathilde, pause to examine the philosophical and etymological implications of the conjunction "and." Yet, despite such pretentious talk and much sham Schopenhauer, the great scene exudes a passion impossible to reconcile with the concept of abstinence. Certainly copulation had never before been so graphically rendered in musical terms. The shattering evaded cadence that sounds as Mark bursts in upon the lovers confirms the flagrant circumstances in which they are surprised, and Isolde's earlier conversation with Brangäne would indicate that other love nights had already been enjoyed whenever Tristan could safely approach the garden. There are limits to what can be even symbolically represented on the stage, and the music must tell the full tale to the audience, too often led astray by the unruffled attitudes of soprano and tenor, usually shaped like Giotto's granite hills, singing at one another while decorously seated on a papier-mâché bench.

The *Liebestod* eventually transmutes the sensual rapture of Tristan and Isolde into a spiritual ecstasy. Similarly, the theme of "The Victors" sustained Wagner and Mathilde in a state of exaltation after Minna had put an end to what was evidently the less abstemious phase of their affair. Mathilde's decision to cease sexual intercourse with her husband during the period of her closest association with Wagner did not mean that she had become all spirit. The fastidious lady probably desired but one lover at a time.

While recasting "The Victors" in the Giustiniani, Wagner wrote that at this particular epoch of his life he had arrived at insights carrying him even beyond Schopenhauer and demonstrating a path to complete pacification of the will through that higher love flowering from a sexual relationship. He could hardly have been more frank. Allied to this conception of a love rising above the carnal instinct, he saw an analogous ascendance of the racial will (*"Gattungs-Wille"*). Thus, he was already preparing that uneasy union in *Parsifal* of his theories of sexual abnegation, Schopenhauerean compassion, and—alas—race.

In Venice Wagner was again studying Schopenhauer. This reading, his perusal of a history of Buddhism, and the events of the preceding months made "The Victors" gravely meaningful to him, and, as the orchestral web of *Tristan* grew, he also strove to come to terms musically with the Indian tale. His lack of success evidently made him reconsider his sketch and discover in it a serious flaw. That the Buddha was perfect and free of passion deprived the plot, he felt, of the dramatic tensions that generated music. Moreover, Ananda, the young monk, though nearer the problems of life, had already overcome the temptations of the flesh. Thus, two of the three leading characters were without those conflicts forming the basis of Wagner's dramaturgy and at the very time shaping the searing music of *Tristan*.

Joseph Kerman has brilliantly described *Tristan* as a drama of progress toward a condition of illumination. The hero's triumph is self-enlightenment, this developing experience forming the material of the uncompromising work. The image of mighty death invoked by Tristan in Mark's garden finally confronts him as he falls purified by a suffering worthy of Isolde's final mystic hymn. *Parsifal* logically proceeded from *Tristan* with Isolde's *Liebestod* and a revised concept of "The Victors" as the fascinating links between. In Karl Friedrich Köppen's book on Buddhism Wagner believed he had found suggestions that might transform "The Victors" into a *Tristan*-like work in which the motive of human growth, of triumph over limitations, might involve the figure of the Buddha himself.

The Buddha originally held that women, captives of the sexual function, were unable to achieve that state of undisturbed concentration and contemplation necessary for redemption. Through observing the experience of Ananda and the maiden, the sage relaxed the stricture and admitted women among the elect. In this gesture Wagner saw his opportunity. By an act of love the Buddha had reached his own perfection. His earthly career was over. Through an intuitive and compassionate emotional experience he disposed of the final problem yet detaining him in existence. So, in a sense, had the Dutchman once redeemed himself.

This intuitive pity was to flow into Parsifal. He is first introduced as an unthinking boy who meaninglessly kills a fowl. And it was precisely the slaughtering of a bird in a Venetian poulterer's stall that incited that letter to Mathilde in Wagner's Venetian diary in which he dilated upon mankind, its road to redemption blocked by an undeveloped or studiously neglected capacity for pity and compassion. He assured her that one day his meaning would be clear in the Good Friday scene in *Parsifal*. Indeed, Parsifal's first step toward maturity is taken when he throws away bow and arrows. The drama that would see the light nearly a quarter of a century later was clearly forming in Wagner's mind as he completed the second act of *Tristan* and struggled to drive a musical wedge into the tale of Ananda and the maiden.

Of course, Wagner would not be himself unless he sowed tares in the often rich field of his Venetian writing. He is embarrassing when describing his flirtation with suicide. And when he compares his borrowings to the devotional mendicancy of a Buddhist monk, he is unintentionally hilarious. His first entry after the flight from the Asyl presents a favorite fantasy of his death, the final scene of *"Hochzeit"* with Mathilde clasping his corpse in view of all. (Otto's and Minna's place in the tableau is not given.) And early in 1859 Wagner set forth in the diary yet another vision of his end; Mathilde, as Brynhild, leaps into his grave of flames, their ashes mingling into one eternal ur-substance (*"ein göttlicher Urstoff der Ewigkeit"*). He idolized her to such a point that, when they met again, he was shocked to discover reality to be far from the Venetian dream. In any case, in March, when the second act of *Tristan* was finished with her gold pen, his Mathilde-fever was already clearly beginning to subside. She had served his purpose.

Suicide had been Tristan's wish as he let his guard fall before Melot's blade. Only through death could he and Isolde crown their yearning with spiritual union. But Wagner himself was gradually casting off the Tristan-Schopenhauer-Buddha mood in which existence was held an error. He was emerging, no longer a figure of despair but of pragmatic resignation. Wagner-Tristan was slowly turning into Wagner-Sachs. His plans for *Parsifal* were set, but the climb to Monsalvat was years in the future. At the moment he seemed sharper than ever for practical and worldly matters.

But "The Victors" remained in the recesses of his mind till his last day. Death found him at work on an essay combining observations on marriage (going back to his notes for "Jesus of Nazareth") with both the racial theories of his late essays and the Buddhistic sketch. His pen was retracing the tale of Ananda and the maid when it fell from his hand.

VIII

Paris: Victory from Defeat

I

With the completion of the second act of *Tristan* Wagner ended his seven-month stay in Venice. A variety of factors brought about his departure. Saxony was increasing pressure on the Austrian authorities to expel him. Moreover, he faced the termination of the allowance that was permitting him to scrape through an awkward period when his wife's needs in Germany had to be answered as well as his own. The Ritters, who came from Narva in Russian Estonia, had suffered severe losses as a result of the Crimean War. Minna indicated that he could no longer lay them under contribution, and he had to make new provision for his sustenance. In addition, hostilities between Napoleon III and Franz Josef threatened—June was to bring the battles of Magenta and Solferino—and Wagner feared being cut off from his own retreat to Switzerland. Milan was already in a state of siege when he embraced Karl in farewell at the Venice station. It was their last meeting; although they corresponded for a while, the relationship began to dissolve with the pension.

Via Milan Wagner made his way to Lucerne, where he arrived on March 28, 1859. The Erard followed him over the St. Gotthard and was set up in spacious quarters at the Hotel Schweizerhof. There the final act of *Tristan,* so impatiently awaited by Breitkopf's engravers, came into being. He journeyed to Zurich to visit the Wesendonks, and they returned his calls in Lucerne, a public show of amicability that helped Mathilde's reputation recover somewhat from the damages of the preceding summer. Otto, now certain of his wife, showed toward Wagner what a neighbor described as "an excessive enthusiasm." In Germany, Minna bristled up when she learned that these relations had been resumed.

Wagner wrote her a letter recalling her flight from Königsberg of over twenty years before. Admitting that as a young husband he had offered only poverty and jealousy, he asked her, nonetheless, to remember his quick forgiveness. He was tacitly entreating for similar pardon and implied that the Wesendonk crisis had been a by-product of his artistic temperament and nothing more. (In his letters to Mathilde the purple Venetian style was yielding to fraternal chattiness.) But Minna, implacable, replied with references to Jessie Laussot and Bordeaux. Obviously she felt that the Dietrich business had been paid for many times over.

Tristan was completed on August 6. The ink of its final notes was still wet when he wrote to Minna of the lovers, "May he rest in peace, and she too!" The Tristan-Wesendonk malady had passed.

Wagner was determined to settle permanently in Paris, for it was imperative that once again he be in direct contact with major musical institutions. Otto provided the means of removing him from Switzerland by purchasing the copyrights of *Rhinegold* and *Valkyrie* for twelve thousand francs.[1] By mid-September Wagner was in Paris, resolved to set himself up in style. Minna was needed, and he had made up his mind to have her back.

In Dresden, Dr. Pusinelli was reluctant to permit his patient to re-enter her husband's world. Recovering slowly, she herself wished the reunion deferred. But Wagner insisted, maintaining that as he could destroy her, so could he save her. However, he took the precaution of urging Pusinelli to make Minna understand that for reasons of her health she must not expect ever to sleep with her husband. There was sufficient money to set up a comfortable household, Wagner told her, describing the Wesendonk advances as those of a benefactor who wished to remain anonymous. If he did not want Minna the wife, after a year of separation he desperately needed Mother Minna. To Pusinelli he painted a new golden age for the poor creature, and on November 17, with many misgivings, good old "Mutz" arrived in Paris with dog and parrot.

2

Ever since Belloni's visit to Switzerland, the possibility that Paris might mount its first Wagnerian opera had hovered before the fee-hungry composer. *Tristan* was now his choice. Its success in France might shame the

---

[1] Otto, so shabbily treated in *Mein Leben,* was at least given a kind of monument in *Meistersinger,* in which he appears as the heavy-footed merchant, Pogner, willing to invest some of his commercial gains in German art. There was a steady improvement in Otto's operatic career. He had first been cast as Hunding, and during the Asyl and Venice days Wagner obviously conceived of him as Mark. All three parts were written for the bass voice.

Germans and perhaps awaken their interest in the *Ring*. But from the beginning the path of *Tristan* toward production was uphill.

Devrient at Karlsruhe had abandoned it as unplayable by his relatively modest company. When Wagner represented the work as highly practical, he had, of course, deceived himself as well as others. He admitted to Mathilde, "The fruit of *Tristan* is not easily gathered." It (and also the future *Meistersinger*) at least would not be at the mercy of machinists, an advantage, to be sure. But, upon reading the score again, he wondered whether it did not overstep the limits of musical performance. At times he himself feared the opera to be inexecutable, and it is all the more understandable that at Karlsruhe, without the composer's guidance, one of the most revolutionary musical creations of the century presented insoluble riddles; and Baden dared not offend Saxony by inviting him into German territory. In Paris, on the other hand, he could personally coach his artists. But first the capital was to be prepared by concerts presenting selections from his earlier works along with the *Tristan* prelude. Then, perhaps, a repertory of Wagner operas might be established in a Parisian theater and finally *Tristan* unveiled. He observed that his role in France seemed fated to be that of the eternal debutant.

On this visit Paris did not ignore his presence. He was to find a local coterie including Saint-Saëns, Gounod, Léon Kreutzer, Stephen Heller, Champfleury (Jules Fleury-Husson), and Gustave Doré. Even the customs inspector assigned to Wagner had proved an admirer. The aging Rossini received him well, and men of the quality of Catulle Mendès, Gautier, and Baudelaire sought him out. Bülow had arrived to assist with the concert rehearsals, and a group of enthusiasts helped concoct a French translation of *Tannhäuser*. Wagner no longer thought much of *Rienzi; Tannhäuser,* a more subtle work but with the same strong aroma of Meyerbeer about it, had, he thought, the best chance of making his local fortune and paving the way for *Tristan.*

The concerts took place during January and February, 1860, in the Théâtre Italien, formerly that Théâtre de la Renaissance in which *Liebesverbot* was to have been performed twenty years before. Despite an unfriendly press and catastrophe at the box office, the series proved a *succès d'estime.* Berlioz, Meyerbeer, Auber, Reyer, Gounod, Gevaert, and Baudelaire had added luster to well-papered houses. Baudelaire wrote Wagner, "I capitulated to you immediately." The composer's attempt to recoup his losses by similar concerts in Brussels during March only aggravated his plight. All his money had been consumed including that more recently advanced to him by Schott and Sons of Mainz, to whom he had sold the *Rhinegold* rights really belonging by previous purchase to Otto Wesendonk. Happily, Countess Kalergis was to step forward and assume the deficit. Gautier had celebrated her beauty as that of a *femme-cygne* in his "Symphonie en blanc Majeur." An old Wagner enthusiast, this figure of international society and politics had attended the *Tannhäuser* première in Dresden. Once a piano pupil of Chopin, she was a rarity for her time—a musical and levelheaded lady-Wagnerite—Delacroix's *Journal* revealing her disdain for Wagner's theories. The latter had once looked upon her with "disgust" (*"Abscheu"*) as a diplomatic intrigante; however, her interest in him and her money helped change this attitude.

In gratitude, Wagner arranged in her honor a private reading in May, 1860, of the second act of *Tristan;* Klindworth was imported from London to preside at the piano, and Madame Garcia-Viardot and Wagner divided the vocal parts. At the conclusion he was disappointed to discover Madame Kalergis sitting absolutely dumb; Berlioz, the only other guest, found his tongue to remark tactfully upon the ardor of the composer's delivery. Wagner blamed his guests' lame reaction on Viardot, suspecting that, as a Berlioz partisan, she had not done her best. Apparently Wagner always remained unaware that his performances as a practical musician often rendered an audience mute. His wrong notes and frenzied howls as he played and sang *Tannhäuser* for Carvalho in the autumn of 1859 had left this worthy Parisian impresario badly shaken, and Wagner could in all innocence and truth proudly write Mathilde of the extraordinary impression he had made. Typically, he passed over his own singing deficiencies to pounce on those of Garcia-Viardot, who had read the difficult music at sight. Though he later praised the skill and expression of her extempore Isolde, at the time he saw enemies everywhere, even taking offense at Berlioz's honest appraisal of his Paris concerts. The French composer, he felt, was merely envious.

Wagner had sent him one of the first copies of *Tristan,* inscribed with gratitude to the creator of *Romeo,* and, despite illness, Berlioz attended all three of Wagner's Paris concerts. On the whole his review was complimentary. If he could make little of the *Tristan* prelude and found a certain blatancy in the *Tannhäuser* music, he did extol the *Lohengrin* prelude as a masterpiece. At these concerts the *Tristan* prelude was performed with its "assuaging" concert ending (composed some weeks before) and the *Dutchman* overture with a freshly created coda in *Tristan* style.

Berlioz had difficulty appreciating the *Tristan* idiom. No doubt his French taste for clarity of texture and of articulation was offended by the prelude's thick impasto and conjoined structure. Wagner himself was frightened by the score's originality and during rehearsals had found himself leading bewildered orchestral players from note to note "as if uncovering gems in a mine," a task made more difficult by the fact that the musicians were confused by his infamous fluid beat. Berlioz cannot be accused of jealousy in voicing a frank opinion. But certainly he grew bitter as rumors gathered that the doors of the Opéra, so firmly closed against his *Trojans,* would soon swing open to *Tannhäuser.* And most aggravatingly, the forces thrusting forward the foreign work were political, not musical.

3

For the moment the Italian War of the preceding summer was forgotten. Magenta lived on gloriously as the name for Verguin's new synthetic dye made fashionable by Eugénie, Empress of the French. At Solferino almost forty thousand lives had been thrown away, and although Louis Napoleon was usually not one to count cost, clearly his army could bleed to death before the strongholds of the defensive Quadrilateral—such as Verona and Mantua—that remained in Austrian hands. Moreover, with Prussia preparing to mobilize on the Rhine, the French flank was menaced. Napoleon and Franz Josef patched together the Treaty of Villafranca. Although Austria ceded Lombardy, *boulevardiers* were soon to quip that a secret clause in turn forced *Tannhäuser* upon the Opéra.

Indeed, the Austrian Embassy was behind Napoleon's surprising command that the work be mounted. Princess Pauline Metternich, niece and wife of the Austrian ambassador, had the Emperor's ear. A close friend of Eugénie, she was a shallow, outspoken aristocrat who indulged a freedom of expression and action that made her one of the most discussed and quoted figures in the capital. She took few pains to disguise her opinion that the court at the Tuileries was more than a few cuts below that of Vienna's Hofburg. Having heard *Tannhäuser* in Dresden, she saw in its composer a controversial German artist she could adopt as her own protégé and enjoy imposing upon Parisian society. Who he really was she was not quite sure, and *Tannhäuser* must have been one of her more cloudy memories. For quite a while she was under the impression that Wagner was a composer mainly of fugues and announced that she would just love to play them on her piano, a Viennese instrument he discovered to be perennially and hopelessly out of tune. He found her a very queer sort, foolish, often asinine. But he treated her as if she were a Socrates and had his reward. To please her the Emperor charged the Opéra to give Wagner authority in all that might concern the proper preparation of *Tannhäuser* (mid-March, 1860). He had observed of Paris, *"Möglich ist hier alles!"* ("Anything is possible here!")

The Prussian and Saxon embassies, somewhat embarrassed by the Fatherland's attitude toward its famous son, suddenly showed interest in his problems. Attempts were made to influence King Johann.[2] It seemed odd that a

[2] Bülow was also using his influence at the Prussian Embassy; moreover, Madame Kalergis was related to Baron von Seebach, the Saxon ambassador.

man to whom an emperor opened the resources of the world's greatest theater might be arrested and perhaps executed should he return home. Not surprisingly, Paris came to look upon *Tannhäuser* as part of a mysterious Germanic intrigue.

Formal rehearsals began at the end of September, and for almost six months Wagner supervised them. Little that he demanded—and he was not shy—was denied. He was happy with the cast. At his request the young leading tenor of the Hanover Opera, Albert Niemann, had been imported for the title role. Bülow, who stood by Wagner during rehearsals, has left his impressions of the marvelous décor, which no other stage could rival. Wagner rejected the scenic plans three times before they were drawn to his satisfaction. The orchestra was without peer, and the entire institution worked with an efficiency and attention to detail that taught him much about the manner in which to run an opera house. Petipa was to design the ballet. And it was here that the first serious difficulties presented themselves.

Because of the habits of the Opéra's subscribers, especially members of the Jockey Club, many of whom had mistresses in the ballet, it was traditional to offer dancing as part of a work's second act, when these gentlemen, arriving from dinner and cognac, were best prepared to admire a shapely calf and a well-turned bosom. For aesthetics of this nature *Opera and Drama* had made no provision. The management remained unimpressed by Wagner's arguments that his second act presented no dramatically valid excuse for introducing dancers and appeared unmoved when he enthusiastically pointed out that, on the other hand, his opening scene, which he described to Julie Ritter as *"etwas schwach"* ("somewhat weak"), would gain by an elaborate extension of the revels at Venus' court. Through the years he had been dissatisfied with his rather tame bacchanal, and he now declared himself delighted not only to create an elaborate ballet tableau but also to rewrite and amplify the ill-defined, flimsy part of Venus, who, he wrote Mathilde, would have to "improve her singing." Deaf to the admonitions of officials who warned that the most influential and vocal segment of the public would be absent during the first act and therefore feel cheated of its ballet, he set about recasting the Venusberg scene in the idiom of *Tristan*.

At this time the subject of Parsifal was stirring in him again, and with marvelous rapidity his pen sketched Kundry's great predecessor, the Paris Venus. Correspondence reveals that his mind was dwelling on the temptress in Klingsor's garden as he transformed the stiff and lifeless Dresden goddess into a wounded, proud woman. And, not content with rewriting and adding to the music of the enchantress and her followers [3] in the flanking acts, he also tightened and retouched other scenes.

[3] Her text was expanded; the old words were largely reset, added material being

The world is richer for Wagner's refusal to compromise and gain an easy success, and for his determination to give Paris his best, even though he must have known it would be rejected. But artists who had prepared themselves from the Dresden score can be forgiven their distress upon learning that to a considerable extent they had to begin again. The Paris orchestra was equal to anything, but Madame Tedesco, the Venus, who had with effort proudly mastered the Wagner of 1843–44, suddenly found herself struggling with a vocal line midway in style between Isolde's curse and Kundry's hysterics.

It was a miscalculation to believe that a production could be kept so long in preparation without all concerned becoming sick of the affair. Over one hundred and sixty rehearsals were held. The orchestra broke into rebellion. The Emperor had given Wagner carte blanche, and, except for some weeks when he fell victim to a fever, he personally drilled the entire personnel.

By March, 1861, it was obvious that *Tannhäuser* must soon come to performance or sink down of its own weight. But by rewriting the opening scene Wagner had left Petipa little time to compose any but the most obvious choreography. As late as mid-December, 1860, Wagner had written Otto Wesendonk, "The first dance scene isn't begun; and I have as yet no idea how I will do it." (In January he was still undecided about abridging the song contest!) Moreover, none of the Opéra's ballerinas would consent to appear in the first act, and with effort Petipa found near the Porte St. Martin, three Hungarian ladies, known for their fairy pantomimes, who consented to mime the Three Graces. Seven years before, when the Pomeranian city of Stettin had mounted *Tannhäuser,* even its provincial critic raised his voice against ballet costumes at Venus' court. In Paris, too, there seemed no way around the tradition of starched gauze, and the Hungarian Graces were outfitted in pink *tutus.*

Minna had misgivings about the new Venusberg and lamented her husband's "hocus-pocus of Venus apparitions." With tenuous precedent, he had declared the Hörselberg near Eisenach—traditionally the haunt of fiery demons—to have been the abode of the goddess of love. A resident of Thuringia, she was addressed as Frau Venus. When Wagner, in Paris, first blocked out the extended revels at her mountain court, he thought much in terms of Nordic mythology. As a mob of bacchantes drove in a menagerie of animal monsters, the Strömkarl was to emerge from whirling waters (into which maenads would perhaps throw the head of murdered Orpheus!)

---

composed directly to French verses. (Later he labored to fit a German translation to this vocal line.) The *"Geliebter, komm"* of 1843–44 was given a new sensuality by a change from duple to triple time and its transposition down half a tone. The meter of the sirens' song was similarly altered. Of course, much was reorchestrated to accord with the voluptuous texture of the new bacchanal.

and accompany the frenzied dancing on his marvelous violin. As **Wagner** developed this Venusberg pantomime, he may have recalled Homunculus' remark to Mephistopheles: "Only the romantic spirits are known to you; a genuine specter can be classic, too." Wagner was obviously attempting his own *"klassische Walpurgisnacht."* Although centaurs, nymphs, fauns, amoretti, the Graces, and the dismembered Orpheus formed a part of the original scheme of the Paris bacchanal—indeed, nymphs had figured in the Dresden ballet—the Mediterranean element grew steadily stronger and ousted the Strömkarl, who had so pleased Wagner in the beginning, and the stage filled with Nereids, Tritons, and elaborate visions of Europa, Leda, and their lover Jupiter in his disguises as bull and swan.

Wagner's tableaux of classical mythologic orgies were, of course, naïve enough, resembling something in the "ancient" manner that Richard Geyer of the Kreuz School might have turned out for Professor Sillig. As a youngster he had been entranced by Genelli's feeble water color, "Dionysius Educated by the Muses," belonging to his brother-in-law Friedrich Brockhaus. (Eventually Cosima acquired it.) To the end of his days Wagner pictured the ancients in terms of such Biedermeier *Kitsch,* which unmistakably pervades Venus' cavern. "I really would like to have Genelli's water colors at hand," Wagner wrote Mathilde while planning the new ballet. "He made these mythological orgies very plausible." Mephistopheles' words fit Wagner's predicament: "I mastered northern witches easily, but over these foreign spirits I've little control." The classical Walpurgis Night of *Tannhäuser* is embarrassingly adolescent, and it was unfortunate that he chose to turn this vulnerable side and show what he himself termed a *"mythologisches Gesindel"* ("mythological crew") to Europe's most jaded, cynical public. The miraculous Venusberg music could not yet redeem the situation; its *Tristan* vocabulary was still beyond the understanding of most.

In general, the book of *Tannhäuser* amused the city even before the première. Why a man would even for a moment consider quitting the goddess of love simply evaded a Parisian's comprehension. In a version of the story by a fifteenth-century Frenchman, Antoine de la Sale, the hero, after quitting the magic mountain, returned to taste its joys for eternity, the cynical ending also found in the German folk tale. Wagner's sanctimonious finale had flown in the face of tradition and aroused resentment in Germany; in Paris it drew gleeful ridicule.

The vast sums involved, the energies expended, and the time consumed—all fed the jokes and tales about *Tannhäuser* that traveled the boulevards. Rumor even spread that the scenery had burned. In the world of opera little is relished as much as another's fiasco. The carrion birds were awaiting the corpse. And since an unbreakable tradition decreed that no composer might conduct his own première, a slow, painful musical demise of the

Paris *Tannhäuser* seemed inevitable during the final rehearsals when the baton passed from Wagner into the hands of Pierre Dietsch,[4] an incompetent routineer; tempi wavered, nuance vanished. But outside forces determined that the victim not linger in agony but succumb quickly to a carefully planned assassination.

4

The three première performances of *Tannhäuser* in Paris (the first occurred on March 13, 1861) take their place among the most shameful events in France's musical history. Members of the Jockey Club not only resented Wagner's flouting their traditions but also detested the Austrian clique surrounding the Emperor. By disrupting *Tannhäuser,* they could show disapproval of Wagner and Princess Pauline in particular and of Germans and Austrians in general. Moreover, many of the Jockeys were Legitimists and looked forward to mortifying Louis Napoleon and Eugénie sitting in state. Armed with hunting whistles and flageolets, which they blew on command, the Jockeys turned the carefully prepared presentations to shambles. Whistling, hissing, shouts, and laughter filled the great hall. When others protested, fights broke out. Many times the stage action was forced to halt as the artists helplessly awaited quiet. At the slightest decrease in volume of chaotic sounds the valiant musicians picked up the thread, and by a miracle of determination all three performances were fought through to the end. Practiced tacticians, the Jockeys had let the opening scene unfold in silence during the first performance, the outburst when the shepherd appeared in the Wartburg valley thus having the success of a sudden strike from ambuscade. Throughout the disorders, they applied the technique of the deceptive calm followed by turbulence. Wagner, who had used a claque to advantage at the initial *Tannhäuser* performances in Dresden, had unwisely eschewed such services in Paris. With organized help he might have routed the enemy. But he was caught without experienced retaliatory shock troops.

Wagner did not attend the third *Tannhäuser*. Like Princess Metternich, Minna, too, had been publicly insulted, and he could take no more. But his demand that the score be returned was only reluctantly acceded to by a management now aware that, once the rowdies tired, the opera might slip into the repertory and prove itself at the box office. Characteristically, Wagner came to believe that the German Jews in the audience had been at the bottom of the tumult.

[4] Ironically, he was the composer who set the Opéra's version of *Dutchman, Le Vaisseau fantôme,* made from the sketch purchased from Wagner in 1841.

But Minna blamed the debacle to a large part on Richard. Her advice had always been to guarantee a Parisian success by first producing the action-filled, spectacular *Rienzi* and then to mount the later operas on this solid base. Wagner had chosen to ignore her practical recommendation. Through with *Rienzi,* he had longed to refashion *Tannhäuser* in the sensuous chromatic idiom of *Tristan.*

Moreover, Minna could never understand why *Tannhäuser* could not have been made compatible with French taste by inserting a ballet in the second act, right before the minstrel contest. (One of Bayreuth's most brilliant postwar productions of *Tannhäuser,* that of 1954, turned the entry of the Thuringian nobles into a highly stylized dance tableau.) From her standpoint, fame and money had been thrown away by her husband's standing aloof from any concession. Another foreigner, Verdi, somehow managed to reconcile varying operatic traditions with his artistic conscience and had eclipsed even Meyerbeer as the most popular and highest-paid composer in Paris. With the help of Scribe, Vaez, and Royer, *Lombardi* had been transformed into *Jérusalem* (1847), its dazzling production meeting Paris' special dance behests with Verdi's freshly composed music; and when *Trovatore* appeared on the Opéra's boards as *Trouvère* (1857), it, too, had offered extended ballets tied into its action.

But Wagner refused to yield, and, to her exasperation, Minna doubtlessly soon realized that he had never really believed in this latest Parisian adventure. A year before the *Tannhäuser* fiasco he wrote to Mathilde, "I have no faith in my operas in French. All that I do toward that end goes against an inner voice that I can stifle only with levity or violence; I believe in neither a French *Tannhäuser* nor a French *Lohengrin* and least of all in a French *Tristan.*" Minna found his "stubbornness" in respect to the ballet hard to pardon, for it was obvious that, had he so wished, his genius could have made a virtue of necessity. She often wondered why she had been dragged to France to observe the imposture in which he was involved. The Paris *Tannhäuser,* a giant machine set in motion by impulses remote from art, pulled him into its complicated mechanism, and he had little time to analyze his attitudes. He did not create the new Venusberg music for detested France. His defiance of Parisian custom and the city's retaliatory attack upon the most German of contemporary composers was to restore him to his homeland.

In July, 1860, the ban on Wagner's return to Germany had been partially lifted. King Johann, Friedrich's successor and a sensitive man known for his translations of Dante, declared himself to have no objection to the composer's entering Germany if he avoided Saxony and traveled with the permission of those princes whose territories he visited. The following month Wagner had crossed the Rhine to fetch Minna from a water cure in the

Taunus and had also visited Baden-Baden to thank Augusta of Prussia, now princess regent,[5] for championing his cause with Johann. Obviously, he also wished to determine how far she was to be relied upon for further aid. After a Rhine journey he and Minna had returned to Paris for the *Tannhäuser* rehearsals.

Immediately after the première, the tale of the disgraceful events at the Opéra spread over Europe. Germany's musical public closed ranks behind Wagner. In Dresden a performance of *Tannhäuser* evoked an unparalleled storm of applause that was clearly a protest against Paris. And this demonstration was in King Johann's theater. Complete amnesty was but a matter of time. The Jockeys had outrun themselves.

5

Their second extended residence in Paris proved to Wagner that he and Minna had no future in common, a fact she had long known. A curious combination of love, duty, need, habit, and perhaps a sadism that pervaded so many of his relationships, had made him insist upon the ill-fated reunion. At first, he had promised the kind of social life in Paris that he knew would delight her. "I'll gather together a cozy little crowd (Germans, of course), for whom I want to be at home every evening as long as the strict lady of the house does not chase us to the devil. Dinner parties in Paris are out; but sitting around in the evening does not cost much." And, on Wednesdays, Wagner's Paris drawing room was open to visitors who, however, could hardly suspect from his lavish hospitality that their host was facing financial ruin. Day by day he was attempting to stave off summonses. Minna sadly reflected that it was ever his way "to start on a high level and end on a low one." In addition to the sums spent on the concerts, he found that clothes, interior decoration, and expenses for a household that included three servants quickly exhausted the money from Wesendonk and Schott. Wagner's methods of gathering more were as unconscionable as ever; observing his hypocritical attitude toward Julie Schwabe, a wealthy Manchester Jewess whom he had arranged to have brought to the receptions for obvious reasons, Minna observed, "She will not escape from Richard's hands unfleeced." Of course, she did not. But Wagner had not heard the last of her.

[5] In 1857 King Friedrich Wilhelm IV had succumbed to a serious mental disorder, and by the following year his younger brother, Prince Wilhelm, Augusta's husband, had assumed the regency. The approaching death of the King, Wagner believed, would be of moment to his cause, for the Prince was as yet not completely his own master. But Augusta's interview with Wagner did not go well, the Princess evidently being dumfounded to discover the poet of *Lohengrin* addressing her in Saxon dialect.

Minna had found herself playing the role of an honored housekeeper who enjoyed the privilege of sitting in the salon with company. And, when alone in her separate suite, she often had reason, as in the Asyl, to wonder what was going on in her husband's rooms.[6]

That Wagner and Liszt's elder daughter, Blandine (Madame Ollivier), were having a liaison was a morsel of Paris gossip.[7] Apparently there had already been talk about them during one of his earlier visits. His explanation to Minna in a letter of January 29, 1858, would seem unnecessary were it not defensive: "Blandine—whom I had on my arm, as it is not possible otherwise in such a locality—naturally was considered to be my wife." He and his new mistress had understood one another almost immediately. Her wit was delightful, and she seemed to him gentler (*"wohl sanfter"*) than her sister Cosima. But Blandine had a brazen streak and, like Mathilde at the Asyl, entered the Wagners' house without paying the least attention to Minna's existence. Ashamed to stay, Minna was equally ashamed to return to Dresden, where old friends had warned that Richard would never change. From Zwickau Natalie wrote to assure her that his "intoxication" would pass and that he would once again be her congenial *"Richard-Mann."* But Natalie did not know that, in accepting as terms of reunion the sexual prohibition communicated by Dr. Pusinelli, Minna had delivered herself into an awkward predicament. And, presciently, she already sensed danger from Cosima.

For a time an outwardly friendly relationship existed between them. After the Wesendonk crisis Cosima had invited Minna to Berlin. She was well aware of the infatuation for Karl Ritter that had seized Cosima within a year of her marriage to Hans.[8] From the beginning Frau von Bülow was

---

[6] In October, 1859, Wagner moved into a house on the Rue Newton. Within the year, the rebuilding of the area according to Haussmann's plans forced him to abandon a home on which he had spent a fortune for prepaid rent, repairs, and lavish furnishings. The landlord had swindled an uninformed foreigner, and the Wagners removed to the Rue d'Aumale in October, 1860.

[7] Liszt and Princess Carolyne were appalled by this development, which made Minna and Liszt's old mother into friends sharing a common misery. Blandine occupies a shadowy place in *Mein Leben* because Wagner dictated the book to her sister. A censored but evocative sentence from Cosima's diary reveals her thoughts a decade and a half later when, as Frau Wagner, she took down her husband's comments about Blandine. "Gay, yet melancholy pictures rise up from the past; my sister hovers between us! . . . It has all vanished."

[8] Alone with Karl in a boat on Lake Geneva, she had suddenly asked him to kill her. Miserable with his new wife, he offered to die, too. This was obviously not the reaction Cosima had hoped for, and she dramatically assured him that the plan must be abandoned to spare his life. After a separation of three weeks she wrote him that the episode now embarrassed her and asked him to forget it. Karl related the tale to Wagner, who, in turn, passed it on to the Green Hill. In later years, on Cosima's orders, these sentences were struck from the edition of Wagner's letters to Mathilde.

not too fastidious in respect to her vows and, like her sister, was considered rather fast. For her own youthful fall Minna compensated by extreme narrow-mindedness, and in her eyes Cosima was a profligate. The wretched look in Hans's eyes pained Minna, but his adulation of Wagner, incontinent as Cosima's, made her lose sympathy. She knew that many begrudged her the titular possession of so great an artist and protested that she would prefer being envied a good husband. One can imagine the levity such homespun remarks inspired among the Wagnerian retainers thronging her house.

Those differences in temperament and intellect that had given Wagner sober thoughts before his wedding in Königsberg almost a quarter of a century before had widened fatally. In earlier years his wife's beauty had bridged the gap, but few traces of the lovely Minna Planer now remained. The couple had become almost strangers to one another. But that at times he still hoped for a life with her is shown by his rapid, marvelous sketch of the tale of Erec and Enide (August, 1860), a combination of *Feen* and *Lohengrin,* in which a doubting wife, having driven her husband to the grave, reawakens him by her grief. But little Fips's death broke the final tie.

IX

New Wanderjahre

I

Wagner's years of restless wandering followed the Paris *Tannhäuser*. He wrote that during this period Goethe's *Wanderjahre* first became meaningful to him. One wonders what he found to admire in this novel of social ethics. His own *"Wanderjahre"* formed a period of outer fame but of inner discontent that steadily eroded an already vulnerable character. The artist preserved his integrity at high cost to the man; love, friendship, and conscience were sacrified without demur to the cause of his works, financial independence being too often gained by corrupt means justified by the concept of the hero's need. His name as a master grew, but so did his reputation for improbity. Earlier, his borrowings had often boasted at least the questionable distinction of being proud, arrogant, inventive frauds; they now degenerated into a kind of sordid larceny and grasping. The creature Deems Taylor called "Wagner the Monster" was stalking Europe.

The German Confederation lay open to him. His first task was to find a suitable birthplace for *Tristan*. Though he frequently returned to Paris, during the following months he mainly roamed through Germany and Austria and, to his delight, was enthusiastically greeted. At Karlsruhe the grand ducal couple received him as a friend in April, 1861, and, despite the limitations of their opera company, reconsidered the abandoned *Tristan* project. A production of *Rhinegold* was also vaguely projected. But it was in Vienna that, seemingly, he found his haven. Its famed Opera had a promising cast for *Tristan* and an administration eager to welcome the work. Special Wagnerian performances were arranged to honor him, and his tears flowed when at a rehearsal in May he heard *Lohengrin* for the first time. The public showed him the highest signs of affection, and during a *Lohengrin* performance applause forced him to rise in his box and bow after each "number"! At a specially scheduled *Dutchman* he was no less vehemently hailed. And, while attending a musicians' congress in Weimar in August, he had to plead with enthusiasts to spare him a torchlight procession.

In Weimar he again enjoyed outwardly friendly relations with Liszt, who had recently avoided him in Paris on account of the Blandine affair and also because he feared being again laid under contribution. Though Liszt's trunks were already packed for his removal from Weimar, he had tarried for the concerts. The Princess' absence from Haus Altenburg—she was in Rome—helped the friends regain something of the old conviviality. Blandine and Ollivier were also with Liszt, and, when the festival came to an end, Wagner enthusiastically accompanied his mistress and her husband to Nuremberg, Munich, and then Reichenhall, where Cosima was taking the saline water cure, Ollivier being obliged to submit all the while to Blandine's and Wagner's joking in German over his head. During this brief August visit to Reichenhall, Wagner first sensed that a liaison with the younger sister was also possible. Fascinated by Cosima's wild disposition, he would soon answer her questioning look.

During July he had finally disposed of his Paris household and of Minna, who was shipped off to Bad Soden in the Taunus with his vague assurances of someday establishing another nest with her. Excusing himself for two Parisian years which weighed on his conscience like a nightmare, he plaintively declared to her that all had been meant for the best. Later in the month he had visited her on his way to Weimar. Soon thereafter she left for Saxony.

Money problems gave him no rest. Minna was again set up independently, and his own needs were far from small. No new income would be forthcoming until *Tristan* was performed and started on the round of German theaters. News from Vienna's great Kärntnertor Opera House was not encouraging. The tenor, Ander, so glorious a Lohengrin, had become terrified of *Tristan's* part and was succumbing to a series of strategic indispositions. By mid-August Wagner was in Vienna and took up residence in the house of Dr. Standhartner, a Wagner enthusiast and physician to Empress Elizabeth. Tausig formed part of Wagner's Viennese circle, as did Peter Cornelius, to whom had been entrusted the copying of those alterations and transpositions in the part of Tristan indispensable to Ander's recuperation.

Wagner worked miracles with the Vienna orchestra and all the members of his cast except Ander, whose continuing protective hoarseness delayed the première repeatedly. Though publicly the tenor attributed his difficulties to a cold, caught while visiting the Kaisers' tombs in the crypt of Speyer Cathedral, nonetheless, little by little, rumor spread that *Tristan* challenged performance. In Leipzig, Breitkopf and Härtel became uneasy over their heavy investment in engraving what Wagner had assured them to be a practical score. In the face of these difficulties Wagner found solace in the charms of his absent host's niece and housekeeper, Seraphine Mauro, known to her admirers, who included Cornelius, as "Doll."

Where was Wagner to get money? During visits to Paris, acquaintances would find excuses not to receive him, having come to see his needs in terms of a bottomless pit. In Berlin even the Bülows were to be terrified by the possibility of his arrival at their home. After the dismantling of his household and Minna's departure, friends at the Prussian Embassy in Paris had taken pity, and for a while he had lived at the residence of the Ambassador, Count Pourtalès. For the Countess, the daughter of Moritz August von Bethmann-Hollweg, he wrote an *Albumblatt* for piano that celebrated the black swans in the Embassy's pool (July). Only a month before, he had written such a thank-offering for Princess Metternich. But it was Countess Portalès who knew how to express her concern in hard cash.

In May a surprise visit to the Wesendonks in Zurich had netted Wagner little, and, when during his Vienna sojourn they invited him to join them on a Venetian holiday in November, he saw the opportunity of striking again. (Fearful of mentioning Mathilde's name to Minna, he wrote her that Dr. Standhartner, summoned to Venice for consultation by Empress Elizabeth, had insisted on his companionship during the journey!) The *Tristan* project, which he described as dangling on the lax vocal cords of a fatigued tenor, was moribund, and his situation desperate; plans to import Schnorr or Tichatschek to Vienna had fallen through. But Otto and Mathilde, at the end of their largesse, were deaf to hints. Poor Bülow, who could barely keep his household together, was soon bothered for a loan.

2

In *Mein Leben* Wagner commented that inspiration to take up creative work again and begin *Meistersinger* came to him in Venice as he contemplated Titian's "Assumption of the Virgin." Otto, evidently shocked to discover that despite months of residence in the city Wagner remained unacquainted with its treasures, did encourage him to do some sightseeing, and he certainly found himself before the altarpiece. (Amusingly, he could not quite remember where the painting hung; the manuscript of *Mein Leben* erroneously places it in the Doges' Palace.) But the autobiography paints an exaggerated scene. Whatever relationships may have joined the two masterworks in his mind are impossible to know; but the notion of reviving his old *Meistersinger* plan had occurred to him well before the Venetian holiday of 1861.

Originally the work had been envisioned as a comic, Aristophanic complement to *Tannhäuser*. When he rewrote this opera for Paris, ideas about the lighter project doubtless revived, to be further stimulated by the visit to Nuremberg with the Olliviers. *Meistersinger* had to be discussed in Venice with Mathilde, for Wagner had given its Marienbad draft of 1845 into her safekeeping and wanted it again. The work's musical and literary outlines appeared before him with remarkable clarity, and on the train from Venice back to Vienna the overture was conceived. Then, not waiting to receive the original sketch from Mathilde's portfolio, he continued work on a *Meistersinger* scenario begun in Vienna the month before his departure for Venice. With Cornelius' help he was permitted to borrow Wagenseil's *Von der Meistersinger holdseligen Kunst* from Vienna's Imperial Library and extracted from it the quaint *Meistergesang* terminology that punctuates the conversation of Sachs, David, Beckmesser, and Kothner. With suggestions gleaned from E. T. A. Hoffmann's "Master Martin the Cooper," [1] hints from Johann Ludwig Deinhardstein's play *Hans Sachs* as well as the opera Lortzing made out of it, and ideas from the same composer's *Waffenschmied*, Wagner fashioned what was to be his most popular work.

In December he was in Mainz reading the scenario to the publisher Schott, from whom he received advances for the rapid completion of a practical operatic comedy suitable to both modest and first-rate theaters. Rather than return to Vienna, where the exasperating Ander seemed permanently out of voice, Wagner went to Paris, tempted by an invitation from the Metternichs, who offered quarters in the Austrian Embassy, where he might work in seclusion. Unfortunately, the unexpected death of Princess Pauline's mother upset the considerate plan, and the *Meistersinger* poem was brought into being in a quiet *hôtel garni* on the Quai Voltaire. After completing *Tristan* and almost two thirds of the *Ring*, Wagner was again writing pure grand opera, a reconversion Paris fittingly witnessed. He wrote Minna how droll it seemed to be occupied with the world of Hans Sachs and Nuremberg, only to look up and behold the Tuileries and the Louvre.

By early February, 1862, he was back in Mainz to recite the completed libretto with great success at Schott's before an intimate company that included Cornelius. In spite of floods and icy weather the latter had made his way from Vienna solely for this reading. He had come to mean much to Wagner, who about this time had suggested that they live together and belong to one another "like a married couple." But the creator of the

[1] In 1859, Bizet, who knew the tale as *"Le Tonnelier de Nuremberg,"* planned a three-act opera based on it. After somewhat reluctantly abandoning the idea, he observed, "One of these days someone will do my *'Tonnelier.'* "

Barber of Bagdad was too aware of Wagner's moral frailties and possessed too independent a nature to surrender to the intellectual enthrallment such an arrangement implied.

The month was not at an end when Wagner was installed at Biebrich in a house on the brink of the Rhine across from Mainz. He wished to be near Schott, whom he looked upon as a new and easily tapped source of revenue. And so important to him was the establishment of a comfortable home that he again decided to call Minna to his side despite their recent unhappiness together. He wrote to her expressing his longing to work unmolested. But their separation grieved him. He left the decision about a reunion entirely in her hands, inviting her to think the matter over thoroughly. "If you feel, after the great hardships which have depressed you and your heart, that . . . your one mission in life now is to make my life easier . . . that you can achieve *your* purpose in life only when you provide me with all possible quiet and cheerfulness for my work so that you can say to yourself that *you,* too, have taken part in my creations—then, I say, come!"

Minna did not reply. But within the week he was shedding tears and almost beheading with his embrace the old comrade who stood at his door. She intended to stay only long enough to put his new household in order. But the first hours passed so happily that they began to make plans for settling together at nearby Wiesbaden. The unfortunate arrival of a letter and present to Richard from "the Wesendonk" changed the atmosphere. Suspicions were reborn, old sores aggravated, the deepest wounds opened. The terrible scenes of the Asyl were re-enacted as quiescent resentments burst forth afresh. After what he described as "ten days of hell" she left. Both were in torment as they parted at Frankfort.

In Dresden she contrived to turn her illness to his advantage in the matter of the Saxon amnesty. Following her advice, he petitioned the King in March to grant it unconditionally because of his wife's poor health. She was liked in Dresden and received those small courtesies that so pleased her, being addressed as *"Frau Kapellmeister* Wagner" and accorded a permanent seat in the royal theater by the court. Her malady and Dresden residence provided the formula through which the King could graciously pardon without reversing his stand toward her husband, who by the end of the month was accorded full forgiveness for his wife's sake. Obviously her health required that she reside near Dr. Pusinelli, who had submitted her medical history to the palace. It was assumed that Wagner was longing to race to her side. Saxony, like the rest of Germany, was now open to him. But Minna, who desired him home, doubtlessly, to show Dresden that despite all storms she was still Frau Wagner, was soon appalled to learn that he wanted a divorce. Hans Sachs had found his Eva Pogner.

3

At first Wagner had attempted to transform Frau Wesendonk from Isolde into Eva. In Venice he had found her reconciled with Otto. Again sharing her husband's bed and obviously content, she would bear him a son the following June. In a sentence Cosima suppressed in the publication of the Wesendonk correspondence, Wagner observed to Mathilde, "Not my wife, but your husband, drove me from your side." After alluding to her pregnancy in a letter from Paris in late December, 1861, Wagner wrote, "I feel compelled to assure you that at last I am completely resigned."

In *Meistersinger* Hans Sachs sings to Eva, "My child, I know the sad tale of Tristan and Isolde. Sachs, being wise, would avoid Mark's fate." For a time Wagner luxuriated in playing Sachs's withdrawing in abnegation when his young love chooses another. In the third act of *Meistersinger* both the textual reference to *Tristan* and the simultaneous quoting of its motif of desire had intense, poignant personal implications for Wagner. Tristan dedicated Isolde to death; it was Sachs's part to step aside so that Eva might embrace life. Play actor though Wagner was, Mathilde's metamorphosis from Isolde to Eva must have cost him suffering during that Venetian holiday. Though Sachs's wisdom made his pain more endurable, it was pain nonetheless. But Mathilde would soon be replaced in the part of Eva. In the more sober atmosphere of Paris and Biebrich Wagner could justify the change.

In Venice he had been offended by the Wesendonks' stubborn refusal to comprehend his latest financial woes. They simply would not listen. He was talking to the wind and had obviously exhausted another account. Beyond respect for genius Otto no longer had any reason to keep him in his pay. After the completion of the *Meistersinger* libretto the Richard-Mathilde correspondence gradually declined to an ever more widely spaced exchange of polite notes, forewarnings of the end sounding from Paris late in 1861. He was beginning his valedictory: "From the depths of my soul to all eternity I thank you for my having written *Tristan*." He soon assured her that she would continue to hear the prosaic facts of his outer existence, but of his inner life there remained only his works. "Nothing more will happen, I assure you, nothing but the creation of art." The muse of the Green Hill was being sent away, but with excellent references.[2]

[2] Mathilde could not lose her taste for this avocation. Rejected by Wagner, she turned to Brahms—she was to offer him the Asyl—and sent him one of her texts (on cremation!) to be set as a cantata. Brahms and his circle were vastly amused by the pretensions of this rather absurd woman who had been wickedly persuaded by

On the Rhine he was soon enjoying the company of a younger Mathilde. He had first met Mathilde Maier at a party given by Schott. The girl's beauty did not exclude a strong and practical mind that inspired many touches in the character of Eva. In Biebrich he could act out his latest work under intimate conditions. He soon became so enamored that he determined in this case to let art and life go their separate ways. The middle-aged master would marry the maiden before some dashing Stolzing appeared.

Pusinelli and Wagner's sister Luise were commissioned to sound Minna about a divorce. Doubtlessly informed that Fräulein Maier was now considered "hostess" at the new "Beaver's Nest" on Rhine, Minna angrily refused and recommended that her husband control his impatience till time ended their union. She knew that her days were coming to a close. Wagner might have forced the issue had not the lovely "Thilde" Maier declined his importunings; a hereditary defect of the ear, she felt, did not fit her to become a composer's wife. Minna was thus spared what would have been to her the disgrace of a divorce proceeding.

Wagner soon found assuagement at the Frankfort theater, where an actress, Friederike Meyer, had caught his eye. It was simple to introduce himself, for she was the sister of Luise Meyer-Dustmann, his Vienna Isolde, whose soulful voice and complete mastery of her role had in some measure comforted him during rehearsals in the face of Ander's incapacity. But Friederike had been repudiated by her family. Her talents in the boudoir secured her engagements on the stage, and she was at the moment the special protégée of the Frankfort theater's director, who maintained her splendid home.

She was soon a regular visitor at the Beaver's Nest, contributing to those gay summer frolics that set the good folk of Biebrich by the ears. Guests came; guests went. The Bülows arrived, as did the young tenor Schnorr von Carolsfeld and his wife, Malvina, both of whom Wagner had so admired in a Karlsruhe *Lohengrin* (May, 1862) that with Hans at the piano he now set about coaching them in *Tristan*. The Biebrich circle also included Liszt's disciple Raff, who had settled in Wiesbaden, his actress-wife (Doris Genast), and Wendelin Weissheimer, who had introduced Wagner to Mathilde Maier at Schott's. When scarcely more than a boy, Wendelin had knocked at the door of the Zurich Asyl to pay his respects. A devoted Wagnerite, he was now at the Mainz Opera, and an allowance from a wealthy

---

Wagner that she possessed poetic genius. He was never fooled. The title page of the manuscript of the Wesendonk songs describes them as *"Fünf Dilettanten-Ge-dichte."* When she sent him some of her writings in later years, he treated them as trash. After hearing of his death, she composed a poem (ending with *"Heil dir, Heil! Es ist vollbracht!"*) which, though it must have cost the lady tears, reads like a satire on Wagnerism.

father and a natural generosity made him doubly welcome at the Beaver's Nest.

Wagner made little progress on *Meistersinger*. After a spirited beginning, inspiration came spottily. Only the overture (later called "prelude"), the *"Wach' auf"* chorus, and the third-act prelude, which grew from this chorus, were fully conceived. He was obviously wasting himself. The first act advanced laboriously, and when Leo, his landlord's bulldog, bit his right thumb, causing it to swell, the score was put aside for weeks. Franz Schott, increasingly uneasy about his large investment and the composer's unkept promises to deliver manuscript, denied all new requests for funds. Wagner was furious; he had only settled in Biebrich in order to enjoy what he called Schott's financial protection. Frau Betty Schott, who had formerly taken Wagner's part, was now scandalized by the Friederike affair and fed her husband's resentment. Matters were at an impasse. Schott would not pay; Wagner could not compose.

Life on the other side of the Rhine was even more complicated than worthy Frau Betty imagined. Bülow was in a deep depression, and Cosima and Richard were again exchanging Hoffmannesque glances. Hans, who had once declared himself willing to be Wagner's bootblack, masochistically grieved over his inferiority to him and bemoaned his own second-class talent. Cosima expected much from him, and his songs seemed so paltry and lamentable that he could not find the heart to read the proofs sent by his publisher. Crushed by the immensity of genius as he contemplated what had been written of *Meistersinger*, in misery he sank down passively and worshipfully before the altar as Cosima prepared to mount toward the god.

The Bülows' union was not happy. Duty rather than love had drawn them together. As Cornelius observed, the marriage was a sacrificial act of gratitude on the part of Hans, who wished to lessen the anxieties of his revered teacher Liszt by giving his bastard daughter a distinguished name. Suitors had flocked around lovely Blandine. But, in finding a husband, Cosima lacked the physical advantages to offset her illegitimacy. Despite the good face she put on, there was much about her marriage mortifying to a spirited young girl. Not surprisingly, she soon sought release in affairs.

Her early reserve toward Wagner had been due in part to a still inadequate German. After her episode with Karl Ritter on Lake Geneva in 1858, she had returned to the Asyl and, when leaving, had fallen at Wagner's feet, covering his hands with tears and kisses. (Cosima later insisted that Wagner's not entirely sympathetic accounts of her extraordinary behavior be struck from the edition of the Wesendonk letters.) Her glances at their more recent Reichenhall encounter could not have surprised him. And from the beginning it must have been clear to many that it would take more than a husband to satisfy her sexually. Moreover, by the time of the

Biebrich sojourn she had come to realize that professionally, too, Hans was destined to disappoint her imposing demands. Her intimacy with Wagner may well have begun at Biebrich. Hans's irritability, complete loss of confidence in himself, and talk of suicide possibly proceeded from a domestic as well as an artistic crisis.

To comprehend the forces that were ineluctably reshaping the lives of Wagner and the Bülows, it is necessary at this point to turn from events on the Rhine to consider Cosima's background and personality.

4

Like Wagner, Cosima had been born illegitimate. Her mother, Marie d'Agoult, left her aristocratic husband, Count Charles d'Agoult (whom she had wed in 1827 with Charles X and Louis Philippe, then Duke of Orleans, as witnesses), to become Franz Liszt's mistress. She bore him three children, of whom Cosima was the second.

An unusual pedigree helped give rise to Cosima's renowned anti-Semitism, which was already vigorous during the Biebrich visit, the presence of Jews in nearby Wiesbaden causing her much distress. The insane bigotry of her later years cannot be attributed to Wagner's influence alone. The vice had grown in him through fears that his own background might be, in part, Jewish; Cosima had similar anxieties of her own, but with a more tangible basis.

Her mother's father, Viscount de Flavigny, a product of the *ancien régime*, had been a page to Marie Antoinette. Both his parents had perished by the guillotine, and the impoverished young émigré re-established himself by marrying the daughter of Simon Moritz Bethmann, a Jewish banker of Frankfort on the Main. There Marie was born in 1805. Four years later, Flavigny returned with his family to France, where he died when Marie was thirteen. For a while the child again lived in the Frankfort household of those Jewish ancestors who were to prove so embarrassing to her own daughter, Cosima. Well does one grasp the defensive purpose behind Cosima's vehement description of Frankfort as "abominable" because of its Jews. Ashamed of her descent from the patriarchal Schimsche Naphtali Bethmann, she spent a lifetime seeking to deny it through such abuse.

Cosima was born in Italy during the idyllic love between Marie and Liszt and, like her mother, was raised mainly in France. Her childhood was difficult. When her parents' liaison came to an end, hastened by Liszt's affair with Lola Montez, Marie returned to her husband.[3] Liszt gave the

---

[3] Lola Montez delighted in relating the spurious tale of that easily bewildered bibliophile the Count d'Agoult, who, having sought out his children to present them to a visitor, discovered five instead of the two he thought he had.

children into the care of his mother, Frau Anna, who lived in Paris. When he entered his involvement with Princess Wittgenstein, she, a noblewoman accustomed to command, began to maneuver the children's affairs in order to counter the influence of Marie.[4] From her residence in Weimar's Villa Altenburg, the Princess ordered the strict tutor of her youth, Madame Patersi de Fossombroni, to leave St. Petersburg and proceed to Paris. The heartsick Anna Liszt was forced to deliver her grandchildren into the hands of the seventy-two-year-old tyrant. The lessons in submission, restraint, and tact that Cosima learned from this fearsome instructress were to stand her in good stead during her years with Wagner.

Cosima's mother turned to writing and under the name of Daniel Stern attempted to achieve renown. Liszt was amused to observe that the rise of George Eliot, considered by critics the only female author comparable to Sand, was a sore point with Marie. But she enjoyed a certain vogue for her historical works, and with her example and that of the ambitious Wittgenstein, whose last years were to be dedicated to the twenty-four volumes of her *Causes intérieures de la Faiblesse extérieure de l'Eglise,* Cosima, too, determined to make herself into a literary figure.

From the earliest days of her marriage to Bülow she set aside a writing salon for herself and contributed to the *Revue germanique.* The Princess' influence on her was paramount. Although in later years it was the policy of Wahnfried to deprecate Sayn-Wittgenstein, clearly this powerful woman, addressed as "Mother" by Cosima,[5] provided the prototype of the latter's career. In the Princess she found her model.

Marie, her real mother, was beautiful. Cosima, nicknamed "Stork," was as plain as the Princess, whose strength had nonetheless succeeded where Marie's delicate charms had failed. Wittgenstein had bound Liszt to herself by links which to him seemed silken but which were forged from the iron of her Slavic will. Her haughty rule over the Altenburg was re-created a generation later by Cosima at Wahnfried. Born with Marie's determination and complete lack of humor about herself and adopting the manner of the Princess—especially her soft-spoken ruthlessness—Cosima determined to eclipse both. But misled by her father's and Wagner's overenthusiastic estimates of Bülow's abilities as a composer, she believed he had genius to be shaped.

For a while Bülow, as a good Wagnerian, imagined that after Beethoven nothing more could be expressed in purely instrumental forms, the music

[4] This granddaughter of Moritz Bethmann disparagingly referred to the Princess as a Jewess; quite evidently, Marie passed many of her own problems on to Cosima.
[5] For her marriage to Bülow, Cosima required the Princess' consent as well as Liszt's.

drama offering the composer his only field. He had flirted with the Tristan legend in his earlier days, as had his friend Karl Ritter, and then turned to the most dramatic figure of Arthurian romance—Merlin. When Richard Pohl proved unable to shape a libretto on the subject, Cosima, in secret, helped by her friend Ernst Dohm, sketched a scenario which she presented to her husband on Christmas Eve, 1858. He attempted to work on it, but the project came to nothing. Quite simply, Hans had little feeling for the theater. Though he developed into a more finished and technically sure conductor than Wagner himself and in Munich was to preside over the only two Wagnerian productions the composer ever judged worthy of his works (the *Tristan* and *Meistersinger* premières), it was Bülow's musical mastery that triumphed. He paid little attention to the stage. (One can understand his later enthusiasm for Brahms.) For years the Merlin affair and what it symbolized corroded the relationship between Hans and Cosima. Her demands on him proved too great.

These were powerful, masculine women—Marie, the Princess, and Cosima. They mothered lovers in the hope of fathering their artistic productiveness, the niceties of bourgeois morality taking second place to a driving need to create, even if vicariously. Each was determined to emulate that cigar-smoking descendant of Augustus the Strong, George Sand. Yet, although she had Musset and Chopin as lovers, in the end it was Sand's own gifts that raised her monument. In contrast, the three other ladies with their literary and philosophic pretensions appear quite foolish at this distance.

Marie d'Agoult had become reconciled to giving up Liszt when she felt herself mistaken in the belief that an interpreter might develop into a significant creator. Her resentment was born when the tone poems began to issue from him under the Princess' tutelage. Cosima, in her turn, vainly waited for her husband—her father's favorite pupil—to compose something of substance. Once certain of his incapacity, she did not hesitate, regardless of price to husband and family, to follow what she felt to be a higher duty by allying herself to one of the giants of the age. She would not risk a second mistake.

It would be unfair to suggest that her public betrayal of Hans was an act of pure calculation or that she was insensitive to the sufferings her decision engendered. She carried a gnawing guilt to the grave. But she felt endurance for the sake of Wagner's art to be a kind of sacrament. Moreover, her union with him delivered a blow to the father from whom she was seeking retribution for the misery of her childhood.[6] Ironically, her

---

[6] Cosima never forgot those terrible years when Liszt forbade his children to mention their mother's name in his presence. It had been primarily to check her

plans were successful because in a homely, masculine girl, almost a quarter of a century his junior, Wagner came to find the mother-sister of his dreams.

5

At Biebrich, Wagner had exhausted Schott's advances by the end of the summer, and the publisher adamantly refused any new subsidy, even after receiving the Wesendonk lieder in lieu of more *Meistersinger* manuscript. He paid for the songs but would not invest further in an opera whose composer blithely maintained that only more money could keep him in the mood to carry it through. In desperate need of funds, Wagner tracked him to his cure room at Kissingen and found Frau Betty at the door on guard against any new Wagnerian assault. Herr Schott was declared too ill to receive. Nor could an abusive letter from the composer change his attitude. He acidly and prophetically wrote to Wagner that his needs could not be met by a mere publisher, but only by a banker or a prince with millions.

Somehow money had to be scraped together. To young Weissheimer of the Mainz Opera now fell the privilege of meeting the financial emergencies at the Beaver's Nest. Moreover, this young composer's plan to give a concert of his own compositions in Leipzig was expanded to include Wagner as well as Bülow. At Frankfort *Lohengrin* was conducted by its composer in September for the first time and in an uncut version, a performance arranged by the theater's manager, who was Friederike Meyer's official protector. The evening almost ended in disaster when, during the orchestral interlude between the scenes of the final act, a wrong cue brought in, simultaneously, a pair of off-stage trumpet fanfares written a half tone apart and meant to sound successively. Helpless, Wagner put down his baton and covered his ears in view of the audience. Yet despite this near catastrophe, the opera impressed Frankfort.

To Bülow's distress, Wagner and Cosima were now openly frolicking together, indulging in the kind of pranks associated with the first days of

---

ascendant influence that they were given over to Madame Patersi, who even censored their mail. In order to cut all contact with Madame d'Agoult, Liszt eventually ordered the girls to Prussia, where they were put in the care of Bülow's mother. There were, of course, moments in later years when Cosima felt close to Liszt—moments Wagner deeply resented. But her real attitude toward her father was shown at the time of his death in Bayreuth during the festival of 1886. In her mind the event was not sufficiently important to occasion a change in schedule. This shabby behavior was her way of indicating to the assembled faithful her opinion of Liszt's place in the Wagnerian firmament that he, more than any other, had helped shape.

romance. When Wagner sang Wotan's farewell before friends in Frankfort, he was symbolically saying good-bye to Cosima, whose face, as she listened, appeared to him "serenely transfigured." He wrote, "Here all was silence and secrecy." His belief that she now was his led him to moods of "eccentric excitement" and "unruly high spirits." Bülow somberly watched his wife and friend at play, his "often excessive ill-humor" drawing "involuntary sighs" from the composer, whose account of these incidents in *Mein Leben* is remarkably candid. Late in October he quit the Rhineland for Leipzig and the concert with Weissheimer.

On November 1, 1862, Wagner led the première of the *Meistersinger* overture in the Gewandhaus. In general, Leipzig's public believed his music to be *nicht Gewandhausfähig*—not meriting performance in the famous hall. It was nearly empty; clearly, Leipzig wanted no part of this native son, although the orchestra, at first unfriendly toward him, did warm to the genius of his music. There were, of course, no profits from the undertaking, Weissheimer bearing heavy losses. At this time his limited talents as a composer were indulged by Wagner; but when new sources of revenue opened to the latter, poor Weissheimer was to discover just what value he really had in the great man's eyes. At the moment an unexpected gift of fifteen hundred marks from the Grand Duke of Weimar had been secured by Cosima through her father and helped Wagner quiet his most aggressive creditors.

He was elated to find Cosima at the Leipzig concert. She was in mourning for her sister, Blandine, who had died at St. Tropez after confinement. To Wagner, this death was a blow aimed at himself alone! He believed fate to be striking one he loved simply to ruin *his* happiness and therewith *his* capacity to create. His concept of the universe was completely egocentric. Since misfortune seemed to pursue his friends, he declared them victims of those mighty forces set in motion simply to torment *him*. In this mood he had sophistically expressed fears to Hans in a letter of September 6, 1862, that it was perhaps his turn to suffer some ordeal. The weeks with Cosima at Biebrich and Hans's moodiness must certainly have led Wagner to foresee misery as his disciple's lot. *Mein Leben* indicates that a very special relationship already existed between Wagner and Cosima when they met again at Leipzig.

According to Wagner's outrageous phrase, he proceeded from Leipzig to Dresden to do Minna the "honor" of a visit. He had warned her that he could stay only a few days, so urgently was he expected in Vienna, where *Tristan* rehearsals were to be resumed.

In the capital from which he had last exited as a revolutionary he found Minna comfortably established. She had embroidered "Salve" on the doormat and—pathetically—had set aside a bedroom and study to accommodate him during what his fictions had led her to hope would be frequent visits. Questions and explanations were skillfully avoided, for they usually found themselves in the company of others. Only at his departure did the anguished wife, sensing that little time was left her, break down and voice a fear that she would never see him again. It was, in fact, their last meeting, their final parting.

6

In many ways Wagner's life was a heroic struggle to impose his art on an indifferent and often reluctant world. Yet he frequently spent his energies surmounting obstacles he himself had willfully placed in his own path. The abandonment of *Tristan* in Vienna was to a large extent his own fault.

Ander had recovered both courage and voice. All would have been possible had not Wagner foolishly decided to bring Friederike with him to Vienna[7] (November 14) and had he not also premeditatedly insulted Hanslick, that most influential of the city's music critics.

Frau Dustmann had been a summer guest at Biebrich. Although Wagner observed that Friederike awakened her hostility, he chose to ignore its consequences to his fortunes in Vienna. She was outraged by Wagner's tactlessness in bringing to town her notorious sister and implied that he not only exploited Friederike sexually but was also taking her money. And who in the theater was unaware of the sources of Friederike's income? Furious, Madame Dustmann joined the anti-Wagner clique, and the composer discovered that, though he now had a Tristan, his divine Isolde was doing her best to wreck the production. Ostensibly, Friederike had come to Vienna to join the Burgtheater, where Wagner's old friend Laube had become director. But her trial performance proved so incompetent that the pretense had to be dropped. When the damage his thickheadedness had caused finally became clear to Wagner, he quickly shipped his mistress off to Italy.[8]

---

[7] Despite the pleasure of Friederike's company, he could not dispel thoughts of that farewell to Minna. From Vienna he sent her a telegram: "Believe me, dear Minna, I think of you, even if anxiously. Hope for good news!"

[8] Her health had suffered grievously. She had become very thin, and though her hair had suddenly almost entirely fallen out, she resolutely refused to wear a wig. One can imagine the impression she made at the Burgtheater! Wagner really no longer wanted her, and eventually she returned contritely to her former protector in Frankfort, after a pathetic attempt to build an independent career at the tiny Coburg theater.

But the situation in Vienna was almost beyond repair. Not only had the Friederike scandal undermined his position at the opera house, but, in addition, a certain reading of the *Meistersinger* poem in the presence of Hanslick had already completely alienated this powerful figure from Wagner.

Wagner and Hanslick had first become acquainted in Marienbad during July, 1845. The Bohemian student, only twenty, knew the piano scores of *Rienzi* and *Dutchman,* and Wagner, delighted, asked him to attend the forthcoming première production of *Tannhäuser.* After hearing the work in Dresden, where he had also been invited by Schumann, Hanslick wrote a lengthy and perceptive essay on the opera serialized in the *Wiener Musikzeitung* (late in 1846). He had gone to the imperial capital to complete his studies at the university. Though examining the shortcomings as well as the merits of *Tannhäuser,* he unreservedly hailed Wagner as the leading dramatic composer of the day.

With the production of *Lohengrin* in Vienna in 1858, Hanslick, by this time the city's outstanding critic, parted company with Wagner's aesthetic. An admirer of Meyerbeer, he had seen in *Tannhäuser,* constructed around the nucleus of the contest on the Wartburg, the promise of development along the path of historical grand opera. The supernatural Venus adventure had taken its place within an imposing historical framework. *Lohengrin,* however, despite the fact that Wagner had set the miraculous tale against the background of Henry the Fowler's uneasy truce with the Hungarians, pointed in the direction of the symbolic myth, in Hanslick's view a hazardous path.

From the first, Hanslick had criticized Wagner's overindulgence in the chord of the diminished seventh and the tremolo—Berlioz, too, had taken exception to Wagner's abuse of these devices—and recognized that the composer often lost all sense of proportion, pursuing ideas to immoderate lengths. The Swiss essays had further estranged Hanslick. He regarded their egoism and bombast with distaste. It was clear to him that they claimed as universal law only that which suited Wagner's own abilities. Nietzsche, too, was to observe that, where Wagner lacked a faculty, he would posit a principle outlawing it. Furthermore, Hanslick perceived the appeal of Wagnerism to be least of all musical and recognized the movement as a dangerous cultural phenomenon. In a tribute to Wagner after his death, Hanslick maintained that he had joined battle not so much against the artist as against the repulsive idolatry of his adherents. Though always aware of Wagner's genius, Hanslick deplored an influence he believed to be leading opera on a treacherous bypath and correctly foresaw that after *Lohengrin* Wagner's way was for himself alone and that followers must inevitably meet disaster. Considering Wagner the last of the romantic line, an end rather than a beginning, Hanslick could not accept him as continuing the tradition of Beethoven. Their brilliance and moments of exaltation notwithstanding, Wagner's creations represented, in his opinion, not an enrichment but a distortion of music. He saw Wagner as adjacent to his art rather than of it, the master of the superlative, a grammatical form without a future.

Moreover, as a writer with a truly distinguished style, Hanslick could not abide Wagner's prose or most of his so-called "poetry," nor could he take very seriously the assertion that the librettos were self-sufficient works of art. In his review of *Lohengrin,* Hanslick declared himself sufficiently merciless to hope that those who recognized such a claim might someday be required to undergo its test.

Though harsh, his estimate of Wagner is closer to modern criticism than is the undiscriminating adulation of the Wagnerites. As a partisan of the Leipzig school, Hanslick was deaf to many beauties in Wagner's scores, and in respect to Wagner, Berlioz, and Liszt (and later Bruckner and Richard Strauss) was unable to surmount an innate conservatism and a prejudice against "literary" music. Nonetheless, he could never be accused of intellectual dishonesty. One may disagree with his complaints about Wagner's unvocal writing, boring declamation, orchestral din, clumsiness, monotony, exaggeration of expression, and perpetual modulation; yet, considering the hysterical excesses of the Wagnerites, he generally kept his temper, his logically presented opinions being based not on emotion but on a thorough study of the score in question. He had had four years of theory, composition, and piano with Tomaschek and was thoroughly professional at the keyboard.

Though he fought Wagner vigorously, he never denied him; if he found little to praise in this music, he nonetheless could extol the beauty of a strong, sincere effort; if he detested Wagner the man, he found him invulnerable in respect to artistic morality. If Hanslick was at times wrong, he was not unrighteous.

Wagner's attitude toward Hanslick was less dichotomous and generous; after the *Lohengrin* review he thoroughly loathed him.

The Vienna Opera was well aware of Hanslick's writings on Wagner. Its optimism in planning a production of *Tristan* was an echo of clinking coin at the box office on Wagner nights. The Viennese public read and respected Hanslick but usually formed its own judgments. Yet, in the case of the novel and uncompromising *Tristan,* the management, and especially the cast, felt from the beginning that a Wagner-Hanslick rapprochement would be advantageous. Efforts had been made in this direction by Ander and Frau Dustmann. Even Laube was besought to use his influence. But at arranged "chance" encounters Wagner was uncivil.

Only when Hanslick gallantly remarked to him upon the relationship between misjudgments and personal limitations and declared himself willing to learn, did Wagner seem to respond. But to this call of the critic for
social intercourse and friendship he was to give strange answer when he
returned to Vienna from the Rhineland. Ironically, it was probably because
of their supposed reconciliation that the Kärntnertor Opera House had
summoned Wagner back.

Hanslick was subsequently invited to the home of Dr. Standhartner to
hear Wagner recite the *Meistersinger* poem (November 23, 1862). At this
time the pedantic, narrow-minded character now known to the world
as Beckmesser appeared in Wagner's manuscript under the name of Hans-
lich. Wagner had maliciously trapped the critic in a barbarously contrived
situation. Pale and upset, Hanslick fled the reading as soon as he could,
Wagner doubtlessly finding the whole affair vastly amusing. As Hans Sachs
he had acted out the last act of *Meistersinger* and sent the cantankerous
Marker fleeing the scene of contest. He wanted no mercies from the critics.
Success would come from the Folk, from those with no knowledge of the
musty Tabulatur.

7

Meistergesang interested Wagner not only as a particularly German art
expression, but also because its practitioners, like himself, wrote both their
texts and music. In *Meistersinger,* Hans Sachs, symbolizing the worthiest
aspects of this national tradition, became Wagner's spokesman on aesthetics,
adroitly parrying the jabs of quibblers and, when aroused, thrusting the
blade deep. So delighted was Wagner with playing the role of Sachs in
everyday life that during the long period of *Meistersinger*'s creation he
took to wearing a velvet Dürer beret, encouraged his entourage to address
him as *"Meister,"* and assigned his tailors the task of giving his already preposterous wardrobe an added *"altdeutsch"* look.

Desiring the public to be aware of only the genial side of Sachs's complicated character, Wagner, in the final act of *Meistersinger,* took pains to
clear him technically of complicity in the ruin of Beckmesser. But legalistic
sophistry remains sophistry nonetheless. Though Sachs is careful to convey
to Beckmesser only the paper on which the prize song is written, making
no mention of the poem itself, this hairsplitting does not free him from
guilt in a clear case of entrapment. Beckmesser's understandable assumption is that the freshly penned verses in Sachs's handwriting on Sachs's
table are the work of Sachs. The cobbler wilily gives assurance that he will
never claim authorship of the lyrics but neglects to add that, only moments

before, he had written them down from Walther's dictation. If his victim had had a lawyer's ear for words, he would have realized that he was being presented with only the piece of paper and not its content.

Musically and dramatically the scene is one of the marvels of the century's comic opera literature, in which one must turn to Berlioz's *Beatrice and Benedict* or Verdi's *Falstaff* to find its equal. Nevertheless, it brings to mind uncomfortable recollections of Wotan's business transactions with the giants; even in glorious, golden *Meistersinger,* morality rests upon the idea that any means justifies a Wagnerian end.

Sachs's benignity is limited to a rather select group. Beckmesser, rejected and repudiated, is Alberich in transition to Klingsor. (The amazing psychological interrelationships among certain Wagnerian themes are shown by the fact that the musical idea representing the Mephistophelean in the *Faust Overture* anticipated Beckmesser's motif.) Perhaps, as he wanders in fury and frustration from the Nuremberg meadow, the process begins in the course of which he eventually mutilates himself, becomes an enchanter, and seeks the destruction of the closed society that has excluded him. As Klingsor he returns in *Parsifal* to menace a fellowship that is the ultimate manifestation of the restricted, elite Wagnerian community. Vainly attempting to gain access to the elect and making a last effort to deny his strain through self-castration, Klingsor is nonetheless disdainfully rebuffed by the Grail Knights; he is not of their breed, and no stratagem will change the fact.

Wagner's humor is cruel; it requires a victim. Certainly there is no balance between Beckmesser's offense and his punishment. Is his pedantry more worthy of castigation than that of his colleagues? His faults are all too human: doubts expressing themselves in seeming conceit and overconfidence, a lack of creative talent seeking remedy in reliance upon rule, and the misery of wooing a younger person who finds him thoroughly ridiculous. When he is tricked by Sachs, first into making a complete fool of himself before the townsfolk and then into unmasking himself as a plagiarist, pity must be felt for the grotesque little man choking with impotent rage and brandishing his lute as he disappears. Sachs's work of destruction is complete.

Wagner-Sachs saw himself as a heroic figure, defender of German tradition, a poet-composer, made wise by the storms of life, who would lecture the world on the aesthetics of word and tone and the preservation of national identity. No longer believing in revolution and without confidence in even the most sympathetic princes, he kept his trust in the strength of the German Folk and German art and wished to preserve both uncontaminated by Franco-Judaic influences. The noble Sachs of the *"Flieder"* and *"Wahn"* monologues, the Sachs to whom are addressed two of the most moving apostrophes in literature—Eva's *"O Sachs! Mein Freund!"* and the citizens' *"Wach' auf"*—could at the same time deserve Beckmesser's sharp comment, "With all your show of virtue, you're still a rogue." In the fluctuations of the cobbler's personality Wagner but reflected the dynamics of his own. Nor could he resist flattering himself in the opera by reversing the proportions of his own virtues and frailties.

In his autobiography Hanslick observed that, when the Wagnerites called him "Beckmesser," they showed complete misunderstanding of a character representing the pedant absorbed in trifles. His criticism of Wagner, he remarked, never indulged in a discussion of piddling detail but rather concerned itself with general principles of operatic aesthetics, and he pointed to the Wagnerites as Beckmessers in reverse, finding every sixteenth rest in their master's scores an occasion for glorifying his genius. Hanslick rightly insisted that the enormous and rather foolish Wagnerian literature really exemplified the quintessence of "Beckmesserism."

It is sad to observe a genius descending to the level on which Wagner chose to engage Hanslick. Of course, the reason for this critic's obstinacy and wickedness was discovered. He was a Jew, and Wagner took special pains to expose the culprit in an addition (1869) to *Jewry in Music,* an "explanation" written in the form of an open letter to Madame Kalergis (then Frau von Mouchanoff), who did not deserve the embarrassment this distinction brought her.

Apparently Hanslick's mother descended from a prosperous Jewish merchant family, and he was not particularly desirous of having the fact known. The Nazi regime honored all he stood for by proscribing his books. Such anti-German outsiders had to be chased from the meadow before Nuremberg. The grand opera trappings of *Meistersinger's* final act and its musical mastery often make one forget that its imposing shadow fell over events at later Nuremberg festivals.

That the Nazis chose to mount *Meistersinger* in celebration of their annual party day in Nuremberg made many well-meaning people lament the evil purposes to which scoundrels can put great art. However, in this case no distortion was necessary. For example, Richard Stock in his *Richard Wagner und die Stadt der Meistersinger* (1938), an elaborate propaganda effort blessed by those in Wahnfried, had only to quote and paraphrase Wagner to have the result come out pure Julius Streicher. As he wrote Bülow on February 20, 1866, Wagner wanted *Meistersinger* produced in the city it celebrated because he saw this ancient seat of German tradition as a bulwark against Jewish influences. Wagner was outraged by the erection in Nuremberg, opposite the monument to Hans Sachs, of "an imposing synagogue in purest Oriental style." His indignation was to find redress some decades later when the Nazis demolished this structure stone by stone. Herr Stock could in all conscience—if that is the word—proclaim the life goals of Wagner to be fulfilled on that day when the Führer set forth the Nuremberg race laws in the new capital of the war against Jewry. Nor did Stock forget to condemn the *"Halbjude"* Eduard Hanslick, and to quote in derision his review of the *Meistersinger* première.

8

In the final act of *Rosenkavalier* that elegant Viennese aristocrat the Princess von Werdenberg turns to Lerchenau, her country cousin, and wryly asks, "Can't you see when a matter has come to an end?" This was fast becoming the attitude of Vienna toward *Tristan,* which had lost the dignity of being seriously discussed. Though for a while it had provided amusement as the background for a bedroom farce, as the months wore on, everyone, except Wagner, was becoming weary of the whole affair. Gradually even the pretense of interest in bringing the opera to performance was being abandoned. And Frau Dustmann would soon conclude the comedy by declaring herself too ill to sing. But Wagner refused to believe that all the preparations had been in vain. For Vienna formally to relinquish the work would be catastrophic confirmation of the widespread suspicion even held by some of his friends that, despite their beauties, the works he had composed after *Lohengrin* simply defied performance. *Rhinegold, Valkyrie,* two thirds of *Siegfried,* and *Tristan* seemed doomed to be silent scores. And what of this new so-called "practical" *Meistersinger,* which he seemed unable to compose and whose few completed pages again called for tremendous instrumental resources?

Any thought of fees from *Tristan* was now out of the question, and, despite his unparalleled genius for divination, at the moment he could locate no flowing money wells in the immediate landscape. His solution was to organize a concert tour that, he hoped, would be remunerative and would also stimulate interest in his unperformed works. Orchestral parts had to be abstracted from the scores of what was completed of the *Ring* and *Meistersinger,* and in this work Cornelius, Tausig, and Weissheimer were joined by the famous young composer Brahms.

Throughout 1863 Wagner roamed Europe as an itinerant conductor. Like Berlioz, who had earlier set a pattern for such journeys, he was welcomed in musical and aristocratic circles. The series started in Vienna's fabled Theater an der Wien with three concerts in December, 1862, and January, 1863, patronized by Empress Elizabeth. At the suggestion of Madame Kalergis, she sent Wagner a thousand gulden. The enterprise had started well. His only real dissatisfaction had been with three students from Marchesi's classes, who sang the Rhine Daughters, the Flosshilde, "a highly offensive Jewess," remaining long in his mind.

February found him in Prague, where he met Marie Löwe-Lehmann, an old friend from Leipzig days and once his and Minna's colleague at Magdeburg and Königsberg. Her voice having long since gone, she was now turning to account her considerable talents as a harpist and played in the orchestra under Wagner at a highly successful concert. The most delightful memory he carried from Prague was of her lovely young daughter, Lilli Lehmann.

Triumphs in St. Petersburg and Moscow in March and April brought lavish compensation and contact with Anton and Nicholas Rubinstein. Wagner made a deep impression on the German-born Grand Duchess Helene, to whom he read his *Meistersinger* and *Ring* poems at a series of tea parties. For a brief time he felt she was the understanding, limitlessly wealthy patron of his dreams. Had he not frightened her by pressing for money too quickly and too vehemently, a pension might have been his. She did send him a gift of a thousand rubles. There had been interest in his work in Russia even before this visit. In 1860 he had been offered fifty thousand francs to give concerts and mount *Tannhäuser* in St. Petersburg, but his agreement with the Opéra had compelled him to remain in Paris. Amends were now made for a former disappointment, and he exited from Russia with a good deal of money and a gold snuffbox, on which members of the Moscow orchestra had ordered engraved *"Doch Einer kam,"* from Siegmund's cavatina in *Valkyrie.*

There were summer concerts in Pest, where he was invited on Reményi's initiative. November brought new successes in Prague, which honored him with a special performance of *Dutchman,* and later in the month he conducted at Karlsruhe before the Grand Duke of Baden and his mother-in-law, Augusta, since 1861 Queen of Prussia. At Baden-Baden Wagner relaxed as the guest of Madame Kalergis, recently become Frau von Mouchanoff. (She had arranged his invitation to Russia.) In Pauline Viardot's villa he met Turgenev, who had admired the orchestral excerpts at the first Karlsruhe concert but evidently couldn't abide the singing. Vocal solos, such as "Wotan's Farewell," were usually included to give the public a taste for the new style.

After his final Karlsruhe appearance, Wagner hastened to Zurich in an attempt to extract another loan from the Wesendonks. But their deafness to his laments had, if anything, increased since the Venetian trip. They saw no sense in aiding a man who had obviously let a fortune in concert fees and gifts filter through his fingers. By night he traveled to Mainz to assault the house of Schott for new advances but retreated disappointed. He had promised to visit Minna in Dresden on the way to Silesia, where he had engagements. But he changed his mind and, avoiding the city, wandered to Berlin, tarried with the Bülows, and parted from Cosima with an understanding that a serious affair between them was but a question of time and place. In the public edition of *Mein Leben* [9] she took care to strike

[9] Wagner distributed copies of his private edition of *Mein Leben* to close friends with the understanding that they never discuss the contents of the book. After his death, Cosima recalled these gifts, even King Ludwig's set. Evidently most were destroyed, the Bayreuth archives preserving only two complete copies and part of a third, relics hidden from the curious obviously because cosmetical changes were to be worked upon the eventual public edition. This appeared in 1911 and has proved surprisingly faithful to the now available private print, Cosima having insisted on relatively few omissions and alterations. She had been inhibited from using her blue pencil freely by the enterprise of Mary Burrell, who in 1892 had secured and locked in her formidable collection of Wagneriana a hidden extra copy of the first three quarters of the autobiography. The mystery with which Wagner in the eighteen-seventies surrounded the preparation of these three sections for the press (the final part was printed at Bayreuth in 1881) and his repeated pleas for extraordinary discretion lest a proof or copy slip out had led the printer, Bonfantini of Basel, to realize how valuable a prize lay in his hands. Not surprisingly, he did what Wagner most feared and, in addition to the eighteen copies ordered, clandestinely struck off a nineteenth for himself, laying it aside. The unbound and uncut sheets passed to Bonfantini's widow, from whom Mrs. Burrell purchased them. The completed sections of the latter's biography of Wagner, published in 1898, the year of her death, clearly revealed a contraband copy to be in the Burrell archives, and Cosima, facing the danger that one day private and public print might be collated, restrained her editorial hand. In general, the changes she introduced into the public edition attempted to soften some of her husband's observations on personalities, an aim the very opposite to that attributed to her in respect to the private print by Mrs. Burrell, who had seen her as blackening others to make Wagner shine the brighter. Unwilling to believe him guilty of the crudities of *Mein Leben*, Mrs. Burrell had mistakenly imagined Cosima its true author.

In 1963 the Munich publishing house of Paul List brought out an edition of *Mein Leben* based directly upon the manuscript Cosima wrote from Wagner's dictation. This scholarly work not only makes available their emendations and marginal glosses and considers the differences among manuscript, private print, and public edition but also includes Wagner's Annals.

These were cryptic memoranda extracted from the red notebook in which, since 1835, he had jotted down the main incidents of his life. Wishing to prevent future comparison between his frank, contemporary estimates of men and events in this Red Book and their frequent post-factum manipulation or suppression in the autobiography, he started in February, 1868, to transfer from the Red Book into a so-called "Brown Book" the information needed to jog his memory while completing *Mein Leben*. These Annals entered, he destroyed the potentially compromising Red Book except for its four opening pages, which, being uncontroversial, provided a fine memento. The replacement of the Red Book by the synoptic Brown Book Annals is to be regretted; one longs, for example, to know how the Red Book treated the Laussot affair, so utterly misrepresented in *Mein Leben*. But the Annals are, nonetheless, valuable records, especially for the clarifying but quickly vanishing flashes of light they sometimes throw upon the Richard-Cosima-Hans-Ludwig tangle.

Prudently, Wagner brought *Mein Leben* only to May of 1864, the date of his

out his statement in the private printing that during the visit, sobbing and weeping, they acknowledged that henceforth they belonged to one another alone.

From Berlin he journeyed to Löwenberg, where he was to conduct the private orchestra of the Prince of Hohenzollern-Hechingen, an enthusiast for the new music of the Liszt school. Bülow had conducted the *Faust Overture* for him in 1858. Unluckily, the generous prince was really too old and financially exhausted to be of much use to Wagner. But the neighborhood offered another opportunity.

Nearby was the estate of Henriette von Bissing, the wealthy widowed sister of his old Zurich friend, Frau Wille. Henriette had been among the company that heard Wagner's first reading of the *Ring* poem at Mariafeld in 1852. To this good woman he opened his heart and sang the old, well-rehearsed saga of his miseries. Deeply touched, she was soon to promise him sufficient income to guarantee his independence. She joined him at his hotel in Breslau, where he conducted a final concert before returning to Vienna. Apparently, he hinted to her that they would one day marry. During this period he confided to friends that his salvation lay in a good match, and in one of his most shocking letters (March 21, 1864, to Pusinelli) he was to speak of Minna's mere existence as the cause of his difficulties. This Napoleon felt that the time had come to exchange an old Beauharnais for a Hapsburg.

The Breslau concert on December 7 had been organized by Leopold Damrosch, whom Wagner had met in Weimar some two years before. The composer was perplexed to find Breslau's musical life almost exclusively in the hands of Jews, who treated him with great politeness. A confidante of Cosima's, Marie von Buch (later Countess von Schleinitz), appeared in the

---

summons to Munich. It was to be Cosima's task, with the aid of the final entries in the Annals—they do not go beyond 1868—and her own diaries, to complete the tale to the composer's death. But his wish that she finish *Mein Leben* was never carried out, and only Wagnerian party members were given access to her journals.

Yet, with the decades, Cosima herself had been slowly changing. This highly intelligent woman began to realize that her inability to call back all the widely dispersed Wagnerian documents made it impossible to edit her ideal Wagner into paper existence. She had, for example, forced the deletion of compromising material from the publications of Wagner's letters to Mathilde Wesendonk and from the Uhlig correspondence. But such manuscripts, or copies of them, lay beyond her grasp. Her strongbox, as the cataloguers of the Burrell Collection observed, had often doubled as incinerator. (Though drafts of some of the Nietzsche letters she destroyed survive in his papers, her burning of Cornelius' letters to Wagner can never be made good.) Time was on the side of truth, and in the end Cosima had to content herself with postponement. Her journals mysteriously vanished from the Bayreuth archives and just as mysteriously became the property of Eva (Frau Houston Stewart) Chamberlain. At the latter's death they disappeared into the recesses of a Munich bank from which they are scheduled to emerge sometime during the next decade.

rather tawdry beer parlor that had been transformed into a concert room. Matters were becoming incredibly complicated. On December 9 Wagner quit Silesia and returned to Vienna. Henriette and Cosima were apparently to await the hour when fate would unite them with the hero. In the path of the first was Minna, still stubbornly alive; Cosima's obstacles were Hans and the demands of her Berlin home, which now included two daughters, Daniela and Blandine. It is not improbable that Wagner hoped one day simultaneously to enjoy the security of Henriette as a wife and the pleasure of young Cosima as his mistress.

But Henriette was soon up in arms and retracted her promise. Fantastic tales were circulating about the household Wagner had set up during the preceding spring and which drew him back to Vienna. Doubtlessly the Wesendonks had heard the gossip, too. Here was the secret of the disappearance of his funds, his increasing indebtedness. He had embarked upon a folly that would almost lead him to a second term in jail.

9

Wagner's fifth and final concert in St. Petersburg on April 17, 1863, had been a benefit for unfortunates close to his heart—those imprisoned for debt. He was back in Vienna at the end of the month. Seemingly, Minna had hoped that he would return by way of Dresden, but he wrote, "You would be wise, dear Minna, no longer to concern yourself with what I do or don't do . . . ; only in this way could you contribute to my peace." On May 12, two days after sending this sullen message, he moved into new quarters.

They comprised the upper story and parklike garden of a stately house in suburban Penzing. In Biebrich his architect-landlord had taken over the Beaver's Nest for his own purposes, and Wagner had to establish a new home. He anticipated future invitations to Russia, and the Austrian capital seemed a convenient place between East and West. Moreover, the musical taste of the Viennese public was the most highly developed in Europe, and their enthusiasm at his concerts had deceived him into believing that the *Tristan* plan might be resurrected. Siccardsburg's and Van der Nüll's splendid opera house was rising on the newly created Ringstrasse, and so great was Wagner's interest in their work that he issued a pamphlet on the artistic mission of such a theater, recommending that it adopt many of the rehearsal procedures of the Paris Opéra. He had come to love the Viennese and their city, where he now hoped to take up the *Meistersinger* score again.

With a reckless enthusiasm for luxury and an equally reckless optimism about a Russian tour that never took place, he poured all his assets and much borrowed money into his new establishment, being intoxicated with a preposterous interior decorating scheme—with matching wardrobe—that was to provide Vienna with delicious material for satire. He took the caretakers of the house, the Bohemian Franz Mrazek and his wife, Anna, into his personal service, as well as a maidservant. A crew of decorators and the seamstress Bertha Goldwag labored to achieve his exacting demands.

Walls vanished behind hangings of silk and velvet. Violet and red dominated a costly profusion of heavy carpets, deep cushions, plush chairs, and poufs, the whole accented with garlands, passementeries, and decorative braidings of lace. And through these outlandish settings he flitted in satin pants with matching slippers and jackets, almost everything being padded and lined with fur. For his most relaxed moments, he had Bertha stitch for him twenty-four silk dressing gowns of various colors.

In Prague, the fifteen-year-old Lilli Lehmann had been aghast at Wagner's manner of dress. He had appeared in a yellow damask dressing gown, pink tie, and voluminous black velvet cape lined with rose satin. Thoroughly frightened by this apparition and its impetuous hugs and kisses, she had to be quieted by Mamma Marie, who later joked with her old friend about his bantering proposal to adopt the talented young charmer. For both Marie and Richard it must have been a case of *ridentem dicere verum*. She had known his inflammable personality since he courted her during his wild student days in Leipzig and guessed that her daughter's voice was not what most interested him. His choice of a playmate for his Penzing nest some months later showed that Lilli's tearful panic arose from sound instincts.

Desiring company at mealtime—so he declared—he tried out as companions two daughters of a pork butcher in the Josefstadt. Lisbeth, the younger and only seventeen, seemed unable to grasp the full extent of her duties. But Marie was more knowing. Answering to "sweetheart," she learned how to heat his study, to perfume it with heavy scent, and, sporting the pink drawers that so delighted the master, to await his arrival, doubtlessly in one of Bertha's two dozen padded silk and fur marvels.

Having exchanged eternal vows in Berlin with Cosima and concluded an arrangement in Breslau with Henriette, he had rushed back to Vienna and the young embraces of Mariechen. He also tried to persuade Mathilde Maier to come and supervise his household! To Minna's daughter Natalie he had written from Penzing, "I'll stay by myself, and no one shall take her [Minna's] place. . . . My lot is loneliness, my life—work!"

Friends like Cornelius had long foreseen calamity in the Penzing adventure, and by the spring of 1864 it was clear even to Wagner that he was approaching no ordinary financial crisis but perhaps final ruin and disgrace. Silence on the part of Grand Duchess Helene answered his entreaties, his last request (March) having been that she allow him a pension for Minna's support, a responsibility soon shifted to the long-suffering Pusinelli. At times of stress Wagner resented the necessity of providing for her, although he felt it quite natural to keep one hundred bottles of champagne in his cellar.

Castles in the air, and the very material one in Penzing, had been built on unrealized hopes. Unable to meet expenses and raising money at ruinous rates with no prospect of repayment, he was finally reduced to asking young Tausig [10] to endorse a note. Borrowings and mounting interest were reaching staggering sums. His worries became unendurable. Moreover, as an artist he seemed written out; *Meistersinger* stood still. What few musical ideas came displeased him, and he often believed that the opera would have to be abandoned. He must have been in a state not far from deranged when he penned that shocking letter insinuating that his salvation lay in Minna's death. Nor, sadly, was she unaware of his impatience to hear news of her end.

By the third week in March his creditors were moving toward what seemed the only solution of their problem; Wagner's person and possessions were threatened with immediate seizure. Quickly assigning his furnishings to Mariechen, he fled Vienna on March 23, leaving behind silks and satins, ribbons and bows, laces and poufs, sweetheart and wine cellar, and a recently acquired brown hound named "Pohl." Because of the note [11] Tausig found himself in a dangerous position, and he, too, was forced to avoid the city.

Wagner again escaped to Switzerland, this time by way of Munich, a city mourning the death of King Maximilian. He paused before a shop window to admire a picture of the new Bavarian monarch, a dark, handsome youth. Mariafeld, the Willes' estate near Zurich, was Wagner's goal. [12] From Penzing he had written Frau Wille, urging her to persuade the Wesendonks to make their mansion or the Asyl available to him. He required "only food and service" and would be "in no way a burden." But Otto Wesendonk, having no intention of once again hazarding the control of his household, had declined to put the composer up at the Green Hill. Fortunately for him, Dr. Wille was away in Constantinople, and his wife, once called "Fricka" by Wagner because she left the première reading of the *Ring* poem to attend her sick child, welcomed the fugitive, who was comfortably installed for several weeks.

Upon his return Wille was appalled to find in his home the man who had

---

[10] The two of them had given a joint recital in the large Redouten-Saal (December 27), Wagner conducting the *Freischütz* overture among other selections.

[11] Wagner rarely made such matters good. Kietz, for example, had never recovered financially from his attempts to help Wagner during the early days in Paris.

[12] Wagner had also thought of living with Mathilde Maier and her family if only they might be persuaded to quit Mainz.

taken such liberties in Otto's. The latter in the meantime had offered Wagner a modest monthly pension as long as he remained in remote Mariafeld. Frau Wille wrote, "Wagner's stay at Mariafeld was not an unmitigated joy." Realizing that the kind of money and adulation he required were no longer to be had from his old Swiss friends, Wagner left for Stuttgart on April 28. A sigh of relief rose from Zurich.

Karl Eckert was *Kapellmeister* at Stuttgart's court theater. He had once helped bring *Lohengrin* before the Viennese public and recently had journeyed to Karlsruhe to hear Wagner conduct. Perhaps this enthusiast would now mount *Lohengrin* in the Württemberg capital; or he might find the composer a refuge in which to turn out sufficient *Meistersinger* manuscript to justify another financial foray against Schott. Wagner was clutching at phantoms.

To Cornelius he had written that only a miracle could save him. He was tired, confused, and bitter. Not only did he believe himself indebted to no one but, on the contrary, held the world in arrears to him for the beauty he was bringing it. Luxury was a Wagner's due; he demanded beauty and brilliance. The Wanderer in *Siegfried* sings of himself as the "Alberich of light" ruling from cloud-hidden heights. But the world was thankless. Wagner saw himself a victim of man's ingratitude, of feigned friendship, of benefits forgot. Yet his was not the resigned irony of Arden Forest but the fury of the stormy heath. In Mariafeld he had dreamed that he was King Lear wandering through the raging tempest as the fool sang him derisive songs.

As Wagner sat in Eckert's hospitable home rehearsing his problems, a Herr Pfistermeister's card was brought in. On it was written, "Secretary to the King of Bavaria." Answer was immediately sent that Wagner was not there. Obviously, the "secretary" was a decoy set afloat by creditors. At his hotel Wagner found an urgent message from the mysterious visitor. A morning appointment was set up, and Wagner spent a sleepless night pondering what new disaster threatened.

Pfistermeister entered his room at ten. He bore a photograph and ring of the Bavarian king and handed these relics to the dumfounded composer whom he had tracked to Stuttgart after seeking him at Penzing and Mariafeld. It was the King's desire that Wagner proceed to Munich, where, under royal protection, he was to live free from material care and bring his artistic mission to completion.

A miracle, indeed! Wagner's own Lohengrin had appeared. As he was taking his meal at Eckert's before departing, news was brought confirming the dawn of a new operatic day. Black Alberich, the archfiend, was no more. With bells attached to hands and feet to signal any sign of life, Meyerbeer, who had feared being buried alive, lay dead in Paris.

X

Power Politics and Love in Munich: Wagner-Ludwig

After an emotional meeting with Wagner in Munich's Residenz Palace, King Ludwig rented Villa Pellet on Lake Starnberg for him so that they might pass the summer near one another. From this new home the royal carriage brought him to the castle at Berg within minutes. He hastened daily to Ludwig "as to a sweetheart," and they talked of their artistic plans. Looking at the "glorious" youth, Wagner felt himself in the presence of a miracle, "that precious reward of my genius . . . born for me out of the womb of a queen." Ludwig, believing that to succor this man gave his new authority its only meaning, could scarcely believe his own good fortune and wrote him, "Now, oh wonder, the moment has come, now that the royal purple enfolds me! Since the power is mine, I will use it to sweeten your life. . . . The most beautiful moments of my life I have received from you, everything, everything from you, every joy, every rapture!" Wagner informed Frau Wille that he and Ludwig would frequently sit together by the hour, lost in mutual contemplation.

Ever since Ludwig's governess, Baroness Sibylle Meilhaus, had inspired him with tales of the Munich première of *Lohengrin,* his enthusiasm for Wagner had grown,[1] a development heartening in a prince hitherto with few enthusiasms. Tutors could interest him in little. They included two famous professors from the University of Munich, Ignaz von Döllinger, the great Bavarian theologian and historian, and the chemist Justus von Liebig. Their pupil could rarely sustain concentrated thought, and the court was concerned to observe the royal heir lost in solitude, reverie, and daydreams and struggling to remain apart from the real world. A natural intelligence

---

[1] Years later he wrote Wagner, "Through this work there began to glow in me the holy, eternal love for you which blesses me and feeds the fiber of my being."

and sensitivity often gave him an intuitive comprehension of men and events, but a sickly torpor hindered his pursuing any idea consistently. This magnificent physical specimen was devoid of energy. Even his piano studies were followed with lassitude, for, indeed, music itself did not particularly arouse him. The theater alone could do this—especially the impassioned dramas of Schiller. But not until he encountered the *Schwärmerei* of *Lohengrin* did the moody, oversensitive adolescent feel that his melancholy had found its ideal artistic counterpart. Through Wagner he suddenly experienced "heavenly joy midst earthly pain."

After attending his first performance of the opera in 1861, he had embarked upon a program of self-education based upon a study of Wagner's writings, considering him his best instructor. He later wrote to Cosima that when still a boy he passed joyfully through the woods and meadows near Hohenschwangau, carrying Wagner's image in his spirit and heart, and on the mirrorlike Alpine lake read the *Ring*. Such indoctrination was not without hazards to an already strange mind. But, though Teutonic myth fed Ludwig's neurotic strain, he imbibed the romance of Wagner's tales while rejecting the drossy didacticism of his essays. It is doubtful that he ever took Wagner's lectures more seriously than Döllinger's or Liebig's. Wagner learned this fact slowly and reluctantly, perhaps because the boy at first seemed so utterly his own and had even adopted a kind of ecstatic Wagnerian prose, the styles of Uncle Adolf Wagner and Professor Weisse, those literary mentors of the composer's youth, reaching in Ludwig an unforeseen royal culmination.

Wagner spoke and wrote of the King with a delirium causing some to wonder whether the glorifier of the German woman had not suffered a sexual change of direction not unknown to middle age. Such was not the case. What seemed a propensity toward homosexuality evidently remained sublimated, although he wrote to Mathilde Maier that his first interview with Ludwig was a "love scene both seemed reluctant to end" and their relationship a kind of liaison. Wagner was heady with his new position and its opportunities for artistic achievement and political power. Everything seemed unreal, magical. Only a month before at Mariafeld he had dreamed of being summoned by Frederick the Great to join Voltaire at Potsdam! Was he now awake or asleep? Contrast with the immediate past was too great for him not to lose his balance for a while. And the King's exquisite beauty conquered everyone; even Bismarck felt its force. In the very first lines Wagner sent Ludwig, the correct note had been struck, and throughout the ups and downs of a tortured relationship, both men rarely departed from this overcharged manner of address when dealing with one another, their impassioned arioso being thoroughly Wagnerian and knowing no *secco* recitative. Every idea and emotion was through-composed.

Wagner seemed concerned lest his good fortune vanish as suddenly as it had come. Bülow was no doubt amazed to learn from him that he would immediately expire should the beloved princeling die. To Eliza Wille he communicated fears that the "beautiful and gifted, spiritual and noble" young king seemed so remote from the vulgar world that he was perhaps destined to fade "like a fleeting dream of the gods." Alarmed, Wagner determined to nourish what at times seemed more vision than reality.

He declared that Ludwig loved him "with the ardor and glow of a first love," and, tragically for the boy, the boast was true. To maintain the temperature of this infatuation it was imperative for the composer to present himself in the role of a virtuous philosopher much buffeted by an ungrateful world. He was quick to cast Ludwig as Parsifal, a male vestal, and "Parsifal" did, in fact, become his secret nickname in Wagner's circle. He, of course, wished to appear as Gurnemanz, wise advisor to the young Grail King. Certainly he saw danger in his new situation from the first; if Ludwig was not yet fully conscious of the homosexual stirrings within himself, the worldly-wise Wagner must have recognized his fate and the problems an increasingly publicized friendship might raise. Ludwig was to act out his Wagnerian fantasies with mounting boldness, the *Lohengrin* and *Parsifal* libretti becoming the very pivots of his existence. Not content with dressing himself and his favorites as Wagner heroes, he would one day command an army of workmen to raise a Monsalvat-like sanctuary on a high mountain,[2] where in all-male company he could retire from the world to brood. The light illumining this temple—not surprisingly, planned by Jank, Munich's leading designer of operatic scenery—was reflected from Wagner's poetry. When with passing years the King, like Amfortas, succumbed to the snares of the flesh as before his eyes Klingsor's Flower Maidens took the shapes of enchanting equerries, soldiers, and actors, he turned in his guilt to these libretti for consolation and strength. He strove for the renunciatory strength of Parsifal but died an unredeemed Amfortas. Nonetheless, Wagnerian drama, not Wagner, was the loadstone of this tragic life. With pain Ludwig slowly learned that the artist, while ostensibly playing Gurnemanz, often slipped into the part of Kundry, that complicated creature who simultaneously built and destroyed.

[2] As early as the spring of 1868 the King was planning to erect Schloss Neuschwanstein over the medieval ruins near the Pöllat gorge "in the authentic style of the old German knightly strongholds." While at Paris during the preceding year for the Exposition, he had visited the castle of Pierrefonds near Compiègne, which the architect Viollet-le-Duc had "restored" to a Gothic condition it had never known. Napoleon and Eugénie delighted in his work, and Ludwig doubtlessly saw in the Pöllat site the opportunity for a similar creation. The exterior of Neuschwanstein was to be one of the most evocative fantasies of the Gothic Revival.

2

In addition to assurances of bounty to come, Ludwig had straightway granted Wagner thousands of gulden with which to settle pressing debts. But the composer intended to pocket what he could by keeping creditors ignorant of his turn in fortune for as long as possible and then, the news becoming known, to belittle it as exaggerated by absurd rumor. It is rather sickening to observe his deception of an old creditor and benefactor like Pusinelli, whom, along with Frau Tichatschek, he asked to continue Minna's support for a while. The latter was informed that he was living on "a small salary" from the King. He claimed to have just enough to manage, a Wagnerian concept of modest means permitting him to contact his Viennese seamstress, Bertha, concerning quantities of heavy satin in deep rose, pale pink, blue, crimson, dark yellow, and light brown. Those dressing gowns abandoned in Penzing had to be replaced. A journalist was to refer to the bombastic poem of praise [3] Wagner penned for Ludwig that summer as "a rhymed receipt."

Wagner had visited Vienna for a few days in May and June to gather up his servants (the Mrazeks) and the dog, to pay the most urgent debts, and to repurchase what could be located of his auctioned possessions. In a fury against friends who had faithfully acted to protect what they could of his property from the Viennese deluge he himself had let loose, he blamed them for his losses and wrote Mathilde Maier of their "unbelievable stupidity." Cornelius especially aroused his ire by refusing an invitation to settle permanently with him in Bavaria. In his strange way he loved Peter. During the dark hours at Mariafeld he had gloomily written to Dr. Standhartner in Vienna, "One thing! Send *Peter* to me soon! . . . He must share all sorrow with me. . . . Only death must he leave to me alone; he need only be close by!" Now he found it incomprehensible that Peter preferred work on his opera *The Cid* to the post of jester at the new Wagnerian court. Wagner was becoming more and more intractable. The opposing side of a problem had never been within his vision; now even the middle ground was blurring. One was either for or against him, and to be for him implied a complete sacrifice of personal desires. Cornelius reflected that he was treating old friends "like bootblacks." In a mood of deep resentment Wagner had stormed Wotan-like from Vienna to take up residence at Villa Pellet.

He was lonely; the house was desolate, his bed unshared. The rarefied air enveloping his interviews with the King left him gasping. He could

---

[3] The fifth stanza of *"Dem königlichen Freunde"* echoes *Valkyrie,* its imagery evoking an embarrassing picture of Wagner-Sieglinde awakened by Ludwig-Siegmund.

write that the dear lad was "everything" to him—"wife and child, friend and brother"—and that communion with his photograph helped stifle desire for a female companion. "Ah! this sweet youth!" he cried. But such literature was meant for others; the demands of reality would not be put down.

Cosima, among other ladies, was obviously on his mind, but for a time he hesitated to embark upon a course that would end in Hans's ruin. Perhaps he thought affectionately of the rain-soaked boy who years before had presented himself in Zurich at Villa Rienzi. Wagner summoned Mariechen from Vienna and Mathilde Maier from Mainz, but neither was eager to enter a domestic alliance with him. (Not even a personal appeal from the Bavarian King could make the lady of the pink drawers change her mind.) Early in June Wagner had evidently resolved to put aside sentimental hesitance; he invited the Bülows with their children and maid to vacation at Villa Pellet. He would be without company during the second half of June and early July, when Ludwig was going to Kissingen. It was a propitious time to put Cosima's Berlin avowals to the test.

All except Hans journeyed to Lake Starnberg at the end of June. He followed a week later, a week that shaped the rest of his life. Cosima had come to give herself to Wagner. By meeting his need she consecrated herself to his art. She had looked upon Frau Wesendonk's reluctance to take a stand with him as pitiful. No "pale and sickly" Mathilde repressed by bourgeois considerations, she dared all. In her opinion, Mathilde, "very nice, although a bit sentimental," had borne herself poorly in respect to the composer. But Hans, too, was necessary to Wagner's plans. An important place awaited him in the musical program being formulated with the King. It was a bold game to steal the wife while keeping the husband bound in duty and devotion. But Siegfried had done it; the motive of the wife exchange had a venerable Eddic tradition, and Hans seemed born for the part of Gunther.

Probably the lovers soon told him of their relationship. He had arrived exhausted and overwrought. Certainly he remembered those wretched days at Biebrich and, not unlikely, had from the first suspected the purpose of an invitation described to him by Wagner as the product of "lengthy deliberations." Run down, his nerves in shreds, for a while Hans may have fought his fate. But, despite a blustering Prussian exterior and caustic tongue, he was weak, and Wagner skillfully exploited the masochism of a man who could sign himself "vassal and servant" and close a letter with "at your feet." [4]

---

[4] Some months after Blandine's and Cosima's arrival at his mother's Berlin home, Hans wrote to his old friend Jessie Laussot that he was embarrassed by the girls' superiority and was sure he seemed terribly uninteresting to them. He was self-possessed only in front of an orchestra or at the keyboard.

Richard Wagner during the
Munich period (1865)

Ludwig Geyer, Wagner's father

Albert Wagner,
the composer's eldest brother

Cäcilie (Geyer) Avenarius,
Wagner's youngest sister

The Leipzig market place as it appeared during Wagner's youth. His uncle Adolf lived in the taller house (left) at the end of the square.

Rosalie Wagner,
the composer's eldest sister

"The Red and White Lion," the birthplace of Wagner (demolished in 1886), on the Brühl in Leipzig

Wilhelmine Schröder-Devrient

Cosima (Liszt) von Bülow in 1863

Minna (Planer) Wagner as she looked when the composer first met her (oil portrait by Otterstedt in the Burrell Collection)

Minna (with Peps) and Richard Wagner during the early years of his Swiss exile

Otto Wesendonk in 1860

Mathilde Wesendonk, by C. Dorner

Princess Carolyne Sayn-Wittgenstein

King Ludwig II of Bavaria
in his coronation robes

Ludwig II with his fiancée,
Duchess Sophie Charlotte of Bavaria

Ludwig II with Josef Kainz

The Munich Hoftheater, scene of the premières of *Tristan, Meistersinger, Rhinegold,* and *Valkyrie*

Malvina and Ludwig Schnorr von Carolsfeld in the title roles of *Tristan and Isolde*

Cosima during the Triebschen period

Wagner in 1865 with Pohl

Wagner in London, 1877

Wagner during his visit
to Munich, autumn, 1880

Wagner as drawn by cartoonists of his time:

Left: The tag on Pecht's portrait of Wagner alludes to its cost to Ludwig II; Wagner is shown as a modern Orpheus able to charm gold from King Ludwig's treasury; the "monk," a symbol of Munich, warns the composer that his arrogance betokens a fall.

Below: André Gill's famous statement on Wagnerian music

RICHARD WAGNER, par GILL.

Franz Betz as Wotan
in the first Bayreuth festival

Joseph Tichatschek as Rienzi

The Bayreuth Festspielhaus, side view: The highest section is the stage house, the auditorium being to its right

Theodor Reichmann as Amfortas
in the second Bayreuth festival

Albert Niemann as Siegmund
in the first Bayreuth festival

The interior of the Festspielhaus before the turn of the century

Cosima Wagner, as seen by cartoonists,
protecting the *Parsifal* score: *Above:* A satyr—
Heinrich Conried, manager of New York's
Metropolitan Opera—attempts to wrest it from
her; *right:* Cosima, "guardian of the Grail,"
sits on the score.

The garden façade of Wagner's house in Munich

The last photograph,
taken by Adolf von Gross
in 1883

The Palazzo Vendramin, scene of Wagner's death, in Venice

The Wagner-Bülow family in 1894
Left to right: Siegfried, Biagio Gravina (Blandine's husband), Blandine, Daniela, Isolde, Eva, and Cosima

Wagner's grandchildren, Verena and Wieland, greet the Führer at the entrance to the Bayreuth Festspielhaus.

A bit past the middle of August he suffered something not unlike a stroke, possibly the result of being forced day after day to face the fact and the cause of his radically changed domestic situation. His wife had taken a second husband. He lay paralyzed for days at the Hotel Bayerischer Hof. Did he have himself brought there from the lake because, as Wagner insisted, Munich offered better medical service or, rather, because, for the moment, he could not bear to be under the composer's roof? To use Wagner's own adjective, Hans was not only ill but "enraged."

Cosima was not at his side. Apparently wishing to disclose the predicament to her father and to seek his advice, she had rushed off to Karlsruhe, where Liszt was attending a music festival. From there he returned with her to Munich, where over Hans's sickbed his eyes met Wagner's for the first time since the Weimar concerts of three years earlier. Liszt must have been thoroughly dejected. Wagner observed how gray he had become. His son Daniel had died of tuberculosis at the end of 1859; Blandine had given her life shortly after bringing another Daniel into the world; and now Cosima's marriage was shattered. He spent some hours with Wagner at Starnberg, and, though his heart was lifted by what he read of *Meistersinger* at the piano, his conversation probably also touched upon the less sunny subject of Cosima.

She was pregnant. One wonders whether she knew whose child she was carrying. At a trial in 1914 concerning the disposition of the Wagner inheritance, the family's dirtiest linen was publicly aired. Cosima found herself testifying that from June to October of 1864 she had had sexual relations only with Wagner. But his housekeeper, the then ancient Anna Mrazek, deposed that during Hans's stay at Villa Pellet Cosima shared his bedroom. That the child Isolde, born in April of 1865, was Wagner's would perhaps not have been legally denied could it have been established with certainty that Hans made no demands upon his wife during the weeks at Starnberg. Indeed, he was ill much of the time. But can one believe that this blunt Prussian was play acting when he greeted Isolde's birth with joy? In his Berlin way he announced that for the third time he had become "a mother." He must have had some reasonable hope that his wife's latest child was his. Most likely no one was really certain of the infant's paternity until the passing weeks saw the development of that unmistakable domelike brow, aquiline nose, and protruding jaw.

In the light of Anna's statement it would seem that Wagner and Bülow shared Cosima during the summer. She certainly was openly to pass back and forth between them throughout the coming months. Evidently Wagner had forced Bülow to accept and make the best of a *fait accompli*. Cosima's testimony at the trial implied that after October she was again sleeping with someone other than Wagner, and, of course, during the early autumn she was separated from him and back with her husband.

The very novelty of the *à trois* arrangement at Villa Pellet seemed to exhilarate the lovers. Wagner started a string quartet. The form was unusually intimate for him, and his ideas for the piece did not reach full expression until put to use later in a chamber work on a larger scale—the *Siegfried Idyll*. This same thematic material from the Starnberg quartet also survives in the final act of *Siegfried*. When Cosima bore Wagner a son in 1869, he celebrated the event by inserting these melodies designed for the quartet into the opera's monumental final duet. But major surgery was needed for this graft, and the scars never healed. A section of Brynhild's text was altered, and, in a mangled prosody and tortured syntax, she was enabled to sing her tenderest entreaties to tunes originally conceived for the quartet in honor of Cosima. For decades, until the secret of the insert became known, critics remained perplexed by the great passage, whose text begins with *"Ewig war ich"* and ends with *"vernichte dein Eigen nicht!"* Its simple lyricism contrasts strangely with the relatively turgid texture of the surrounding music. The episode seems to have dropped into the score from another musical world. And so, indeed, it had.

Though the Starnberg melodies recalled blissful hours to Richard and Cosima, for Hans they must have been wormwood. From the time of his stay at Villa Pellet he was permanently ill and wretched. But he danced to Wagner's call to the bitter finale and, characteristically, ended by excusing himself to Cosima.

Wagner's diary reveals his pain at separation when early in September a very sick Hans took Cosima and the children back to Prussia to wind up affairs and prepare for the move to Munich. Miserable in Berlin, where his career was an unending war with the critics, he could not resist what Wagner was offering—an unparalleled opportunity to rise in the new order of art about to be called into being by the King. During the summer Wagner had sent Hans to Berg castle to play for Ludwig, with whom he had dined alone, an extraordinary sign of royal favor. Obviously, his talent would be properly esteemed in Bavaria. Wagner no longer wished to conduct more than occasionally. He tired easily, and his memory, one suspects, was no longer dependable. Hans was to hold the baton in model performances in Munich that would astound the world. Professionally much was to be gained by allying himself with his betrayer and master, whose art he would worship to his last day. A descendant of the composer-hero of Waterloo, Count Friedrich Bülow of Dennewitz, Hans was ready to suffer any humiliation in his private life to avoid a public scandal and damage to the military name he revered. Moreover, he was responsive to Wagner's and Cosima's sadism and probably would not have sought escape even had he found an opening in the net being woven about him.

Wagner, too, was eager to keep the Bülow name unsoiled; above all, King

Parsifal's faith in Gurnemanz had to remain unshaken. Upon the royal good will now rested the incomes and artistic hopes of all. A trio of operatic conspirators had formed at Villa Pellet. The half-willing baritone looked uncomfortable in his costume and was in miserable voice; but Cosima and tenor Richard were adept at improvising a descant and at effecting fast changes of costume and mask. Their higher voices would carry the performance. Writing to Frau Wille, Wagner declared that it had been easy to persuade Ludwig to appoint Hans his pianist and that he had snatched his protégé from insanely nerve-wracking employment in Berlin to find him a nobler field of work! A poem he wrote for Cosima early in October ecstatically asked, "What new world is taking shape?"

3

In October he returned to Munich and occupied a splendid mansion, the Hôtel Jôchum on the Briennerstrasse.[5] This street, a continuation of the Nymphenburgerstrasse, connecting the neoclassic Königsplatz with the palace, held an important place in the program of Wagner and Ludwig. As axis and ceremonial way of the Wagner movement, it was to be prolonged through the royal gardens, pierce the St. Anne quarter, continue across a heroic bridge to be thrown over the Isar, and terminate at a Wagner theater dominating the terraces of the far bank.[6] By the end of December, Semper was in Munich, summoned from Zurich by the King to plan the ambitious undertaking. Ludwig I, an indefatigable builder, had raised Munich's classic gateways and museums and given the city the composite Greek-Roman-Florentine face it still shows; this Athens on Isar his grandson was now to crown with a monument to all the Muses, the temple of the *Gesamtkunstwerk*.

To prepare for performances in the new theater, the composer began to organize his ideas about a special conservatory to train singers, instrumentalists, and conductors in his style. Public taste would be guided both by a weekly journal of Wagnerian polemics, issued by the school's faculty, and by an allied newspaper elucidating the concept of civic rejuvenation through the Wagnerian drama. He took for granted that his artistic enterprises in Bavaria were to be part of the nation's political life. Thus, channels of communication free from the anti-Wagnerian attitudes so often found in a metropolitan press were to link the artist, his academy, and the layman.

[5] At first, the house was rented for him by the King, who later purchased it for what was hoped would be Wagner's lifelong use.

[6] On November 26, 1864, the King wrote Wagner of his decision to construct "a great stone theater," a plan which had already been thoroughly discussed by them.

If these projected organs of propaganda threatened an unimpeded flow of the usual Wagnerian nonsense on aesthetic, social, and political subjects, Wagner's sensible plans for the school did reveal a man aware, as few of his countrymen were, of the deficiencies in German music education and its faulty relationship to professional life. Many of the ideas advanced for the Munich school recall details of his "Draft for the Organization of a German National Theater for the Kingdom of Saxony" of his Dresden days. There, too, he had envisioned an institute that was "an organic whole," renewing itself and evolving "out of its own being." In both schemes, once the cycle was set, the school would nourish the theater with personnel, as the theater, in turn, provided the school's faculty. The spirit of *Meistersinger* pervaded the Munich plan with its exercises and competitions.

In Wagner's opinion, the vocal art was the prop needed to shore up musical pedagogy. Throughout his career, he had deplored the technique of the average German singer, and he was now resolved that, in Munich, song was to be the basis of all musical instruction. He hoped to oblige every instrumental and conducting student to take at least elementary instruction in singing. Study of Italian pieces in the original language was to be included in the curriculum in order to help students attain *bel canto* (*Gesangswohlklang*). The portato "Bayreuth bark" that has become the respected model of a widely imitated Wagnerian elocutionary style was a creation of Cosima's period; Wagner would be appalled by what often passes for singing in his operas today.

His immediate task was to complete the *Ring*. Toward this end a contract was drawn up, according him lavish compensation, maintenance allowances, and special grants so that he might find the peace of mind in which to conclude the work within three years. In return for Ludwig's munificence the tetralogy became royal property.

Early in 1865 the King agreed to Semper's suggestion that a provisional Wagner theater be erected in a wing of Munich's exhibition building, the Crystal Palace. The plan would enable the architect to work out many technical problems beforehand. They included new stage machinery and lighting devices, acoustic considerations, and, mainly, the method of constructing a hollow under the stage that would serve to envelop the instrumentalists without at the same time impairing their tonal quality. "Not too deep," Semper was to warn. Wagner realized that some such construction to reduce the volume but not the quality of sound had to be devised if his singers were to be heard easily through the massive orchestration of his latest scores. He remembered a small pit of this type at the Riga theater; it was to be the point of departure for Semper's experiments. Moreover, not only sound but sight concerned Wagner. He found the orchestra a distracting spectacle. As early as his Parisian short story

"A Happy Evening" (1841), he had inveighed against those who pressed toward the first rows in order to see the instrumentalists and remarked that "nothing is more prosaic and depressing than the sight of frightfully swollen cheeks . . . unaesthetic grabbling . . . wearisome bowing."

While awaiting the growth of the building schemes from paper to stone, Munich's existing musical facilities had to suffice for his older works. On December 4 *Dutchman* was performed under his baton. The Bülows had arrived in November and were comfortably settled in a house on the Luitpoldstrasse. But the threat of complete paralysis still hung over Hans. His health as well as the fact that the sick man had nonetheless to prepare a Christmas piano concert at the Odeon for the King (it included the "Emperor" Concerto, as well as works by Mozart and Bach) may have compelled Wagner's reluctant return to the operatic podium. *Kapellmeister* Franz Lachner did the spadework during the *Dutchman* rehearsals in order to spare the composer's energies. It was too early for Wagner to reveal his intention of supplanting such regulars of Munich's musical life with his own people.

Interestingly, when his artists found the *tessitura* of the finale taxing, he lowered it by half a tone, the spirit of a performance always being more important to him than the letter.

4

At first, Wagner recognized the wisdom of moving cautiously. But his egoism and tactlessness could not long remain disguised. In the beginning the jokes heard from palace to beer hall were indulgent; if the King wished to keep a composer rather than the more usual ballerina, it was his own affair. But Wagner refused to read the signs about him. Old Ludwig I was still alive and an object lesson. Not twenty years before, the pretensions of his mistress, the notorious Lola Montez,[7] had raised a public cry that

---

[7] Lola's origins were not as mysterious as she wished others to imagine. Variously rumored to have been stolen by Gypsies from her cradle, and to have come from Spain, Turkey, or India, and even believed to have been an illegitimate daughter of Lord Byron, she had, in fact, been born Eliza Gilbert in the city of Limerick. Her talents as dancer and actress were minimal, but beauty, wit, intelligence, an imperious nature, and a rebellious, indomitable will carried her to Europe's highest social and intellectual circles. Ludwig I elevated her to the Bavarian nobility as Baroness Rosenthal and Countess of Landsfeld, a composite of Landshut and Feldberg; her friends included Balzac, Hugo, Dumas, Sainte-Beuve, Gautier, Lamartine, Sue, Delacroix, Chopin, Rachel, and Mademoiselle Mars. She met Wagner when Liszt brought her to the Dresden performance of *Rienzi* specially scheduled for him early in 1844. Her astounding life spanned an unhappy youth in India and a phenomenal postlude to

brought to pass his abdication. As Wagner's native arrogance gradually showed itself more openly and his demands upon the treasury grew, he gained the popular nickname of "Lolotte." Since it was becoming common gossip that the young king had no interest in women, such remarks had unmistakable implications. At this time, through his own incredible indiscretions, Wagner gained a reputation still clinging to his name, that of being an active homosexual.

He called Bertha, his Viennese milliner, to Munich, and, with an army of decorators and upholsterers, she transformed the Briennerstrasse house into a whorish fantasy of silks, satins, velvets, and laces. The wonders of Penzing were re-created on a huge scale, Bertha alone furnishing fancy stuffs costing ten thousand gulden. To explain her imports to astounded customs men, she felt it wise to declare the bolts of finery and gorgeous costumes as intended for a countess in Berlin! Once again she created a grotesque Wagnerian wardrobe to harmonize with the décor.

As reports of such self-indulgence spread through Munich, indignation against Wagner's support by the royal treasury mounted. Peacocks roaming his garden seemed to confirm tales of Oriental opulence behind the baroque-style façade of the house. Was history repeating itself? It was on the Barerstrasse, not far from the Hôtel Jôchum, that Ludwig I had ordered architect Metzger to raise a palace in Italian style for Lola Montez, a dwelling filled with sculptures taken from the Glyptothek and paintings—among them a Raphael—pulled from the walls of the Alte Pinakothek. Lola's Pompeian drawing room, marvelous stairway of glass, mantelpiece of Sèvres porcelain, and perfumed fountain had been the talk of Munich. Magnificently clad, she passed through the city in a carriage bordered with gold, lined with ermine, and with crimson cushions. So great was her ascendance over the King that, when he joined her in the royal loge at the opera, she alone remained seated as the audience rose. With some reassurance, young Ludwig's advisors must have recalled the day when a seething mob had appeared before Lola's residence, smashing windows and battering the doors as she fled through the garden.

---

her career in America's Far West, where she became the most glamorous entertainer of California's gold-rush era. In the United States she performed *Lola Montez in Bavaria,* a play written especially for her, from New York to San Francisco, acting this anti-Jesuit drama against a painted cloth representing the glories of her Munich palace. An inveterate reformer and lecturer, she offered to instruct leaders of New York's Tammany Hall on the Jesuit danger! As "Fanny Gibbons" she settled in Brooklyn toward the end of her life and could be seen carrying copies of Pope's *Essay on Man* on her evening walks to the dairy farms of Flatbush, stopping at what is now Prospect Park to distribute them to young people. She lies in Brooklyn's famed Greenwood Cemetery. When informed of her death in misery and poverty, Wagner remarked, "Such daemonic and heartless beings are not to be pitied and regretted."

For the moment, the fantastic household of the "Lolus" or "Lolotte" of the Briennerstrasse was to be suffered and the *"roi jeune fille"* humored. Though his government was not particularly delighted with either Wagner's drain upon the exchequer or his projected building schemes and educational programs obviously intended to serve private ends, much was tolerated because of the King's youth. His steadfast devotion to Wagner's art was as yet not understood by courtiers who, confident that his enthusiasm would lower with time, possessed a multitude of devices for procrastination. In any case, they had no intention of permitting Munich to be reorganized and rebuilt according to a Wagnerian design. They would make certain that the grandiose plans remained unrealized. Poor Semper fashioned sketches and models and engaged in endless negotiations, discussions, and correspondence; but not a spade was ever turned for either the provisional or the permanent theater. Time, the court felt, was on its side; dissemble and delay were the watchwords; in general, royal favorites had short reigns, and Ludwig was easily bored. And if, as was expected, Wagner dared follow Lola's scenario to the end and attempted to interfere in politics, there was little doubt that Munich would rise to drive him out. Ludwig's ministers smiled, bowed, and waited.

5

Wagner's notorious involvement in the Dresden rising had not helped endear him to the court. Early in their friendship, Ludwig requested him to define his contemporary political thinking. The result was the essay "On State and Religion," of July, 1864. Its infrangible syntax does not yield much sense, but Ludwig loved this kind of thing and probably quoted what could be communicated of its vaporous contents to startled ministers, some of whom may have caught in it echoes of the Vaterlandsverein speech of 1848.

The essay hailed the King as a kind of superman, the representative of the "purely human" (*"der Vertreter des rein menschlichen Interesses"*); relaxation from his heavy burdens was to be found in the Wagnerian music drama, which would uplift him as it discoursed upon the Schopenhauerean nullity of reality. Ludwig was assured that Wagner had "never descended to the province of politics proper" and had been mistakenly branded a revolutionary by such limited creatures as police officials, who judge only from outward appearances; a statesman like Ludwig, however, could not be similarly misled. Perhaps Wagner knew that, fired by Schiller's *Don Carlos* and resentment against King Maximilian, his father, Ludwig himself had once planned a revolutionary drama.

Early in 1865 a soothsayer, Frau Dangl, assured Wagner that his destiny was to protect the young king from evil counselors. He hung upon her words, for she was repeating what little by little he had come religiously to believe. He wrote Frau Wille of "the King's wonderful, deep, foreordained affection." In a sense he was reliving those feverish, optimistic Dresden days before he turned against Friedrich of Saxony, and he now believed Ludwig to be that redeeming monarch described years before in his impassioned Vaterlandsverein address. Persuading himself that he faced a terrible choice, which he dramatized in letters to friends, he asked whether he could shirk his heaven-imposed duty to instruct and thus save Ludwig. Why was this cup directed to the artist's lips, to him who longed only for the repose in which to create? Why had there been placed in his hands the destiny of a nation—indeed, of greater Germany itself? He was in a highly agitated state and by September could write in his diary, "I am the most German of beings (*der deutscheste Mensch*); I am the German spirit. Consider the incomparable magic of my works."

Did he realize how closely he was following Lola's path? She, too, had seen her relationship to Bavaria's monarch in terms of a political charge, feeling that her moral obligation was to mold his mind by expounding the social theories of Lamennais, whom she had met in George Sand's salon. But there was a difference; in contrast to Wagner's, her ideas had been clear enough for old Ludwig to attempt their practice. She was whispered to be an agent of English Freemasonry and of Benjamin Disraeli! Her sharp thinking on public affairs brought her into direct contact with the framing of governmental policy. Lola's ideas, though radical, were intelligible. But during his life Wagner's foggy writings and utterances on matters of state served merely to stimulate heroic reveries in his followers, especially the royal neurotic adolescent. It was left to a later, darker age to convert these murky political thoughts into actions.

That politicians with special interests were seeking to make use of Wagner's influence at the palace helped strengthen his sense of mission. Moreover, the celestial Wagnerian city could be founded only in a sympathetic political atmosphere, and he knew that beneath their official politeness Ludwig's ministers were far from friendly. During the summer he advised the King to limit the authority of Cabinet Secretary Pfistermeister over artistic matters by appointing "an intendant of all departments of the royal household having to do with art," in short, a kind of special minister of Wagnerian affairs, someone who would pursue wholeheartedly the program drawn up by Ludwig and himself. This recommendation he reiterated in November, while spending a romantic holiday with the King in the mountain fastness of Hohenschwangau castle.

That same autumn of 1865 for Ludwig's edification he had begun a political journal, printed in censored form during Bayreuth days under the title, "What Is German?" Carefully copied out by Cosima from the original sketches, it scorned the "blustering" political disturbances of 1848 as "un-German," democracy in Germany being "a completely translated thing," a French concept foisted upon the nation by its Jewish press. It is amusing to observe the draft dodger of 1833 recommending universal military service to Germans as "no burden, but a beneficial branch of body culture." He saw some hope for making the Jew lose his Jewishness by conscripting him into a German Folk army modeled on that of Switzerland. He would "either vanish or be transformed into a true German."

As for the king, his role was to be more positive than that outlined in the Dresden Vaterlandsverein speech, where he was to abdicate and automatically to become the first republican of the land. Now he was simply to rise up and lead Germany to redemption. *Meistersinger* warned that German princes had so lost touch with native art that the task of preserving German culture was falling to the Folk alone. But Wagner refound in Ludwig the springtime of his political days in Dresden. Miraculously, *the* prince had appeared. Reciting Brynhild's "To new deeds," Wagner was sending his hero forth as savior of the German world. (But tenoring would avail little against Bismarck, as Ludwig soon discovered.) The journal hurled brickbats at Prussia and, of course, at the parasitic Jews, "the completely alien element" at bottom responsible for the corruption of the German spirit. "The German . . . sees himself . . . squeezed between Junker and Jew."

Evidently, Ludwig was to put the Prussians in their place, sort out the Jews, and then (perhaps attired as Lohengrin)[8] lead all worthy Germans down the Briennerstrasse and across the Isar to the new Nibelung theater. The lights out and music started, a thankful nation would find itself redeemed. Wagnerian thought was really very simple; his metaphysics and politics, hailed as a new revelation by his disciples, boiled down to a few preposterous ideas, repeated and slightly varied through the decades of his writing.

While orchestrating the Wood Bird scene in *Siegfried,* he had, in September, 1865, during a mood of "prophetic clarity," addressed a letter to Ludwig, his hero, the Siegfried of his life. He discoursed upon the meaning of their love and proclaimed the royal power and the heroic deed to be one—"the

[8] The King and his intimates enjoyed appearing in costume; his favorite, Prince Paul von Thurn und Taxis, arrayed as Lohengrin, was pulled across the lake at Hohenschwangau in a swan boat. An entry in Prince Hohenlohe's diary remarked that Ludwig had a special theatrical wardrobe tailored for himself and would slip it on in the privacy of his room. This delight in masquerading was yet another temperamental link to Wagner.

awakening of the noble bride through him; Germany is his Brynhild! I sing the song of this bride's awakening. It is a serious, solemn song, and yet intimate and deep. It is the meaningful promise (*Wort*) of the *German spirit*." Though this imagery compared Ludwig with Siegfried, a vision of the young king as Parsifal, the noble and chaste youth who redeems a racially debased realm, was obviously already before the composer's eyes. *Parsifal* was to set forth his ultimate ideas about a German ruler's duties. It was to be his final sermon to Ludwig and the one most filled with peril for posterity.

6

Autumn found him feeling quite secure. In contrast, the early part of 1865 had been a season of alarms. A scandal had arisen over the fee for a portrait he sat for and then sent to the Residenz; the King was startled to discover payment expected for what was ostensibly a gift.[9] Moreover, Wagner had referred to him with unbecoming familiarity as "my boy" in the presence of the Cabinet Secretary, the incredible blunder apparently confirming the worst of Munich gossip. Ludwig, sensitive to any sign of discourtesy toward his position, was angered and denied the composer audience. Rumor of his disgrace spread. Comments, charges, denials, and lampoons filled the newspapers.

An anonymous article by the poet Redwitz spoke respectfully of Wagner's art but, denouncing his luxurious living at public expense, advised that limits be set to an intimacy impairing the King's relationship with his subjects. Ludwig's displeasure, however, quickly faded, and tender notes and poetic exchanges continued between the palace and the house on the Briennerstrasse. Wagner knew the depth of his friend's emotional dependence upon him. The slightest hint that, Lohengrin-like, he might depart was sufficient to bring the boy to heel.

In Dresden, Minna read Redwitz's article and the satires on Wagner's ways, which she justifiably feared might "have very bad consequences, considering German standards. It is true that many small exaggerations are based on envy, but nevertheless I've heard the most fantastic little stories from eyewitnesses. . . . Let us pray for the poor soul of Rumorhäuser, as he is called."[10]

[9] The artist was Wagner's old friend Friedrich Pecht.
[10] This letter to Kietz is misdated March, 1864, in Macmillan's edition of the Burrell Collection. Minna refers to Wagner's summons to Munich "nearly a year ago" and to publications and events confirming the year as 1865. The German edition of the Collection rightfully questions the earlier date.

The spring had witnessed the emergencies accompanying the mounting of *Tristan*. The Schnorrs arrived from Dresden to sing the title roles, and Bülow received an appointment as special *Kapellmeister*. He worked himself to the bone. In an unguarded moment during a rehearsal he referred to the Munich public as *"Schweinehunde."* The Prussian's disparaging remark about the Bavarians, tossed out in a passing fit of pique, was gleefully picked up by the press and the indiscretion inflated to a major scandal threatening the entire production. Josephine Kaulbach, the painter's wife, observed that "since the Lola story, Munichers have not been so enraged." For a while it seemed that Hans might have to exit in the manner of La Montez. He apologized publicly.

The première had been set for the middle of May, and Wagner invited friends from afar. Frau Wesendonk declined, as did Eliza Wille; he felt vexed and abandoned, not possessing sufficient sensitivity in personal relationships to grasp how painful it would be for Mathilde and her circle to observe the secrets of her Zurich garden unfolding on the stage.

Pusinelli, too, was summoned, but at the same time cautioned to say nothing to Minna. Her appearance in Munich would be extremely awkward. Cosima had given birth some weeks before at the time of the first orchestral rehearsal of *Tristan,* and heads were already shaking over the question of little Isolde's paternity. Nor could Wagner have been eager for his wife to view the splendors of his establishment. Informed about his affair with Cosima and his extravagant manner of living, she had written Kietz, "Every three months I receive a crumb from R's abundance." As matters ended, Pusinelli could not leave Dresden; on the eve of the scheduled performance he was obliged to inform the Hôtel Jôchum that Minna lay fatally ill.

May 15 was an extraordinary day for Wagner. Not unexpectedly, Ludwig sent a hysterical letter, mainly patched together with extracts from *Tristan*. He could hardly contain himself until evening and the performance. Freely varying Isolde's part, he declared, "Born for you, fated to be yours, this is my mission!" A second communication from Pusinelli arrived in the morning, announcing that Minna had passed the crisis and would survive.

But the day's commotion was only beginning. Police officials entered Wagner's house with warrants to attach his furnishings for failure to settle the claims of Madame Schwabe, the English Jewess who had once generously lent him money in Paris. Despite his efforts to quash the idea that the King's coffers were at his disposal, old creditors, not fooled, were pressing their demands. Julie Schwabe quite justifiably expected to be repaid, and her attorney had given ample notice. Wagner had lamented that in such matters he never seemed to meet with "more high-minded, finer natures" and felt himself the victim of "the most shameless ruthlessness." He looked into mankind's heart and beheld only "an abyss." Cosima sped to the royal treasury and came away with twenty-four hundred florins to settle the matter.

Next came utterly calamitous news; sudden hoarseness had seized Malvina Schnorr. The *Tristan* performance was put off. Was its Viennese history to be repeated in Munich? Malvina was Germany's foremost dramatic soprano, with a voice of range and power. The talk that no vocal cords could survive Wagner's new style seemed confirmed.

"Perhaps tomorrow?" Ludwig optimistically wrote when learning of the postponement. But Madame Schnorr's indisposition lingered. She attempted to cure her catarrh at Reichenhall. In answer to a message from the distraught composer, she asked that "so absurd a telegram" not be sent again, for she and her husband "were suffering sufficiently." Not until June 10 did Munich give the first Wagnerian première in fifteen years. It demonstrated that his so-called "impossible" scores were indeed possible. Although the four performances were poorly attended and, understandably, a good part of the audience found the revolutionary work incomprehensible, Wagner's high opinion of the interpretation permits one to gauge its quality. Public reaction was more of bewilderment than hostility. The importance of the work as a seminal force on contemporary music can be compared with that of Stravinsky's *Sacre du Printemps* at the beginning of the present century.

Among the few who grasped the magnitude of what they heard were Edouard Schuré, who wrote the composer a moving letter of appreciation, and Anton Bruckner. The latter displayed the kind of slavish adoration Wagner had come to expect of disciples. In Bruckner's personal hierarchy Wagner sat between God the Father and the Bishop of Linz, and in the presence of the musical member of this trinity he remained standing. (Later, he once fell to his knees.) But, although happily surrounded at the première by a reverent group, Wagner was all the more infuriated that those he most wished to see held themselves aloof.

Not only had Mathilde Wesendonk and Frau Wille excused themselves, but Cornelius played truant in Weimar, where his *Cid* had been performed the month before,[11] and Liszt could not be coaxed from Rome. Many once close to Wagner could not bear to behold the monster of conceit he had become. (Cornelius' Barber of Bagdad is asked by the Caliph whether his claim to be a "total and universal genius . . . the barber of the future" justifies his stealing from contemporaries.) The eighteen-sixties represent a critical point in the deterioration of his character. Photographs, especially from the Munich period, reveal signs of change and tension appearing on

---

[11] Although Cornelius obviously desired to shun the *Tristan* première, he was so badly off at the time that he probably could not have afforded the fare to Munich even had he wished to go.

the once unassailable marblelike mask. Friends from better days did not wish to be near him. Nor would Liszt, who had recently received minor orders, have been especially happy to contemplate the Richard-Cosima-Hans triangle at close range.[12] Wagner felt embittered by the many absences; in the presence of *Tristan's* greatness, personal considerations seemed to him petty. But not all those who came were rewarded with unfailing courtesy. Poor Mathilde Maier faithfully hastened to Munich to discover that Wagner had cooled considerably toward her.

Ludwig was the happiest disciple. Searching for words, he ended by stammering the closing lines of the *Liebestod,* "To sink unconscious in the highest rapture." He always looked back upon these *Tristan* days as the most glorious of his reign. *Lohengrin* yielded its place to *Tristan* as his favorite opera. In 1872 he was to write Wagner, "Of all your works that I yet know, this one is dearest to me; . . . it seems as if fashioned for me and strikes the most sympathetic chords in my soul!"

A student of the text, he knew it by heart, and little could have escaped him in color and nuance. Certainly he was aware of the aura of homosexuality vibrating throughout. The Tristan-Melot-Mark relationship, into which Isolde not unknowingly intrudes, could not but awaken his compassionate response. This aspect of the plot should be explored; though more implied than clearly delineated, it is nonetheless broodingly present and must have made Ludwig all the more vulnerable to the opera's sorcery.

7

In the second act Brangäne seeks to put Isolde on guard against Melot's jealousy, inspired, she believes, by his desire to rise at court. She fears that Melot would betray his friend, Tristan, in order to supplant him in King Mark's favor. In the course of this warning she lets fall some fascinating observations: During the confusion as the king had boarded the ship to welcome Isolde, Brangäne noticed Melot's eyes seeking out Tristan's; if Mark believed Isolde's fainting, overwrought condition to be the result of the sea voyage, Melot was not taken in; nor was Brangäne's mistrust allayed by his subsequent behavior—frequently she has discovered him spying.

Isolde's reply to her adds further suspicions: "Do you mean Sir Melot?

---

[12] Liszt was deeply sympathetic to Bülow, though he, on the other hand, had little right to criticize Wagner or Cosima. Nonetheless, his own amours had been characterized by a romantic swagger and openness, as when he pulled Marie d'Agoult from her husband's palace and the Princess from her homeland. Unlike Wagner, he did not derive Venus from venality; from the time of his shabby liaison with Friederike Galvani in Würzburg a certain grossness was present in all Wagner's affairs.

Oh, how wrong you are! Is he not Tristan's truest friend? When my beloved must avoid me, he stays only with Melot." Here Isolde, sure of Tristan and in a gentle, yielding mood, is dismissing something she was unable to contain during her opening-act fury. Then, not yet having tasted the potion and still torn between love and hate for Tristan, she blurted out to him a rather nasty rationalization of her reason for having tended his wounds in Ireland. Earlier, she had told Brangäne that, wishing to be freed from his anguished glance, she had cured him only to speed his return home. But to Tristan himself she scornfully disclosed, "I cared for the injured man so that when recovered he might be slain in vengeance by the man who won him from Isolde." Taunting him, she recognized his love for her, though still refusing to acknowledge her own emotions, and correctly predicted that his resentful comrade would be the agent of her own revenge. Tristan, who after his cure had sworn to her "with a thousand oaths . . . eternal thanks and fidelity," had been back in Cornwall since their first encounter, and evidently she was not ignorant of his companionship with Melot. Her prophetic words must ring in Tristan's ears when at the close of the second act he lets his sword drop before his friend's and rushes forward to fulfill the augury.

Ernest Newman attempted to explain away Isolde's remarkable lines by appealing to a syntactical confusion in Wagner's mind. If the ablative pronoun *"ihm"* were substituted for the given accusative *"ihn,"* then the verses might possibly express Isolde's hope that Tristan meet his death at the hands of one of her future lovers. But, though Wagner's grammar was at times weak, he did know the difference between *"ihn"* and *"ihm,"* and, as Newman himself admitted, the passage appears in Wagner's manuscript and was printed in poem and score for all the world to see. Furthermore, Wagner read the work aloud to friends, sang it, heard it time and again during rehearsal and performance, and yet let the remark stand unchanged. Perhaps it was a Freudian slip that his mind refused to reconsider,[18] this jab that the clever, enraged woman directs toward the

---

[18] Similarly, though he repeatedly heard the "errors" in the *Ring* text, Wagner did nothing to repair them. In respect to his verse, he evidently could reach an uncritical state in which early and late drafts merged in his mind to form a fluid shape meaningful, of course, to himself but not to others, unless they knew his preliminary studies. Newman seems to treat Isolde's *"Ich pflag des Wunden"* as one of Wagner's typical errors or oversights and offers an untenable interpretation of the passage, which, if one thus willfully distorts its meaning, must then strike the ear as utter nonsense, forming part of no comprehensible pattern. Such an attitude hardly does justice to Wagner, who was a careless, at times an inept, but not a thoughtless dramatist. E. P. Dutton's new edition of the *Tristan* poem (1965), which offers a new translation into English alongside the German text, seeks to escape the challenge of the strange lines by tampering with the original verse; with no indication of a substitution, a reassuring *"ihm"* replaces Wagner's offending *"ihn."* This is hardly playing the game.

vulnerable hero whom she loves and who is about to hand her over to another man. Turning to sarcasm, she pursues the idea further, asking, "If men get on so well with Tristan, who then will kill him?" At this point he hands her his sword; he is utterly defeated.

At the end of the opera Melot, cut down by Kurvenal while attempting to reach Tristan's side, dies gasping his name. (Strikingly, the King's most intimate companion, young Prince Paul von Thurn und Taxis, was known as "Melot," among other pseudonyms, in the Wagner-Ludwig circle.) Considering all these hints, not surprisingly, Ludwig, as he matured, found Tristan, sexually tormented and yearning, replacing the rather neuter Lohengrin as the Wagnerian hero most sympathetic to him.

Tristan's relationship to his uncle, Mark, reinforces Isolde's revelations about the knight and, in addition, suggests a morbid variation on the theme of Wagnerian incest—an inverted counterpart of the situation that made Isolde, like Brynhild, her lover's aunt.[14] Moreover, Ludwig's and Wagner's friendship had elements of the attachment between Mark and Tristan, with the peculiarity that the ages of patron and protégé were reversed.

Wagner's version of the Tristan tale is most completely disclosed in his prose sketch; when he turned this scenario into poetry, his diction frequently became laconic, his syntax contorted, his purpose devious. The language of *Tristan* is erratic, capricious, private. Too often, little can be gleaned from the verse, and to gather even part of its meaning one must examine the roots from which the odd drama grew.

The freakish and obscure dialogue often seems to curve promisingly upward—like those stairways in mannerist painting that, though leading nowhere, are nonetheless mounted by hopeful figurants, evidently doomed to fall—evasive phrases appearing to be tenable as single units, but not in context. Indeed, the wavering, unstable atmosphere of *Tristan* is akin to that of mannerist art, restless chromatic harmony rarely permitting points of repose in recognizable tonalities, and a thick orchestral impasto—the colors, as if prepared from bitumen, are generally dense and dark and only fitfully luminous—creating an unceasing viscous movement that strains the nervous system; *Tristan* is a great but exhausting experience. One wanders in a world of calculated eccentricities, indirections, and seeming irrationalities, where repressed underplaying may immediately follow hysterical overresponse, where the spectator's call for clarity is overwhelmed by the intensity of the immediate emotion, where the resolution of shifting dissonance is endlessly postponed, where mystic forces propel neurotic protagonists through settings to which they seem strangely unrelated.

[14] It is not plain how much time has elapsed between the first two acts of *Tristan* nor whether Mark has already married Isolde or is delaying matters through a protracted betrothal. The aunt-nephew relationship, so dear to Wagner, is in any case clearly implied.

Wagner achieves a fluid coherence of disharmony in his characters, and through their perverse world one must pick his way carefully, for a relationship is rarely what it seemed at first glance. There come to mind those figures of a Pontormo, Bronzino, or Beccafumi that rise from spaceless chairs able to accommodate no human, or stand within smaller-scaled portals through which they could never have passed. In such art, elements from a more logically constructed universe often assume a dreamlike ambiguity; in *Tristan* they are seen through a heavy sea of iridescent music that changes their shapes and significance as the flood washes over. At times certain contours seem to firm, but in general little can be seen clearly as forms emerge and quickly vanish.

Often a fascinating contradiction arises between the spare dialogue of *Tristan* and its abundant orchestral vestment, seamlessly pieced together with motifs whose pliant edges enable them to interlock; nor is the contrast any less between the abstract verse and the substantial scenery Wagner had in mind. One thinks of the enchantment of those ascetic medieval carved saints decked out on feast days in sumptuous, bulging upholstery fabrics.[15]

Wagner achieved his kind of verbal dissociation or disintegration not directly but by a process of reduction. His prose sketches were realistic scripts which, as in the case of *Tristan,* he gradually broke down into puzzling, frequently almost meaningless alliterations and rhymes. Happily, however, the original scenario preserves clues to allusions that otherwise would have remained hopelessly buried in the finished poem. The prose version, for example, tells just what Tristan had in mind when singing of his earlier dedication to "the glory of honor and the power of renown." The prose account, combined with narratives in the opera, yields the following tale of particular pertinence to the Wagner-Ludwig friendship:

Left a childless widower, King Mark, out of affection for his nephew, has refused to consider remarriage. But political opposition has developed to Tristan as royal favorite, and, when the latter returns from his first Irish adventure singing Isolde's praise, Mark's courtiers think her both a worthy match for their master and a means of diminishing Tristan's influence. The King is urged to send the knight after her. If Tristan consents to undertake the mission, Isolde will become queen, and in time an heir will bypass the nephew's succession; if he refuses, his desire to maintain his own precedence will stand revealed. To protect name and knightly honor, he lets himself be goaded into becoming part of the plan. At first Mark resists, but,

[15] In *Tristan* this collision of the poetic and musical imaginations goes beyond a librettist's obvious need to keep lines short because music is long; in this clash Nietzsche in all likelihood recognized an Apollonian-Dionysian antithesis. As to décor, the productions of postwar Bayreuth have shown that *Tristan* fares well when performed on an almost bare platform filled with pulsating light.

under the threat of leaving forever, Tristan wrings his approval. For the sake of bolstering his waning prestige, the knight will sacrifice the woman who has saved his life and the uncle who loves him above all else.

In order to keep Tristan near, Mark is thus forced into approving the marriage expedition. Not surprisingly, after Isolde's arrival, "awed and timid" (*"ehrfurchtscheu"*), he holds back from sexual contact with her. Even before laying eyes on him, she knows of his limitations, scornfully calling him "Cornwall's vigorless king." When he discovers the lovers together in the garden, his imposing lament is directed to Tristan alone, his references to the lady being, in fact, rather gallant. He is not angry with her because he does not really care how she passes her time. By Tristan alone does he feel outraged and abused; only the beloved is worthy of castigation.

For all practical purposes Isolde might well vanish from the garden with Mark's entry. She is almost superfluous. Indeed, not a few directors have despaired of what to do with a leading lady suddenly abandoned by the author to figure among the supernumeraries. And how many Isoldes have desperately rearranged their veils a thousand times while awaiting those few lines near the end of the act! In the disjointed, spiraling, sprawling middle act of *Tristan,* with its sudden shifts and discontinuities—it has not one axis but three, of different proportions, about which the action revolves—the commanding, decisive crisis is suddenly played between Mark and Tristan. During those years when Wagner repeatedly betrayed him, the cries of the Cornish king must have echoed in Ludwig's ears: "Tristan, this —this—to me?"

The phosphorescent, glimmering phrases and tones of the garden scene, the turbulent, neurotic, grinding sounds of the hero's suffering at Kareol, the bewitching commingling of symbols for ideal love, raw sex, and death, the intimations of meanings beneath meanings—all these elements formed that *Tristan* atmosphere in which Ludwig discovered he most comfortably breathed. As a pioneer of Wagnerism and certainly as its most dramatic victim, he led the way for a generation that was to sink itself into this dissolving, shadowy, alienated world.

If much of *Tristan* partakes of mannerism's characteristic disorientation, the opera at its end does achieve a fulfillment which, though qualified, is nonetheless untypical of this art of tribulation without recompense. After his confrontation with Mark and wounding by Melot, Tristan sinks into a dream that frees his will from paralysis. As he half-awakens from a deathlike sleep, the *"alte, ernste Weise,"* the melancholy tune piped by the shepherd on his shawm, serves as Tristan's Proustian *"petite madeleine,"* helping him to summon the past. He not only suffers, but also learns. The man who at first seemed a marionette steadily begins to comprehend his tragedy. He submits, but with knowledge. This is his reward and the kind of private victory in which a coming generation of disturbed Wagnerites could share with the help of their analysts.

Tristan attempts to reconcile self and life; his deed is thus introspective, personal, intimate. Alone on stage, he rips the bandage from his wound, lets the blood flow, and, not far from madness, exultantly calls for the death that is approaching him across the waters in the shape of Isolde. She enters the stone gates of Kareol, an archetypal goddess—Cosima was to recognize her as such as she extinguished the torch in the second act—bringing the only peace Wagnerian man can know, the promise that alone can finally resolve his tensions, doubts, and crises, her incomparable litany hymning in sensuous imagery the beatitude of self-dissolution, of sinking into the flooding waters of the world soul, of being swallowed and drowning in watery nothingness.

Ludwig was, in fact, discovered one day floating face downward on his beloved Lake Starnberg. Cosima had written him some weeks after the funeral of Schnorr, whose death had followed soon upon the *Tristan* première, "Our art—I dare say it—is religion; its bearers are martyrs." No less than Schnorr, the King died of too much *Tristan*. Even before laying eyes on him, Wagner had written Ludwig's elegy; when this Lycidas met his watery grave, his Milton was already dead.

In the *Liebestod* there is a kind of purging, but no true catharsis.[16] Despite the fact that the aria finally reaches the elusive B major on which the lovers had set their sights in the royal garden, the general impression is nonetheless inconclusive, equivocal. The text really tells little, its words having more effect than sense. The awaited tonality, so long teasingly postponed, and the liquescent, shimmering orchestral sound, dissolving with the final magnificently spaced chord, alone indicate that the tragedy has ended in some kind of vague accommodation.[17]

The bread and wine of the Wagnerian ritual are romantic harmony and

---

[16] The finale does not give the exhilarating effect of heroic release, of breaking through, as in, for example, Beethoven's *Fidelio,* but rather the sensation of floating into the infinite—an experience beautiful, romantic, but uncertain.

[17] Wagner does not clearly state what happens to Isolde. "As if transfigured, she sinks gently into Brangäne's arms upon Tristan's body." Does she physically die or will she, like St. Theresa, having had a spiritual experience, live to write a book about it? Kurvenal is stowed away with Scribe-like efficiency, but Brangäne lingers on among the unemployed while Mark, *faute de mieux,* administers a blessing as the curtain falls. Amusingly, as Mark and his soldiers hacked their way with difficulty through the gateway, Brangäne, a better strategist, quite easily vaulted the side wall. With details of this kind Wagner was perfectly helpless. They are unimportant; yet, if one calls into play the stereotyped situations of boulevard stagecraft, one should be able to handle them. But, no matter; overpowering music makes everything plausible.

the romantic orchestra, a Eucharist in which the presence is complete under the first but not the second element. The composer offers the faithful an easy spiritual experience on an intensely physical level. Wagnerians could dream of purity and renunciation as they embraced the flesh. Here was the secret of Wagner's power, and in this respect he has not unjustly been called jesuitical. The King, whose passion for the corporal was cleansed both through sacraments of the holy Church into which he was born and those of the Wagnerian rite he helped establish, built for this art its Franconian sanctuary and led Europe to its steps. Bayreuth is also Ludwig's monument, and from the day of its première *Tristan* shed the mysterious light that showed his way.

8

Wagner appeared so firmly entrenched in Munich that any hope of dislodging him must have seemed vain. At the Residenz Palace the painter Michael Echter was decorating a corridor with scenes from the *Ring* and quotations from it in letters of gold.[18]

With the *Tristan* triumph behind him, Wagner determined to stabilize his financial position for life. In August, 1865, under veiled threats to depart, he proposed to Ludwig that his arrangements with the crown be amended. "And now, my friend," he began, "we must also composedly set my personal situation in order." He intended to talk directly to his patron, without the courtly use of intermediaries, and turned to Ludwig his friend, depending upon him to negotiate his latest request with Ludwig the king. Wagner's letter and its enclosed schedule of demands formed a masterful symphony of sophistry and arrogance. He even ended by dragging in the pathetic figure of his poor wife, "unfortunately living apart from me," implying that her sustenance was a burden. His new needs required another two hundred thousand (!!) gulden, of which a modest forty thousand were to be given him immediately, the remainder to form a capital sum under government control but yielding him five per cent interest in quarterly payments! Wagner's demands upon Ludwig call to mind Winckelmann's shabby financial dealings with the young Muzel Stosch.

Even had the request been less astounding, the King was in any case reluctant to hand over large sums. Like Otto Wesendonk, he had learned that the control of money merely inspired Wagner to fall deeper into debt, his

---

[18] Soon Ludwig would be planning to commission the singer's father, the venerable Schnorr von Carolsfeld, Wilhelm von Kaulbach, and perhaps Bonaventura Genelli to do cartoons of Wagnerian scenes. Wagner made poor Echter alter some of his compositions as many as three times.

line of creditors seemingly never becoming shorter. The giant capital sum—it represented about two thirds of the moneys annually available for the King's personal pleasure from the Civil List—was, of course, not set aside, the demand being completely unrealistic, even considering Ludwig's generosity. But by autumn Ludwig, capitulating in respect to the outright cash gift, granted the forty thousand gulden, and, in addition, raised Wagner's annual allowance to equal the interest on the requested reserve fund. Wagner had assured him, "I have . . . estimated . . . very closely, as trifling as at all possible." In October, Cosima was dispatched to the royal treasury, where hostile officials sought to embarrass her by paying out the forty thousand gulden in sacks of coin. As unabashed as Fafner gathering the hoard, she arrived back at the Briennerstrasse in command of two cabs filled with silver, a treasure Wagner would half deplete by the end of the year.

She now completely enveloped his life, regulating his correspondence and appointments. The womanish side of his nature, ever more pronounced with advancing age, was taking shelter in her youth and strength; he now suffered fits of hysteria with which she alone could cope. Like Wagner, Bülow was also subject to attacks of raving and admitted that his nature inclined toward the unmanly and erratic. Cosima had been well schooled in sailing through emotional squalls. In a sense, Minna, Jessie, and Mathilde had been too passive and feminine for Wagner. The articulate, aggressive Cosima, always in control of a situation even when wrong, came to fight many of his battles. Indeed, he gradually allowed her to sway him to an astounding extent, not only in practical but also at times even in artistic decisions. An entry in his diary during September of 1865 presents two ways of developing incidents involving the Holy Spear in *Parsifal;* he asks, "Which is better, Cos?"

Quietly and determinedly striving to possess him completely, she resolved to alienate him from such comrades as Cornelius, who at the end of 1864 had finally succumbed to invitations and joined the Munich circle. The way to Wagner now lay solely through Cosima, called "the Delphic Oracle" by his old friends. She must have realized that Peter saw through her posturing as the noble, platonic amanuensis. He guessed that Hans had handed her over to Wagner on some understanding. Although she ostensibly lived at the Bülow residence, secretarial duties seemed to keep her in the Hôtel Jôchum at all hours.

9

Despite formidable opposition from the royal family, led by Queen Mother Marie Hedwig and old Ludwig I, Wagner seemed firmly in the saddle at the time of his November visit to Hohenschwangau. While affairs of state occupied the young king during morning hours, sentimental *billets* and poetry traveling the gothic halls kept the friends in touch. Fully aware of how delicate an instrument Ludwig was, Wagner nonetheless did not hesitate to peg the strings tighter and draw the bow recklessly. "Patience!" he advised on November 11. "I am in your angelic arms! We are near one another, and my earnest joy tells you that I am happy!" But on the next day Ludwig experienced what was evidently to become a recurrent dream foretelling that Wagner and he would go their separate ways. His note of the twelfth recounted a scene clearly related to *Lohengrin;* to the sound of music a boat approached and bore him away from the shores of a lake where he had been in conversation with the composer.[19]

But omens still appeared favorable to Wagner. Despite controversy about his character, influence, and demands, extraordinary appreciation of his worth as an artist was nonetheless shown by his sharpest critics even at court. Munich was not Paris, where Empress Eugénie confused Offenbach with Beethoven because, after all, both were Rhinelanders.[20] Relatively few in Paris had really comprehended Wagner's genius or even thought of him seriously; his resentment against the city could to some extent be justified. His patroness, Princess Metternich, had been addicted to the vaudeville chanson, and the Jockeys opposed him not as an artist—this would at least have implied some concern with higher values—but as a political symbol. When these gentlemen, dedicated to the *corps de ballet* and the improvement of horse breeding, ruined *Tannhäuser,* it was in their eyes only a piece of furniture, smashed during an amusing skirmish with the imperial court. But in Munich Wagner's works were honored even by those who did not understand them, and by his political antagonists. In 1867, when the Wagner question was no less momentous, Redwitz told the sculptor Zumbusch that *Lohengrin* was the most sublime work he knew. Palace and public recognized that in their midst was a link in the great line of German composers, and, though Wagner spoke darkly of enemies and Bülow raged about *"Schweinehunde,"* it was difficult to discover ill will in the applauding audience at the Munich theater. As previously in Vienna, it was Wagner

[19] Although Ludwig's similar dream of early 1866 included Cosima, but not, as far as is known, the idea of separation, it was obviously a return of the Hohenschwangau picture. Again the King discovered himself on the Vierwaldstättersee in discussion with Wagner. In October of 1865 he had made his first journey to Switzerland and had taken the boat ride from Brunnen to Flüelen that had so delighted Wagner in former years.

[20] After an opening at the *Bouffes Parisiennes,* she asked the waggish maestro whether he was, in fact, that famous composer from Bonn. Acknowledging a Cologne origin, he then paused, seemingly to search his mind for the name of the lesser light the Empress had in mind.

himself who brought everything down by his incredible conduct, of which one may observe, as Monsieur Thiers did of the contemporary French political scene, that no faults were left to commit.

Ludwig kept his head in the clouds and assured his friend, "All obstacles will now be overcome; I see clearly; the malice of the world cannot prevail against the two of us." Their correspondence immediately following the Hohenschwangau idyll obviously recapitulated many of their discussions in the castle, where Wagner had even ventured to lay before him a plan for reorganizing the Bavarian cabinet. This done, the young king, having followed Siegfried's victorious path, would "know all, accomplish all," while dexterous Wagner, having played the part of the helpful Wood Bird chirping suggestions into the hero's ears, would next throw the Wanderer's cloak about his shoulders and "peacefully and blissfully contemplate the Twilight of the Gods." The deed was the hero's to perform. "As the hopeful Wanderer and good-humored Wood Bird, I can and may not proceed further." The fire of Brynhild's rock blazed in the background, but Ludwig felt that in this particular case Siegfried and the Wanderer must go on together. "Siegfried . . . wishes always faithfully to stand at the Wanderer's side; . . . he must approach the Twilight of the Gods with the Wanderer—without him, life is death." Here was a hero who really did not care to awaken the maid, at least not alone!

To carry out the ideas of his mistress, Ludwig I had once created the so-called *"Lolaministerium."* Would a *"Lolotteministerium"* now be called into being by his grandson? His government watched Wagner quietly. At such junctures a political amateur, puffed up with a sense of his own importance, often stepped high and tripped. The day Lola was goaded into announcing her intention of closing Munich University marked the beginning of her fall. And might not a snare or two now be artfully stretched across Wagner's way? The clatter was heard sooner than anyone had dared hope.

A bit past mid-November he left Ludwig at Hohenschwangau and returned to Munich. Late in the month, in reply to a newspaper attack, he sent an anonymous contribution to the *Neueste Nachrichten.* He denied authorship, but few were fooled; as Pfistermeister observed, the style, the grammatical constructions were unmistakable. According to Cornelius, the impulsive Cosima had set in motion the strategic and moral misstep. The self-same day he dictated the piece to her, Wagner righteously declared to the King that he "never in any way instigated . . . a newspaper article." [21]

[21] The draft of the *Nachrichten* article survives in Cosima's handwriting. Though Wagner was clearing himself of complicity in inspiring a piece that had appeared in the *Anzeiger* of Nuremberg, his statement to Ludwig remained no less dishonest. In a

Of course, he painted himself as an injured innocent. Playing the role of an objective bystander, he wrote to the *Nachrichten* under an assumed initial as one desiring to set the record straight. He decried the situation in Munich, where all Wagner's "artistic inclinations were most uncouthly opposed by personal interests!" Wagner, he declared, "therefore believed it necessary to express himself composedly and instructively, and toward this end wrote a report to the King concerning a German music school to be erected in Munich"; the surprisingly well-informed reporter lamented, "Not a single critical voice of any significance whatsoever made itself heard concerning this published report. On the contrary, from this time on, there appeared symptoms of an ever-widening plot whose goal was clear . . . to ruin Wagner's position in Munich completely." Wagner, describing himself in the third person, went on to moving heights: Conspirators had undertaken to pour slander about him into the ears of the Folk, the main purpose of this calumny being to frighten the King and thus deter him from pursuing his Wagnerian program; the Folk had been led astray by the nobles and clergy. "These people, whom I need not name . . . perceive a final means of saving themselves . . . by representing the King's unshakable (*unerschütterliche*) friendship for Wagner as ruinous." And the truth was, this self-advocate pleaded, poor, misunderstood Wagner, who stood distant from every political party, longed only for tranquillity.

He was completely sincere; his mind was a simple mechanism. What was good for Wagner was good for everybody, and to cross him was to move against the public welfare. During the summer of 1865 the old Munich conservatory of music had been closed as a step toward establishing his academy. The event stirred resentment. That he looked upon the national treasury as his own purse and planned to rearrange Munich artistically, physically, and politically seemed to him a most natural state of affairs. Those whom his projects would inconvenience or oust were the Nibelung and Rhine Daughters of the realm, and not worthy of attention. At the end of *Rhinegold* Loge recommends that the river maidens, lamenting the loss of their gold, seek consolation by basking henceforth in the gods' new splendor. The *Nachrichten* article concluded with an analogous solution to Munich's difficulties. How simply a god could dispose of problems. With obvious reference to Cabinet Secretary Pfistermeister and his associates, Wagner—anonymously, so he thought—assured his readers that "with the withdrawal of two or three individuals enjoying not the slightest esteem among the Bavarian Folk, the King and the Bavarian Folk would once and for

---

letter to Wagner of December 15, Herr Lutz, one of Ludwig's officials, made it clear that the court was well aware who had made the fatal *Nachrichten* contribution and that its intemperate phraseology had contributed toward the composer's fall.

all be freed from these tedious disturbances." Wagner little suspected that with this last sentence he determined his own removal.

Not only did the article picture the King as in his vest pocket, but his use of the royal name had been unmannerly, insensate. Ludwig was shocked, especially by the phrase "unshakable friendship." He had read the article before quitting Hohenschwangau for Munich and realized that Wagner's position was now imperiled. Exploitation of their intimacy through journalistic polemics was an almost unthinkable blunder. Wagner had been successfully tricked into a fatal indiscretion.

Ludwig enjoyed Wagner's misty theorizing on Germany's artistic and historic destiny. However, in the realm of hard, practical politics he listened forbearingly to his friend's harangues, but went no further. Wagner admitted that, when he held forth on such matters, Ludwig examined the ceiling, whistling to himself softly. He was neurotic, but no fool. Now he could not wait indulgently for the tempest of nonsense to spend itself in private. What could be tolerated in interviews and letters was intolerable in public print. Moulin-Eckart, Cosima's rather confused biographer, wondered why the King was displeased with the article, which, after all, had nothing in it save such ideas as recur time and again in the Wagner-Ludwig correspondence. Indeed, here was precisely the reason Ludwig felt betrayed.

To Röckel, his old friend of the Dresden revolt, Wagner had written that he considered the King's reputation as a musical enthusiast to be "a Brutus mask for him; behind it . . . something quite singular ought quietly to grow and develop." He deluded himself into believing that Ludwig was "burning" to see political Wagnerism a reality. But things were turning out quite differently. It had proved impossible to make an anti-Semite of him, and, despite affection for Wagner and devotion to his art, Ludwig in his calmer moments was coming to view the man more and more dispassionately.

Frau Dangl had publicly foretold that Wagner would not remain long in Munich. Others without her gift of prophecy were coming to the same conclusion.

The capital was seething with the Wagner question, especially the matter of the forty thousand gulden. The King had to choose between the dignity of his throne and the continuance of a relationship that to many appeared morally and politically unhealthy. The affair was turning him into a figure of international ridicule, and from Vienna famous old Grillparzer sent a poem advising the people of Munich to seize the *Salbader* (someone who talks boringly and interminably) and cast him into debtor's prison.

Alarmed by his increasingly shaky position, Wagner had named the Hôtel Jôchum "the ship." Upon completing the orchestral score of the second act of

Siegfried (the *Partiturerstschrift*) on December 2, he wrote on the manuscript, perhaps with surprise, "Still on the ship." Within four days it was to capsize.

The cabinet, the royal family, and even the Archbishop brought pressure. Wagner's treachery to former patrons and friends was recalled to Ludwig, who was told of the populace's resentment at observing his generosity rewarded by arrogance. "Lola! Lola!" was the warning. Prince Karl, the King's great-uncle, feared revolution.

On December 6 Ludwig resolved that Wagner had to quit the kingdom for several months. He had no intention of sacrificing his crown to Wagner's concupiscence and wrote him that circumstances forced the decision; their love, like that of Siegfried and Brynhild, would be eternal: "Though sundered, who can separate us?" Had not Wagner used this quotation from *The Twilight of the Gods* some months before, when threatening Ludwig with his departure? Thus was he forced to digest his own treacle as he prepared to flee yet another city. It was believed that the temper of the populace was such that his personal safety was endangered. Lola Montez had had to seek refuge from angry crowds by running into the Theatiner Church. Cosima, perhaps overdramatizing the danger, lived in fear of his being murdered!

His departure was a double blow to her. She was dining at the Hôtel Jôchum on the evening of the sixth when news of his banishment arrived. In his words, "She was at the point of fainting; with difficulty I helped her regain her composure." She had been the force behind the article. It had miscarried, and she was unable to join her lover in exile. Frau von Bülow could not publicly travel and live with Richard Wagner. The masquerade had to continue. Somehow the financial and artistic expectations of the trio would be salvaged. The King still believed in Wagner's sincerity, if not his prudence. Ludwig's love had not been lost—nor had the allowance.

XI

Banishment from Munich:
The Triebschen Intrigues

Separation was painful. During the preceding August, when Cosima had gone to Pest with Hans to attend the première of Liszt's *St. Elizabeth,* Wagner quit Munich to seek solitude in one of the royal Alpine lodges. There, in a diary, the so-called "Brown Book," he recorded his unhappiness. Cosima was at the disposal of two husbands, and by this time Wagner considered her his wife alone. For a moment he thought that Bülow must be made to renounce his rights completely. "Stay with me; don't leave again. Tell poor Hans candidly that I can't get along without you. Oh God! if only you might safely (*ruhig*) be my wife before the world! This perpetual coming and going . . . is horrible!" But, though Hans, despite moments of defiance, could be forced to do whatever was demanded of him, two considerable obstacles to Wagner's open union with Cosima remained—the King's idealism and the tenacious purpose with which Minna recovered from her heart seizures.

With Ludwig's surprising decision, a parting of unpredictable duration confronted the lovers. Cosima seemed inconsolable as Wagner's train left the Munich station on December 10. And he, suddenly gray of face and hair, looked more than his fifty-two years. He had not yet recovered from the shock of Schnorr's death. A brief illness, and the young tenor had died unexpectedly within a month of the fourth *Tristan* performance. That many held the physical strain of the part responsible for the tragedy wounded Wagner doubly. The Schröder-Devrient of his later years had appeared and vanished. Schnorr's singing of *Tannhäuser* at a quickly arranged performance in Munich during March had given Wagner "a glimpse into my own creation . . . such as has been seldom, perhaps never, yet vouchsafed an artist"; he described the role as "this most difficult of all my dramatic tasks for the singer." The young man who had sung both it and Tristan and who had even started to learn the Nibelung music was no more. "In him I lost . . . the great granite block needed to raise my building and now found myself directed to seek his replacement in a pile of bricks." Who was there to sing Tristan, Walther, and, above all, Siegfried? Chances of achieving satisfying model performances seemed seriously impaired. Once again Wagner was dejectedly turning toward Switzerland with shattered hopes.

Ludwig, too, suffered. He wrote Cosima, "Need I tell you what I have endured in these last days and that I decided upon the step with a bleeding soul? And yet, believe me, I had to act thus." In the hope that, with time, old resentments and animosities would spend themselves, he had found strength to exile the man for whom he had longed since boyhood. But Baron Pfordten, who in 1848 had formed part of the cabinet of Friedrich of Saxony, was Ludwig's foreign minister. Considering Wagner a danger to the state, he made it known that the composer's reappearance would signal his resignation. The King needed him: "At least for the moment it would greatly injure the country to let this man go." Bavaria was sailing toward a severe international crisis.

During Cosima's summer absence (the Bülows returned to Munich on September 13), Wagner had again taken up the theme of *Parsifal* and worked on its scenario, a development no doubt inspired by his reading of the *Ramayana* in Adolf Holtzmann's translation at the King's mountain lodge. But aside from this sketch and some scoring of what had already been composed of *Siegfried* he had shamefully misspent his genius in Munich.[1] Early in 1865 the musical outlines of the final act of *Siegfried* had begun to emerge during his "good hours," but amorous and political involvements had left him few of these. He had indulged in idiotic intrigue long enough. Somewhere behind that enormous forehead, *Meistersinger,* the climax of the *Ring,* and *Parsifal* were pressing toward birth.

Attacks on Wagner did not end with his exit from Munich. In January, in reply to a charge that he had left his wife in penury, Minna, in a wavering hand, wrote a public denial to the press. She performed this final act of loyalty to her absent husband even though her few remaining days were being embittered by gossip naming him father of Cosima's latest child.

After brief stays at Bern, Vevey (where he took long walks along the lake with the Grand Duke of Baden), and Geneva, he settled near the latter city in a handsome but draughty house called "The Artichokes." Its furnishings and decorations had seen better days, and, although the property

---

[1] Ludwig had been distressed that Wagner, in the face of bold assurances to the contrary, made little progress on the *Ring*. "Are you now composing again, dear friend? Has Siegfried the Awakener pierced the fire?" was the kind of inquiry he repeatedly made. Like its creator, he held the *Ring* libretto "above every poem ever written."

was let for only three months, Bertha was nonetheless summoned from Vienna to hang his rooms in silk and satin. Most important, at The Artichokes he again took up *Meistersinger,* resuming at Beckmesser's question in the first act: "Are you ready now?"

What he had heard about the climate and beauty of the French Riviera made him consider it a promising place for a permanent haven. On January 22 he left on an exploratory trip to seek, he wrote Cosima, "the nest of our repose" and by way of Lyons, Toulon, and Hyères made his way to Marseilles. There he received a telegram from Pusinelli announcing that Minna was dead. Awakened during the night, she had opened the window to relieve a feeling of suffocation and had evidently just returned to bed when the stroke came. Pusinelli plaintively asked, *"Que faire?"* Wagner was in a stupor. He should have hastened to Dresden, as he had upon hearing of Schnorr's death; at that time he had been seized by the desire to press a final kiss upon his tenor's cold brow, and though he missed the obsequies, the race against time had itself been a gesture of devotion. Now, he simply requested Pusinelli to arrange the burial.

Clad in white and with her morning cap, Minna Planer Wagner was put into her coffin and carried to rest on the twenty-eighth. Members of the Royal Orchestra, friends, and relatives formed the dignified cortège. Her "Richel" did not arrive. Troubled by an inflamed finger (!), he returned from Marseilles to The Artichokes. One obstacle had disappeared into the earth.

Minna left her possessions to her daughter-sister, Natalie. Aside from trifles, Wagner made claim only to his correspondence with his wife. The preceding May the King, having read with pleasure Wagner's "Autobiographical Sketch" of 1843, requested him to prepare a "detailed description" of his "spiritual progress and also external life." Two months later he had begun to dictate *Mein Leben* to Cosima. Some of the fantasies he planned to spin for Ludwig and posterity were at odds with much evidence in his own handwriting, and from this time on he strove to repossess his early correspondence. Natalie acted cleverly, sending him a quantity of letters and evidently pretending that the remainder had been lost or destroyed. From her, one hundred and twenty-eight of Wagner's letters to Minna eventually made their way into the possession of Mrs. Burrell.

Upon his return to Switzerland he found that his old hound had died and been hastily dug into the earth. At his order the pet was unearthed and laid in a specially built coffin. In so emotional a state that he almost lost consciousness, Wagner wound a collar about Pohl's neck and a coverlet around his already decomposing body, and then reburied him midst a grove of trees. A monument of Jura stone was ordered to perpetuate his memory.

One cannot help believing that, despite his well-known sentimentality concerning animals, in this extraordinary rite the composer was observing solemnities and experiencing emotions associated with old Minna as well as old Pohl. The strange ritual seems to have been meant to cleanse his guilt in having failed to walk with his wife to her grave. Certainly he was shattered by her death, expected and often desired. Symptoms of his skin and gastric maladies reappeared. During the final year of her life Minna had written him, "At the bottom of your heart you are good after all; I always knew it; it is only from your mind, in which so much beauty and splendor dwells, that sometimes there also comes much harm for those about you—all that shall now be forgiven and forgotten."

2

Toward his highly strung young patron Wagner occasionally experienced something not far from hostility, even contempt, and felt a need to wound, to exact penance for a surprising show of independence. Before quitting Munich he had hurled the charge of "fickleness" at Ludwig, who deeply resented the slur. But indignation changed to heartache when he received from Marseilles the composer's dramatic vignette of Roland's death. Here every stop on the formidable Wagnerian console was pulled:

The traitorous Ganelon (Pfistermeister) deludes Charlemagne (Ludwig) into believing that the horn calls of Roland (Wagner) do not signal distress but are echoes of the hunt. As the betrayed hero's life bleeds away in the valley of Roncevaux, he decides to destroy his sword, "Durandal," lest it fall into unworthy hands. He attempts to smash it against the mountain, which splinters while the weapon remains whole, shattered rocks being "his final art-works." Roland then gathers his last strength to hurl the wonderful blade into the depths of a lake. Wagner closed the symbolic recital with a warning: "No one shall wield it again!" The King was being threatened with the thunderbolt he most feared; Wagner was clearly hinting that as a result of the Munich imbroglio the *Ring* might remain unfinished.

He enjoyed imagining a terrible revenge when Ludwig came to his senses. "Now the king [Charlemagne] discovers that he was deceived. The traitor suffers frightful punishment. Four hundred thousand enemies must fall; three hundred cities are burned." Significantly, in the sketch of this fantasy written in Wagner's diary the "enemies" were called "unbelievers." In his version for Ludwig he toned down the vulgar allusion, his purpose being to pain, not antagonize, a prince who refused to view every unhappy effect as the result of a Jewish cause. While in Lyons late in January Wagner had observed the night sky with Orion's sword, its point turned toward

Munich. He wrote in his Brown Book, "Cut, cut, my sword, that a king's heart may feel what true sorrow is!"

When Munich rejected Wagner, it immediately became un-German in his eyes. He railed at toy monarchs playing at Louis XIV in the mock French palaces of their "rotten un-German courts," and liked to believe that the Philistinism of foreigners and of natives prizing alien ideas had forced him from the capital. In his mind the Jews, as always, were working the destruction of everything truly German; with their plots he now associated the Catholics, for the clerical party had vigorously combated his influence on the King. In a hysterical reverie he blended the two enemies into one and denounced Munich, "where baptized Jews, won over by the Jesuits, unpunished, instruct the Folk and, unhindered, are able to pursue the King's friends—because they are so loved by him—with the most shameful calumnies."

At the time of her flight from Munich Lola Montez had seen herself as a kind of well-dressed, worldly Joan of Arc, vainly attempting to counter the Jesuits with the revelations of "St. Lamennais." Wagner, too, held himself a victim of the black cloth. Actually, both royal favorites had gone down before the new concepts of public decency demanded of rulers by Germany's rising middle class. Moreover, Ludwig had become a less-than-perfect Wagnerite and could write heresy to Cosima early in 1866; "he [Wagner] judges without knowing intimately and precisely the circumstances of which he speaks. . . . About many matters, I concede, the dear one may be right, but not about all, not about all!" Ludwig was beginning to recognize in him the suspicious petulance of Goethe's Tasso. To Cosima, who accepted the composer's every utterance as revealed truth, this royal heterodoxy must have been shocking.

Wagner now realized that his theater would never rise on the Isar. His thoughts were turning away from Catholic-Jewish Munich and toward Nuremberg, described by his own Hans Sachs as "lying in the heart of Germany and through deeds and works peacefully confident of true tradition." Though within Bavarian territory and thus a possession of Ludwig, Nuremberg was Protestant and historically a dominion of the Hohenzollern whom the Hohenstaufen had invested as its Burgraves in medieval days. The city's fortress was one of King Wilhelm's ancestral homes, and after the War of 1866 his colors as well as Bavaria's were to fly from it as Ludwig's gesture of reconciliation toward this uncle of Prussia.[2] In this city recalling the Reformation, Wagner now hoped to see the première of *Meistersinger*

---

[2] The privilege was wrested from Ludwig by King Wilhelm, who demanded co-ownership of the castle. Since the Prussians had the power to annex the entire town, Ludwig showed a pleasant face about a matter that thoroughly enraged Wagner.

and to establish his school of German art. Nearby, and also within Ludwig's domain, was Bayreuth—it, too, an ancient Hohenzollern seat—where Wagner contemplated using one of the royal pavilions as a retreat.

These were plans for the future. Soon The Artichokes would have to be relinquished, and his immediate need was a comfortable home. Early in March, while Hans was on a concert tour, Cosima with her daughter Daniela joined Wagner in Switzerland for three weeks. Considering himself done with Munich and judging the King still sufficiently naïve and under his spell, he dared brave the newspaper tattle the visit inevitably awakened.

Only a day before her scheduled return to Munich—it was Good Friday—Cosima and Wagner discovered a perfect estate on the outskirts of Lucerne while on a steamboat excursion. The house, called "Triebschen," was built on a peninsula jutting into the Vierwaldstättersee, the property, girt with poplars, boasting a superb Alpine panorama as a background. Ludwig, who would have preferred his favorite to settle in Bavarian territory, nonetheless paid the rent as a gift. Once again Bertha, Wagner's Viennese seamstress, was called upon to work costly miracles upon the interiors, this time with pink satin and cupids. He moved into Triebschen on April 15, to be joined within the month by Cosima and her three daughters.[3]

Wagner's return to Munich appeared increasingly unlikely, and on May 15 Ludwig wired and wrote to Switzerland that life without his friend was intolerable; he contemplated joining the exile as soon as an abdication could be arranged. It was not clear whether the boy was in an operatic mood or a deep depression. He cried out, "Torture! Despair! My grave is near. . . . If I cannot live with and for him, then death is welcome."[4] Pfistermeister pointed out to his young monarch that "Herr Wagner would be the first to turn his back upon the 'Royal Friend' as soon as the latter could give him nothing more or not enough to cover Wagnerian needs." And, indeed, Wagner and Cosima were appalled by Ludwig's latest game. There was always the chance that his epistolary fantasies might become realities; a Ludwig without power, spending day after day with them, loomed as a petrifying possibility. Wagner recommended patience and devotion to princely duties. "Give up, I implore you, every concern with art and with our plans for this half year. . . . In exchange, turn your attention most energetically to affairs of state . . .; remain midst your people, show

[3] Daniela, Blandine, and Isolde were respectively and affectionately called Lusch, Boni, and Loldi.

[4] As early as his letter to Cosima of January 2, 1866, Ludwig had dramatically offered "now joyfully to abandon country and people and follow him!" These gestures were certainly not meant to be taken seriously. It is reported that in later years, when Ludwig learned that he must forfeit the crown, he sobbed and murmured how much he had loved being king.

yourself to them. . . . Out of love for me, nobly endure for half a year."

The politically crucial summer of 1866 threatened the very independence of Bavaria. Prussia was challenging Austria's supremacy in the German Confederation, which Bismarck was prepared to smash and then rebuild around the concept of Hohenzollern hegemony. The Wittelsbach, caught between the ambitions of two powerful dynasties, could easily be crushed. During this period Ludwig was two people—the hysterical boy seeking release by writing reams of nonsense to his exiled favorite and, at the same time, the calm young statesman surveying the limited resources of his land and intuitively attempting to follow a reasoned political course. If the Bavarian throne in the end owed its survival to Bismarck's generosity, Ludwig's conduct nonetheless helped sway the decision.

For the moment he felt the need to be strengthened. He would see Wagner, even if briefly. Sending ahead to Triebschen his favorite and aide-de-camp, Prince Paul von Taxis—called the *"treue* Friedrich" as well as "Friedrich Melot"—he followed to celebrate the composer's fifty-third birthday on May 22. The two young men obviously enjoyed the intrigue, incognito, and disguises of the adventure. In his fanciful costume of extravagant hat and sweeping Byronic cape Ludwig was, of course, recognized. At the door of Triebschen he had told the servant to announce the arrival of Walther von Stolzing. Within two days the romantic pilgrimage was over, and he was back in Bavaria. But even this short absence during a period of international tension was taken in bad part by press and public. Abuse was hurled after him in the streets, and, when he opened the parliament, his reception was, as he put it, "ice-cold." Moreover, Munich's general indignation was deepened by a legal action started against Wagner at the end of May for twenty-six thousand gulden of debt on bills of exchange. Why, many wondered, had the lord of Bavaria visited this notorious defaulter and passed two nights in the same house with a woman now referred to by the newspapers as "Madame Hans," "carrier pigeon," and little short of a whore?

Since Minna's death Wagner's income from the King was larger than ever, and he determined to silence wagging tongues by again settling the entire Wagner-Bülow family under his roof for the summer. Hans followed Cosima and the children to Triebschen. His wife's indiscreet stays with Wagner were giving rise to discussion of the very questions his self-sacrifice was supposed to have quelled. Certainly the point would be reached where even Ludwig's naïve idealism would be undermined. News of Cosima's latest imprudences had reached as far as Liszt in Rome. Hans spent over two miserable summer months living with the lovers in a futile effort once again to give the lie to scandal. All that remained to him was an official position in Munich, becoming increasingly difficult to maintain in the face of the latest embarrassing developments. In view of the gossip reported in the newspapers, he had felt it necessary to offer his resignation. But, if the talk refused to die, Hans's presence at Triebschen did give the proper "family" background to a new and dangerous intrigue Wagner and Cosima were spinning, this time around the figure of the King. Only a drastic and dramatic move on their part could, they thought, prevent his eyes from being opened to the facts.

3

A flood of gossip was reaching Ludwig, who, nonetheless, struggled to maintain his belief that Wagner's association with Cosima did not infringe upon the boundaries of comradeship. Coincident with Bülow's arrival in Triebschen at the beginning of June, Wagner moved to end the crescendo of vituperative comment pouring from the press and to buttress the King's good will. He dispatched one of his most extraordinary messages to the palace. Climbing upon a pedestal and assuming a patriarchal pose, he assured Ludwig that Cosima was being publicly dragged through the mud simply because of her "most compassionate devotion to her father's friend, her husband's mentor (*Vorbild*), the highly esteemed protégé of her . . . king." The latter was asked to abandon his royal silence by writing a letter to Hans that would commend his artistic achievement in Munich, express indignation at observing him the victim of scurrilous journalism, urge him to remain at his post, and compliment the character of his noble wife. She sent Ludwig her own appeal, begging him to provide this letter, which, she claimed, alone might vindicate her husband's honor. For the sake of her three children (the last of whom was Wagner's), she implored the King by this act to restore to them the Bülow name unstained! She who was at the time carrying Wagner's second child proclaimed her innocence in the manner of Elsa and looked toward Ludwig as her Lohengrin. To guarantee his appearance in the lists, Wagner by telegram let Prince Paul, the royal adjutant and intimate, know that, should the letter not be forthcoming, Ludwig would probably never again hear from him. "Should he [Bülow] be denied the one valid satisfaction I have requested, then henceforth must I . . . be dead even to the exalted friend." Wagner had sent a draft of the proposed letter to the King, who had merely to copy it and affix his signature. For some unfathomable reason the Triebschen plotters imagined that this document, when published, would make opposition to them vanish.

Their seemingly heartfelt pleas filled Ludwig with new confidence, and from the idyllic Roseninsel, where he was celebrating the first anniversary of the *Tristan* première with his beloved Prince Paul, he dispatched the letter to Hans with the understanding that it might be made public. It was straightway delivered to the press.

The Triebschen plot to weave the prestige of the royal name into a net of lies was both criminal and cruel. Rather sooner than later the truth had to come out. Wagner was certainly harboring the idea of kicking over the traces of public opinion by taking Cosima openly whenever Hans's usefulness was over. Since Minna's death it was possible to consider rewriting the trio as a duet and dismissing the baritone. Merely to gain temporary respite from the clamorous press, Wagner was willing to make Ludwig's signature witness perjury. Not only was the young man exposed to ridicule, but, far worse, his sensitive nature never recovered from the betrayal. For a long time he had closed his eyes to much that was disappointing in Wagner's character and fought to remain asleep, enjoying a dream that was his only reality. Wagner was to awaken him roughly, and Ludwig, a child of *Tristan*, could not bear the light.

The Bülows' part in the fraud presents them in characteristic roles; Cosima was remarkable for a ruthless, driving spirit but not integrity, while Hans had become the pathetic tool of powerful personalities. At Triebschen he was reading the second act of *Meistersinger* as it came from Wagner's pen and again prostrated himself before the man he considered the genius of the age.

The King's public declaration of faith in Cosima's virtue did not have the effect hoped for. Again the unique prose betrayed Wagner's hand. Moreover, the nation was occupied with more serious matters than Frau von Bülow's sleeping habits. By the middle of June Bavaria joined Austria in war against Prussia. Early in July Moltke's new needle-gun brought disaster to General Benedek's Austrian army at Königgrätz in Bohemia; Vienna lay vulnerable.

Only Bismarck's reluctance to humiliate the Imperial City spared her streets the tread of foreign boots. The whole affair was ending so quickly that Europe, especially France, was amazed. Austria bought peace at Prussia's terms, which, like those offered Bavaria, were generous. Unlike the troops of blind George of Hanover, Ludwig's army by its incompetence and relative inaction had made matters rather easy for Prussia; if Bismarck let Ludwig keep his crown for reasons that were to Prussia's advantage, he did so with a magnanimity that only occasionally graces the mighty.

But, despite Berlin's urbanity, Prussian hegemony was a clear fact. Franz Josef, that ceremonial heir of the Holy Roman Emperors, had submitted, and the smaller German rulers were being reduced to ciphers. The gap between the two parts of Prussia closed; she swallowed Hanover, Hesse-Kassel, Hesse-Homburg, the Duchy of Nassau, and the free city of Frankfort, seat of the brilliant diets of the past and the parliament of more recent years. The unity dreamed of in the church of St. Paul was being realized, but through fratricidal strife—the *Bruderkrieg*. Despite Bismarck's benignity, the German palate tasted of blood and iron. Europe's map was changing and —astoundingly—without France's complicity. The fiat of "the Great Nation" was no longer law, and Paris was quick to recognize Königgrätz as a disaster for French policy and prestige. Prussia was in the ascendant, and Wagner was keenly aware of the shift in the political balance. Within not too many months he would be pondering an expedient change to the side of power. By July, Wagner, Cosima, and Hans were toasting Bismarck at Triebschen and crying out in unison, *"Delenda Austria."*

The summer was difficult for Ludwig. He was thoroughly depressed. His pathetic troops, led by operetta generals, had made a very bad show. Eduard Vogel von Falckenstein's Army of the Main was mopping them up throughout July, and by the third week of the month the main Prussian force was outside Vienna. Ludwig wrote to Wagner, "The spirits of darkness rule; alas, everywhere deceit and betrayal. . . . God grant that Bavaria's independence may be preserved; if not, if her foreign representation is lost, if we come under Prussian hegemony, then away; I will not be a powerless shadow-king!" To Cosima he wrote three days later (July 21) that "not the difficult political situation" tortured him—"that would be cowardice"—but separation from Wagner, "who is all to me." Ready to flee from ugly reality back into the dream, he was again talking of abdication. "It can't go on like this. No, no! Without him the strength of my life wastes away; I am alone and abandoned. . . ."

Once more Wagner counseled patience and, as a diversion, recited the Nuremberg plan hatched some months before. Munich's very name, derived from *Mönch* (monk), was distasteful to him. He pictured the King forsaking its Residenz and sallying forth to dwell at Bayreuth castle. Nearby Nuremberg would become Bavaria's new seat of government; there Wagner's academy would rise and his model performances, "offered as a gift to the nation," take place. *Meistersinger* mounted *in* Nuremberg would liberate Ludwig from Munich. That the King had been well applauded by his troops and subjects during a recent journey through Franconia probably inspired Wagner to rekindle this Nuremberg fantasy in which certainly neither he nor the King really believed, though the latter sent word that once again his mentor's communications had strengthened him to endure. Fortunately, like Cosima, he had neither sense of proportion nor humor where Wagner was concerned, else their correspondence would have been of short duration. Obviously, Wagner grasped Ludwig's almost desperate homosexual craving for a fatherly friend—he had grown up estranged from both his parents— and mercilessly exploited this advantage in his letters.

These had achieved an intensely intimate tone, despite a tireless exchange of extravagant, stilted compliments. The pattern had been set quite early; Wagner's messages repeatedly hailed the King as Germany's savior by reason of his beauty, sensitivity, and devotion to Wagnerian ideals, and Wagner was in turn greeted as a god come to earth to redeem through his art. These salvos of mutual homage fired, the pair turned to the business at hand, if there were any, aside from the usual exercise in panegyrics. Yet through the paraphrases of Wagnerian poetry and expressions of excessive esteem that so often make the collection of letters read like a wicked anti-Wagnerian parody, a tide of reciprocal affection nonetheless flowed. Ludwig, the friend, loved Wagner—or, rather, the idea of Wagner—with an enthusiasm he sought to strengthen by writing as if unaware of the less lofty aspects of the composer's character; Ludwig, the monarch, left to secretaries the task of communicating unpleasant truths about money and manners to his master when such reminders were necessary, and, when particularly vexing subjects had to be broached, Cosima was the intermediary.

From the start of his friendship with the King, Wagner played a role that with time had broadened and grown increasingly demanding. At first he satisfied as Gurnemanz and then, to his delight, discovered that he was also expected to pull on the robes of deity. Ludwig required that Wagner himself be an operatic work of art; he wished into being the faultless musician-philosopher of his dreams. The actor, eager to please and earn swelling fees, spoke the expected lines eloquently, on occasion sinking himself so deeply into his part that his own identity came into question. Ludwig, on his side, played the novice to perfection, though he was keenly aware that the master in whom he so delighted was largely a theatrical illusion. Fearing some accident might reveal the player strutting in paint and costume, he took precautions against this cruel day; as far as possible nothing was allowed to disturb the pretense of complete, idyllic harmony between the friends. No one worked harder than Cosima to keep this strange play on the boards. A tireless prompter, she kept feeding the performers their cues even when it appeared that the theater was collapsing about them.

For his part, Wagner loved Ludwig as sincerely as he could love anyone. In his eyes, every friend was a potential candidate for sacrifice, and to each he offered unlimited opportunities of martyrdom. Yet one often senses his unfeigned concern for the adolescent so completely conquered that he could write, "Deeply and from my heart I love no woman, no parents, no brother, no relatives, none but you!"

The letters break through all but the final barrier between ruler and subject. Wagner called the boy "my Ludwig," and one senses their reaching toward that familiar ultimate "*du*" which etiquette forbade Wagner to initiate and shyness held the King from proffering in letters that would obviously one day be published. At times, it seemed that both were really corresponding with posterity. As if to compensate for the endearing pronoun, each outvied the other in inventing salutations of the most romantic sort, such as "My beloved, beautiful wonder! My lord! My friend!" from Wagner, and "Unique one! Lord of my life!" from Ludwig.[5]

After the Prussian blitzkrieg in the "Seven Weeks' War" it was idle for either, even in their fanciful letters, to pretend that Bavaria had any immediate future in German political affairs. By autumn, Wagner had redefined Ludwig's mission mainly in artistic terms. He formulated "a ringing antithesis"—on one side Prussian rule equated with ballet and Italian opera (evidently he was unaware of Bismarck's refined appreciation of Mozart and, especially, Beethoven), on the other, German majesty synonymous with Wagner's creations. As opposed to Prussian materialism, Bavaria, through possession of the Wagnerian art-work, was to become "the protecting rampart of German honor." The score of *Meistersinger* was growing at Triebschen, and Wagner foresaw its première in Nuremberg as "a difficult day for Count Bismarck and the North German Bund but a proud, beautiful one for Ludwig the German and his Richard!" But this seemingly inexhaustible ingenuity in contriving fables for the boy was about to be put to a problem it could not overcome.

At the time of Ludwig Schnorr's death Wagner observed, "Now I have only one Ludwig left!" But during this difficult fall of 1866, when he was striving to cope with the young king's confused state of mind, news came that the great tenor's spirit was abroad and seeking contact with him. Again there were two Ludwigs. Wagner found himself caught in a grotesque intrigue, amazing in even his eventful life.

4

From the time of Schnorr's funeral his widow, Malvina, had intimated her conviction that the special bond uniting the couple with Wagner during the *Tristan* production had not died with her husband. Schnorr on his deathbed had instructed Malvina to go to Munich. Wagner wrote Ludwig, "There, with us, she was to help complete what we had begun with him," for Schnorr had told her, "Help Richard! He, too, will help you and care for you!" However, Wagner did not come to know the intensity of Mal-

---

[5] Occasionally, in an excess of emotion, Wagner availed himself of the *"du"* for a moment but then fell back into the formal *"Sie."* See his letters to the King of November 22, 1866, and March 31, 1867. In the latter he cries, *"O Parzifal! Wie muss ich Dich lieben, mein trauter Held!"* When Wagner on October 6, 1866, closed a letter with "your subject," Ludwig protested that he was the "servant" in their relationship.

vina's sense of mission until the end of 1866, when he received her alarming news: Until he fulfilled certain behests, Schnorr's ghost would find no rest.

The tenor's death lay heavily upon him; his diary reveals the deep responsibility he felt for the tragedy. An enormous girth belied a fragile constitution. As early as November, 1864, the King had expressed to Wagner his fear that Schnorr's obesity betokened a short career. During his Karlsruhe days Schnorr had dreaded the exertion of Tristan's role. Malvina had prevented his undertaking it and at the same time shielded his pride by declaring herself unequal to Isolde's demands. But at Biebrich, under Wagner's inspired coaching, his confidence grew, and by the time of the Munich première he was in an ebullient state, sustained by contact with the composer and his incomparable work. Today it is difficult to gauge the score's mesmerizing and literally maddening effect upon many who first heard it. Herr Eberle, one of the assistant conductors working under Bülow on the revival of 1869, actually broke down from overexcitement during rehearsals and left for an asylum. The highly emotional Schnorr burned himself out with the première performances and, after the last one, fell an easy victim to a fever, described as *"Springende Gicht* [leaping gout] . . . that traveled from his knee joint to his brain." He tore his hair, which had to be sheared, and roared like a lion. At the end, three people were required to restrain him. Frau Tichatschek reported to Minna his doctors' private view that he died of *Tristan* (spelled *"Triestan"* by the good Pauline), a highly simplified diagnosis, but probably not farther from the truth.

Malvina desired to build upon this sacrifice. She had a right to think herself worthy of Wagner's friendship. Esteeming her artistry no less than her husband's and comparing her to Schröder-Devrient, he paid his highest compliment. During the *Tristan* rehearsals she already surpassed anything expected; ecstatically he wrote Ludwig, "From her, one will be able to learn what a tragedienne is!" And shortly before the scheduled performance he observed, "Frau Schnorr is perfect; no living artist of her sex may in any way be placed beside her." In all Germany she alone possessed the range, stamina, and dramatic qualities necessary to project the incandescent Isolde.

After Schnorr's death Wagner maintained a cordial relationship with her. She was to take part in future model performances of his works and join the faculty of the new Munich music school. Schnorr had died a soldier in the Wagnerian campaign, and his wife was ordered to the front of the continuing battle. Wagner wrote, "In truly every respect her influence on our young female singers would be the finest I might imagine." Certainly he did not anticipate any personal entanglement with her. But, though Malvina had no desire to take over duties in his bedroom, Wagner failed to recognize her fanatical craving for the role Cosima proudly played before the world, the helpmate to genius.

In March of 1866, thanks to Wagner's and Cosima's efforts, King Ludwig granted a pension to Malvina, and she moved to Munich. Triebschen was unprepared for the storm it thus unwittingly unleashed.

After Minna's death Frau Schnorr evidently judged the time approaching for the fulfillment of her Wagnerian destiny. She had come under the spell of one of her singing pupils. This Fräulein Isidore von Reutter was a medium and exploited an interest in spiritualism the diva had shown even before her husband's death. Dying in Dresden, Schnorr had called out with his last breath to the absent Wagner, "Richard, don't you hear me?" After the funeral Malvina asked Wagner whether these anguished cries had reached him in Munich. Isidore easily convinced the emotional woman that Schnorr's troubled shade not only demanded that his widow guide Wagner's artistic destiny but also advocated her gifted medium's marriage to Ludwig of Bavaria! The latter's meeting with his fate-destined bride was, of course, to be arranged by Wagner, who had so lavishly praised the prognostications of Frau Dangl that Isidore perhaps hoped to find her own talents no less esteemed.

Her revelations were communicated to him in November, when she and Malvina descended upon Triebschen for a nerve-shattering visit. But Wagner accepted only spirit messages confirming his own desires, and Cosima filled the role of his clairvoyante in residence. On June 25, 1865, he had written Ludwig of her sinking into "ecstatic fits of slumber, which take her unawares from time to time and in which, out of deepest sleep, she soon speaks clearly and coherently, imparting visions of which she has not the slightest remembrance upon awakening." Cosima saw such wondrous images as Wagner's enemies catapulting to eternal damnation as Ludwig hovered above like Christ in the "Last Judgment" of Michelangelo. "Oh, how terrible! I can't look!" the sensitive lady cried out in her sleep. But Isidore offered no such enticing pictures, and Wagner admonished Malvina to rid herself of an imposter and intrigante. Clearly, Isidore was ill-informed about the basic traits of the King's personality. And, if supernatural forces could make him fall in love with a woman, she was certainly not this vulgar, uneducated amazon who had, Wagner told Röckel, the "figure of a military policeman." Moreover, Isidore undiplomatically quoted Schnorr's specter as urging Wagner to write less strenuous vocal parts. This was the kind of irritating advice his brother Albert used to give him. He needed no such psychic recommendations. Schnorr's pragmatic ghost also advised him to compose more songs and thus become really popular! The *"Wahn"* ("madness") of *Meistersinger's* second act seemed to be erupting at Triebschen.

Malvina looked upon Wagner's rejection of her communications as the act of a misguided soul and soon let loose the wrath of the spurned upon Cosima, whom she recognized as "the unclean spirit" perverting Wagner's mind. "Woe to that devilish being who has bound your noble soul in shameful fetters." Unbalanced by Schnorr's death, overexcited by Isidore, and enraged by Wagner's disbelief, she determined to destroy the wicked Cosima by denouncing to the King her illicit relationship with Wagner, obvious to anyone visiting Triebschen. Cosima was well advanced in pregnancy.

That Malvina's position as an intimate of both might give the indictment unusual weight filled Wagner with anxiety. Yet he soon realized that little could be added to what had been repeatedly put through the press and felt it the wisest course to stress his conviction that poor Frau Schnorr was hopelessly deranged. *"È pazza, amici miei!"* was Don Giovanni's desperate answer to Elivira's accusations. And indeed, at first, Triebschen's bizarre involvement with a pair of spiritualists diminished whatever credence the tale might otherwise have found with Ludwig, to whom, moreover, Wagner, without any evidence, denounced Isidore as a tool of his Munich enemies. He was striving to put sufficient pressure on the King to force Frau Schnorr's exile from Bavaria under threat of withdrawing her pension.

The episode left Ludwig with much to think about. Wagner had intimated that he might best understand the affair in terms of *Lohengrin*. The King was Elsa, into whose ears Ortrud and Telramund were pouring calumnies about her savior. Ludwig might have reflected that Lohengrin, a master of the fatuous and the cliché, could abide only as long as he resisted giving direct answers and that, when a "higher" duty called, this knight sailed away, leaving his beloved prone on the ground. (Within not too many months the Wagnerian skiff was to point its prow toward Bismarck and Prussia.) Obviously, Ludwig's patience was at last being worn thin by Wagner's shabby adventures. He was coming to realize that, though eccentric, Malvina was not mad, and openly faced the fact of his friend's formidable capacity for mendacity and duplicity.

5

Though Ludwig toyed with the idea of moving his government to Nuremberg, clearly Munich, a Wittelsbach capital for over six centuries, would not lose its status to accommodate the composer of *Meistersinger*. Almost apologetically the King reminded Cosima that he did have some attachment to the city of his boyhood. Wagner, who had resolved never to reside in Munich again, was obliged to reconcile himself to occasional visits in connection with his royal duties.

His situation had eased; Munich's press, occupied with the war and its consequences, had neglected the campaign against him, and a governmental reorganization resulted in the departure of several hostile officials. The new foreign minister, Prince Hohenlohe, who took office on the last day of 1866, looked upon him as a harmless extravagance. Moreover, his distant residence in Switzerland for a time softened misgivings concerning his intrigues and scandalous love life. Now that the composer could hazard a return to Munich, Ludwig desired the *Meistersinger* première at the court theater and commanded model performances of *Lohengrin* and of *Tannhäuser* in the Paris version as soon as practicable. Wagner could write reams about the noble German traditions of Nuremberg, but its operatic resources were in reality miserable, and, to his horror, the city had put on performances of Meyerbeer's *L'Africaine* and Verdi's *Trovatore* [6] during Ludwig's recent visit. Such was the cosmopolitan taste of the Nurembergers whose Teutonic purity Wagner had lauded. *Lohengrin* had recently been done with great success at Pest, which Wagner briefly considered as a possible site for the *Meistersinger* première. But Ludwig declared to Cosima that he "would sink into the ground should this happen," and Wagner quickly readjusted to the idea of Munich.

Bülow, increasingly refractory, had moved to Basel in September of 1866, and so firmly was Cosima ensconced at Triebschen that she could write the King, whom she and Wagner still believed to be virginally naïve, of plans to "visit" her husband, who was set up *en garçon*. Ludwig learned from Wagner that, since he was financially better off than Bülow, it would be easier for all if Cosima was cared for and awaited her confinement at Triebschen!

But independence was not yet to be given Hans; Wagner had sensibly concluded that composition was his primary task, especially at a time when his pen flew with inspiration. The main labor of mounting his operas in Munich had to pass to Bülow's dependable hands. That he return to Bavaria was imperative.

It was not easy to lure him back. He was weary of scandal. But Wagner moved to secure for him a new rank of *Kapellmeister* with extraordinary authority, the directorship of the Wagnerian academy, and, as balm and delight to his wounded Prussian soul, a royal decoration, the Grand Cross of the Order of St. Michael, first class. Wagner knew every weakness of Hans, who had recently come to speak of himself as "a Prussian nobleman." Even Ludwig, the Wittelsbach scion, found his manner somewhat "excessive." But, indeed, what other illusions were left him?

February, 1867, saw the completion of the composition sketch of the final act of *Meistersinger* and the birth of Wagner's and Cosima's second

---

[6] Wagner considered Verdi beneath contempt; Ludwig, however, was to become a Verdi enthusiast.

daughter, Eva, whom the public was encouraged to consider a Bülow child. Hans hastened to Triebschen for her birth, not only to preserve appearances, but also because a possibility remained that the child might be his.

By March, direct consultation with the King over the new projects was necessary, and Wagner crossed the Bodensee to Bavaria. Optimistic, he happily observed what he took to be a friendly look on the face of the great stone lion guarding Lindau harbor and relished the sobs of joy with which proprietor Schnaufer greeted him at Munich's Hotel Bayerischer Hof. In addition to seeing Ludwig, he met with Prince Hohenlohe, whom he lectured on politics, and had an interview with Duchess Sophie of Bavaria, the youngest sister of Austria's Empress Elizabeth. Astonishment and approval had greeted news that Sophie would become Ludwig's queen on the day of the *Meistersinger* première.

Ludwig had known her since childhood, and they came to enjoy a friendship based upon a mutual enthusiasm for Wagner, sharpened in both young people by her father, Duke Maximilian. Ludwig believed that he and Sophie shared Wagner as their salvation: "We live as if on an oasis in the sandy sea of the desert." Though Ludwig looked upon her much as a sister, her parents, especially Duchess Ludovica, perhaps not without self-interest, came to view his confidences, correspondence, and visits to their castle at Possenhofen as preliminaries to courtship. Moreover, Sophie fell deeply in love. Out of pity for her and a desire to prove his manhood, he let himself be borne toward the altar. In the beginning the game was entrancing; Ludwig played the gallant. But, as the wedding drew nearer, his masquerade became a wretched business, and, feeling increasingly threatened, he began to show toward his fiancée a hysterical, violent, even cruel side. He had been in his element when planning ceremonies and selecting wardrobes and new furnishings. But as the time approached to celebrate the climax of these preparations in the royal bed, Ludwig gave way to despair and determined to end his life with cyanide if the engagement could not be broken. He wondered how he had let things go so far. Wagner sensed his anxieties. A compassionate letter of September 22 shows the composer at his finest: "Open your heart to me! . . . Tell me what oppresses you! I am told by an inner voice which I can nonetheless only answer if it reaches me through you." In October the betrothal was dissolved by mutual consent; Sophie awakened from a bad dream, and Ludwig felt he had risen from the dead.

She had made every attempt to please, writing reverently to Wagner, whose superior claim to her groom's heart she openly acknowledged. Had not Ludwig warned her that their union would be relatively short, since his own death would follow closely upon Wagner's? Her letters even attempted vain but nonetheless courageous flights of Wagnerian hyperbole dutifully sprinkled with quotations from the holy texts, her efforts showing that same good will and industry evident in her needlework. Obviously, she and her parents had not been unaware of Ludwig's psychological problems, nor were they guiltless of a certain amount of intrigue in their efforts to gain the throne; yet doubtless she loved him and, had he not given in to panic, would perhaps have guided his life and her own to a happier end. In 1897, as Duchess of Alençon, she was to burn to death in Paris at the ghastly charity bazaar fire.

The tragicomic events in Bavaria were to unfold some months in the future. During the spring of 1867 Sophie and Ludwig still appeared the ideal young lovers, and Triebschen saw fit to co-operate in his plan to draw the handsome young princess securely within its circle. But her interview with Wagner in Munich was prepared with utmost secrecy. She felt it wise to keep far from the brush with which Munich tarred Wagner's friends until after the crown was firmly on her head.

Early in April Wagner brought confirmation of the royal recall to Hans in Basel, and that same month Herr and Frau von Bülow again set up house in Munich. Wagner had given up the Hôtel Jôchum, and their apartment on the Arcostrasse was spacious enough to accommodate him on visits. Cosima passed back and forth between the two with great ease. The myth of a happy Bülow ménage had to be preserved. But to even so astute and initiated a friend as Cornelius it appeared that perhaps she had definitely returned to Hans. Her reciprocal motion was mystifying, and Peter finally renounced attempts to solve the intriguing puzzle. But, not improbably, Bülow was as obliging a husband as ever when Wagner occupied his guest suite. Despite his reproaches that Wagner and Cosima were again leading him to ruin, he had not sufficient strength to resist their trap. The bait was too savory.

Though the fortunes of the trio had been re-established beyond anything that might have been anticipated some months earlier, two clouds hung over Wagner's sunny victories: Since Triebschen remained his permanent home,[7] he bewailed the separations from Cosima the new arrangement imposed; in addition, he inwardly recognized that his personal influence with Ludwig had seriously declined. Their encounters had been kept to a minimum even during Wagner's birthday visit to Lake Starnberg.[8]

The royal forbearance with Wagner the man had been frayed threadbare. Triebschen's reaction to the Malvina affair had awakened suspicions; the alarmed calls for her banishment forced Ludwig to focus his eyes on what he had preferred to contemplate with hazy idealism—the singular position

---

[7] The baby, Eva, remained with Wagner and his servants at Triebschen; he took to having her dressed in the same shade of pink satin he wore about the house.

[8] As a gift the King gave him the famous piano-desk combination.

of Frau von Bülow in Wagner's household. Now, Ludwig's earlier image of the creator of *Lohengrin* could be conjured only in emotional letters. Reality brought an ill-mannered egomaniac whose main concern seemed to be with gulden, and who, apparently incapable of learning from experience, still believed himself fated to direct Bavarian politics. To the exquisite Ludwig's horror, he would pound on the furniture when making his points.

Nonetheless, there were still dreams of mighty undertakings. Whatever he came to think of Wagner's character, Ludwig remained constant in his devotion to the composer's works. October was expected to witness the laying of the Wagner theater's cornerstone, the opening of the music school, and the first *Meistersinger,* along with the royal wedding. Wagner desired the première to take place on the nuptial day as a sign to the world that he and Ludwig were born for one another; it would be one of those "coincidences that alone are the lot of those sent by God." But, though ostensibly voyaging together toward the same lofty goals, their way was rocky and lined with unsuspected pitfalls.

Wagner precipitated a catastrophe by inviting old Tichatschek to play in Munich's so-called "model performance" of *Lohengrin* under Bülow. It was almost a dozen years since the singer had called Wagner's attention to young Schnorr as his successor! At a rehearsal in June, Ludwig beheld with repugnance the swan knight of his fantasies embodied in the beery corpulence of a time-worn tenor. The sudden royal order to postpone the performance and engage a new hero [9] was a blow to the composer's judgment and pride. He abruptly quit Munich for Triebschen, a punishment Ludwig felt he did not deserve. Although Ludwig placatingly wrote, "I kiss the hand that has chastised me," when *Tannhäuser* was mounted at the beginning of August, Wagner moodily remained away.

Even a development promising to realize one of his and Ludwig's earliest dreams ended in disaster. Prince Hohenlohe called upon Julius Fröbel, whose politics Wagner had long regarded with enthusiasm, to establish a new government newspaper, the *Süddeutsche Presse.* It was to have a daily column devoted to Wagnerian affairs. His old plan for uniting an aesthetic journal and related political paper was to be realized in this one publication. However, he was expected to confine his activities to the artistic *feuilleton,* the paper being an official Bavarian organ toward whose costs government funds as well as Ludwig's personal contribution were subscribed.

In September, 1867, coincident with work on the last act of *Meistersinger,* Wagner began for the *Süddeutsche* a series of fifteen anonymous articles

[9] Sentiment certainly played a part in Wagner's hiring of Tichatschek. The role had been written especially for his silvery tenor, which still preserved much of its old luster. The youthful Heinrich Vogl assumed the role after his elder colleague's pathetic withdrawal.

called "German Art and German Politics." Reproachfully, Wagner wrote Ludwig that this latest literary effort was a "substitute for our conversations at Hohenschwangau, to which you now no longer summon me!" The articles were an expansion of Hans Sachs's final address in the opera, but, alas, without transfiguring music. The old Wagnerian clichés were rehashed; belaboring French degeneration and the shallowness of French culture, Wagner hailed the contrasting vigor and innate virtue of the German Folk, whose God-given mission was the civilizing of the world through the instrumentality of a revitalized German theater.

The articles included many other observations hardly befitting a government paper. As in the political journal for Ludwig, he praised the Burschenschaft, those university fraternities of gymnasts brought into being through the efforts of the proto-Nazi, Friedrich Ludwig Jahn. Two years earlier (September, 1865) at the time of the jubilee celebration of the Burschenschaft at Jena, a sketch of Pastor Riemann, a Nestor of the organization, had caught Wagner's eye in the *Illustrierte Zeitung*. In his diary he extravagantly praised the Burschenschaft's ideals. He had burst into tears at the sight of Riemann's head. "There is German ideality. Completely indescribable! Little movement, no Hungarian, Polish, or French suppleness, somewhat heavy, inelegant; but this meditating spirit! The naïve look, the wonderful faith in it, the fanaticism! This Burschenschaft! Is there anything more singular? With what in the world is it to be compared? Thoroughly unique." He asked Ludwig, "Is this facial expression still to be found only in old men? No, I have a friend in manhood's most youthful bloom who is more beautiful than Riemann, and in his appearance I read everything that again makes the German Folk dear to me!"

Wagner had been a Burschenschaft member during his student days in Leipzig, and in his newspaper series of 1867 he eulogized the insane student, Karl Ludwig Sand, who in 1819 had murdered the famous playwright Kotzebue in a ghastly manner. The international Kotzebue had been detested by Jahn's youth corps, fed on their leader's diet compounded of hatred for the French and Jews and exaltation of Germany's Folk. Though it could hardly have been a secret that Wagnerian political theory rested on foundations put in place by "Father Jahn," many readers of the *Süddeutsche* must have been shocked to find Wagner, whose authorship was obvious from the first, extolling the murderer in his ninth contribution. Kotzebue, renowned for his Gallic facility and particularly Parisian flair for the theatrically effective, was dismissed by Wagner as "a German buffoon" and, echoing Sand, as "the seducer of German youth, the betrayer of the German Folk." (Wagner preferred not to think of all the "German" incident he had culled from Kotzebue's *Die deutschen Kleinstädter* for use in the second act of *Meistersinger!*) According to Wagner, the "lad in old-German gown"—the uniform worn by Jahn and his followers in protest against the importation of French fashions [10]—could only answer Kotzebue with the dagger, "an unexampled deed, remarkable in what it presaged, a completely instinctive deed." However, Wagner's attitude toward the terror and violence of the Jena "unconditionals" presaged the most!

Nor could it have escaped the notice of readers that among other tender points he was gratuitously mixing in Germany's Catholic-Protestant conflict. And in the thirteenth installment he served up Jahn's theories concerning the creation of a new nobility based on duty to the state. Many in authority must have realized that somehow the articles had to be stopped. The opinions of Jahn, once thrown into jail by Prussia on charges of conspiracy, were being resurrected in an official Bavarian publication and at a time when ties between the kingdoms were still delicate.

Wagner had already touched upon much of the dangerous nonsense of this series in his political diary for Ludwig.[11] The printing of such material in a government publication was, however, a different matter. By a bit past mid-December, when the thirteenth installment had been issued, the King's order came to break up whatever of the remaining type had been set and to discontinue what had become an intolerable affair. Although the articles had earned the standard mechanical royal compliments, Wagner's extreme anti-French bias was evidently having disturbing repercussions on the nation's foreign policy, and the Residenz came to look upon this latest diatribe as "suicidal" (*"selbstmörderisch"*). When Bizet eventually read it, he was sickened, a reaction that must not have been unusual.

Wagner's meddling was becoming increasingly distasteful to Ludwig, who, moreover, recognized the sorry figure he cut in his subjects' eyes for having been duped into giving Cosima that official amende honorable. He knew that Frau Schnorr was speaking the truth. Only a month before (November, 1867), Wagner, terrified by Malvina's tongue, had again overreacted by threatening to boycott Munich until she was banished.

6

The King's growing disaffection had prompted Wagner to seek a resolution to the trio's problems. The Cosima issue would be faced. He was

[10] Wagner frequently inveighed against the influence of French mode on German dress. In this he was a true son of Jahn, some of whose disciples wore animal skins to stress their Teutonic heritage.

[11] There Wagner had commented upon the "misunderstanding" that had prompted the Austrian Chancellor Metternich—father of the Ambassador to Paris during the *Tannhäuser* affair—to move against the Burschenschaft after Kotzebue's murder. The Chancellor had not been unhappy over the political possibilities the assassination opened up.

miserable at Triebschen without her, and her own situation in Munich was increasingly trying. Late in September he had written Hans recommending that he find the strength not to sink down beneath the immensity of the tasks fate had assigned him; these could be read in the eyes of his friend. Shouldering such duties courageously, the martyr was to have as reward an awareness of his own noble sacrifice. In short, he was soon to be disposed of; Wagner would no longer share Cosima. "So, my dear Hans, that is settled," Wagner buoyantly declared.

Liszt's autumn visits to the Bülows in Munich and to Wagner at Triebschen were attempts to help them sort out their tangled lives. He found time to play *Meistersinger* from the manuscript as Wagner sang, and was again captivated by the work. The interview, so feared by Wagner, ended with a reconciliation through art, well prepared by the Munich performances of *Tannhäuser* and *Lohengrin* Liszt had recently attended with Cosima. Yet, like many others, he desired the least possible contact with Wagner the man. Nor was he particularly fond of his daughter.

Meistersinger was completed by the end of October. To clear his head Wagner took a Parisian holiday to see the Exposition, where the big Prussian cannon made by Krupp of Essen was the most prophetic display. By the end of the year he was in Munich to celebrate Christmas with the Bülows, bringing all kinds of toys from Paris for the children. He was cheerful despite his recent defeat in respect to the *Süddeutsche* articles. The tears of 1867, Cosima assured the King, would be transformed into pearls during the new year; 1868 promised an unprecedented victory with *Meistersinger*.

By the end of 1867 Ludwig was obviously weary of Wagner, but during the following spring they enjoyed a sentimental rapprochement through resumed correspondence. It was essential that their estrangement end before the *Meistersinger* production.

On March 9, 1868, the King first broke the silence that had lasted months: "I no longer can bear being so completely without information about you!" And after tenderly inquiring about the composer's health, he dared ask, "On what part of *Siegfried* are you working at the moment?" Wagner immediately let fly; the discontinuance of the *Süddeutsche* articles still rankled deep. "Why . . . these old magic sounds of a love which—alas!—must now press through my veins like intoxicating poison? Yes! It was beautiful!" An old threat was revived. "About *Siegfried*—ask me no more! Wreckage will one day witness to the world who I was and what it is!" Ludwig hastened to send the expected lines. Their play was running again. "Oh God, it has come to this: everything, everything is to pass away, the hallowed work, what was so nobly begun, is thus to go down, end so lamentably; never will, never can this happen. . . . Have I really become another, do you no longer recognize Siegfried joyous in victory, no longer know the true Parsifal? . . . There was a time when my word had so much power over you, when it healed deep wounds; has it then lost its old miraculous sound? . . . I am who I was from the beginning; God has chosen me." Ecstatically admitting his guilt, he declared that he had suffered and emerged purified and strengthened. The hero had but slumbered and now stood ready for battle. A certain royal firmness is felt toward the end of the letter. Beneath the gushing verbiage Ludwig made it clear that he expected an immediate and forgiving answer and wished to hear no more about "wreckage." Having already paid for *Siegfried* many times, he wanted to see a finished score, now that *Meistersinger* was out of the way. For him, the latter had been an unwanted luxury, an interruption in the realization of the *Ring*. His enthusiasm for *Meistersinger* always appears somewhat manufactured.

Wagner, already in Munich, where the King's letter was forwarded from Triebschen, replied that he was like a seaman who, drifting on the ocean, had caught a glimpse of the sun and found his bearings. *Siegfried* would be finished within the year; this was his vow.

The romantic reconciliation remained literary. As far as possible the King avoided disillusioning physical encounters with Wagner. Though the latter spent much time in the capital in connection with the preparations for *Meistersinger,* Ludwig did not appear eager to receive him. And when they celebrated the composer's fifty-fifth birthday together on the Roseninsel, the meeting was not an unqualified success. The golden days had fled. And in Munich tension was high as the *Meistersinger* rehearsals progressed, Hans's waxing animosity toward Wagner showing that the latter had repossessed Cosima. Between Wagner and the King and among members of the trio matters were close to the breaking point. At the time the composer jotted down a melancholy theme he planned to use in a mourning symphony for Romeo and Juliet, the subject of the star-crossed lovers certainly having reference to himself and Cosima. The musical idea later came back to him several times and was finally set to work in *Parsifal* as the processional music accompanying Titurel's coffin.

The *Meistersinger* première under Bülow's baton on June 21 was a triumph. Wagner considered the work his finest. Its appeal to nationalism could not have been advanced at a riper moment, feeding as it did that flood of emotion that would in not many months send German armies toward Paris. Hans Sachs's great tirade ended the work with what many recognized as a summons to a racial war on the Latins.[12] To acknowledge

---

[12] There are various approaches to this troublesome passage. One is to cut it from the opera, a practice met with more often than not at the Metropolitan, for example. Another is to claim that there is nothing offensive in a speech that shows Wagner's

the audience's applause, Wagner rose from his place beside the King and stepped to the front of the royal box. Court etiquette lay shattered. In concert with the masterpiece a new era was being born; young Ludwig was the past, the aging Wagner the ominous future.

Ludwig signed "Walther" to a letter of homage to Wagner written in the morning hours after the performance. And though, pathetically, its quotations from the opera revealed that he really thought of himself as Eva, he heroically ended, "Hail German art! In this sign we shall conquer." He would have been stunned to know that Wagner would not stand before him again until the general rehearsal of the first Bayreuth festival some eight years later.

7

For a while Cosima had again felt so sure of herself in Munich that she attempted to get a position at court as reader to Ludwig's mother, hoping in this way to gain Queen Marie's confidence and win her over to the Wagnerian party. But by summer, gossip about the trio had regained its former pitch. On June 24 Wagner returned to Triebschen, and within a month Cosima followed. He wrote the King that she simply could not bear the filth being raked up. "The righteous pride of the woman has been injured." But not even Wagner's famous *"Suada"* (blarney) could screen so exposed and indefensible a position. She was quitting her husband's home to take sanctuary with the man with whom her name had been linked in scandal.

By the time Ludwig warned that her permanent departure would only serve the cause of their enemies and make the gossip mills turn faster, Cosima and Wagner were preparing to take their stand. During August he sketched a play about Luther and his decision to marry, clearly seeing himself as the great reformer and Cosima as the golden-haired Katharina von Bora!

In September the lovers left for a holiday together in northern Italy—he, perhaps with intended irony, had told the King that Cosima's doctors recommended a milder climate—and passed over the St. Gotthard to visit Stresa,

---

politics rising from the practical to the ideal, a text maintaining that, even if the holy German Kaiser Reich itself were to go down, German art would remain holy and indestructible. However, the means of achieving this blessed Teutonic state are clearly indicated—the obliteration of French cultural influences simply because they are essentially base (*"welschen Dunst mit welschem Tand"*), a program Hitler eventually implemented. This text is not a passive observation but rather an active plea—a warning and an incitement that was so received by contemporary audiences. Not surprisingly, Wagner clothed these deeply felt sentiments in music of extraordinary power.

Wagner's beloved Borromean Islands, Genoa, Milan, the shores of Lake Como (Cosima's birthplace), and Lugano. In early October they were back at Triebschen, having returned via the Val Leventina of the Ticino. From Faido she had evidently written Bülow of her decision henceforth to devote her life exclusively to Wagner. In a letter to Hans of the following June, she was to describe her consternation to perceive that "a life *à trois* proved unrealizable." The arrangement had finally to end. She was carrying Wagner's third child and no longer wished to deny his offspring their father's name. Moreover, the two mountebanks were tired of their juggling and tricks.

Accompanied by her four daughters, Cosima returned to Munich in mid-October to discuss with Hans the possibility of divorce. He was no longer indispensable to Wagner, who had been grooming a substitute for months. In the fall of 1866 a twenty-three-year-old Hungarian musician, Hans Richter, had arrived at Triebschen to do score copying. Wagner recognized his unusual talent and by the end of 1867 had placed him as a coach in the Munich Opera. There he worked under Bülow on *Meistersinger* and did yeoman service knocking the part of Walther into tenor Franz Nachbaur's head. Though Richter was unknown and untried, Wagner felt him capable of assuming Hans's position.

Wagner could not have been unaware that Bülow considered his musical task in Munich to be that of conducting fine music of all types and composers, an apostasy that probably descended to him from Liszt. Following the latter's example at Weimar, he was contemplating a production of Byron's *Manfred* with the music of Wagner's bête noire, Schumann. With the young, fawning Richter, Wagner would have no such problems of independent thought. Moreover, that Bülow looked upon him with repugnance had not made their recent artistic co-operation easy. Probably the only person poor Hans found more loathsome was himself. As far as Wagner was concerned, his old pupil was now expendable, the divorce a necessity. His only real fear was the King's resentment at being mercilessly revealed the dupe his subjects had long thought him.

But Hans was unwilling once more to sacrifice his career to Wagner's needs. He was never a popular figure with the public, but his abilities were recognized, and his work in Munich gave him immense satisfaction. To fall in with the plan to drop all pretenses and divorce Cosima could only result in an explosion of scandal that would again force him from the city. By this time, in whose bed Cosima slept was probably a matter of indifference to him. He had lost her completely and was now struggling to keep the sole indemnity his complaisance had earned—his work.

Early in November, while Cosima discussed matters with Hans, Wagner, for the first time in years, felt a curious need to visit his family in Leipzig.

He proceeded there after a hurried visit to Munich, probably not unconcerned with his fears about Ludwig's reaction to the latest developments. A request for an audience, preferably at Hohenschwangau, was denied; *"De profundis clamo . . .* I await your sign!" Wagner wrote, but none came. From hints in his October communications the King had certainly gathered that he finally wished to confess. Offended by the whole ugly business, the young man obviously wanted to spare himself this ultimate embarrassment. Except for a rather sober New Year's greeting he did not write Wagner until February, a long and significant silence. Cosima's guile, too, had deeply pained him, for, even after recognizing Wagner's weaknesses, he had clung to belief in her. Had she not piously assured him that she could never do otherwise than tell him the whole truth about everything? It had been a second shock to learn that obsequious Cosima was cut from the same bolt as Wagner.

Upon the latter's return from Leipzig, she and his two daughters joined him at Triebschen on November 16 after sorrowfully taking leave of Bülow's children, a parting, she told her diary, to be endured then and at any time, since destiny had imposed a higher duty. No clear understanding about the divorce had been reached. Apparently, Hans wished her to separate from Wagner if any legal proceedings were initiated, perhaps during this period to live in Rome with her father, whose advice, moreover, he wanted before taking any step. Liszt had taken clerical vows, the first four Franciscan orders, during the spring of 1865. Cosima was willing to shed her Catholicism and proceed, but Hans held back, realizing how wounding such a scandal would be to the devout Abbé Liszt, whose apartment in the Vatican had been steps from the Sistine Chapel. Indeed, Princess Wittgenstein's efforts to obtain a divorce in order to marry him had come to nothing despite his personal friendship with Pius IX. But now Cosima had only one religion. She had once written Ludwig that, if necessary, she would accuse her own child for Wagner's sake.

At Triebschen all was calm. Like Walther at the end of *Meistersinger,* Wagner had won the maid through art: "I boldly courted earth's loveliest image, chosen by my heart, consecrated as my muse, as noble as she is gentle; in sunlight's bright day through the victory of song, Parnassus and Paradise have been gained." Tristan's shadow realm was a universe away, and soon Siegfried would claim his Brynhild in an atmosphere of blinding effulgence. Serenity came to Cosima for the first time in years. She knew her place would be at Wagner's side until his death.

But in Munich, Bülow, undecided and frantically striving to hold on to his professional position, was reduced to painting a rather amateurish camouflage. He spread the tale that Cosima had left for France to visit her stepsister, the Countess de Charnacé. It was a desperate act.

Unable to care for Daniela and Blandine, a task also beyond his aging mother, Bülow found himself forced to send them to join their sisters at Triebschen in the spring of 1869. He had to write to his daughters, "be very happy that you are at Triebschen and thank good Uncle Richard often for permitting you to live there with Mama." In his pathetically stilted letters to little Daniela, the pretense was maintained that all four girls were his and that their mother had to live in Switzerland for reasons of health.

The well-bred courtesy of his letters to Cosima and Wagner notwithstanding, Bülow found ways of exasperating them under the cover of self-sacrifice and unctuous solicitude. Despite Isolde's remarkable Wagnerian profile, he insisted to the end that she was his daughter. When discussing his will with Cosima in 1875, he wrote of *"nos trois filles en commun,"* and had even rather archly declared his inability to remember the dates of their births. That he provided an inheritance for Isolde was to help bring to pass the trial of 1914 and with it the tale of Cosima's nocturnal peregrinations at Villa Pellet.

In June of 1869 he learned that his wife, frankly described by the press as Wagner's mistress, had borne the latter a son, Siegfried. During the preceding months, when Hans had asked her whether she was again pregnant by Wagner, she had denied the fact with protestations. Now Bülow bitterly declared his cuckoldry most splendidly crowned.

He no longer had the strength to play a part. The newspapers did not spare him. His revival of *Tristan* [13] during the summer was praised for the devotion the conductor brought to the work of his wife's lover. He could no longer stand his ground. There were few who doubted that, despite his obvious ability, he owed his position to his complaisance as a husband. He was physically and emotionally shattered. His was the mood of the dying Tristan, and he saw the only remedy for his misery in "absolute personal resignation." To Wagner he wrote in English, "It must be so." What he called "fatal" *Tristan* ended as it had begun his Munich career. He cried to Cosima that the work had literally finished him: *"Le Tristan m'a donné le coup de grâce."* Leaving his daughters to her care and relinquishing his post, he quit the city in which he had sacrificed to Wagner everything but his life. Minna had been more obliging.

---

[13] This was the famous production witnessed by d'Indy and Duparc. The title parts were taken by Heinrich and Therese Vogl, another married couple thus succeeding to the roles first sung by the Schnorrs. There were a few transpositions in the second act and discreet cuts in the third. Wagner opposed this revival, commanded by the King, and was furious with Bülow for conducting it rather than seizing the opportunity to resign for "artistic" reasons and thus camouflage the real cause of his impending departure.

XII

Aesthetic Change of Heart

I

Wagner would never flee again; his days as Wanderer were past. Over the years he had roamed the world, his drooping cap set against the storm; "Such is Wanderer's fashion when he goes counter to the wind," Wanderer-Wotan explained to a puzzled Siegfried questioning his taste in millinery. As "way-weary guest" he had sought shelter at many strange hearths, paying for his stay by lecturing. "Companionably I rested with good folk; many gave me gifts." Thus did the god describe his social successes of the past as he forced his way into Mime's rocky living room despite the latter's protests and, much like Wagner in Otto Wesendonk's parlor, went about rearranging the life of an unwilling host. Unbidden, the Wanderer seated himself majestically before Mime's fire and compelled him to enter a contest of words upon which his life depended. So had the tempest-driven, desperate Wagner often inflicted his overpowering personality on those he desired to use; the game over, he, like Wotan, left them to their fate.

But the god no longer wished restlessly to bestride the world. The "well-appointed, stately home" with which Fricka-Minna had so many years before vainly sought to content him now answered his need. And the bewitching motif to which Fricka in *Rhinegold* first sang of this *"herrliche Wohnung, wonniger Hausrat"* winds through the scene of Brynhild's awakening by Siegfried, written during Wagner's joyous 1869 with Cosima at Triebschen. "Do you know," he asked her, "what I was thinking about in connection with Brynhild's great arpeggio? Of the movements of your fingers when you are dreaming, when your hand moves through the air."

He began the closing act of *Siegfried* on the first of March, and was working on its full score by the end of summer. Its love music, dazzling and somewhat overweening, has none of the neurotic ecstasy of *Tristan* and the Venusberg scene in the Paris *Tannhäuser,* but rather moves with the self-satisfied strut of Nuremberg's burghers. Having started as revolutionists in the political ferment of Dresden following Louis Philippe's fall, Siegfried and Brynhild are united over two decades later in bourgeois German Switzerland during the heyday of Bismarck. Social and artistic improvement is far from the minds of a pair whose interest is in establishing a workable sex life,[1] details of which they argue at length until the curtain falls on the unrestrained physical consummation of their discussion. Walhall can fall to pieces, the order of the universe be wrecked—they will to bed! A blinding carbon arc was to illumine the carnal climax of what had started under soft gaslight as an idealistic, romantic adventure in governmental reform! The music exults. This hero does not have to run over to the Venusberg for a professional or slip into a shadowy garden to enjoy his friend's wife. In broad daylight, before the world, Wagner took his mate as Siegfried enfolded his eternally young aunt.

2

This final act of *Siegfried* represents a decisive change in Wagner's attitude toward the *Ring*. With Erda's descent in the opening scene much of the cycle's allegorical apparatus sinks into the stage. What symbolic odds and ends are left, Wotan soon gathers up and carts away after being routed by Siegfried.[2] Once the hero plunges into the fire to claim his bride, a different spirit prevails. As Shaw observed, what follows "is opera, and nothing but opera." Siegfried and Brynhild embrace in an artistic environment not new to Wagner, but newly rediscovered.

With Wotan's overthrow the composer abandoned any pretense of con-

---

[1] At first Brynhild resists the hero with a graceful aria, *"Ewig war ich."* Here the Biedermeier imagery and sentimentality of Wolfram's *"Blick' ich umher"* from *Tannhäuser* form the substance of a text set with superb irony to a melody from the Starnberg quartet. The words speaking of the spirit bend to the contours of a tune that arose during a period of sexual fulfillment. The passage is charged with a private symbolism amazing even in Wagner.

[2] The meeting between Siegfried and the Wanderer, although built around another cumbersome question game involving excessive biographic recapitulation, nonetheless does mount toward that fine climax in which the god is symbolically maimed by his grandson. Wagner had already treated a not dissimilar situation in *Meistersinger*, as Sachs in his workshop formally gave way before the young Walther. But Wotan, representing a sterner paternal authority, is unwilling to withdraw with the cobbler's grace. His soul bursts with a terrifying mixture of love, hate, pride, self-pity, and a dichotomous desire to destroy and be destroyed. Like the priest-king at Nemi, he raises his weapon against his successor. The awkwardly constructed encounter rises to the level of a profound psychological revelation. In Wotan's relationship to Siegfried Nietzsche saw a striking representation of Wagner's turbulent nature.

tinuing the tetralogy in the spirit of *Opera and Drama*. The phase of his career that began in the second act of *Lohengrin* and continued with *Rhinegold* and *Valkyrie* was closed. Though conceived in the Zurich of his *Gesamtkunst* speculations, *Tristan* developed after he had outgrown them. The work was a rambling free coda capping the stricter forms of the early *Ring* dramas, and its very convulsiveness betokened a stylistic emergency to be ended by that drastic reaction known as *Meistersinger*. Upon the latter's foundations the final scene of *Siegfried* and the remainder of the *Ring* were to rest. The idealistic dream of Dresden and those first months in Zurich ended when Wagner turned to *Tristan*. Fascinated, he almost detachedly observed the dramatic change in his aesthetic course.

He recognized how far *Tristan* overstepped his own rules. Intuitively he knew that it revealed the Swiss essays as pseudo-aesthetic jargon, though to the end of his life he never quite gave up attempts to reinterpret them as if they were embarrassing passages in Scripture somehow to be harnessed to theological purpose. At the time of *Tristan* the eternal lecturer could not yet grasp what he had done in his newest work or communicate to others what had befallen him artistically.

At first, he could only observe with wonder this creation in which he admitted having thrown all theory to the winds. While composing the third act, he wrote to Mathilde Wesendonk in despairing admiration of himself, "Child! This Tristan is becoming something terrible!" Overwhelmed by the freedom with which his pen moved, even Wagner required time to understand *Tristan*. Yet from the beginning one thing was clear: The apodictic judgments once thundered from Zurich were no longer valid for their author, who wrote "completely without critical deliberation." System had been left so far behind that principles and practice could in no way be reconciled.

At the première, disciples who had studied their lessons discovered that the first Wagnerian work unveiled after *Opera and Drama* departed most radically from this essay's code by exhibiting a purely musical autonomy and daring for which no one had been prepared. What had this unconstrained Lisztian symphonic poem with vocal parts to do with the prescriptions of the Swiss writings? The word, there venerated as the regulating element in the composite art-work, had now sunk to a position of subservience to the music. The Zurich *Ring* operas had not reached the stage; the public could not know that, before *Tristan,* this tendency toward musical dominance had already begun to show itself in the still unperformed final act of *Valkyrie* and more boldly in what was completed of *Siegfried,* where, indeed, the aria had made a swaggering re-entry. (Despite all the Wagnerian talk, the Swiss *Gesamtkunst* aesthetics govern only *Rhinegold* and the first two acts of *Valkyrie*.) And in the love duet, Tristan and Isolde abandoned the *Gesamtkunst* injunction to sing alternately, and joined their voices. Moreover, to provide text for his impassioned musical outbursts in *Tristan,* Wagner, as a substitute for the word repetitions of Italian and French opera, had in many places strung together appositives and synonyms in staggering series. This "poetry," happily swallowed by sweeping musical tides, communicated no more profundity than the unselfconsciously reiterated phrases of the most pedestrian operatic poetaster. In *Tristan* music was clearly the master. Intuitively, Wagner had acted to protect his musical imagination from self-imposed intellectual restrictions. His relationship to his thematic material became unrestrained, at times even profligate. (Chapter XIV, on the leitmotif, will in part concern itself with the specific technical changes his musical style underwent at this period.)

Subconsciously, Wagner recognized his predicament as a theorist. After sending *Opera and Drama* into the world, he had come to accept Schopenhauer's estimate of music as the unique, highest, and liberating art, which, penetrating the heart of the metaphysical will, directly expressed its essence without the help of intermediary ideas. Wagner's earlier concept of the fellowship and impersonality of the individual arts under the leadership of the word had developed during his Dresden days along with an interest in communism. Then a desire to merge the egoism of the individual unit into a kind of directed collectivism characterized his thinking about both aesthetics and politics. But as his belief in this particular social system waned, so had his enthusiasm for the corresponding art theory, and he finally acknowledged, at least to himself, what every opera composer instinctively takes for granted—the supremacy of music.[3] Like most composers, on this point he had been an intuitive Schopenhaurean early in life.

In his complimentary article on Halévy's *La Reine de Chypre* for the *Gazette musicale* in 1842, he had claimed that to music alone was reserved the task of revealing primal elements and the secrets of the soul, and as early as his first contribution to the *Gazette*—"On German Music" of 1840— he had lamented, "Through what a rubbish of extras from other art forms must one not first wade when hearing an opera, in order to arrive at the real drift of the music itself!" The article extolled purely instrumental composition as the genre representing music at its "most independent and characteristic." The idea of music's superiority even ran deep beneath the artificially contrived landscape of the Swiss essays, where it unexpectedly welled up from time to time.

[3] Avowedly, Gluck, too, had once wished "to reduce music to its proper function, that of seconding poetry." He believed in theory "that the relation of music to poetry was much the same as that of harmonious coloring and well-disposed light and shade to an accurate drawing, which animates the figures without altering their outlines." But, like Wagner, he was—as Berlioz happily observed—unable in practice to keep music a vassal to the word.

After *Tristan* he was unwilling publicly to face the fact that endorsement of music's superiority over her sister arts contradicted his writings on the reciprocal relationships within the *Gesamtkunstwerk*. He strove to bring his Swiss speculations into harmony with a view which actually attacked their very basis, for Schopenhauer's theory of music and the Wagnerian synthesis were irreconcilable. Though inwardly Wagner must have recognized the illogic of the effort, long before the *Tristan* première he was nonetheless attempting to chart this new and unnavigable theoretic course. Early in 1857, only two months after he had conceived the first musical themes for *Tristan,* his famous open letter to Princess Marie Wittgenstein on Liszt's symphonic poems made public a sentiment already confided to Liszt in correspondence; Wagner declared as an article of faith that "into whatsoever alliance music may enter, it never ceases to be the highest, the most redeeming art." With this statement he planted a banner with a changed Wagnerian device. But, embarrassed by the word "opera," he refused to pronounce the name of the territory he claimed or to admit that he had visited it before.

In "Music of the Future," written in September, 1860, a year after the completion of *Tristan* and during the creation of the Parisian Venusberg score, he again acknowledged music as the more powerful agent in its union with poetic drama. The latter was now held to play a mediating role between the metaphysical, ideal world of music and the conceptual, material world of the listener, the play being a "plastic expression" meant to clarify music's abstract language of feeling. No longer, as in *Opera and Drama,* was music to be a more intense but parallel expression of the words. Poetry would perceive that her inmost longing and ultimate goal was to blend with, "to ascend to," music, which, nonetheless, as far as an audience was concerned, lacked an essential that only poetry could provide—the capacity to reply to the question, "Why?" "This disturbing and yet so indispensable question" could be answered when poetic drama joined music and related it to phenomena. And, together, these arts had the power to transport auditors into an ecstatic state in which inquiries were no longer made and all answers given. Wagner, of course, was thinking of the intoxicating effects of the music of *Tristan.* Some years later, before a public reading of *The Twilight of the Gods* in Berlin, he would stress the role of the composer even more strongly by declaring that German music gave to the dramatic action an "ideal freedom, that is a deliverance from motivation through contemplative thought . . . the characters having no need to express their impulses (*Beweggründe*) in the sense of reflecting consciousness." The "Why?" was really unimportant to Wagner. Reason had no place in a universe ruled by intuition; music, a mystic reverberation of the world soul, told the auditor all he needed to know.

"Music of the Future" declared that the poet was to be measured by what he left unsaid. The musician, echoing these silences, was to speak the unutterable. He could dare plunge boldly into the sea of tone, for his hand gripped that of the poetic dramatist; thus enclasped, they joined music's ideal realm and the material world of the public.[4]

Wagner liked to imagine that "Music of the Future" pictured a *Gesamtkunst* structure in which the planes of music and dramatic poetry mutually penetrated and supported one another. But the essay really described a fabric held aloft mainly by the musician. The poetic dramatist was clearly in his service. The relationships established in the Swiss essays were set tail over head; Wagner's attempt in "Music of the Future" to justify in theory music's predominance over the text in *Tristan* and in the Paris Venus scene, ended by denying his earlier essays, even though he somehow managed to persuade himself that he was confirming them. Understandably, he was reluctant to admit that his polemic tracts of a decade before were largely inapplicable to his work. Perhaps sensing the inconsistency of his position and intuitively wishing to cover whatever embarrassing queries might arise, he stressed the "abnormal" state of his mind during those Zurich days. But the Swiss essays, waggishly called "the books" by the English critic Davison, continued to stand as the gospels of Wagnerism, and because of the composer's ambivalence the apocryphal "Music of the Future" did not shake faith in them. More perceptive disciples perhaps consoled themselves by reflecting that even the Evangelists were not always in agreement; with patience, good Wagnerians awaited further revelation.

Three years after the première of *Tristan, Meistersinger* was first heard. In the face of their master's dogmatic assurances that myth alone could provide themes worthy of the German stage—he had declared Shakespeare's greatest error to have been the use of chronicle material—startled disciples beheld a historical opera in the manner of Meyerbeer. Moreover, *Meistersinger* boasted a libretto obviously modeled on the practice of Wagner's detested French foeman, Eugène Scribe; and there were distinct arias, marches, choruses, a rousing crescendo finale, a ballet, and elaborate ensembles capped by—*horribile dictu*—a quintet! All the closed Italian forms on the Wagnerian Index were shamelessly exhibited. End rhyme, though berated in earlier theory, had first quietly returned to mingle with alliterations in *Tristan* and now openly prevailed. And again, as in *Tristan,* the text was for the most part submerged in a sea of gorgeous musical sound. Dis-

---

[4] Apart from the difficulties of swimming hand in hand, after their plunge into the "great waves," the poet and musician find themselves "ever on the ground of the dramatic action" thanks to the poet's links with the world of phenomena. According to this infamous image, they are really wading palm in palm all the time.

ciples must have wondered whether all the interdictions had been amended. Perhaps they confidently hoped that the *Ring* would yet accommodate the composer's works to the Swiss pronouncements—*Rhinegold* and *Valkyrie,* completed over a dozen years before the *Meistersinger* première, still remained unperformed—and set his world aright, for the new Wagnerian paradise, beautiful as it was, strangely resembled his old descriptions of hell.

3

Wagner's essays written during the long period of *Meistersinger*'s creation reveal increasing uneasiness about his vulnerable position as a theorist. (They were not only political discussions but also aesthetic harangues; for Wagner, the two subjects were one.) Obviously, he wished to avoid the touchy issue of the relationship between poetic drama and music which in *Meistersinger* was essentially that of Scribe and Meyerbeer. For the moment, he turned to obfuscation; through a more general consideration of his latest work he sought to bestow some vague, metaphysical status upon the reborn Wagnerian grand opera. Schopenhauer, who had rejected the form as a monstrosity, was again twisted to an alien purpose, especially his evocative suggestion that the criterion of philosophical ability is an aptitude for viewing men and things as phantoms or dream-pictures. Wagner, in turn, would bestow this philosophical gift upon the artist.

"On State and Religion" (1864) touched upon Wagner's return to the theater of action which "does not really depart from life, but rather remains within it, exalts it, and reveals life itself as a play which, even if it have a serious and terrible appearance, yet is but a dream image (*Wahngebilde*) and as such comforts and beguiles one from the sordid reality of distress." He had come back to the theatrical genre of *Rienzi,* but now the action play was to be seen as if in a dream. (By the time of *Parsifal* the dream would turn to phantasmagoria.) Reality was not to be represented by symbolic correlatives, but rather by illusion—or better, delusion—Schopenhauer's ultimate revelation about reality.

The idea of art and life as mutually reflecting dream mirrors dominates *Meistersinger.* ("On State and Religion," like "German Art and German Politics," was an image of the opera seen through the distorting glass of Wagner's prose.) Walther dreams the prize song and with Sachs's help coaxes it from the world of half-forgotten images to paper. Sachs assures him that art and dream are one, for "poetry is nothing but the expounding of prophetic dreams." Walther wonders where the boundary between dream and poetry lies. "They're friends," Sachs assures him, "always happily near one another." Beckmesser's attempt to make Walther's dream his own gives it a nightmarish quality, and, when in the festival meadow the latter converts his dream song into the prize song, he reinterprets the dream once again, a good part of the closing act of *Meistersinger* being consumed by successive readings of the same dream.[5]

This concern with dreams owes much to Volume One of Schopenhauer's *Parerga and Paralipomena,* which Wagner had first read during his Zurich days. Here, in an extensive chapter (*"Versuch über das Geistersehn . . ."*), Schopenhauer accounted for visions and prophetic dreams. The latter occurred when what he termed "the dream organ" was more than usually stimulated. It then led the sleeper into contact with the metaphysical will, which, since it was inaccessible in terms of the phenomenal world, spoke indirectly through allegory. During that strange state between sleep and wakefulness when this roundabout communing took place, the sleeper's mind might also confusedly mix metaphysical shapes with phenomenal ones and thus give rise to apparitions. In this manner Schopenhauer explained the visions and clairvoyance of seers and prophets. To them Wagner added the artist, who, through the workings of a prodigiously stimulated dream organ, also had the power to communicate with the Universal.

Such thoughts, derived from the *Parerga,* formed the substance of Hans Sachs's sermons to Walther on the framing of a master's song. In *Beethoven,* an essay of 1870, Wagner was to extend the *Parerga's* pages on clairvoyance into the area of musical aesthetics by declaring that parallel to the dream world of sight was a similar mystic realm of sound (*"eine Schallwelt neben der Lichtwelt"*) providing telepathic aural experiences which, corresponding

---

[5] For the romantic artist, dreaming was a state that, paradoxically, could awaken creative powers. Hölderlin remarked that "man is a god when he dreams, a beggar when he ponders." Schiller called this young poet "the dreamer." Throughout Wagner's works, sleep and dreams play prominent roles. In a dream Erik foresees the Dutchman's arrival and Senta's fate. Both Wotan and Tannhäuser are first discovered slumbering, the former enjoying a vision of the completed Walhall as he mumbles of honor, power, and renown, the latter, amid the revels of Venus' grotto, dreaming of springtime in Thuringia. At Eisenach he sinks into a dream of Venus during the festivities in the castle as Wolfram sings an aria in itself an evocation of a dream image. In the meadow before the River Scheldt Elsa recounts the phantom vision of Lohengrin that came to her while she slept, and Sieglinde relives in a harrowing dream the burning of her childhood home. Erda, the seeress, gains knowledge through dreams, and her daughter Brynhild is condemned to sleep. In a dream Herzeleide speaks the symbolic name of her son, Parsifal, and Kundry, whom he redeems, suffers a kind of catalepsy, her entire existence being a succession of trances. Through the medium of dream she travels from incarnation to incarnation, much as Arindal in *Feen,* by means of "approaching slumber," made his way from "a wild, rocky desert" to Ada's fairy palace. And the song, "Dreams," is Wagner's most famous study for *Tristan,* whose lovers flee from day's delusion to the truth of night and dreams.

to the phenomena of clairvoyance and visions, enabled music to enter the consciousness.[6] The final act of *Meistersinger* and much in the articles written during its composition show a groping toward this abstruse theory of music drama, which would come to paper at Triebschen, but only after fruitful hours of conversation with Nietzsche.

In his address on the day of the foundation-stone ceremony at Bayreuth, Wagner was to speak of "scenic pictures that appear to manifest themselves . . . out of an ideal world of dreams." These specters of the universal will, released through the artist's dreaming, were to set before the viewer "the complete reality of a noble art's subtlest illusion." To capture on stage the atmosphere of dream phenomena, Gottfried Semper suggested for the Wagner theater in Munich that double proscenium in receding perspective eventually built at Bayreuth. Characters so framed appeared larger than life, yet, at the same time, mysteriously remote; as music rose from the invisible, sunken orchestra pit, "the mystic abyss," Wagner saw the scenic picture attaining the superreality of a clairvoyant vision and becoming "the truest copy of life itself."

He was depending upon Semper's architectural disposition of the festival theater to help him, through perspective tricks, lighting, and the mysterious source of the orchestral sound, so to bewilder an audience's senses that for it, as for the sleeper in the *Parerga,* dream and reality would merge into a single revelatory experience. Through these concepts that took shape during the writing of *Meistersinger* Wagner saw a way of fitting out grand opera with metaphysical attachments. "On State and Religion" of Wagner's Munich period was in part an attempt not only to explain the naturalistic, "operatic" action of *Meistersinger* and that uneasy alliance of dream and reality characterizing his work in general, but also tentatively to play with ideas from the *Parerga* in which he glimpsed a path out of his theoretical difficulties—a fantastic vision of the opera house as ontological academy.

"German Art and German Politics" of 1867 hailed German music as the art that would give birth to a drama surpassing in expressiveness even that of the ancient Greeks. Wagner attached great importance to actors, the intuitive virtuosos of illusion, and, in an incredible image, declared the mime —a term he used primarily to signify the accomplished singing actor such as Schröder-Devrient [7]—to be related to the poet much as the monkey is to man in Darwinian theory. The poet organized abstractly, artistically, and in a higher, more selective manner what the mime intuitively achieved through

---

[6] Professor Jack Stein indicates that the romantic attitude toward dreams may have made *Beethoven* appear less strange to Wagner's contemporaries than it does today.

[7] In his *Actors and Singers* of 1872 Wagner was to pay final tribute to the influence upon him of Schröder-Devrient's mimetic art.

a physical imitation of reality. Since Wagner was beginning to think of his drama in terms of Schopenhaurean apparitions proceeding in part from the universal will, it was necessary to confer some ideological distinction upon his actors, the shadows of these shadows.

It all made debatable sense. Madame de Staël observed that "a Frenchman can speak even when he has no ideas, but a German always has in his head a little more than he can express." Wagner was playing with concepts that would one day appear a bit better organized in *The Destiny of Opera* —an essay pendent to *Beethoven*—wherein his final comprehensive views on dramatic theory were to be expounded. Throughout the *Meistersinger* period his thoughts about the *Gesamtkunstwerk* were in flux, and he sent them forth disorderedly, sporadically, and somewhat penitently. To the end of his days he attempted through his essays to expunge his guilt about having exchanged the dialectic of *Opera and Drama* for the pragmatic art of the Rue Le Peletier and refused to admit to his intellectual consciousness the fact of this desertion. Vainly he sought to explain the embarrassing theoretic posture in which he found himself in terms of either his old Swiss essays or Schopenhauer, whom he turned, twisted, and, finally, "improved."

One might ask whether there was ever any real identity in spirit between Wagner's operas and Schopenhauer's teaching, apart from the composer's superficial enthusiasm for the idea of self-denial, a concept that had already attracted him in Goethe's works. Wagner disparaged reason and exalted instinct. Should doubts arise about the correct rendering of compositions from earlier periods in musical history, he wished students of his proposed conservatory to seek the advice of the lay public, "unprejudiced by formal study." The unconscious, intuitive, and involuntary were for him the necessary and creative. Thus Hans Sachs in *Meistersinger* called upon the Folk to judge the music contest. In the *Ring* the thinkers—Fricka, Loge, Alberich—are enemies to be routed by the natural and "redeeming" perceptions of inherent wisdom. Mime learns, to his amazement, that not his knowledge but Siegfried's natural stupidity alone avails to forge the hero's sword. (*"Hier hilft kein Kluger . . . hier hilft . . . die Dummheit allein!"*) Wagner celebrated the amateur. Wotan's main frailty in Wagner's eyes seems to be his habit of sinking into analytical thought. However, in the end, he becomes a good Wagnerian by rising above this fault to attain a state of redemptive renunciation through an instinctive act of the will, the prospect of ruin no longer filling him with dread once "desire wills it." From this point of view it would be difficult to find a work more antagonistic than the *Ring* to the spirit of Schopenhauer, for whom instinct and the will, synonymous with error, had to be subjected by the intellect, not the other way around. In the intellect he saw an avenue through which one might escape the tyranny of the will and its desires. One sees that it was not a poor literary style alone that made the philosopher ignore the writings Wagner sent him. In *"Heldentum,"* an essay of the *Parsifal* period, Wagner eventually attempted to come to terms with the Schopenhauerean relationship between intellect and will, but ended with the hooligan Siegfried and the cretin Parsifal as his pathetic examples of mental power.

That theoretical scribbling through which Wagner sought to justify his works to himself and his disciples betrays the enormous effort it cost him to bring his relatively undistinguished intellect to bear upon the marvelous workings of his artistic intuition. The essays always forced him to adopt a completely anti-Wagnerian point of view, that of explaining instinct in terms of reason. Hans Sachs had to some extent succeeded with this approach in *Meistersinger;* but, of course, he sang, and very beautifully. However, in unaccompanied prose, Wagner croaked. Moreover, he now found it impossible to state his case convincingly, because he refused to face his situation honestly; the cloudy waters of his speculative writings turned increasingly muddied, his always unwieldy syntax often becoming trackless. The late pamphlets are fascinating, but painfully contrived and at times hysterical. As has been observed, the Wagnerian movement refused to accept them. If disciples could not openly reject what came from their master's pen, they could nonetheless choose quietly to ignore these strange offerings and even decline to acknowledge that with *Tristan* and *Meistersinger* he had undergone an aesthetic change of heart.

4

The aesthetic crisis of *Tristan,* which was resolved in *Meistersinger,* was essentially musical. A strong dose of diatonism restored a patient weakened by chromatic fever. The cure also included a recuperative journey to scenes of his past, the middle-aged master joyfully re-exploring the haunts of youth. *Tristan* had been his final exhausting search for the fugitive *Gesamtkunstwerk;* purged by his mighty labor, he turned back to grand opera; his remaining triumphs were to be in this genre. The final scene of *Siegfried* (a short opera in itself), *The Twilight of the Gods,* and *Parsifal*—works whose method had been implicit in *Rienzi* and *Tannhäuser*—were in the mainstream of Wagner's artistic development. Ironically, at the end it was he who, through repossession of his Paris heritage, approached the aesthetic of Verdi. Shaw was being neither cantankerous nor outrageous when he suggested that aesthetically and intellectually *The Twilight of the Gods* and *Un ballo in maschera* have much in common.

The Twilight of the Gods was *Siegfried's Death* of 1848. Wagner's old revolutionary friend, Röckel, had observed, much to the composer's annoyance, that despite its new name and ending the final evening of the *Ring* had essentially little to do with what had gone before. Few changes had been introduced when the poem was superficially revised to harmonize with the three libretti later prefaced to it. The work first envisioned in Dresden as a heroic grand opera remained just that in its creator's mind during the difficult period when he vainly strove to reconsider its material in terms of those *Gesamtkunst* theories that had assisted at the birth of *Valkyrie* and *Rhinegold*. This dilemma must have played the largest part in his decision in Zurich to discontinue work on the *Ring*, and even King Ludwig's cajoling could not make him pick it up until he had worked out his aesthetic and musical problems in *Meistersinger*. Indeed, the score of the first two acts of *Siegfried* had already shown him at cross-purposes. That unfailing confidence of *Valkyrie* is missing; there text and music were born under the same aesthetic star. But *Young Siegfried* had first appeared to him in the guise of a light comic German opera. Not only the notorious failings of the libretto but also the composer's inability to reconcile an "operatic" conception with his incongruous aesthetic theory accounts for much that went wrong in those opening acts made up of incompletely realized and unartfully dovetailed fragments. The hero's brilliant tenor arias mix uneasily with the *Gesamtkunst* brooding of his dwarfish companion, and one finds grim reminders that originally Wagner thought of the Mime scenes as amusing.

Proof that Wagner fully realized his quandary was his sudden refusal to proceed with the work. Acts one and two of *Siegfried* form a fumbling score forged more by a genius' will than by his inspiration, though they are filled with inspired details. The final act was the crucial link to the heroic grand opera depicting the hero's tragedy, and by the summer of 1857 Wagner must have felt that his relationship to his material had grown too puzzling and ambiguous to permit his safe passage through the flames. He had to work out his instinctive rebellion against *Opera and Drama* on other levels in order to find himself again. Chafing under self-imposed aesthetic restraints that inhibited his inspiration in *Siegfried*, he fully embraced Schopenhauer's theory of music's sovereignty among the arts, wildly fought his way to freedom in *Tristan*, and then more calmly rediscovered his true artistic personality in *Meistersinger*.

The ability to laugh at oneself is a sign of maturity. The code of the Meistersinger as presented by Kothner and David at least subconsciously parodies the precepts of *Opera and Drama*, and the intense chromatic agitation stirring Walther in his earlier scenes is certainly a satire on the *Tristan* fever. By the end of the opera the knight has calmed down and wins the maid with a diatonic song firmly rooted in C major. Sachs teaches that neither frenzied freedom nor unnatural constraints will win the day but a logical unfolding of the artist's ideas in forms that give shape but do not bind. And this aesthetic lesson Wagner chose to present within the framework of Parisian grand opera! *Meistersinger* achieved, he was ready to turn to the renamed "Siegfried's Death" with its poisoned drinks, conspirators' ensemble, massed chorus, and Scribe-inspired *coups de théâtre*. But before returning to this practical Parisian kind of "show," he paused to bid an emotional, sad farewell to the elusive ideal that had tantalized musicians since the days of the Camerata—the *Gesamtkunstwerk*.

5

The first scene of the closing act of *Siegfried,* played at the foot of Brynhild's fire-rock, is the composer's superb *ave atque vale* to the music drama—to all he had once hoped to achieve in the *Ring*. Using a powerful magic, a final effort of his will, Wanderer-Wagner constrains the seeress, Erda, to cast off meditating, cosmic slumber, to rise and carry to the surface the spirit of the long-abandoned saga. In impassioned song the god invokes the world he once strove to master and then forsook: "Awaken! Out of long sleep . . . from caverns of mist . . . from secret depths, rise up! I sing you to wakefulness." The shadows of the *Ring*'s music obey the command. During the melancholy conversation between god and prophetess the old motifs, sleeping for so long, pass in ghostly review and form a specter bridge between the old part of the cycle and the new, as Wagner summons up, makes peace with, and finally buries his Nibelung past. With his hero he is ready to push on toward that rediscovered goal of the ultimate grand opera [8] on which his eyes had once been firmly set in Riga. The ancient goddess cannot grasp what is happening. Her godly wooer of olden days lapses into a strange new accent (his *"ein kühnester Knabe, bar meines Rates"* clearly derives from Hans Sachs's musical idiom), and throughout the interview swirl the old motifs, but in varied hues, values of light and shade, and color intensities as unfamiliar to her as the dense orchestral web itself. Confused by a universe that seems to her wild and disordered (*"Wild und kraus kreist die Welt!"*), she longs to subside into the earth whence she came.

---

[8] It is no disparagement to call *The Twilight of the Gods* grand opera. Like Verdi's *Aïda,* it combines all the Parisian theatrical tricks of Meyerbeer with superb music that functions equally well when accompanying scenic effects or underlining romantic sentiment, though evocative relics of Wagner's earlier musico-dramatic methods remain throughout. In his *The Destiny of Opera* (1871) Wagner defined his *Gesamtkunstwerk* as a *"durch die höchste künstlerische Besonnenheit fixierten mimisch-musikalischen Improvisation von vollendetem dichterischem Werte,"* a very long way of saying "a well-made, action-filled opera," a description best fulfilled among his works by *Meistersinger.*

She and the Wanderer are apparitions. "You are not what you call yourself," she tells him, summing up Wagner's difficult position as an aesthetician, and he sorrowfully concedes that she herself no longer has any reality. A ghost has called up a shade to discuss a world in which neither exists. Both must vanish, and they take with them the vision of the Wagnerian *Gesamtkunstwerk.* The god no longer desires to strive for what cannot be. "To sleep, then, close your eyes; in dreams behold my end!" Wagner never created anything more noble and moving than this scene of farewell to an ideal.

That strange dream of the Hellenic art-work in which the Teutonic gods would be resuscitated had passed. The heart had really gone out of the whole jejune experiment years before, when Wagner had cast off self-imposed rules and given the reins over to his creative genius. But, ironically, he almost seemed to approach his goal of forging a new mythology in the very act of renouncing the attempt. As wraiths, Wotan and especially Erda— so wooden, archaic, and futile in *Rhinegold*—suddenly become charged with a powerful symbolism, and with frenzied rites the Cosmics, a curious offshoot of the curious cult of Stefan George, were to call upon her at the beginning of this century.

But the gods of the *Ring* were really dead. In grotesque pageants George's young men would hopefully masquerade as the Great Mother.[9] But their master produced for their edification not the ancient prophetess but Maximin, a stripling of unsurpassed beauty whom he declared to be divine. The veneration of George's beloved young Maximin is an extraordinary link between the monastic homosexuality of *Parsifal,* centered around the leadership of an intuitively inspired youth, and the not dissimilar fellowship of Ernst Röhm's troopers. Not the *Ring* but *Parsifal* was the Wagner work whose mythology was powerful enough to leave an indelible mark on Germany. Not the vision of the ur-matriarchy but an image of the Germanic Ephebus was to help lead the nation to ruin, when the composer released a daemon that had always lurked deep in his soul.

[9] Nietzsche disliked the Erda-Wotan interview intensely, seeing it as "a scene full of mythological horrors, which makes the Wagnerian feel himself a visionary."

XIII

Reichsdeutsch *Wagner:* *Musical* Realpolitik, *Aesthetics,* *Nietzsche, and Bayreuth*

I

From the day she joined Wagner to stay at Triebschen, Cosima felt new-born. He never ceased to overwhelm her, and, if one believes her diary, in his presence she was perpetually on the point of dissolving into tears or swooning. Hers was a doglike fidelity. When he raged, she took cover only to race back to lick his hand as soon as it was benevolently extended. She asked, "How should I ever presume to forgive him? It is my duty to be good and amiable to Richard just as the hours come round and strike."

But even staunch Cosima looked upon his reissuing of *Jewry in Music* in March of 1869 as an indiscretion. The theme of Jewish perversity formed a staple of his conversations with her early in the year and had certainly fallen upon appreciative ears. However, she doubted the wisdom of further involvement in controversy. To many, the reprint appeared the act of a fanatic courting antagonism. He had been unable to suppress this urge. The Jewish problem possessed him increasingly and ever more obsessively until his death, giving him no rest, tenaciously invading his conversations, letters, and articles, prejudice ripening into unreasoning hatred and finally settling into a diseased leitmotif. He honestly believed his attitude on this question to be "remarkably objective," this consciousness, he observed, en-abling him to withstand the arrows of outraged Jewry. Nonetheless, years before, in a letter to Liszt (April 18, 1851) he had called this hatred necessary to his nature "as gall is to the blood."

Because of his reputation in this area, at times evil was suspected even when he intended none. Beckmesser's serenade was hissed at the Vienna première of *Meistersinger* in February, 1870; the song was wrongly believed to parody synagogue chant. But the incident underscores how clearly Wagner's contemporaries judged just what his Marker was intended to represent. There were cries of "We won't hear it!" Wagner saw in this incident at the imperial Opera a Jewish affront to Franz Josef's authority, an interpretation typical of his Humpty Dumpty outlook. " 'When *I* use a word,' Humpty Dumpty said, in rather a scornful tone, 'it means just what I choose it to mean—neither more nor less.' "

Less abstract concerns also fretted Wagner's otherwise joyful hours, fears that Ludwig might terminate the pension maintaining Triebschen with its staff of over half a dozen servants and its satin and gilded chambers, landscaped acreage, badly trained dogs, and aviary filled with rare specimens. From Munich, Cosima had brought Wagner's favorite peacocks, Wotan and Frigge, who strutted proudly about the garden. But despite hurt and moments of anger, the King did not falter in service to Wagner. Since the latter pretended to be in touch with Cosima through the mail, Ludwig could feign ignorance of her residence at Triebschen, the subterfuge, which obviously could not long be sustained, at least enabling him to resume correspondence. However, from this time on, his epistolary relationship with Wagner was that of a disillusioned though still devoted lover, uneasy silences of weeks and months being broken by overwrought letters of reconciliation.

Ludwig asked for fresh installments of *Mein Leben*—taken down by Cosima with a wonderful gift from Wagner, Mathilde Wesendonk's golden pen!—and showed himself eager to mount the completed portions of the *Ring* as soon as possible. Wagner—and Cosima, too—had never objected to the latter idea, at times seeming to favor a year-by-year, successive unveiling of the component dramas as a method of accustoming artists and public gradually to the difficulties of a new style. But now he was compelled to think realistically about the *Ring* and Munich. His behavior had forced the city's gates to close against him. Until his alliance with Cosima was legalized and sufficient time had passed to take the edge off scandal, he could not comfortably return to the capital for any length of time either with her or alone. Among formidable obstacles to their marriage were Hans's reluctance to divorce and Liszt's disapproval.[1] Moreover, the affair was kept alive by an antagonistic press, gleefully exploiting every particular that came its way. Wagner's attitude of postponement toward the projected *Rhinegold* première was born of the Cosima dilemma; Munich was impossible for him,

---

[1] Wagner had created the Paris Venus under the stimulus of Blandine, Liszt's elder daughter; the younger was now his mistress as he completed another musical portrait of a passionate goddess. Through the Liszt girls he doubtlessly experienced a kind of vicarious communion with their father, memories of whom meant more and more to him. He delighted in recognizing in Cosima traits of the old friend, who remained bitterly estranged.

and for a while he even flirted with the idea of abandoning Ludwig and turning to the Prussians as new protectors. He thought of writing to Johanna Bismarck, who might persuade her husband to step forward as a Wagnerian patron. But Cosima warned against the step; the moment was not ripe.

Ludwig could not be swayed from his own resolve. During the summer the stage of the court theater was rebuilt and the pit lowered to meet the sonorous instrumental demands of the tetralogy. Realizing that maneuvering for time was futile, Wagner agreed to co-operate with the preparations for *Rhinegold* from the distance. Singers, designers, and machinists from Munich made their way to Triebschen for consultations, as did Richter, who was to conduct. Officially, he occupied a subordinate position on the theater's musical staff. He was to hold the baton only in deference to Wagner's and Bülow's wishes and possessed neither the musical authority nor those extraordinary powers in the theater granted the latter by royal mandate.

Were Richter provided with such authority, then through him Wagner might well be able to control the Munich Opera even from afar. Without this advantage he would certainly have to discuss matters with the theater's administrator, Baron von Perfall, and perhaps even be civil to him. But Richter was a twenty-six-year-old unknown and as yet too puny a musical figure for Bülow's mantle. Realizing that only unexpected, drastic action could secure the needed power, Wagner plotted a *coup d'état;* he would create chaos, play upon fear, and then take over by placing this puppet in command. On August 21, 1869, Wagner wrote Otto Wesendonk that the *Rhinegold* would be "very respectable, nothing having been spared to fulfill all . . . technical requirements," and urged him to attend what would obviously be a success. Wagner, however, intended to use the troubles often attending a première as a means of reasserting his authority in Munich.

The monumental preparations for *Rhinegold* had reached the final full rehearsal, which took place on August 27, in the presence of the King and a select company. (The performance had originally been planned for two days earlier, the royal birthday.) Snags developed in the stage machinery, a not surprising occurrence during the first mounting of so difficult a work. The staff gave assurances that the trouble could be quickly corrected by a few special rehearsals.

Wagner, who had been previously informed of the décor's imperfections and of an obviously impending mechanical mishap, depended upon it to trigger his plot. On the day after the marred dress rehearsal, Richter, acting upon Wagner's orders, asked to be relieved of conducting a production he claimed would discredit his master. Insolently the raw novice denounced Perfall as ultimately responsible for the breakdown by reason of his general miscomprehension of the composer's greatness! Simultaneously, from Switzerland Wagner dispatched a telegram to the King urging him to cancel the performance because of the faulty scenery. According to Wagner's plan, Ludwig was to be caught in this pincerlike movement; panic-stricken by the prospect not only of dishonoring the work but also of seeing long and costly rehearsals about to go for naught, he was expected suddenly to grasp the only way of saving the situation: He would docilely request Richter's return after arming him with full authority in the theater and then trust that the *Meister* himself would deign to appear and set things right.

But Wagner and Richter never anticipated that the machinist, Carl Brandt of Darmstadt, who was later to rescue the first Bayreuth festival from many a similar catastrophe, would so rapidly remedy the scenic disorder, and, above all, that Ludwig would rebelliously refuse to follow the Triebschen scenario. He saw through the intrigue—Richter's resignation had an unmistakable Wagnerian cast—and burst into rage at Wagner's double-dealing and Richter's presumption. The young nobody, who for a while imagined himself successfully terrorizing the King and his opera, was suspended for insubordination; Ludwig announced his royal intention of witnessing the *Rhinegold* première in September and ordered a new conductor to be found. Another Wotan was summoned, too, for the baritone Betz, also an agent of Wagner, had been encouraged to add to the turmoil by his own withdrawal.

At the moment Ludwig's resentment against Wagner blazed highest, he fleetingly experienced the emotions of Friedrich of Saxony, and considered halting all monetary favors to the ingrate and closing the theater to his works should he persist in his mischief and plots. Annoyed and hurt, the King left for his Alpine retreat. *"J'en ai assez!"* he remarked.

Naïvely certain that his intrigue—Newman called it a *"Putsch"*—would succeed, that he could force Richter's way and simultaneously destroy the theater management, Wagner, following his script, appeared in Munich and to his astonishment found the *Rhinegold* rehearsals closed to himself as well as his vassal. In utmost perplexity he retreated to Triebschen, where by the end of September he learned of the opera's successful performance under Franz Wüllner's baton. Moreover, the complicated *mise en scène* had been maneuvered faultlessly. Although Wagner liked to pretend ignorance of any details of the affair, Cosima's old friend Alfred Meissner was to upset the Triebschen household with his description of the production's scenic wonders. Indeed, within a month of the première (September 22), the King was discussing the machinery for *Valkyrie* with Carl Brandt. It was the policy of Wahnfried historians to depreciate the *Ring* premières at Munich, and as recently as 1965 Geoffrey Skelton described their end "in ridicule and failure," an assertion derived from the tales circulated by such overwrought and prejudiced Wagnerites as Judith and Catulle Mendès, but not the judgments of less partisan auditors like Cornelius and Liszt. (Judith declared that her circle had "the fanaticism of priests and martyrs—even to the slaying of . . . adversaries!") It would seem that in many ways, especially scenically, these Munich performances surpassed the level of the first Bayreuth festival.

2

Ludwig's contemplated production of *Valkyrie* and Wagner's first vision of the Bayreuth festival coincided. In a sense, Cosima's adultery called the latter great project into being. Her earlier entreaties to Ludwig to postpone building the Semper theater had been born of her and Wagner's realization that Munich would be impossible for them when they finally took their stand together.

Hans had still made no decisive step toward a divorce. Though Richard's and Cosima's life at Triebschen seemed sweet and their overweening pride helped them make a show of indifference to the world, their situation nonetheless had its strains. Wagner was known at times to break forth with the coarsest expressions concerning his relationship with her. They urgently wished to marry and legitimize their bastard children. The birth of their son, Siegfried, on June 6, 1869, spurred this desire. Occasionally, Wagner joked rather strangely about Cosima and her four daughters, calling them the entire "Bülowiana," as if he himself had doubts as to who was who. (One recalls those fanciful tales about the Count d'Agoult, the husband of Cosima's mother, who simplified his life by blandly referring to the youngsters about the house as "my wife's children." After his marriage to Cosima, Wagner was to use this device in his letters to the King.) Field glasses were often turned upon the Triebschen peninsula; boats and coaches filled with tourists attempted to enter the property as part of excursions that also included the ascent of the Rigi and the promenade to the Lion of Lucerne. And there were such mortifications as the demand of the neighboring parish of Horw that the infamous couple be expelled on moral grounds. The mail brought anonymous offensive notes.

But the most serious vexation was that Wagner's irregular relationship with a now notorious woman prevented his supervising the *Ring* premières in Munich. His attempts to play for time were without effect on the King, whom he exhorted to stop further Nibelung productions in letters that either gave no valid reason for doing so or advanced impossible conditions for his participation. He tried pathos; he tried threats. "Perhaps only over our graves, in another nobler time, will the martyred Nibelungenring be redeemed from its curse, from that curse whose redeeming magic word a predestined king himself holds back from uttering." "Without me, without my omnipresent guidance and co-operation, my new works . . . can only be abortions." Certainly his presence would be incomparably helpful, but everyone was aware that he had locked himself out. Even Ludwig now spoke openly to his courtiers of "the Bülow scandal." He wrote Wagner that he simply had to forgive "youthful impetuosity"; *Valkyrie* would be given. Finding unique exaltation and refreshment in Wagner's works, he had no intention of bearing the consequences of the composer's indiscretions by depriving himself of artistic pleasures for which he had sacrificed so much. That Wagner's machinations had caused the departure of both his musical lieutenants from Munich and left him without reliable contact with the royal theater was not its fault. Moreover, he had shown characteristic discourtesy toward its staff, having written a note of incredible blackguardism to Wüllner in an effort to intimidate him and prevent his conducting *Rhinegold*. Nor did he lose any opportunity of insulting Director Perfall. At Triebschen the Munich Opera was scornfully called the "Perfalleum." When the King, unmoved by Triebschen's intimidations, ordered the *Valkyrie* première to be followed as quickly as possible by that of *Siegfried,* Wagner grew thoroughly alarmed.

Even should he be able to marry Cosima, Munich would remain antagonistic. To mention their names was to open a catalogue of off-color jokes. And by the opening months of 1868 it had been obvious that the plans for the Semper theater would come to nothing. For years of labor on studies, sketches, estimates, and models, the architect gained only knowledge of the professionally charming refractoriness of courtiers. And since his flight from Munich in 1865 Wagner's interest in the project had cooled. Now it was agonizing for him to reflect that his mighty Nibelung works, intended to regenerate German civilization, were entering the world of performance as part of the general repertory. Since the days of his correspondence with Uhlig some twenty years before, he had dreamed of the very special nature of the *Ring*'s presentation.

Simultaneously with Munich's preparations for *Valkyrie,* there again arose in his mind the idea of a theater of his own in some small town where he might not only be the artist but also play the king, a place so modest that his desires could not be thwarted by interference from other individuals or institutions. His scheme was akin to that outlined in 1863 in the preface to the first public printing of the *Ring* poem. He dreamed of creating a new center for his drama, what he was to describe as "a kind of Washington of art."

Bayreuth, which had first interested him as perhaps providing a quiet residence near Nuremberg should he have succeeded in persuading Ludwig to transfer the Semper theater there, now possessed in his eyes the over-riding advantage of having no cultural resources other than its monuments.[2] Its vanished Margraves had thoughtfully left behind a theater designed by Giuseppe Galli da Bibiena that boasted the deepest stage in Germany. Here Wagner would assemble his artists and produce the *Ring* without having to go through the travail and expense of building. And, being without thermal springs, Bayreuth was not frequented in summer by a public unsuited to his serious purpose. (He was to turn down offers to build his theater from such prosperous watering-places as Baden-Baden and Reichenhall.) Moreover, Bayreuth lay within the confines of Bavaria, thus keeping him under Lud-wig's protection. That the town had once been included within the Kingdom of Prussia[3] would not be disadvantageous should Wagner wish to seek Hohenzollern support, an idea with increasing appeal for him. Carlyle's *History of Frederick the Great* had appeared in German translation in 1869, and Wagner devoured the masterpiece that no doubt helped him make a poetic transition to the idea of Prussian puissance. Indeed, the superb play-house had been built for Frederick's sister Wilhelmine.

Wagner did not know how diminutive an auditorium opened upon the mammoth stage. Otherwise he would have recognized the very acoustical problem that had driven him to move the *Tristan* rehearsals from the gem-like Cuvilliés theater in Munich's Residenz to the larger court Opera. Dur-ing early sessions in the small hall he had rejoiced in his artists' clear diction and in the fact that every emotion crossing their faces could be plainly observed from the farthest seat. Hoping to give the première in this intimate environment, he tried to ignore Ludwig's opinion that the opera and the theater were irreconcilable as to scale. In April of 1865 the King had observed, "For the performance of a large work of this type the Residenztheater appears to me completely ill-suited." Later rehearsals with full orchestra proved deafening, and Wagner was compelled to transfer the production to the bigger house.

Serious problems of balance were arising in his works. As his orchestral technique evolved and his contrapuntal textures became thicker and more complex, his words and indeed the very sound of the voices were being throttled with a curtain of instrumental resonance. His desire to sink the orchestral players beneath the stage of the Semper theater—an arrangement he had known in miniature at the Riga Opera—had been only in part a device to increase the theatrical magic by making the source of instru-

[2] Most of Wagner's information on Bayreuth seems to have come from the Brockhaus encyclopedia, the *Konversations-Lexikon.*

[3] After Prussia's victory in the War of 1866, King Wilhelm had contemplated tak-ing back from Bavaria the ancient Hohenzollern territories of Ansbach and Bayreuth.

mental sound invisible; primarily, his hopes were to dampen the sonority of the instruments so that his singers might be more easily heard. Certainly, he could not have suspected Bayreuth's Bibiena theater to be even without a modern pit, or his plans would not have soared with such optimism. But to announce them to the King was as yet inopportune. He feared for his allowance.

3

Valkyrie had its triumphant première under Wüllner on June 26, 1870. After two performances it alternated with *Rhinegold,* three half *Ring* cycles being given. Despite fine performances, audiences acquainted with *Tristan* and *Meistersinger* remained disappointed in *Rhinegold.* Over fifteen years had passed between the composition and performance of a work that bore the scars marking an effort in a transitional style. But with *Valkyrie* composer and artists conquered. Public and press lavishly praised Wagner's genius. Nonetheless, Triebschen, which would have preferred that fiasco punish the King's show of independence, remained wrapped in clouds of hostility.

The international guests gathered in Munich for the brilliant festival (they included Brahms, Joachim, Saint-Saëns, and Liszt) had not yet scattered when Europe was gripped by crisis. A militant undercurrent had been felt during the performances. Brynhild's battle cry was wildly applauded and a similar storm of approval greeted Wotan's "Where bold spirits stir, I openly foment war." The long-feared conflict between France and Prussia erupted on July 19 with the vote of the Chamber in Paris. Ludwig had no choice but to join a pan-German effort under Prussian hegemony. His army fought under the command of the Hohenzollern crown prince, later Kaiser Friedrich III. The irresistible force of Prussia would inevitably propel Bavaria into membership in the new German Empire. Though retaining more autonomy than other constituent states, the Wittelsbachs' ancient lands were to become fiefs held on Hohenzollern suffrance. Prussia was no longer the future but the present, and Wagner saw this clearly.

Only a day before hostilities began, the Vatican Council, summoned by Pope Pius IX, defined papal infallibility. But this Jesuitical, Ultramontane victory had bitter opponents among Catholic churchmen, especially in Bavaria. Ludwig supported a leading dissentient, his old tutor, the theologian Döllinger, who in August convened a congress at Nuremberg to repudiate the Council's action.[4] The clerical party in Munich began an intrigue

---

[4] Within the year he was excommunicated. From the violent reaction against the work of the Council the Old Catholic community was born.

that it hoped would end in the King's deposition. Ludwig, however, weathered the storm, and a law expelling the Jesuits from Bavaria was proclaimed in September of 1871. The spirit of Lola Montez had triumphed. But for a while Wagner—who, though not an admirer of Döllinger, endorsed German resistance to the Council's decisions—feared that Ludwig and with him the allowance would be swept away.

Apart from its threat to Ludwig's power, the Ultramontane issue did not greatly concern Wagner; nor, despite his melodramatic remonstrances, did the *Valkyrie* affair appreciably disturb Triebschen's peace. Realistically, he and Cosima admitted to one another that Ludwig's enthusiasm for the *Ring* kept them in luxury. With some disquietude she was learning just how quickly Wagner consumed vast sums and conceded the hopelessness of prevailing upon him to economize in the slightest way. She wrote, "Richard really lives by grace of the Nibelungs. He owes them his existence, and so we must also thank God that a being such as the King should have such a queer whim in his head and simply will see and have the things." Nothing if not practical, she was unwilling to kick up too much of a pother over a so-called "violation of principles"—the year-by-year unveiling of the dramas —about which Wagner was really indifferent. Only when a new source of income was evident would it be practical to gallop about on this particular aesthetic high horse.

Not the *Valkyrie,* not the Döllinger dissension, but the war deeply affected Wagner and drew forth his worst. The old hatred of France burst out anew. He who had once heaped contumely upon the Prussians for the benefit of Ludwig now could not find words sufficiently laudatory to describe them. His letters to Röckel in the opening months of 1867 had already shown a growing admiration for Prussia as a counter force to Hapsburg and thus Jesuitical influence; "great, great thanks are due Prussia's achievement." Not many weeks later he was recommending to Ludwig a "firm and honorable alliance with Prussia." Now he extolled the war as something sublime and holy, a dance that would have a Beethovenian finale. Once more there arose before him that long-cherished vision of Paris in ashes. Paris, that "abyss of utter vulgarity," the *"femme entretenue"* of the world, would go down in ruin, and with its destruction—so he assured Cosima, who had been raised in the city—mankind would be freed from evil. Thus ran the latest version of the typical Wagnerian scene of fiery redemption. Obediently Cosima agreed that the French must be humbled, and set about rolling bandages for the troops. Triebschen's uncompromising, flag-waving chauvinism was gauchely communicated to such French Wagnerites as Mendès, his wife, Judith Gautier, Villiers, Saint-Saëns, and Duparc; returning from the Munich festival, they had felt sufficiently above nationalism to pay their respects to the master. Saint-Saëns later observed that Wagner's lack of discretion was equaled only by his genius.

On July 18, the day belief in the Roman Pontiff's infallibility was elevated to dogma, a Berlin court had declared Cosima von Bülow guilty of deserting her husband and dissolved their marriage, Hans having resigned himself to the procedure during the spring. In the modest Protestant church at Lucerne the Wagner-Bülow children and a curious crowd watched Pastor Tschudi marry Cosima to Richard on August 25, the King's birthday, a concurrence planned by Wagner as "destiny's hallowed sign . . . happily greeted as a blessed token." Whatever Ludwig could make of this elucidation, the ceremony was certainly another blow to Pius IX's friend Liszt, who perhaps still had hopes of becoming director of the papal chapel. Her father's generally uncomfortable position did not displease Cosima. She held him, along with her mother and Princess Wittgenstein, responsible for the death of her beloved brother, Daniel. For his part, Liszt, like the Princess, found the lovers guilty of "the moral murder of Hans" and was to instruct his Paris bankers to continue sending Cosima her stipend under the Bülow name—it was open war. As events undermined Liszt's idols one by one, Cosima crowed to her diary, "And so the three figures whom my father honored are in an enviable position! Mazzini in prison, the Pope in a thousand troubles, and Louis Napoleon in the gutter." [5]

The latter had gambled and lost. Early in September the Second Empire fell at Sedan. Wagner cried, "This is a christening present for Fidi. . . . God in heaven, what a destiny! I am fatal to the Napoleons. When I was six months old, there was the battle of Leipzig, and now Fidi has made mincemeat of the whole of France." But little Siegfried seemed hardly cognizant of his imposing victory and chortled innocently as Pastor Tschudi baptized him on September 4. Everything was being put into good bourgeois order—not for Munich as Ludwig hoped, but for Berlin.

Well before that impressive moment on January 18, 1871, when in Versailles' Hall of Mirrors Wilhelm of Prussia was declared Emperor of the reborn German Reich, Wagner knew with whom he wished to cast his lot. Ludwig, who had been forced by his position as the most important of the smaller German princes to offer his uncle the imperial crown, was a relic. His banner dipped before the Hohenzollern kaiser. Wagner's jingoistic poem, "To the German Army before Paris," dutifully dispatched via Lothar Bucher

---

[5] Napoleon's difficulties were producing an immediate effect in Italy. After his declaration of war he had withdrawn from Civitavecchia the French garrison that had helped maintain papal authority over Rome. Visconti-Venosta announced the Italian government's intention of occupying the city. The Pope refused to yield his temporal power and attempted resistance. But by September 20 the Porta Pia was breached, and the green-white-red tricolor flew from the Capitol. The Eternal City was liberated. Mazzini, who had left England for Sicily, found himself arrested at sea, taken to Gaeta, and confined for several weeks.

to Bismarck early in 1871, and an evil farce, *A Capitulation,* begun in November, 1870, ridiculing the horrors of hunger during the siege of Paris—he wanted Richter to set this dreadful doggerel to music in Offenbach style—show not a patriot, but rather a man throwing away even the pretense of decency. Typically, he sent forth the latter effort anonymously.

In a preface written for its later publication in his *Collected Works,* Wagner maintained that the piece really made the Germans look more ridiculous than the French, for Gallic follies at least had the quality of originality, while in this area, too, the Germans could only imitate their neighbors. And, indeed, the capitulation is twofold, the surrender of the French to the Germans and of the latter, once again, to Parisian artistic leadership, especially in the theater. "And the Germans?" asks the French chorus, and Gambetta answers, "They're peacefully sitting with the others; they've capitulated and are in transports at being able to attend our theaters again." It is Offenbach, "the most international individual in the world," who arrives to save the day with his dance tunes.

Wagner was upbraiding his countrymen for still following the frivolous artistic example of a capital that had been in their hands to destroy. (Only now, he told Cosima, could he understand what had confused him as a youth—Blücher's desire to level Paris.) Gambetta proclaiming the "rats' republic," the chorus singing "rats with sauce! sauce with rats!" the description of Offenbach as "the Orpheus of the underworld, the estimable rat-catcher of Hameln," the transformation at Offenbach's command of the giant rats into French ballet dancers, and the satire on Victor Hugo and *Les Misérables,* as the poet keeps popping up out of the sewers and crawling through the drains, are so repulsive, so tasteless, and so completely unfunny that the violent antipathy the would-be comedy awakened in France could not have been surprising. (Wagnerites are able to see Aristophanic greatness in it all.) But Wagner pretended amazement at the furor. After all, he always claimed that there was nothing personal in his anti-Semitism.

4

He wished to make an opportunistic gesture of gratitude to the soldiers of the Reich in a "Mourning Symphony for the Fallen" to be played during a defile of the victorious troops in Berlin. Sounding the capital on the project, he was told that no such depressing ceremony was contemplated. The *Einzug* of the troops was to be gala and gay. From his statements in later years, when the plan came back to Wagner, it is clear that his threnody was to put to use the Romeo and Juliet theme of 1868. Not only the idea of obsequies but also the figure of Berlioz and his *Romeo* and *Funeral* symphonies were entangled in the concept. Wagner had never forgotten the superb effect of the latter work, written for the martyrs of the July Revolution, the excitement of the massed military bands, and the drama of Berlioz presiding over this *fête funèbre* in the Place de la Bastille. He especially wished to create something analogous to the close of Berlioz's symphony, an easily grasped melody the populace could immediately embrace and sing. Wagner's second offer to compose special music for the return of the soldiers dwelt upon this intention to cap the affair with a national hymn. His services were again declined. Wahnfried biographers have seen in this stand the opposition of the Jew Joachim, who occupied an influential position in Berlin's musical life. But Bismarck was handling the touchy Ludwig and his participation in the new Reich with utmost delicacy and obviously did not want the Wagner issue to obtrude itself. Caution was the watchword in triumphant Berlin.

Though officially rebuffed, Wagner was determined publicly to display his new political attachment. Toward spring, 1871, he turned the *Kaiser March,* written for band in anticipation of the Berlin ceremony, into a concert piece. Masterfully orchestrated, it was at least less mechanically contrived than the truly dreadful *March of Homage* created for Ludwig some seven years before. During the summer Wagner was to ask permission to orchestrate this latter piece for concert use as the *King Ludwig March,* tactfully but not very convincingly informing Munich that the German nation was pining to hear it played along with the *Kaiser March.* Wagner expected the Prussian work to prove more than a politic *pièce d'occasion;* he hoped it might be used as a coronation march and to see its closing vocal section in praise of Emperor Wilhelm become the anthem of the Reich.[6] The popular *"Wacht am Rhein"* exasperated him.

Clearly, his main desire during this period was to let the Hohenzollern know where his loyalty was. He told Cosima of a recurring dream in which the Prussian royal house overwhelmed him with favor. He would counterbalance the defeat and humiliation of the *Rhinegold* and *Valkyrie* premières in Munich; the *Ring* in Bayreuth was to be achieved through and performed for the glory of the renascent Reich. Nietzsche, who foresaw the decline of the German spirit with the rise of the Empire, was to remark, "What have I never forgiven Wagner? That he condescended to the Germans—that he became a German Imperialist (*reichsdeutsch*)." But he had always had a particular instinct for marching in step with ideas in vogue.

There remained the delicate operation of cutting his artistic ties to Munich carefully and gradually, so that the vital artery linking him to a royal

---

[6] How little he thought of it is shown by his converting the hymn to the Kaiser into a song in praise of Cosima, sung by her children at the family's Christmas party of 1871. On purely musical matters the great composer rarely fooled himself.

treasury would remain intact until a new passage from Berlin could safely maintain the essential flow. As usual, he used not Siegfried's blade but Mime's craft.

Seemingly, the King could expect Wagner to visit Munich to discuss the *Ring* productions within a reasonable time after his marriage to Cosima. But by the spring of 1871 his intention of depriving Ludwig of his moral and legal right to the cycle was made mercilessly clear. The final notes were put to the *Siegfried* full score on February 5, 1871. That Wagner immediately proceeded to occupy himself with the *Kaiser March* symbolized his desertion of his friend.

In return for maintaining the composer in luxury, the King's reward was to have been the possession and mounting of the Nibelung scores. But after the completion of *Siegfried,* Wagner lied, claiming that it could not be delivered to Munich because the orchestration of the final act remained unfinished. Once a completed score was in Ludwig's hands, orchestral parts could be abstracted and a performance made possible. This Wagner was determined to prevent. By the summer Schott had brought out Klindworth's piano version of *Siegfried.* It could only have been made from the completed full score whose existence the unembarrassed Wagner had the temerity to deny. His correspondence reveals conscienceless double-dealing, although Cosima's diary indicates that the deception may have occasionally unsettled him. But with his new inclination toward Berlin he was coming to view his dependence upon the King as "outrageous." In an attempt to call his bluff, Ludwig had indicated willingness to mount only the first two acts of *Siegfried* if the third were really incomplete.[7] Wagner then let him understand that he would prefer to burn the whole business and go begging.

At this point the King gave up. Concerning Wagner's bad faith he was no longer capable of surprise. During the spring of 1871 he had learned of the Bayreuth project with displeasure (*"Der Wagner'sche Plan missfällt mir sehr"*). Its success would cheat him of his childhood dream of making Munich the Wagner capital. Obviously, the final operas would be held back for the new project. Wagner had informed him that it was now his goal "to call forth a German national undertaking" whose direction naturally would be exclusively in his hands. Since Berlin's Royal Academy of Arts had extended membership to him and he was to deliver an address before it, he wondered aloud to Ludwig whether the occasion might not be oppor-

---

[7] Ludwig's idea was not as inartistic as might appear at first glance. As a libretto, acts one and two, badly constructed as they are, constitute a complete unit. Of course, he could not know that Wagner's change of musical style in the closing act also made it into what is a separate opera. In the hope that Wagner might change his mind about surrendering the full score, the Munich theater prepared scenic plans for *Siegfried,* and by autumn the work was in rehearsal with the help of Klindworth's piano arrangement.

tune to announce the new enterprise. But the summons actually went out in April in the form of a brochure outlining the Bayreuth idea but as yet withholding the name of the town, first revealed publicly in a communication of May 12.

Few deserved better of Wagner than Ludwig, and few did he treat more shabbily. But the aristocratic gentleman knew when a game was over, and he sadly drew back, refusing to use his power to retaliate. The manuscript of the full score of *Valkyrie,* not yet engraved, was in his possession; short of writing the work out again, Wagner would have been unable to produce the opera without it. Indeed, as owner of the *Ring,* the crown had the right to forbid its performance. An attempt was made to barter *Valkyrie* for *Siegfried*, but, knowing the King would not descend to his level, Wagner demurred. Eventually the *Valkyrie* score was sent him, and Ludwig declined to assert his legal rights. *Noblesse* obliged that genius be served; moreover, in this spirit Wagner's allowance was continued. But as far as the new adventure was concerned he was financially on his own. Not wishing to name the Hohenzollern court, Wagner informed Ludwig through Hofrat von Düfflipp that "private persons" would step forward with funds simply out of "their great devotion" to his art.

During the period this aesthetic *Realpolitik* was developing, Wagner had found himself again involved in speculative writing. Both the birth of the Reich and the Beethoven centenary had been celebrated in 1870. The coincidence stirred Frau Cosima. "The war is a Beethoven festival," she announced.[8] Wagner's essay *Beethoven,* if not, as Newman amazingly implies, "among the most suggestive documents in musical literature," is nonetheless significant for its rigorous disavowal of the basic tenets of *Opera and Drama* through a highly personal adaptation of Schopenhauerean theory and, most important, gives evidence that the conversations Wagner was enjoying with a new young friend were not without influence on his thinking. Almost simultaneously both were to be evolving twin aesthetic treatises. Destiny had brought him into intimate contact with an extraordinary intellect.

5

Nietzsche remarked, "All things considered, I would never have survived my youth without Wagnerian music." He and two other sixteen-year-old

---

[8] It should be remembered that Cosima's dead sister had been the wife of that Emile Ollivier who headed the French ministry in office at the war's outbreak. (By early August news of French military catastrophes had driven him from his post, and he sought refuge in Italy.) Cosima's relationship with someone so high in the enemy's counsels may have led her, defensively, to an almost lunatic jingoism.

boys founded and constituted a proud and uncompromising aesthetic society called "Germania," which, by pooling its members' allowances, was eventually able to buy Bülow's piano arrangement of *Tristan,* the opera Nietzsche always considered "absolutely Wagner's *non plus ultra.*" Ecstatically they hammered it out at the keyboard. While a student of classical philology at Leipzig University, Nietzsche finally heard the full sensuous effect of the prelude as played by an orchestra, and his every nerve responded to what he later called in *Ecce Homo* "the fifty worlds of strange delights." Soon after this concert of the Euterpe Society, in October, 1868, Wagner made that puzzling incognito visit to his native city and stayed at the home of his sister and brother-in-law, Ottilie and Hermann Brockhaus. There he met young Nietzsche, who was enchanted by his wit, awed by his greatness, and overjoyed to hear him discuss his debt to Schopenhauer. The brilliant boy, less than a year older than Ludwig of Bavaria—Nietzsche's dead father and Wagner had been born in the same year—in turn made an extraordinary impression on the composer, who encouraged him to visit Triebschen to continue their discussion of music and philosophy. Hans Sachs was in need of a new Walther; Ludwig was obviously weary of the role, and not often did Wagner receive such intelligent homage.

Within months Nietzsche, upon the recommendation of his master, Ritschl, was appointed a professor of classical philology at Basel. Being near Triebschen, he sought Wagner out during the spring of 1869. As he approached the house for the first time, he heard Wagner composing at the piano the harmonies of Brynhild's lament in *Siegfried,* "He who has awakened me has wounded me."

And Wagner did become Nietzsche's awakener, who, by subsequently failing to live up to the youth's ideals, dealt him wounds which, though they never healed, yet played a salutary role in his development into one of history's most formidable philosophic writers and thinkers. Like King Ludwig, he at first placed Wagner upon so high a pedestal that the concussion of the idol's fall shattered not only it but the shocked worshiper, too. Little by little, the youth detected the extent of Wagner's intellectual and moral charlatanry, and learned, in Mencken's phrase, that actors make bad philosophers. Overthrowing false idols was to become Nietzsche's business; he later warned his readers against veneration. "Be on guard lest a statue crush you!"

But no clouds shaded those early bewitching and refreshing days at the lake, where Nietzsche, submissively lost in adoration, passed golden hours stolen from his duties at Basel. Years after his break with Wagner, he observed, "I pass over my other relationships lightly; but at no price would I have my life bereft of those days at Triebschen, days of confidence, of serenity, of sublime flashes, of profound moments." Wagner, who in the beginning showed his most Olympian, Goethean side, became the young man's "mystagogue for the secret doctrines of life and art." Like Faust, Nietzsche called for the moment to abide; it was so beautiful.

Though Cosima never found Nietzsche really sympathetic, she nonetheless treated him charmingly, radiating a mysterious, aloof fascinaton that was her specialty. Predictably, he fell in love with her. She was his senior by seven years, and the unequivocal homeliness of her youth was changing to a kind of bizarre beauty. She as well as Wagner drew him to Triebschen, which he called his "isle of the blessed." Despite a taxing schedule at the university and a load of private studies, he became her errand boy. How amusing to think of Nietzsche doing her Christmas shopping and discussing the children's toys with the salesgirls of Basel. Wagner, so irresistible when he wanted to please, also inflicted his own commissions on his new friend, the most onerous being that of seeing the early chapters of *Mein Leben* through the press. He was soon relieved of the proofreading, perhaps because Wagner suddenly realized that many pages might offend and perhaps alienate the highly bred, chaste young man. Certainly what he did read helped open his eyes.[9] In general, Cosima and Wagner, despite their protests, acted as if Dr. Nietzsche had no purpose but to serve their needs.

Wagner liked him enormously. But completely disinterested friendship was a luxury he permitted himself infrequently. He sensed Nietzsche's abilities as a writer and wished to yoke them to his cause. The title of Professor in Ordinary of Classical Philology (conferred on Nietzsche by the university faculty and the Swiss government in April, 1870) dazzled the composer, who had never found much support from savants. The company of Nietzsche and his brilliant philological colleague Rohde (Ritschl had nicknamed them "the Dioscuri") was a matter of great pride to him, and he was to cause much unwitting amusement by his pompous references to "my friends, the two university professors!" He expected Nietzsche's writings to establish Wagnerism in academic circles, where enthusiasm for it had so far been conspicuously restrained. The composer felt himself swinging into a wider intellectual orbit. The average Wagnerite was all emotion, his brain power none too high. The more flattered by the attentions of the superior young scholar, Wagner determined to bind him closely to the Triebschen household. He was admitted into Wagner's secret plan to awaken Cosima on her birthday on Christmas Day, 1870, with a performance on the stairway of his *Triebschen* (later *Siegfried*) *Idyll* by a group of musicians

---

[9] The installments of *Mein Leben* sent to the palace interested King Ludwig greatly, but one wonders whether he, too, found the tale, even after Wagner's editing, disillusioning. Understandably, Otto Wesendonk advised Wagner not to go into details of his life minutely in the autobiography. Otto may well have suspected what was in store for him.

brought from Lucerne.[10] Nietzsche had been in the house when Cosima gave birth to Siegfried. Realizing the unlikelihood of living to raise him to manhood, Wagner contemplated appointing his young friend the boy's legal guardian. The relationship between the two men grew increasingly close, and during the war year of 1870—the high tide of their intimacy—each labored at a work reflecting this happiest time of their friendship, a brief period Richard Strauss considered one of the century's most significant moments.

6

Nietzsche's first book was, as his sister wrote, the product of "a wealth of aesthetic problems and their solution . . . fermenting in his mind for years." As a means of developing them, he gave two public lectures at Basel early in 1870, "The Greek Music Drama" and "Socrates and Tragedy." At Triebschen, the content, especially of the second, at first caused something of a commotion on the part of Cosima, agitated to discover Socratic and Euripidean rationalism treated as inimical to tragic art. During a summer visit to the Wagners Nietzsche read aloud his article on "The Dionysian Viewpoint." These studies were to ripen into his first large-scale work, a dissertation on the Greeks eventually called *The Birth of Tragedy from the Spirit of Music,* a project over which he brooded during his war service as a medical orderly.

By the end of 1870 he was back in Switzerland, recovering from serious illnesses contracted while on duty. His manuscript proceeded haltingly. In April, he finally read part of it at Triebschen and was hurt to recognize Wagner's disappointment; the book was not about him! The draft of Nietzsche's proposed *The Origin of the Tragic Idea,* sent to Cosima for Christmas, had evidently led Triebschen to hope for something quite different from its faithful disciple, who thereupon set about fulfilling these expectations by entangling his theory of Greek tragedy with a glorification of the Wagnerian drama. Tragedy, once born of music, would be described as reborn with Wagner; the patch seemed easy to make and was certainly contemplated with sincerity and devotion. The completed work came out early in 1872.

Revisions had been undertaken and an extended postlude in praise of Wagner and *Tristan* attached. Yet the book's conversion into a specimen of Wagnerian propaganda was less than smoothly accomplished; Walter Kaufmann observed, "Even that part of *The Birth of Tragedy* which deals with

---

[10] Even after rejecting the *Ring* music, Nietzsche continued to love the *Idyll.*

the Greek drama could probably never have been written without Wagner's work." The book's famous concept of the Apollonian and Dionysian conflict and reconciliation in Greek drama—the struggle of twin Hellenic divinities who strove and yet united in necessary interdependence [11]—was inspired by the tragic art of *Tristan*. Its intoxicating, orgiastic music had revealed to Nietzsche the terrible power of the Dionysian impulse and that strange antithesis of pain begetting joy, joy engendering agony. Of Beethoven's setting of Schiller's "Ode to Joy," the very foundation stone of Wagnerian theory, he wrote, "The Dionysian is approached as, awestruck, the millions bow down to the dust." This frenzy joined to stately, plastic Apollonian dream images together generated great drama, a marriage of *Rauschkunst* and *Traumkunst*.

In a freshly written "Foreword to Richard Wagner" introducing *The Birth of Tragedy,* Nietzsche remarked that he was planning the book just at the time the composer's essay *Beethoven* originated. And not only did Nietzsche spatchcock the famous quotation from *Meistersinger* on *Wahrtraum-Deuterei* into his opening section on Apollonian dreams, but also, later in the book, called upon Wagner's *Beethoven* as witness to the eternal truths of Schopenhauer's theory of music. These references, along with the great tribute to *Tristan,* had their desired effect; Wagner and Cosima suffered paroxysms of delight.

That the work was rewritten to give it a Wagnerian bias was considered absurd by most of Nietzsche's colleagues, and jeopardized his career. When the next winter semester opened, he was humiliated to discover no students registered in his courses. For a long time he was academically dead. Wagnerism was generally considered the pastime of hysterical ladies, effeminate men, French decadents, and anti-Semites. For a young professor of Nietzsche's promise to turn his first book into a polemic for so widely mistrusted a cause seemed complete folly. Perhaps fear of this very aftermath had first made him design it without excursions into the Wagnerian drama. Openly called one of Wagner's literary lackeys, he paid a high price for his loyalty. But at least he had the sympathy of the great Professor Burckhardt, who, though he despised Wagner, admired what his young colleague wrote of the Greeks.

---

[11] Nietzsche borrowed this antithesis from ideas in the writings of numerous forerunners, especially Goethe, Schiller, and Heine. Such predecessors notwithstanding, it was through *Tristan* that the young man actually experienced the Dionysian and found the inspiration to write about it. Existing in a strange limbo touching the borders of history, philology, philosophy, and music, *The Birth of Tragedy* seems forbidden entry into the heartlands of any of these disciplines. Its scholarship was of an imaginative, evocative kind that took some decades to find wide appreciation. Yet the book's language, though at times excessively Dionysian, revealed the master from the first.

How complete was Nietzsche's early thralldom to Wagner? The young man must have been flattered to discover in *Beethoven* a style, dialectic, and poetic concept of Schopenhauer, all obviously benefiting from his hours of attendance at Triebschen; but neither pride nor awe made him blind to the fact that the essay was a hopeless attempt to reconcile the irreconcilable by building principles of opera upon the foundation of a philosophic theory really denying the form. Nietzsche himself had fallen into the same trap and later was to recognize in his own "impossible" first book, "burdened with every fault of youth," a painful effort to express, in Schopenhauer's terms, values fundamentally opposed to Schopenhauer's spirit and taste. In this respect his letter to Wagner of November 10, 1870, acknowledging receipt of the *Beethoven,* is significant; one senses an inward awareness of the dilemma. He wrote that most students of Schopenhauer would find difficulty perceiving the harmony between the latter's ideas and Wagner's, and emphasized that in *Beethoven* chiefly "those to whom the message of *Tristan* has been revealed" would be able to follow Wagner. There was more truth in the observation than Nietzsche was himself willing to admit at the time. Emotion, not reason, was the key to both Wagner's book and his own; an Apollonian mind availed little when approaching their Dionysian prose.

7

Beethoven pursued the turn Wagner's *Gesamtkunst* theory had taken a decade earlier in "Music of the Future." But now he was no longer pretending to restate the Swiss essays in abbreviated form. "On State and Religion" of 1864, looking back at the decisive "Music of the Future," had described it as the result of "pondering" (*"überdenken"*)—not summarizing —his old point of view, a significant admission. In *Beethoven* all pretense was thrown away; *Opera and Drama* was a thing of the past; aesthetic theory was finally catching up with artistic practice.

Poetry was cashiered and now accorded a position humbly subordinate to a main synthesis of dramatic music and stage action, the relative positions of these ingredients in *Meistersinger. Gesamtkunst* theory now embraced Schopenhauer's comments on symbolic dreams and visions, music paralleling the former, drama the latter. But music, with its clairvoyant, revelatory character, was hailed as possessing unique power and towering above the other arts, the musician being "entitled to a position of holiness." Drama was music's visible counterpart, and dramatic verse itself was of relatively trifling importance. *Beethoven* described the relationship of music to poetry as "thoroughly illusory." Reiterating that a union of poetry and music must always end in the subordination of poetry, Wagner observed that in the

Ninth Symphony Schiller's text was really not very scrupulously set—one senses an attempt to justify the often haphazard vocal lines in *Meistersinger* and in *The Twilight of the Gods,* on which he was at work—and that the great hymnlike melody itself, significantly first presented in purely instrumental guise, was the element that stirred the listener. (Wagner would soon rewrite the passage, correcting [!] its prosody, for his performance of the Ninth at the Bayreuth foundation-stone ceremony.) A text now appeared to be regarded simply as a stimulant to evoke a mood and thus draw music from the composer. Intuitively Wagner had long considered this *volte-face.* Fifteen years before writing *Beethoven*—that is, soon after his first exposure to Schopenhauer—he had confided to Liszt his new opinion of the finale of the Ninth Symphony as its weakest movement, a judgment already in conflict with his teachings enshrining the word.

The Destiny of Opera (1871), a direct outgrowth of *Beethoven,* stressed the free character of the new twofold synthesis of music and dramatic action. Music was released from all compromise, the composer's contribution being the principal ingredient of the art-work. The drama was molded by tone and mimetic action, and, following their inspiration, the poet but drafted the work's plan. Through musical means such as melodic line and tempo, the composer communicated directly with the audience. He was the true mime of all the roles, the margin of caprice so often possible to performers in the spoken theater being reduced in the music drama by the existence of the score. Wagner saw the composer as a ventriloquist speaking through the orchestra and singing actors, whose passivity, thanks to his creative exertions, ironically gave an impression of complete spontaneity. He believed he not only had come to terms with the consequences of espousing Schopenhauer's speculations on music but also had gone beyond the philosopher in this field. In comparison to the improvisatory nature of the new theory, in which the ideal drama was to have the character of an extempore mimetic-musical expression, *Opera and Drama* of twenty years before seemed a musty manual of *Gesamtkunst* arms. At last Wagner had explained the impromptu genius of *Meistersinger* to himself.

Schopenhauer would certainly have been horrified by this use of his theory of music, and perhaps the result was in some ways painful to Wagner himself. After years of dialectic rambling and reams of paper, he had ended by defining grand opera. *Sicut erat in principio.*

Wagnerians again paid little attention to the revisionist avowals of their master, driven by ambivalence to embed his new thoughts within essays touching many other subjects. His changed attitude remained largely unnoticed, misunderstood, or disregarded. *Beethoven* and *The Destiny of Opera* were relatively modest in scale. No new magnum opus appeared to replace *Opera and Drama,* which Wagner had, in fact, reissued in 1868 in a new edition with a special foreword. He did not appear eager to make the general public aware of how completely his work and thinking had altered. Quite the contrary, unsure of himself, he added to the confusion. The preface to *The Destiny of Opera* sophistically referred the reader to *Opera and Drama,* described as in complete agreement with the new work, which, however, offered some fresh points of view. He ended *Beethoven,* in which poetry had been reduced to complete obeisance, by picturing Goethe's Eternal Feminine as the spirit of music leading the poet to redemption. Seemingly, he called to mind the Swiss essays and their celebration of music as the womanly principle in the *Gesamtkunstwerk;* but those disciples who lingered over this coda to *Beethoven* would perhaps realize that to Wagner deliverance was dissolution. For the Wagner of *Beethoven* a piece of music retained its character even when the most varied texts were sung to it. To such a position had the author of *Opera and Drama* really come, though to the end of his days he oscillated on this theoretic point.

His "Reminiscences of Auber," written in the autumn of 1871, suggested a dialectic relapse by explaining Auber's musical genius in *Masaniello* as having proceeded in part from Scribe's libretto—along with Auber's music a remarkable and explosive manifestation of the Parisian folk spirit. The book was the fecundating partner in its union with music, Wagner's diction here implying the vigorous role for drama described in the Zurich writings (*"unmittelbare Befruchtung durch das Drama"*). Again, in "A Glance at the Condition of Contemporary German Opera," a biting and often amusing survey of Germany's theaters published early in 1873, Wagner spoke of an opera's text as "the effective material substance of a work." At the very same time, before his Berlin reading of *The Twilight of the Gods,* he somewhat inconsistently followed a panegyric on the power of music with a request that his audience judge his poem by the standards applied to spoken plays because, so he claimed, it avoided the usual operatic arrangement of inserted numbers, being constructed as an extended dramatic dialogue. Of course, the work really abounds in operatic solos, ensembles, and innumerable Parisian "situations." But more interesting than Wagner's self-deception on this matter was his positive attitude toward the text. The ingeniously formulated synthesis of *Beethoven* was ignored, and Wagner seemed happily riding his favorite hobbies of two decades before.

Some of his articles of the same period, however, helped spread the newer gospel. "The Name 'Music Drama'" of 1872 portrayed music as ready to reassume "her ancient dignity as the very womb of drama . . . not its rival, but its mother"; he toyed with the idea of defining his drama as "deeds of music made perceptible" but, observing the overpowering role of music in *Tristan,* humorously admitted there was not much to see in this work, especially its second act, in which "little more than music takes place."

Yet in his essay of 1879, "Operatic Poetry and Composition in Particular," again music suddenly fell from its high rank. Wagner very deliberately wheeled about to present his old image of poetry as the masculine, formative principle in the music drama. (He had been rereading *Opera and Drama* at the close of 1878.) A year later, in "Religion and Art," in the course of a discussion of church music, he turned back and spoke of music's unique position among the arts: Music "dissolves" the words, which vanish, leaving only "the pure emotional content . . . the most secret essence (*das eigenste Wesen*) . . . a world-redeeming incarnation of the divine dogma of the nullity of the phenomenal world." Here, in a welter of Schopenhauerean "Parsifalisms" one recognizes the message of *Beethoven*.

In Wagner's vacillations is sensed the proud desire to pretend that his pronouncements could never be out of date; he wished somehow to persuade himself and others that, though all was different, nothing had changed. To the end he persisted in the ungainly attempt simultaneously to take possession of two widely spaced aesthetic chairs, a maneuver beyond even the gymnast of Eisleben.

8

The Destiny of Opera formed the lecture Wagner delivered before the Berlin Academy on April 28, 1871. He had snatched at an invitation from this rather insignificant society in order to justify a diplomatic visit to the capital. Although he conducted a concert in the presence of the Kaiser and Kaiserin on May 5, two days earlier he had achieved his real purpose, an interview with the mighty Chancellor, who later told Lothar Bucher that he had yet to encounter such conceit. Wagner was certain Bismarck would immediately grasp Bayreuth's significance to the Reich could he be prevailed upon to read "German Art and German Politics." Since the war the composer had believed that "such a powerful mind must see the importance of the theater at once." Prestigious support was needed; the character of the Bayreuth enterprise had changed abruptly.

A visit to the town in mid-April had revealed the inadequacies of the old opera house; moreover, in Wagner's opinion, its Franco-Italian style would provide an infelicitous setting for his truly German art. Cosima wrote Nietzsche how "impossible" it would be "to have Siegfried and Wotan appear midst amoretti, shells, and the whole apparatus of the eighteenth century." At Bayreuth Wagner now purposed to build the essentials of the Semper theater, omitting architectural embellishments (they would appear later in Semper's and Hasenauer's superb Burgtheater in Vienna) and leaving to the German nation the future task of turning the structure into a monument; it would be posterity's duty to encase his simple provisional theater in marble. (One recalls how Santa Maria degli Angeli encloses the "Porzi-uncola" of St. Francis!) The visit to Berlin was the climax of an extended tour through the new Reich; taking advantage of a wave of nationalism and of gratitude toward Prussia, he intended to fire enthusiasm for the Bayreuth venture as a pan-German effort centered in Berlin and then to turn this enthusiasm into money.

Wherever he appeared—Leipzig, Dresden, Darmstadt, Berlin—he was ad-mired as the leading composer of the ascendant Empire. Though chagrined to discover his celebrity resting mainly upon the gimcrackery of the *Kaiser March,* he seemed nonetheless eager to yoke himself and his *Ring* to the Prussian chariot and was beginning to resemble that description of his fellow citizens once offered in the anti-Prussian journal of his Munich period: "In his longing for 'German grandeur,' the German can usually dream of nothing other than a kind of revival of the Roman Kaiser-Reich, an idea filling even the most good-natured German with an unmistakable appetite for mastery and a craving for supremacy over other people." But now he hoped that the recent war had been but a stage in a larger Hohenzollern design that would result in the destruction of the Catholic Hapsburgs.

Great forces were compelling him to identify his work with an authori-tarianism always close to his heart. In terms of Darwin, Prussia had proved the favored race in the European struggle and, according to Gobineau, the superior entity dominated by right. For all its sublimity, there is in the *Ring* a brutality making it perhaps the ultimate artistic expression of the premises and tendencies of the time. Prussia was not one of those creaking, reactionary regimes whose weaknesses had been laid bare by the liberal surge of the century's earlier years, but, rather, a new, disciplined, and mechanistic tyranny. Wagner rejoiced in the German officers' unquestioning obedience, the outcome, he believed, of profound instinct and intuition. "The German . . . indulges in no chimerical visions. . . . I have been through all these illusions and have now reached the point of being able to understand the meaning of this narrowly defined sense of duty." Nietzsche, who at-tempted to stand against his times, maintained in the first of his *Untimely Meditations* (1873) that "strict war discipline, natural courage and endur-ance, superiority of the leaders, unity and obedience among the led . . . have nothing to do with culture." But Wagner embraced the era. The German General Staff's account of the war was to be his favorite reading during the Bayreuth rehearsals, and, when contemplating the completed theater, he was to tell Cosima that the only thing he yet honored and loved was the army. The idealism of the romantic age had fled. Brynhild awoke in the ponderous, materialistic, negative world of romantic realism. Wagner observed, "If the *Ring* . . . coincides with the victories of Germany, this will be no mere coincidence, whether we live to see it or not."

9

With the devoted help of Countess Marie von Schleinitz, an old friend of Cosima's (while still Marie von Buch, she had approached Wagner in 1863 at his Breslau concert) and wife of an influential courtier, Berlin became the business center of the Bayreuth movement.

Tausig, who had settled in Berlin, at first shared management of the enterprise with the Countess. In July he succumbed to typhoid fever at the age of twenty-nine. His death was a blow to Wagner, for whom he filled the place occupied in former years by Kietz and Karl Ritter. Wagner reflected upon the way Tausig had "felt the curse of being a Jew" and wrote a touching epitaph for the gravestone of a young man who had been strangely dear to him. Cosima, never really sympathetic to Tausig, explained to Countess von Schleinitz that he had been *"metaphysically* ruined by his connection with the family from which he had sprung. His inward unrest, his instability were due to the consciousness of his origin."

At the suggestion of Emil Heckel, a Mannheim music dealer, plans were under way for the founding of Wagner clubs in all towns and cities where enthusiasts could be mustered. The festival was exalted as the Reich's noblest cultural undertaking, in which individuals and societies were invited to participate through the purchase of certificates of patronage. In his best Zurich manner Wagner was to announce that, in the construction of his Festspielhaus, architecture might well be reborn out of the spirit of music and a new German building style discovered; the unique contributions of German designers were to be to the theater, and Wagner saw himself as the modern counterpart of Amphion, at the sound of whose lyre huge stones formed themselves into the city of Thebes.

Despite anger over the composer's mendacity in the matter of the *Siegfried* score, the ever-forgiving Ludwig subscribed to the extent of twenty-five thousand thaler, a fortune he later put at Wagner's personal disposal for the building of Wahnfried, his new Bayreuth home. For the latter, Wagner had his heart set on some land communicating with the Hofgarten behind Margravine Wilhelmine's palace, the same area where the Festspielhaus was to be constructed. Wagner asked Ludwig to send him the plans for the Munich theater. In 1869, Semper had finally been paid—or, rather, underpaid—for his heroic labors, and the sketches were royal property. They were eventually adapted to Bayreuth conditions by Carl Brandt and Otto Brückwald, an architect from Leipzig.

In the Bayreuth banker Friedrich Feustel Wagner found a necessary link to the town council. It resolved to place a plot for the theater at his disposal.

But difficulties in connection with the terrain and problems of acquisition caused the site to be shifted twice before the historic structure, named the "National Theater" in the council proceedings, began to rise beneath the eminence called the "Bürgerreuth." The hospitable city fathers were eager to attract money and tourists to their corner of Franconia, but most of the population seemed less than enthusiastic about a new neighbor who had earned such a notorious reputation in Dresden and Munich.

Preliminary diggings for the theater were under way when, at the end of April, 1872, Wagner, Cosima, and the children were settling at the Fantaisie, a hotel close to the Duke of Württemberg's handsome estate at Donndorf and situated but minutes from Bayreuth. It had not been easy to quit Triebschen's seclusion, and at the last moment Wagner instructed that all his green curtains be brought along. He carried with him the composition sketches for *The Twilight of the Gods,* completed at the lake less than two weeks before his departure. Well aware that this was his most monumental creation, he had written to Pusinelli during work on the Norns scene, "Whatever I write down is all just 'superlative.' "

On the morning of his fifty-ninth birthday, in a gloomy downpour, he laid the cornerstone of the Festspielhaus before a throng of drenched Wagnerites, most of them having their first adventure with the Franconian climate. They dried out in the Bibiena theater, where Wagner spoke, declaring that on the cornerstone rested the edifice of Germany's noblest hopes. Later in the afternoon the guests reassembled in the small theater to hear him conduct an orchestra and chorus of volunteer musicians, with Wilhelmj as concertmaster, in the *Kaiser March* and Beethoven's Ninth. Among the vocalists was Wagner's niece Johanna. Although she had but a shadow of the voice that had embodied the first Elizabeth and for which Elsa and the *Valkyrie* Brynhild had been written (already in 1856 Liszt reported her loss of the notes above the staff), Wagner had asked her to sing the solo alto part in the symphony as she had done twenty-six years before, when he first led the work at Dresden.

He was seeking links with the past on this historic day. Nietzsche observed him silent, turned in upon himself. Ghosts must have crowded around him—Rosalie, Lehrs, Uhlig, Frau Ritter, Schnorr, Tausig . . . Minna. And, to his sadness, many who had played important roles in his life stayed away. Ludwig had let Wagner know that he preferred not to receive an invitation. But most painful was the absence of Liszt, who had recently received one of the most persuasive, indeed, beautiful, letters ever to come from Wagner's pen. Although Liszt had generously subscribed to Festspielhaus certificates, he preferred to remain away, sending to Bayreuth his blessing and vague hopes for a not-too-distant reunion. Wagner, however, insisted upon forcing a reconciliation, and in September he and

Cosima sought Liszt out at his retreat in the Hofgärtnerei at Weimar, where he had re-established himself for several months a year at a ducal invitation. The friends had not met since Liszt's visit to Triebschen in October of 1867, and Liszt again beheld the woman he both feared and admired, Cosima, whom he called *"ma terrible fille"* and later *"Cosima unica."*

From the time of Bayreuth a certain softening was at times to be sensed in Wagner, as if he occasionally desired some adjustment to a world he had always confronted exclusively on his own terms. He was growing old and could no longer ignore those quickly vanishing spasms that choked his heart.

10

Despite meetings, toasts, and hurrahs, a sober glance at the books of the Bayreuth company showed relatively little money coming in. And, even before the cornerstone had been set, it was rumored that the theater would cost substantially more than the three hundred thousand thaler budgeted. Early in 1873 the lag in the sale of certificates forced Wagner to endure the fatigue of yet another tour to whip up enthusiasm by concerts and personal appearances. And he had but returned from a journey through Germany (November 10 to December 15, 1872) to take stock of both large and small theaters in his search for artists for the *Ring*. In Dresden he saw old friends—Tichatschek, Pusinelli, and also the Wesendonks, who had settled in Saxony after leaving Zurich in the wake of anti-German sentiment provoked by the siege of Paris. Dresden feted and serenaded its old *Kapellmeister*. A regimental band of the Royal Infantry played excerpts from his works outside his hotel, and he leaped through the lower-floor window to thank the musicians. In Berlin on January 17 he read *The Twilight of the Gods* before a distinguished company that included Adolph Menzel, Helmholtz, and Moltke, in whom he perceived, as in Bismarck, traits of Frederick the Great. After conducting in Hamburg and visiting Schwerin, where the Duke of Mecklenburg bought six certificates, he returned to Berlin for a concert to be performed before the imperial couple.

He was able to draw more applause than money from the Prussian aristocracy. Bayreuth was Bavarian, and Kaiser Wilhelm and Bismarck, still looking upon him as King Ludwig's favorite, hesitated to do anything that might unnecessarily offend the sensitive boy. The Chancellor did not want Prussia to appear to be poaching in a "hunting preserve" of the young monarch, whose animosity toward Crown Prince Friedrich was problem enough. Had Wagner been disposed to forget Bayreuth and transfer his activities completely to Berlin, no doubt a splendid Wagner theater would have risen on the Spree. A Wagner society was founded by a Herr Löser, who interested many in certificates on the mistaken understanding that the *Ring* would be given in the Prussian capital. But Wagner was attempting to play Berlin and Munich against one another, while hoping that at the end a decisive leap from either direction would land him with both feet squarely in Bayreuth. His posture threatened, at the least, a tumble. He knew that his activities in Berlin had aroused the displeasure of Ludwig, who had warned him "never to lend a willing ear to foreign offers." But Ludwig's jealousy and sentiment might yet be turned to advantage should all else turn out badly.

On February 8, 1873, he and Cosima were back in Bayreuth. In April there was another trip, this time to Cologne, Kassel, and Leipzig. On the way to his native city he had paused in Eisleben to revive memories of his boyhood stay with Papa Geyer's brother. He somehow found the strength for the endless traveling, speeches, dinners, and conducting chores while the scoring of *The Twilight of the Gods* coursed through his brain. Outwardly, he appeared to have the health and vigor to carry through work needing several lifetimes. But his heart was paying the heavy price, and to Cosima he had confessed fear that it was damaged. After the concert for the very first Wagner club (Mannheim, December, 1871), he had written Ludwig, "Unfortunately, recent experience has but proved to me that I can no longer engage in orchestral conducting without exhausting myself excessively. To be sure, people are astounded by the magic I appear to practice on the musicians; but no one understands what the practice of this magic power costs me." Amy Fay, the American pianist, who observed him in Berlin in 1871, wrote, "When he conducts, he is almost beside himself with excitement. . . . The orchestra catches his frenzy, and each man plays under a sudden inspiration. . . . Every sinew in his body speaks. . . . His whole appearance is of arrogance and despotism personified." Despite such exertions, by the summer of 1873 considerably less than half the capital necessary for the theater had been promised. He had told Cosima that with Bayreuth he was putting his fatherland to the test. It had unqualifiedly failed. He later wrote Ludwig, "My Bayreuth festival was my last inquiry of the 'German spirit'; I was answered; the Grand Duke of Baden even paid for half a certificate for his son and successor. Can I desire more?" There was nothing to do but denounce the Jews and the Jesuits (who, it seems, were getting German money that was rightfully his) and call to King Ludwig for help.

But, abandoned by Wagner, Ludwig had turned to building projects of his own on a scale more suitable to a Louis XIV than the ruler of a declining principality. Years before, he had quickly apologized to Wagner for showing enthusiasm for the beauty of Cologne Cathedral, the completion of which was one of his grandfather's concerns. Ludwig hastened to observe that "architecture itself should be nothing but a means toward the one great goal." He had learned the Wagnerian catechism well. But after his rift with Wagner he was seized by the Wittelsbach passion for building and, spending his way to financial disaster, declined to guarantee a loan for Bayreuth. (At the height of his annoyance over the *Rhinegold* intrigue of 1869, he had—almost symbolically—asked Court Secretary Düfflipp to send to Berg castle "that book of Viollet-le-Duc's . . . which contains the views of the rooms.") The twenty-five thousand thaler deflected toward Wagner's mansion was, he indicated, his first and last contribution toward an affair hardly in his interest. It was a glum little group of sponsors and delegates from the Wagner clubs that inspected the shell of the theater at the end of October, 1873, in the mud, fog, and darkness of a classic Bayreuth rain.

By the opening of 1874 the festival appeared doomed. Even the outer structure was somewhat short of completion, and there was no money for the interior amenities, to say nothing of the stage equipment planned by Brandt, the scenery, and the costumes. Wagner strove to bring his plight to the attention of the Kaiser, who still hesitated to intervene in what he believed to be essentially a Bavarian affair. At this point Ludwig relented. He could not stand by and watch all go down in ruin. The old idealism and affection stirred again. On January 25 he informed Wagner that Parsifal, aware of his mission, would do "what lay within his power." He asked for a photograph of the composer, Cosima, and the children. (She sent the gift with a well-phrased note that spoke of the "past trial-filled years," thus breaking her long silence to him.) Within the week Düfflipp was able to write Wagner that the winds from Hohenschwangau were decidedly more favorable toward Bayreuth. By the end of February, 1874, Ludwig agreed to advance one hundred thousand thaler of credit from his private exchequer to the Bayreuth theater. The sums drawn were to be repaid from box office receipts, Wagner's original plan for an "invited" audience of enthusiasts at the festival having fallen victim to financial reality. In the meantime, funds from the sale of certificates were to be allocated toward the reduction of the loan, and materials purchased by it were to be the royal secretariat's property until the indebtedness was discharged. Wagner's failure to meet these obligations was to make Ludwig legal owner of the decorations, gas appliances, and machinery of the Festspielhaus.

On February 3 Wagner had prepared one of those political shifts that he could accomplish so quickly and, above all, without embarrassment. His Hohenzollern hopes had proved illusory. Done with the *Kaiser March,* he struck up the old familiar strain: "Oh, my gracious King! But behold all the German princes and recognize that toward you alone does the German spirit still hopefully glance. You, who called forth the confederation of the Empire [it is to be recalled that Ludwig was compelled to offer the

Kaiser crown to Wilhelm], are the final hope of the German spirit abandoned to horrible corruption, and are summoned by destiny to achieve what no one save you can." Apparently Ludwig never tired of this thick orchestration.

With the King now deeply committed, Wagner kept pressing for more. In money matters he was a master tactician. He negotiated a more advantageous system of receiving his royal allowance, and Ludwig was repeatedly importuned to ignore the letter of the recent contract and for the sake of immediate building needs to permit the composer occasionally to dip into funds from the certificates. By the autumn of 1875 the King yielded on this point. He had become champion of an undertaking originally planned to rob him of his rights and often must have asked himself how it had happened.

Nonetheless, 1875 drew to a close with little hope that the festival could take place. Even if the building were somehow completed, where would the two thousand marks per day needed for rehearsals be found? During the autumn Wagner had shifted back to Berlin, where it soon appeared that his request for a subsidy of thirty thousand thaler would be handed from the Kaiser to Bismarck to the Reichstag. Wagner had utter contempt for the latter body, which in 1871 had granted equality of citizenship to the Jews, a development that made him turn violently from Bismarck. He later wrote in "Shall We Hope?" (1879), "Where our un-German barbarians sit, we know; elected by *suffrage universel,* they are found in the parliament that knows everything save the seat of German power." Moreover, this assembly was certain to make his affairs a matter of open legislative discussion. Finding such a situation abhorrent, he held back from petitioning. The idea was "unbecoming," he told Ludwig in a letter of January, 1876, thus feeding him a cue that remained unanswered for several months. Wagner's refusal to approach the Reichstag irritated Bismarck, for he had been prepared to lend his authority to the request. When the composer arrived in Berlin in March, he learned from Frau von Schleinitz that nothing more was to be expected from the displeased Chancellor.[12] But in June Ludwig again saved the situation by granting the festival authorities what was, for all practical purposes, free access to the certificate money, thus relinquishing a security which had, in any case, proved fictitious; only a fraction of the projected sale had been subscribed. By this time his financial involvement in Bayreuth approached a quarter of a million marks.

[12] Wagner had sent Bismarck "German Art and German Politics," which opened with a tribute to Konstantin Frantz, an anti-Semitic political writer who had had a serious falling out with the Chancellor. The latter may have taken amiss the reason for the gift, which remained unacknowledged by a statesman notorious for his courtesy. In such matters Wagner was extraordinarily clumsy.

II

That Wagner never completely despaired of obtaining from either the Kaiser or Ludwig the funds an uninterested German Folk was loath to contribute is shown by the assurance with which he lavished money on Wahnfried, his new Bayreuth home. In September, 1872, he had quit the Hotel Fantaisie for a rented house in Bayreuth on the Dammallee. There he remained until the end of April, 1874, when he removed to the almost completed Wahnfried, whose cryptic name alluded to a retreat from life's illusions. The King's contribution toward the building having proved insufficient, Wagner had extracted ten thousand florins more from Schott against future delivery of some purely orchestral works he had in mind. Unfortunately for Schott and posterity, they were never written, though the firm eventually received the *Siegfried Idyll,* whose performance the composer had originally hoped to restrict to his family circle.

At Wahnfried he took up a baronial style of life, surrounded by many servants and those gewgaws and gauderies of Second Empire decoration he so admired. "The tomb is all we want," Cosima assured her diary. But evidently she and Wagner had agreed to welcome death in the indefinite future and in high style. In these new surroundings he felt vigorous enough to live "to an absurd age" and predicted that he and Cosima would die together "in a sort of euthanasia." For this purpose he arranged a sofa in his room on which they might one day gently expire. Their tomb was prepared at the end of the property, and during its construction he would often descend into the excavation to speak to the workmen about death. He and Cosima enjoyed contemplating this simple monument and scattering food on its surface for the birds. (She outlived him by almost half a century.) Russ, the most venerable of their dogs, good-naturedly ruled the garden until his death in May of 1875. And there were two other giant Newfoundlands— Marke and Brangäne, an unusual pairing of names, though the latter answered to "Branke"—several terriers, and a spitz named "Putzi." A Swiss housemaid, Asra, kept her master supplied with his beloved dressing gowns. In the basement of Wahnfried he had secreted large boxes of colored satin, and Asra had as model for her labors a spring-green creation decorated with pink bows, possibly a relic of Viennese Bertha's handiwork. At times Wagner enjoyed pulling on his old German-style *Meistersinger* costume, probably not dissimilar to the Netherlandish painter's outfit with beret that Nietzsche's sister had observed him wearing at Triebschen. In Cosima he had found someone who shared his love for dressing up. And not only did she let him help plan her magnificent wardrobe, but she, too, adopted an archaic manner of attire.

And play acting, to a large extent, dominated domestic relationships at Wahnfried. Its *nouveau riche* ceremonial makes one think of Faninal's household in *Rosenkavalier*. Georg, the valet, addressed the baby son as "Herr Siegfried." The children rose when their parents entered a room, and Cosima's hand had to be kissed. Her purpose was to make them learn to love Wagner "as a god." Judith Gautier observed Cosima's annoyance when Wagner joked familiarly; she wished him "to be more reserved, more Olympian." But the Olympian was easier for him in some spheres than others. The formality of Cosima's dining room—Wagner loved the cooking of the decadent French—contrasted strongly with her husband's unreconstructed table manners. It was hard to educate a man in his sixties, Lilli Lehmann observed.

Of course, there were relaxed moments when he would join in a game of hide-and-seek or horse and wagon, or would permit Fidi to ride him. Or he might crawl under the piano, where the children loved to conceal themselves. But they were completely dutiful and, like Cosima, learned to trim sail quickly in the face of sudden Wagnerian squalls. He would become violently jealous if she devoted too much time to them, and they came to know that supernumeraries performed on call and then vanished. For assembled guests they were required to sing from the hall gallery the hymn of praise to Cosima's charm and beauty Wagner had first composed for Christmas of 1873, the *Children's Catechism for Cosel's Birthday*. (It was enlarged and set for small orchestra the following year.) They were summoned by a servant—perhaps Cosima's factotum, a hairdresser who, incredibly, answered to "Schnappauf," a name worthy of Sheridan—announcing to the governess, *"Fräulein, der gnädige Herr wünscht dass die kleinen Herrschaften auf der Galerie singen möchten."* (The affectation of this invitation to sing for company is not easily translated.) Their governess reported that "they got much applause and ran away giggling."

Susanne Weinert, governess at Wahnfried from the summer of 1875 to the spring of 1876, left a diary chronicling some of the folk ways of the household. One cannot forbear quoting the note Mrs. Burrell attached to the manuscript, which came into her possession: "Ludicrous Journal of an innocent idiot Governess at Wahnfried, Bayreuth, unconsciously describes the inhabitants to the very Life—all their pomposity, impudence, and impecuniosity." Fräulein Weinert's background was Saxon, and this may in part have accounted for her replacement. Wagner was particularly eager to shield the youngest, still impressionable, children from Saxon dialect, which he knew had not benefited his own social career. He sometimes bantered in the broadest Saxon as if to stress that it was a charming joke. Nietzsche's sister Elizabeth found *die kleinen Herrschaften* extremely well-spoken and well-behaved. In later years, Cosima recommended Daniela to

Marie von Schleinitz's care by stressing her daughter's obedience and "unconditional submissiveness." The educational methods of Princess Wittgenstein and Madame Patersi were continued at the Wahnfried. In 1875 Bülow's daughters were enrolled at the Luisenstift at Niederlössnitz and thus were only occasionally at Wahnfried. Making every effort to compensate for the separation from their father, Wagner always treated them as his own. But his favorites were unmistakably Isolde and Siegfried, who belied his stage namesake's personality by being angelic, fine-grained, intelligent, not surprisingly, rather timid, and thoroughly his mother's boy. Four months after her death at the age of ninety-two in 1930 he followed her to the grave.

Emotionally, Wagner was never anything but a child himself and felt neglected if all faces were not continually turned in his direction. (As late as 1881, Cosima warned Daniela to greet Wagner specially in every letter.) His worst shows of ill temper followed any sign of affection on Cosima's part for her father, now a frequent guest at Wahnfried, for whom a special room was set aside. Having at his own insistence resumed contact with Liszt, Wagner—like Cosima—could not tell whether he loved or hated him. Visitors noticed this strange ambivalence. Lilli Lehmann recalled a revealing incident: She was singing Liszt's "Mignon's Lied" for Cosima when Wagner entered the room, listened self-consciously, and then remarked to his wife that he had been unaware of her father's having composed "such pretty songs." He further observed that hitherto his estimate of Liszt's contribution to music had been restricted to the realm of piano fingering! Cosima forced herself to laugh, but obviously Lilli did not pretend to be entertained. Moreover, Wagner's attempt to prohibit French in Wahnfried was less a display of nationalism than a hostile gesture toward Liszt's and Cosima's personal conversations. On the very day the *Ring* was completed she handed him a letter from Liszt, and the innocent act caused Wagner to raise so vehement a scene that the great event became for her a trial of almost unbearable pain. A message from her father, and all sympathy for her husband vanished, Wagner cried. His manner could suddenly change from an overdone Faninal-like etiquette to ugly scenes in Saxon dialect that sometimes struck her dumb. Elizabeth Nietzsche remarked upon the equanimity with which Cosima received the outbursts of wrath Wagner, without the slightest cause, would often turn upon her. She suffered deeply. On the eve of her conversion as a Protestant (October 31, 1872)[18] he had discussed Liszt in terms so savage that she wrote in her diary, "I must indeed have been guilty of some neglect. . . . But it seems to me that it is not right of him to fly out at me so violently time after time." Nietzsche theorized that Wagner felt com-

---

[18] It took Frau Cosima little time to start making unpleasant observations about "the Catholics."

pelled to set upon the spirits of enemies he felt ever hovering about him. However, his tantrums subsided as quickly as they arose, and then he could not apologize sufficiently. During one of these contrite moods at Triebschen he had remarked to Cosima that she ought to know that everything about her was high and holy to him; if he occasionally permitted himself certain expressions, it was like the ancient Saturnalia, when a man might jest with the gods. This was the kind of cajolery that used to send Minna into a rage of her own. But Cosima reacted by weeping violently for joy, and told her diary, "I simply cannot understand or endure that he should set such store by me." Certainly there were times of utter contentment and profundity, as when they would walk together through the incomparable Franconian countryside or when he would lecture on music. He told her she was "in the morning the priestess of Apollo, in the evening, Sappho." He loved her to his utter capacity to love another.

12

Though essentially she saw her task as one of standing by and taking whatever tenderness or abuse came her way, through forbearing patience and constancy she exercised considerable control over him. All the techniques of unblushing flattery, pretended helplessness, and extravagant reactions that he applied to his relationship with Ludwig she in turn, but more subtly, used on him. He predicted her future title of "Margravine of Bayreuth," and, indeed, she had appropriated it well before his death. Her myth had been forming since Triebschen days. Not only did he hail her as a clairvoyante, but also celebrated her gentle hand as having the power to recall a man from death. She apparently believed her touch had cured a servant's child.

At those rare times when she thought Wagner about to commit an artistic error, she shed her usual meekness in his presence and argued until he submitted. She wished to be a Caroline Weber, called by her husband his "gallery"; upon her insistence he had done away with the opening scene in *Freischütz* between Agathe and the Hermit and had begun instead with the "Victoria" chorus. Cosima had already forced Wagner to retain Hans Sachs's address at the end of *Meistersinger* and to add to it the infamous "Beware!" passage. She importuned him until, at two in the morning, he got out of bed to sketch its words and music. Now she insisted he shorten the finale to the *Ring.* "I begged him to leave out *Wunschheim* and *Wahnheim* [home of desire and home of illusion], which sound a little artificial." He yielded.

At her urging not only were these arcane references jettisoned, but also all earlier versions of the coda of the immolation scene. Ironically, these elided sections contained the verses most admired by Ludwig, especially the lines beginning *"Verging wie Hauch"* and ending with *"die Liebe nur sein."* Already ecstatically quoting the latter passage in his second letter to Wagner (May 28, 1864), he had declared, "These words seem to me to have been written out of my innermost being." He learned from a rubric in the sixth volume of the composer's *Collected Writings* that the verses would not be set, and in September, 1874, wrote him, "I would find it lamentable should you not compose the concluding words of Brynhild . . . that were poetized earlier, for Brynhild's words of farewell are certainly of a thrilling, holy power." By the following spring he was reduced to pleading: "I beseech you, dearest Master, to set to music for me . . . those words you once allotted to Brynhild, which I so passionately love. . . . It would delight me extraordinarily could I hear resound in the performances to take place before me [deceptively, Wagner had encouraged his belief that three private *Ring* cycles would reward his building of the Festspielhaus!] those words so deeply significant, so full of truth, that glorious, sublime gospel of love that Brynhild bequeaths the world before her departure!" Wagner assured him that the lines would be composed and "inserted by the singer in these performances." But on January 11, 1876, Ludwig was still plaintively asking, "Is the composition of those heavenly words completed?" Cosima had won, though as a sop Wagner vaguely sketched a separate setting and sent it to the King for his thirty-first birthday (August 25, 1876). It was a souvenir.

This text also provided the favorite *Ring* quotations of Liszt and Princess Wittgenstein. Forces of which Cosima was perhaps unaware had made her come to look upon these very strophes as affected. They are no more so than many other sections of the tetralogy. For the Wittgenstein-Liszt relationship she felt white hate, and she was not without jealousy of the letters Wagner sent the King.

She painfully pondered the nature of their friendship, an entry in her diary of October, 1878, revealing what a torture it was to her. After perusing Wagner's latest letter to him, she wrote, "A most strange and indescribable feeling came over me when I read at the end of it that Richard's soul belonged forever to the King. It was like a serpent's tooth at my heart, and I really do not know what I should prefer. I should not like what he has written to be a mere phrase, yet I should not like it to be true, and even if it were in my power to do so, I would not have it unwritten; for all he does is well done. Yet I suffer and pine in the effort to conceal my suffering. All hail, sorrow, I am ready to greet thee as a guest!"

The quotation is one of the most revealing in a diary so far available only in a censored and obviously manipulated form.

13

The irascibility that the mention of Liszt's name, the sight of his handwriting, or the fall of his foot could at times arouse in Wagner was born not only of their terribly complicated domestic interrelationships but also of an artistic problem. The religious element already present in much of Liszt's early work and growing steadily stronger as he aged had come both to exasperate and to attract Wagner. While visiting the house on the Dammallee during October, 1872, Liszt had played his *Christus,* Wagner and Cosima having already perused the score together. Despite her derogatory remarks about "the singsong of priests," certainly an echo of Wagner's comments, the oratorio must have nonetheless interested him, especially after hearing it from Liszt's fingers. It was not just a sense of duty, as Cosima's biographer, Moulin-Eckart, implied, that made him journey to Weimar with her and Daniela to attend its performance under the composer on May 29, 1873. Wagner was eager to hear its full effect. Cosima's impression of the work as she left Weimar's Stadtkirche was of something "thoroughly un-German," whatever that might mean. He, however, remarked that it seemed to reflect belief without faith, a fascinating observation from the composer in whose mind the poem and music of *Parsifal* were already coursing.

Certainly there was much about Liszt's religion to amuse the skeptical. The shocking anti-Semitism of his *The Gypsies and Their Music in Hungary* (1861), an echo of Wagner's *Jewry in Music,* contrasted strangely with his sentimental piety. And the handsome Abbé, clutching his breviary and Book of Hours and posturing in his cassock before his mistresses, made many suspect that he could throw off his superstitious, paper-flower Catholicism as easily as his ecclesiastical garb. But, unlike Wagner, doubtless he had some kind of genuine Christian experience. The persuasive way in which his life and works blended the sacred and profane recall those baroque ecclesiastical structures wherein mystical piety and sensual gratification mix inextricably and easily, the pulpit and pews becoming opera boxes, the sanctuary a stage. As Madame Mouchanoff observed to the Grand Duke of Weimar, many disdained Liszt's religious compositions as ridden with genuflections and heavy with theatrical ostentation. But this was, she said, all part of his frantic struggle to take heaven by storm.

The depth and sincerity of religious belief could really have made little difference to Wagner, who, despite the hocus-pocus of *Parsifal,* thoroughly detested Christianity as Judaic error perpetuated, a situation he was determined to correct. His displeasure with Liszt's later works may well have proceeded not only from their curious artistic unevenness and memories of the fanatically devout Princess Wittgenstein (for him the evil daemon of his friend's personal and artistic life), but also from the fact that he himself, preparing to lay hands on Catholic ritual for his own histrionic purposes, had come to consider the Christian subject much as he looked upon the Nibelung material, that is, as his property alone.[14] In Nietzsche's phrase, he was about to "adjust" Christianity for Wagnerites. He contemplated creating a new religion that would use the old symbolic trappings but not the old faith. Cosima, summing up his attitude toward the drama before him, wrote that "the Grail and its legend express the longing of the Christian soul to commune with the Redeemer apart from the Church and without any hierarchy—not a protest, but the creation of a contrasting ideal." Wagner was preparing in *Parsifal* that concept of Aryan Christianity his future son-in-law Houston Stewart Chamberlain (Eva's husband) was in turn to bequeath to Alfred Rosenberg and the Nazi movement. Moreover, during his career the composer had more than once sought to cover the traces of his borrowings by disparaging compositions to which he was indebted. *Parsifal* would have been a different work if *St. Elizabeth, Christus,* and *The Bells of Strassburg Minster* (for chorus, orchestra, and baritone, and based on a text taken from Longfellow's *Christus*) had not preceded it. After receiving the poem of *Parsifal,* Nietzsche wrote, "First impression on reading it: There is more Liszt than Wagner. . . ." Throughout the Liszt-Wagner relationship there can be observed what Huneker called the "seizure of the weaker by the stronger man."

14

Wagner's flaring temper was as old as his childhood nickname of "Cossack." But the years immediately preceding the festival of 1876 placed an almost unbearable load upon his shoulders, often strained to the breaking point. In addition to the financial vexations accompanying the building of Wahnfried and the theater, he had to gather and train a cast and staff and at the same time devour time and energy with wearying activities connected with fund-raising, while over all loomed his principal task, that of completing *The Twilight of the Gods*. And ever more frequently a tightening around the heart intimated that even Richard Wagner was mortal.

As he proceeded with the orchestration of *The Twilight of the Gods,*

---

[14] Wagner despised the works of Hebbel, not only by reason of his reputation as one of Germany's greatest dramatists (born the same year as Wagner, he had died in 1863), but also because his cyclic trilogy, *Die Nibelungen* (completed in 1860), successfully used some of the very material of the *Ring* in dramas of elevated poetic expression.

he regretted being cut off from any opportunity of trying out his work and often wondered whether he was using too many instruments. The problem troubled him deeply. He remembered that in the past he had found it necessary to rescore passages after hearing them. Even after all the corrections he still found parts of *Dutchman* "noisy" and hoped to revise it once again. And he longed to thin the brass in the second act of *Tristan*. He seemed strangely unsure of himself on this technical point of orchestral density.

For the mechanical labor of extracting, copying, and proofing parts, and also for the more creative work of accompanying and coaching artists, he assembled a group of talented young zealots. This so-called "Nibelung Chancery" included Felix Mottl, Hermann Zumpe, Anton Seidl, and the neurotic Russian Jew Joseph Rubinstein, for whom Wagner felt enormous affection. The morbid young man, who became his rather unhealthy substitute for Tausig, committed suicide soon after Wagner's death, finding existence impossible without him. The first three "Chancery" members were to become important conductors, the Hungarian Seidl and the Austrian Mottl bringing the benefits of their Bayreuth experience as far as the stage of New York's Metropolitan Opera.

By the summer of 1874 some of the principal singers were visiting Wahnfried for instruction. Most had sacrificed fees and had come to this preliminary study out of a sense of dedication. Association with serious artists usually brought forth Wagner's most admirable qualities. He could show amazing patience, indulgence, and kindness if he felt the recipient capable of eventually grasping his intent. But tranquillity has never characterized an operatic enterprise. Strife arose between Joseph Hoffmann, who designed the scenery (his sketches were approved by Lenbach), and the Brückner brothers of Coburg, who were executing it. Hoffmann, a pupil of Karl Rahl, had created scenery for *Magic Flute* and *Freischütz* at the new Vienna opera house, but since he was at the time without a studio and assistants, the execution of his *Ring* sketches was given over to the Coburg firm recommended by Carl Brandt. Changes introduced when translating them into actuality evidently greatly upset Hoffmann; the Brückners exploited the most pompous aspects of the style of Hans Makart, Wagner's favorite painter.

Every day in Bayreuth brought emergencies draining Wagner's stamina. There were problems of staging for which he had no solution, and to Professor Döpler of Berlin, who was to design the costumes, he could only offer the negative advice that whatever their style, it must avoid both the high medieval and Greco-Roman, a request denied in the productions of postwar Bayreuth, whose gods are closer to Olympus than to Asgard. Wagner knew of the Professor's highly praised costumes for Franz Dingelstedt's famous première of Hebbel's *Die Nibelungen* at Weimar in 1861. But at

Bayreuth Cosima meddled in Döpler's work and, in the end, they almost came to blows; the costumes, she wrote, "absolutely remind one of Indian chiefs." The Professor had evidently made an odd ethnographical compromise. And not only were there such matters as the Cosima-Döpler conflict to arbitrate, but the creator of the *Ring* had to find means of housing and feeding in an ill-equipped provincial town a personnel of hundreds and almost two thousand daily visitors. Yet in the face of untold difficulties and distractions the last notes of the *Ring* were written on November 21, 1874, that day of incomparable triumph and sorrow for Cosima. The work, begun more than a quarter of a century before, was complete.

During the first half of 1875 Wagner searched for singers in Leipzig (where he attended a performance of Schumann's *Genoveva*), Hanover, and Braunschweig, and conducted in Vienna, Pest, and Berlin. The purpose of the concerts was not only to benefit the building and rehearsal funds but also to provide opportunity of trying out excerpts from *The Twilight of the Gods*. He urgently wished to test the balance of orchestra and singers and also to discover whether his artists could cope with their music under performing conditions. His Brynhild, the Austrian soprano Amalie Materna, distinguished herself, riding the crest of his orchestral flood with consummate ease. And in Berlin Niemann sang handsomely. But Wagner wanted him only for the part of Siegmund. Siegfried had to be sung on the stage by a younger man, and Wagner thought he had found him. But in Vienna and Pest this hope had come crashing to the ground.

The problem of discovering a singer equal to the inhumanly difficult double role of Siegfried had proved insurmountable from the very beginning. Twenty years before, while working at *Valkyrie,* Wagner had asked himself in a letter to Schindelmeisser why he wrote for heroic tenor, wondering how tasks like his were "even remotely to be solved by such eunuchs." As early as 1872 Cosima made mention of Franz Diener, recommended by Schott, as already preparing the young Siegfried in Bayreuth, she, in fact, regularly attending his rehearsals. But, like many a later aspirant, Diener—who angered Wagner by accepting a highly profitable contract from the Cologne Opera—gradually passed from sight. A year later Richter presented to Wagner Herr Glatz, a Hungarian doctor of laws. Young, outrageously handsome, of enormous stature, an accomplished athlete, musical, and the possessor of a tenor voice Wagner described as "one of the most powerful and noblest" he had ever heard, Glatz seemed ideal material. But in April of 1875 Wagner wrote King Ludwig that the young man, whose carriage caused him to be frequently mistaken for his Majesty of Bavaria, had proved incapable. During the course of the concerts at Vienna and Pest, in March, 1875, he had attempted Siegfried's forging arias, the duet with Brynhild from *The Twilight of the Gods,* and the scene of the hero's death. The results must have been catastrophic, for at the second

Vienna concert it was the Swedish tenor Labatt who struggled with the notes. Hans Richter's coaching had ruined a fabulous voice. Wagner's and Cosima's enthusiasm for Richter (he had married a singing teacher, who contributed her share to the vocal vandalism) cooled considerably after this affair. Moreover, they were incensed when his honeymoon interfered with his obligations toward them. And after Cosima heard him conduct a cut, orchestrally retouched, and polylingual (Hungarian and Italian) *Dutchman* at Pest, the disenchantment seemed complete.

After a vain attempt to engage Hermann Schrötter, whom the Braun-schweig Opera refused to release, Wagner fell back upon Georg Unger for the part of Siegfried. Looking at photographs of this fleshy and black-bearded tenor, one finds it hard to realize that his vocal deficiencies were tolerated at Bayreuth because Wagner saw in him an exemplary embodiment of volatile youth! His recalcitrant vocal cords caused anxiety right up to the final act of the opening *Ring;* his sound was baritonal and his range short, even the G's turning "white." But he fought his way through, his earnestness of purpose helping endear him to Wagner.

His artists assembled again in Bayreuth during the summer of 1875, and on July 20, amid scaffolds, lumber, and the workmen's tools, singers and orchestra tried out the unfinished Festspielhaus. The acoustics justified the unusual arrangement of the building. A new instrumental sound, though muffled, nevertheless did not obscure detail, even though the players were depressed half beneath the stage in a deep cave like a submerged amphi-theater. The singers were able to project their voices relatively easily over a subdued tonal volume. A compromise offered vocal strength and clearer comprehension of the text at the price of orchestral brilliance. As in most fine auditoriums, whether the acoustical success owed more to planning than accident can never be determined. (The light materials chosen to build what was to be a provisional structure evidently gave the hall its noble resonance.) Wagner's followers, who glorified him as Shakespeare and Beethoven in one, now sang his praises as Palladio reborn.

And the singers were not only audible but also visible from most of the chairs, which, rising in tiers of increasing width, formed a fan-shaped auditorium, an arrangement Wagner remembered from the tiny Riga Opera. The disposition of seats had the character of a classic arena, tiers of boxes on the side walls being excluded because from their height the instru-mentalists could be glimpsed in their grotto. No spectator was to be per-mitted to measure the perspective of the décor or the costumed actors against the orchestra and its conductor.

The creation of such illusion had been a special concern of Semper. His double proscenium dominated the auditorium. In a letter to Wagner of November 26, 1865, he had discussed plans for the contemplated provisional Wagner theater in Munich, his comments perfectly describing the appearance and functions of the stage end of the Bayreuth Festspielhaus: "According to our agreement, I have placed two prosceniums, separated by the sunken orchestra, one behind the other. The architecture of the more narrow second proscenium is a repetition of the large anterior one, but on a smaller scale. Thus there will come about a complete displacement of scale from which will follow both an ostensible enlargement of everything happening on the stage and also the desired separation of the ideal world of the stage from the real world on the other side of the boundarylike orchestra. The latter is to be completely invisible but by no means too deeply set." This final admonition was disregarded at Bayreuth, and it is to be doubted that Semper would have sanctioned the extreme depth of the Festspielhaus pit, which reminded Hanslick of a steamship's engine room. He, feeling that Wagner had "gone too far, or to put it better, too deep," missed the full splendor of the Wagnerian orchestral sound.

The double proscenium became the focus of a perspective trompe l'oeil decoration. From the flanking walls projected a series of paired abutments, each taking the shape of a base supporting a Corinthian column and entablature. Shallow at the back of the auditorium, these projections, between which doors were pierced, increased in depth as they advanced toward the front, making the hall appear to be a funnel, its apex at the stage opening. The frontmost pair of abutments was joined to the ceiling cornice by acanthus scrolls echoing, in bigger scale, those of the proscenium piers, the cornice itself repeating, in an enlarged version, the flattened arches of the double proscenium. Thus the first pair of columns actually supported a third and largest proscenium thrown across the stage aperture.[15] Wagner gratefully wrote Carl Brandt, "The extension of the proscenium was an inspiration on your part, which crowns the entire idea of the interior of the theater."

The other columns, terminating below the ceiling, served as decorative pillars for lighting fixtures. The back wall of the hall was taken up by a row of simple boxes with a private gangway behind for the use of the family, royalty, and those "high-ranking personalities" Governess Weinert generally distinguished as *"die vornehme Welt in Wahrheit und Dichtung."* The canvas ceiling, painted to represent an awning laced against the cornice, patches of sky showing through, evoked that Zurich plan of decades before to present the *Ring* in a kind of open-air festival in the manner of the ancients. The Corinithian order was to have been the motive unifying the modest decoration of the building, but in the end much was sacrificed to a tightening budget. Originally, the proscenium piers were to have been

---

[15] The past tense is appropriate for this description of the Festspielhaus. Today much of the carefully calculated perspective effect is obliterated by the gray-black paint shrouding the entire proscenium area.

enriched with Corinthian elements, and a gallery of related columns had been planned for the main exterior façade.

In July, tests of the scenery and machinery also started. Here Brandt and his son were pillars of strength, for behind the father lay the experience of the Munich half *Ring*. Working with them was the ballet master Richard Fricke, whose choreography Wagner had so admired during a performance of Gluck's *Orfeo* at Dessau in December, 1872, that he summoned him to Bayreuth to work out the swimming movements in the Rhine scenes as well as the grouping of vassals in *The Twilight of the Gods*. Fricke's advice was put to use throughout the production. In addition, the poor fellow was to find himself conscripted as dancing master and tutor in etiquette to Cosima's children. Every morning before their reading lesson he drilled them in the *Kaiserschritt* and the *Promenadenschritt* and taught the art of bowing "with an amiable smile," accompanying these ludicrous exercises himself on the violin. Such was life at Wahnfried.

Clashes of temperament made the summer something less than the ideal period of devoted study Wagner had hoped for. Cosima's growing haughtiness and sense of self-importance rubbed artists the wrong way. Her second marriage had not undone her reputation as a lady of easy virtue, and as a reaction she was wrapping herself ever more thickly in the mantle of the *grande dame* and moral censor. But she was not yet old enough to carry off the part.

The tenor Niemann, like Betz and Lilli and Marie Lehmann, had refused to consider an honorarium for his services; nonetheless, Cosima treated him condescendingly, and he had to rebuke her severely for criticizing his behavior at a Wahnfried garden party. He was in a wretched state after a rehearsal at which he had behaved rather boorishly. Evidently Wagner's Erda, Frau Jaïde, attempted to raise his spirits. That she good-humoredly offered him some cold cuts from her own plate so appalled Cosima that she dispatched Schnappauf with a message summoning the lady for a lecture. Madame Jaïde stalked out, and Niemann exploded. The vulnerable Cosima's foolish meddling almost cost Wagner his Siegmund and an artist who sang not only Erda but also Waltraute and whom Wagner described to Carl Brandt as "the biggest artistic talent and most sensible artist in our ensemble." Moreover, Niemann was his main hope should Unger falter as Siegfried. The incident so upset Betz, who had stood by Wagner throughout the *Rhinegold* affair in Munich, that he threatened to resign the role of Wotan and quit Bayreuth. It took weeks to restore calm.[16]

[16] This is how Cosima's biographer, Moulin-Eckart, covered the affair: "When Niemann returned the part of Siegmund, after behaving in a perfectly foolish way, this was only one of the many everyday incidents that no director and nobody familiar with theatrical affairs would take seriously, nor did they do so at Bayreuth."

Cosima could not grasp the necessity for serious artists to relieve their stretched nerves by cutting up. Wagner's score imposed upon them tasks of unheard-of difficulty. They had to struggle to achieve what today is a matter of routine. Wagner wove his magic spell, patiently coaxing and gradually unchaining within them powers whose existence they had never suspected. After exhausting rehearsals they sought release in a kind of capering utterly alien to Cosima, who expected all concerned with the eternal art-work to imitate her show of permanent exaltation.

But despite her noble example, Gunther and Fasolt wrapped themselves in the linen of the Hotel Sonne and executed savage war dances in the streets, and the time was coming when the twenty-year-old Felix Mottl would be frequently observed shopping for sweets dressed in Madame Materna's gown, hat, and veil. And scandal erupted when the "Chancery" boys were discovered experimenting with hashish. In 1875 and 1876 the town was turned upside down by the antics of the inhabitants of the cardboard Walhall on the hill, and, like Cosima, the natives had little sympathy for what they observed.

Wagner, of course, understood. To show appreciation for a thoroughly mad evening of pranks by his artists, he stood on his head, and this, in Lilli Lehmann's significant words, "in spite of Cosima's presence." During the festival year Wagner was to make her apologize to the performers for slighting them at her Wahnfried social evenings, which, to his pain, they had learned to avoid. Cosima was only in her element when holding court, flattering aristocrats, and condescending to others. But she could not establish her tyranny over Bayreuth artists until after Wagner's death.

Autumn of 1875 found him in the Austrian capital superintending productions of an uncut *Lohengrin* and a *Tannhäuser* in the Paris version. Old Tichatschek was a special guest in his box at the Vienna première of the latter on November 22. Three and a half years before, during a concert in this city for the Bayreuth building fund (May 12, 1872), Wagner had given the first performance of a new introduction to *Tannhäuser* in which the original Dresden overture dissolved into the Paris Venusberg music (at the Paris performances the old overture had come to its full close, the new Venus scene then following) and had awakened a public appetite for the reworked score. At the 1875 production this composite was first used as part of a staged performance. Wagner had no desire to devote himself to such revivals. But he was under obligation to Vienna for the services of Madame Materna and felt it diplomatic to propitiate a management that had the power to wreck the Bayreuth *Ring* by canceling her summer leave.

In the metropolis he had the opportunity, increasingly rare for him, to hear important contemporary works. But by this time he was almost completely uninterested in the compositions of others (Liszt and Bruckner were exceptions) and probably attended in the hope of chancing upon a voice possibly of use at Bayreuth. Cosima's correspondence repeated his pronouncements on what he heard: Bizet's *Carmen* was reported to be repellent but not without signs of talent; but to find an adequate description of Verdi, whose Requiem Richter conducted on November 2, the reader was referred to Spontini's term for Italian musicians—*"cochons"* ("swine"). [17] In an open letter to Friedrich Schön (1882) Wagner was to declare sarcastically, "I am no musician and realize it immediately when anyone brings me a famous composition of one or another of our celebrated music masters of the day and I just simply cannot perceive any music in it. Obviously, it is a question of an infirmity which burdens me and makes me unfit to participate in our musical progress." Sounding much like Rossini's Doctor Bartolo, he complained to Cosima that young composers no longer knew how to write melodies.

He bestrode Vienna like a conquering kaiser even though the capital was not of one opinion concerning him and his works. The press was generally hostile, but what Cosima called "a somewhat Semitic public" thundered its appreciation. Talk of Wagner filled the streets and coffee houses, and he made a convert of a lad who was to be one of the few of the coming generation of composers capable of turning the Wagnerian musical heritage to significant account.

From his habitual spot in the Court Opera's fourth gallery, fifteen-year-old Hugo Wolf listened to *Tannhäuser*. Fired by enthusiasm, he shouted himself hoarse and would not rest until he had met Wagner. He loitered in the streets, at the stage door, and in the lobby of the Imperial Hotel, hoping to catch a glimpse and perhaps the eye of his idol. Through the connivance of the Wagners' servants, whom he managed to contact, one day Hugo was smuggled into Wagner's magnificent suite in the Imperial and found himself in the presence of the master, who was attired in one of his fantastic velvet and fur creations. The boy managed to request an opinion of some of his compositions, which he clutched. Wagner treated him charmingly, though he declined to look at the music. He wished his visitor much joy in his career, urging him to diligent work. It was an encounter showing Wagner at his best—light, full of humor, and generous to the young interloper. Wolf has left his impression of the overbearing, arrogant Cosima. She was not amused.

The Bavarian king could not have been happy to learn of Wagner's operatic activities in Vienna. After all, he had declined to do anything in Munich on the ground that he would never again traffic with the com-

[17] Spontini was so quoted in Wagner's article on the composer; the reference was clear.

mercial repertory theater, having only recently refused an invitation extended through *Kapellmeister* Hermann Levi to conduct a *Tristan* at Munich. What, then, was he doing in Austria? True, conducting was now almost beyond his powers. (At Bayreuth his failing memory, especially of his texts, forced him during rehearsals to keep a "Chancery" boy at his side as prompter.) Nonetheless, his physical presence and suggestions worked wonders on musicians. But the theater on the Max Joseph Platz no longer existed for the composer, who hastened to the new house on the Ringstrasse, although he was as dependent upon Munich's money as upon Vienna's personnel. Wagner, having learned to have absolute confidence in Ludwig, treated him as the world usually treats the considerate.

Wagner returned to Bayreuth for Christmas. Early in the festival year of 1876 he earned a five-thousand-dollar fee from the United States by composing on order a special march to be played at the celebration of the first hundred years of the nation's independence, the Philadelphia Centennial. As he worked on this potboiler, musical ideas for the second act of *Parsifal* kept obtruding themselves. He quipped that his Flower Maidens apparently wanted to be American. Early in March he was back in Vienna, taxing his strength to conduct a performance of *Lohengrin* for the benefit of the Opera's chorus,[18] which, along with its orchestra, he judged incomparable. The next evening the grateful musicians crowded the railway station to sing in tribute the great chorus in praise of Luther and the Reformation from *Meistersinger* as Wagner departed for Berlin much like a monarch. He had become an institution. Indeed, when he entered a public place, people rose and shouted *"Hoch!"* His greatness was undeniable; even those who loathed him as a person admitted as much.

In the Prussian capital he oversaw the city's first production of *Tristan,* which took place on March 20 with Karl Eckert conducting. At the suggestion of Wagner's old enemy, Director von Hülsen, the net proceeds of the première, some fourteen thousand marks, were contributed to the festival fund by the Kaiser, whose seventy-ninth birthday the performance had celebrated, though two days early. In Berlin Wagner not only finished his march for Philadelphia but also evidently attended to problems pertaining to a lawsuit instituted by Adolf Fürstner, who had followed Meser and Müller as publisher of the Wagner operas first printed in Dresden some three decades before. From his earliest days, whatever Wagner touched sprouted difficulties that never ceased multiplying.

[18] Ernest Newman was in error when he described Wagner's Vienna *Lohengrin* as "the solitary occasion in his whole life when he conducted this work of his." At the close of his Biebrich period, he had led an uncut *Lohengrin* in Frankfort on September 12, 1862 (see page 214).

During the spring of 1876 final rehearsals for the *Ring* started in Bayreuth, and care and labor attended them until the last moment. There had been changes in cast. Therese Vogl, the Sieglinde, quite in character had found herself pregnant and had been forced to step aside, while the Hagen, Emil Scaria, true to the Nibelung heritage, had demanded a special fee. Wagner bowed gracefully to the superior force of love, but not to blackmail. Scaria withdrew, taking with him the First Norn. New artists were being tutored, Johanna Wagner assuming the contralto Norn as well as the part of Schwertleite, which she had already undertaken.

Madame Scheffzky, to whom the role of Sieglinde fell, has a more secure place in the annals of royal anecdote than in musical history. Wagner hired her *faute de mieux*. She was a member of the Munich Opera, and her powerful voice evidently pleased King Ludwig, for she sang for him privately. Intrigued by the handsome young man, she joined the ranks of those ladies determined to draw some romantic response from him. While singing Elsa's "dream" in Ludwig's swan boat, which floated on the shallow artificial lake in his Venusberg grotto at Linderhof, she was inspired to fall into the water and call to him for help. With his elegant forefinger he summoned a valet, calmly asking him to fetch and dry the lady. As far as Ludwig was concerned her disadvantages were twofold—she was female and quite homely. Whether because of the latter failing or vocal deficiencies or both, at Bayreuth she earned a secure place on Wagner's list of artists not to be re-engaged.

Anxieties mounted. Wagner's stage directions would vary from day to day. Although he frequently indicated to his artists that a problem might be approached in various ways, obviously, at times, he himself was uncertain and floundering. Tempers grew shorter. The complicated mechanisms did not always function, and, in fact, at the opening *Rhinegold* a mishap caused the very first transformation to fail, the river bed resolutely refusing to yield place to Walhall. Except for a dazzling electric light that played upon figures during the numerous night scenes and the installation of steam machines to emit tinted vapors, the Bayreuth stage, despite publicity, was in no way unusual for its time. The miracle was that the Brandts and Fricke were able to accomplish anything at all in the midst of the Franconian woods. Problems that might have been resolved simply in a large city remained unanswered in a town without resources. A musician with a damaged instrument could not find a craftsman to repair it.

Tantalizingly, the papier-mâché mechanical dragon ordered from London [19] was arriving one section at a time. His anatomy was never com-

---

[19] London was famous for its theatrical machinery. When Verdi had doubts about how to manage the appearance of Banquo's ghost in *Macbeth*, he sent inquiries to London.

pletely assembled. The neck went astray, and there was no shop adequate to contrive a reasonable substitute. It was a foolishly comic Fafner, his head resting upon his shoulders, that Herr Unger slew at the première of *Siegfried*. Evidently the dragon came whiffling and burbling, the hero's blade went snicker-snack, and the audience, alas, giggled, as it is still wont to do today. Hanslick said, "Wagner has composed the scene in deadly earnest, but the effect is comical," and Nietzsche soberly remarked that the dragon lost much when visualized!

The highly artistic Fricke was distressed by the puerilities of Wagner's stagecraft in this scene and suffered to observe the lofty drama and music of the score often accompanied by theater effects not far from those of a provincial children's pantomime. Even Hanslick would be benevolent enough quickly to pass over both the ludicrous pair of mechanical rams that wheeled out the queen of the gods for her superb confrontation with Wotan and also noble Grane, an "aging nag . . . led by the bridle and held fast by a cord beneath the stage." A glance at Haus Wahnfried gave the measure of Wagner's eye for beauty, and from the beginning of rehearsals the cast and staff came to know his limitations. From the man who set his wife and son in allegorical garb over the lintel and chiseled pompous enigmas concerning his destiny on the façade, little could be expected. Lilli Lehmann indicated that the front of Wahnfried offered artists and townsfolk a perennial source of amusement.

Moreover, Wagner lacked knowledge as well as taste in the area of scenic design. From the time of the Munich *Rhinegold*, it had been clear that the absent composer sulking in Switzerland had little idea how his fantastic visions were to be disclosed in an opera house. His uncertainties had led him to contact the famous theater machinists and designers, Mühldorfer of Mannheim and Gropius of Berlin, to ask whether the stage directions of the *Ring* poem were practicable. Their affirmative answer had evidently encouraged him to demand the impossible. He wished every detail realized on painted canvas or with props and stubbornly resisted any attempt to simplify. When Fricke suggested that the Norns do without heavy ropes and instead express their task through gesture alone, Wagner cried, "No, never with gestures," although at times circumstances forced him ruefully to such concessions. Conferences on décor could end with him in tantrums or with his sullen withdrawal.

Fricke especially despaired of the botched spectacle representing the collapsing Gibichung hall and the cataclysm of the finale. Here was the ultimate operatic extravaganza, combining the doomed Asgard of the Edda with the burning Capitol of *Rienzi*, the exploding Münster castle in *Prophète*, and the crashing palace and rising floods of Lortzing's *Undine*. It was meant to "out-Meyerbeer" Meyerbeer, but the effect on the Bayreuth stage was rather mean. Fricke foresaw the criticism this failure would awaken. Even Cosima was depressed by "archeological trivialities . . . to the detriment of the tragic and mysterious," the Fenimore Cooper Gibichungs especially shocking her. (Ironically, she and Wagner had been the first to hamstring Döpler by raising absurd "archeological" questions.) Hanslick, who was to compare the crudely painted and stitched canvas waves of the mighty Rhine to "the Red Sea in a provincial production of Rossini's *Moses"*—by this time he knew just where to hit Wagner the hardest—was justifiably to ask whether performances unable to fulfill the requirements of the libretto should be labeled model productions. The wall of magic fire, brilliantly successful at the 1870 production, was, according to the sympathetic Angelo Neumann, utterly unconvincing at Bayreuth. Scenically, *Rhinegold* and *Valkyrie* had fared much better at Munich, and obviously the rest of the *Ring* would also have benefited from the conveniences of a great court theater. By the time of the première the Brandts were reduced to distemper, the good Fricke to despair.

15

Outwardly the festival (August 13–30) was a success. Kaiser Wilhelm had attended the opening *Rhinegold* and *Valkyrie,* and Ludwig, though increasingly misanthropic, was so entranced by the relatively private final dress rehearsals that with "a burning desire . . . once again to plunge into exalted fervor" he returned to brave the crowd at the third and last cycle. With the final curtain Wagner hailed him as having shared in the *Ring's* creation, the most welcome compliment to Ludwig, who had always looked upon himself as a partner in the "eternal work." Other German princes suddenly realized that they had let slip an opportunity of adding to their fame. The Grand Duke of Weimar was to lament his failure to follow Liszt's advice to make of Weimar what Bayreuth had become.

But the presence and opinions of royalty seemed insignificant in the new atmosphere. Few knew to what an extent the Festspielhaus was a creation of Ludwig's generosity. That a composer, seemingly by his own efforts, had succeeded in erecting and operating a private opera house solely for performances of his own works seemed a miracle, and enthusiasts felt part of a unique moment in cultural history. One of the festival guests, Peter Ilich Tchaikovsky, watching Wagner pass in his sumptuous carriage rolling directly behind the Kaiser's, wrote, "What pride, what overflowing emotions must have welled up at this moment in the heart of that little man who, by his powerful determination and great talent, has defied all obstacles to the final realization of his artistic ideals and audacious beliefs!" If Tchaikovsky's reports on the *Ring* praised Wagner's industry and symphonic technique more than his operatic achievement, the King in a letter to Wagner from Hohenschwangau, written three days after the dress rehearsals, sounded what was to be the characteristic tone of the coming decades of Wagnerism. He declared the composer to be god and man and infallible. Pope Pius IX had an equal in matters aesthetic, who soon, by means of his final work, would attempt to occupy the *cathedra* itself, there to legislate faith and morals.

Though many fell by the wayside, the staunchest disciples endured with stamina comfortless lodgings, an infamous cuisine, and other staggering inconveniences. Transportation was inadequate, and many were exhausted by the long ascending walk to the distant theater, whose barren approaches were unfinished. Tchaikovsky wrote, "At three o'clock we took our way to the theater, which is on a hill some distance from the village. Even for those who have managed to find strength in a good meal, that is the hardest part of the day. The way is uphill with absolutely no shade, so that one is directly in the scorching rays of the sun. Waiting for the performance to begin, the miscellaneous crowd camps on the grass near the theater. Some dawdle over a glass of beer in the restaurant. . . . On every side one hears complaints of hunger and thirst mingled with comments on current or past performances." He observed that "throughout the whole length of the festival, food formed the chief interest of the public. The artistic performances took second place. Chops, baked potatoes, and omelets were discussed much more eagerly than the music of Wagner." Though delightful breezes from the Fichtelgebirge accompanied the guests' descent after dark into the town, the way was hardly lit. Nor was the building without its hazards. The gas fittings in the auditorium, only completed on the day of the *Rhinegold* première, were not yet functioning properly. Repeatedly and inopportunely the house was plunged into darkness. And water had not yet been properly piped to the hill.

Imperfections notwithstanding, the greatness of the cycle made itself felt. But rows of empty seats bore sad witness to the dissuasion worked by an unfriendly press and high prices. The first cycle was sold out, but many tickets remained for the rest of the festival. The opening *Ring,* with its unsteadiness and stage accidents, was treated severely by the critics, and no rush to Bayreuth developed. (Wagner was furious that little public notice was taken of the improvement in later performances.) For months newspapers had magnified every difficulty and predicted calamity. Moreover, both Lilli Lehmann and Nietzsche recorded their astonishment at the specially raised tariffs greeting the visitor. As Nietzsche's sister had observed, the townsfolk showed interest only in the externals of Wagner's art! Their brisk business in the sale of complimentary passes hardly benefited the box office. No idealism had led the city fathers to grant the composer a terrain. The Folk for whose redemption the *Ring* had been called into being evidently had to be rich, a situation so vexing Wagner that before his death he called into being a fund to enable a certain number of students and enthusiasts of modest means to attend future festivals.

Musically, the performances must have offered superb moments. The orchestra was made up of Germany's finest instrumentalists, with Wilhelmj as concertmaster. Had Wagner not feared the strain on his heart, he would certainly have taken the baton. He often thought of Bülow, who himself regretted an absence enforced by pride. If the composer was unhappy with what he held to be Richter's inflexible beat, he was perhaps unfairly measuring his protégé against a genius' inner vision. Susanne Weinert, who had sat near Wagner at the Vienna *Lohengrin* of December, 1875, reported his distress at Richter's tempi. "Sometimes he wanted to have the tempo slowed up, but sometimes he murmured, 'Miserable dragging—hurry it up!' " During the *Ring* the King observed his restlessness. Without Wagner behind him tapping and singing, Richter evidently lapsed into a detailed, four-square approach reflecting his own stolid temperament.[20] And Cosima's comments had for some time attempted to whittle away Wagner's confidence in him. She found it hard to forgive his having married without consulting them and his being, like her father, Hungarian. Not even the gesture of baptizing his daughter "Richardis Cosima Eva" had succeeded in allaying her hostility.

That Wagner was truly ecstatic over most of his singers—especially Materna, Niemann, Betz,[21] Jaïde, Hill (Alberich), Siehr (Hagen), and the Lehmann sisters (Woglinde and Wellgunde)—was praise beyond praise. Unhappily, at the end Wagner had had to instruct Unger to sing Siegfried

---

[20] Seidl eventually emerged as the conductor for whom Wagner showed something close to the respect he reserved for Bülow. The composer wrote to Angelo Neumann of Seidl, "No one of all the conductors understands so well my tempi and the union of the music with the action." With Seidl in the pit during New York's great seasons of German opera in the eighteen-eighties and eighteen-nineties (such artists as Lehmann, Niemann, Vogl, Reichmann, Materna, and Marianne Brandt were in the company), the Metropolitan Opera could boast a Wagner tradition more authentic than that of Cosima's days at the Festspielhaus. Seidl died in 1898, and his funeral service was held at the Metropolitan.

[21] Wagner admired Betz's artistry. But he really wanted a "black" bass sound for Wotan, and Betz was a baritone. (Don Carlos in *Ernani* had first brought him his fame.) Yet the compromise species of high bass often fails during Wotan's long stretches over the staff, and, in general, baritones have handled the too wide-ranging part more successfully, weak low notes being less disturbing than cracking high ones. There are clear indications that the role would have been rewritten for the normal bass compass had Wagner lived to mount the *Ring* a second time.

with full voice throughout. A tolerable *mezza voce* eluded his sincerest efforts. His scene beneath the linden tree must have been a trial.

The novelty of the musical style, with its extended passages of arioso and the unrelenting length of some episodes, extinguished the glow in not a few zealots (the middle act of *Valkyrie* seems to have undone many). And the visual side of the performances disillusioned and even excited ribaldry among the less reverent. Ludwig was appalled by the Brückners' realization of Hoffmann's sketches. Except for *Rhinegold,* he thought it a terrible botch, especially the forest scene in *Siegfried,* though it took him almost five years to gather the courage to tell Wagner of his disappointment. Something must have gone terribly wrong. Hanslick thought the scenery well painted, blaming the general disenchantment on poor lighting. Whatever the cause, the beauty of Hoffmann's sketches was hardly realized on stage. Elizabeth Nietzsche summed up the atmosphere of the festival as "tragicomical," a description also applicable to the décor. Many for whom *Opera and Drama* was a Bible suffered chagrin. The mystic equation for the *Gesamtkunstwerk* fell from even a pretense of equilibrium in the domain of stage decoration. Had the graphic and plastic arts to renounce their independent lives to achieve fulfillment in the Brückner brothers of Coburg? Fortunately, the impressionists were continuing work, unaware of Wagnerian theory proclaiming that painting and sculpture had perfected themselves only to enter the service of the scenic designer. Wagner had once literally put his hand on the problem when he advised Nietzsche to take off his glasses and listen to the orchestra if he would gain the most from *Tristan.* When Cosima staged the next *Ring* at Bayreuth twenty years later, she claimed fidelity to the 1876 production, while at the same time departing drastically from its example. Faithful to her husband's memory in word, she attempted to go beyond him in deed. That she failed [22] reflected upon her abilities, not her motives. The most fanatic of Wagnerites recognized that the first *Ring* had been, on the whole, a visual fiasco.

A few scenes, however, did come off well, especially those of the Rhine with the gamboling maidens and also the settings in which, in addition to the pulsating gas illumination, colored steam and electric light created theatrically thrilling effects.[28] Moreover, following the example of Riga and,

[22] Lilli Lehmann decried the muddle Cosima made of the 1896 *Ring,* whose scenic aspects offended even the pontiff of French Wagnerism, Edouard Dujardin.

[28] Electricity in the form of the carbon arc lamp had been used to represent the rising sun in the production of Meyerbeer's *Prophète* at the Paris Opéra. Not only had Wagner attended the Opéra's *Prophète,* but he had also observed the magic King Ludwig's technicians could achieve through electric light at royal illuminations and pageants. (Probably these spectacles were at the bottom of popular tales about his arranging for artificial moonlight when he roamed his domains at night.) As a

more notably, of London, where since about 1856 theaters had begun to extinguish their house lights when the curtain rose—a procedure strengthened by Sir Henry Irving—Wagner kept the auditorium completely dark during performances. As a result the stage presented a series of dramatically lighted pictures framed by the double proscenium. Nor did the prompter's activities take away from the spectacle; the disturbing silhouette of his box had vanished along with the orchestra, his work being done behind the scenes. What one saw and heard seemed guided by invisible, magic hands. And not only did the curtain rise vertically, but could also part in the center to sweep up diagonally in graceful folds.

The festival left Wagner completely dispirited. But he believed better performances of the *Ring* would take place during following summers, when, he hoped, his artists might be properly compensated for engagements sacrificed in the interest of the Bayreuth adventure. Before Munich took up its rights to the complete *Ring*, he wished to improve and polish the "model" representation.

He also had in mind the eventual mounting at Bayreuth of all his other operas from *Dutchman* on. Ludwig especially longed for *Tristan*, the work of Wagner's that was still closest to him, "that poem and music of *Tristan* which agitates the innermost being, convulses to the point of annihilation, redeems and exalts!" And Ludwig hoped Madame Materna might include that birthday scribble of Brynhild's deleted text "only once" in a coming performance of the *Ring* finale. "Oh, promise me this, truly beloved friend!" The idea, so naïve, must have made Wagner smile. The boy had actually believed him! But they were both full of mutual hopes and plans; their relationship was moving to a more serene level, Ludwig's letters, in particular, becoming moving expressions of filial love. Those tensions, stratagems, and devices, bred of marks and gulden, were forgotten. The sight of Wagner after eight years must have disquieted Ludwig. The head was still high and the eyes flashed, but signs of wear were unmistakable. "You must yet live many, many years for the glory and as the highest pride of the German nation . . . above all, for your true friends, who love you deeply."

The poem and music of *Parsifal* were not yet begun on paper. Much remained to be done in the theater on the hill. But, when in mid-September

---

result of Edison's discovery of the incandescent lamp, three years after the first Bayreuth festival, the stage eventually had a more flexible and regular source of illumination. In its use the Opéra again pioneered (1880 and 1881), and within half a decade many of the world's great theaters, following the lead of Paris, abandoned their gas systems. The mammoth apparatus purchased for the Festspielhaus by King Ludwig's generosity was thus unfortunately outdated within a few years of its installation.

the exhausted composer set out with his family to convalesce in the Italian sun, he was not yet fully aware that the calamitous financial condition of the festival precluded its continuance.

The news soon traveled over the Alps. Bankruptcy threatened; the deficit approached one hundred and fifty thousand marks. Help from the King seemed unlikely, his own exchequer being embarrassed by Bayreuth's failure to repay its loans. After visiting Verona, Venice, Bologna, Naples, Sorrento, Rome (which he disliked), and Florence, Wagner was back in Wahnfried at the end of the year to wrestle with money problems that had cast a disturbing shadow over his journey. During it he had had two meetings of great symbolic importance: In Rome he met Gobineau,[24] who was his brief future; at Sorrento he bade farewell to Nietzsche, the best of his past.

16

Just when Nietzsche's reservations about Wagner and his works began to form is difficult to determine. But in all likelihood doubts were already growing by the time of the move to Bayreuth. The golden atmosphere of Triebschen had awakened cheerfulness and confidence; in gloomy, gray Bayreuth the dream was broken. (Countess von Schleinitz, Cosima's closest friend, was to call Bayreuth "the grave of friendships.") Wagner, playing his role of father substitute too realistically, took offense at his disciple's unwillingness to run to him whenever summoned. But even during Triebschen days Nietzsche had ever more frequently excused himself from calling. Like Liszt, Cornelius, and King Ludwig before him, he, too, began to feel an imperative need to preserve his freedom in the face of Wagner's arrogations. (Cornelius had once written, "Wagner consumes me. . . . He burns and leaves me no air to breathe.") An avoidance of too frequent personal contact with him was becoming what Nietzsche called a "sanitary" necessity. And the composer's vulgar jokes and tantrums shocked this clergyman's son from whom Wagner wisely hid *A Capitulation.*

Early in April, 1873, Nietzsche and Rohde came to Bayreuth for Easter and visited the house on the Dammallee. Wagner was disappointed to learn that Nietzsche's newest philosophic study did not concern itself with him. It was the young scholar's duty, he felt, to devote his energy to the Bayreuth undertaking, which was in serious difficulties.

[24] Wagner and Gobineau had an admirer in common, Emperor Dom Pedro of Brazil (see page 177). A French diplomat, the Count had been minister at Rio. Traveling in Europe with the Emperor in 1876, he stopped at Rome in November on his way back to France.

Nietzsche was among those woeful delegates meeting in Bayreuth in October of 1873 to survey what seemed a doomed enterprise. His public appeal asking the nation to support the festival was not used by its committee only because his petulant tone appeared unlikely to win new donors. Yet, despite an outward espousal of the cause, he was coming to see it as typifying the very materialism Wagner castigated in theory. From the point of view of the Bayreuth committee, the building of Wahnfried with funds originally destined for the theater was a strategic blunder discouraging the sale of certificates. It appeared that financial sacrifices were expected of everyone except the composer, and descriptions of the villa, opulent as it was, were, of course, exaggerated in newspaper reports. Even Ludwig was disturbed by what he heard. Although Wagner had his permission to divert the funds, the maneuver led to fantastic stories and rumors.

There was, moreover, an unmistakable odor of Philistinism about Bayreuth's certificates, clubs, jingoism, and anti-Semitism, and the new *reichsdeutsch* Wagner was difficult to stomach. Suddenly he appeared to epitomize the era. "He knows what our age likes . . . idealizes our age, and thinks much too highly of it," observed Nietzsche, who was fretted by gnawing doubts about the *Gesamtkunstwerk*. An early awareness of the fundamental oneness of the Wagnerian drama and grand opera was ripening into certainty. He came to see Wagner's work as a stupendous effort to assert and dominate, bringing together anything and everything—the neurotic, the ecstatic, the magnificent, the clamorous, all thrown pell-mell within the prodigious frame of grand opera—an art so determined to convince at any cost that all means, coarse and refined, were used to create effects. "Alarming tendencies," Nietzsche remarked.

Such judgments were perhaps too severe. But with the new Bayreuth era he was obviously viewing the Wagnerian world with different eyes. "There is something comical about the whole situation. Wagner cannot persuade the Germans to take the theater seriously. They remain cold and unresponsive —he becomes impassioned, as if the whole salvation of Germany depended upon this one thing." Essentially, Nietzsche was psychologically out of tune with Wagner, who entered through the nerves, while the path to the maturing philosopher was by way of the mind. For Nietzsche, the will had to be strengthened, not annihilated. He was preparing to take leave of Schopenhauer, a tendency already implicit in *The Birth of Tragedy,* where the conciliation of Apollo with Dionysius had been imposed by Apollo—the positive conquering the negative, the builder subduing the destroyer. But for Wagner of the *Parsifal* era, "suicide was the supreme assertion of the will." Schopenhauer, the prince of denial who had originally drawn the friends together in Leipzig, was to become one of the forces pulling them apart.

Tensions were felt early in 1874, when *Of the Use and Disadvantage of History for Life,* the second of Nietzsche's *Untimely Meditations,* reached Bayreuth. Piqued because it was not concerned with Wagnerian matters, French-Hungarian Cosima, born in Italy and educated in France, took it upon herself to offer one of the supreme masters of the language suggestions for improving his German! (During a coming visit to Vienna she was to lecture Semper on architecture!) Although Nietzsche smiled at the presumption of a woman whose speech and writing were adequate for a foreigner and no more, he did once permit himself the heresy of suggesting that her eagerness to improve literary style might be more efficaciously directed toward her husband's well-known transgressions in this area.[25] The Triebschen days were indeed past, and more and more Wagner must have feared that Nietzsche was slipping away.

In the course of 1874 the pair came close to an open break. Nietzsche, who had heard Brahms's *Song of Triumph* in the minster at Basel, took a copy of the score to Bayreuth and left it on Wagner's piano when he visited in August. Wagner reacted like a bull to a red cloth, later confessing to Elizabeth that he had surmised that her brother was saying symbolically, "See here! Here is someone else who can also compose something worth while!" The suspicion was well founded. Wagner admitted, "I let go of myself, and how I did rage!" Nietzsche, who didn't say a word, stared "with a look of astonished dignity." He was probing, testing, and discovering the full extent of Wagner's tyranny. Walter Kaufmann has remarked that Wagner afforded Nietzsche a singular and firsthand opportunity to study the will to power.

Nietzsche was well aware of the origin of those headaches thwarting his departure for the Bayreuth rehearsals of 1875. He wrote, "there is something so undignified about sicknesses of all sorts, as they cannot even be regarded as accidents." To Rohde he was pleased to observe that, though not in Bayreuth, he was not despondent. "Has this any rhyme or reason? Do you understand it?" he asked, really knowing the answer; 1875 passed without his setting foot in Wahnfried.

[25] Ernest Newman missed the point of a remark about language dropped by Nietzsche in Bayreuth some months later. Claiming no longer to find pleasure in German, he expressed his intention to speak Latin, obviously a reference to Wahnfried's criticism of his latest book. Cosima set about repairing the damage in a letter sent to him after reading *Schopenhauer as Educator* (1874), the third of the *Meditations.* She wrote him, "when you affirm that you take no pleasure in the German language, you are magnanimously punished by the noble muse, who has endowed you with a gift of persuasion and impressiveness, to be attained through the medium of no other language. . . . Do you not see, dear friend, that this *is* German . . . *felt* as a German would feel it, *spoken* as a German would speak it?" Bayreuth did not want to lose him.

For the occasion of the festival Nietzsche composed a final compliment, really a farewell, to the master to whom he owed his greatest aesthetic experiences—the fourth of the *Untimely Meditations,* called *Richard Wagner in Bayreuth*. Sections of it betrayed the contradictory emotions at war within the author, who felt that his work "should not be spoken of among the living; it is for the shades." An era was closing. But Wagner did not hear the note of doubt and pronounced the book "simply tremendous!" and asked—how ironic it seems today—"Where did you learn so much about me?" Indeed, a warning sound had already been perceivable in the earliest of the *Meditations*—the book entitled *David Strauss, the Confessor and Writer,* issued in 1873—which Wagner, too, had enthusiastically commended.

It was perhaps with conflicting hopes of either confirming his skepticism or regaining a lost faith that Nietzsche had set out for the final festival rehearsals of 1876. (Early in the year he had written: "Alas, Bayreuth! I either dare not or cannot go there. . . .") But his health was wretched. Difficulties with his vision and migraines forced him to flee the Festspielhaus for Klingenbrunn, a tiny town in the Bohemian forest, an incident so oddly interpreted in Ernest Newman's *Life*.

Newman's brilliant detective work, inspired by the revelations of Hoppe and Schlechta, revealed Elizabeth Nietzsche as a shameless manipulator of facts who, like Cosima, did not scruple to misrepresent documents in order to maintain a myth. She concocted falsified versions of Nietzsche's letters in an effort to make the escape to Klingenbrunn appear solely the result of artistic disillusionment and not of illness. But Newman, engrossed in the ugly growths and parasitic creepers infecting the dense Wagner-Nietzsche forest, quite lost his way. Having exposed Elizabeth's knavery, he was determined to substantiate the very claim she had sought to bury and, in the face of evidence to the contrary, declared Nietzsche's departure to have been for "reasons purely and simply of health, not of a revolt . . . against Wagner's mind and work." Some pages after the above quotation, the jury having been harangued and swayed and the prisoner sent to the gallows, Newman completely reversed himself, declaring, "This is not to imply that his [Nietzsche's] sudden revolt against Bayreuth was the result purely and simply of his bodily malaise." Such a reading of his case, Newman declared, would be "superficial." One couldn't agree more, and this statement (as graphic a Freudian compulsion as one can find) really invalidates much of his chapter called "The Realities of the Matter." Newman's writing on Nietzsche is constructed of such contradictions.

Clearly, Nietzsche's headaches, eye trouble, and retching were not unrelated to the emotional crisis through which he was passing in respect to Bayreuth. Newman uncharitably described this wretched man's behavior as that of "a sick spoiled child" and "a skeleton at the feast." Nietzsche later wrote, "Sickness is always the answer when we are disposed to doubt our right to *our* task." Newman would probably dismiss this with his favorite disclaimer—*construction faite après coup,* but analysis most often comes after the event. According to Newman's main thesis, Nietzsche "left Bayreuth in a fit of pique—excusable to a great extent by the physical sufferings he was undergoing—fled to Klingenbrunn, there begun [*sic*] to self-justify his pettish flight by committing to his note-books resentful reflections on Wagner and his art, and then in after years, having realised that his behaviour in Bayreuth presented him in anything but a dignified light, had begun to weave a legend of his own about it all and to impose that legend on others. And to establish that legend he no more balked at unveracity than his sister did later."

What was pettish or undignified about a sufferer's eagerness to exchange crowds for solitude Newman does not reveal, unless his evidence is Schuré's highly debatable interpretation of the young man's melancholy air during rehearsals, performances, and Wahnfried receptions as jealousy of Wagner. Schuré thus described him at Bayreuth: *"L'œil fixe trahissait le travail douloureux de la pensée."* It was the same philosopher's glance before which Keats's Lamia melted. A heavy heart, not envy, made him uncommunicative. Is one really expected to believe that the iconoclastic work first sketched at Klingenbrunn was the result of headaches, pettishness, and a sense of embarrassment, and not ultimately of gnawing doubts about his erstwhile idol? Newman's case is simply untenable, and another of his amazing reversals demonstrates his inner rejection of it.

Concerning that summer visit to Wahnfried in 1874, Newman observes in Chapter XXI of the *Life,* "It seems clear, then, that Nietzsche had been brooding discontentedly over the subject of Wagner's 'tyrannical' nature and his dislike of Brahms for some time before he went to Bayreuth in August. . . . The Basel performance of the *Triumphlied* (under Brahms himself) took place . . . on the 9th June; and, as we now know, Nietzsche's note-books were packed by that time with memoranda that show how far he had diverged by now from Wagner." But in his crucial Chapter XXV these observations had to be ignored, for they destroyed his theory. There one reads, "Now nothing is more certain than that in 1875 Nietzsche was still heart and soul with Wagner in all essentials." Newman was incapable of willfully juggling facts, but apparently could willfully forget them. He had no love for Nietzsche and despised Elizabeth. Seemingly, this pair made the great man lose his objectivity and, with it, his memory.[26]

[26] At one point, Newman's fury against Elizabeth also made him lose plain common sense. He pounced upon her for describing the Basel performance of the *Song of*

This prejudice leads to some curious byways in the *Life*. To maintain that those rehearsals the ailing young man attended "could have given him only an imperfect idea of the totality of the *Ring* even had he been in a normal state of health at the time," Newman had immediately to forget his scrupulous listing of them—*Rhinegold, Valkyrie, The Twilight of the Gods* (one act a day and without costumes), and, possibly, *Siegfried!* Nietzsche, even with his indisposition, returned determinedly to the theater and, despite the starts, stops, and wrangling during the rehearsals, must have left for Klingenbrunn with a complete impression of the cycle. Though Newman struggled to stack the cards against Nietzsche, his integrity repeatedly prevented him from suppressing the very evidence damaging his claims.

His resentment of Nietzsche seems to rest upon the fact that this man of naïve and often dilettante musical tastes dared challenge a master in his own area. But Nietzsche's challenge was essentially ethical, not musical. Moreover, despite his genius, Wagner's opinions of contemporary composers— Brahms and Verdi, for example—seem no less foolish than those of Nietzsche, whose enthusiasm for Peter Gast and August Bungert Wagner equaled with his recommendation of Giovanni Sgambati as the only modern composer of genuine talent he had come across. And what is one to say of those lectures on history, politics, philosophy, aesthetics, and even philology that Wagner visited upon the young professor, or of the pretensions of the Wagnerian drama to philosophic significance?

The overriding fact is that at Klingenbrunn Nietzsche started sketches he was one day to develop into *Human, All too Human,* the first open skirmish in what was to become his holy war against Wagnerism. In the preface to his *Toward a Genealogy of Morals* (1887) he described the period 1876–1877 as one during which he gazed "over the broad and dangerous territory" his mind had up to that time roamed. The values that had sustained him for years were dissolving. Yet, though his heart had already taken farewell of Wagner, he returned to Bayreuth for the first cycle. He did not renounce love easily.

Once he had hoped to see Bayreuth almost in terms of his future Zarathustra, of "that *great noontide* when the chosen among the chosen dedicate themselves to the greatest of all tasks." He had had a vision of human dignity, but instead found himself surrounded by the kind of common German he loathed. Bayreuth, he had believed, would signify the "morning sacrament on the day of combat." There he had expected to find

---

Triumph as having taken place "in the spring," triumphantly revealing the date as the ninth of June. But, astronomically, summer begins with the solstice, and there is nothing in her statement to dispute.

kindred spirits expectantly awaiting a new consecration in an atmosphere like that of Berlioz's ideal city of music, Euphonia. Instead, he beheld an offensive crowd of wealthy first-nighters and the curious, smelling of tobacco and stale beer. The patrons en masse appeared self-important, terribly bored, and unmusical to boot—"culture Philistines." He observed with horror the frivolous rich who had found a new pretext for idling, a new sport, grand opera with obstacles, a welcome change from the Baden-Baden races. And there were the Wagnerites, the club members who in the pubs threatened violence to anyone daring to disagree. Talking of Wagner and Schopenhauer and singing *"Gaudeamus igitur, Wagneristes sumus,"* while raising high their pints of beer (*Schoppen*), they were quickly dubbed *"die Schoppenhauer"* by the natives. In *Ecce Homo* Nietzsche was to sum up all Wagnerites by crying, "My kingdom for one sensible word!" and went on to suggest, "Eventually, for the edification of posterity, one ought to have a genuine Bayreuthian stuffed, or, better yet, preserved in spirit—for spirit is exactly what is lacking—with this label: 'An example of the spirit on which the "Reich" was founded.' "

For Nietzsche, Bayreuth had turned out to be a "contemptible little German affair." Even the faithful Wagnerite Feustel described the audience as "by no means that receptive body for which Wagner had hoped." The few dedicated souls present were lost in a sea of vulgarity which washed even over Wahnfried, where Wagner, like some schismatic Pope, gave mass audiences and blessed these cultural vagrants who, for his own sanity, he had to pretend were pilgrims. The spectacle of the Wagnerites' triumph over Wagner unfolded before Nietzsche's eyes—"Wagner bedecked with German virtues."

The performances confirmed Nietzsche's doubts. And Wahnfried's paranoiac anti-Semitism frightened him. It became one of the major issues over which he broke with Bayreuth. He carried into his infinitely sad future the best of the great German heritage symbolized by Lessing. After his sister married a leader of the anti-Semitic movement, Bernhard Förster, Nietzsche wrote, "Your association with an anti-Semitic chief expresses a foreignness to *my* whole way of life which fills me ever again with ire or melancholy. . . . It is a matter of honor to me to be in relation to anti-Semitism absolutely clean and unequivocal, namely *opposed,* as I am in my writings."

Nietzsche's sister, not surprisingly, remained an intimate of the Wahnfried household after her brother's break with it and into the Nazi era. To Cosima, she had cried out at the beginning of the new century, "how wonderful that two women stand at the head of, and to a certain extent represent, the two intellectual tendencies ruling the modern world." Not the least tragic irony of Nietzsche's tragic life was the role of the unscrupulous Elizabeth as trustee and editor of his works. Under her aegis and following her example the Nazis embarked upon their monstrous perversion of his writings. In Nazi Germany Wagner's prose was printed with no changes while Nietzsche's had to be cut, trimmed, adjusted, and ripped from context,[27] Bäumler, moreover, advancing the convenient idea that the philosopher really didn't mean what he said. The Wagner-Nietzsche antithesis is symbolically impressive—two overwhelming geniuses, one representing the worst and the other the best of the German ethical tradition, the latter's final madness seeming somehow both ironic and ineluctable.

During the *Ring* performances Nietzsche felt as if he had come to his senses. He saw it all as "the death agony of the *last great art.*" There were tears in his eyes when he left. But, while journeying, he must have wondered how he had sustained a serious intellectual relationship with the man who had just announced his immediate project before poetizing *Parsifal*—"to reread universal history."

Nietzsche's health had seriously declined. Granted a leave from the university, he set out for Italy. At the cornerstone ceremony, Cosima had introduced him to Malwida von Meysenbug, an old friend of Wagner's, who arranged for his accommodations in Sorrento, where he arrived in October. He had been upset to learn that the Wagners, too, had chosen this town for a sojourn. But the friends met with great cordiality despite Wagner's antipathy toward Nietzsche's companion, the philosopher Paul Rée, a Jew. As yet Wagner had no idea that Nietzsche had parted from him intellectually and artistically. And to the end Nietzsche was grateful for the transfigured moments Wagner's music had given him. The festival was not mentioned. Each had his reasons for being melancholy and silent about it.

At the close of October they took their last walk together. In view of the bay and islands, admired since antiquity, Wagner suddenly began to speak of *Parsifal* in terms of his own religious experience, dumfounding to someone well aware of the depth of his atheism. Nietzsche already knew the drama; Cosima had read the prose scenario to him on Christmas Day of 1869 and recorded his "frightful impression" (*"furchtbarer Eindruck"*), a most ambiguous observation. At Sorrento, Nietzsche, who had long before recognized how large the actor bulked in Wagner, was nonetheless shocked to discover the extent of his theatrical need to play out his dramas in life. And if Wagner was performing his part so fervently before an old friend who remembered the sarcastic comments with which he put down Cosima's mawkish flights of religiosity, where then was the beginning and end of the

---

[27] A German postwar edition of selections from Wagner's prose carefully edits out his anti-Semitic observations. The technique once used to turn Nietzsche into a proto-Nazi now serves to make Wagner a humanist.

posing? What Princess Wittgenstein called the composer's "godless senti-ments" (*"gottlose Gesinnung"*) were known to all his acquaintances. And how insufferable this make-believe, pious Wagner seemed to a young man who admired intellectual integrity above all other qualities. A philosopher cannot act; there was nothing for him to say. "Why are you so silent, my friend?" asked Wagner. The two never met again.

By the end of 1877, they had become further estranged by an almost in-credible incident. In October Wagner took it upon himself to suggest to Nietzsche's doctor that the young man was essentially suffering the ef-fects of excessive masturbation and recommended a water cure! Nietzsche, upon hearing of this meddling, naturally became enraged. Westernhagen, who published the correspondence between Wagner and Dr. Otto Eiser of Frankfort, saw loving concern in Wagner's opening the subject; others might perceive a fearsome destructiveness. The letters go far to explain Nietzsche's later references to Wagner's "perfidy" and "murderous insult."

With his *Human, All too Human* (the first volume appeared in 1878), sketched at Klingenbrunn and given its main outlines at Sorrento, Nietzsche purged himself of everything alien to his new attitude. He called his work "a book for free spirits." Originally, he had hoped to send it out under a nom de plume. But, since his publisher demanded the prestige of the Nietzsche name, Wagner's was in turn suppressed throughout. The initi-ated would have no doubts that the inhabitants of Wahnfried were the target of many an aphorism, and open scandal might perhaps be avoided. It was Nietzsche's fantastic hope that the relationship might somehow survive. In *Ecce Homo* he described the book as "war, but war without powder or smoke, without warlike gestures, without pathos and contorted limbs. . . . One error after the other is calmly laid upon ice; the ideal is not refuted— *it freezes.*" After dispatching two copies to Bayreuth with a droll inscription in verse "to the *Meister* and the *Meisterin*" (*"ridendo dicere severum"* be-came the motto of his later *The Wagner Case*), he awaited news that Wagner would permit a friend to differ. But such was not Wahnfried's way. Apostasy would not be tolerated.

Late during the summer of 1878, Wagner, without mentioning Nietzsche's name, thrust at him and his book, in the third installment of the article "Public and Popularity," a brisk, modest sally, not meant to draw blood. But the wrathful Cosima let Elizabeth know just what she thought of her brother. It was quite clear to the Wahnfried circle that a disciple's defection evidenced mental derangement. And a more obvious explanation was at hand. Cosima wrote, "Many things went into the making of this miserable book! Last of all Jewry, in the person of one Dr. Rée." That a sympathetic Wagnerite like Schemann could be overwhelmed by the sheer beauty of Nietzsche's style was all the more exasperating to her because it was a weapon Wagner could not wield. She feared for the Faith. Wagner declared that the young Nietzsche had budded and bloomed, but now only the bulb was left—"a really disgusting object."

Nietzsche suffered. To turn his back on "Father" Wagner and "Mother" Cosima, whom he never ceased adoring, to disentangle himself from Wagnerism were acts not only of self-mastery but of self-denial. He continued to love what he had come to hate and see as a danger. In *Ecce Homo* he wrote of Wagner's music, "The world must be a poor place for one who has never been sick enough for this 'voluptuousness of Hell'!" And though Triebschen and Bayreuth had cost him almost a decade, yet, by knowing Wagner, he had touched the hand of genius, discovered that he was no less one, and found his way. He saw his relationship to Wagner as that of Shakespeare's Brutus to his Caesar, the greatness of the victim being answered by the greatness of his destroyer. Nietzsche, commenting on the marvelous way Wagner represented Wotan's relationship to Siegfried—"his love, the obligatory hostility, and the joy in pure destruction"—further added, "All of this is symbolical of Wagner's own nature." In *The Gay Science* (1882) he wrote, "Independence of the soul—that is the issue here! No sacrifice can then be too great. For it, one must be willing to sacrifice even one's dearest friend, be he the most glorious human being, ornament of the world, genius without equal."

Nietzsche wrote in the "Sanctus Januarius" of *The Gay Science,* "The law governing us *decrees* that we must live as strangers; by very reason of this, we shall become more sacred to one another!" In *Ecce Homo* he spoke of "the holy hour of Richard Wagner's death in Venice," and Lou von Salomé has given a truly touching picture of a visit with Nietzsche to Triebschen, his gentle voice recalling times past as his eyes filled with tears. Even in his late and heated anti-Wagnerian polemics one always senses awareness of Wagner's immensity. One wonders, however, whether Wagner ever really suspected how close he had been to the mind of the age.

XIV

Leitmotif and Wagner's Musical Architecture

I

The interval between *The Twilight of the Gods* and *Parsifal* provides a convenient space from which not only to survey certain aspects of Wagner's development as a composer with particular reference to the leitmotif—a device with which his name is inextricably linked—but also to consider what formal design techniques, if any, articulate his enormous musical structures. *The Twilight of the Gods* is Wagnerian architecture at its most ambitious, Wagnerian technical dexterity at its most dazzling. From here one looks backward upon an extraordinary musical development, which his aesthetic theorizing reluctantly but inevitably followed, and forward toward his final work, in which the symbolist tendencies growing since his middle years reached an ultimate expression.

Though Wagner's very first attempts at opera turned the leitmotif to account, he was hardly its inventor. Allusive references to chorale tunes enrich many Bach works, Gluck toyed with thematic recall, Grétry put the device to ambitious use in *Richard Coeur de Lion* (1784), and, soon after, Mozart provided the Commandant in *Don Giovanni* with music similar in chordal structure, mood, and color to accompany his two ghostly manifestations. The leitmotif as unifying element was exploited by Méhul (*Ariodant*, 1799) and, a generation later, most effectively by Löwe in those ballads for which Wagner admitted to Lilli Lehmann a special fondness. In E. T. A. Hoffmann's *Aurora* (1811-1812) and especially his *Undine* (ca. 1813-1815), an ingenious leitmotif technique may be observed. Weber wrote recurring music to symbolize the spell of the diabolic Samiel in *Freischütz* and employed thematic reminiscence in *Euryanthe,* as did Marschner in his operas. The fabric of Mendelssohn's *Elijah* is interlaced with returning phrases whose original textual associations are significantly recalled at later appearances. Schumann was a master of melodic reminiscence, as in the telling final moments of *Frauenliebe und -leben,* and Berlioz in his early cantata *The Death of Orpheus* (1827) composed a subject representing the Bacchantes, the germ of the flexible *idée fixe* of his maturity, later slowly elaborated by Wagner into the formidable musical system of the *Ring.*

Thus many composers admired and imitated by the young Wagner had experimented with leitmotif technique, and by the time of *Lohengrin* Schumann was also artfully binding together an opera, *Genoveva,* with a number of reminiscence themes. Even before *Lohengrin* and *Genoveva,* Verdi had used leitmotifs in *Ernani* and *I due Foscari,* and as early as 1836 Glinka had employed the device liberally in his *A Life for the Czar.* Moreover, Meyerbeer's recourse in *Huguenots* to a chorale as both identifying tag and musical bond must certainly have made a strong impression on Wagner, who in Triebschen days observed to Cosima that a Jew had made an opera out of a Lutheran hymn. Not only did romantics enjoy that mixture of the literary and musical which is the essence of the leitmotif, but also the reiterating of themes furthered their tendency toward homogeneity of structure, as opposed to classical musical architecture built upon principles of contrast.

Wagner's earliest operas show him contriving associative themes of such remarkable immediacy that they could be easily identified and recalled in respect to the person or idea musically depicted. It was his genius to arrive at a significant tonal *Gestalt* corresponding to his dramatic concept; often both occurred to him simultaneously.

After *Lohengrin,* when his poetic style adopted an Eddic laconism and his newly formulated synthesis announced the obliteration of boundaries between aria and recitative, his leitmotifs abandoned their former Berlioz-like length and lyricism. Becoming trenchant, they took the form of a harmonic complex, a rhythmic configuration, a melodic outline, or any combination of these. Unlike the earlier type of motif that he had inserted here and there into the musical texture as a kind of label, these new themes, succinct enough to make their descriptive points without interrupting the constant flow of changing poetic images, began to constitute the very tissue of his score. They could succeed one another quickly, could be combined, and were also fertile organisms capable of being transformed by rhythmic, harmonic, and instrumental alterations that either painted the shifting status of their conceptual correlatives in the drama or hinted at meanings beneath the surface of the words. *Lohengrin* reveals Wagner remodeling motivic material to fit the mood of a dramatic situation. In later works he brought this technique to heights of virtuosity, as when the flowing triple meter of young Siegfried's motif changes to a more staid duple time with strong offbeat stresses to picture the mature hero of *The Twilight of the Gods;* the melodic line remains basically unchanged, yet the metamorphosis is complete.

Rienzi has a most arresting early example of the leitmotif used to underline psychological complexities, although there is as yet no question of altering the motif for this purpose. After the unsuccessful attempt upon the tribune's life, he is warned by his enemy, Colonna, that his fall is nonetheless near. Rienzi is visibly shaken. His answer is sung to the contour of that sepulchral phrase that opens the overture—more correctly, it follows the line of the motif's second appearance (bars twelve, thirteen, and fourteen of the overture) with its tense, altered interval. Rienzi's reply is a question, "Gloomy reminder, what do you want of me?" the query being directed to Colonna, to himself, and—most fascinatingly—to the orchestra, which, beneath the vocal part, with its note values changed to accommodate the words, is sounding the motif in its original broad form.

In the middle act of *Meistersinger* there is an analogous moment when the orchestra, through motif, talks to a character on stage. Eva hears the poignant theme of Sachs's renunciation sounding through the notes of his outwardly gay shoemaker's song. Suddenly aware of her neighbor's love, pain, and sacrifice, she cries, "The song—I know not why—fills me with grief; . . . Oh best of men! That I should cause you distress!" And beneath this vocal line the orchestra again combines the themes.

This last example shows motifs being contrapuntally interlocked to create an intricate literary symbolism, conflicting forces being expressed through contrasting linear movement. Yet one must not overemphasize this aspect of the Wagnerian drama, which has been credited too long with a descriptive explicitness its creator longed for in theory, but which the musician in him happily precluded from complete realization.

2

Opera and Drama described motifs of reminiscence derived from the vocal line; when later reiterated by voice or instrument, they were to represent ideas germane to the words originally sung. But a musician whose most characteristic gifts were of harmonic and instrumental color could not limit the *Ring* to so confining a system. The very first motif in *Rhinegold* is not a vocal melody, nor does it even underlie the voice. It rises as an arpeggio in the orchestra while the stage curtain is down. Being without textual reference, it becomes a relatively vague musical-literary symbol associated throughout the tetralogy variously with primordial matter, Father Rhine, his witless daughters, nature in general, its mother goddess in particular, her children the Norns, and, by further extension, fate; inverted, it symbolizes the end of a cycle—the fall of the gods. But for this comprehensiveness, such a motif of purely orchestral origin pays with the clarity that only direct association with the word can yield.

The allusions attributed to the Rhine-Nature theme are nonetheless bound together by a sweeping and coherent poetic concept, the motif transforming itself as it takes on new implications. A source of wonder in Wagner is not only such subtle interrelationships linking apparently unconnected points in the text to manifestations of the same motif,[1] but also the manner in which motifs generally considered to be distinct and separate are, in fact, closely united by means of musical resemblances if they express diverse aspects of the same basic idea or emotion. Thus, for example, the onomatopoetic ditty of the Rhine Maidens (*Rhinegold,* Act I) is metamorphosed into the Wood Bird's song (*Siegfried,* Act II), Woglinde's ichthyoid "Weia" becoming an ornithoid "Hei"; these elemental creatures really share the same theme,[2] but with rhythmic differences to contrast movement in water and air. Motifs, moreover, may grow out of fragments and combinations of others, as, for example, when the music depicting the Norns' weaving is formed by twisting together the outlines of the Ring and Rhine-Nature motifs. And the listener's mind is crowded with associations all the richer for such an instrumental theme's breadth of reference.

Wagner certainly sensed that themes of orchestral origin upset his theory of deriving music from verse. Defensively and obscurely he explained their function as that of kindling presentiments or preparing for what was yet to materialize, of manifesting the instinctive desire of perception to take objective form. A clearer exposition would have undermined his theoretic insistence on literalism. But in practice, once such a musical presentiment had attached itself to dramatic concepts, however vague, it was thereafter often manipulated in precisely the manner of a reminiscence motif, its poetic ambiguities thus being compounded.

Indeed, Wagner's reminiscence themes were themselves not always rigorously applied. Frequently, the use of a reminiscence at a particular point in the drama may seem farfetched in respect to its original text. The listener is often forced to resolve apparent inconsistencies on the surface by seeking a symbolic plan beneath, and it is a tribute to the composer's genius that many orderly and reassuring patterns have been traced using elements from disciplines as varied as politics, economics, and psychology.

Wagner's marvelous orchestra also plays its part not only in transforming but also in forming the "word-born" reminiscence. Although a motif's first version may have the melody in the vocal line alone (Alberich's curse), the

---

[1] Concerning his use of motifs to paint similar situations in different works, see note 7 of Chapter IV and note 15 of Chapter VII (pages 80 and 166).

[2] It might be argued that Wagner simply wished to stress their artless nature by means of triadic themes. Yet the similarity of their material remains too great to be ignored. The bird tune first appears in the orchestra for the very special reason that until Siegfried tastes Fafner's blood, neither he (nor the audience) can decode the warbler's message.

orchestra may also double the voice during such a maiden appearance and simultaneously provide harmonic and instrumental color (the Ring). Many a reminiscence motif is essentially a harmonic structure whose highest strand supports the words. At a later point, a suggestion of this uppermost part in a vocal or instrumental melody or a touch of the harmonic flavor is sufficient to call back the initial dramatic situation. (The first chord in *Tristan* epitomizes a tragic dilemma; critics like Ernst Kurth have referred to Wagner's *Leitharmonie.*) Moreover, the melody of a reminiscence motif may at its first appearance travel between voice and orchestra, instruments completing the tune as well as supplying harmony and color. For example, this union in which neither voice nor orchestra makes an entire statement characterizes the phrase depicting the hero as free agent first heard in *Siegfried* when Wotan tells Alberich that the young stalwart will stand or fall his own master. Voice and orchestra together form a melodic-harmonic complex so firmly yoked to the dramatic concept announced in the text that, when Siegfried and Brynhild ring their rapturous changes on this theme during the close of the love duet in *The Twilight of the Gods,* one feels pity for an optimism based upon their godly relative's limitless capacity for self-deception. Through the motif's exuberant elaboration in voice and instrument one remembers the words of Wotan in that gloomy scene before Neidhöhle.

An exclusively instrumental passage may also function as a clear reminiscence if introduced concurrently with some specific event on stage (the awakening of the gold or Walhall first looming up through the mists), and a theme may appear in the orchestra so briefly before its dramatic counterpart materializes on stage that it seems to fall between presentiment and reminiscence. For example, the melody usually called Siegfried's horn call (actually first heard as a string passage) sounds a moment before the hero enters to take up the tune and lead it to a high C.

The freedom with which Wagner could approach the motif, even while he was under his own theroretic spell, is suggested by his exploitation of a brief orchestral phrase first heard in the opening act of *Valkyrie*. This fragment of three notes in rising intervals that bridge a minor sixth ends the passage for low strings leading directly to Hunding's denunciation of the Volsung clan (*"Ich weiss ein wildes Geschlecht"*). In the second act this upward thrust (but now with wider thirds) seems to be the force impelling the meandering line to which Fricka, supported by the first violins, begins to inform Wotan of her awareness that he has fathered the illicit Volsung twins (*"Doch jetzt, da dir neue Namen gefielen"*). Later in the act the same sinuous contour returns in the muted violas to accompany Sieglinde's dream of her childhood in the Volsung abode (*"Kehrte der Vater nun heim!"*). (Here the figure's span has shrunk, but the short middle note of its first appearance recurs.) In the third act the phrase in the woodwinds and second violins surrounds the words with which Wotan acknowledges inward approval of Brynhild's defiant attempt to save his Volsung son (*"So thatest du"*). The motif is defined mainly by contour; though its intervals and rhythmic organization vary, seemingly its *Gestalt* had for Wagner a musical symbolism touching Wotan's mortal family, its home, and its race. At first an impalpable presentiment, with the addition of a text it ends having the character of a reminiscence. (Wagner has been unjustly accused of stealing the motif from the opening of Liszt's "Faust" Symphony. Actually, both gentlemen borrowed it from a common source—Schubert's piano Sonata in B flat.) Though Wagner put it to use in Wotan's passionate censure of Brynhild in the final act of *Valkyrie* (*"Wunschmaid war'st du mir"*), in this case, as Ellis has pointed out, the suggestion is the general one of Wotan as father, an allusion not in conflict with the above references but illustrating the vagaries of association into which themes originating as presentiments may frequently fall.

3

Though using motifs both of reminiscence and of presentiment (and hybrid derivatives), Wagner tended increasingly toward the second, purely musical in inspiration and less confined in reference. Every shift in his position as an aesthetician resulted from some change in his attitude toward music, and it was his new "symphonic" manner of treating thematic material that led to the essays "Music of the Future" and *Beethoven*. From the time of *Tristan* many of his themes had only the most general associations. Compilers of motivic charts were hard put to agree upon appropriate names for motifs that were becoming primarily a reserve of pregnant thematic material. An ever-growing technique of orchestral counterpoint intertwined them in complicated structures faithful in mood to the coincidental stage situation but frequently indifferent to specific dramatic relevance, a development especially confusing in Wagner's use of motifs originally precise in meaning and debasing to the poetic nuances of his orchestral themes as well. This insouciance is already observable in the first act of *Siegfried* where the hero's mention of a fish is accompanied by two bars of the Rhine-Nature arpeggio! Only an instant before, Wagner was serenely painting a stream with a shifting dominant-tonic relationship in the tradition of Beethoven's "Pastoral" Symphony. For the expediency of the moment he padded his score with a gratuitous pictorial touch. Fish, water, and, therefore, Rhine seems to have been the careless thought process. What indeed had this association to do with the profundities of the motif of primordial images? Such accommodations for effect, which became more and more frequent in Wagner, are as worthy of dispraise as those in Puccini, whose orchestra at times, in Kerman's inspired phrase, "screams the first thing that comes into its head."

4

A species of reminiscence motif results when Wagner, for dramatic purposes, translates sections of the vocal line from one place in the score to another. The technique is that of the reminiscence, but in these instances a single transference is usually involved; in any case, there is no question of the abundant restatements of most motifs. In *Lohengrin,* for example, Elsa inadvertently reveals to what depth Ortrud's caustic *"Kannst du ihn nennen"* (Act II) has burned itself into her mind by ending a plea to her husband (*"sei Schweigens Kraft bewährt,"* Act III) with the villainess' closing melodic phrase (*"die Frage drum verbot"*) pitched a tone higher. At this point Lohengrin becomes a stern admonisher, fearfully sensing Ortrud's spirit behind his wife's entreaties. In the first act of *Siegfried* the hero derisively mimics Mime's whining vocal line; and in *The Twilight of the Gods* (Act II) Brynhild's *"Lehrt ihr mich Leiden,"* set to far-off echoes of her *"War es so schmählich"* from the third act of *Valkyrie,* achieves a terrible irony as she begins that moral descent which prepares her redemption. Perhaps the most striking use of this technique occurs during the last act of the *Ring;* escorting Siegfried's body into the Gibichung hall, Hagen sings almost note for note the melody of his father's outburst in *Rhinegold,* *"Kein Froher soll seiner sich freu'n,"* that mid-section of his curse on the gold derived from the motif of the Ring.

But not all interrelated phrases of this type have such clear dramatic implications. It has been observed that Wagner's attitude toward his thematic material seems definitely to have begun to change early during the composition of *Siegfried; Valkyrie* remains the high point of his art for the manner in which text and motif are counterpoised in artful equilibrium.[8] Thus any seeming incongruity appears doubly disturbing in this work. Max Friedlander has convincingly explained Wagner's hitherto puzzling use of the renunciation motif at the end of the first and third acts. Throughout the *Ring* the motif symbolizes relinquishment and demission in their widest sense. In *Valkyrie,* Siegmund grasps the handle of the sword and

---

[8] "The Victors," based upon the idea of reincarnation, tempted him to consider a use of reminiscence motifs to link individuals with their former existences, a plan apparently involving multiple themes for each character.

repeats the melody first sung by Woglinde in the depths of the Rhine. It is the moment for Wotan to fulfill his promise to yield the weapon, an act propelling his Volsung son toward a fate that in turn sunders the god from his favorite daughter. Significantly, the motif sounds again during their parting as Wotan kisses her into penitential sleep. The concept of ceding, withdrawal, and an acceptance of consequences is common to these incidents. A theme originally a true reminiscence has turned about and become a presentiment. The motif becomes meaningful in *Valkyrie* only when taken in the broad, associative sense.

But in *Valkyrie* a strange transference of vocal line resists elucidation. Why, during this farewell, does Wotan sing the melody of Siegmund's *"Selig schien mir der Sonne Licht"* (Act I) to the phrase *"wenn kindisch lallend"*? Is the god's backward glance at happier days really sufficient dramatic justification for calling back the picture of Siegmund meditating upon the radiance of Sieglinde? (However, with fine dramatic pertinence this vocal phrase first sung by Siegmund begins his son's *"Nahrung brachte zum Neste das Männchen"* in the first act of *Siegfried,* the young hero availing himself of the grace note added to the melody by Grandfather Wotan.) And why in *Siegfried* does a vocal phrase from the farewell (*"zum letzten Mal letz' es mich heut'"*) suddenly emerge in the orchestra as Wotan rides from his meeting with Alberich at Fafner's cave? (When the moonlight first reveals Wotan at the rocky entrance, his simple declaration that he has journeyed by night is also set to a reminiscence of this phrase.) That an analogy was intended between the two leave-takings is suggested by Donington's poetic reconciliation of the incidents in terms of Jungian psychology. But, to many, this poignant reminiscence seems to function in *Siegfried* as pure musical padding, the kind of effect without cause for which Wagner took Meyerbeer mercilessly to task.

5

Wagner's methods of achieving musical and dramatic unity included not only the repetition of individual motifs and phrases but also, occasionally, the transference of whole stretches of orchestral tissue. In *The Twilight of the Gods* the hero recounts his boyhood adventures to substantial segments taken from *Siegfried,* and, as he dies, portions of Brynhild's awakening scene reappear. Most remarkable in this respect is Isolde's *Liebestod,* essentially a fresh vocal counterpoint with new words set over a recapitulation (differently notated) of the coda of the second-act duet. The love-death is thus represented as the ultimate aspect of the love night. When that dominant seventh chord, whose resolution was interrupted by Mark's arrival, finally dissolves into B major, the closing act's dramatic symbolism is expressed in purely musical terms. That Isolde's abstruse and knotty text is swallowed in a surge of transfiguring sound is of comparatively little importance. After *Valkyrie,* Wagner's word and tone no longer lived together in balance but, rather, in an increasingly uneasy state of accommodation in respect to relative density and, most important, poetic intent.

Even though from *Siegfried* on it is still possible most of the time to establish a general connection between the dramatic situation and simultaneously sounding motifs (with either precise or hazy connotations), the relationship between verse and music has actually become increasingly superficial in terms of specific motivic relevance. No longer, as in *Valkyrie,* can the appearance of motifs almost invariably be vindicated by a particular dramatic need for reminiscence or presentiment; they are often merely musical tags loosely attached to objects, persons, or ideas even casually mentioned in the text, and really serve to provide matter for orchestral manipulation. They form the floods and ebbs of a symphonic tide and reappear so often that their efficacy as mediums of reminiscence is quite blunted. Moreover, their frequent superposition makes it difficult to sort out particular poetic functions, for, as Hanslick remarked, "Where every little sequence of notes is supposed to lead somewhere and signify something there can be no guidance and no significance."

At times Wagner's employment of motifs in the *Ring* became reckless. Not far from the absurd is that *locus classicus* in the final act of *Siegfried* where Brynhild's sudden wild passion, burning glance, and enfolding embrace are painted by the dragon motif (Donington hears in these growls a reminder of the destructive element in Brynhild); and those two bars in the prelude to *The Twilight of the Gods* where Siegmund's and Sieglinde's love theme underlines Brynhild's devotion to her horse seem equally irresponsible. The integrity of *Valkyrie* gradually yielded to a kind of glorious musical opportunism.

In *Meistersinger,* Wagner for pages on end freely wove motivic patterns into extended passages justified more by musical beauty than by their miscellaneous relevance to the situation on stage or in the dialogue. Essentially, he was again pursuing characteristic orchestral figures throughout an aria or scene in the old operatic tradition that he had begun to desert after *Rienzi.* At times he seemed unable to let his motifs go without having lovingly teased them into symphonic play. In that delicious interweaving under Sachs's and Eva's conversation in the second act, phrase repetition and sequential patterns (with alterations in harmonic and instrumental color) mix with the decorating devices of classical variation technique. Significantly, the two orchestral motifs here exploited are spread beneath so much text that they cannot be accurately named, and the vocal lines themselves have sunk to a rather formless chatter. Music no longer interprets the word; instead, the vocal lines rather reticently annotate upon the main action, now transferred to the pit.

Hanslick observed: "Given the text and the orchestral accompaniment, a good musician, well versed in Wagner's music, would be able to insert suitable vocal parts in the empty spaces, just as a sculptor can restore the missing hand of a statue. But one could as little restore the lost orchestral accompaniment to Hans Sachs' or Eva's vocal parts as create the whole statue with only the single hand to go on." The ultimate capitulation of the voice to the growing demands of the orchestra was predicted by the very concept of the symphonic leitmotif opera. By this time Wagner no longer believed in *Opera and Drama.* Moreover, he had never given heed to its strange limitation of motif to moments of lowered emotional intensity in the poem. Even *Rhinegold,* his only work showing evidence of having been composed with an eye on the rule book, pursues an opposite course.

There are many instances in the later "orchestral" operas in which Wagner's combinations of motifs have extraordinary dramatic pertinence. Though superposition of themes into contrapuntal structures often tended to tangle literary allusions, yet, when Wagner was able to yoke the constructional, musical task of his motifs and their symbolic significance to a single purpose, they could coalesce into passages attaining a literary articulateness disturbing to those who feel that musical considerations alone must govern tonal combinations. Actually, musical purposes are most often supreme in Wagner. His most dazzling "literary" superpositions of themes— for example, the piling up of motifs in the *Meistersinger* prelude or in the finale to *The Twilight of the Gods*—are admired by many who have not the slightest knowledge of their dramatic import.

Did calculation or intuition play the larger part in Wagner's selection and development of motivic material in those great revelatory moments in his dramas? On this point it is best to let him speak through a letter to Uhlig of January, 1852:

I have again looked a little at the music of *Lohengrin.* . . . Would it not interest you, since *you* always write things of this kind, to discuss the thematic web and show how the path I have struck out must lead to ever fresh developments of form? Among other things, this came into my mind. . . . Just at the beginning of the second scene of this [the second] act—when Elsa steps onto the balcony—it struck me how in the prelude for wind instruments . . . where Elsa appears by night, a theme is heard for the first time which later on, when Elsa advances toward the church in bright daylight and full splendor, is presented in complete development, broad and bright. Thereupon it became evident to me that my themes always originate coherently and with the character of plastic phenomena. Perhaps you can express this better than I.

Wagner was perhaps making rather much of his expansion of the melody that was to accompany Elsa's progress from the *Kemenate*. But only after perusing his composition did he realize that he had first inserted the phrase in the balcony scene in order to depict her anticipation of the ceremony. Clearly, he was expressing to Uhlig delight with the inspiration of his subconscious.

6

It is profitless to consider Wagner's techniques of thematic exploitation from the point of view of the classic Viennese school; in the romantic era the lines between repetition, sequence, variation, and development became increasingly shadowy. In fact, Wagner successfully incorporated both classic and romantic methods of thematic manipulation, the one, following Beethoven's example, including the devices of fragmentation, augmentation, diminution, and combination, the other resembling the manner of Schubert, whose developments often recapitulate entire melodies, a procedure that was to stand Anton Bruckner in good stead. (The romantics tended to say many times what the preceding age would have spoken once.) At his best Wagner elaborated his material with a conciseness that gives the illusion of organic growth, his sense of climax being not inferior to Beethoven's; at his worst he shared with Schumann the habit of capriciously idling and pottering with motifs until the effect produced is that of inspiration being cranked rather than followed.

However, what Wagner mainly took from the past were formulas and procedures; there is no point of contact between Beethoven's strict thematic and tonal relationships and the relatively rhapsodic approach of Wagner. From the classic standpoint there is something downright untidy about his starting *Tannhäuser* with the pilgrims' theme in E major and ending the opera with the same tune in E flat.

The apposition and opposition of key as an element of form received little attention from him despite Gerald Abraham's precipitate pronouncement —not typical of his brilliant *A Hundred Years of Music*—that "tonality plays as important a part in the great *Ring* 'symphony' and its successors as in the symphonies of Mozart, Beethoven and Brahms." To demonstrate his claim Abraham cited Lorenz's observation that Siegmund enters and leaves the action of the *Ring* to the same key. But between the Volsung's arrival in Hunding's hut and his death on the mountain the auditor has sat over two hours in the opera house, heard numberless modulations, and probably been out for a generous intermission! With such time spans the idea of key as a constructional element—its role in the classic symphony—becomes extravagant; at most, the D minor functions as a reminiscent tone color for those with long memories. Wagner claimed the thematic manipulation of the Beethoven sonata as his inheritance, not its harmonic stresses.

In her *Challenge to Musical Tradition,* Adele Katz persuasively analyzed Wagner's methods of tonal organization. But the only extended illustration she permitted herself to construe was a purely orchestral prelude. She observed: "In the music-drama, with a constant shift of scene and action, it would be impossible to achieve the structural unity that sustains the larger motions in a movement of a sonata or a symphony." Frequently a joint between analyzable sections is without structural or tonal implications. Examining the conflicting elements in Wagner's musical technique, she lit upon only one aspect she held to be consistent throughout—"the fidelity of the music to the text and action."

Wagner would have agreed. *Opera and Drama* describes modulation as a function of poetry, the purpose of key changes being to mirror the fluctuating emotions of the text; such an approach must result in tonal adventitiousness in terms of over-all structure. Changes of key for the dramatic purpose of the moment necessarily affect only small areas. In a famous example from *Rhinegold,* Wotan, by taking up the melody of Fricka's *"Herrliche Wohnung"* a whole tone lower in pitch, indicates opposition to her sentiments. But such effects, though notable, are fleeting and have nothing to do with musical architecture. For real modulation, Wagner substituted what Hanslick called "incessant" total undulation. He never hesitated to sacrifice clarity of tonality to an immediate dramatic need, to court the pathos of sequential repetition at the cost of lucid harmonic progression, to call into play what Katz called "a purposeful co-ordination of abnormal intentions that sets forth the mood."

Wagner's writings are sprinkled with startling misconceptions of classical symphonic principles, especially of Mozart's. In "Music of the Future" he declared that Mozart "usually fell into banal phrase construction which frequently shows his symphonic movements in the light of so-called 'table music' (*Tafelmusik*), that is, music which, between the unfolding of attractive melodies, also offers an attractive bustle intended to accompany conversation." As far as Wagner was concerned, "the steadily recurring and noisily swaggering half cadences of the Mozart symphony" seemed a musical setting of "the sound of dishes clattering (*das Geräusch des Servierens und Deservierens*) on a princely table." Mozart's gifts as a symphonist were also treated patronizingly in Wagner's report on the planned music school in Munich. Not surprisingly, throughout his career excited critical protests followed his conducting of such works, their subtle tonal equilibrium being obviously incomprehensible to him.

In fact, Wagner's mission was to grind tonality to bits by continuing certain tendencies in the harmony of Schumann, Chopin, and Liszt. The four augmented triads that open the latter's "Faust" Symphony prophesied the coming of a world in which there would be neither major nor minor. At almost the same time Wagner was working on *Valkyrie,* whose motif of magic slumber is a drooping succession of chords ambiguous and uncommitted as to key. Though, in general, his chromatic alterations, suspensions, appoggiaturas, and passing notes enrich a still recognizable diatonic understructure, they nonetheless helped build a new tonal system in which harmonic combinations formerly considered harsh and ugly began to satisfy. And not only did his works make chords of the seventh and ninth seem consonant and reposeful, but his chromaticism gradually led musicians to look upon all steps of the twelve-tone scale as having equal generative force. After *Tristan,* the erstwhile powerful notes of diatonism lost their prerogatives.

Though his last opera abounds in diatonic passages, with almost his final creative strength Wagner pursued his war on key. The impressionistic prelude to the closing act of *Parsifal* sets foot in atonal territory as it re-explores the melancholy, disjointed polytonal idiom of the introduction to the third act of *Tristan*—ruined Kareol and the neglected Grail domain are really the same landscape [4]—wandering into areas of strangely modern thematic fragmentation and tonal disintegration. Ever enlarging the diatonic tonal framework for his expressive needs, he eventually burst it; building upon traditional techniques, he ultimately negated their historic roles. Directly ahead lay Debussy and Schönberg.

On the whole, Wagner's so-called "thematic developments" are essentially passages of motivic variation. Musically he expressed the psychological unfolding of character by means of thematic metamorphosis, and toward perfecting this technique Liszt's example undoubtedly helped lead his way. Wagner, of course, borrowed technical formulas from Beethoven's development sections. But without contrasts of stable tonality, no real development in the Beethoven sense can take place. Mozart may present the illusion of the tensions and conciliations of sonata form in his operas, but not Wagner, whose harmonies often shift with each successive melody note, in the manner of Chopin. Brahms, the master of the variation (who even succeeded in accommodating it to sonata form), recognized its significance in Wagner's

---

[4] One is reminded of the close connection in Wagner's mind between the Parsifal and Tristan legends. Originally, he planned to lead Parsifal, in the course of his search for Monsalvat, to the castle of the dying Tristan. The final *Parsifal* prelude depicts the hero's sorrowful wandering, the very journey that was to have brought him to this domain of Kareol. Musically and spiritually, the composition is related to the one composed decades before. The prelude to the final act of *Tannhäuser* is also a tone poem depicting a knight's pilgrimage in search of redemption.

work; it was not by chance that he chose to play his *Handel Variations* at their famous encounter in Vienna.[5]

It is a pity that Wagner died before creating those last symphonies he contemplated. Perhaps some clue as to what they might have been may be found in that chef-d'œuvre of sequential variation, the *Siegfried Idyll,* whose Brahmsian tone, meditative, oscillating, and lullabylike, is so striking. Brahms was well aware of how much he and Wagner had in common. It is fascinating to observe in *Meistersinger* the Brahmsian manner in which the theme, borrowed from Mendelssohn, to represent Sachs's renunciation seems to be "constructed" as counterpoint to the melody of his song about Mother Eve. Echoes of this latter ditty, so humorous and superficial on the surface, are exploited as material for the profound prelude to the final act.

Among the first sections of *Meistersinger* composed, it includes both the renunciation motif and a fragment of the second half of the Eve strophe though, significantly, these melodies are not dovetailed. Apparently it was a later inspiration to make the pair of musico-dramatic ideas interlock in the middle act. But in this overwhelming moment the renunciation theme remains unaltered and is fitted against the rhythmically modified melody of the *first* half of the Eve stanza. The original material was not meant to work in combination, the prelude being, in fact, a masterly example of Wagner's more usual technique of simulated polyphony.

In general, to approach his synthetic counterpoint with the symphonic models of an earlier day in mind is idle. His interlockings depend more upon juxtaposition than conjunction, overlappings often being effected by the most obvious juggling of note values, as, for example, in those highly contrived vocal lines of the closing moments of *Siegfried.* And in this finale, not only are the singers' parts clumsily blended, but also the orchestra stubbornly forces together themes that resist combination. Yet, in the theater, few can withstand the overwrought, compelling effect of the whole. Examining *Tannhäuser* in his study, Schumann was disturbed by what he held to be its harmonic and contrapuntal solecisms. But after seeing the opera, he wrote to Mendelssohn, "I have to take back some of the things I wrote to you after reading the score; from the stage everything strikes one very differently. I was quite moved by many parts of it." Even that Brahms who thirty times invoked the *passacaglia* theme in the final movement of his Fourth Symphony respected Wagner's technique for what it was.

[5] This meeting between the two greatest German musicians of their age was arranged in Vienna during February of 1864. By some miracle, the evening turned out well. After Brahms had played his *Handel Variations,* Wagner managed the outwardly polite but double-edged observation, "One sees what can still be done with the old forms in the hands of one who knows how to deal with them."

7

Harmony became Wagner's primary musical means of interpreting his texts. Although in his early work motifs were usually imbedded unmodified within convenient chordal configurations, with time the motifs themselves became increasingly harmonic in character. Through the device of harmonic transformation, they were used, as *Lohengrin* attests, with growing flexibility. Though much traditional orchestral accompaniment survived in *Valkyrie,* its harmony and motif showed signs of coalescing, and by the time of *Tristan* the harmonic web was being spun largely of motivic strands and counterpoints to them. In this interlinked texture, motif and harmony had become one, the voice part, which in *Opera and Drama* had been seen as the source of motif, becoming something quite different.

The vocal line in the mature works of Wagner is the verbally articulate and thus conceptually intensified thread of the dense orchestral network, what Bekker termed a lyrical heightening of the harmonic process. As an outgrowth of harmony, the singer's part occasionally takes on the character of those piano and orchestral recitatives of Chopin, Liszt, and Berlioz which, ironically, came into being through efforts to give instruments a kind of speech. The idiosyncratic style of that main carrier of Wagnerian motif, the romantic orchestra, influenced the vocalist's contribution, especially to the later operas, a development forecast by Wagner's predilection for the presentiment and also by *Opera and Drama,* which had pointed the way of the reminiscence from the larynx to the pit. Often the voice became an obbligato instrument differing from other instruments only in that it bore a text.

That harmonic-melodic, instrumental-vocal organism called the leitmotif —Wagner's own term, *Grundthema,*[6] better describes its musical function— provided the composer with the main material out of which he built larger formal units. These, though at times fashioned from some single motif or a fragment of it, were usually pieced together with the elements of more than one such theme, motivic material being placed occasionally in the voice, frequently in the orchestra, and sometimes in both alternately or simultaneously.

Oddly enough, the easiest route toward grasping the nature of these compound units lies through a consideration of Wagner's writing for the voice, which, despite its instrumental traits, persistently and longingly strove for songlike expression.

The singer's part, though it may at times derive directly from motif, more

[6] According to Wagner himself, the term *"Leitmotif"* was coined by Wolzogen.

often is a counterpoint governed by harmony and prosody. Despite attendance on their claims, this vocal line frequently exhibits an intrinsically beautiful and symmetrical contour, not only at those moments of tension when the pliant arioso rises to impassioned song, but also in more neutral sections. Balance, however, is at times sacrificed to dramatic effect; or, as in *Meistersinger* and the penultimate and final dramas of the *Ring,* a conversational quality is achieved by means of jagged, brisk musical dialogue or through vocal ornament sometimes ironically at odds with the poetic meter.

In the construction of Wagner's arioso, parallel phrases find an important place, even if they do not play quite the salient and consistent role predicted by *Opera and Drama.* The vocal line as a function of the harmonic-motivic complex often flows along with and imitates the matching patterns of an orchestra whose main devices are repetition, sequence, and close variation. Yet complementary phrases abound even when the voice seems to strike forth on its own, riding freely above the instruments. Seemingly alert only to harmonic and prosodic demands, it may suddenly mirror the shapes of preceding phrases or seek symmetry by pursuing some contrasting or parallel course suggested by the constructional or alliterative patterns of the verse. Its generally instrumental disposition of intervals notwithstanding, Wagner's vocal phrasing remains, on the whole, remarkably faithful to the example of the early romantic masters, particularly Schumann's, and serves as a strong unifying element amid the shifting moods of the dramas. The strophic principle of the German aria and lied, though disguised, makes itself felt; Wagner's "through-composed" abandon is, to some extent, a cleverly devised illusion through which a general squareness may be perceived. The section in *Opera and Drama* detailing the fine points of musical prosody that were to characterize Wagner's new art was essentially a description of devices used by composers from Bach to Schumann, although, typically, Wagner spoke as a prophet. Schumann's word-tone synthesis, albeit governed by stricter meters than Wagner's, obviously provided him with an important model. The winged spirit of the *Dichterliebe* breathes through the noblest pages of *Lohengrin,* whose lyricism and stanzaic structure persist, in the form of answering phrases, even in the musical setting of the *Ring*'s ferocious *Stabreim.*

Perhaps one should regret that Wagner did not pursue with even more consistency *Opera and Drama*'s recommendation of repeated phrases as an ideal unit for constructing the vocal line. *Rhinegold,* his only opera lacking a confident musical diction, owes its finest vocal moments to the device. In fact, one suspects that only the fulminations of *Opera and Drama* against the ensemble prevented a concerted number from growing out of that phrase (derived from the suffix to Freia's motif and associated with the idea of flight) sung in turn by the mortified gods as they behold Fafner and Fasolt amassing the hoard. Moreover, Alberich's curse in *Rhinegold* sets rolling paired and spacious vocal phrases, whose silhouettes remain stamped on the mind. And Loge's *"Um den gleissenden Tand,"* brief though it and its repetition are, helps firm the arch of his narrative much as Parsifal's *"Ich sah sie welken"* adds profile to the scene of Kundry's weeping.

For Wagner, parallel phrases constituted a miniature musical form. *Opera and Drama* held their repetition necessary to confirm a melody's first impression. Of innumerable examples it is awkward to fix upon any as more suitable for citation than others; in the first act of *Siegfried* Mime's parallel snippets lyrically voice his cajolery and identify him with a characteristically spare melodic outline. At the opposite emotional extreme, Wotan's expansive and deeply etched paired phrases in the final act of *Valkyrie* delineate godly dignity. And analogous phrases provide welcome equilibrium in *The Twilight of the Gods,* counterbalancing those long stretches where symmetry of vocal line succumbs to the relatively amorphous and essentially instrumental dialogue style characterizing much of *Meistersinger.* (Here, the impassioned orchestra takes upon itself the function of song while the voice enunciates the text as dry obbligato.) The set pieces of *Meistersinger* demand mirrored phrases, and the vocal parts of *Tristan,* with their rhyming units, revel in them. And, as has been indicated, parallelism relieves the relatively disjunct declamation of *Parsifal,* also wisely tempered by its almost complete eschewal of *Stabreim.*

Paired phrases form the heart of that song form somewhat exaggeratedly claimed by Alfred Lorenz [7] to be one of the ultimate supports of Wagner's musical architecture. Its role, if not quite so momentous, should nonetheless be considered, this musical form providing a convenient frame in which to examine certain of Wagner's constructional techniques.

The venerable *Bar,* a descendant of the *canzo* of the medieval troubadours, consists of two *Stollen,* a pair of verses sung to essentially the same melody, and a concluding *Abgesang,* an epode with a different but not necessarily unrelated tune (schematically, AAB). Lohengrin's warning to Elsa never to ask about his origin is an example of a brief *Bar,* whose matching *Stollen* and contrasting *Abgesang* make up a motif, that of the forbidden question. In the opening scene of the *Ring,* Woglinde's vocal line that specifies the price of gaining the Rhinegold is a *Bar* constructed of two motifs, the renunciation theme being announced and then repeated to form the *Stollen,* that of the Ring (first sung only a page earlier by Wellgunde) contributing

---

[7] Joseph Kerman has called Lorenz's monumental *Das Geheimnis der Form bei Richard Wagner* "infuriating as a *reductio ad absurdum* of certain valid insights." The present writer learned more from the twenty-five pages on *Tristan* in Kerman's *Opera as Drama* than from Lorenz's protracted and tortuous study.

to the *Abgesang.* The above-cited complementary phrases sung by Parsifal and Loge are the *Stollen* of miniature *Bare* set in their arioso. In the illustration from *Parsifal,* voice and instruments build their parallel *Stollen* from a narrow chromatic figure associated with Kundry as enchantress (it derives from Klingsor's theme); a motif first heard in the prelude and depicting Amfortas' and Christ's suffering provides material for the orchestral part of the *Abgesang.* In the twin *Stollen* of his *Bar,* Loge sings a version of the Nibelung hammering motif while the orchestra in somber harmonies simultaneously sounds the first phrases of the Rhine Daughters' song to the gold, its second section being exploited in the *Abgesang.* Sometimes small *Bare* are gathered into bigger units. During Brynhild's awakening the orchestral accompaniment to her famous semaphore—a pantomime now abandoned, and happily so, in most theaters—is cast as a *Bar,* which is then repeated with the addition of her vocal greeting. These two *Bare* in turn form the *Stollen* of a larger *Bar,* whose *Abgesang* extends from *"Lang war mein Schlaf"* to the modulation to E major and Siegfried's reply.

On a larger scale the *Bar* was the form into which Walther was obliged to cast his prize song in *Meistersinger.* Both Kothner and Sachs lecture him extensively on the requirements of *"Ein jedes Meistergesanges Bar."* Untypically, when creating Walther's solo in the final act, Wagner, winking at his published doctrines, wrote the melody first, later forcing verses to its contours. But his more usual practice of working out a musical composition after completing its text invited a treatment of the *Bar* free enough to prevent the phrase repetition inherent in the form from interfering with the niceties of prosody and dramatic expression.

As sections of Wagner's chordally punctuated recitative demonstrate, a *Bar* need not have motivic material in either voices or instruments. Moreover, many of the above procedures were called into play when he composed freely or in other forms.

The *Bar* was hardly the only song form in which he cast his musical sections.[8] One finds a variety of *da capo* or bow forms (schematically, ABA), ranging from Brynhild's brisk war cry (*Valkyrie,* Act II) to Mime's sustained and rueful *"Zwangvolle Plage!"* (*Siegfried,* Act I). The concept of the rondo's unifying refrain is applied on a modest scale to Siegmund's monologue, *"Ein Schwert"* (*Valkyrie,* Act I), as the sword motif returns in the orchestra between the sections of his text and in heroic dimension the same rondo principle gives shape to Siegfried's scene with the Forest Bird.

[8] Much as Machaut had done centuries before, Wagner adapted patterns originally monophonic to his many-voiced idiom. Brangäne's warning song in *Tristan* was his graceful bow to the German medieval tradition of the *Wächterlied.*

As suggested by the *Bare* from Brynhild's awakening, purely orchestral segments of Wagner's operas show a similar use of song forms. Consider the passages immediately following Sieglinde's *"wo Unheil im Hause wohnt!"* (*Valkyrie,* Act I): The D-minor motif of Volsung sorrow announced in the cellos and double basses is sequentially repeated. Tempered by the thirds of the Sieglinde motif in the violins and violas, this reiterated phrase constitutes the *Stollen* of a *Bar*. A *Fortspinnung* or melodic development of the sorrow theme by the low strings opens the *Abgesang* (historically, as in Walther von der Vogelweide's famous *Palästinalied,* this final section of the *Bar* often availed itself of material from the *Stollen*), which closes with Siegmund's announced decision to await his host. The *Bar* is then repeated by the orchestra alone, starting with a superb excursion into the parallel major. The instruments develop the material by means of melodic and harmonic enrichments, woodwinds and four horns being added to the instrumentation, which during the first *Bar* was for strings alone except for a touch of horn color at the mention of Hunding's name. For the hero's words this orchestral *Bar* substitutes a coda built on the love motif, which, weaving through the bass, modulates toward the scene of Hunding's arrival.

The opening unit of the *Bar,* with its structure of paired verses set to the same or similar music, offered Wagner opportunities to explore his delight in sequential repetition and variation; moreover, the form was easily expanded. In the second act of *The Twilight of the Gods,* for example, he ingeniously fashioned the scene of the oaths by turning to use the historical precedent of the "duplicated" *Bar* (related to the *Leich* of the minnesinger), but freely enough to encompass the emotions of an entire scene. Siegfried sings two pairs of *Stollen*. (The repetitions are varied, the reprise of the first *Stollen* preserving only its general contours and characteristic intervals, that of the second being very close to its model.) His *Abgesang* ends with a deceptive cadence leading to a reiteration of the entire *Bar* by Brynhild with new variations to accord with the fury of her text. This expanded and repeated *Bar* may be schematically represented as AA'BB'C/A''A'''B''B'''C', a variety of motifs making up its harmonic and melodic material.

8

Thus, not only do various song forms in miniature help shape Wagner's arioso (lying in the ebb and flow of his speech-song, they often constitute those delicious cantilenas which suddenly shine forth and then as quickly vanish—in Hanslick's unsympathetic phrase, "all too quickly stifled in the quicksands of declamation"), but frequently in larger proportion they may embody a vocal solo, an orchestral utterance, or an entire scene. Moreover, holding them to be the architectural basis of entire acts and even operas, scholars like Lorenz consider, for example, the closing scene of *Parsifal* to be two bows and a *Bar* forming a big *Bar,* or see, in the opening act of *Siegfried* and the whole of *Tristan* and *Parsifal,* the symmetry of enormous bow forms, or even regard *Meistersinger* itself as a giant *Bar,* its first two acts forming paired *Stollen* and the final act an *Abgesang.* And Lorenz disciples cannot decide whether the whole *Ring* is a Brobdingnagian bow or a Gargantuan *Bar,* so splendid a case being possible for either interpretation. Analysis of this sort often depends more upon wresting symmetries and contrasts of dramatic incident from the text than upon musical considerations, and the forcing of dramatic matter into the catalogue of song forms seems a dubious pastime. Many portions of Wagner's scores defy filing in the dossier of traditional designs, although there are analysts who somehow stuff them into such compartments.

By expanding and joining freely composed sections and formal song units —the "little unities" Nietzsche so derided—Wagner developed his larger architecture, the whole achieving continuity through his remarkable technique of avoiding full cadences, the boundaries between the parts being suppressed. The theory that his art was an evolutionary one of eternal "becoming" rests upon his genius for chromatic harmony and the deceptive cadence. He told Mathilde Wesendonk that the secret of his musical form lay in his art of transition (*"die Kunst des Überganges"*) and significantly observed in *On Conducting* of 1870 that "the intrinsic weakness of the variation form as a structural principle is revealed whenever strongly contrasting parts are placed side by side without link or reconciliation" (*"Verbindung oder Vermittelung"*), an obvious reference to Brahms.[9] The fre-

---

[9] The essay was in part a derisive attack upon the *Handel Variations* of Johannes Brahms. Writing of their meeting in Vienna and the young composer's performance of the piece, Wagner damned with pianissimo praise someone he numbered among the "odd guardians of musical chastity": "Considered *per se,* there is little to take exception to in these musicians; most of them compose perfectly well." Brahms's technical mastery on paper and at the keyboard obviously unsettled him—Brahms was twenty years his junior—and the essay not very subtly attempted to equate such classical virtuosity with "primness," "woodenness," and, by innuendo, with the impotence of the castrated. The genius he referred to as "St. Johannes" annoyed him terribly. His own incompetence at the piano, especially the inability to translate from full score to keyboard, made it difficult for him to forgive such abilities in others—Liszt was the great exception—for he was embarrassingly dependent upon assistants to play anything complicated for him. Both he and Cosima decided that in the proposed school at Bayreuth students should learn to play piano but only up to a certain point lest mechanical skill destroy their talent! It was always his way to elevate his shortcomings to virtues worthy of imitation.

Ernest Newman believed Wagner's abilities as a pianist to be generally under-

quently stated and, at first consideration, paradoxical observation that Wagner, in spite of the vastness of his works, was essentially a miniaturist, a view first set forth by Nietzsche, is attributable to the fact that his building modules were essentially the lied and the aria. One must marvel at the imposing arches he threw up with their modestly scaled material. The great spans of the first two acts of *Siegfried* are constructed essentially of a succession of joined song-form solos, thinned cadences providing the fluid mortar; musically, something of the Singspiel clings to these scenes.[10]

Although Wagner's delight in tarrying to refine the expression of a passing emotion is typical of romantic composers, he to some extent surmounted at least one of their shortcomings, that tendency to lose the picture of the whole when building up larger forms. On this point Nietzsche was perhaps unjust. Perspicaciously he observed that Wagner, unable to cut from the block, was obliged to create in a patchwork manner, and, indeed, Wagner's method was essentially that of Schumann and Chopin, who would construct an extended composition by stringing together a series of small ones. But, whereas with Schumann and Chopin the result was often a succession of superb lyric moments that interpreters must struggle to bind into a cohesive entity, Wagner was generally more successful in keeping his over-all plan in view. Moreover, his involved network of cognate themes helped give his scores unity, *Tristan,* for example, exhibiting a Beethoven-like compression of motivic resources. And, though acutely remarking that Wagner built by patching and that his theoretic writing was largely a gigantic apologia for this procedure, Nietzsche failed fully to credit the ingenuity with which the master craftsman dovetailed, hinged, and mitered. With a kind of resolve, patience, self-assurance, and appreciation of his own ability that were pre-eminently Victorian, he stubbornly fabricated his mammoth structures. Nietzsche's pity for all this trouble—he compared Wagner's methods to those of the Goncourts—seems strangely misplaced. Unlike

---

estimated because of an admission in 1842 of his incapacity at the keyboard. The early date left him ample time in which to improve, thought Newman, who, however, was evidently unaware of a letter Wagner wrote to Ludwig on February 10, 1878, during the creation of *Parsifal*. The composer spoke of young Anton Seidl, who "plays piano well enough to play from my composition sketches for us, for I myself—unfortunately—never learned to play the piano properly." When he was without assistants, Cosima would hammer out the upper parts while he labored at the lower. Judith Gautier has left an amusing picture of the composer attempting to play his scores at Triebschen as Richter stood by striking notes "between the master's hesitating fingers."

[10] From the literary point of view has not the old Viennese clown, the Hanswurst-Casperle, crawled into Mime's costume? Moreover (its Eddic origin notwithstanding), a papier-mâché pantomime serpent is assaulted in the best Schikaneder tradition. As remarked earlier, the Viennese magic opera greatly influenced Wagner.

Schumann, Wagner inwardly recognized his own limitations as well as his gifts, and cannily refused to be drawn into the subtle dialectics of the sonata. Not the greater musician of the two, he was certainly the cleverer; he knew the rules by which he would play best. And, though he raised Walhall by laboriously piling up and cementing stone on stone, his dogged determination to achieve big architecture succeeded in producing a reasonable simulacrum within the limits of his essentially decadent style.

The latter adjective is not used in a pejorative sense. Wagner's art is decadent in that too frequently the whole seems in danger of being forgotten amid the exquisite detail of the parts. But most often he saves the day; his tectonics represent a victory of will over nature, and penetratingly Hanslick commented upon the "truly beelike industry" with which *The Twilight of the Gods* was executed. Wagner's expedients were those of such colossi of contemporary architecture as Scott, Semper, Hasenauer, and Garnier. Not infrequently, the operas betray their segmental construction when a less-than-gifted conductor holds the baton. The "big line" that critics rightly clamor for in Wagner is achieved only by a musician who knows how to keep the joints concealed.

9

Wagner had observed to Uhlig that harmony and instrumentation were inseparable in his music. He continued the work of Berlioz in refining the orchestral palette, the poetic implications expressed by his harmonies being yet more subtly shaded by effects of timbre. In order to achieve certain tone colors in the *Ring,* he introduced additional brasses into the orchestra, the most famous of them being the so-called "Wagner tubas" (really a consort of instruments intermediate between horn and tuba) later used by Bruckner and Strauss. Again following Berlioz's example, Wagner frequently demanded instrumental resources that can rarely be completely realized. The *Ring* orchestra calls for sixteen woodwinds and seventeen brasses. In *Rhinegold* eight harps were in the pit at the Bayreuth première, and, according to Wagner's instructions, eighteen anvils in three sizes were supposed to ring out from the caverns of Nibelheim. One thinks of the battery of sixteen kettledrums prescribed by Berlioz for the *Tuba mirum* of his Requiem.

Wagner's orchestral color also functioned as yet another unifying device. At a desired moment he was able to evoke the particular shades of a past scene. And tone color is often a characteristic element of his motifs. His hues, like Rubens', embrace the entire spectrum, the values scaling the ladder from pitch dark to blinding light, the chroma ranging from subtle neutrals to utmost brilliance. Midst the swirling shapes on his canvas single figures may be illuminated, dramatically emerging in relief against a somber background. So, for example, Gutrune shines with a silvery, lunar glow that detaches her from a throbbing, shadowy environment.

IO

Even after considering the interrelations and unifying techniques in the Wagnerian opera, it is not easy to say just what holds it together in the way one may describe the dynamics of sonata form or define the *chaconne*. The judgment of Hanslick and his followers that Wagner's "endless melody" represents "formlessness raised to a principle" or "the formless infinite" is obviously harsh and biased. (In the tinted steam that became the most powerful weapon in Wagner's new theatrical arsenal, Hanslick saw an effect whose combination of formlessness and sensuous appeal showed a special affinity with what he held to be the composer's musical principles.) At the other extreme, Lorenz's overzealous reduction of Wagner's world to the symmetries of song forms is equally unreasonable. Somewhere between, the voice of Tovey—like Gerald Abraham's—consoles with the false hope that Wagner's form may be analyzed as intelligibly as Beethoven's; Tovey found no time to illustrate this appealing thesis, merely stating that "a mature Wagner opera is organized as highly, and almost as purely musically, as a Beethoven symphony," Wagner's scores being "architectural" and "on a scale actually from ten to twenty times larger than anything contemplated in earlier music." Tovey tantalizes; he suggests the dimensions of the case but shies from presenting it for the very good reason that promising bits and pieces of evidence do not constitute a legally rigorous brief.

Like most romantic composers, Wagner often deliberately buttressed his art with formal apparatus taken from the past, a practice reassuring to those who, despite much talk of artistic "progress," felt theirs to be an age of social and artistic disintegration. The romantic century was the first that found itself compelled self-consciously to seek a style. London's Whitehall and Vienna's Ringstrasse bear witness to the parade of architectural revivals that attempted to exhibit the spirit of the times; ironically, only *in toto* did they express their perplexed age. In music, the newly born study called "musicology" was beginning to offer for adaptation a corresponding hoard of tonal artifacts. Among the many ambivalent characteristics of romanticism was the artist's desire for shelter in the objective security of an adopted style and his simultaneous yearning for subjective release through a revolutionary break with tradition. Liszt could not survive this conflict; Wagner put it on the stage as *Die Meistersinger*.

In its final act, Walther, having learned the masters' rules, excites their admiration in the festival meadow as he sings his prize song. But perceiving its manuscript fall from the spellbound Kothner's hand, he suddenly feels liberated and begins to improvise. What was written in the past no longer constrains. His composition has paid homage to tradition; rule has helped to a point. Suddenly unfettered, he responds to the impulse of the moment. His is a romantic vision, born of feeling, impetuosity, yearning, and reverie. To communicate its loosely but subtly connected images a relaxed, highly personal expression is needed, one answering only to the individual's sensitivity. Walther returns to the dream world that first gave his inspiration birth.

Wagner's music as a whole presents an analogous contention between the strict and the free. Abstract musical patterns cannot be reconciled *pari passu* with the business of drama, especially one whose ideal is of continuous flow. It was not Wagner's intention to attempt such an adjustment; in fact, in his opinion, Beethoven did violence to the dramatic concept of *Fidelio* by the recapitulation in the third *Leonore* Overture. There, Wagner felt, the development section with its trumpet call leads the listener to expect a theatrical conclusion, not a reprise; moreover, the customary change of key in this returning material gave him the impression of insufficient forward movement. His own solution to Beethoven's problem in *Fidelio* would certainly have been closer in spirit to the second *Leonore,* which anticipates the tensions of the drama by following the fanfare with the coda of hushed thanksgiving and then jubilation.

Wagner's musical form is essentially free, a kind of romantic tone poem bending to the dramatic needs of the text. In his attempt to describe the constructional principles of Liszt's symphonic poems, he admitted that his thoughts were not easy to make clear, for the "secret" lay in the artist's ability to behold the poetic subject in a way serving to shape intelligible musical forms. This was his own method, too, but all the more subtle and complicated in his case because dramatic poem and music often came to him simultaneously. His *The Destiny of Opera* defined the *Gesamtkunstwerk* in terms of extemporizing, and in his mature operas his composing technique had the character of a musical stream of consciousness, the ideal resembling that of the impromptu, not the sonata, whose essence he was never able to grasp.

Though at times he scoffed at Mozart's instrumental works, especially those in sonata form, *Don Giovanni* aroused his enthusiasm; as a theater composer Mozart was less bound to formal patterns than as a symphonist. (Wagner found the opera somewhat deficient dramatically and, when mounting it in Zurich, had felt obliged generally to touch things up.) And even though Wagner rejected the tradition from which Beethoven's methods grew, the bolder architecture, intenser expression, and more romantic, extrovert drama in the latter's symphonic scores drew his admiration. Their style appeared to him still bedeviled by traditional foursquare phrase construction (!); yet he found in their spontaneity and vital melody that craving for freedom which he imagined finally fulfilled only in his own creations. These, he declared, encompassed the Beethoven symphony, gave it a new formal liberty, and, ironically—in a not untypical Wagnerian resolution—thus ended its existence. He believed that he had married the Beethoven symphony to the Shakespearean drama's "sublime irregularity" (*"erhabenen Unregelmässigkeit"*), thereby reaching "perfection of musical form through its final emancipation from every remaining fetter." This *Liebestod* to the traditional symphony (it had really died decades before) appeared in *The Destiny of Opera,* in which the ideal music drama (obviously *Meistersinger*) was described as a fixed improvisation. That improvisation, once fixed, is no longer improvisation did not disturb Wagner. Though contradictory, the description communicated the very spirit of his musical method. He stood forth in a favorite role. The Beethoven symphony, though born with the original sin of classic form, was yet deemed worthy of redemption by Senta-Wagner, who, strengthened by thoughts of Shakespeare's untrammeled genius and armed with motivic techniques for swimming through heavy seas of tone, selflessly plunged into the amorphous floods of the romantic orchestral style.

II

Traditional patterns that stud his work certainly aided him—like Walther —to a point, providing convenient support for his kaleidoscopic motivic material, that system of interrelated themes upon which he relied to give the whole coherence. For Wagner, motivic repetition and transformation meant form, though at first glance it may seem illogical to describe the shape of an edifice in terms of the varied character of its brickwork; discussing the end, he seemed really to talk of the means toward it. His musical structure was patched together out of units whose occasionally traditional plans were for the most part called into use, molded, and modified by the requirements of drama. Motif, the musical flesh of these units, was (ideally), for Wagner, a direct function of his unfolding poem. Through the metamorphosis of motifs he explained a *modus* of musical *operandi* that was in itself his concept of form, a musical stream reflecting the vicissitudes of the libretto, a music that became drama because drama shaped its moods despite the motifs' frequent questionable relevance to specific points in the text.

As early as 1852 his letter to Uhlig quoted above showed him explaining his musical form in terms of the reiteration of motifs within the orchestral web. Nearly three decades later, his essay "The Application of Music to Drama" of 1879 described his musical unity not in terms of tectonics but as proceeding from the "web of motifs (*Grundthemen*) pervading the entire art-work, themes which, as in a symphonic movement, contrast, complete, reshape, separate, and intertwine." He stressed the fundamental difference between the manipulation of motifs in a symphony on the one hand and a music drama on the other, theatrical situations at times permitting eccentricities of modulation that would appear unmotivated in a piece of absolute music. Since symphonic forms descended from the dance, he had held their essential principles to be those of change, repetition, and alternation rather than development. In the relative freedom of Beethoven's development passages he had liked to imagine dramatic music releasing itself from the stricter symmetries of dance. But, though always preaching music's liberation and proud of his extraordinary achievement in heightening music's emotional power to the point of ecstatic abandonment, nonetheless, at the end of his days he appeared to fear lest the expressive weapons he had forged end by destroying the very integrity of the tonal art, should they fall into the hands of the less gifted. The hybrid Wagnerian music drama, created by a master, had opened the door to the rankest amateurism. Even Nietzsche took to writing titanic pieces in chromatic harmony. Perhaps Wagner's talk of turning to quartets and symphonies in the twilight of his career was not unrelated to the problem. Obviously disturbed by young composers who, in attempting to ape his style, strove for farfetched harmonic changes, he urged them to remain in a key so long as they had something to say in it. And he seemed to regret that there was more interest in the literary implications of his motifs than in their significance as musical structures.

Apart from observing, as in *Opera and Drama,* that a unified musical design proceeds from loyally paralleling a poetic plan through tone, Wagner indicated no belief in any overarching, abstract patterns informing his scores. (These patterns are, nevertheless, proved for Lorenz's disciples—including the many who have not struggled to read him—their arguments often seeming theological in spirit, in that they depend upon the very special insights of faith.) Attempts to diagram the weave of this marvelous musical cloth remain forced and futile; too much is freely worked. Warps and wefts may for a while duck in and out in some recognizable manner only suddenly to skip or twine irregularly, unprecedently. What is analyzable in such sections is usually so in terms of some dramatic need. Scenic effect and all those extramusical considerations that are part of the operatic convention also make demands upon the music. Wagner was no more innocent of musical padding than other opera composers.

In the end it must be admitted that often one can feel, not demonstrate, the strength of his formal logic, a musical vitality that could translate his operose poetic drama into an expansive art of overwhelming presence and persuasiveness. The high priest of intuition had only one "secret"—free-ranging romantic genius. He wrote, *"Kein Schema gibt's für meine Kunst . . ."* ("My art cannot be diagramed"); his creations will never happily yield to the chart maker.

XV

Parsifal *and Polemics:*
Eroticism, Vegetarianism, Racism,
and Redemption

I

A weary Wagner had returned from Italy to celebrate Christmas of 1876 at Bayreuth. His health had not improved. The festival's failure and the fall of Periclean Athens seemed to him analogous. Longing desperately to devote his remaining energies to *Parsifal,* he appeared eager to hand his theater over to almost anyone willing to assume its monstrous debt. Bayreuth was to be delivered to "the lasting care of a ruling social power." Lawsuits impended, and the day seemed not distant when unpaid contractors might strip the building of its movables. He toyed with the plan of selling Wahnfried to appease his creditors and moving to America, or of asking the Kaiser to take over the festival in the name of the Reich, ideas probably advanced as part of the old strategy to alarm the King, incite his fears and jealousy, and thus encourage his help. And Ludwig was to be appropriately horrified by the idea of Wagner in the New World; "in that obstinate American soil your roses cannot prosper, there where Mammon is lord of selfishness and lovelessness."

He was the cause of Wagner's latest quandary. Without royal consent the composer could not raise funds by selling the *Ring* to opera houses clamoring for it; legally the work belonged to the crown, which, in fact, also had a lien on the scenery and machinery Wagner hoped to rent to other theaters. But the niceties of contracts never impeded him when it was in his interest to ignore them, and, true to form, he was soon negotiating with Leipzig and Vienna. Like Otto Wesendonk before him, Ludwig, who never stopped the composer's munificent allowance, had long become resigned to his methods. Wagner was permitted to peddle the giant score for

389

his own profit if, at least, Munich's priority of performance was respected.[1]

Wagner saw his financial tangle most easily unsnarled could he persuade Munich to take over the Festspielhaus as a branch of its court theater, an admission that his former repudiation of the city and its Opera had had nothing to do with artistic standards, his objections and tirades having been raised only to mask the embarrassing Cosima problem. In fact, the Munich *Tristan* and *Meistersinger* remained the only productions of his works he consistently praised. (With close friends he did not dissimulate and spoke and wrote of his *Ring* performances in unhappy terms.) Supposedly, he had called Bayreuth into being because of Munich's deficiencies; now he was asking its personnel to join him at the new theater. Ironically, Bayreuth was to be saved by the Munich Opera and by the good will of its director, Perfall, whom he had so maliciously maligned during the *Rhinegold* crisis of 1869.

The grants Wagner had received and his continuing allowance entitled Munich to perform his works without paying royalties. However, the composer's genius, popularity at the box office, and need suggested to Perfall a special favor—a ten per cent commission on the gross receipts from Wagnerian works performed at the royal theater to be earmarked for the creditors of the Bayreuth festival. Banker Feustel, too, viewed such a concession as "a sole possibility of avoiding catastrophe." On the last day of March, 1878, the King acceded to the arrangement, which was to last until the liquidation of all debts. Furthermore, he guaranteed a yearly minimum payment of royalties, a commanding warranty enabling the festival committee to borrow sufficient funds to pay off contractors and workmen, the new loan being discharged by the royalty installments. When the loan was erased, the royalties were then to be credited to Ludwig's exchequer until his own advances were refunded. Thus, he not only freed Bayreuth from outside debt by diverting sums from his court theater's treasury, but then also proceeded to satisfy his own claims by transferring money from one of his pockets to another. The efforts of the Wagner clubs had produced little. Ludwig in reality built both the Festspielhaus and Wahnfried and then rescued the concept of Bayreuth from oblivion, a concept in which he never really believed. He, moreover, agreed that, should the composer's al-

---

[1] Some theaters wished to mount only *Valkyrie*, widely—and quite accurately —believed to be the only part of the *Ring* with a chance of survival in the general repertory; other houses thought it wise to start with *Valkyrie* and then, having won an audience, to move on to the rest of the cycle. From the beginning, *Valkyrie* commanded attention as the best constructed of the *Ring* dramas. Moreover, its scenic effects would not tax the capacities of any small theater equal to mounting *The Magic Flute*. And, above all, a Meyerbeer heroic tenor was not required, the part of Siegmund being negotiable by an ordinary dramatic tenor.

lowance cease after the discharge of the deficit, then the court Opera would be obliged to pay him or his heirs full legal commissions on performances, a move designed to strengthen his family's position upon his or the King's death. On the very day following the financial settlement, Perfall turned up in Wagner's correspondence as "highly gifted," the latter offering advice on the coming production of *Siegfried* in Munich, which he hoped would in some respects improve upon what had taken place in Bayreuth, an attitude that must have inspired wry smiles in those who remembered the storm he had raised over the capital's *Rhinegold* and *Valkyrie.*

A major point in the contract of 1878 was a stipulation lending the personnel of the Munich theater to Bayreuth for the production of *Parsifal* —guest artists, however, were not ruled out—Munich in return receiving the right to perform the work without paying royalties other than the gratuitously bestowed ten per cent. Obviously, in the interest of liquidating all obligations, *Parsifal* was to be completed and performed as quickly as possible. Thus, even before the work was finished, Wagner assented to public performances of it outside his own theater, their future receipts playing an important part in his financial arrangements with the King.[2]

Wagner had not been idle as others sought a formula to save Bayreuth. In the spring of 1877, after completing the poem of *Parsifal* (April 19), he had journeyed to London in an effort to raise money by giving concerts. Since his last visit Captain Fowke and General Scott had built their mammoth and improbable Albert Hall facing Kensington Gardens, and its ten thousand seats inspired enthusiasts to entice Wagner across the Channel with promises of rich profits. Several Bayreuth singers appeared with him, as did Richter, who conducted half of each concert (except that of May 19, which was led by Richter alone), Wagner fearing the strain of sustaining an entire program. But in his state of health he should never have undertaken the exertion of public appearances. Even close friends admitted he did not come out well in the taxing series, whose purpose was to summarize his development as poet and musician. He fatigued easily, his beat was more nervous than usual, and a once extraordinary memory now played

---

[2] At one point in his *Life* Ernest Newman would have it that the agreement of 1878 was a broad instrument designed to cover all possible contingencies, public performances of *Parsifal* in Munich, however, never being seriously contemplated. But the contractual details about just what royalties the King's theater would pay on the opera were obviously designed in reference to something quite specific, and Newman later admits in one of those reversals characteristic of his fourth volume: "Manifestly the Bayreuth production and the consequently ensuing performances in Munich were vital factors in the liquidation of the debt, so it is not to be wondered at that the Committee was perturbed by the implications of a postponement of the festival." In effect, a Munich production in Bayreuth was to be transplanted to the capital. Private performances of *Parsifal* in Munich for the King alone involved no question of receipts.

him wicked tricks. To add to his woes, the singers were plagued by laryngitis. Attendance, though large, fell well below expectations, and he felt happy to emerge from the experience with a relatively whole skin. In proportion to the energy expended, Bayreuth profited little.

He and Cosima left London on June 4 and proceeded to Bad Ems with its hot alkaline baths and draughts. They were joined by the children, little Siegfried evidently having need of a cure, too. The Kaiser was at the Kurhaus, and Fidi was sent off with a bouquet for him. Isolde, the only outspoken and unrepressed child of the group, was not along, having been left for treatment at an orthopedic institution at Altenburg. (She appeared to be the most gifted of the children and, in the great tradition, was to set to music her own text on the subject of the Newfoundland Marke, an opus the master himself would at times be heard singing.) Wagner rested at the Villa Diana, where, among others, Mathilde Wesendonk, with her daughter Myrrha, called.

After a month, the Wagners left the Rhineland for Heidelberg. There Siegfried fell seriously ill of a throat infection. The family tarried at the Hotel Schloss, which also housed Ulysses S. Grant. His meeting with Wagner ended in some embarrassment; the composer commanded only a few English phrases helpful at rehearsals, and the American statesman knew not a word of either German or French. Following an outing to Mannheim, the Wagners journeyed to Lucerne—with a sentimental visit to Triebschen—and then traveled on to Munich, where Wagner had a disheartening conversation about money with Herr Düfflipp. The family proceeded to Nuremberg and then to Weimar to see Grandfather Liszt (Loldchen had been picked up at the Altenburg clinic), and, after an excursion to Eisenach and the Wartburg, returned to Bayreuth at the end of July.

Of London, Wagner perhaps remembered with pleasure the Germanophiles George Henry Lewes and George Eliot. Cosima had read Lewes's biography of Goethe. One wonders whether Miss Eliot, who had recently written *Daniel Deronda,* discussed it with the author of *Jewry in Music.* He had met Browning, too, and been received at Windsor by Queen Victoria. For her part, Cosima had reveled in London's artistic riches, the monuments, galleries, and museums, and had made the acquaintance of Watts, Burne-Jones, and Herkomer. But, alas, the sight of a portrait of Joachim at Watts's studio seems to have ruined one of her days.

2

In September, 1877, the composition sketch of *Parsifal* was begun. Wagner seemed in a mellow mood when, on the fifteenth of the month, he lectured delegates of the Wagner clubs gathered in the Festspielhaus. What they lacked in money they balanced with enthusiasm, and many displayed a "Bayreuth ribbon" in the manner of a royal decoration. Wagner stressed his hopes of making the town an educational center of national art, where through training and lectures a new generation of instrumentalists, singers, and conductors might be developed to give model performances of German masterpieces, especially of his own works from *Dutchman* to *Parsifal.* The plan came to nothing. Even his most ardent followers must have sensed the tenuousness of his talk. And, embarrassingly, as he later admitted, no applicants answered his open invitation to join him in Bayreuth for practice sessions (*"Übungen und Ausführungen"*).

From this academic mood of late 1877 did come the establishment of his infamous journal, the *Bayreuther Blätter,* originally planned as the proposed school's literary organ. Its pages, sponsored by the newly reorganized patrons, provided a forum from which he could hold forth on any topic entering his head. Attempts to found a Bayreuth Academy having failed, Wagner looked to the *Blätter* as an instrument in which to apprise subscribers of "the obstacles to a noble development of the German artistic capacity . . . and the efforts necessary to conquer them." Considering this program, it is not surprising that his main contribution to the publication was a series of anti-Semitic tracts in which he at times descended to a vulgarity marking the *Bayreuther Blätter* as an ancestor of Rosenberg's *Der Völkische Beobachter* [3] and even Streicher's filthy *Stürmer.* The wealthy young Prussian Hans von Wolzogen, one of the most fully indoctrinated of Wagnerites, was summoned to Bayreuth to edit this new propaganda sheet. He was to become a somewhat pitiable substitute for the traitorous Professor Nietzsche—Wagner rather naïvely assuring the King, perhaps to help reassure himself, that Wolzogen, too, had studied philology! In the direction of the periodical, Cosima, however, was the *éminence grise;* from her Wolzogen humbly took his marching orders. She was under no illusions and after almost two years of struggle with the publication could write Hermann Levi, "Wolzogen can certainly not vie with Nietzsche as a stylist at present [!], but I most decidedly hope that he will train himself to be a writer; I agree with you that he is not a born one. Wolzogen has one of the most curious natures I have ever come across, a life so completely absorbed in an idea would seem incredible had one not seen it." And this quality justified all in Bayreuth.

[3] Rosenberg shared editorial duties with Dietrich Eckhart (also spelled Eckart), who is frequently confused with Cosima's biographer, Richard, Count du Moulin-Eckart. Dietrich, often called "the spiritual father of National Socialism," died of alcoholism late in 1923.

Amazingly, the *Blätter* project got under way at a time when it appeared doubtful whether the Festspielhaus stage would again be used for anything more ambitious than sessions of the Wagner clubs. Wolzogen settled in Bayreuth in October (the maiden copy of the *Blätter* appearing in February, 1878) while the first moves toward rescuing Bayreuth were only started by Perfall in November, 1877, to reach fruition the following spring.

There was always something of the frustrated schoolmaster about Wagner. If he had to go down, he would do so discoursing. The journal was a consolation to him during his last years. Germany had done worse to him than reject the externals of Bayreuth's art; it had remained indifferent to the significance of his movement intended to regenerate the nation's spirit. And in the pages of the *Blätter* he could bring his salon harangues to a wider public and have the pleasure of printing denunciations of apathetic Germans who would not stir themselves to assert an innate racial superiority (by attending performances at Bayreuth, one supposes) and of publicly raging against the perennial wickedness of the Jews.

By the close of 1877, when Munich was first giving hope of saving Bayreuth from bankruptcy, Wagner was deep in the first act of *Parsifal*. He was coming to see in Christ's self-sacrifice upon the cross the ultimate symbol of the reversal of the will to live—Jesus as the greatest Schopenhauerean. That he had achieved being without natural fecundation was to Wagner further evidence of a mission of world-denial and symbolic of the nullity of phenomena. The idea derived from Schopenhauer himself, who had equated Christ's freedom from sin with his rejection of life and saw the virgin birth as a sign of disaffirmation. In *Parsifal* Wagner's canon preaching the identity of denial, death, redemption, and love was to amalgamate with racism to reach a strange apotheosis. As he toiled at the marvelous score, he was to deliver himself of much philosophic feculence, out of which would grow the essay "Religion and Art," published in the *Blätter* in 1880. But his initial impulse to start work on *Parsifal* had been incited by something quite far from abstract maunderings.

3

During the festival of 1876 Wagner had had his final grand affair. Filled with thoughts of *Parsifal,* the aging voluptuary sought to quicken the erotic senses—now failing—that in former years had always liberated his inspiration. What Rosalie, Schröder-Devrient, Minna, Jessie Laussot, Mathilde Wesendonk, Mathilde Maier, and Cosima in their various ways had once done for him, became the mission of Judith Gautier, a voluptuous

French beauty, daughter of the famous poet who had been an early champion of Wagnerian opera.

In the company of her husband, the poet and critic Catulle Mendès (a Sephardic Jew who in the year of the Paris *Tannhäuser* had asked Wagner to contribute to his new—and short-lived—*Revue fantastique*), and of their friend Villiers de l'Isle-Adam, she had visited Triebschen several times during the period of the *Ring* productions at Munich. Dazzled by her beauty, Wagner had made a bit of a fool of himself, climbing trees and scaling the façade of the house to belie his years and prove his fitness and manliness, the boy acrobat of Eisleben offering her his accomplishments while the guests cried out in admiration and mock terror.

Both she and Mendès turned up at the Bayreuth festival, although they had separated two years before. Offended by the crudities of *A Capitulation,* he had repudiated Wagner the man and walked glumly past the entrance to Wahnfried. Judith had no such scruples and wished a significant place in the Wagnerian chronicle. She gave herself to the genius almost forty years her senior. Cosima, of course, knew of their trysts at Judith's lodgings, but, aware of her husband's special needs, diplomatically turned her head. She had become what Minna had been to him during their middle years together, someone who saw to his comfort and well-being, Cosima's sense of mission and iron control, however, never permitting her to voice, except in her diary, the sense of injury that life with him could occasionally kindle even in her. But she realized he could not break into the atmosphere of a new work if restricted to the well-ordered routine with which she surrounded him, a kind of wisdom poor Minna had completely lacked.

Whereas in his younger years his love affairs were first by-products of his artistic energies and then furnished a reciprocal excitation of his sensibilities, the brief liaison with Judith was a stimulus in reverse (really in reverie) to *Parsifal*. The fires no longer flared; sparks were now precious. And the fresh fuels banking the flames had to be ever richer and rarer. His needs for silks, satins, furs, and perfumes had reached the fetishistic. A strange compulsion forced him to pull on ludicrous travesty. That his skin was extremely sensitive may explain his silk chokers and underwear but hardly those quilted, shirred, bowed, laced, flowered, fringed, and furred gowns he dragged through his private rooms. In a famous letter to Bertha, his seamstress, he once poetically described and sketched a sash five yards in length to be made for a fantastic pink satin robe of his own design. Considering his height of little over five feet, one must wonder how he managed to walk in these costumes without tripping.

Coincidently with his work on the first act of *Parsifal* he wrote frankly to his *"douce amie,"* Judith, whom he also called *"geliebtes Weib,"* of certain childish indulgences (*"enfantillages"*) he wished to permit himself. From

Paris, hated capital of *"welsch"* degeneracy, she was to send him rich fabrics and exotic scents. His letters to her were not unlike those of the eighteen-sixties to Fräulein Bertha, except that Judith received her orders for merchandise mixed with references to her smothering kisses and warm arms. When Daniel Spitzer printed Wagner's letters to Bertha in the Vienna *Neue Freie Presse* in 1877, he expressed fears that the world's satin reserves were inadequate to fill the bottomless gulf of the composer's needs. Indeed, the latter confessed to Judith the enormous pleasure satin woven of silk gave him. But though he required vast quantities of it, alas, Judith's suppliers seemed unable to come up with *his* shade of "pale and delicate" pink. (The difficulties of getting this color had caused a crisis or two with Bertha.) And he wanted a yellow silk lampas with embroidered pink flowers, which he would call "Judith" and use as a cover for his chaise longue. Reclining on "Judith" he would be able to conceive music for his sacred work, *Parsifal.*

In the late years, with the decay of the senses, his erotic interest in perfumes grew even stronger. He asked Judith to ship limitless amounts of amber, Milk of Iris (he poured half a bottle of it into his daily bath), and Rose de Bengale, and he called for powdered scents to sprinkle over fabrics. Kundry was sending him "balsam from Arabia" along with an eagerly awaited pair of Turkish slippers. As he conceived the music to Amfortas' progress to his healing dip, Wagner may well have pictured Kundry in terms of Judith and her exotic salts and minerals. With this knowing Parisian he seems to have lowered some of the barriers masking lifelong compulsions. His study in Wahnfried was directly over the bath, which he would inundate with rare odors. Seated at his desk and attired in incredible silk and fur outfits douched with sachet, he breathed in the aromatic fumes rising from below and with them memories of Judith's glowing embraces. Amid scenes worthy of Huysmans' Des Esseintes,[4] the first act of the "religious" drama, *Parsifal,* came into being.

Early in 1878 he contemplated the world and cried out in distress and with unwitting humor to Ludwig, "Then German decadence is no longer to be arrested." Though he denounced degeneracy in others, his own odd methods of titillation seemed to him really quite charming. The old passions had to be stimulated under a kind of voluptuous duress. In his original French he had called Judith his *"superflu enivrant,"* his *"Abondance."*

---

[4] Des Esseintes, hero of Huysmans' *A Rebours,* studied perfumes as one would languages. Count Robert de Montesquiou, whose character furnished, in part, the model for Des Esseintes and for Proust's Baron Charlus, was known to intimates as "Chief of Fragrant Odors," and Dorian Gray, an ardent Wagnerite, was also a scholar of scents. Wagner told Judith that perfumes could make him do "silly things."

(She later commented on "the freedom and audacity" of his French.) Feeling the current flowing in reverse he knew *Parsifal* to be his final creation. Siegfried had welded a weapon; Parsifal was to break his.

So steadily and intensely did Wagner work that Cosima feared for his health; his problem was not to find ideas but to set limits to those that came to him. He archly observed, "I am composing all day now, like Raff or Brahms." For him, the true German composer was not what he considered Brahms—a craftsman and no more—but a priest of music, "demonically suffering, godlike." In his caustic "On Poetry and Composition" of June, 1879, he wrote with obvious reference to Brahms's eclecticism, "Compose, compose, even when you have no ideas! Why is it called 'composing'— a putting together—if invention, too, is considered necessary? . . . I know famous composers whom you can meet at concert masquerades, today in a ballad singer's disguise . . . tomorrow in Handel's Hallelujah wig, another time as a Jewish czardas player, and then again as genuine symphonists decked out as a number ten," the last a bitter reference to Bülow's having welcomed Brahms's First Symphony as "Beethoven's Tenth." Wagner thought of his own works as ethical and political revelations in the medium of tone; Brahms, with his diligence in all instrumental forms and his opus numbers, seemed to him a musical mechanic, a worthless survivor of another age.

By the end of 1878 Wagner had reached the composition and orchestral sketches for the third act of *Parsifal*. But a doubt lingered in his mind. The instrumentation was to differ completely from that of the *Ring,* in which, despite the sunken pit, more than occasionally his singers had struggled unequally against the volume of orchestral sound. (Just before the curtain rose on the first *Ring,* he had instructed his instrumentalists, "Piano, pianissimo, and then all will be well!") In *Parsifal* the instrumental web was to be spun of "cloud layers" (*"Wolkenschichten"*). Frightened by his frequent heart spasms, Cosima urged him to rest. Pretending to stop and divert himself with reading, he secretly completed the orchestration of the prelude, borrowed the Duke of Meiningen's orchestra of fifty men,[5] strengthened them with some wind players from the local regimental band, rehearsed at the Hotel Sonne, and on Christmas morning awakened Cosima with the harmonies of this incomparable tone poem rising from the hall of Wahnfried. (In 1881 a change was made in bars ninety-nine and one hundred, a weak progression being eliminated.) Along with those mummings in which the children in costume recited poems in his praise, he

[5] Early in 1877, before departing for the London concerts, Wagner and Cosima had attended some of the famous performances at the Meiningen theater—Grillparzer, Molière, and Shakespeare—and charmed Duke Georg II.

loved arranging such serenades. They could hardly have been kept secret. Possibly Cosima was surprised by the "Triebschen Idyll," but she must have put her considerable histrionic talent to the test in registering astonishment at a full symphony orchestra in her front hall. The family wept in delirium as the piece unfolded. Sobbing with the others, Wagner then burst with joy. How it sounded! The opera had long been generating its own momentum and La Gautier forgotten; months before, he had turned his correspondence with her over to Cosima. His final communication to Judith, on February 10, 1878, had ended, *"et enfin nous nous reverrons un jour!"*

4

In the seclusion of Wahnfried the opera grew—easily, inevitably. Early in 1878, when it was clear that Munich would free him of debt, he had written Ludwig, "The days flow by, one very much like the other; but each day advances my work. I am now living the happiest time of my life."

The composition and orchestral sketches of *Parsifal* were completed at the end of April, 1879. He sent Ludwig some verses on May 3, the date on which the summons to Munich had come fifteen years before:

> *Dritter Mai! Holder Mai!*   Third of May, gracious May!
> *Dir sei mein Lob gespendet:*   To you be praise extended:
> *Winters Herrschaft ist vorbei*   Winter's rule has had its day,
> *Und Parsifal vollendet.*   And *Parsifal* is ended.

Work on articles (especially "Shall We Hope?," an ambitious attack on the Reichstag and the press) and an excursion to the Fränkische Schweiz early in summer (Pegnitz, Pottenstein, Gössweinstein, Muggendorf, and back to Bayreuth via Streitberg) provided some diversion. And at the beginning of August he started to rule the bar lines of his full score, a labor revealing how clearly instrumental details were envisioned. There remained the formidable mechanical job of putting them down between the neatly drawn verticals, and he began it before the month was over.

Despite almost unrelenting work, his understanding with Munich to produce the opera in 1880 could not be realized. Certainly he must have recognized this goal as unattainable when the agreement of 1878 was ratified. However, he never took clauses not to his advantage very seriously and, for the most part, looked upon contracts as providing some momentary advantage and then to be modified or ignored. The arrangement of 1878 had furnished the means of quieting the immediate and threatening demands of contractors. It was time to renegotiate. Ludwig, always understanding, consented during July of 1879 to an amendment leaving the date of the première entirely to the composer, the only answer from the artistic point of view, for Wagner could never function within time limits. But the change could hardly have reassured those concerned with the festival loan, for receipts from the Munich *Parsifal* were to play their part in its reduction. Moreover, Wagner, in defiance of his obligation, was openly talking of restricting the work to Bayreuth.

The existence of the *Bayreuther Blätter* had stirred him to renewed literary activity, ironically at a time when Cosima remarked of her friend Malwida von Meysenbug, "I marvel that those who have been through a great deal do not really grow tired of expressing their views—and printing them. . . ." Orchestrated, as usual, with sounding brass and tinkling cymbals and boldly ranging the arts and sciences, his articles, for the most part, clearly pertained to *Parsifal,* especially his vigorous denunciation of vivisection, most obviously an offshoot of this drama in which a lifelong love of animals was finding expression. In *Die Feen,* the mad Arindal imagined himself shooting a beast which then, to his horror, looked back with the same "broken eye" Parsifal was to observe almost half a century later in the slain swan. Since that day in Venice when a bloody poulterer's establishment had caught his glance, Wagner had guarded a vision of the Grail domain, wherein all creatures would be sacred. Inevitably, he also embraced vegetarianism, a practice he had formerly censured in Nietzsche and which, Weingartner observed, despite spirited recommendations to others, remained without visible effect on his own diet. *"Wie steht es denn mit den Vegetabilien?"*—"How is the vegetable affair coming along?"—Cosima had ironically asked Nietzsche in September, 1869. But now vegetables were a solemn matter to Wagnerites, commanded by their master to become herbivorous. Darwin's *Descent of Man* of 1871 (almost immediately translated into German by Carus) was one of the consolations of Wagner's final years; by revealing man and beast to be of the same substance, it gave him hope for a new religion in which vegetarianism and antivivisectionism were to play a part.

His public condemnation of vivisection (autumn, 1879) took the form of an open letter to Ernst von Weber, former African explorer and diamond miner and now author of *The Torture Chambers of Science.* Wagner's article offered an incredible motley of elements. Jesus and Darwin somehow joined forces to point the way. Examining the relationship of the human race to animals, Wagner discovered the latter to be morally superior creatures, subject to man only because he possessed a quality they lacked—deceit. But since it had been demonstrated that man descended from the beast, man and beast were one. By mixing evolutionary theory with the New Testament, Wagner brought salvation to the animals, for, he stressed, Christ died for all who breathe. What prevented the world from grasping the full splendor of this Wagnerian revelation was the Pentateuch, the books of the Jews preaching animal slaughter and sacrifice. "The Old Testament has won the day, and the predatory beast has become a beast of prey who does sums." (This image of the Jew so appealed to Wagner that he repeated it in his article "Know Thyself.") Incomprehensively, Ernst Newman summed up the letter to Weber as "an eloquent pleading of the cause of suffering animals that cannot plead their own."(!) More perspicaciously, Nietzsche in *The Gay Science* traced Wagner's preaching of pity in dealing with animals to Schopenhauer and, ultimately, Voltaire, and commented on the ability "to camouflage hatred of certain men and things as pity for animals." (Heinrich Himmler, too, was known to speak tenderly of the virtue of love for animals.)

In the course of Wagner's preposterous ramble on vivisection, in which he not only railed at the books of Moses but also hurled brickbats at Nietzsche and Brahms—there are obvious allusions to Nietzsche's disavowal in *Human, All too Human* of Schopenhauer's concept of pity, and the sorry affair ends with a slap at Brahms's *A German Requiem*—one recognizes the Good Friday discourse of Gurnemanz in the last act of *Parsifal,* wherein all creation (including vegetation!) shares the redemptive wonders of the holy day, and in the references to Darwinism are to be glimpsed links to the notion of Parsifal as a redeemer of race. In "Religion and Art" of the following year Wagner was to join even more closely the concepts of vivisection and flesh eating, an association already evident in the open letter. (To him vivisection was clearly born of the brutality of Jewish doctors.) He was to divulge a new text for the Last Supper, according to which Christ, the supreme symbol of slaughtered flesh, "offered his disciples wine and bread for their daily meal," saying, "Taste such alone in memory of me," an ordinance directing his followers to become vegetarians!

Asininity had never been foreign to Wagner's essays, but with the open letter appear the first signs of a frightening irrationality, a clouding of the mind, a general corruption of the faculties evident and increasing throughout 1880 and patently manifesting itself in "Religion and Art." More and more often he was gripped by heart spasms. Unable to pick up his score again until the end of September of that year, he was barely able to finish ruling his bar lines, and only two months later, on November 23, could he resume orchestrating. The year had been spent in a long, futile search for health in Italy.

5

On the last day of 1879 he had fled to Italy with his family to escape the rigors of Bayreuth's winter and the depressing sight of the empty theater, which he called "a madman's whim" (*"eine Narrenlaune"*). Drawn toward the Neapolitan sun, for seven months he occupied the luxurious Villa Angri at Posilipo. By summer, a severe outbreak of facial erysipelas, which had been plaguing him again, made a change of climate expedient. Sea bathing was to be exchanged for mountain air, and doctors recommended his immediate return to Germany for a rigorous cure at Gräfenberg in Silesia's Reichensteiner Gebirge. But refusing "to be fool enough to abandon Italy in her most beautiful months for evergreens, rain, and a heavy overcoat," he chose to resettle somewhat northward. After an exploratory tour, including a rest in Perugia, he established himself at Siena in what Liszt called a "princely" palace, the Villa Torre Fiorentina. It had once housed Pope Pius VI, and Wagner delightedly reposed in the enormous papal bed.

During the Italian sojourn he would not stir without a retinue of friends and servants, and Cosima was often appalled by the expenditure. Wagner did not move; he "progressed." Happily, Ludwig specially augmented his ill and aging friend's allowance so that no luxury might lack. In all was an unspoken fear; the full score of *Parsifal* was somewhere in his head, but the ruled measures remained empty. That miraculous mental concentration of old refused his summons, a disastrous condition for someone who had described composition as recollection; he was failing. The completion and mounting of *Parsifal* were to become a race with death. Cosima, watching anxiously, could not bear to believe him subject to physical laws. Was not his genius great enough to exempt him from the eternal processes? The death of Anselm Feuerbach in Venice on the very day Wagner entered the Villa Angri was a frightening omen.

Social intercourse was Wagner's salvation. He visited the conservatory of Naples to meet Francesco Florimo, who in 1876 had brought Bellini's remains back to his native soil from Paris, a service similar to that performed decades before by Wagner in respect to Weber. *The Destiny of Opera* had disdainfully called Bellini's music "insipid and threadbare." But now Wagner was returning to a love of his youth; crying, "Bellini! Bellini!" he embraced the octogenarian musical scholar, both old men trembling with emotion.

A parade of guests passed through Wagner's grandiose Italian salons. Unable to work, he found his need greater than ever for submissive souls to lecture and then dismiss when done with them. Though he read aloud and expounded the *Oresteia* to his followers on three successive evenings, he fatigued easily; to Ludwig he wrote, "What I require is only a deep sleep with complete forgetfulness . . . for my weariness is boundless. . . ." The resumption of work on *Mein Leben* filled him with depressing memories. He was not easy company. With Liszt, who joined the family for ten days at Siena, he dared not assume those despotic airs that now came so naturally.

Beneath shaggy brows the Abbé's eyes still flashed with independence, and from the beginning he had never taken Wagner the diatribist very seriously. But new bondmen danced attendance, among them Sgambati, a Liszt pupil Wagner had met in Rome in 1876 and hailed as an unusually gifted composer. A Russian painter, Paul Zhukovski, had quickly become a part of the Posilipo household, where the young Rhenish musician Engelbert Humperdinck was also welcomed. Both were to follow Wagner back to Bayreuth. (Ironically, Humperdinck had come to Italy through funds from Berlin's Mendelssohn Foundation.) The moody Joseph Rubinstein, whom Wagner called "my Wahnfried court pianist," appeared and was at the keyboard when the first Grail scene from *Parsifal* was performed at Villa Angri on Wagner's sixty-seventh birthday, the composer, Humperdinck, and Martin Plüddemann singing the Grail Knights and Cosima's daughters the voices from on high. And there was Siegfried's tutor, handsome, dashing Heinrich von Stein, a pupil of the ferociously anti-Semitic philosopher Dühring [6] and a friend of Malwida von Meysenbug's.

Most of all, Wagner enjoyed the presence of this highly bred spinster from Kassel, long a staunch fighter in the Wagnerian ranks. He had first met her during his visit to London in 1855,[7] when she, too, was an exile. Malwida had first brought Frau Schwabe to his Paris drawing room and during the pandemonium at the Opéra's second *Tannhäuser* had at the top of her voice delivered an opinion of France's musical culture that made Minna fear for her courageous friend's safety. Doughty Malwida, notorious as a friend and confidante of Mazzini, had attended all performances, ready to do battle. Time and again she proved her devotion to Wagner and his cause, even making the effort to take up residence at Bayreuth, though the raw climate soon drove her away. His description of her as "unbelievably ugly" and as "a democratic old maid," though discreetly cut by Cosima from the published Wesendonk letters, may be excused as a simple factual report. Malwida was one of the few for whom he could find no unkind words, and this despite her friendship with Nietzsche.

[6] In Stein, Nietzsche saw a fine intellect to be rescued: "This excellent person, who, with all the impetuous artlessness of a young Prussian nobleman, had waded deep into the Wagnerian swamp (and into that of Dühringism besides!)." Engels called Dühring "the Richard Wagner of philosophy—but without Wagner's talents."

[7] In London, Malwida had been companion and tutor to the children of Alexander Herzen, the famous political writer who had established his "Free Russian Press" in the English capital, Madame Herzen having years before decamped with the poet Georg Herwegh, a member of Wagner's Zurich circle. In her final years Malwida became Wagnerian catechist to the youthful Romain Rolland. The autobiographical *Memoirs of an Idealist* are an interesting record of her determination to play a role in artistic and intellectual life.

Wagner's long line of young male disciples that had started in Paris four decades before with Kietz ended with another ineffective artist, Paul Zhukovski. The son of a German mother and of the Russian translator and poet Vasili Zhukovski, who had been the Czar's tutor and close to Goethe, Paul spoke German fluently. A member of the international artistic colony, a friend of Turgenev and of Henry James, he was a mere dilettante painter, his great gift being a personality of extraordinary winsomeness and the manner and conversation of someone raised at the imperial court of St. Petersburg. The elegant Liszt paid him his highest compliment: "Personally he is very much of a gentleman, and not at all boring." Renoir, who was to meet him in Palermo, declared, "This Russian is charming." In Paris, Henry James had found him "a most *attachant* creature," and they had vowed eternal friendship. Indeed, James thought he had discovered a soul friend. But fate had brought Zhukovski to a house but minutes from Villa Angri; the Paul-Henry relationship was to founder on Wagner.

Certainly James had no illusions about Paul's artistic or even intellectual abilities; he was the wealthy amateur, an eternal dabbler, "a lightweight and a perfect failure," with the softness often characterizing the son of a father's old age. But if a visit to Posilipo confirmed James's estimate of this "impracticable and indeed ridiculous mixture of Nihilism and bric-a-brac," the change that contact with Wagner had worked upon his friend's once so enchanting personality repelled him. The discerning visitor to the 1876 festival was now a Wagnerian flunkey. His sweetness and delicacy, once so winning, had turned to self-abasement; Paul had found his cause and sunk down in complete humility, speaking of the composer in terms of ultimate greatness and ultimate wisdom. Turgenev had once described Paul as a "naïve epicurean," but his personality now seemed ruled by a rather sophisticated servility. In Wagner he found someone born to command and felt himself destined to obey (most of Wagner's relationships with men were sado-masochistic), though he was aware of the composer's daemonic power either to build or destroy. Not only did the new Zhukovski unsettle James, but he could not stomach Wagner's entourage with its "fantastic immorality and aesthetics." Evidently Cosima was not his idea of a lady. After three uncomfortable days, he fled Posilipo for Sorrento.

Wagner wished Paul to design settings not only for *Parsifal* but also for all the operas to be eventually mounted at Bayreuth. There the young man was to settle and make his art collection the nucleus of a local museum. The composer clung to him with incredible tenacity, later taking offense when he dared leave for a holiday of a few days. During their happy excursions together in Italy the general outlines of the *Parsifal* scenery took shape. From the Saracenic courtyard and exotic park of the Palazzo Rufolo in Ravello (some miles northeast of Amalfi) came inspiration for Klingsor's magic garden, and in the superb domed cathedral of Siena they saw a vision of the Grail temple. On Wagner's side, this vision certainly grew from recollections of Dresden's cupolaed Frauenkirche, where his *Love Feast of the Apostles* had first been heard. Its thematic material, particularly the "architectural" disposition of its voice parts, returned in *Parsifal*.

Desiring to possess Paul completely, Wagner came to speak of him as a son of his first marriage—a very strange fantasy; for his part, the artist adopted a Neapolitan fishing lad, Peppino, whom he took along to Bayreuth when setting out to dedicate himself to the eternal work.

6

During ten months in Italy Wagner produced nothing save the foolish "Religion and Art" and a brief and murky supplement to it. At first, the essay appears to promise an exploration of the power of music to reveal the essence of religious symbolism. (What Wagner essentially intended to convey was succinctly put by Cosima in a letter to Hermann Levi, "Believe me, my friend, our art is a religion. It has been made possible for art to rescue what is most holy to us from all dogmatism and rigid formalism.") But Wagner pulls the reader into a labyrinth of irrelevant, convoluted thought; vegetarianism, vivisection, racial decline, alcoholism, Schopenhauerean metaphysics, geology, trade unionism, folk migrations, socialism, Jehovah's villainy, penal reform, ethnology, zoology—all are touched upon with the aplomb of ignorance. The twaddle is readable only because each succeeding idiocy plays its part in building a kind of fascinating surrealistic fantasy —Wagnerian reality. One learns, for example, that the Japanese are strict vegetarians, that in certain American prisons the most hardened criminals have been completely reformed simply by putting them on a vegetarian diet, that the cult of the Virgin Mary arose as an expression of opposition to the dreadful Jewish Jehovah, that a painting of this tribal god cannot possibly have any effect on the devout, that on the brackish shores of the Canadian lakes survive species of vegetarian panthers and tigers. Perhaps the most impressive revelation is Wagner's latest plan to save the world: He would encourage vegetarianism by a migration of the population from those northern lands whose climate encourages man to eat flesh to the more temperate zones of South America and Africa. Humanity was to be redeemed by a vegetable diet.

The most extraordinary thing about the whole affair was that there were those to take it seriously at the time and later. Members of the Italian entourage could only shake their heads in wonder at a wisdom soon to be shared with all the patrons, thanks to the existence of the *Blätter*. The Bible of Elizabeth Nietzsche's husband, Bernhard Förster, was "Religion and Art" and its supplements.[8] In one of the latter, "Know Thyself" of 1881, Wagner declared Germany fallen—"exposed defenseless against the incursions of the Jews." In 1886 Förster and Elizabeth quit Germany for Paraguay and, with a group of adherents, founded Nueva Germania, a colony that attempted to live Wagner's teachings, especially his anti-Semitism. (The composer had watched Förster's public agitations with sympathetic interest but with little confidence in their success.) The settlement was a failure, many followers accusing the Försters of swindling them of their money, a Wagnerian detail evidently added to the program. Förster committed suicide in 1889, and Elizabeth returned to Germany. For a while the financial scandals growing out of this Paraguayan adventure in applied Wagnerism damaged the anti-Semitic movement in Germany. However, it recovered. Like Hitler, another and somewhat later student of Wagner's prose, Förster had become an ardent vegetarian. And if the Wagnerian vivisection reform did not sweep South America and failed to come into being in Germany under Ludwig or the Kaiser, Hitler, as Walter Kaufmann observed, "later copied Wagner's antivivisectionism and enforced it by law."

Wagner himself delighted in toying with the notion of emigrating to America to found a "new society." Bound to ideas of racial purification and vast sums of money, the plan became one of the most comforting fantasies of his old age. Years before in Zurich he had met Carl Schurz; moreover, impressions of visiting German-Americans had recently so encouraged him that startling visions rose before his eyes—a million dollars raised by subscription and a theater, school, and home in Minnesota. Americans, among them his dentist, Dr. Jenkins, attempted to cool his ardor. Certainly the United States would welcome the great composer, but that religious attitude toward Wagnerian opera he demanded and which had not developed in Germany was even less likely to grow across the seas. But Wagner insisted that the best Germans were leaving for the United States, where they were preserving the racial stock in its purity as the old Germany with the rest of Europe sank into decay. Heinrich von Stein was instructed to procure a map of North America and to educate Siegfried for a future as an American. The idea came and went, and was but one of the many reveries of Wagner's dotage. (He also dreamed of the boy's becoming a combination of doctor and veterinarian, evidently some kind of healer able to cure both wounded swans and ailing Grail kings.)

[8] Wagner called "What Avails This Knowledge?" a *Nachtrag* or supplement to "Religion and Art"; the later "Know Thyself" and *"Heldentum und Christentum"* were termed *Ausführungen* or amplifications of "Religion and Art." "Supplement" here covers all three essays.

Early in October, 1880, the Wagners, turning homeward, pressed farther north toward Venice. After two days in the Hotel Danieli, they set themselves up in the splendor of the Palazzo Contarini on the Grand Canal. During his month in Venice Wagner pursued his friendship with Count Gobineau, pored over the latter's *Essay on the Inequality of Races,* and completed his first supplement to "Religion and Art," called "What Avails This Knowledge?"

It is a terrible fog of words—though a mercifully small patch—out of which peers his concept of art providing what debased religion could no longer bestow. The noblest art-work (he does not name *Parsifal*) through its "enrapturing effect" (*"entrückende Wirkung"*) on the spirit would bring the spectator images of the archetypical Christian virtues whose order he arranges as Love (*Liebe*), Faith (*Glaube*), and Hope (*Hoffnung*), this new disposition following the motivic construction of the *Parsifal* prelude. When he conducted two private performances of it for King Ludwig on November 12, less than three weeks after completing the article, Wagner provided a special program note describing the composition as being built upon his newly reordered trinity of virtues, the final *Hoffnung* being followed by a question mark, realized in music by the unresolved chord of the seventh with which the piece ends. This questioning hope, to be confirmed by the drama of *Parsifal,* was for Germany's racial regeneration.

He arrived in Munich at the end of October. *Kapellmeister* Levi had arranged to give a series of Wagner operas. At a private performance of *Lohengrin* for Wagner and Ludwig, they sat together in the royal box. Wagner called Lohengrin "the magician" of their love, who had first brought them together, and, fittingly, the work was the occasion of this, their last intimate meeting.

Stormy and emotional ovations greeted the gray-haired, stooping composer wherever he appeared in Munich. The power-drunk royal favorite of the sixties was forgotten; there were only the works. His artistic magnitude now seemed part of his presence as he gradually began to shed his mortality. At the special renditions of the *Parsifal* prelude he laid eyes on Ludwig for the last time. November 17 found him at Wahnfried, and within the week he was bending over the unfinished orchestration of *Parsifal's* opening act.

And *Parsifal* was now his own. He had played and won a final game with Munich and the King. Grieved that what he termed the "last and holiest" of his works was, according to the agreement of 1878, to share the *Ring's* fate and end on the common operatic stage, he had determined to scrap the offensive clause. As early as August, 1879, when the instrumentation of *Parsifal* was only begun, Ludwig was warned that the work might not be produced during the composer's lifetime. (It is to be remembered that the King had relinquished any say in the matter of the première's date only the month before; Wagner was never slow to press an advantage.)

He would lovingly work at the orchestration, lock the finished score "under seven seals," and leave it to his son to determine when the time was right for its performance. "What then is the place of this most Christian of all artworks in a world that in cowardice succumbs to the Jews!"

His laments at the prospect of releasing *Parsifal* to this degraded, evil society had reached a climax in a letter to Ludwig from Siena dated September 28, 1880. The resounding Wagnerian bombarde voiced the composer's often repeated threat to quit Europe and tour the United States, where a quickly earned fortune would make him independent. October had not passed when Ludwig renounced his theater's rights to *Parsifal*, except for private performances for himself.

From some reserve of genius Wagner summoned strength to continue its instrumentation at Bayreuth. He worked so as to profit by the unique acoustical qualities of his theater. The dampening effect of the deep and covered pit, which had robbed the *Ring* orchestra of its luster, was turned to advantage in the gossamer and aloof quality of the score. The Festspielhaus was built to house the *Ring* after most of it had been conceived and written, the pit functioning mainly as a corrective device. *Parsifal* alone was created specially for this theater and, not surprisingly, still gains something exceptional—apart from sentimental atmosphere and historical associations—from the hall's architecture. The world of musical impressionism arose from the opera's wondrous orchestral textures. *Pelléas* was to be its child, though a son who reacted against the father he so resembled. Wagner, an artist who in general had built upon and summarized the achievements of his contemporaries, was in his old age following new paths.

But, as he labored, there was that tightening around his heart; death was stubbornly at work.

7

Increasingly Wagner looked upon *Parsifal* as a testament bequeathing the sum of his knowledge to the Germany he never ceased to berate and yet love. This consciousness of mission had furthered his persistent maneuvers to reserve the work for Bayreuth. "Religion and Art" observed that the "poet-priest, the only one who never lied, was always sent to mankind as mediating friend at its direst periods of terrible error," and to Wagner the times seemed supremely perilous. In a letter written to the King from Villa Angri on March 31, he had followed a long jeremiad with a paragraph filled with hope drawn from this sense of destiny: "I rejoice in one thought and consideration, the results of which might yet bring a great salvation to the world. It really seems to me that I should be able to make clear to miserably degenerate man the reason for his degeneracy and for his redeemer, Christ. In my various articles in the *Bayreuther Blätter* my gracious friend [Ludwig] has certainly already observed my serious and consuming interest in discussing that perception which discloses to me the cause of mankind's ever-increasing decline from godliness."

Essentially, the *Blätter* articles were confused expressions in terms of Christian symbolism of his views on racial degeneration. *Parsifal* used these very symbols to present this problem allegorically; Wagner's final gift to his countrymen offered an ultimate solution in the form of a mystery for which he scorned even the term "music drama." *Parsifal* was to be a *Bühnenweihfestspiel,* a festival play designed to consecrate a stage, and with this prodigious verbal construction he dedicated Bayreuth to a new and strange cult.

His relentless efforts to trick the Munich Opera out of *Parsifal* by beguiling Ludwig were, however, not solely idealistic. Aware of death's nearness, Wagner was eager to assure his family's financial future. The matter had consumed him for some time. When Ludwig politely asked for news of little Siegfried, he could hardly have expected the complete outline of the boy's economic future that had come his way early in 1879. Above all, Wagner informed him, Siegfried must not have to work for money—"with this constraint modern slavery begins." For thirty years after his father's death he would enjoy royalties. These he was to divide, using half and putting aside the remainder to form a capital which, by the time the rights expired, would produce an income sufficient for his maintenance.

Though at first glance Siegfried's financial future might have appeared strengthened had the circulation of *Parsifal* to other theaters been encouraged, this step in turn would have destroyed whatever hopes remained for the big empty theater on the hill. The *Ring* was on its way to becoming part of the regular German repertory. Remembering those stacks of unsold tickets for the first festival, Wagner reasonably concluded that, with the work no longer a novelty, even fewer enthusiasts would undertake the expense and trouble of visiting Bayreuth for any future cycle. And he had similar anxieties concerning *Parsifal;* once produced in Munich, inevitably it would be taken up by other theaters. Sound business judgment made him wrest *Parsifal* from Ludwig as Bayreuth's exclusive property; without this privilege, the Festspielhaus seemingly had no · future. *Parsifal* festivals promised greater immediate returns than *Parsifal* royalties. Wagner made his decision. In his open letter to Wolzogen on the termination of the society of patrons he frankly declared the "earning power" of *Parsifal* to depend upon its restriction to Bayreuth.[9] His idealism rested upon a firm foundation of German marks.

[9] On December 24, 1903, *Parsifal* was staged at New York's freshly gilded Metropolitan Opera House, the first time publicly on any stage other than that of the

8

Those provisions of the 1878 contract benefiting Wagner were still in effect and placed the Munich Opera's resources at Bayreuth's disposal for the *Parsifal* production. The services of many associated with the 1876

Festspielhaus. (Private performances for King Ludwig had taken place in Munich. London had heard a concert performance in 1884. Two years later New York also experienced the work in concert form under Walter Damrosch with Marianne Brandt as Kundry, and a famous reading took place at the Brooklyn Academy of Music on March 31, 1890, with Lilli Lehmann, Kalisch, Reichmann, and Fischer in the cast, Seidl conducting.) Wagnerians denounced what they called the Metropolitan's "rape of the Grail." Julius Kniese, Cosima's musical factotum and Siegfried Wagner's conducting coach, cried out against "un-German greed for profit in New York. . . . There they know not what they do." Professor Wolfgang Golther lamented this "sin against the Holy Ghost of German art." Cosima vainly sought legal means to stop an event made possible by the vagaries of international copyright law. Not only had Schott obligingly printed the score, which was freely sold outside of Bayreuth, but also Mottl, engaged by the Metropolitan, brought to New York his own copy preserving Wagner's comments. As Kolodin observed, obviously Mottl helped prepare the historic première conducted by Hertz. Wahnfried wondered how deep the treachery lay. Heinrich Conried, manager of the Metropolitan, had been born in Austrian Silesia, the son of Josef and Gretchen Cohn. Could Mottl, after all, be a Jew, too? Wagner had perhaps at times thought him racially suspect. One day the unfortunate young Austrian mispronounced *Sieglinde,* putting the stress on the second syllable. He recorded Wagner's resulting abuse of Austrians as un-German. "Half of them are Slavs, half Italians!" Cosima had come to believe firmly in Mottl's Jewishness and did not keep her thoughts private. (In order to chase this shadow from his name, Otto Strobel, the Wahnfried archivist, published during Nazi times a family tree of twenty-three large pages proving "beyond question that Felix Mottl was of pure Aryan descent.") From Wahnfried she hurled her thunderbolts, threatening those participating in the Metropolitan *Parsifal* with banishment from Bayreuth. And the jealousy of German impresarios, who had another decade to wait until this box office gold mine was legally theirs, expressed itself in pious indignation. The Metropolitan *Parsifal* was a triumph, and especially in the second act and transformation scenes the stage, newly rebuilt by Lautenschläger of Munich, permitted effects impossible at Bayreuth. The uproar over the "desecration" of a "holy" work seems ludicrous when one studies its libretto and the shabby intrigue leading to its first production. Moreover, special considerations made Wagner contemplate releasing *Parsifal* to a touring troupe organized by Neumann. Though the composer stressed the maintenance of standards so that the opera might do its missionary work to the full, obviously ten per cent on net profits plus another special ten per cent on gross receipts made him consider the matter seriously. From Neumann one gathers that, had Wagner lived, the work eventually would have been given to his company. Clearly, Wagner wanted to study the attendance figures of several *Parsifal* seasons at Bayreuth before committing himself. Neumann was not refused, but was merely asked to wait, with the assurance that no one else would get the monopoly. Jewish business acumen did not disturb Wagner when the profits poured into his own coffers.

Ring were again sought, and, to Ludwig's horror, the Brückner brothers prepared to construct and paint Zhukovski's scenery. Munich's theatrical workshops, among the finest in Europe, were available to Wagner for *Parsifal;* that he spurned them for the services of two provincial painters aggravated Ludwig. In this area the composer's judgment was highly questionable. "Religion and Art" had assured Wagnerites that the plastic arts had "fallen to total ruin," a statement Ludwig was not ready to dispute when he thought back on what the brothers Gotthold and Max had accomplished in 1876. Carl Brandt and his son Fritz again had the stage machinery in their care, though the senior Brandt died at the end of 1881, leaving Fritz to carry the project through. Early that year Wagner dispatched a piano version of the magic garden scene to Lilli Lehmann, asking her to recruit and train a band of Flower Maidens with secure and pleasant-sounding high B flats. (She had prepared the Rhine Maidens for the *Ring*.) But her unhappy love affair with Fritz Brandt finally made her decline to appear herself. Though plans were upset, Wagner understood this disappointing absence. However, in order to be independent of fits of operatic temperament and feigned or real illnesses—during the first festival, Betz, furious because Wagner had forbidden solo bows, had shown his power to wreck the undertaking by affecting hoarseness—he decided upon multiple casts that would also permit a large number of performances and involve many leading artists in what would be a school of Wagnerian style. And, though inevitably a war of precedence broke out over the première, in general, his ideas were more realistic than in 1876. He faced the fact of his permanent dependence upon the regular ticket-buying public. The rather useless society of patrons reorganized in 1877 was to be dissolved. He held them in ill-concealed contempt. They had failed, and for the powerless he had only scorn.[10]

Since Ludwig had granted him the use of the Munich orchestra and chorus, it was understood that the royal *Kapellmeister* would conduct *Parsifal*. Through devotion to Wagner's works and extraordinary performances of them, this man had forged a strong and sympathetic relationship with Cosima. Her letters to him are among her warmest. The two new friends had become confidants on artistic and also on highly personal matters, despite the embarrassing fact that the gentleman was Hermann Levi, son of the Rabbi of Giessen. She considered him "a most excellent person, with real delicacy of feeling." He moved in the artistic circles congenial to her, for he had been an intimate of Anselm Feuerbach's and was close

---

[10] The dynamics of Wagner's and Hitler's psychology were astoundingly similar. One thinks of the latter's utter disdain for the little group of Munich Nationalist Socialists he first joined. He later wrote, like Wagner of the patrons, "Terrible, terrible; this was club-making of the worst kind and manner."

to Lenbach and Wilhelm Busch. Only illness had prevented Levi's accepting Cosima's fervid invitations to visit during the last Italian sojourn. She even felt constrained to interpret to him Wagner's latest racist writings and thus soften their blows, especially "Know Thyself," a rabidly anti-Semitic supplement to "Religion and Art." During the early years of their friendship Levi's charm drew from her an uncharacteristic charity.

Wagner had the highest opinion of the young conductor's abilities. Weingartner remarked upon the spiritual nature of his interpretations and a baton technique so perfect that gestures were reduced to a minimum. (Weingartner's musical approach owed much to his example.) But although Wagner declared his respect for a Jew who clung to the Biblical *Levi* and did not change to *Löwe* or *Lewy* (a rather nasty glance at Lilli Lehmann's maternal name), this was about the extent of his enthusiasm for installing Israel in the Bayreuth pit; the conductor's Jewishness was a bitter pill for him. He even flew at King Ludwig for commenting that confessional differences were unimportant, considering the essential brotherhood of men, anger, as will be remarked, being reinforced by sudden awareness that Ludwig had rejected the racial message of the *Parsifal* poem. That he shared the Hohenzollerns' revulsion from anti-Semitism was infuriating. The nation was seething with the agitations awakened in the seventies by financial failures and swindles for which the Jew provided a scapegoat. The reference in "Know Thyself" to the Jew as "the darling of liberal princes" was not only Wagner's sneer at the protests of the Prussian Crown Prince Friedrich and his wife, Princess Victoria of England, against this rabble-rousing movement but also an unfriendly jab at Ludwig and Levi. Bismarck had in him much of that traditional sympathy of Prussian officialdom for Jewish emancipation; his doltish tolerance of a decade before, Wagner was sure, would yet bring the Reich down in ruins. In "Know Thyself" Wagner expressed outrage that the Reichstag's bestowal of full citizenship upon Jews permitted them to "consider themselves in every conceivable respect to be Germans—much as Negroes in Mexico were authorized through a carte blanche to look upon themselves as whites."

During the War of 1870 the German command's reluctance to bombard Paris had made Wagner impatient, and he had wanted to send Bismarck a note on the subject. Yet news of the burning of the Tuileries by the Commune drew from the composer a cry of pain. And though he never stopped denouncing the Jews and calling for their destruction in theory, unlike Bülow he could not bring himself to sign Bernhard Förster's anti-Jewish petition of 1880 to the Reichstag.[11] He disclaimed any altruistic motives,

---

[11] Bülow's signing of the petition contradicted much of the blunt Prussian liberalism of his earlier days. He had been a disciple of Proudhon and a close friend of the

maintaining that, after the failure of the antivivisection plea to which he had put his name, his support would be withheld from all such organized efforts. Yet one would like to believe that other than practical considerations stayed his hand (Ludwig and the Hohenzollerns would have been horrified, and he was dependent upon Levi and Rubinstein, author of the piano reduction of *Parsifal*) and that Wagner would have been appalled by the ghastly consequences his political and religious intolerance helped engender —the burning of cities and of humans. When Bavaria entered the War of 1870 on the side of Prussia, Dr. Pusinelli had cried out to him, "You noble sower, now see your harvest." But at the same time a different and truly deadly crop was slowly maturing, fed by Wagnerian utterances and well tended by people like the worthy doctor for whom *Jewry in Music* was prophecy. This fearful harvest was to be of flesh and blood.

Ludwig's broad-mindedness, unlike the worldly Bismarck's, Wagner blamed on naïveté; the King was told that, lacking experience of Jews in everyday situations, he naturally could idealize them. Wagner blustered, but Munich stood firm. Since no artistic reason could be advanced to justify Levi's removal, Ludwig resolved that without his royal *Kapellmeister* there would be no royal orchestra, no royal chorus, and hence no *Parsifal*. It is a tribute to the young man's character that, like Nietzsche, he felt this point important enough to defy Wagner's tyranny.

And the latter had pushed matters to the point of crisis. During the preparations for *Parsifal* in 1881, Levi had on occasion journeyed to Bayreuth, where he resided in Wahnfried. So offensive did Wagner's conduct toward his guest eventually become that Levi, his veneration of genius notwithstanding, had felt compelled late in June to flee the house and wrote Wagner asking to be relieved of conducting *Parsifal*. Not only had there been Wagner's tasteless efforts to persuade the Rabbi's son to undergo baptism so as not to profane the temple scenes of the opera, but during the summer Wahnfried had been thrown into turmoil by an anonymous letter

---

Jew Ferdinand Lassalle, a founder of German trade unionism. To please him, Bülow, under the pseudonym of W. Solinger, had set Herwegh's text for a German labor anthem, the *"Arbeiter-Marseillaise."* Bülow had, in fact, been instrumental in bringing Wagner and Lassalle together in 1864 at Lake Starnberg. The latter, seeking aid in his love affair with Helene Dönniges, hoped that, through Wagner's influence, King Ludwig might be prevailed upon to persuade Wilhelm von Dönniges, a member of the Bavarian diplomatic corps, to soften his stern opposition to his daughter's relationship with a flamboyant Jewish socialist. Dismissing Lassalle as a Jew and a poseur, Wagner showed little sympathy for him and wrote Frau Wille, "this was a love story of pure vanity and false pathos." Conveniently for everyone, Lassalle soon died of wounds suffered in a duel over the fair Helene. (George Meredith's *The Tragic Comedians* [1880] derived from these events.) Despite the vigorous prejudices of his later years, Bülow preserved warm memories of Lassalle.

to Wagner accusing Levi of being Cosima's lover. Did Wagner for a moment look at both his wife, almost a quarter of a century his junior, and her special friend, the handsome, soulful Jew, two years younger, and, remembering her vagabond nocturnal habits at Villa Pellet, wonder whether he had finally been cast as a Hans von Bülow?

His behavior was compulsive, beyond control. With many Jews—Tausig, Rubinstein, Levi, Lilli Lehmann and her mother, and Neumann (who was just entering his life)—he could never disentangle genuine affection for the individual from a general, consuming hate in which sadism played an ugly part, a sadism calculated and raw in the case of Levi, a cruel ritual Theodor Adorno compared to a cat's play with a mouse. Despite the sham Christian piety of *Parsifal,* Wagner remained a nonbeliever to his death. Yet he delighted in tormenting Levi with plans for his baptism and even enjoyed painting the insolent picture of their going to Communion together! (In later years it hurt Weingartner to observe the contempt with which the Wagner family treated Levi behind the mask of friendship; the cats kept the mouse frisking.)

It was essential to coax Levi back to Bayreuth, for reports of Wagner's baiting would not be well received in Munich, and the conductor's absence would tend to confirm the gossip about Cosima. And, since Wagner's hatred of Levi's people did not exclude an admiration for his artistry, while Levi's appreciation of Wagner's genius outweighed his disgust at the man's ill-breeding, a rapprochement was effected, Cosima no doubt contributing her diplomatic best. Levi admitted that he had become a Wagnerite "through long detours and after many inner battles," his letters from Bayreuth to his father revealing a struggle to forgive the composer his faults and to believe him essentially free of "petty prejudice" (*"kleinliches Risches"*) in respect to individuals. However, what was written to calm the worried Rabbi does not agree with Levi's later confidences to Weingartner, to whom he remarked of Wahnfried, "It is easy enough for you in that house, Aryan that you are."

Though behind the scenes Wagner was doing his utmost to rid himself of Levi, he finally on September 19 felt it politic to write Ludwig that, after all, he would accept the head of the Munich orchestra without asking his religion, a letter often naïvely trotted forth to demonstrate Wagner's essential tolerance! In answer, on October 11, Ludwig made his remark about the brotherhood of man and voiced his opinion that racism was loathsome (*"nichts ist widerlicher"*). This was more than Wagner could stand. He realized how utterly he had failed with Ludwig. No longer able to control his rage, in a letter dated November 22, 1881, he read the King that famous lecture on the Jews as the congenital enemies of humanity and all that is noble in it (*"dass ich die jüdische Race für den geborenen Feind der reinen Menschheit und alles Edlen in ihr halte"*). And this foulness he vented on the King, who early in his reign (1866) had visited the synagogue in Fürth and pledged to follow his father's example in working toward Jewish emancipation. Moreover, during the summer of 1881 Ludwig had enjoyed a romantic friendship with a twenty-three-year-old Hungarian Jewish actor of the Munich theater and taken him on a trip to Switzerland. (This young man—Josef Kainz—was to become one of the glories of the German-speaking stage.) To Wagner's outburst Ludwig made no reply until over two months later, when he subtly referred to the faithful Jews with whom the composer surrounded himself. It was too late to discuss openly and reasonably a subject on which Wagner was completely deranged. (Nietzsche had described him to Seydlitz as "an *old*, unchanging man.") In such an atmosphere of hate and rancor the "Christian" drama *Parsifal* was completed and prepared.

9

Wagner's bigoted explosion reached Ludwig from Palermo. Badly in need of sun and quiet, the composer had left for Sicily with his family on the first of November. Some ten days before, he had completed orchestrating the second act of *Parsifal*, and the strain of overexertion was evident. For months severe chest pains had been tormenting him almost every day. Confronted by his almost insupportable irritability and nervousness, Cosima somehow maintained her famous composure. Acknowledging his gift for saying things that were "very wounding and offensive," she nonetheless believed he did so "innocently," though unavoidably observing his "daemonic instinct" to go "straight to the point"; she lamented, "It is the fact that one is defenseless against it that makes one feel so uncomfortable."

Doctors had assured him of his organic soundness and, to clear up his chest congestion, recommended those daily promenades the Bayreuth weather, however, made impossible. His troubles, they said, were abdominal and digestive, and Italy was his remedy. Above all, he regretted having built his capital in a climate in which the sun hardly dared appear. "This is my present grief!" He had come to hate Bayreuth. But there were compensations. To his enormous pleasure, Cosima, as a birthday surprise, had ordered the ceiling of his library decorated with the arms of those cities boasting successful Wagner societies.

During the year not only had his health been further drained by intensive preparations for the *Parsifal* production (he wanted all the scenery and machinery in the theater by autumn), but, in addition, the excitement accompanying four cycles of the *Ring* in Berlin during May, 1881, had exhausted him. This series had been the charge of the impresario Angelo

Neumann. His brilliant mounting of the *Ring* in Leipzig in 1878 had attracted the admiration of the composer, who, having realized considerable profit from a production of uncompromising standards, eagerly put himself into the hands of a scrupulously honest man with a unique understanding of both art and business. In 1882 his touring *Ring* company, using some of the Bayreuth apparatus, was to get under way and prove highly remunerative to Wagner and his heirs. That someone of Neumann's energy and integrity should be a Jew puzzled Wagner, and Cosima could not overlook this basic flaw once pardoned in Levi.

For a time the Royal Opera House appeared to be the likely scene of Neumann's Berlin *Ring*. But friction between director Hülsen and Wagner ended in its transference to the Viktoria Theater. Hülsen, wishing to produce *Valkyrie* alone, had named this future privilege as the price of opening the royal theater to Neumann's production of the entire cycle. Wagner refused in a manner offensive to both Hülsen and the Kaiser. There was little sorrow over the incident among members of the regular Berlin company, unhappy about another troupe singing in their hall.

The Viktoria *Ring* was a brilliant success, and in the end the octogenarian emperor, renowned for his common sense, put in an appearance, attending the last two acts of the third *Siegfried* and the final *Twilight of the Gods*. Wagner had kept watch over rehearsals, during which he frequently took the baton, and attended the opening and closing cycles. (In between, he had returned to Wahnfried, where Count Gobineau was visiting.) In this regular theater without a covered pit he feared the singer would drown in orchestral sound. Neumann recorded his special plea to the instrumentalists: "Gentlemen, I beg of you not to take my 'ff' too seriously!" He asked all dynamics to be scaled down lower than written. "Remember, you are a hundred against one!" had become his motto in dealing with his opera orchestra.

The strain and excitement exhausted him. After the final curtain, while standing on stage to receive the traditional speech of praise and laurel wreath, he was struck by a severe cramp in his heart and quickly walked into the wings to avoid falling in view of the audience. But few of his outraged artists, so often witnesses of his notorious bad manners, would believe his later explanations. It was generally assumed that, by this exit from the court's presence, the impossible composer had seized an opportunity to insult the royal house.

Only Daniela, who early in October had gone off with Grandfather Liszt to Rome,[12] was missing when the family set out for Sicily on the first of

---

[12] Daniela had also been seeing her father, Bülow. Inevitably the question of Isolde's paternity had been revived and was disturbing the children, now becoming aware of their strange family history. Of Daniela's visit to Rome and the Liszt-Wittgenstein

November, 1881. Rubinstein was awaiting the weary travelers. With difficulty a bed had been procured for Wagner on the boat from Naples; Cosima and the children passed the night on deck surrounded by fellow passengers, human and animal. In Palermo Wagner had taken sumptuous quarters at the Hôtel des Palmes and, revived by the sun, almost immediately began the final act of his full score, which he completed on January 13. Exactly a year and one month of life remained to him. His work was accomplished, and he felt death had been cheated.

Christmas was enlivened by a visit from the faithful Zhukovski, and early in February the hotel was given up for the Villa Gangi on the Piazza dei Porazzi. Here Wagner jotted down an ending to a fragmentary phrase written for *Tristan* nearly a quarter of a century before and then abandoned. This curiosity in A-flat major and thirteen bars in length, now known as "the Porazzi theme," possibly symbolized the links between *Tristan* and *Parsifal*. It was left on Cosima's table as a kind of mystic gift, whose private meaning, though hard to fathom, obviously had to do with a rounding out—a completion.

Early in the new year Daniela arrived from Rome. Fidi recovered from a severe case of typhoid fever, and Wagner seemed to improve in the sun. He was delighted to find himself in the land of the Hohenstaufen, the city of his *Liebesverbot,* a capital heavy with German history, where Manfred had been crowned and Friedrich II lay buried. From such soil, rich in Swabian lore, had grown that strange tale of Fatima the Sarazenin, first conceived in Paris and then finished in Dresden for Schröder-Devrient. He upbraided fate for having put her in another generation. It was for the daemonic, Hoffmannesque art of this woman he had called "slut" (*"Sauluder"*) behind her back that Kundry had been written. It is difficult to resist the conjecture that at one time Schröder-Devrient had revealed to him some secrets of the sophisticated love-making for which she was celebrated. The notorious epistolary novel *Memoirs of a Singer,* influenced by de Sade's *Justine,* is supposedly in part an autobiographical work of the great diva. This was the Kundry he dreamed of in Palermo. To describe the kind of singer required for the role he borrowed Voltaire's remark to Mademoiselle Dumesnil at a rehearsal of *Mérope:* She needed, the philosopher observed, *le diable au corps.*[18]

---

circle, Cosima remarked in alarm, "what she told me simply made me shudder. All the things I do not mention before her were discussed in her presence; she saw all personal relations in an almost horrifying light, and, even in quite insignificant matters, the verdict was almost always diametrically opposed to mine."

[18] Wagner's search for a singer with this quality led him to Marianne Brandt. Though dramatically she was to be the finest Kundry of the festival, evidently Wagner's personality repelled her. Bayreuth proved an unpleasant experience for La Brandt.

In Palermo, Wagner walked, talked, rested, and thought of the past. Beyond the *Parsifal* production and vague plans for writing some purely instrumental pieces, there was no mention of a future. The King still hoped for "The Victors," but what Wagner could use from it had been absorbed into *Parsifal*. In the brilliant Sicilian sun the shadows were deepening.

Pierre-Auguste Renoir, made famous by his success at the salon of 1879, had been in Italy since autumn. Wishing to make a portrait of Wagner, he journeyed from Naples and, two days after the completion of *Parsifal*, succeeded in persuading the exhausted man to sit for a quick sketch. The latter gave small praise to the effort and jestingly compared the face to a Protestant clergyman's. The artist had captured what the composer and the faithful felt compelled to deride and dismiss. Renoir's pencil had traced the contours of that marvelous head with its bulging brow; but the flesh drooped, the narrow eyes could barely focus, and the expression was of infinite weariness. Death looked out of the rubber mask Wagner's face had become. From the sketch, Renoir made that painting, now in the Bibliothèque de l'Opéra, which Julius Meier-Graefe described as "a picture of merciless psychological insight." Renoir has also left a written impression of the declining master, who engaged him in "the silliest conversation" in a mixture of German and guttural French, punctuated with expletives and climaxed by a tirade against the Jews. To make the old man happy, Renoir contributed some derogatory remarks about Meyerbeer.

On March 20, 1882, the Wagners quit Palermo for Acireale, escorted by the young Sicilian Count Gravina, who had become engaged to Blandine. From his hotel balcony Wagner witnessed the nocturnal passage of Garibaldi through the city and the emotional greeting the population gave its dying idol, whose procession to Palermo celebrated the Sicilian Vespers. Just six hundred years before, the island had risen against the French. Those bloody final pages of Hohenstaufen history, always so fascinating to Wagner, were before his eyes—the wrath of Pope Urban IV, who damned Tannhäuser and the Hohenstaufen, the fall of Manfred, the beheading of Conradin by Charles of Anjou, the tragic end of the Hohenstaufen line, the revolution against Angevin authority begun at the hour of Vespers on Easter Tuesday of 1282; and now this modern folk hero, on a stretcher in a railroad car—a Rienzi with only weeks to live—saluted with religious awe. The centuries seemed to roll together. History and myth appeared one. Wagner was deeply affected.

But at Acireale he suffered so violent a heart spasm that Cosima fainted upon viewing him. His condition gradually improved, and by April 10 they were at Messina after visits to Catania, Giarre, Riposto, and Taormina. As they stood on the heights of this last town with Etna above and land and sea stretching beneath, he said to her that it was here they ought to have fled in 1858 and spared themselves "many, many useless agonies." His escape to Italy during August of that year had, of course, been the terrible climax of the Wesendonk affair. A kind of gallantry made him frequently persist in pretending to her that he had never been emotionally involved with the lovely Mathilde. Cosima could not have believed his protestations but, nonetheless, enjoyed hearing them.

On this magic island he thought much of Shakespeare's *Tempest* and those words with which Prospero resigns his marvelous powers. More and more his talk was of death, and Cosima feared being left behind. They embarked for Naples and, after a visit to Posilipo to see the superb Villa Angri once again, left for Venice, where they arrived on April 15 to stay two weeks. On the thirtieth the party reached Munich and, via Nuremberg, arrived home on the first of May. But Wagner could not be without company for long. Ten days later Count Gobineau again visited Wahnfried.

10

During the *Meistersinger* days at Triebschen the political writings of Konstantin Frantz had intrigued Wagner. They seemed learned corroboration of his anti-French, anti-Semitic, and growing Reich-nationalistic sentiments. For a while Frantz provided the measure of Wagnerian political thinking and, as his reward, received the dedication of the 1868 edition of *Opera and Drama*. Cosima called him "one of the renowned unknowns." Similarly, Joseph Arthur, Count de Gobineau, also one of those *berühmten Unberühmten,* became the validating spirit hovering over the completion of *Parsifal*.

His *Essay on the Inequality of Races* threw its strange shadow over Wagner's final years. The work, written over a quarter of a century earlier, had remained relatively unexplored until Wagner helped make it famous and eventually a pillar of Nazi racial theory through its enthusiastic adaptation by his disciples, especially Houston Stewart Chamberlain's ambitious refashioning. In the frail, almost blind French intellectual, Wagner thought he had found a scholarly and scientific corroborator of his own scribblings on race, and the Count, whom Wagner had taken to Berlin for the fourth *Ring,* imagined his ethnological thesis come alive on the stage of the Viktoria Theater.

After seeing the first Berlin *Ring* cycle, Wagner had cried out in his newly acquired Gobineau vocabulary, "It is certainly the most characteristic work of the Aryan race . . . this strain of the once purest white peoples of the Asian highlands. One may hope, when experiencing the success of such a work among us!" Gobineau's enthusiasm is more difficult to fathom; his famous epigram, *"Nous ne descendons pas du singe, mais nous y allons"*

("We do not descend from the ape but are headed in that direction"), sums up his pessimism, and, ironically, in the hands of his disciples from Wagner to Hitler *Gobinisme* did lead man back to the beast. For the Count, man's certainty was death in degradation. In addition, he disputed the Aryan qualities of the Germans; it was the Teutonic tribes of the ancient days and early Middle Ages he idealized, not his German contemporary, whom, in fact, he found racially impure and supremely contemptible. However, the persuasiveness of Wagner's music cannot be overestimated, and, as Oscar Levy suggested, Gobineau's long *Essay* might well be called *The Twilight of the Aryan.* It was, like the *Ring,* a tale of decline and fall. But, as Barzun observed, "Wagner's optimistic nationalism overlooked this point, just as he overlooked Gobineau's denial that the Germans were Nordic and his affirmation that music was the gift of the Negro race to the hopelessly mixed Europeans. The vision of Wagner and Gobineau implicitly agreeing in the Villa Wahnfried that Wagner must be more Negro than Nordic gives the story of their friendship a much-needed touch of high comedy." The final volume of Glasenapp's biography of Wagner religiously preserves fragments of their fatuous conversations.

They were essentially an ill-mated pair. Even if Gobineau was a poseur—his title has been questioned (he may have been a kind of solvent Baron Corvo [14])—his elegant and aristocratic ways were ingrained, and Wagner's Teutomania, mock Christianity, pie-in-the-sky redemption, and rowdy anti-Semitism must have been abhorrent to him. But after decades of neglect he was being "discovered," and, if his host really had a most limited grasp of what he had written, the luxury of being admired must have been nonetheless pleasing to a sick old man near death.

His writings influenced Wagner in much the way Goethe's and Schopenhauer's had. In all of them were found seeming confirmation of ideas long entertained, and from analytically superior minds convenient phrases could be abstracted and adapted for personal purposes. The catchwords of Wagner's early and middle periods were "redemption" and "renunciation." To these the dying composer added the arresting war cry—"racial decline." It was the rather ambitious duty of *Parsifal* to provide a framework in which all three could be expounded and reconciled. As such, the work succeeds

---

[14] One of the most fantastic manifestations of *fin de siècle* decadence, Baron Corvo, author of the strange and impressive novel *Hadrian the Seventh,* was born of very modest origin in London in 1860 as Frederick Rolfe. Count Gobineau located his ancestral home in Asgard, and the no less pretentious Baron, who explained "Rolfe" as a derivative of "Rollo," an ancestor common to himself and William the Conqueror, developed a family tree showing the English throne to be rightfully his. As Wagner adopted the vulture or hawk (*Geyer*) as his device, so Rolfe used the raven (*corvo*). Like Wagner, he died in Venice.

extraordinarily well. It is Wagner's most ingeniously wrought libretto, and Nietzsche thought its situations to be "of the highest poetry."

Wagner's views on the subject of race, thoroughly stimulated by his discussions with Gobineau—having attended a Swiss school where courses were conducted in German, the latter spoke the language fluently—were crystallized in what was yet another postscript to "Religion and Art," an essay completed early in September of 1881 and called *"Heldentum und Christentum"* ("Heroism and Christianity"). For Gobineau, Christianity and its child, democracy, by teaching equality had stimulated racial mixing and brought Europe to the path of irreversible decline. The *Essay* preached doom and despair. But, although embracing Gobineau's ideas about man's degeneration, Wagner could not accept a scenario lacking a redemptive finale. He tacked an apotheosis with clouds and colored lights to the Count's gloomy thesis. Racial mixture was not ineradicable; adulterated blood could again be made pure. At hand was a savior long hinted at, Wagner's most ludicrous creation—the Aryan Jesus, whom the vaticanations of *"Heldentum"* first revealed in full theoretical splendor. The article must be considered by anyone desiring to penetrate at least one layer of *Parsifal*'s meaning.

XVI

Moral Collapse: "Heldentum" and Parsifal

"*Heldentum*" was built upon an article of Wagner's Dresden period, *The Wibelungs,* written as a study for the *Ring* scenario and remarkably anticipating the later development of his symbolism and racist theorizing. He frequently brooded over its ideas, working them into final form in *Parsifal* and its explanatory essay, "*Heldentum.*"

The Wibelungs singled out the ancient line from which the Frankish-German and Hohenstaufen kaisers had sprung as that "one chosen race" rightfully claiming universal rule. Indeed, Wagner said, such a tradition had persisted among the Folk even during its periods of degeneracy. Through descent from the hero-god, Siegfried, the great German kaisers had succeeded to the right symbolically to strive for the Nibelung gold and its power to confer dominion over the world. These inheritors of the hoard had to perform mighty deeds, for the hero-god's conquest of the dragon was to be repeated ever again, the gaining, possession, and maintenance of authority becoming a ritual for these royal heirs of Siegfried dedicated to the symbolic rewinning of the token.

In *The Wibelungs* Wagner declared the Nibelung hoard to have ascended in the course of history and to have assumed a more mystical guise as the Holy Grail. Similarly, he regarded Christ as Siegfried manifest in a more spiritual condition. In chivalric days kaisers such as Barbarossa—himself an extraordinary example of the reborn Siegfried—pursued the transfigured hoard known as the Grail, then no less a "talisman of mastery" than at its first appearance as the dwarf's gold. The hoard-Grail remained the exclusive inheritance of Siegfried's descendants, the German kaisers, who formed a master race fated to subject all.

How closely the Nibelung and Grail legends were related in Wagner's mind is shown by a notation of September, 1865, for the *Parsifal* libretto.

Originally, he thought of making the Grail Knights perform the dragon ritual: "When the Grail was delivered, the lance, too, was promised to the knights; but it had first to be won through difficult battles." The severe trials Parsifal undergoes between acts two and three are a remnant of this idea.

Picking up the thread of *The Wibelungs* in "*Heldentum*" and pursuing a piquant bit of Wagnerian ethnological-mythological anthropology, the composer described the Aryans, the great Teutonic world leaders, as sprung from the very gods, in contrast to the colored man, to whom he conceded the rather lowly Darwinian descent from the monkey. This was Wagner the scientist, evolutionary theory having arisen during the years between the two essays. As a devout anti-Semite he found unacceptable the Biblical explanation of mankind's origin in an act of the Jewish God. Sweepingly, he declared Aryan and human history to be one, for, without fortifying themselves with an admixture of godly white blood, the colored races could achieve nothing. In this way, Wagner believed, inferior peoples had through the ages drained Aryans of an indigenous purity, their distinguishing godly features being sucked out. It was his purpose in "*Heldentum*" and its artistic counterpart, *Parsifal,* to confront Germany with the seriousness of its racial crisis—to outline the perfection, decline, and hopes for regeneration of the debased Aryan.

He had lost "faith in constant progress," in Spencerian optimism. "Shall We Hope?" of 1879 had decried the man who "surrenders to the comfortable guidance of the theory of constant human progress. Let him do or leave undone what he will, he is sure of marching ever forward. Seeing great efforts come to nought, he judges them to have been of no value to constant progress; for example, if people prefer to see the *Nibelungenring* in comfort at the theater in their own centers of commerce instead of setting out upon the somewhat troublesome visit to Bayreuth in order to attend carefully worked out festival performances, it will be seen as a sign of contemporary progress that one no longer has to strike forth on a pilgrimage to something extraordinary, but, rather, the extraordinary, comfortably transformed into the usual, is brought to one's door." The failure of the first festival had helped turn Wagner from belief in inevitable advance toward higher forms, a path he had so confidently trod in *Opera and Drama.* He had abandoned his old concept of Darwinism.

Surveying the world from the heights of Monsalvat, the Grail community in *Parsifal* was alarmed to observe natural selection working against its distinctive Aryanism. At its expense, others were growing more adroit, and the gods' very own appeared headed toward erasure. Something was terribly wrong; the evolutionary machinery was malfunctioning, confusing the fit with the unfit. Instead of working toward endless improvement and Aryan perfection, it was producing racial corruption. The knights were confronted with an enemy gaining upon them every day. Here was the decisive racial crisis that grew into an uncompromising struggle for power. *Parsifal's* false façade of Christian abnegation masks this almost insane conflict.

The earlier Wagnerian romantic rebel had contended with a society to which he could at times and at least to some degree adapt. Siegfried became a Gibichung chief and Walther a bourgeois. Even Wotan and Alberich met in a strange, poetic truce before the dragon's cave, acknowledging themselves opposite faces of the same coin, though remaining no less determined to exterminate one another. But the final act of *Meistersinger* had indicated changing times; soon even dialogue between adversaries would be impossible. In *Parsifal,* Klingsor's currency was valueless, its mottos, its very metal, false. Monsalvat was Wagner's paranoiac concept of a small self-contained elite group, uniquely possessed of the truth, obsessed with its "purity," and struggling with an outside world it held worthless. Redemption was promised the hard-pressed knights, but, obviously, the Wagnerian redeemer was not to be found among Jewish craftsmen or lepers. Not by accident did Gurnemanz almost immediately remark upon Parsifal's noble, highborn appearance. He knew what signs to read. Racial heredity and strict breeding, not natural selection, formed the new mechanism of salvation. Wagnerian eugenics had come into being; in his latest writing the composer had embraced the darker implications of Darwinism. Gurnemanz, obviously a subscriber to the *Bayreuther Blätter,* had studied *"Heldentum."*

2

Here Wagner celebrated the Aryans as the globe's noblest race, their rule and exploitation (*"Beherrschung und Ausbeutung"*) of lower breeds being justified by ethnologic superiority and thus by natural law. But, he lamented, the Aryans' age of gold had passed, their godly purity having been vitiated not only by the supplanting of their natural vegetable food by flesh eating (an evil brought about by the Jews, "former cannibals, educated to be the business leaders of our society"), but also because an innately noble Aryan strain had been enfeebled by crossbreeding. Gobineau, who had handily separated the races into *maîtres* and *esclaves* and who had devised for himself a family tree showing his own godly and direct descent from Odin(!), was cited as a scientific authority corroborating this now painfully familiar theory appropriated by Nazism. Echoing *"Heldentum,"* Hitler in *Mein Kampf* was to contrast the materialistic instincts of the Jews and the idealism of the Aryan drive for mastery.

Wagner conceded to all races one factor in common, a capacity for conscious suffering. But only the Aryan, an instinctive Schopenhaurean, possessed the overpowering intellect permitting him to master his will. In contrast, lower strains remained victims of the senses, servants of their blind cravings. Since the Aryan alone could subdue the will, he alone was capable of metaphysics and of rising to the heroic.

Wagner had arrived at a kind of Schopenhaurean Siegfried! But somehow he had to turn a paradox into a parallel, Siegfried into Parsifal, the hero into the hero-saint. Contemplating the holy men of early Christianity, Wagner perceived a likeness between their renunciation of the world and Siegfried's drive toward arduous deeds. By the energy of his Aryan intellect, the saint overcame self, heroic pride here finding its equivalent in holy humility. Wagner wondered whether the saint did not, after all, rival the worldly hero in endurance and suffering. If this transition from Siegfried to Parsifal puts the reader in a state of wonderment, what follows must leave him stupefied; for, after nasty references both to the Roman Church and to Nietzsche's discussion of cowardice and humility in the thirty-eighth aphorism of his *Dawn,* Wagner turned to consider a problem taxing even his ability to send up a fog of words—the racial character of Christ's blood.

For Wagner and his followers the problem was enormous. He had set *Parsifal* within the framework of a medieval Christian tale, Christ's blood being the agent of the various characters' redemption. Benighted historians, lacking Wagnerian insight, had gulled the world into believing Christ a Jew. "Public and Popularity," a series of articles by Wagner appearing in the *Blätter* during 1878, had declared the identification of Christ's God with the tribal God of Israel to be "one of the most terrible derangements of world history." How could that Jewish blood Wagner condemned as infectious at the same time be the source of mankind's deliverance? There had followed a bolder pronouncement to the effect that "it remains more than doubtful that Jesus himself was of Jewish stock," saving tidings broadcast to the Wagnerian flock in "Religion and Art" of 1880, in which Wagner also announced that Judaic elements had been incorporated into Christian doctrine to its ruin.[1] Moreover, "Religion and Art" once and for all unmasked the jealous Jewish god, Jehovah, as the force behind opposition to vegetarianism. Adam and Eve had fallen, Wagner pointed out, not because they had tasted animal flesh—the bloody Jehovah would have delighted in this— but because they ate fruit. And did not Jehovah find Abel's fatted lamb more tasty (*"schmackhafter"*) than Cain's offering of the field's produce? (This was the essay revealing Wagner's idiosyncrasies turning to serious aberrations.) But though a great Wagnerian storm was raised against Jehovah

---

[1] In *The Gay Science,* Nietzsche commented on Wagner's refusal to credit the Jews with what he called their greatest achievement, as "the inventors of Christianity." Hitler, for whom the Old Testament was "Satan's Bible," followed the teaching of *"Heldentum"* that Jesus was not a Jew, and, in fact, declared him to have been the son of a certain Pantherus, a Greek soldier in the Roman army.

as the Klingsor of the stockyards, seducing pure Aryans with beefsteaks rather than flower maidens, in contrast, Wagner's award of Aryan citizenship to Jesus seemed hemmed with hesitations. The faithful could breathe somewhat more easily after "Religion and Art" appeared, but obviously doubts still gnawed at the master's mind. "More than doubtful" plus a subjunctive could not satisfy truly devout Wagnerites. In *"Heldentum"* he determined to settle the issue, and none too soon—the première of *Parsifal* was less than a year away.

For a moment he appeared to be taking a sane approach. Ignoring the point of view of "Religion and Art," Wagner asked in *"Heldentum"* whether there were anyone sufficiently sacrilegious to inquire concerning the racial composition of Christ's blood. The device was that of *reculer pour mieux sauter,* and a dazzling leap brought Wagner forward with a new revelation. In Christ's veins flowed a kind of superblood, which, though above individual race, was yet an archetypical manifestation of the Aryan species. As epitome of all humanity's conscious suffering, this blood symbolized the ultimate Aryan conquest of the will—its complete abrogation, leaving only the will to redeem. Christ's blood was the fountainhead of pity streaming through all mankind, a divine substance capable not only of refreshing the Aryan fallen from grace by commingling with inferior breeds, but also of raising the latter from their innate debasement. The Redeemer's blood was thus both a miraculous antidote to racial decline and an agent of racial improvement. By contemplating this blood, mongrels might rise (though there was obviously a limit to their ladder of redemption) and fallen Aryans could wipe away the sin of crossbreeding. Wagner saw Christ's blood as part of an "utmost endeavor" to rescue the world's noblest race from sinking down, the Crucifixion having been arranged to provide a formula for rescuing the Aryan.

Only the Jews remained without hope of salvation in the Wagnerian cosmology. "Know Thyself" called the Jew the "daemon of man's downfall" and noted that "even interbreeding does not harm him." The Jew was outside the cycle of racial betterment, and in the same essay Wagner noted that "if a Jew or Jewess intermarry with the most extraneous races, a Jew will always be born." Hitler proved more liberal! Despite extreme efforts, Klingsor could never become a member of the Grail fraternity, even his ultimate gesture of self-castration being unacceptable; the stratagem was insolent, his presumptuousness rebuffed. Wotan observed to Alberich during their meeting at Fafner's lair, "Each thing has its own nature; this you can never alter." And in *"Heldentum"* Wagner wrote, "Pride is a delicate virtue, suffering no compromise (*keinen Kompromiss*) such as the mixing of blood." Over a decade before, at the conclusion to an open letter of explanation concerning *Jewry in Music,* he had pondered whether the Jews were to be eliminated by "violent ejection" or through assimilation. By the time of *Parsifal* he no longer pondered—*"keinen Kompromiss."* Total destruction alone would suffice.

In the *Deutsch-Französische Jahrbücher* of 1843 and 1844, Karl Marx published a series of articles, "On the Jewish Question," in which he declared, "The social emancipation of Jewry is the emancipation of society from Jewry." For him, the problem was to be solved by the Jews' own repudiation of Judaism and capitalism, ideas found in Wagner's earlier writings. How much of Marx Wagner read is not clear, but certainly he had heard much of him from Bakunin in Dresden. The vulgar, obsessive, vitriolic anti-Semitism of Marx, who descended on both sides of his family from rabbis, grew from the same desire to deny as Wagner's. However, the physical destruction of the Jews never entered Marx's mind; one would like to believe the same of Wagner, but his late essays reveal a complete moral collapse.

The *Parsifal* articles in the *Bayreuther Blätter* and the drama itself provided an outline the following generation filled in with ineffably appalling detail. Certainly Wagner was not the only proto-Nazi with a program for racial regeneration. But his musical genius and the increasing popularity of his works gave his theorizing a unique and fateful power. *Lohengrin* was the twelve-year-old Hitler's first opera, and he was swept away by an enthusiasm knowing no bounds, presumably not only by that tender romantic sentiment popularly associated with the swan-knight, but also by those ferocious passages of nationalism erupting throughout—the German king's impassioned call to end "the need of the Reich" through a crusade against the eastern villains menacing German soil, and the blood-curdling cry of the armed men in the final act (a passage often cut outside Germany), "A German sword for the German land! Thus will the power of the Reich be established!" Indeed, before departing, Lohengrin turns to the king to predict Germany's victory over "the eastern hordes." Hitler moved on to the thick tomes of Wagnerian prose and declared the composer's political writings his favorite reading. Throughout his career he regurgitated their ideas and phraseology, even adopting their convoluted style as his very own. He said, "Whoever wants to understand National Socialist Germany must know Wagner," alas, one of his few true statements. As he awaited death in Venice, Wagner had called his final work "an exhortation of [the world's] inmost soul, prophesying redemption . . . the image of a prophetic dream. . . ."

3

By the time Wagner had finished the full score of the second act of *Parsifal* and departed for Sicily, he had, through his notorious articles written for the *Bayreuther Blätter,* presented and justified the "religious" symbolism of *Parsifal* to himself and his followers. On its darkest level— and one easily accessible to many of these disciples—*Parsifal* is an allegory of the Aryan's fall and redemption. The seemingly ruined Grail King, Amfortas, stands at the very center of the drama, the text of his lament during the first temple ritual being the poetic equivalent of a good deal of material in *"Heldentum."* "Much too much blood" was Nietzsche's comment on the new Wagnerian Communion.

Amfortas contrasts the divine blood of Christ in the Grail with his own sinful blood, corrupted by sexual contact with Kundry, a racial inferior, this criminal miscegenation epitomizing the Aryan dilemma. Both blood streams contend within his own wracked system, the first tide, Aryan and divine, pouring gently into his heart at the very moment its source, the Grail chalice, is awakened and glows,[2] the second and sinful current simultaneously gushing madly out of his body through the wound received as the price of yielding to the degrading seduction. For a moment his Aryan intellect slipped; he lost control of his will and fell from the heroic, a most lamentable position for someone Wagner called "the head of the race."

There is apparently little respite for the poor creature, though he is sprinkled with the latest Gautier bath salts. The evil blood spilling from the wound is fed by a craving to repeat the transgression: "The hot blood of sin flows, eternally renewed from the fount of yearning that, alas, no expiation ever stills!" One might possibly interpret this "fount of yearning" (*"Sehnens Quelle"*) as a longing for redemption did not Parsifal, whose mission was to retrace Amfortas' steps, experience the same erotic surge. Even after rejecting Kundry the young saint cried, "Oh, worldly derangement, midst the burning transports of highest salvation to yearn for the fount of damnation!" (At this point, Kundry, seeing an opportunity to counterattack, cried, "Did my kiss make you see the world so clearly?") Parsifal had momentarily fallen victim to what Heinrich von Treitschke, one of the authors of anti-Semitic history, warned against—a certain non-Germanic "gracefulness of vice," which Treitschke recognized as an alluring specialty of both the French and the Jews.

Indeed, Parsifal had weakened dangerously before Kundry's charms. Having excited his sensuality by extended references to Herzeleide, his mother, the knowing enchantress then enfolded him, promising a sexual union yielding the very joys his father had known "when Herzeleide's inflamed passion poured over, scorching him." The kiss of Kundry, she assured the boy, would be his "mother's final greeting and blessing." Kundry

[2] The Grail, like its antecedent, the Rhinegold, has fits of consciousness and slumber and also gleams when aroused. Wagner's symbols of power had pronounced sexual characteristics.

promised maternal intercourse. Though for a time Parsifal succumbed to the witchcraft, he soon freed himself, unlike Amfortas, who had carried from his shameful coitus with Kundry that terrible wound which would not close.

The uncovering of the Grail in the temple results in the immediate and painful symbolic mixing of blood streams within Amfortas' veins, a torture beyond endurance, and, quite understandably, he calls for death in the last act rather than submit once again to the sadism of the Grail ceremony. The syntax of Amfortas' first aria is perhaps the most forced and convoluted of all Wagner's poetic texts, a characteristic also shared by some of the *Blätter* articles. There is a kind of desperation to present the Wagnerian blood imagery convincingly. The music, however, has a place with the greatest he ever wrote, flowing with its own noble logic. Amfortas, once known under the name of Tannhäuser, hungers for both non-Aryan sex and Aryan salvation and is wisely kept under close surveillance by a brotherhood critically diminished by the weakness of members who have similarly yielded to the blandishments of outsiders.

After the agonies of the rushing blood, the super, archetypical fluid within the chalice gives the king only brief respite. Obviously, something is wanting—a new leader with a new solution, the Wagnerian hero-saint. The motif of pity foretelling his arrival (*"durch Mitleid wissend"*) has a remarkable likeness to that phrase in the opening act of *Siegfried* to which the Wanderer sang his prediction about the hero, "Only he who has never experienced fear shall reforge Nothung." A new master with the steel of Siegfried in him and evincing a ferocious kind of pity is awaited by the dwindling corps of knights, significantly described by Wagner as a "race chosen to guard the Grail." The latter, as *The Wibelungs* revealed, is really the Rhinegold itself, the divine talisman of the master race, now threatened by Klingsor, the villain of the piece. He has already possessed himself of another fateful token of Aryan superiority, the shaft of Wotan, now baptized as the sacred spear that once pierced Christ's flesh, provoking the flow of superblood. The Grail and spear, in Westernhagen's phrase, "ancient Aryan symbols of life-renewal," are the fetishes worshiped in *Parsifal* and have nothing to do with the Jewish carpenter of Nazareth.

Klingsor, thus well on his way to pre-empting Aryan prerogatives, is a remarkable composite of Ortrud, Alberich, and Beckmesser. Earlier it was observed that the latter, long ago relentlessly driven from the charmed circle of Nuremberg, would return as the self-mutilated necromancer. In his *"Gefiel er dir wohl"* one actually hears a characteristic harmonic color of Nuremberg's town clerk. He had, at least for a time, kept one foot in the door of the saved; and, indeed, Wagner occasionally pitied dark Prince Alberich. But Klingsor has never been part of the elect and can never be; nor is he worthy of Wagner's pity. He stands outside the mystical processes of Wagnerian redemption—the Jew as the composer had finally come to see him, the figure he described as "the incarnation of the characteristic evil that brought Christianity into the world." Klingsor represented not only the Jew, Wagner told Cosima, but the Jesuit, too.

Ironically, a deep force made him create in Klingsor an enormous, energetic, heroic figure, a marvelous monstrosity, whom Debussy recognized as the only human and moral character in the drama. It was Wagner's fantasy that all of Europe's Jews and their works might be made to vanish with the wave of an Aryan lance, like Klingsor and his enchanted castle and park falling to ruin and waste before the sign of the cross made by the reclaimed spear in Parsifal's hand. This magic domain represented those Jewish-Jesuit metropolises of the world from which Wagner had fled to establish his sanctuary in the Franconian forest. In this scene his tireless tirades against Mendelssohn and Meyerbeer finally reached the stage; their compositions were artificially contrived blossoms with no roots in Aryan soil, and the hero-saint with power to resist such Semitic snares could discern that the Jew's garden of art was really a desert and that he had only to invoke the symbol of the Crucifixion—itself a symbol of Aryan rescue—to reveal the fraud in its true aspect.

On the other hand, only a month after completing the orchestration of incredibly beautiful music for the garden-desert, Wagner told King Ludwig on November 22, 1881: "By dealing in pictures, jewelry, and furniture, the Jews have an instinct for the genuine and lastingly profitable which the German has so completely lost that, in trading with the Jews, he ends with the spurious." This instinct, the composer informed Ludwig, governed the Jew Neumann's interest in the Wagnerian drama. There is a kind of reasoning in all this. In the world of the looking glass, life can seem real enough, but, as Alice observed, "the books are something like our books, only the words go the wrong way."

Parsifal's sudden insight in the magic garden was the realization that by yielding to Kundry he would dilute his purebred strain. *"Heldentum"* specifically warned that, although inferior races might be raised by Aryan impregnation, the resulting improvement they enjoyed was paltry compared to the catastrophic decline an admixture of their blood worked upon their masters. At the almost fatal moment when the temptress' lips touched his, the youth became the Wagnerian hero-saint.

For Wagner, the first kiss marked the end of individuality. Siegfried gave way to panic before adjusting to the change, but Parsifal was immediately vouchsafed the sense of belonging to Amfortas. Desire was conquered by an atavistic vision of blood warning him to prevent the theft of his sexual force and strengthening him to conquer the will. Parsifal, shrieking, "Am-

fortas! The wound!" remembered the sinfully mixed blood of the Grail
King gushing from his side,[3] and the boy's own bloodstream swirled in
sympathetic commotion. Strengthened by this psychic experience, he was
able to reject the advances of a creature all the more pitiable because she
herself had fallen a victim to Jewry. Ferris, the erstwhile Grail Knight, and
his companions, through whose ranks Parsifal had fought his way into the
magic garden, had sold themselves to Jewish luxury. Depraved Aryans,
weakened beyond help by habitual sexual indulgence with mongrels, they
could only flee before the blade Parsifal snatched from Ferris. But eventually
Kundry was able to take instruction from *"Heldentum."* Learning that the
duty of hybrids was to be the menials of their betters, she spent the final
act of the opera groveling and uttering only the word "service."

Parsifal reclaimed the spear, that holy apparatus of Aryanism outrageously
appropriated by Jewry, and returned this stolen symbol of power to the
temple. Preparing to mount its altar-throne as the new Grail King, he perceived Jesus' blood glowing on the spear's tip and surging longingly to
rejoin its related blood in the cup. His description of this phenomenon triumphantly announced the ultimate lesson of *"Heldentum"*—pure blood
mingles naturally only with its like; Aryan must cleave to Aryan; gods must
lie only with gods. The now complete reservoir of superblood, having
restored Amfortas to health,[4] then granted Kundry the ultimate reward of
helotry—the bounty of death, the question put by the unresolved dominant
seventh chord on E flat ending the opera's prelude—that is, "Shall we hope?"
—being affirmatively answered by the work's closing passage in the tonic A
flat major. The Aryan world was again in splendid diatonic order, the
Volksgemeinschaft once more intact. Like a bad dream, the chromatic, unclean Klingsor had vanished in the ruin of his chimeric castle, his fate having
been sealed in the garden when the blood image appeared before Parsifal,

---

[3] In Wolfram von Eschenbach's *Parzifal,* Anfortas is a lusty Grail King with the
battle cry of *Amor.* He, too, is injured sexually, a poisoned spear piercing his testicles.
For Wagner to take over this detail from Wolfram would have resulted in some
extraordinary stage business, and so the wound was relocated. Amfortas, struck by
Klingsor with the sacred spear, received the gash in his side. In the closing scene
Wagner directs Amfortas to rip open his robe and reveal the wound, but most
artists singing the part appear, for convenience' sake, to be suffering some damage
in the pectoral area. Herbert Janssen, the great German-American baritone (he was
greeted at Bayreuth by Muck as the only true interpreter of the role since Reichmann,
the first Amfortas), told this writer of Daniela's distress to observe the change. He
had vivid memories of her standing in the wings and making frantic gestures to
him in the direction of her side.

[4] In "Know Thyself" Wagner implies that tainted Aryans might also redeem
themselves through study of the German language. One assumes that Wagnerian texts
would be most beneficial.

turning the self-avowal and perception (*"Bekenntnis"* and *"Erkenntnis"*) of sex that Kundry had hoped to awaken in him into a revelation of racial duty and mission.

Wagner ended "Know Thyself" (*"Erkenne dich selbst"*) of 1881 with a mystically phrased observation; only when his countrymen awakened and ceased party bickering, would there be no more Jews, a "great solution" (*"grosse Lösung"*) he foresaw as uniquely within the reach of the Germans if they could conquer false shame and not shrink from ultimate knowledge (*"nach der Überwindung aller falschen Scham die letzte Erkenntnis nicht zu scheuen"*). *Parsifal* showed the way. The shattering *"Erkenntnis"* that came to the hero in the magic garden would be Wagner's final revelation to his countrymen. "Germany, awake!" (*"Deutschland erwache!"*) [5] was the slogan under which Hitler brought the *"grosse Lösung"* to reality.

This painful interpretation of *Parsifal* has been traced largely with its creator's own words. Yet, even though *Parsifal,* more than the *Ring,* was the gospel of National Socialism, Wagner's genius operates on many levels, and, as has been noted, the work may also and more comfortably be regarded as his final treatment of the themes of empathy, growing awareness, and the love-death. But to be completely comfortable one must overlook the fact that, like Hans Sachs's benignity, the compassion extolled in *Parsifal* is restricted to a chosen group. Westernhagen described Wagnerian pity as "aristocratic." The Third Reich overflowed with this particular kind of benevolence. *Parsifal* is not only un-Christian, it is anti-Christian. Nietzsche, who believed racial mixture to be the source of great cultures,[6] recognized the opera as "a work of malice, of vindictiveness, of poison secretly brewed to envenom the prerequisites of life, a *bad* work . . . an outrage on morality." Yet he also acknowledged the ingenuity of its libretto and the incredible beauty of its music.

Max Friedlander [7] observed Wagner's delight in setting up stage situations

[5] The Nazi poem *"Deutschland erwache!"* was written by Dietrich Eckhart.

[6] Many of Gobineau's and Wagner's ideas on race were taken over by the latter's son-in-law Houston Stewart Chamberlain in his *The Foundations of the Nineteenth Century* (1899), one of the seminal works of the proto-Nazi movement and a book the last German kaiser believed to have been sent to his people by God. Like Nietzsche, Chamberlain felt that extraordinary races were the result of blood mixture, and cited the Prussians as an example; however, according to his program, the noble race, once produced, had to be safeguarded through inbreeding. He embraced Wagner's Aryan Christ as revealed in the *Bayreuther Blätter* and declared Him to have been without "a drop of true Jewish blood in His veins. . . . Any further assertion is an arbitrary assumption."

[7] Mr. Friedlander's "A Psychoanalytic Approach to Wagner's Ring" was published in *Connotation* (a journal of Fairleigh Dickinson University), Volume 2, Part 1, Spring, 1963. Unfortunately, his other lectures delivered at Bayreuth remain in manuscript.

whose externals paradoxically project a point of view at variance with his text. At these moments the average spectator, satisfied with what appears to be a conventional operatic situation, settles back to drink in the beautiful sea of sound. A large part of the public, for example, is unaware that the love potion scene in *Tristan* is not a token exchange of magic draughts but the result of a bald plan for murder and then suicide, that the brother and sister Siegmund mentions in his *"Winterstürme"* cavatina in the first act of *Valkyrie* are not himself and Sieglinde but a poetic reference to spring and love, and that Sieglinde's frenzy and flight in this work's second act are caused not by remorse for incestuous adultery but by hysterical regret for not having indulged it earlier. Wagner enjoyed the trick of juxtaposing the seeming and the real. In *Parsifal,* with the help of church bells, snippets of the Mass, and the vocabulary and paraphernalia of the Passion, he set forth a religion of racism under the cover of Christian legend. *Parsifal* is an enactment of the Aryan's plight, struggle, and hope for redemption, a drama characterized not only by the composer's natively obscure and elliptical literary style, but also by the indigenous circumlocutions of allegory, the calculated unrealities of symbolism, and, especially, the sultry corruptions of decadence. The temple scenes are, in a sense, Black Masses, perverting the symbols of the Eucharist and dedicating them to a sinister god. And the Black Mass, so fascinating to the *fin de siècle* decadents, was but one of their obsessions weaving its spell around the aging Wagner and his *Parsifal.*

4

Nietzsche's major attacks on Wagnerism, *The Wagner Case* and *Nietzsche contra Wagner,* were concerned essentially with decadence, and *Parsifal,* in exhibiting the quintessential of the movement and revealing Wagner as its high priest, offered the philosopher his easiest target. A *pasticcio* of freakish elements—at first glance a seemingly serene and ample frieze whose figures under closer examination reveal themselves as grotesques, moving puppet-like before backgrounds realized in a strange discontinuous perspective—*Parsifal,* nonetheless, exhibits the finest grain and subtlest workmanship of Wagner's works, reminding one of the exquisite finish to which Bronzino polished a portrait or Mallarmé a poem. The opera's influence on the French was considerable; Count Axel of Auersburg's fantastic castle, reared by Villiers, combines characteristics of both Monsalvat's domain and Klingsor's dungeons, and the Rosicrucian hero, like Wagner's stripling, is a handsome fellow who eschews sex. In the score of *Parsifal,* a tenuous, fluctuating, impressionistic light replaces the glow of *Tristan* and the hard glare so often glancing from *Meistersinger,* the final scene of *Siegfried,* and *The Twilight of the Gods.* Even the gross seduction scene is modeled in a delicate *sfumato.* The music hovers and evaporates like the kaleidoscopic images of symbolist poetry, although Wagner compensates for what might have become a tendency toward flaccidity, a danger inherent in impressionism, by tightening his musical periods. The atmosphere of the whole work is dreamlike, a brooding nightmare of Aryan anxiety, but the *horror vacui* of the instrumental style of *Tristan, Meistersinger,* and the end of the *Ring* has yielded to a musical texture that is transparent, rare, and vaporous, and, even if the ambiguous drama is constructed of denser elements, the disintegrating world for which Wagner feared is realized in vast and airy tonal vistas.

A consideration of Wagner's musical evolution has already pointed to the nonconceptual tendency gradually gaining in his work, the motif departing from the relative obviousness of the naturalistic and the conventionally allegorical to become, instead, a vague but rich symbol of inexhaustible intimations. Between *Rhinegold* and *Parsifal* his style underwent a change from the explicit to the allusive and evocative. In the *Ring* he had too often felt the need for a threefold identification of a concept in text, orchestra, and action, a technique, as Nietzsche observed, that said a thing again and again until one despaired and then believed. On the other hand, in *Parsifal* little is directly named by the mysterious text or elusive motifs, and the audience is left to divine meanings. Musically and poetically, Wagner was following the path from high romanticism to impressionism and symbolism. When Tristan in his delirium had cried that he could hear light, Wagner was already deliberately mixing images and mingling the senses in the manner of Poe and his European disciples, whose desire for words to share music's indefiniteness was a step toward a complete entanglement of all perception. The idea came to Wagner directly from Goethe, who could saturate his verse with what seem to be simultaneous allusions to color, sound, and odor. The example from *Tristan* obviously derived from the second part of *Faust,* where the light of Homunculus both shines and sounds in the Pharsalian fields.[8] Wagner had at hand in the *Gesamtkunstwerk* an arsenal of reciprocal linguistic, acoustical, and optical devices that were the symbolist's ideal.

In *Beyond Good and Evil* Nietzsche clearly saw Wagner's deep relation-

---

[8] Mephistopheles commands, "Little one, let your lamp (*Leuchte*) shine with sound!" and Homunculus replies, "Thus shall it flash and ring." The stage direction reads, "The glass booms and beams powerfully." Tristan cries, "Do I hear the light? The torch (*Leuchte*) . . . goes out!" As Brandes observed, in such a line as *"Wir säuseln, wir rieseln, wir flüstern Dir zu,"* Goethe anticipated Wagner's Rhine Maidens.

ship to French romantics of the forties, artists to whom he appeared "fundamentally related in all the heights and depths of their necessities. . . . It is certain that the same storm and stress tortured them, that they *sought* in the same way, these last great seekers! All of them plunged in literature to their eyes and ears—the first artists of universal literary culture —for the most part even themselves writers, poets, mediators, and blenders of the arts and the senses (Wagner, as musician, belongs among the painters; as poet, among the musicians; as artist, really among the actors); all of them fanatics of expression 'at any price.' " And by the end of the century Yeats could speak of Wagner as the supreme example of symbolism in Germany, the spirit of Baudelaire's *correspondances,* wherein *"les parfums, les couleurs et les sons se répondent,"* having anticipated the fluid atmosphere of impressionism, of symbolism—of *Parsifal.*

Baudelaire remarked, *"faire l'amour, c'est faire le mal."* Sex had always been associated with vice in Wagner's mind, and Baudelaire's view of guilt as adding seasoning to love doubtlessly helped attract him and his followers to the satanic tale of *Tannhäuser* and eventually make Wagnerism a part of the French decadent and symbolist movements. In *Parsifal* sex became something of an aberration, certainly something to be feared, and abstinence the more usual state of the saved, a condition reinforced and protected by monkish seclusion. In Wolfram von Eschenbach's *Parzifal,* except for the king, who might take a wife, any man pledged to serve the Grail was to renounce the love of women. Nonetheless, according to the Tale of Trevrizent (Book IX) the rule was well honored in the breach through official dispensation and personal whim. In the temple resided twenty-five radiant maidens appointed to care for the Grail, which, moreover, in order to provide future personnel, frequently directed the gentlemen of the company to ride forth and beget offspring. ("God can teach them how to do this," Wolfram charmingly added.) At best, Wolfram's knights strove, and rather unsuccessfully, to "guard themselves against incontinence." The Wagner of *Parsifal* could hardly have approved of such sexual insouciance or, indeed, of the kitchens of their temple, where the Grail provided "whatever game lives beneath the heavens, whether it flies or runs or swims." No doubt sobering vegetable meals were served in Wagner's Monsalvat, where he clearly imposed upon his troop a strict sexual fast to be lifted, not capriciously, but only under immaculate racial circumstances.

In a Germany where Bismarck had conferred equal citizenship on all regardless of confession, it was perhaps safest for Aryan gentlemen to refrain until certain of a lady's papers. In his anti-Semitic pamphlet, "Modern" (1878), Wagner derided the Jews who were changing their names, and, although he professed amusement at the development, one senses his genuine alarm at "the delicious names with which our new Jewish fellow citizens confront us, as much to our astonishment as our delight. . . ." The situation was another threat to Aryan purity.

Does chastity work *miracles?* Nietzsche wondered while contemplating the astounding fact that Parsifal was Lohengrin's father. Yet somewhere Parsifal did find a lady of unimpeachable ancestry worthy of his Aryan attentions. Love between men and women had as its purpose, according to Wagner of the *Parsifal* period, only the perfecting of race, and Parsifal learned his duty. But duty and desire do not necessarily agree; an air of homosexuality hangs heavy over Monsalvat. The single genuinely natural emotion evinced in a work mainly devoted to sexual-racial problems is that of the swan circling the lake in search of his mate just before Parsifal's arrow strikes him down! Nietzsche protested, "Sermons on chastity incite against nature." The adjective Huneker perceptively derived from *Parsifal* was "Parsiphallic," and, as Stanislaus Przybyszewski observed, the mysteries of the Black Mass are dedicated to Satan-Satyr, Satan-Pan, and Satan-Phallus. According to Nietzsche's *The Wagner Case,* the composer "in his closing years was thoroughly *feminini generis."* The adverb is perhaps too restricting, but otherwise the observation should not be dismissed as a mere product of rancor.

In the same book Nietzsche remarked, "Scarcely anyone has character sufficient to resist being undone—being 'redeemed'—when he perceives himself treated as a god; thereupon he *condescends* to woman. A man is cowardly before the Eternal Feminine, and women (*die Weiblein*) know it." The reference was obviously to the Richard-Cosima relationship. Certainly in his final opera Wagner adopted the fierce misogyny of Schopenhauer, the great *Frauenhasser.* Woman is demonic, destructive—a peril. For Wagner, she had become something not unlike Przybyszewski's *dulce malum et vitiosa propago,* "a sweet evil and a corrupt shoot." Yet, whereas the German-Pole drew strength from the vine encircling him, the aged Wagner sought to free himself from its grasp. Much was hard, suffocating—Strindbergian—about Cosima, who, since she so often behaved absurdly, reminds one of Wilhelm Busch's *"fromme Helene."* The heights of deviltry and the depths of atonement between which Kundry travels perhaps echo her creator's frequent and passionate outbursts against his wife.

Wagner's seemingly new attitude toward women had not been entirely absent from his earlier work, his fame as an exalter of the feminine notwithstanding. In his *Toward a Genealogy of Morals* Nietzsche asked, "What is the significance . . . of an artist like Richard Wagner offering homage to chastity in his last days? In a certain sense, he had, to be sure, always done so, but only at the end in an ascetic sense." But this was not really accurate. An attitude that rejected women's sexual favors paradoxically ran through the works of the younger Wagner, and in his final years the old master attempted to turn this latent fear of sex to the advantage of his racial doctrines.

Lohengrin abandoned his wife for the monastery with the pathetic explanation, "The Grail will be angry if I stay." Tannhäuser, the pivotal character in Wagner, and one of the earliest satanists in German literature, was hardly a model of abstinence; yet he was satisfied with neither erotic Venus nor saintly Elizabeth and in the end sought to conquer sex through fierce self-humiliations. He bequeathed his insecurity, debility, morbidity, masochism, and general *Nervosität* to his heir, Tristan. Amfortas, another Tristan, unwittingly impressed these very neuroses upon Parsifal's blank mind.

From the time of that political journal written in Munich, Wagner had seen the hero-saint Parsifal in terms of Ludwig—the young, homosexual prince, the enchanting *Weibjüngling* with political power. Courtly, but standing aloof from woman (the manner adopted by Hitler), he would redeem a debauched kingdom by means of a thorough racial cleansing and thus achieve his destiny as a dragon-fighter, the heir of Siegfried and of the glorious predestined kaiser stock. This was the theme in an almost limitless variety of guises Wagner hammered at relentlessly throughout his correspondence with Ludwig, who patiently ignored the message. Its intent was painfully clear to him.

In a drama on Achilles Wagner had planned at the end of his Dresden tenure, the warrior's mother, Thetis, offered him immortality if he would forswear revenge for the death of his beloved Patroclus. Scorning the gift, Achilles fulfilled his mission, thus achieving a higher divinity. In *Parsifal*, this fascinating interplay of mother love and homosexual attachment returns as Mother-Thetis-Kundry again stands before the hero promising the same reward if he will forget Amfortas: "Completely enfolded in my embrace of love you will attain godhood!" Parsifal rejects the lure, and Kundry, like Thetis, eventually bows down, acknowledging the loftier duty. Wagner felt the close relationship between his "Achilles" and *Parsifal* and, soon after completing the prose sketch of the opera, wrote Ludwig on September 16, 1865, of his hope to finish the abandoned play.

But the King was uncomfortable about *Parsifal* from the day he received the sketch of its libretto early that same month. After expressing to Wagner the expected reaction that "this art is holy, the purest, most exalted religion," he went on to reveal that he suspected it to be nothing of the sort. The Mother-Thetis-Kundry labyrinth opened before him. "I permit myself to put only one question to my beloved friend in respect to *Parsifal*—why is our hero first converted through Kundry's kiss, why does his divine mission become clear to him through it? Only from this moment on can he transplant himself into Amfortas' soul, can he understand his nameless misery, and feel with him!" And Wagner answered, "Darling, that is a terrible secret!" After developing a preposterous parallel between Adam, Eve, and Christ on one side and Amfortas, Kundry, and Parsifal on the other, he informed Ludwig that, when Parsifal's lips touched Kundry's, "with lightning speed he said to himself something like this: 'Ah! That is the poison from which he [Amfortas] sickens, he whose lament I did not understand till now!'"

The "terrible secret" was obvious enough to the King. Parsifal-Ludwig's innocence of and indifference to women was yet to be turned into a force of redemption. Fate had placed him above the temptations of racial pollution, that "poison" of Kundry's lips (after all, the master himself, like Amfortas, still found those of dubious heritage disturbingly interesting), giving the royal youth the opportunity to act freely and decisively toward achieving national purification. Wagner wished to see in Ludwig a divinely ruthless despot of transcendent grace and beauty, sweeping away all impediments with an imperious gesture, that very image of Heliogabalus with which Stefan George was to associate the tragic king—a graceful tyrant gathering up the folds of his purple train and stepping over a corpse on the marble stairway.

Not by accident had Wagner nicknamed Ludwig "Parsifal"; nor can it be believed that the accident of illness or an attack of misanthropy made him decline to attend the Grail drama's Bayreuth première. At private performances in Munich he could approach the work as romantic opera rather than as an exposition of racial doctrine. Though his was the face of a Dorian Gray, his portrait was not decaying. With his usual perspicacity Hanslick, from the time of the first performance, declared it necessary to ignore *Parsifal's* "false religious-philosophical pretensions" in order to "experience in it moments of significant artistic stimulation and brilliant effectiveness." He observed, "The listener sufficiently naïve to comprehend the Wagnerian *Parsifal* as a superior magic opera, as a free play of fantasy reveling in the wondrous, will capture the best side of it and salvage the least troubled pleasure." This was the level on which Ludwig wished to contemplate *Parsifal.* His correspondence with Wagner shows him studiedly disregarding its racial communications and, when pressed, defending himself against them. The Bayreuth atmosphere was not one in which he breathed easily. He desired to see in *Parsifal* only a glorious musical and dramatic counterpart to those scenes of medieval knightly and religious pageantry with which artists were covering the walls of his dream castle of Neuschwanstein.

5

Not only the snobbery of racism but also its inevitable Neronic concomitants of inbreeding, cruelty, depravity, and an atmosphere of exhaustion make *Parsifal* seem to distill the essence of *fin de siècle* mysticism and demonism. The Flower Maidens are specters of Wagner's older female creations, shadows of Wagnerian woman's once effective sensuality, now powerless. (He had at first contemplated placing the figure of Isolde among them.) In the winter of *Parsifal* they sing, "In spring the master (*der Meister*) gathered us." Not wicked because they are not real, weird organisms akin to Odilon Redon's plants whose stems culminate in human faces,[9] these creatures are completely illusory. Kundry in her aspect as temptress has the opera's only role approaching that of a woman, and as the embodiment of antifeminine Satanism became the ancestress of Wilde's Salome much as Parsifal furnished a model for Jochanaan. The attempt of Kundry, the succubus, to ruin the hero by luring him to carnal intercourse forms the drama's crisis, his resistance calling to mind Huysmans' conclusion that the chaste alone can be truly obscene. For all its greatness, the second act of *Parsifal* must be protected by its stage director from resembling a series of satirical drawings by Beardsley or Lautrec.

The obsessive Kundry is not only a vampire who draws her nourishment from a destructive kind of sexual intercourse but also a hysteric suffering mediumlike trances, wavering between, on the one hand, a desire to help preserve certain ritualistic articles in their orthodox place for canonical use and, on the other, a compulsion to help deliver them to a magician for his own Black Mass. (Huysmans himself fought a similar battle.) The "holy" symbols, as has been noted, are the old Wagnerian fetishes neurotically transformed, the Nibelung gold being worshiped as the Grail of superblood, while Wotan's shaft of authority reappears as the venerated spear captured by Jewry with the Reichstag's help.

Thus, scattered through the opera is an extraordinary number of elements beloved of the decadents—the erotic and perverse, exemplified by Kundry, the demonic prostitute, a true Art Nouveau *femme fatale* (her most characteristic motif has the luxuriant swirl of *Jugendstil* and *Secessionsstil* decoration); the intoxication with destruction, criminality, and degeneracy in her, the self-castrated Klingsor, and the hostile Storm Trooper Grail Knights, who in the end shamelessly reveal their sadistic hatred of Amfortas; a delight in the satanic, the occult, and black magic; the yearning for chastity and salvation, so often the intermittent cry of the debauched, those whom Nietzsche described as "hapless (*verunglückten*) swine reduced to adoring chastity . . . oh, with what a tragic grunting and fervor!"; and the flight to solitude and detachment as shields against reality, the basis of the very concept of Wagner's Monsalvat.

[9] More than a decade before *Parsifal,* Tenniel had drawn grave young Alice conversing with such chattering flowers in the looking-glass garden. When describing Klingsor's necromantic gear, Wagner specifies in particular only a magic mirror.

The *mise en scène,* moreover, fluctuates between, on the one hand, the gorgeousness of a dimly lit, incense-filled sanctuary and the Oriental splendor of a harem and, on the other, the black horror of the necromancer's cell. A Gustave Moreau, Beardsley, or Gaudi should have created this décor and a Mucha the costumes and accessories. (Although the superb musical painting of nature in the two placid Pyrenees landscapes suggests an earlier Wagner, one senses in them—to borrow Hauser's phrase—that *Weltschmerz* has turned to *ennui;* a stultifying *taedium vitae* engulfs *Parsifal,* a sense of stagnation.) It remains an enigma of genius that Wagner was able to yoke all this bizarre paraphernalia embracing the catalogue of his neuroses to both an allegory of the fallen and redeemed Aryan and a symbolic representation of the developing human soul, to overlay the whole with a rather cheap and cracking veneer of fake Catholicism, and yet achieve a monumental masterpiece. Nietzsche called the opera's hero "that manly (alas, so unmanly) . . . poor devil and child of nature, Parsifal, whom he [Wagner] finally made Catholic by such captious means."

Indeed, to use in the temple scenes the still recognizable outlines of the Mass while filling them with an alien content close in spirit to the séance was, at the very least, a serious lapse in taste. During Munich days Wagner had studied the Catholic liturgy with Father Petrus Hamp, who baptized Isolde. The Wagnerian rite is, of course, neither Catholic nor Protestant in form, but, exploiting the symbols of Christian Communion and snippets of the Bible, it creates inevitable associations. Wagner called those who protested against this adaptation "converted Jews, who . . . make the most intolerant Catholics. . . ."

Though the journey from crapulence to the altar is often short, it is nonetheless amazing that *Parsifal* was ever considered a Christian work. "If Wagner was a Christian, then Liszt was perhaps a Church Father!" Nietzsche cried. That many find a performance of the opera an offensive experience is easily understood. Attempting to be a heresiarch, to organize a new religion of race and sensation—a sacred rite to himself in his own shrine—Wagner concocted a drama of monstrous virtuosity. (Years before, Fröbel had foreseen his desire to make his theater into a church.) He was asking adherents to carry out a racial ritual in remembrance of their magus and hierophant, a ceremony of self-worship, certainly not without influence on the George circle with its veneration of the poet-priest. As Hanslick observed, "Something from the institution of the Oberammergau Passion Play . . . caught the fancy of the founder of the Bayreuth Festivals."

Parsifal and its creator were clearly on Nietzsche's mind when he wrote in "We Fearless Ones," the fifth book of *The Gay Science* (added in 1887), of "that tyrannical will of someone seriously ailing, struggling, tortured, who would like to sanction as binding law and constraint his most personal, unique, narrowest characteristics, the very idiosyncrasy of his suffering and who, as it were, takes revenge on all things by stamping, forcing, branding upon them *his* image, the image of his torture." The opulent art of *Parsifal* grew from hatred, from growing impotence, and an ever more disturbing sexual ambiguity.

One imagines the old wizard in his Wahnfried study as, dressed in gowns of fur, silk, and satin and under the stimulus of Judith's perfumes, he first summoned up the musical lineaments of the opera. A morbid atmosphere of artificially excited sensibilities and disease envelops a work stimulated by aphrodisiacs. A curious and mystical dislocation of characters and situations, an irrational spirit, and a crepuscular mood—even in the seduction scene—show *Parsifal* the product of an old master, a fantastic male *Venus im Pelz,* given more to fantasies and self-caressing than indulgence.

Yet there is no fatigue in the musical workmanship; in *Parsifal,* bourgeois Wagner shows an unsuspectedly aristocratic hand. He worked lovingly at the orchestration, at times producing only a few measures a day. But one is conscious that the series of marvelous musical visions has been provoked by memories of things past. *Parsifal* takes place in the vacuum of a tired and fanatic decadent's musings, and it is easy to suffocate in this world completely estranged from reality. If *Tristan* ends with the spectator wondering whether he has not drunk too much of heavy wine, *Parsifal* leaves him feeling that perhaps he has been under the influence of drugs. Nietzsche wrote in *The Gay Science,* "Now, by means of works of art, the poor exhausted and sickly are enticed from mankind's great path of suffering for a lascivious little moment; one offers them a bit of ecstasy and insanity." Almost divinely prophetic, the great German often seemed to be warning that the road to Wagner's strangely beautiful Monsalvat was to lead on to unparalleled madness.

In the final moments of *Parsifal,* Wagner joined hands with Huysmans, who was to become a contributor to the *Revue Wagnérienne.* At the end of his *A Rebours,* which appeared soon after the opera, Des Esseintes, the ultimate decadent, drops into a chair and despairingly asks God to pity the Christian who doubts, the skeptic who would believe, and those who put to sea alone and in darkness without the consoling beacon fires of the ancient hope. It was a petition pointing toward Huysmans' coming reconciliation with the Church, a way Wagner could never travel. But as the Grail glows in Parsifal's hands and the light increases above, choirs, ranged from the floor of the sanctuary to its highest dome, although proclaiming Wagner the savior, hopefully whisper a plea for his redemption, *"Erlösung dem Erlöser!"*

XVII

Death in Venice

I

Early in July of 1882 rehearsals of *Parsifal* were under way in Bayreuth. Compared to the first festival, the task was light. Musical and production problems were less imposing than those of the *Ring,* the artists arrived well prepared—some, like Materna and Hill, were veterans of 1876—and money troubles had melted away, thanks to Ludwig.

Wagner liked to pretend that the role of his "pure fool," Parsifal, was more demanding than that of Siegfried. Any tenor with a heroic frame and passable voice—desiderata hardly found once in a generation—could be trained for the young Volsung, he told the King, while to impersonate Parsifal a singer had to be capable of infinitely greater interpretive subtleties. "May God send the *fool!*" was the composer's prayer, to his happy surprise generously answered.

There were, are, and likely will be few tenors with the steel throat needed to survive Siegfried's vocal rigors. But Wagner immediately found many artists able to manage Parsifal's shorter, generally lower, more lyric vocal line, and the part has had a long list of distinguished exponents. As in the popular *Valkyrie,* the composer had freed himself from dependence on a Meyerbeer heroic voice. In the tenor riches that came his way he found no embarrassment, for excessively temperamental candidates could be dealt with independently. And the role of Kundry, though bristling with vocal and interpretive challenges, was also mercifully brief, thus permitting sopranos [1] of less than behemoth stamina and proportions to undertake it. Stamina, however, was the very quality demanded of anyone attempting the garrulous Gurnemanz. But, despite some extraordinary claims on breath

---

[1] Like Venus, Ortrud, and Brangäne, Kundry was written for soprano. Contraltos and mezzos, not infrequently to their vocal ruin, have taken over these roles.

control, the role was free of high altitude hazards, and any reasonable bass with endurance, clear diction, and a pair of comfortable shoes could get through. The notes of Amfortas lay beautifully for high baritone, and his two temple arias were to become celebrated show pieces. All in all, the composer showed a vocal compassion disdained in the *Ring*.

He oversaw the rehearsals, summoning almost incredible vivacity when teaching his artists. Stressing, above all, maintenance of a long melodic line unbroken by accents of false pathos, he demanded not declamation but singing, and magnetically drew it from his cast. But the tensions of such sessions past, he could easily fall asleep in his chair; Cosima's vigil was to ward off death for a little while.

Physically, the production promised greater success than had been the lot of the *Ring*. The Brückner brothers, Wagner was to assure the skeptical Ludwig, reached in their scenery "the full inspiration of artistic power," quite an achievement for Max and Gotthold. Some of the costumes were reworked by Cosima. After trying on Kundry's attire, she wrote Daniela how "truly disappointed" she was. And what had been turned out for the Flower Maidens from Zhukovski's rapid sketches at first horrified her. A second look made her laugh, for there was still time for change. The gifted Isolde sketched a simple design from which mother and daughter fashioned models. (Weingartner, however, was to describe these costumes as showing "extraordinary lack of taste.") Moreover, the stage machinery was finally functioning; the spear flew into the hero's hand, to quote Hanslick, "like a roast pigeon" (*"als gebratene Taube"*), the castle collapsed on cue, and the garden turned to desert. The only real contretemps developed over the transformation apparatus, inspired by Parisian examples and more directly by Mühldorfer's famous moving scenery for *Oberon*.

Somehow Carl Brandt had miscalculated the rate at which the painted landscape was to unfold across the stage during the two orchestral interludes depicting Parsifal's progress along the almost inaccessible paths to Monsalvat. There were yards and yards of excess canvas. The error was discovered at rehearsals, but too late to change the complicated roller mechanism especially constructed for this *Wandeldekoration*. In order to bring pit and stage together, Wagner was obliged to order the first act interlude played twice and with liberal retards. Remarkably enough, he approved a few bars of extra music added by Humperdinck to stretch the passage; they were to be used until the next festival, when the canvas would be trimmed and the mechanism overhauled. But rather than tamper with the poignant transitional passage in the final act, Wagner abandoned the transformation effect and ordered the curtain to fall between the scenes.

At the première, Hanslick found this technical embarrassment a blessing; to repeat, "one and the same device of scenic magic, reminiscent of fairy tales and children's theater," appeared "dubious" to him from the very beginning. The mechanical difficulty doubtlessly helped save *Parsifal* from those effects of a holiday pantomime fatal to the *Ring* six years before. And, to Hanslick's infinite relief, Wagner departed from the directions in his libretto for the final tableau, where ancient Titurel, who had finally died, was supposed momentarily to raise himself up in his coffin and bless all. Mercifully, he remained horizontal, a final disposition of the father motive haunting the composer since *Die Feen*.

The first performance on July 26 included Winkelmann (Parsifal), Materna (Kundry), Reichmann (Amfortas), Scaria (Gurnemanz), and Hill (Klingsor), with Levi conducting the Munich chorus and orchestra, the latter augmented to one hundred and seven musicians. The first two performances were restricted to the society of patrons, a last obligation toward a group officially disbanded. Repetitions of the work with changing casts continued until August 29, when the sixteenth presentation closed the festival. During this final *Parsifal* Wagner slipped into the pit and conducted the closing act from the twenty-third bar of the transformation music to the very end.

A legend quickly grew; Wagner, it was said, sensing that Levi was ill, had hastened to relieve him. But Heckel confirms suspicions that the composer planned to lead the final scene, as does a letter to Rabbi Levi of Giessen from his son. It relates just what happened in the deep pit beneath the stage into which Wagner rarely descended. (Steps had become a problem to him, and a little window, through which he could confer with Levi during rehearsals, had been cut into the curved and hooded canopy covering the sunken orchestra.)

Hermann wrote to Giessen on August 31, by which time he had completely recovered his health. A nervous fatigue, he related, had seized him *after* the final *Parsifal*. This performance had been an overwhelming emotional experience. "During the transformation music the master came into the orchestra, grabbled his way (*krabbelte*) up to the podium, took the baton from my hand, and conducted the performance to the end. I remained standing next to him because I feared he might make mistakes; but this was an idle fear; he conducted with the certainty of one who might have spent his entire life only as a *Kapellmeister*. At the end of the work, the public broke into a jubilation defying description. But the master did not show himself, remained sitting among us musicians, and made bad jokes. And, when after ten minutes the noise would not abate, I cried out with all my might, 'Quiet, quiet!' This was heard up above, people calmed down, and now the master (still on the podium) began to speak, first to me and the orchestra; then the curtain was raised—the entire singing and technical personnel was gathered above—and the master spoke with such affection that everyone started to weep—it was an unforgettable moment!" The Festspielhaus curtain then fell before Wagner's eyes for the final time.

His tempi had been much slower than Levi's, and the wind players later wondered how they had sustained their phrases. The singers, too, had found themselves near the bursting point. Reichmann, the Amfortas, declared he could go through such a thing but once, for only the presence of the master had inspired him to find the necessary breath and pay the extraordinary tax on his vocal resources.

Levi described a public enthusiastically demonstrating its approval. Reports on such behavior during the first *Parsifal* festival vary according to the source consulted, a not surprising fact, for only with time did Wagner make his wishes on the subject known. The music, he announced, was not to be interrupted, as had been the case at the première, but at the fall of the curtain appreciation of the artists might be freely expressed. According to Angelo Neumann, after some indecision owing to Wagner's unclear pronouncements, the audiences of 1882 ended by applauding every act. Yet gradually the custom developed at Bayreuth of applauding only the last two acts, silence following the first temple scene, that finale Hanslick placed "unquestionably among those dazzling musico-scenic achievements in which Wagner has no rival." Today many who applaud a Bach Passion maintain an ecclesiastic silence throughout and after the opera out of a naïve sense of propriety. Wagner himself did not hesitate to treat the middle act in the spirit of pure grand opera by clapping and hurling "bravo" at his Flower Maidens after their lovely *"wir welken und sterben dahinnen."* He was angrily silenced by disciples who in the dark did not recognize the Philistine.

The festival was a success. Life had been made easier for visitors by better rail service, a new paved and lighted road to the theater, an improved restaurant, and a civic committee determined to prevent the townsfolk's greed from claiming too many victims. Wagner's last summer was happy despite the cold and rain prevailing since May. He could forget the gray and chill and those terrible spasms during which he clenched his fists as if to hold on to life itself. His singers fulfilled his desires, the Munich orchestra played divinely even if its leader remained unbaptized, and none of the stage accidents that had plagued the *Ring* recurred. Attendance, however, was uneven, and few celebrities appeared. At the first festival, Tchaikovsky had observed that the greatest musicians were conspicuous by their absence, among them Verdi and Brahms. The latter had meditated a visit to Bayreuth for *Parsifal* but renounced the idea, convinced that it would soon be released to other theaters. (Moreover, he feared that even the anonymity his mighty beard usually provided would be insufficient shield against the fury of the Wagnerites.) The by now familiar gaping rows of empty seats in the Festspielhaus had not been ruinous, since both orchestra and chorus were paid by Ludwig. His failure to appear was the season's only disturbing disappointment.

To protect him from the public gaze, Wagner had ordered architect Brückwald to add to the center façade of the theater a two-story foyer, providing a private entrance and suite leading to the royal box. The little porch, better designed and detailed than the rest of the building, was also meant to remind Ludwig that Wagner expected the nation to "encase the whole [structure] in massive architecture and provide it with monumental ornamentation." (Wagner had not forgotten the model of the Semper theater.) The interior, too, was to be decorated "in noble materials." The theater had been built with no more solidity than necessary to insure against collapse. Only its dimensions were to be retained in the grandiose edifice planned for the future.

On July 1, 1882, Wagner learned of the King's intention not to attend. The *Parsifal* ritual in Bayreuth was more than he cared to face; he preferred to await the completely private performances to be given at Munich. Alarmed, Wagner urged him to experience the work in the Festspielhaus. "And—it is the last thing I will produce. The monstrous overfatigue that today leaves me only strength enough for these few lines reveals the point my powers have reached. Nothing more is to be expected of me now!" He was telling Ludwig that "The Victors" would never be written. "Oh, why wasn't this theater built at one time in Munich—then all would be well!" Ludwig's magnificent eyebrows must have arched high as he stared at this last exclamation.

Illness, Ludwig officially claimed, forbade his journeying to Bayreuth. When Wagner telegraphed him a birthday poem on August 25 beginning: "You scorn the Grail's comfort," a brisk correspondence ensued, the King's secretaries assuring Wahnfried that reasons of health forced his absence and indicating displeasure that the royal word should be so openly doubted. But Wagner was too near the end to bother with diplomatic niceties and again quite plainly admitted his skepticism in a letter to Ludwig of September 8: "If I must now believe, then I am the more inconsolable!" For many of his young men, the idea of Wagner eventually became more agreeable than the reality of his presence. Recently he had been flabbergasted when the disciple of his Zurich days, Karl Ritter, had him turned from his door in Venice. Wagner sent him a note: "What kind of a person are you!"

Most friends realized that the festival was the last great event of Wagner's life. He seemed to fall apart after the final performance. And there had been the extra excitement of Blandine's marriage to Gravina in Wahnfried on the King's birthday. Wagner wished to escape the cold damp of Bayreuth as soon as possible and prepared to set out on his final journey toward the sun. Caressing his Newfoundland Marke in farewell, he observed that they were parting forever. Five months later the dog would greet him with a great howl as his coffin entered the garden of Wahnfried. Before the final *Parsifal* he had told Cosima of his desire for death. She wrote in her diary, "Late in the evening I sat alone . . . and brooded and brooded, till my excited brain fell asleep, and I knew more or less how things will be one day."

2

Traveling through high floods, the family arrived in Venice by way of Verona on September 16 and, after a couple of days at the Hotel Europa, moved into one of Europe's noblest buildings, the Palazzo Vendramin-Calergi, part of the inheritance of the self-styled Henry V, pretender to the throne of France and Count of Chambord. (Most of the palace was occupied by his relative Count Bardi.) Wagner had rented the large entresol consisting of about fifteen spacious rooms with salons and was delighted to think of himself as a "guest of the Bourbons." He indulged a final interior decorating whim by turning his chamber into a blue grotto of shimmering fabrics.

The faithful gathered on the Grand Canal—Zhukovski, Levi, Rubinstein, Stein, Humperdinck—anxious Valkyries huddled at the feet of a doomed and cantankerous Wotan. In October came a gloomy foreboding, news of Count Gobineau's death in Turin. The honeymooning Gravinas arrived the same month, and Liszt, the lone survivor of friends from earlier days, appeared on November 19. As in 1876, Wagner had publicly praised him during the festival as the first to believe in and further the Wagnerian mission. Yet the gap between the old warriors was ever widening. Wagner had become a nagging bore. Liszt preferred visiting the aristocratic salons of Venice to the eternal lecturing at the Vendramin, and Wagner was livid with rage. Yet Liszt was not without fearful presentiments; at the Vendramin he composed his piano piece *"La Lugubre Gondole,"* an uncanny, ghostly elegy to approaching death, cast in an astoundingly modern harmonic idiom. But the familiarity of former days eluded the friends. Since both frequently assumed the airs of monarchy, expecting no one to speak until first addressed, when together they often talked simultaneously in a dissonant, defiant counterpoint. Only when Liszt sat down at the keyboard was something of the old fellowship refound.

There were moments when Wagner felt well enough to plan coming *Parsifal* festivals. The décor was in existence; with the crown bearing the major expenses and the work restricted to Bayreuth, profits sufficient to mount his earlier operas could be amassed. A new intrigue was set in motion, his letters revealing the emerging outlines of a scheme to deprive Munich of its private *Parsifal*. He mulled over the choice of the opera with which to start the series of post-*Parsifal* revivals. Was it to be *Tristan* or *Tannhäuser?* Desperately he longed to live another decade and leave model performances of his life's work in the care of Siegfried, who would then be old enough to become curator of this legacy. Clearly, the idea of Cosima's taking over never entered Wagner's mind. Sadly noting to Ludwig that death was busy about him, he quoted Tristan's entreaty, *"Noch losch das Licht nicht aus!"* ("Do not put out the light yet!") But Cosima, thinking of a different line from the opera, knew that darkness would soon fall on her house.

Her forty-fifth birthday was approaching. Wishing to prepare a surprise, he rehearsed the orchestra of the Liceo Benedetto Marcello in his C-Major Symphony, given its première half a century before under Dionys Weber in Prague and, soon after, its second performance in Leipzig's Gewandhaus. The parts, copied so many years before in Prague, had been recovered from a trunk left behind when the composer fled Dresden, and Seidl had assembled them into a score. Wagner, who always accused Mendelssohn of jealously destroying the copy sent to him, was still pleased with this pathetic product of his twentieth year, though he did feel it necessary to touch up the trio of the scherzo. With unconscious humor Cosima compared the adolescent symphonist to Siegfried: "This was created by someone unacquainted with fear." But not even Levi, a seemingly uncritical worshiper of Wagner's music, could defend the piece when Elizabeth von Herzogenberg aptly described it to him some years later as *"remarkably meaningless."*

Wagner conducted the work on December 24 before a select group of fewer than fifteen guests in the exquisite and gaily illuminated Teatro La Fenice. The effort drained him. There had been five rehearsals, during which he had suffered heart spasms. This jubilee-birthday-Christmas celebration was the last time he held a baton and his most costly gift to Cosima. Doctors fussed, analyzed, and prescribed to no avail. Even walking was becoming an effort. Now only with difficulty could he make his way on the few clear days to his favorite stone seat in the porch of St. Mark's, where he sat, he said, like Hagen. It rained and rained.

Many of his hours in the Vendramin were spent on articles, one on the recent festival having been written in November and another the following month on his symphony. By the end of January he completed an introduction (in the form of an open letter) to Stein's volume of dramatic dialogues in imitation of Gobineau's *Renaissance*. But there was no single work toward which he could direct his energies. Though his mind wandered, the creative force still throbbed fitfully. Nearly a quarter of a century before, he had written Mathilde Wesendonk, "I know I shall live as long as I have work to do. . . . When that is at an end, I will know myself truly safe." But now knowledge that he had outlived his artistic mission made his humor vile and these final months infinitely tragic.

He plunged himself into studies on the Buddha, desperately trying, as he had decades before on this very canal, once again to force a route to "The Victors." But he knew that he had come to the city of decay to die. In his terrible frustration he struck at the familiar targets. Cosima was upbraided, Liszt denounced, Princess Wittgenstein castigated as the source of all evil, the excitement, of course, provoking terrible spasms. It was a time of suffering for all. And his humor was not improved by a reading of Nietzsche's *The Gay Science,* which chided him frequently (especially in the beautiful eighty-seventh aphorism, "The Conceit of Artists") and even warned against the danger of vegetarians, "the promoters of narcotic modes of thought and feeling."

Parsifal and Wagner may well have been on Nietzsche's mind when he discussed in the "Sanctus Januarius" section of the book "founders of religions" and the honesty in matters of intellectual conscience he believed alien to them. But in an earlier section, the famous aphorism ninety-nine on Schopenhauer's adherents, he had urged, "Let us remain loyal to Wagner in that which is *true* and original in him—and especially in this point that we, his disciples, remain loyal to ourselves in that which is true and original in us. Let him have his intellectual moods and convulsions. . . . It does not matter that he is so often wrong as a thinker; justice and patience are not *his* strength. Sufficient that his life is justified, and remains justified, before itself—this life which calls to everyone of us: 'Be a man and do not follow me—but yourself! But yourself!'" This repudiation of the Wagnerian party man, the disciple who refuses to question, was, in fact, a moving tribute to the composer's greatness. But Wagner saw only treachery.

3

Seemingly, Wagner's growing spiritual relationship with Goethe should provide welcome material when searching for that ennoblement and elevation one hopes to observe in the closing days of genius. But this promising reappraisal of Goethe, like so much else, crashed on the rocks of racism, and the few hints of a *Verklärung* to be found in the dying man's friendship with Joseph Rubinstein were also snuffed out in the racial shipwreck. Only his continuing concern with the old problem of "The Victors" suggested what might have been. This disappointing late communion with Goethe,

the bizarre intimacy with Joseph, and a final wrestling with the Buddhistic theme occupied the weary master as twilight came down.

While creating *Meistersinger,* he had first begun to appreciate the true worth of Goethe, whom he had previously contemplated *de haut en bas.* His enthusiasm, especially for *Faust,* continued to grow, certainly heightened by association with a literary scholar of Nietzsche's caliber. Yet a patronizing attitude is still apparent in *A Capitulation.* Toward its close, Victor Hugo, transfigured as the guardian angel of France and hovering over Paris in a balloon, recites (in a kind of pseudo-Alsatian [2] recitative to his own accompaniment on a golden lyre) a none-too-kind satire on the first half of the famous octet concluding *Faust: "Alles Geschichtliche/ist nur ein—trait—:/ das rein Gedichtliche/mach' ich zum—fait."* Naturally, Wagner refrained from parodying the closing quatrain, that source of most of his finales.

Nonetheless, *Actors and Singers* of 1872, an essay he wrote at the Hôtel Fantaisie while working on *The Twilight of the Gods,* spoke of *Faust* as "the single truly original German play of superlative poetic worth," a description in the tradition of *The Destiny of Opera.* He declared that only a theater whose architecture borrowed concepts from the informally arranged Elizabethan stage could do justice to Goethe's masterpiece. The Shakespearean naturalness of the drama's diction delighted him, the fact that God and the devil conversed with good grace. The rapid, lively dialogue, often a foil for moments of introspection and lyric pathos, had provided a model not unheeded in *Meistersinger,* and, while striving to complete the *Ring,* Wagner evidently found its stilted text, inherited from an earlier self, no longer entirely sympathetic. *Actors and Singers* seemed to reflect an unspoken reaction against its affectations, and he did not protest when Cosima complained about its sententious finale.

In the essay one catches the echo of a secret regret that the *Ring* did not epitomize what he called a "bold call for the participation of the spectator's imaginative power . . . in order to transport him into a world of magic. . . ." By this time he had embraced in theory the free aesthetic embodied in *Meistersinger* and codified in *Beethoven* and *The Destiny of Opera.* But it was too late to think of changing the literary structure of the *Ring.* As a consolation, he persuaded himself that his art was directly connected with the "Prelude in the Theater" from *Faust;* "the whole thing is stated there," he grandly observed and, in an extravagant and moving admission, declared his immolation scene, great as it was, to rank below the close of *Faust.* Most important, his study of Goethe had a salutary effect

[2] The loyalty of Alsatians to Paris infuriated Wagner. He even derisively introduced the name of his Alsatian disciple, Schuré, into *A Capitulation* and much mock Alsatian dialect.

upon his own poetic diction. *Parsifal,* though not free from the usual Wagnerian solecisms and tortured constructions—Nietzsche remarked that it reads like a translation from a foreign tongue [3]—nonetheless, at certain moments, achieves an extraordinary lyric flow and beauty of expression in which Goethe's influence may be felt. Parsifal's phrases in the Good Friday episode show Wagner actually becoming a poet.

His attempts to associate Goethe with his concepts of racial regeneration on evidence from *Wilhelm Meisters Wanderjahre* and *Faust,* however, were forced and foolish. He saw in the magnificent concept of the ancient Faust's reclaiming land by pushing back the sea a prefiguration of his own design for a new Aryan society. In his open letter to Stein, completed two weeks before his death, he wrote, "Unmistakably, the idea of the possibility of society's re-establishment upon new soil strongly fascinated him [Goethe]. Clearly, he recognized that little was to be expected from a mere emigration if not preceded by a spiritual and moral rebirth in the womb of the old homeland itself; toward this end he strove to set before us ingenious symbols of soul-searching expression." Wagner recommended to Stein, Dühring's disciple, a march forward "continuing the lifework of our great poet." But in the *Lehrjahre* Lothario exalted the potential of the individual, not the breed, when declaring that "America is here or nowhere!" and Faust's cry, "I open space for many millions," simply cannot be reconciled with Wagner's racial ideal, which was to find expression in Bernhard Förster's Nueva Germania and, ultimately, in the Third Reich. In the end, the nation's glorious poet could draw from Wagner only the same old hoarse, intolerant cry. And, despite appearances, the Rubinstein friendship was but a public enactment of *Jewry in Music,* though pervaded by that counteractive love that so often swept Wagner during such relationships.

Joseph Rubinstein had made an immediate impression; in his first letter to the composer (1872) the distraught youth, a student of Wagner's works, had called to him for rescue from his degraded state of Jewishness. "I am a Jew. This tells you everything," was the startling beginning of a communication from Kharkov setting the tone of a sado-masochistic relationship both were to enjoy to the extreme. Joseph fulfilled the ideal of those cringing, ashamed Jews "seeking salvation" described at the end of *Jewry in Music,* where Wagner had called to them, "Bear in mind that there is

---

[3] Much of Wagner's verse reads in German like a translation from some ancient and foreign speech. From the time he studied Johann Droysen's translation of Aeschylus in the garden of Dresden's Marcolini Palace, his lines showed a completely unidiomatic complexion. During rehearsals at Bayreuth this writer has observed the late Wieland Wagner turning his grandfather's nineteenth-century texts into modern German for the sake of German-born singers much as an English or American director of Shakespeare might explain Elizabethan vocabulary and constructions to his actors.

but one redemption from the curse weighing upon you—the redemption of Ahasuerus—downfall *(Untergang)*!" This "redeeming work" was to be accomplished by the Jews' themselves embracing "self-destruction" *("Selbstvernichtung")*, an exhortation Joseph seemed ready to follow. But Wagner preferred the young man to live with him in a strange symbiotic relationship. Rubinstein offered him, symbolically, the sacrifice of Klingsor, which Wagner accepted. When acknowledging Joseph's help during rehearsals of the first Bayreuth festival, the composer, in Mottl's approximate transcript, ended by declaring, "If up to now we have not drawn much closer as men, the responsibility is not mine, but yours. You are simply of a foreign race that stands no closer to us."

But, during his final months, Wagner's concern grew for the future of someone so dependent, maladjusted, and indoctrinated that, clearly, he would survive the composer's own impending death with difficulty. Even considering Joseph's natural emotional instability, Wagner had played his part in molding the dangerous mental state of a boy who, seeing himself in terms of *Jewry in Music,* had already tried to take his own life. In a masterly letter to Father Rubinstein, Wagner urged him to spare his son, burdened with neuroses *("gewissen krankhaften Dispositionen")*, the necessity of engaging in a concert career; the Rubinsteins were wealthy, and Wagner suggested that the modest means required be provided to free Joseph for higher things. Wagner had nothing to gain from the letter. It was an uncharacteristic gesture late in a life hitherto remarkably free of disinterested favors or grace in human relationships, a strange, futile attempt to revivify what his own hand had long before struck down.

Even Cosima showed surprising good will toward "Malvolio Rubinstein," who, though a slave to Wagner, was highly independent of others in the Wahnfried circle. When, a year and a half after Wagner's death, he committed suicide in Lucerne, where they had first met, his body, redeemed through *"Selbstvernichtung,"* was taken to Bayreuth for burial in the Jewish cemetery. Joseph had remained a doctrinaire Wagnerian to his final deed. Tantalizingly, the last, unfinished effort of Wagner's pen perhaps hints that he himself was considering the possibility of a retreat from his annihilative teachings that were to infect the world.

In Venice, on February 11, 1883, Wagner began a new essay, *"Über das Weibliche im Menschlichen"* ("The Feminine Element in Humanity"), and was working at it during the afternoon of the thirteenth when he died. The article, though it promised to be an ultimate hodgepodge of all his crotchets, was taking a fascinating turn when the last seizure came.

Man, Wagner declared, was in a state of racial ruin, whereas animals— when permitted to breed naturally—had remained pure, being innocent of marriage for convenience and materialism. Although wedlock should have raised man above the beasts, his perversion of it had placed him below them. But, while intercourse in animals was directed toward preserving the species, man was distinguished by a capacity to love an individual, that is, monogamy with its attendant concept of fidelity. Monogamy, the sign of the superior race and the superior individual, though practiced by the noblest whites from their earliest days, had been abandoned when they were seduced into polygamy by those they conquered. Yet, even in the harems of the Orientals, the force of a particular love could appear. Wagner was starting to forge a link to the tale of the Buddha, Ananda, and the Maid as he had related it in the sketch of "The Victors," when he was compelled to ring his bell in alarm. The final attack had gripped him. Cosima hastened to him. He rested, cradled in her arms, and at three-thirty his heart stopped.

In which direction this final Wagnerian effort was meant to drift is, of course, impossible to determine. For a while one fears a theory of Aryan animals to be at hand. But clearly Wagner was confusedly concerned with finding a way out of the position into which *Parsifal* had locked him. Along with *"Heldentum,"* it contributed toward the foundations of what Erich Fromm called "Hitler's crude popularization of Darwinism." Indeed, in *Mein Kampf* the Aryan is the exalted impregnator. *Parsifal* and *"Heldentum"* had advised man to breed, not for personal reasons, but for the sake of the species, precisely the role given, instead, to the noble animal in Wagner's final fragment, which goes on to insist that man is more than the beast, more than the inseminating mechanism in the machinery of racial better-ment—in essence, more than Parsifal.

Wagner had once respected individual passion pursued in defiance of the group, as the figures of the suffering Siegmund and Tannhäuser attest. The latter was banished from communion with the elect by a leader eventu-ally proved completely wrong. But times had changed when Titurel, the venerable Grail King and terrifying father of Amfortas, ostracized Klingsor much as Pope Urban IV had cast out Tannhäuser. In the new era of *Parsifal,* Titurel boasted the infallibility of Pope Pius IX and the relent-less tyranny of Monsalvat, of Wahnfried, of the Wilhelmstrasse Chancellery of the nineteen-thirties. And though by the end of his career Wagner could no longer conceive of such a hero as Siegmund the revolutionary defiantly spurning the glories of Wotan's Walhall, nonetheless, in the last essay he seemed determined to regain at least something of this old freedom of choice while at the same time desperately striving to hold fast to his racial shibboleths. The attempt was hopeless yet especially fascinating because he sought his route through a gate so long prevailing against his advances— "The Victors." In *Parsifal* he had built a structure plainly exhibiting the nihilistic, authoritarian, and racial concepts of Nazi ideology. But the af-firmative, creative dynamics of "The Victors" again returned to trouble him.

Immanent in the tale was one element which, more than any other, had inhibited him for so many years. "The Victors," as he had found it in Burnouf's history of Buddhism, set forth an allegory of the stupidity of caste. The humble maiden of despised chandala stock, possessed by love for a young monk of a higher strain, had, in another life, herself been a Brahman princess whose royal father disdained her wooing by a chandala prince. What is the meaning of such divisions, the Buddha asked, in a world in which all must keep changing their identities until perfection is reached? Surprisingly, Wagner's sketch of 1856 had strengthened this humane factor by turning the monk, Ananda, into a reincarnation of the scorned prince and by making the princess, rather than her father, first haughtily reject his suit. "The Victors" was Wagner's noblest dramatic concept, though, unhappily, he had never been able to come to terms with it emotionally, dramatically, or musically.

"The Victors" refuted the concepts glorified in *Parsifal*—human value as a function of blood and the myth of the master-slave relationship. Race and position were shifting and meaningless in a universe governed by mysterious cycles of transmigration. The individual, not the species, possessed the potential of rising to greatness. Through self-mastery and the mechanics of eternal recurrence, Ananda and the maid become elevated, heroic figures, Zarathustrian *Übermenschen* achieving the superhuman dignity of the artist and philosopher. For years Wagner had been haunted, perplexed, and tormented by this scenario created by his better self and containing within it the germs of Nietzsche's ethical principles. During his final hours Wagner again drew near the threshold his former friend had already passed and, like the Empress in *Die Frau ohne Schatten,* stood before the bronze-gold portals leading to "the water of life," to the affirmation of creative human values. He, too, could say with the Empress that those gates were not unknown to him.

Throughout his last Venetian sojourn "The Victors," *Faust,* and the *Ring* flowed together in his mind. The evening before his death he sat at the piano in the Vendramin playing the Rhine Daughters' lament that truth is theirs in the deep while guile encompasses those exulting on the heights. Such creatures of the depths filled with longing had always been dear to him, he remarked, a point of view strangely like that of Hauptmann but hardly true. Wagner knew, as Nietzsche observed in *The Gay Science,* "the lower depths of human happiness . . . that weary shuffling along of the soul which can no longer leap and fly, or, indeed, even walk." But his was "understanding without solace, leave-taking without avowal." He had dedicated one of the great talents of the century to ignoble ends. The beauty of the means notwithstanding, Nietzsche, in a letter to Malwida von Meysenbug, called him "a genius of the lie"; "The Victors" was a private truth he had lacked the strength to face, the possibility of a purposeful, spiritual choice, an option for human dignity.

During the early days of the Bayreuth enterprise, Cosima, parroting Wagner, described his career in Faustian terms, voicing a hope that he might, like Faust, acquire "a sphere which no one else desires and then build dikes to cut it off, leaving the rest of the world to spread itself out according to its needs. . . ." But neither Faust nor Wagner carved out their empires without destroying those occupying the coveted lands. Faust ordered his gentle old neighbors, Philemon and Baucis, removed by an assault that left them burning in their home, Mephistopheles consolingly reporting, "The couple was not tormented long but fell dead from fright." Wagner, too, wishing to survey his world without obstructions, had fired many such cottages blocking his view. But Faust's final words form a lofty hymn to man and his destiny to strive as an individual; as he sinks into the grave, his blind eyes see a vision of "free men on free ground." For all his faults, he had concerned himself with what the Pater Profundus called *"Was ewig schaffend uns umwallt"* ("the eternally creative surrounding us"). The Buddha, Ananda, and the Maid alone had beckoned Wagner into these deep regions.

"Creatures of the depths" had never really consciously concerned him, though the Alberichs and Klingsors in his works achieved a grandeur that perhaps surprised their creator. At the end of his life, reproachful spirits risen from the ashes of his hatreds may have stood before him; in the caverns of Nibelheim Wotan-Wagner had answered Mime's sobs and howls with laughter, and, standing before Walhall, had replied to the Rhine Daughters' wails with derision and then mirth. But "Care" had already breathed upon him, and not far behind walked her brother "Death."

The subject of compassion consumed his last days, not the counterfeit pity of *Parsifal*, but the humanity of "The Victors." During those final hours was he at last approaching the infinitely wise Buddha? Did he stand at a moral crossroads as he pulled the cord of his warning bell? Death, long graciously waiting, claimed him at the moment he again confronted that strange tale of love and tolerance sketched almost three decades before.

4

The youthful D'Annunzio may well have helped bear the coffin from the Vendramin to the black gondola waiting to convey it to the station. (His *Il fuoco* depicts the episode.) If so, this laying on of hands was ominous. The remains, traveling back to Germany, were escorted and honored like a monarch's. A colossus had fallen; the world was shocked.

The men Wagner had most despised received the news with genuine sorrow. Nietzsche was at work on his poetic masterpiece, *Zarathustra,* when a report of the event reached him. He wrote Cosima a moving letter of sympathy and in *Ecce Homo* called the hour of the composer's death "holy."

Brahms's immediate impulse had been to send a wreath to the grave, and he was shocked to find the gesture misinterpreted at Bayreuth as one of scorn and mockery. He sadly observed, "It is wonderful to what lengths men's tactlessness and blindness are capable of going." He had remarked of Wagner, "Everything else disappears in a moment before his importance, which nobody is so quick to comprehend or appreciate as I am—the Wagnerites certainly least of all."

When Verdi heard of Wagner's death, he wrote to Giulio Ricordi of the powerful mark the composer would leave upon the history of art. But he reconsidered his observation; his pen canceled "powerful" and in its place wrote "most powerful"—*"potentissima."*

To Hanslick, the death came as a painful surprise. He remarked, "We have yet to encounter a musician sufficiently purblind or vehement to fail to appreciate Wagner's brilliant talent and amazing art, to underrate his enormous influence, and, even in the case of an avowed antipathy, to gainsay the greatness and genius of his works. . . . Not long ago it was his lot to awaken his last great work to life in Bayreuth, day by day to delight in its special preparation, and to luxuriate in the full sunlight of a success such as has lighted upon no artist in any time or nation. We happily cherish the memory of our last view of him upon the balcony of his Festspielhaus . . . triumphantly exulting in the all-mastering power of his will. And, if one were to remind us of his mortal frailties and violent emotions, we would find no trace of them in our memory, for with Grillparzer we say that death 'is like a bolt of lightning which transfigures what it consumes.'"

Selected Bibliography

ABRAHAM, GERALD. *A Hundred Years of Music.* Chicago: Aldine, 1964.

—— "The Influence of Berlioz on Richard Wagner." *Music and Letters,* Vol. 5, No. 3 (July, 1924), pp. 239–46.

—— "Marschner and Wagner." *The Monthly Musical Record,* Vol. 70 (June, 1940), pp. 99–104.

ADORNO, THEODOR W. *Versuch über Wagner.* Frankfort-on-Main: Suhrkamp, 1952.

AGOULT, MARIE CATHERINE SOPHIE (DE FLAVIGNY). *Meine Freundschaft mit Franz Liszt.* Trans. (into German) by Egas von Wenden. Dresden: Reissner, 1930.

ALLEN, WARREN DWIGHT. *Philosophies of Music History.* New York: Dover, 1962.

ANDREAS-SALOMÉ, LOU. *Lebensrückblick: Grundriss einiger Lebenserinnerungen.* Ed. by Ernst Pfeiffer. Zurich: Niehans; Wiesbaden: Insel, 1951.

ARENDT, HANNAH. *The Origins of Totalitarianism.* New York: Harcourt, Brace, 1951; rev. ed., 1966.

ASHBROOK, WILLIAM. *Donizetti.* London: Cassell, 1965.

BAINVILLE, JACQUES. *Louis II de Bavière.* [Paris]: Fayard, 1964.

BARTH, HERBERT. *Bayreuth in der Karikatur.* Bayreuth: Musica, 1957.

—— *Internationale Wagner-Bibliographie: 1945–1955.* Bayreuth: Musica, 1956.

BARZUN, JACQUES. *Berlioz and the Romantic Century.* 2 vols. Boston: Little, Brown, 1950.

—— *Darwin, Marx, Wagner.* 2nd ed., rev. Garden City, N.Y.: Doubleday Anchor, 1958.

BASCH, VICTOR. *Schumann: A Life of Suffering.* Trans. by Catherine Alison Phillips. New York: Tudor, 1936.

BAUER, MARION. *Twentieth Century Music.* New York and London: Putnam, 1933.

Bayreuther Festblätter in Wort und Bild. Munich: Autotype, 1884.

BEETZ, WILHELM. *Das Wiener Opernhaus: 1869 bis 1955.* 2nd ed. Vienna: Panorama, 1955.

BEKKER, PAUL. *The Changing Opera.* Trans. by Arthur Mendel. New York: Norton, 1935.

457

——— *Richard Wagner, Das Leben im Werke.* Stuttgart: Deutsche Verlags-Anstalt, 1924.

BÉLART, HANS. *Richard Wagner in Zürich, 1849–1858.* 2 vols. Leipzig: Seeman, 1900–01.

——— *Richard Wagners Beziehungen zu François und Eliza Wille in Mariafeld bei Zürich (1852–1872) und sein Asyl auf Mariafeld (1864). Ludwig Geyer, der Schauspieler und Maler, als leiblicher Vater Richard Wagners.* Dresden: Reissner, 1914.

BENARY, PETER. "Liszt und Wagner in Briefen der Fürstin von Wittgenstein." *Die Musikforschung,* XII Jahrgang, Heft 4 (Oct./Dec., 1959), pp. 468–73.

BERLIOZ, HECTOR. *Memoirs, from 1803 to 1865.* Trans. by Rachel (Scott Russell) Holmes and Eleanor Holmes. Ed. by Ernest Newman. New York: Tudor, 1932.

——— *Evenings with the Orchestra.* Trans. and ed. by Jacques Barzun. New York: Knopf, 1956.

BITHELL, JETHRO. *Modern German Literature, 1880–1950.* London: Methuen, 1939.

BÖHM, GOTTFRIED VON. *Ludwig II König von Bayern, sein Leben und seine Zeit.* Berlin: Engelmann, 1922.

BÖHME, ERDMANN WERNER. *Richard Wagners Werk in Pommern.* Berlin-Halensee: [Selbstverlag], 1934.

BORY, ROBERT. *Liszt et ses Enfants.* Paris: Corrêa [1936].

BOUCHER, MAURICE. *The Political Concepts of Richard Wagner.* Trans. by Marcel Honoré. New York: Exposition, 1950.

BOURNOT, OTTO. *Ludwig Heinr. Chr. Geyer, der Stiefvater Richard Wagners, Ein Beitrag zur Wagner-Biographie.* Leipzig: Siegel (Linnemann), 1913.

BRAHMS, JOHANNES. *The Herzogenberg Correspondence.* Ed. by Max Kalbeck. Trans. by Hannale Bryant. London: Murray, 1909.

BRANDES, GEORG. *Wolfgang Goethe.* Trans. by Allen W. Porterfield. 2 vols. New York: Frank-Maurice, 1925.

BRINK, LOUISE. *Women Characters in Richard Wagner: A Study in "The Ring of the Nibelung."* New York and Washington: Nervous and Mental Disease Pub. Co., 1924.

BROGAN, D. W. *The French Nation.* New York: Harper, 1957.

BÜLOW, HANS VON. *Neue Briefe.* Ed. by Du Moulin Eckart. Munich: Drei Masken, 1927.

——— *Letters of Hans von Bülow.* Trans. by Hannah Waller. New York and London: Knopf, 1931.

BUKOFZER, MANFRED F. *Music in the Baroque Era.* New York: Norton, 1947.

BUTLER, E. M. *The Tyranny of Greece over Germany.* Boston: Beacon, 1958.

CAMPBELL, THOMAS MOODY. "Nietzsche-Wagner to January, 1872." *PMLA,* LVI (1941), pp. 544–77.

——— "Nietzsche's 'Die Geburt der Tragödie' and Richard Wagner." *Germanic Review,* XVI (1941), pp. 185–200.

CHAMBERLAIN, HOUSTON STEWART. *Die Grundlagen des 19. Jahrhunderts.* Ungekürzte Volksausgabe. 2 vols. Munich: Bruckmann, 1932.

———— *Richard Wagner.* 11th ed. Munich: Bruckmann, 1942.

———— *Richard Wagner.* Trans. by G. Ainslie Hight. London: Dent; Philadelphia: Lippincott, 1897.

CHERNOWITZ, MAURICE E. *Proust and Painting.* New York: International University, 1945.

COEUROY, ANDRÉ. "Gérard de Nerval et Richard Wagner." *Le Guide du Concert,* VIIIᵉ Année, No. 1 (October, 1921), pp. 17–18.

Connotation. Wagner issue. Vol. 2, Part 1 (Spring, 1963).

CORNELIUS, CARL MARIA. *Peter Cornelius, der Wort- und Tondichter.* 2 vols. Regensburg: Bosse [1925].

CORNELIUS, PETER. *Ausgewählte Briefe, nebst Tagebuchblättern und Gelegenheitsgedichten.* Ed. by Carl Maria Cornelius. Vols. 1 and 2 of *Peter Cornelius literarische Werke.* Leipzig: Breitkopf and Härtel, 1904–05.

CROCE, BENEDETTO. *History of Europe in the Nineteenth Century.* Trans. by Henry Furst. London: Allen and Unwin, 1953.

DAUBE, OTTO. *"Ich schreibe keine Symphonien mehr." Richard Wagners Lehrjahre nach den erhaltenen Dokumenten.* Cologne: Gerig, 1960.

DAVID, HANS T., and MENDEL, ARTHUR. *The Bach Reader.* New York: Norton, 1945.

DEAN, WINTON. *Bizet.* New York: Collier, 1962.

DELACROIX, EUGÈNE. *The Journal of Eugène Delacroix.* Trans. by Walter Pach. New York: Grove, 1961.

DONINGTON, ROBERT. "On Rehearing Wagner." *Music Survey,* Vol. II, No. 1 (Summer, 1949), pp. 31–35.

———— *Wagner's "Ring" and its Symbols.* New York: St. Martin's, 1963.

DORN, HEINRICH. *Aus meinem Leben.* 3 vols. Berlin: Behr (Bock), 1870–72.

———— *Ergebnisse aus Erlebnissen.* Berlin: Liebel, 1877.

———— *Ostracismus: Ein Gericht Scherben.* Berlin: Behr (Bock), 1875.

DU MOULIN-ECKART, RICHARD. *Cosima Wagner.* 2 vols. Munich: Drei Masken, 1929, 1931.

———— *Cosima Wagner.* Trans. by Catherine Alison Phillips. 2 vols. New York: Knopf, 1931.

Edda, Die; die ältere und jüngere. Trans. (into German) by Karl Simrock. 10th ed. Stuttgart: Cotta, 1896.

The Poetic Edda. Trans. by Henry Adams Bellows. New York: American-Scandinavian Foundation, 1923.

EDEL, LEON. *Henry James: The Conquest of London.* Vol. 2 of *The Life of Henry James.* Philadelphia and New York: Lippincott, 1962.

EINSTEIN, ALFRED. *Gluck.* Trans. by Eric Blom. (The Master Musicians Series.) London: Dent; New York: Dutton, 1954.

———— *Music in the Romantic Era.* New York: Norton, 1947.

EISER, OTTO. "Richard Wagners 'Der Ring des Nibelungen': Ein exegetischer Versuch." *Bayreuther Blätter,* November, 1878 (Elftes Stück), pp. 309–17.

ELLIS, WILLIAM ASHTON. *Life of Richard Wagner.* 6 vols. London: Kegan Paul, 1900–08.

ENGEL, ERICH W. *Richard Wagners Leben und Werke im Bilde.* 2nd ed. Leipzig: Siegel (Linnemann), 1922.

FAY, AMY. *Music-Study in Germany in the Nineteenth Century.* New York: Dover, 1965.

FEHR, MAX. *Richard Wagners Schweizer Zeit.* 2 vols. Aarau and Leipzig: Sauerländer [1934].

FIECHTNER, HELMUT A. "Neugefundene Wagnerbriefe." *Das Musik Leben,* Heft 6, Jahrgang 3 (June, 1950), pp. 165–68.

FINCK, HENRY T. *Wagner and his Works.* 7th ed. 2 vols. New York: Scribner, 1904.

FÖRSTER-NIETZSCHE, ELIZABETH. *The Nietzsche-Wagner Correspondence.* Trans. by Caroline V. Kerr. New York: Boni and Liveright, 1921.

FRICKE, RICHARD. *Bayreuth vor dreissig Jahren: Erinnerungen an Wahnfried und aus dem Festspielhause.* Dresden: Bertling, 1906.

FRIEDHEIM, ARTHUR. *Life and Liszt.* Ed. by Theodore L. Bullock. New York: Taplinger, 1961.

FROMM, ERICH. *Escape from Freedom.* New York and Toronto: Rinehart, 1941.

FUCHS, HANNS. *Richard Wagner und die Homosexualität.* Berlin: Barsdorf, 1903.

GAL, HANS. *Richard Wagner: Versuch einer Würdigung.* Frankfort-on-Main: Fischer, 1963.

GATTI, CARLO. *Verdi: The Man and His Music.* Trans. by Elisabeth Abbott. New York: Putnam, 1955.

GAUTIER, JUDITH. *Wagner at Home.* Trans. by Effie Dunreith Massie. London: Mills and Boon, 1910.

GEIRINGER, KARL. *Brahms: His Life and Work.* New York: Oxford, 1947.

GILMAN, LAWRENCE. *Wagner's Operas.* New York: Farrar and Rinehart, 1937.

GLASENAPP, CARL FR. *Das Leben Richard Wagners.* 6 vols. Leipzig: Breitkopf and Härtel, v.d.

GOBINEAU, JOSEPH ARTHUR, COMTE DE. *Essai sur l'Inégalité des Races humaines.* 4 vols. Paris: Firmin Didot, 1853–55.

—— *The Renaissance.* Trans. by Paul V. Cohen. Ed. by Oscar Levy. New York: Putnam, 1927.

GOTTFRIED VON STRASSBURG. *Tristan and Isolde.* Trans. by Edwin H. Zeydel. Princeton, N.J.: Princeton, 1948.

GRAND-CARTERET, JOHN. *Richard Wagner en Caricatures.* Paris: Larousse [1892].

GRAY, CHRISTOPHER. *Cubist Aesthetic Theories.* Baltimore: Johns Hopkins, 1953.

GROUT, DONALD JAY. *A Short History of Opera.* New York: Columbia, 1947.

GUGGENHEIMER, HEDWIG. "E. T. A. Hoffmann und R. Wagner." *Richard Wagner Jahrbuch,* II (1907), pp. 165–203.

HANSLICK, EDUARD. *Aus dem Opernleben der Gegenwart.* (Der "Modernen Oper," III. Theil.) 4th ed. Berlin: Allgemeiner Verein für Deutsche Litteratur, 1889.

—— *Musikalisches Skizzenbuch.* (Der "Modernen Oper," IV. Theil.) 3rd ed. Berlin: Allgemeiner Verein für Deutsche Litteratur, 1896.

—— *Vienna's Golden Years of Music, 1850–1900.* Trans. and ed. by Henry Pleasants III. New York: Simon and Schuster, 1950.

HAUSER, ARNOLD. *Mannerism: The Crisis of the Renaissance and the Origin of Modern Art.* Trans. by Eric Mosbacher in collaboration with the author. 2 vols. New York: Knopf, 1965.

————— *The Social History of Art.* 2 vols. New York: Knopf, 1951.

HEIDEN, KONRAD. *Der Fuehrer.* Boston: Houghton Mifflin, 1944.

HEUSSNER, HORST. "Ludwig Spohr schreibt an Richard Wagner." *Neue Zeitschrift für Musik,* Jahrgang 119, Heft 10 (October, 1958), pp. 586–87.

HEWETT-THAYER, HARVEY W. *Hoffmann: Author of the Tales.* Princeton, N.J.: Princeton, 1948.

HILDEBRANDT, KURT. *Wagner und Nietzsche, ihr Kampf gegen das Neunzehnte Jahrhundert.* Breslau: Hirt, 1924.

HILL, RALPH. "On Hanslick and Wagner." *The Chesterian,* Vol. XII, No. 95 (June, 1931), pp. 188–93.

HILLER, FERDINAND. *Musikalisches und Persönliches.* Leipzig: Breitkopf and Härtel, 1876.

HITLER, ADOLF. *Mein Kampf.* Jubiläumsausgabe. Munich: Zentralverlag der NSDAP; Eher, 1939.

————— *Mein Kampf.* Boston: Houghton Mifflin, 1943.

HOLDREDGE, HELEN. *Lola Montez.* London: Redman, 1957.

HUNEKER, JAMES. *Franz Liszt.* New York: Scribner, 1911.

HURN, PHILIP DUTTON, and ROOT, WAVERLEY LEWIS. *The Truth about Wagner.* New York: Stokes, 1930.

HUSSEY, DYNELEY. *Verdi.* (Great Composers Series.) New York: Collier, 1962.

HYMAN, STANLEY EDGAR. *The Tangled Bank.* New York: Atheneum, 1962.

IRVINE, DAVID. *Wagner's Bad Luck.* London: Watts, 1911.

JACOB, HEINRICH EDUARD. *Felix Mendelssohn and His Times.* Trans. by Richard and Clara Winston. Englewood Cliffs, N.J.: Prentice-Hall, 1963.

JACOBS, ROBERT L. *Wagner.* (The Master Musicians Series.) London: Dent, 1947.

JULLIEN, ADOLPHE. *Richard Wagner: His Life and Works.* Trans. by Florence Percival Hall. Philadelphia: Presser, 1900.

KAPP, JULIUS. "Paralipomena zu R. Wagners Leben." *Neue Musik-Zeitung,* Jahrgang XXXIII, Heft 13 (October, 1911–September, 1912), pp. 273–76.

————— "Der Privatdruck von Richard Wagners Autobiographie." *Die Musik,* Jahrgang XXII, Heft 10 (July, 1930), pp. 725–31.

————— *Richard Wagner: Eine Biographie.* 32nd ed. Berlin-Schöneberg: Hesse, 1929.

————— *Richard Wagner: Sein Leben, sein Werk, seine Welt in 260 Bildern.* Berlin-Schöneberg: Hesse, 1933.

————— *Richard Wagner und die Frauen: Eine erotische Biographie.* Berlin: Schuster and Loeffler, 1912.

————— "Unterdrückte Dokumente aus den Briefen Richard Wagners an Mathilde Wesendonk." *Die Musik,* Jahrgang XXIII, Heft 12 (September, 1931), pp. 877–83.

————— "Unveröffentlichte Wagnerbriefe." *Der Merker,* Jahrgang 6, Heft 4 (February, 1915), pp. 133–37.

————— *The Women in Wagner's Life.* Trans. by Hannah Waller. London: Routledge, 1932.

————— and JACHMANN, HANS. *Richard Wagner und seine erste "Elisabeth."* Berlin: Dom, 1927.

KARPATH, LUDWIG. "Richard Wagners Wohnhäuser in Wien." *Musikbuch aus Österreich,* Jahrgang VI (1909), pp. 45–54.

KATZ, ADELE T. *Challenge to Musical Tradition: A New Concept of Tonality.* New York: Knopf, 1946.

KAUFMANN, WALTER. *Nietzsche: Philosopher, Psychologist, Antichrist.* Cleveland and New York: Meridian, 1962.

KERMAN, JOSEPH. *Opera As Drama.* New York: Knopf, 1956.

KIENZL, WILHELM. *Richard Wagner.* Munich: Kirchheim, 1904.

KIETZ, GUSTAV ADOLPH. *Richard Wagner in den Jahren 1842–1849 und 1873–1875.* Dresden: Reissner, 1905.

KLOSS, JULIUS ERICH. *Zwanzig Jahre "Bayreuth": 1876–1896: Allerlei Betrachtungen.* Berlin: Schuster and Loeffler, 1896.

KNIESE, JULIE. *Der Kampf zweier Welten um das Bayreuther Erbe.* Leipzig: Weicher, 1931.

KOLODIN, IRVING. *The Story of the Metropolitan Opera, 1883–1950.* New York: Knopf, 1953.

KREHBIEL, HENRY EDWARD. *Studies in the Wagnerian Drama.* New York and London: Harper, 1898.

KREOWSKI, ERNST, and FUCHS, EDUARD. *Richard Wagner in der Karikatur.* Berlin: Behr, 1907.

KURTH, ERNST. *Romantische Harmonik und ihre Krise in Wagners "Tristan."* 2nd ed. Berlin: Hesse, 1923.

KURTZ, HAROLD. *The Empress Eugénie.* Boston: Houghton Mifflin, 1964.

LÁNG, PAUL HENRY. *Music in Western Civilization.* New York: Norton, 1941.

LANGE, WALTER. *Richard Wagners Sippe.* Leipzig: Beck, 1938.

LASSERRE, PIERRE. *The Spirit of French Music.* Trans. by Denis Turner. London: Kegan Paul; New York: Dutton, 1921.

LAVER, JAMES. *The First Decadent: Being the Strange Life of J. K. Huysmans.* New York: Citadel, 1955.

LAVIGNAC, ALBERT. *The Music Dramas of Richard Wagner.* Trans. by Esther Singleton. New York: Dodd, Mead, 1898.

LEHMANN, LILLI. *Mein Weg.* Leipzig: Hirzel, 1913.

Leipzig Die Geburtsstadt Richard Wagners feiert den 125. Geburtstag des Meisters. Leipzig: Böttcher, 1938.

LEMAÎTRE, GEORGES. *From Cubism to Surrealism in French Literature.* London: Oxford, 1945.

LIPPERT, WOLDEMAR. *Richard Wagners Verbannung und Rückkehr, 1849–62.* Dresden: Aretz, 1927.

—— *Wagner in Exile.* Trans. by Paul England. London: Harrap, 1930.

LIPPMAN, EDWARD ARTHUR. "The Esthetic Theories of Richard Wagner." *The Musical Quarterly,* Vol. XLIV, No. 2 (April, 1958), pp. 209–20.

LISZT, FRANZ. *The Letters of Franz Liszt to Marie zu Sayn-Wittgenstein.* Trans. and ed. by Howard E. Hugo. Cambridge, Mass.: Harvard, 1953.

—— *Die Zigeuner und ihre Musik in Ungarn.* Ed. by Peter Cornelius. Pest: Heckenast, 1861.

LOCKSPEISER, EDWARD. "The Renoir Portraits of Wagner." *Music and Letters,* Vol. XVIII, No. 1 (January, 1937), pp. 14–19.

LOEWENBERG, ALFRED. *Annals of Opera, 1597–1940.* 2nd ed. Ed. by Frank Walker. Geneva: Societas Bibliographica, 1955.

LOOS, PAUL ARTHUR. *Richard Wagner: Vollendung und Tragik der deutschen Romantik.* Munich: Lehnen, 1952.

LORENZ, ALFRED OTTOKAR. *Das Geheimnis der Form bei Richard Wagner.* 4 vols. Berlin: Hesse, 1924–33.

LUKÁCS, GEORG. *Studies in European Realism.* New York: Grosset and Dunlap, 1964.

MANN, THOMAS. *Essays of Three Decades.* Trans. by H. T. Lowe-Porter. New York: Knopf, 1947.

MARCUSE, LUDWIG. *Das denkwürdige Leben des Richard Wagner.* Munich: Szczesny, 1963.

MAYER, HANS. *Richard Wagner in Selbstzeugnissen und Bilddokumenten.* Reinbek bei Hamburg: Rowohlt, 1959.

MEHRING, FRANZ. *Karl Marx.* Trans. by Edward Fitzgerald. Ed. by Ruth and Heinz Norden. New York: Covici, Friede, 1935.

The Meister. The Quarterly Journal of the London Branch of the Wagner Society. Ed. by William Ashton Ellis. Vol. I (1888).

MELLERS, WILFRED. *Romanticism and the 20th Century.* Fair Lawn, N.J.: Essential Books, 1957.

MENDELSSOHN, FELIX. *Letters.* Ed. by G. Selden-Goth. New York: Pantheon, 1945.

MENDÈS, CATULLE. *Richard Wagner.* Paris: Charpentier, 1886.

MEYSENBUG, MALWIDA VON. *Memoiren einer Idealistin und ihr Nachtrag: Der Lebensabend einer Idealistin.* 2 vols. Berlin: Schuster and Loeffler [1917]; Stuttgart, Berlin, and Leipzig: Deutsche Verlags-Anstalt, 1927.

MILLENKOVICH-MOROLD, MAX. *Cosima Wagner: Ein Lebensbild.* Leipzig: Reclam, 1937.

——— *Richard Wagner in Wien.* Leipzig: Reclam, 1938.

MOSES, MONTROSE J. *The Life of Heinrich Conried.* New York: Crowell, 1916.

Neue Wagner-Forschungen: Veröffentlichungen der Richard-Wagner-Forschungsstätte Bayreuth. Ed. by Otto Strobel. Erste Folge (Autumn, 1943). Karlsruhe: Braun.

NEUMANN, ANGELO. *Erinnerungen an Richard Wagner.* 2nd ed. Leipzig: Staackmann, 1907.

——— *Personal Recollections of Wagner.* Trans. from the 4th German ed. by Edith Livermore. New York: Holt, 1908.

NEWMAN, ERNEST. "The Burrell Collection and Its Lessons." *The Musical Times,* May, 1952, pp. 203–06.

——— *Fact and Fiction about Wagner.* London: Cassell, 1931.

——— *Hugo Wolf.* London: Methuen, 1907.

——— *The Life of Richard Wagner.* 4 vols. New York: Knopf, 1933–46.

——— *A Study of Wagner.* London: Dobell; New York: Putnam, 1899.

——— *Wagner as Man and Artist.* New York: Knopf, 1924.

——— *The Wagner Operas.* New York: Knopf, 1949.

NIEMANN, WALTER. *Brahms.* Trans. by Catherine Alison Phillips. New York: Knopf, 1935.

NIESSEN, CARL. "Wagner und seine Bühnenbildner." *Musik und Szene,* Jahrgang 4 (1959–60), pp. 157–61.

NIETZSCHE, FRIEDRICH WILHELM. *Briefe,* vols. 1–4. *Historisch-Kritische Gesamtausgabe.* Munich: Beck, 1938–42.

—— *Werke in Drei Bänden.* Ed. by Karl Schlechta. Munich: Hanser, n.d.

—— *Unpublished Letters.* Trans. and ed. by Kurt F. Leidecker. New York: Philosophical Library, 1959.

O'DEA, WILLIAM T. *The Social History of Lighting.* New York: Macmillan, 1958.

OREL, ALFRED. "Richard Wagner in Vienna." *The Musical Quarterly,* Vol. XIX, No. 1 (January, 1933), pp. 29–37.

PEACOCK, RONALD. *Goethe's Major Plays.* New York: Hill & Wang, 1959.

POURTALÈS, GUY DE. *La Vie de Liszt.* [Paris]: Gallimard, n.d.

—— *Wagner: Histoire d'un artiste.* Paris: Gallimard, 1932.

Programmhefte der Bayreuther Festspiele, v.d.

PRÜFER, ARTHUR. "Novalis 'Hymnen an die Nacht' in ihren Beziehungen zu Wagners 'Tristan und Isolde.'" *Richard Wagner Jahrbuch,* Vol. I (1906), pp. 290–303.

Richard Wagners Photographische Bildnisse. Foreword by A. Vanselow. Munich: Bruckmann, 1908.

RÖCKL, SEBASTIAN. *Ludwig II und Richard Wagner.* 2 vols. Munich: Beck, 1913–20.

ROSENBERG, JOHN D. *The Darkening Glass.* New York and London: Columbia, 1962.

RÜTZOW, SOPHIE. *Richard Wagner und Bayreuth: Ausschnitte und Erinnerungen.* 2nd ed. Munich: Knorr and Hirth, 1943.

RUNCIMAN, JOHN F. *Richard Wagner: Composer of Operas.* London: Bell, 1913.

SACHS, CURT. *The Commonwealth of Art.* New York: Norton, 1946.

—— *Our Musical Heritage.* New York: Prentice-Hall, 1948.

——*Rhythm and Tempo.* New York: Norton, 1953.

SAINT-SAËNS, CAMILLE. "The Wagnerian Illusion." *Music,* Vol. XVII, No. 1 (November, 1899), pp. 22–30.

SAMAZEUILH, GUSTAVE. *Richard Wagner, Vues sur la France.* Paris: Mercure de France, 1943.

SCHAEFFNER, ANDRÉ. "Richard Wagner et l'opéra français du début du XIXᵉ siècle." *Revue Musicale; Wagner et La France, Numéro Spécial* (October, 1923), pp. 111–31.

SCHEMANN, LUDWIG. *Gobineaus Rassenwerk: Aktenstücke und Betrachtungen zur Geschichte und Kritik des Essai sur l'inégalité des races humaines.* Stuttgart: Fromann (Hauff), 1910.

—— *Meine Erinnerungen an Richard Wagner.* Stuttgart: Fromann (Hauff), 1902.

SCHEVILL, FERDINAND. *History of Europe.* New York: Harcourt, Brace, 1954.

SCHMIDT, HEINRICH, and HARTMANN, ULRICH. *Richard Wagner in Bayreuth, Erinnerungen.* Leipzig: Klinner [1909].

SCHOPENHAUER, ARTHUR. *Parerga und Paralipomena: Kleine philosophische Schriften.* Ed. by Julius Frauenstädt. 2 vols. Berlin: Hayn, 1862.

SCHUMANN, ROBERT. *On Music and Musicians.* Ed. by Konrad Wolff. Trans. by Paul Rosenfeld. New York: Pantheon, 1946.

SCHURÉ, EDOUARD. "L'individualisme et l'anarchie en littérature, Friedrich Nietzsche et sa philosophie." *Revue des deux Mondes,* August 15, 1895, pp. 775–805.

SCHWEITZER, ALBERT. *J. S. Bach.* Trans. by Ernest Newman. 2 vols. New York: Macmillan, 1949.

SERAUKY, WALTER. "Die Todesverkündigungsszene in Richard Wagners Walküre als musikalisch-geistige Achse des Werkes." *Die Musikforschung,* Jahrgang XII, Heft 2 (April/June, 1959), pp. 143–51.

SERVIÈRES, GEORGES. *Richard Wagner jugé en France.* Paris: Librairie illustrée, [1887].

SHAW, GEORGE BERNARD. *The Perfect Wagnerite: A Commentary on the Nibelung's Ring.* 2nd ed. New York: Brentano, 1911.

——— *Shaw on Music.* Ed. by Eric Bentley. New York: Doubleday, 1955.

SHIRER, WILLIAM L. *The Rise and Fall of the Third Reich.* New York: Simon and Schuster, 1960.

SIEGEL, LINDA. "Wagner and the Romanticism of E. T. A. Hoffmann." *The Musical Quarterly,* Vol. LI, No. 4 (October, 1965), pp. 597–613.

SIEGFRIED, WALTHER. *Frau Cosima Wagner: Studie eines Lebens.* Stuttgart: Union Deutsche Verlagsgesellschaft, 1930.

SITWELL, SACHEVERELL. *Liszt.* London: Cassell [1955].

SKELTON, GEOFFREY. *Wagner at Bayreuth.* London: Barrie and Rockliff, 1965.

SMOLIAN, ARTHUR. *Richard Wagner's Bühnenfestspiel Der Ring des Nibelungen: Ein Vademecum.* Berlin: Schlesinger; Vienna: Haslinger, 1901.

SNORRI STURLUSON. *The Prose Edda.* Trans. by Jean I. Young. Berkeley and Los Angeles: University of California, 1964.

STEBBINS, LUCY POATE, and POATE, RICHARD. *Enchanted Wanderer: The Life of Carl Maria von Weber.* New York: Putnam, 1940.

STEIN, HERBERT VON. *Dichtung und Musik im Werk Richard Wagners.* Berlin: Gruyter, 1962.

STEIN, JACK M. *Richard Wagner and the Synthesis of the Arts.* Detroit: Wayne State, 1960.

STEIN, LEON. *The Racial Thinking of Richard Wagner.* New York: Philosophical Library, 1950.

STEMPLINGER, EDUARD. *Richard Wagner in München (1864–1870): Legende und Wirklichkeit.* Munich: Knorr and Hirth, 1933.

STERNFELD, RICHARD. "Hat Richard Wagner 1840 im Pariser Schuldgefängnis gesessen?" *Die Musik,* Jahrgang XV, Heft 2 (November, 1922), pp. 127–30.

STOCK, RICHARD WILHELM. *Richard Wagner und die Stadt der Meistersinger.* Nuremberg and Berlin: Ulrich, 1938.

——— *Richard Wagner und seine Meistersinger: eine Erinnerungsgabe zu den Bayreuther Kriegsfestspielen 1943.* Nuremberg: Ulrich, 1943.

STRAVINSKY, IGOR. *An Autobiography.* New York: Norton, 1962.

—— *Poetics of Music.* Trans. by Arthur Knodel and Ingolf Dahl. Cambridge, Mass.: Harvard, 1947.

STRECKER, LUDWIG. *Richard Wagner als Verlagsgefährte.* Mainz: Schott, 1951.

STROBEL, OTTO. *Richard Wagner: Leben und Schaffen: Eine Zeittafel.* Bayreuth: Verlag der Festspielleitung, 1952.

SUARÈS, ANDRÉ. *Musique et Poésie.* [Paris]: Aveline, 1928.

SULLIVAN, J. N. *Beethoven: His Spiritual Development.* New York: Knopf, 1958.

SYPHER, WYLIE. *Four Stages of Renaissance Style.* Garden City, N.Y.: Doubleday, 1955.

TAYLOR, ARCHER. *The Literary History of Meistergesang.* New York: Modern Language Association; London: Oxford, 1936.

TOVEY, DONALD FRANCIS. *Beethoven.* London, New York, and Toronto: Oxford, 1945.

—— *The Main Stream of Music and Other Essays.* New York: Oxford, 1949.

TOYE, FRANCIS. *Giuseppe Verdi: His Life and Works.* New York: Vintage, 1959.

TRUSCOTT, HAROLD. "Wagner: The Growth of an Art." *The Listener,* Vol. LXIX, No. 1781 (May 16, 1963), p. 849.

TSCHUDI, CLARA. *König Ludwig II von Bayern.* Trans. from Norwegian into German by Carl Küchler. Leipzig: Reclam, n.d.

VALENTIN, VEIT. *The German People.* New York: Knopf, 1952.

VENTURI, LIONELLO. *Impressionists and Symbolists.* Trans. by Francis Steegmuller. New York and London: Scribner, 1950.

VIERECK, PETER. *Metapolitics: The Roots of the Nazi Mind.* New York: Capricorn, 1961.

VOGEL, MARTIN. *Der Tristan-Akkord und die Krise der modernen Harmonie-Lehre.* Düsseldorf: Gesellschaft zur Förderung der systematischen Musikwissenschaft, 1962.

Volsunga Saga. Trans. by William Morris. Ed. by Robert W. Gutman. New York: Collier, 1962.

WAGNER, COSIMA. *Briefe an Ludwig Schemann.* Ed. by Bertha Schemann. Regensburg: Bosse, 1937.

—— *Cosima Wagners Briefe an ihre Tochter Daniela von Bülow, 1866–85.* Ed. by Max Freiherr von Waldberg. Stuttgart and Berlin: Cotta, 1933.

—— *Die Briefe Cosima Wagners an Friedrich Nietzsche.* Ed. by Erhart Thierbach. 2 vols. Weimar: Nietzsche-Archiv, 1938, 1940.

WAGNER, RICHARD. *Sämtliche Schriften und Dichtungen.* 5th ed. 12 vols. Leipzig: Breitkopf and Härtel [1911].

—— *Gesammelte Schriften und Dichtungen in zehn Bänden. (Goldene Klassiker-Bibliothek.)* 10 vols. Berlin, Leipzig, Vienna, and Stuttgart: Bong, n.d.

—— *Gesammelte Schriften und Dichtungen.* 4th ed. 10 vols. Leipzig: Siegel (Linnemann), 1907.

—— *Richard Wagner's Prose Works.* Trans. by William Ashton Ellis. 8 vols. London: K. Paul, 1892–99.

—— *Bayreuther Briefe.* Ed. by C. Glasenapp. Berlin and Leipzig: Schuster and Loeffler, 1907.

—— *The Story of Bayreuth as Told in the Bayreuth Letters of Richard Wagner.* Trans. and ed. by Caroline V. Kerr. Boston: Small, Maynard, 1912.

—— *Briefe, Die Sammlung Burrell.* Ed. by John N. Burk. Commentary trans. into German by Karl and Irene Geiringer. Frankfort-on-Main: Fischer, 1953.

—— *Letters of Richard Wagner: The Burrell Collection.* Ed. by John N. Burk. New York: Macmillan, 1950.

—— *Briefe an Hans Richter.* Ed. by Ludwig Karpath. Berlin, Vienna, and Leipzig: Zsolnay, 1924.

—— *Briefe an Hans von Bülow.* Jena: Diederich, 1916.

—— *Briefe Richard Wagners an eine Putzmacherin.* Ed. by Daniel Spitzer. Vienna: Konegen, 1906.

—— *Richard Wagner and the Seamstress.* Trans. by Sophie Prombaum. New York: Ungar, 1941.

—— *Briefe Richard Wagners an Emil Heckel.* Ed. by Karl Heckel. Berlin: Fischer, 1899.

—— *Letters of Richard Wagner to Emil Heckel.* Trans. by William Ashton Ellis. London: Richards, 1899.

—— *Die Briefe Richard Wagners an Judith Gautier.* Ed. by Willi Schuh. Zurich and Leipzig: Rotapfel [1936].

—— *Briefe Richard Wagners an Otto Wesendonk.* Berlin: Duncker, 1905.

—— *Briefe Richard Wagners an Otto Wesendonck.* Ed. by Albert Heintz. Charlottenburg: Algemeinen Musik-Zeitung, 1898.

—— *Richard Wagner: Letters to Wesendonck et al.* Trans. by William Ashton Ellis. London: Richards, 1899.

—— *Briefwechsel zwischen Wagner und Liszt.* 2 vols. Leipzig: Breitkopf and Härtel, 1900.

—— *Correspondence of Wagner and Liszt.* Trans. by Francis Hueffer. 2 vols. London: Grevel, 1888.

—— *Familienbriefe von Richard Wagner, 1832–1874.* Berlin: Duncker, 1907.

—— *Family Letters of Richard Wagner.* Trans. by William Ashton Ellis. London: Macmillan, 1911.

—— *König Ludwig II und Richard Wagner: Briefwechsel.* Ed. by Otto Strobel. 5 vols. Karlsruhe: Braun, 1936–39.

—— *The Letters of Richard Wagner to Anton Pusinelli.* Trans. and ed. by Elbert Lenrow. New York: Knopf, 1932.

—— *Lettres Françaises.* Ed. by Julien Tiersot. Paris: Grasset, 1935.

—— *Mein Leben: Erste authentische Veröffentlichung.* Ed. by Martin Gregor-Dellin. Munich: List, 1963.

—— *Mein Leben.* 2 vols. Munich: Bruckmann, 1911.

—— *My Life.* 2 vols. New York: Dodd, Mead, 1911.

—— *Nachgelassene Schriften und Dichtungen von Richard Wagner.* 2nd ed. Leipzig: Breitkopf and Härtel, 1902.

—— *Neun unveröffentlichte Briefe Richard Wagners an Malwida von Meysenbug. . . .* Ed. by Adolf Zinsstag. Basel: n.d.

WAGNER, RICHARD (cont.).

—— *Richard Wagner an August Röckel.* 2nd ed. Leipzig: Breitkopf and Härtel, 1912.

—— *Richard Wagner's Letters to August Roeckel.* Trans. by Eleanor C. Sellar. Bristol: Arrowsmith; London: Simpkin, Marshall, Hamilton, Kent [1897].

—— *Richard Wagner an Ferdinand Praeger.* Ed. by Houston Stewart Chamberlain. 2nd ed. Berlin and Leipzig: Schuster and Loeffler, 1908.

—— *Richard Wagner an Freunde und Zeitgenossen.* Ed. by Erich Kloss. Berlin and Leipzig: Schuster and Loeffler, 1909.

—— *Richard Wagner an Mathilde Maier.* Ed. by Hans Scholz. 2nd ed. Leipzig: Weicher, 1930.

—— *Richard Wagner an Mathilde und Otto Wesendonk: Tagebuchblätter und Briefe.* Ed. by Julius Kapp. Leipzig: Hesse & Becker [1915].

—— *Richard Wagner an Mathilde Wesendonk: Tagebuchblätter und Briefe 1853–1871.* 16th ed. Berlin: Duncker, 1904.

—— *Richard Wagner to Mathilde Wesendonck.* Trans. by William Ashton Ellis. New York: Scribner, 1905.

—— *Richard Wagner an Minna Wagner.* 3rd ed. 2 vols. Berlin and Leipzig: Schuster and Loeffler, 1908.

—— *Richard to Minna Wagner: Letters to His First Wife.* Trans. by William Ashton Ellis. 2 vols. New York: Scribner, 1909.

—— *Richard Wagner an seine Künstler.* Ed. by Erich Kloss. Berlin and Leipzig: Schuster and Loeffler, 1908.

—— *Richard Wagner an Theodor Apel.* Leipzig: Breitkopf and Härtel, 1910.

—— *Richard Wagner über Parsifal: Aussprüche des Meisters über sein Werk.* Ed. by Edwin Lindner. Leipzig: Breitkopf and Härtel, 1913.

—— *Richard Wagner über Tannhäuser: Aussprüche des Meisters über sein Werk.* Ed. by Edwin Lindner. Leipzig: Breitkopf and Härtel, 1914.

—— *Richard Wagner über Tristan und Isolde: Aussprüche des Meisters über sein Werk.* Ed. by Edwin Lindner. Leipzig: Breitkopf and Härtel, 1912.

—— *Richard Wagners Briefe.* Ed. by Wilhelm Altmann. 2 vols. Leipzig: Bibliographisches Institut [1933].

—— *Letters of Richard Wagner.* Ed. by Wilhelm Altmann. Trans. by M. M. Bozman. 2 vols. New York: Dutton; London: Dent, 1927.

—— *Richard Wagners Briefe an Frau Julie Ritter.* Munich: Bruckmann, 1920.

—— *Richard Wagners Briefe an Theodor Uhlig, Wilhelm Fischer, Ferdinand Heine.* Leipzig: Breitkopf and Härtel, 1888.

—— *Richard Wagner's Letters to his Dresden Friends, Theodor Uhlig, Wilhelm Fischer, and Ferdinand Heine.* Trans. by J. S. Shedlock. New York: Scribner & Welford, 1890.

—— *Richard Wagners Briefe nach Zeitfolge und Inhalt.* Ed. by Wilhelm Altmann. Leipzig: Breitkopf and Härtel, 1905.

—— *Richard Wagners Briefwechsel mit seinen Verlegern.* Ed. by Wilhelm Altmann. Vol. I, Leipzig: Breitkopf and Härtel, 1911. Vol. II, Mainz: Schott, 1911.

—— *Richard Wagners Gesammelte Briefe.* Ed. by Julius Kapp and Emerich Kastner. 2 vols. Leipzig: Hesse & Becker, 1914.

—— *Skizzen und Entwürfe zur Ring-Dichtung, mit der Dichtung "Der junge Siegfried."* Ed. by Otto Strobel. Munich: Bruckmann [1930].

WAGNER, SIEGFRIED. *Erinnerungen.* Stuttgart: Engelhorn, 1923.

WAGNER, WIELAND, ed. *Richard Wagner und das neue Bayreuth.* Munich: List, 1962.

WALLACE, WILLIAM. *Liszt, Wagner, and the Princess.* London: Kegan Paul; J. Curwen, 1927.

—— *Richard Wagner, As He Lived.* New York and London: Harper, 1925.

WALZEL, OSCAR. *Richard Wagner in seiner Zeit und nach seiner Zeit.* Munich: Müller & Rentsch, 1913.

WEINGARTNER, FELIX. *Bayreuth (1876–1896).* Berlin: Fischer, 1897.

—— *Buffets and Rewards: A Musician's Reminiscences.* Trans. by Marguerite Wolff. London: Hutchinson, 1937.

WEINSTOCK, HERBERT. *Donizetti.* New York: Pantheon, 1963.

—— *Tchaikovsky.* New York: Knopf, 1943.

WEISSHEIMER, WENDELIN. *Erlebnisse mit Richard Wagner, Franz Liszt, und vielen anderen Zeitgenossen nebst deren Briefen.* Stuttgart and Leipzig: Deutsche Verlags-Anstalt, 1898.

WESTERNHAGEN, CURT VON. *Gespräch um Wagner.* Bayreuth: Edition Musica, 1961.

—— *Richard Wagner: Sein Werk, sein Wesen, seine Welt.* Zurich: Atlantis, 1956.

—— *Vom Holländer zum Parsifal: Neue Wagner-Studien.* Zurich: Atlantis, 1962.

WHITTAKER, W. GILLIES. "Wagner's Version of Gluck's Iphigenia in Aulis." *Collected Essays.* London: Oxford, 1940.

WILLE, ELIZA. *Fünfzehn Briefe von Richard Wagner nebst Erinnerungen und Erläuterungen von Eliza Wille, geb. Sloman.* Berlin: Paetel, 1894.

WILSON, EDMUND. *Axel's Castle.* New York and London: Scribner, 1931.

WOLFF, WERNER. *Anton Bruckner: Rustic Genius.* New York: Dutton, 1942.

WOLFRAM VON ESCHENBACH. *Parzival.* Trans. by Helen M. Mustard and Charles E. Passage. New York: Vintage, 1961.

WOLZOGEN, HANS VON. *Erinnerungen an Richard Wagner.* Leipzig: Reclam [1892?].

—— *Richard Wagners Heldengestalten.* 2nd ed. Leipzig: Schloemp [1886].

—— "Suche dir, Gänser, die Gans!" *Bayreuther Blätter* (November, 1878; Elftes Stück), pp. 326–34.

—— *Thematischer Leitfaden durch die Musik zu Rich. Wagner's Festspiel Der Ring des Nibelung.* Leipzig: Schloemp, 1876.

ZAREK, OTTO. *The Tragic Idealist, Ludwig II of Bavaria.* Trans. by Ella Goodman and Paul Sudley. New York and London: Harper, 1939.

ZUCKERMAN, ELLIOTT. *The First Hundred Years of Wagner's Tristan.* New York and London: Columbia, 1964.

Index

Index

Index

Goethe, Johann Wolfgang von, 27, 31, 41, 46, 96, 116, 123, 318n, 392, 403, 449; as dramatist, 151–155, 167; influence on W., 16, 88–89, 419, 448–449; motives, 88, 116n, 117, 184, 296, 321; symbolism, 433; works, 6, 17, 19, 20, 95, 151–152, 154, 203, 264, 450, see also Faust
Götterdämmerung, Die, see Twilight of the Gods, The
Götz von Berlichingen (Goethe), 17, 151, 154
Goldwag, Bertha, 227, 233, 240, 262, 265, 330, 395–396
Gollmann (Wagner), Elise (W.'s sister-in-law), 112
Golther, Wolfgang, 409n
Goncourt, Edmond, 382
Goncourt, Jules, 382
Gottfried von Strassburg, 163, 166
Gottschalk, Mme., 49, 52–53
Gounod, Charles François, 70, 153, 192
Gozzi, Carlo, 41–42
Grabowsky, Mme., 52
Gran (Esztergom) Cathedral, 173
Grand opera, 59, 62, 67–69, 76, 89–90, 103, 121, 132, 142, 153–154, 168, 185, 206, 217, 221, 293, 295, 297–299, 320, 353, 444
Grant, Ulysses S., 392
Gravina, Biagio, 417, 445–446
Gravina, Blandine, see Bülow, Blandine von
Greece, 45, 134
"Greek Music Drama, The" (Nietzsche), 317
Greek theater, 119–120, 138–139, 167–168, 205–206, 295, 300, 317–318
Grétry, André Ernest Modeste, 10, 97–98, 362
Grillparzer, Franz, 258, 397n, 455
Grimm, Jakob, 35, 85, 102–103, 116
Grimm, Wilhelm, 35, 85, 116
Gropius, Karl Wilhelm, 346
Grosser, Henriette, 56
Grossgraupa, 112
Grüne Heinrich, Der (Keller), 173
Gutzkow, Karl, 47, 61, 113
Gypsies and Their Music in Hungary, The (Liszt), 335

Habeneck, François Antoine, 67, 72–73
Hadrian the Seventh (Corvo), 419n
Hähnel, Ernst, 94
Hagen, Friedrich von der, 163

Halévy, Jacques Fromental, 185; works, 59, 68, 82, 185, 290
Hamburg, 92, 103, 326
Hamp, Petrus (Anton), 439
Handel, George Frederick, 172
Handel Variations (Brahms), 375n
Hanover, 268, 338
Hans Heiling (Marschner), 44, 104, 106–107, 113, 160n
Hanslick, Eduard, xv, xvi, 161n, 219, 221–222; on Bayreuth, 340, 346–347, 350, 439; on W., 26, 94, 217–218, 455; on W.'s composition techniques, 37, 370–371, 373, 380, 383–384; on W.'s operas, 104, 169, 217–218, 437, 442–444
"Happy Evening, A" (Wagner), 96n, 239
Hapsburg line, 309, 323
Harold in Italy (Berlioz), 72, 75
Hart, Ted, xx, 166n
Hartwig, Friederike Wilhelmine, 2, 10
Hasenauer, Karl, 322, 383
Hasse, Johann Adolf, 11
Hauptmann, Gerhart, 453
Hauser, Arnold, xviii, 439
Haussmann, Georges Eugène, 66, 201n
Haydn, Joseph, 32, 101
Hebbel, Friedrich, 94–95, 336n, 337
Hebrides Overture (Mendelssohn), 90
Hecatommithi (Giraldi), 54
Heckel, Emil, 324, 443
Hegel, Georg Wilhelm Friedrich, 27
Heidelberg, 392
Heiden, Konrad, xii
Heim, Emilie, 176–177
Heine, Ferdinand, 85–86, 93, 127, 130, 133
Heine, Heinrich, 26, 70, 72, 82, 113, 120, 318n
Heine, Wilhelm, 127
Heinse, Wilhelm, 45, 134
"Heldentum und Christentum" (Wagner), 297, 405n, 420–425, 427, 429–430, 452
Helene, Grand Duchess, 223, 227
Hell, Theodor, 81, 90
Heller, Stephen, 192
Helmholtz, Hermann von, 326
Henry V of France, 446
Henry the Fowler, 217
Herder, Johann Gottfried von, 139
Herkomer, Sir Hubert von, 392

Hermann and Dorothea (Goethe), 95, 154
"Heroism and Christianity," see "Heldentum und Christentum"
Hérold, Louis Joseph Ferdinand, 35, 55
Hertz, Alfred, 409n
Herwegh, Georg, 147, 149, 402n, 412n
Herzen, Alexander, 402n
Herzogenberg, Elizabeth von, 447
Hesse-Homburg, 268
Hesse-Kassel, 268
Heubner, Otto Leonhard, 124
Hildebrandslied, 160
Hill, Karl, 349, 441, 443
Hiller, Antolka, 94
Hiller, Ferdinand, 94, 102
Hiller, Johann Adam, 28
Himmler, Heinrich, 400
Hirsch, Karl Friedrich, 52
History of Frederick the Great, The (Carlyle), 307
Hitler, Adolf, xiv, xvii, 222, 283n, 405, 410n, 419, 423–426, 431, 436, 452
"Hochzeit, Die" (Wagner): and other W. operas, 39–41, 76, 77, 151; composition, 36, 39, 77, 148; leitmotif, 55; love-death, 79, 189; poem, 39; sources, 38–39
Hölderlin, Friedrich, 294n
Hoffmann, E. T. A., 13, 15, 20–21, 79n, 81, 83, 85, 160, 206, 362
Hoffmann, Johann, 62–63, 177
Hoffmann, Joseph, 337, 350
Hofmannsthal, Hugo von, 43
Hogarth, George, 97
Hohe Braut, Die (König), 59
"Hohe Braut, Die" (Wagner), 59, 83, 85–86, 119
Hohenlohe, Prince Chlodwig, 243n, 275–276, 278
Hohenschwangau, 231, 242, 243n, 254–256, 258, 279, 285, 348
Hohenstaufen line, 2n, 34, 82, 264, 416–417, 421
Hohenzollern line, 264–266, 307n, 308, 310, 312, 314, 323, 328, 411–412
Holtei, Karl von, 58, 60–63, 113
Holtzmann, Adolf, 261
Homosexuality, 63, 70–71, 140, 175, 184, 231–232, 240–241, 247, 269, 273, 276–277, 300, 334, 345, 404, 414, 435–436, 440
Hopp, Friedrich, 160
Hoppe, Wilhelm, 355

475

Index

Index

69, 84–85, 102–103, 124–127, 129, 134–136, 142–144, 149–150, 171, 179, 182, 190, 199–200, 204, 214–215, 229, 261–263, 265, 276, 283–284, 323, 352, 359, 391–392, 398, 401–404, 406–407, 415–418, 446

Works:

analysis of:

motives and subjects:
Apollonian-Dionysian concept, 318–319, 353; autobiographical elements, 152, 160–161, 164–166, 186, 189, 207–209, 219–221, 229, 232–234, 236, 243–244, 249, 251, 256–257, 270, 274, 285, 287, 315, 359, 396; art, regeneration through, 121–122, 129, 138, 143, 237, 241, 243, 279, 306, 349, 394, 406; art as religion, 404, 448; blood symbolism, 424–425, 427–430, 453; castration, 425, 428, 438, 451; Christian symbolism, 116n, 406–407, 419, 424, 429; compassion, 79–80, 179, 188, 400, 425, 428, 431, 454; Crucifixion, 425, 429; curse, 43–44, 78–80, 107, 368; day and night symbols, 165, 178, 181; decadence, 383, 432, 434, 438, 440; demonism, 437–438; doubting wife, xi, 108–109, 202; dreams, 108, 293–296, 299–300, 318–319, 385; Eternal Feminine, 88, 116, 152, 162, 184, 321, 435; Eucharist, 336, 400, 413, 427, 432, 439; father figure, 6, 9, 42, 57, 443; fire, 77–78, 119, 126, 130n, 132, 158, 309, 412, 454; the Folk, xiii, 117, 119–120, 138–139, 220, 243, 257, 264, 279, 296, 330, 349, 353, 421, 430; Führer concept, xiii, xv, 77, 121, 139, 220, 241, 243–244, 420–424, 427–428, 436; goddess become woman, 42, 151–152, 177, 195; Grail, 120, 122, 132, 421–422, 427–428, 438; humor, 155, 167n, 183, 219–220, 269, 298, 311, 343; imperialism, 40, 312, 322–324, 353, 389, 411, 418–419; incest, 78–79, 83, 186, 249,

288, 427–428, 432; instinct vs. reason, xi–xiii, xvi, 296, 353, 388; love concepts, xiv, 39, 163, 394, 452, 454; love death, 78–79, 109, 179, 187–189, 252, 369, 431; misogyny, 435; mother concept, 78, 214, 427–428, 436; mutilation, 42–43, 132, 157, 220, 288n, 425, 428, 438, 451; mysticism, 437–438; pilgrimage, 78–79, 88, 185, 374n, 422; poet-priest concept, xii, 139, 220, 242, 407, 439; political and social theory, xiii–xvi, 6, 117–120, 147, 156, 158–159, 237–238, 242–244, 276, 278, 280, 282–283, 288, 290, 357, 405, 418, 426; presentiment, 365, 367, 370; redemption, xv, 56, 78–80, 88, 116, 153, 156–157, 165, 184, 186, 188, 243–244, 368, 374n, 394, 400, 404, 419–420, 422–425, 427, 432, 435–438, 440, 450–451; reminiscence, 364–370, 376; riddle contests, 287, 288n; ring (magic), 43, 131–132, 159; saints, 424; sex and power, 427n; sexual abnegation, 109–110, 187, 251, 429–432, 434–438; Siegfried, 120–121, 134, 136, 142, 158, 165n, 421, 424; sister motive, 77, 83, 186, 214, 432; spear, 422, 428–430, 438; suicide, 189, 353, 451; superblood and superrace, 425, 427–430, 438, 453; symbolism, xiii, 164–165, 408, 433–434; theater as temple, 121–122, 295, 322, 408, 439; theater reform, 119–120, 126, 226, 238; transmigration, 79, 185–186, 368n, 453; vegetarianism, 399–400, 404–405, 424–425, 434, 448; vivisection, 188, 399–400, 404–405, 412; will and renunciation, 116–117, 152–153, 156, 158–159, 164–165, 179, 184–189, 208, 252–253, 286, 288n, 296, 353, 368–369, 375, 394, 419, 423–425, 427, 429, 432, 451; *see also* Christianity, Evolution, Homosexuality, Jewish problem, Myth,

Names, Racial theory present estimate of, xvi–xviii technical and artistic aspects, 19–20, 25, 29, 36–37, 39–40, 55–56, 146, 148–149, 217, 362–388, 397, 401; *Abgesang,* 378–381; altering and transposing parts for particular singers, 68, 86–87, 101–102, 106, 204, 239, 286n, 349n; animals in opera, 345–346; aria form, 377, 382; ballet, 195–196, 199, 341; *Bar,* 378–381; bow form, 379–381; chromaticism-diatonism, 29, 32–33, 297, 374, 381; classical unities, 168; counterpoint, 27, 29, 34, 36, 55, 194, 364, 367, 371, 375–377; cuts, 86–87, 137, 339; dramaturgy, 11, 54–55, 153; ending problem, 106–108, 156, 158, 177; formal structure, xix, 362–388; *Gesamtkunstwerk,* xvii, 69, 121, 138–139, 237, 289–292, 296–300, 319–321, 350, 353, 385, 433; harmony, use of, 376, 383; *Leich,* 380; *Leitharmonie,* 366; leitmotif, xix, 44, 55, 76, 139, 362–372, 375–376, 386–387; Lied form, 377, 382; magic opera, 35, 40, 167, 382n, 437, *see also Feen, Die;* manipulation of themes, 29–30, 386–387; *Meistergesang,* 206, 219; miniaturist, W. as, 380–383; motif of presentiment, 364–367, 370, of reminiscence, 364–370, 376; music drama, 39, 113, 139, 212–213, 363, 386–387, 408; orchestra-voice balance, 307–308, 338, 370, 415; orchestration, xi, 29, 69, 76, 82, 87–88, 97–98, 101–102, 105–106, 138–139, 170, 196n, 218, 222, 238, 249, 253, 336–338, 383–384, 397; parallel (repeated) phrases, 377–378, 386; poet, W. as, xvii, 14, 20, 55, 77–78, 104–108, 112, 133, 138–140, 144, 154–158, 166–170, 188, 197, 218–219, 248–250, 252n, 313n, 321, 428, 449–450; practicableness of the

488